Foundations of Reading
Acquisition and Dyslexia

Implications for Early Intervention

D1260136

CONFERENCE PARTICIPANTS

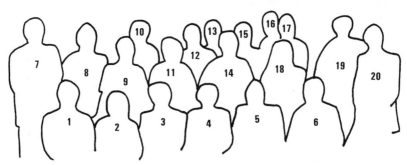

1. Tom Nicholson
2. Susan Brady
3. Benita Blachman
4. Barbara Foorman
5. Linnea Ehri
6. Keith Stanovich
7. Drake Duane
8. Joseph Torgesen
9. Rebecca Treiman
10. David Francis
11. Maggie Bruck
12. Jack Fletcher
13. Brian Byrne
14. Peter Bryant
15. Frank Vellutino
16. Alvin Liberman
17. William Tunmer
18. Maryanne Wolf
19. Richard Olson
20. Paula Tallal

Foundations of Reading Acquisition and Dyslexia

Implications for Early Intervention

Edited by

Benita A. Blachman
Syracuse University

LEA LAWRENCE ERLBAUM ASSOCIATES, PUBLISHERS
1997   Mahwah, New Jersey   London

Lawrence Erlbaum Associates, Inc., Publishers
10 Industrial Avenue
Mahwah, New Jersey 07430

Library of Congress Cataloging-in-Publication Data

Foundations of reading acquisition and dyslexia : implications for
  early intervention / edited by Benita A. Blachman.
    p.   cm.
  "The chapters in this volume are based on presentations made at a
conference on 'Cognitive and Linguistic Foundations of Reading
Acquisition: Implications for Intervention Research. The
conference was sponsored by the National Dyslexia Research
Foundation (NDRF) and held in Kauai, Hawaii, from May 27 to June 1,
1995"—Pref.
  Includes bibliographical references and index.
  ISBN 0-8058-2362-X (cloth : alk. paper). — ISBN 0-8058-2363-8
(pbk. : alk. paper).
  1. Reading—Congresses. 2. Dyslexic children—Education—
Congresses. 3. Dyslexia—Congresses. 4. Reading—Remedial
teaching—Congresses. 5. Word recognition—Congresses.
6. Orthography and spelling—Congresses. I. Blachman, Benita A.
LB1050.2.F69 1997
428.4—dc21   96-53068
                                                            CIP

Books published by Lawrence Erlbaum Associates are printed on acid-free paper,
and their bindings are chosen for strength and durability.

Printed in the United States of America
10 9 8 7 6 5 4

For my father

Morris Blachman

with love and appreciation for his friendship and support

and in loving memory of my mother

Rosalee Bloom Blachman

August 25, 1924–October 10, 1995

Contents

Preface

The chapters in this volume are based on presentations made at the conference, "Cognitive and Linguistic Foundations of Reading Acquisition: Implications for Intervention Research." The conference was sponsored by the National Dyslexia Research Foundation (NDRF) and held in Kauai, Hawaii, from May 27 to June 1, 1995. This was the third in a series of meetings sponsored by NDRF on the subject of brain development, language acquisition, reading, and dyslexia, with the overarching title of "The Extraordinary Brain." The first meeting, "Neurobiological Issues in Developmental Dyslexia," was organized by Albert Galaburda and held in Barcelona, Spain, in June 1990.[1] The second conference, organized by Paula Tallal, "Neural and Cognitive Mechanisms Underlying Speech, Language and Reading," was held in Santa Fe, New Mexico, in May 1992.[2] I had the pleasure of organizing the third conference.

The researchers who participated in this conference have all made contributions to our theoretical and empirical understanding of how children learn to read. Due to the usual budgetary constraints on conference organizers, many other researchers who have also made contributions to the research in this area could not be included in the conference, but their work is represented indirectly by inclusion among the references cited by the participants. All presenters made a commitment not just to share their

---

[1]See *Dyslexia and Development: Neurobiological Aspects of Extra-Ordinary Brains*, edited by A. M. Galaburda and published by Harvard University Press in 1993.

[2]See *Developmental Dyslexia: Neural, Cognitive, and Genetic Mechanisms*, edited by C. Chase, G. D. Rosen, and G. F. Sherman and published by York Press in 1996.

ongoing research but to participate in an intense, 5-day dialogue about the research in reading acquisition and the implications of this work for early intervention. Researchers were asked to address not only what they have learned from their research programs, but also to discuss unsolved problems. This dialogue prompted numerous questions of both a theoretical and applied nature, generated heated debate, and fueled our optimism about the important gains that have been made in our scientific understanding of the reading process, especially our understanding of the critical role played by phonological abilities. The contributions to this volume are sometimes different from the original presentations, in part because they reflect the exchange that took place among conference participants.

This book is divided into the following four sections: Theoretical Foundations, Subtypes of Dyslexia, Beginning to Read and Spell, and Implications for Intervention. It should be noted that the separation between sections is somewhat artificial, and several of the chapters could have been presented in more than one of the sections

PART I, THEORETICAL FOUNDATIONS

The first section of the book includes four chapters that explore theoretical foundations and begins as did the conference, with a presentation by Alvin Liberman, based on his eloquent keynote address. Liberman first describes the relevance of a theory of speech for understanding reading acquisition, and then explores the implications of opposing views of the biology of speech for understanding what makes reading and writing hard to acquire. As Liberman explains, the constituents of speech are articulatory gestures (not sounds) managed by a biologically specialized phonologic module that coarticulates the gestures and makes it possible for the speaker-hearer to produce and perceive speech at a rate that would be impossible otherwise. These gestures evolved with language to serve only a phonetic purpose—no other. Unlike the visual percepts evoked by the letters of the alphabet, articulatory gestures are phonetic by their very nature, requiring no cognitive translation to make them so. But, as Liberman told his audience at the conference, a consequence of coarticulation is that

> Awareness of phonologic structure [needed to understand how print represents speech] is hard to come by: The module spells for the speaker and parses for the listener, leaving both in the dark about phonologic process; coarticulation destroys all correspondence in segmentation between acoustic and phonologic structures, making most consonantal segments unavailable

in isolation; and, most important, the gestural percepts that are immediately evoked by the module are already phonetic in nature, precluding the cognitive translation that would bring them to notice. Special difficulty in reading might well be caused by a weakness of the phonologic module, for that would produce primary representations of a fragile sort, with the consequence that they would be that much harder to bring to awareness.

The chapter by Brady builds on the foundation laid by Liberman. Brady discusses the impact that deficits in phonological processing can have on reading acquisition, and explores the possibility that differences in the ability to encode phonological representations are responsible for many of the language weaknesses of poor readers. She reviews the evidence that individual differences in speech perception might influence a child's ability to gain access to the phonemic structure of words, and provides a critical analysis of the hypothesis that a general auditory deficit might underlie phonological processing difficulties.

The next chapter presents a theoretical perspective that differs from that of the previous two chapters. Tallal, Miller, Jenkins, and Merzenich examine the relationship between deficits in temporal processing (especially deficits in processing rapidly changing acoustic cues) and disorders in speech, language, and reading. Tallal and her colleagues review two recent studies designed to investigate whether children with specific language impairment profit from a training program that incorporates listening exercises using acoustically modified speech and computer games developed to alter temporal integration rates.

In the next chapter, Wolf explores the role of naming-speed deficits in dyslexia, and posits that naming-speed deficits should not be subsumed under the larger category of phonological processing problems but instead represent a separable source of difficulty for poor readers and reflect different underlying mechanisms. Wolf suggests that children who are the most significantly impaired in reading, and possibly the most resistant to treatment, are those who have a "double-deficit"—that is, both a phonological deficit and a naming-speed deficit.

PART II, SUBTYPES OF DYSLEXIA

This section includes two chapters on subtypes of dyslexia. Fletcher and his colleagues review the historical interest in subtyping and the problems that have plagued this research. In a recent study using cluster analysis, these researchers found that a common factor among four of the five identified "specific" reading-disabled subtypes was a deficit in phonological awareness, with variation among the groups on whether or not subjects were also slower in naming speed and impaired in verbal short-term memory.

Stanovich, Siegel, Gottardo, Chiappe, and Sidhu also identify problems that have negated the value of much of the previous work on the identification of subtypes, and delineate a strategy for distinguishing between phonological and surface dyslexics by comparing the performance of dyslexic and reading-age-matched controls on pseudoword and exception word reading. Interestingly enough, when reading-age-matched controls are used for comparison—rather than controls matched on chronological age—surface dyslexia is very infrequent, whereas phonological dyslexia remains a robust subtype.

PART III, BEGINNING TO READ AND SPELL

The four chapters in this section explore the beginning stages of learning to read and spell. Bruck, Genesee, and Caravolas report the results of a cross-linguistic study of English- and French-speaking children in which kindergarten measures of phonological awareness, letter-name knowledge, parent–child reading habits, and nonverbal cognitive ability administered in kindergarten were used to predict end-of-first-grade reading. Although the phonological characteristics of the English and French languages differ, measures of awareness of phonologic structure and letter-name knowledge were the most important predictors of early reading acquisition for both groups of children.

Ehri provides a thorough theoretical account of the phases of development (i.e., prealphabetic, partial alphabetic, full alphabetic, and consolidated alphabetic) that children go through as they develop fluent word recognition. A critical component in the process is learning to use spellings as "phonemic maps that lay out the pronunciation of words visually." Ehri presents evidence to show that children with reading disabilities have less complete representations of words in memory and spend more time at the partial alphabetic stage than normal readers.

In Treiman's chapter, we turn our attention to the development of spelling, beginning with the precursors of alphabetic writing and a review of the changes that occur in invented spelling as the alphabetic principle emerges. Treiman explores how an understanding of the spelling development of typical learners can help us understand the problems dyslexics demonstrate in grasping the alphabetic and morphological basis of English spelling.

Bryant, Nunes, and Bindman explore the child's understanding of the syntactic connections between spoken and written language and point out, for example, that more than phonological sensitivity is needed to understand why the similarly pronounced endings of *kissed* and *fist* are spelled differently. Bryant and his colleagues present the results from the first year of a 3-year longitudinal study investigating the relationship between children's spelling of morphemes and their morpho-syntactic awareness.

PART IV, IMPLICATIONS FOR INTERVENTION

The final section of the book includes chapters with a primary focus on intervention. Foorman, Francis, Shaywitz, Shaywitz, and Fletcher provide evidence to show that children who are not making progress in reading have a deficit in reading skills rather than a developmental lag and, as such, will not "catch up" on their own *and* are in need of early intervention. Foorman and colleagues also report the results of two intervention studies, one with kindergarten children and the other with second- and third-grade reading-disabled children.

Byrne, Fielding-Barnsley, Ashley, and Larsen review studies they have conducted that address several areas of concern, including children's early assumptions about how print represents speech, the role of phonemic awareness and letter knowledge in reading acquisition for both typically developing children and those at risk for reading failure, and the contributions of print exposure and decoding of nonwords to the development of word-specific knowledge (as measured by irregular word reading). In each area, Byrne and his colleagues describe both what is known and what is not known.

The next four chapters focus on intervention studies conducted with at-risk or reading-disabled children. Torgesen, Wagner, and Rashotte report the end-of-first-grade results from an early intervention study with children identified in kindergarten as low on letter-name knowledge and low on a phoneme awareness task and, consequently, at risk for reading difficulty. Three treatments are compared that differed according to whether the participating children received *explicit* phonological awareness training and phonics, *implicit* phonological awareness and phonics, or individualized instruction that supported the regular classroom reading program.

Olson, Wise, Johnson, and Ring review behavioral-genetic evidence to support the strong contribution of phonological deficits to reading and spelling difficulties, and describe a series of computer-based training studies that emphasize the remediation of phonological deficits. Olson and his colleagues have found significant improvement in word recognition among children taught to request speech feedback for unknown words while reading stories on a computer and have, in the research reported here, combined this program with more explicit computer-based instruction in phonological awareness.

Greaney, Tunmer, and Chapman describe two studies conducted with disabled readers and younger normal readers matched on reading age in which the authors found that although the dyslexic children demonstrated onset-rime sensitivity (e.g., in the word *trip*, the onset is /tr/ and the rime is /ip/), they didn't appear to use that knowledge to read unfamiliar words. In two follow-up intervention studies, the authors explore the use of rime-based orthographic analogy training.

Vellutino, Scanlon, and Sipay provide the first in-depth look at the characteristics of children resistant to treatment, and find that children who made the least growth in reading during two semesters of individual tutoring (provided during spring of first grade and the fall of second grade) differed from normal readers prior to the intervention on phonologically based skills, including phoneme segmentation, rapid naming, and verbal memory tasks. Children who made the most growth during the tutoring experience performed more like the normal readers on these preintervention tasks.

The final two chapters focus more specifically on issues related to phonological awareness. Nicholson reviews the evidence that children with limited preschool literacy experiences who come from low-income families are at a particular disadvantage in learning to read. He then makes the case that the early reading instruction these children receive is especially critical to their success and should include instruction in phonological awareness and the alphabetic code.

Blachman discusses unanswered questions related to developing, implementing, and assessing the impact of intervention programs that heighten phonological awareness. She suggests, for example, that we need to know more about the way in which problems in various aspects of phonological processing interact to influence the effectiveness of reading instruction. She concludes with a cautionary note to readers regarding potential pitfalls now that "phonological awareness" has become one of the educational buzzwords of the 1990s.

The chapters in this book represent the progress that is being made in basic and applied research with respect to our understanding of how children learn to read and why many children fail. One goal of the conference was to explore "what we know and what we don't know" (to borrow the words of Byrne and his colleagues). This volume provides an opportunity to share that dialogue with a wider audience.

—*Benita A. Blachman*
Syracuse, New York

Acknowledgments

The conference on which this book is based was sponsored by the National Dyslexia Research Foundation (NDRF) and would not have been possible without the tireless efforts of William H. Baker, Jr., Executive Director of NDRF, and the generous support of Helen U. Baker, the Fisher-Landau Foundation of New York, the McNichols family, Robert G. Hall, and Assets School in Honolulu, Hawaii. My job as conference organizer was made easier by Albert Galaburda and Paula Tallal, who shared valuable information about their experiences organizing earlier conferences sponsored by NDRF, and Colleen Osburn, who handled the myriad on-site details that made things run so smoothly for the rest of us. Heartfelt thanks also go to Carol Baxter and Joan Simonetta of the Reading and Language Arts Center at Syracuse University, who graciously handled much of the paperwork and correspondence for the conference. I would like to extend my appreciation to the conference participants for outstanding presentations and lively debate. The presenters included, in addition to myself: Susan Brady, Maggie Bruck, Peter Bryant, Brian Byrne, Drake Duane, Linnea Ehri, Jack Fletcher, Barbara Foorman, David Francis, Alvin Liberman, Tom Nicholson, Richard Olson, Keith Stanovich, Paula Tallal, Joseph Torgesen, Rebecca Treiman, William Tunmer, Frank Vellutino, and Maryanne Wolf. On behalf of all of the contributors to this book, I would also like to thank Ray O'Connell and Kathy Scornavacca at Lawrence Erlbaum Associates for their assistance and support throughout every phase of this endeavor. I also owe a special debt of gratitude to Jerry Kelly for his support, wise counsel, and good humor while I worked on this project.

Benita A. Blachman

Contributors

Luise Ashley
Department of Psychology
The University of New England
Armidale, New South Wales, Australia

Miriam Bindman
Department of Child Development
    and Learning
Institute of Education
London, England

Benita A. Blachman
Reading and Language Arts Center
School of Education
Syracuse University
Syracuse, New York

Susan Amanda Brady
Department of Psychology
The University of Rhode Island
Kingston, Rhode Island
and
Haskins Laboratories
New Haven, Connecticut

Maggie Bruck
Department of Psychology
McGill University
Montreal, Quebec, Canada

Peter E. Bryant
Department of Experimental
    Psychology
University of Oxford
Oxford, England

Brian Byrne
Department of Psychology
The University of New England
Armidale, New South Wales, Australia

Markéta Caravolas
Department of Psychology
McGill University
Montreal, Quebec, Canada

James W. Chapman
Faculty of Education
Massey University
Palmerston North, New Zealand

Penny Chiappe
Department of Human Development
    and Applied Psychology
Ontario Institute for Studies in Education
University of Toronto
Toronto, Ontario, Canada

Linnea C. Ehri
Program in Educational Psychology
The Graduate School and
    University Center
The City University of New York
New York, New York

Ruth Fielding-Barnsley
Department of Psychology
The University of New England
Armidale, New South Wales, Australia

Jack M. Fletcher
Departments of Pediatrics
    and Neurosurgery
University of Texas—
    Houston Medical School
Houston, Texas

Barbara R. Foorman
Department of Educational Psychology
University of Houston
Houston, Texas

David J. Francis
Department of Psychology
University of Houston
Houston, Texas

Fred Genesee
Department of Psychology
McGill University
Montreal, Quebec, Canada

Alexandra Gottardo
Psychology Department
Birkbeck College
University of London
London, England

Keith T. Greaney
Faculty of Education
Massey University
Palmerston North, New Zealand

William M. Jenkins
W. M. Keck Center for
    Integrative Neurosciences
    and Coleman Laboratory
University of California
San Francisco, California

Mina C. Johnson
Department of Psychology
University of Colorado
Boulder, Colorado

Len Katz
Department of Psychology
University of Connecticut
Storrs, Connecticut
and
Haskins Laboratories
New Haven, Connecticut

Kim Larsen
Department of Psychology
The University of New England
Armidale, New South Wales, Australia

Alvin M. Liberman
University of Connecticut and
    Yale University, Emeritus
Haskins Laboratories
New Haven, Connecticut

G. Reid Lyon
Human Learning and Behavior Branch
National Institute of Child Health
    and Human Development
National Institutes of Health
Bethesda, Maryland

Michael M. Merzenich
W. M. Keck Center for
    Integrative Neurosciences
    and Coleman Laboratory
University of California
San Francisco, California

Steven L. Miller
Scientific Learning Principles
    Corporation
San Francisco, California

Robin Morris
Department of Psychology
Georgia State University
Atlanta, Georgia

Tom Nicholson
Education Department
University of Auckland
Auckland, New Zealand

Terezinha Nunes
Department of Child Development
    and Learning
Institute of Education
London, England

Richard K. Olson
Department of Psychology
University of Colorado
Boulder, Colorado

Carol A. Rashotte
Department of Psychology
The Florida State University
Tallahassee, Florida

Jerry Ring
Department of Psychology
University of Colorado
Boulder, Colorado

Donna M. Scanlon
Child Study and Research Center
State University of New York at Albany
Albany, New York

Donald P. Shankweiler
Department of Psychology
University of Connecticut
Storrs, Connecticut
and
Haskins Laboratories
New Haven, Connecticut

Sally E. Shaywitz
Department of Pediatrics
Yale University School of Medicine
New Haven, Connecticut

Bennett A. Shaywitz
Department of Pediatrics
Yale University School of Medicine
New Haven, Connecticut

Robindra Sidhu
Department of Human Development
    and Applied Psychology
Ontario Institute for Studies in Education
University of Toronto
Toronto, Ontario, Canada

Linda S. Siegel
Department of Educational Psychology
    and Special Education
University of British Columbia
Vancouver, British Columbia, Canada

Edward R. Sipay
Department of Reading
State University of New York at Albany
Albany, New York

Keith E. Stanovich
Department of Human Development
    and Applied Psychology
Ontario Institute for Studies in Education
University of Toronto
Toronto, Ontario, Canada

Karla K. Stuebing
Department of Pediatrics
University of Texas—
    Houston Medical School
Houston, Texas

Paula Tallal
Center for Molecular and Behavioral
    Neuroscience
Rutgers, The State University
    of New Jersey
Newark, New Jersey

Joseph K. Torgesen
Department of Psychology
The Florida State University
Tallahassee, Florida

Rebecca Treiman
Department of Psychology
Wayne State University
Detroit, Michigan

William E. Tunmer
Faculty of Education
Massey University
Palmerston North, New Zealand

Frank R. Vellutino
Child Study and Research Center
State University of New York at Albany
Albany, New York

Richard K. Wagner
Department of Psychology
The Florida State University
Tallahassee, Florida

Barbara Wise
Department of Psychology
University of Colorado
Boulder, Colorado

Maryanne Wolf
Eliot-Pearson Department
  of Child Study
Tufts University
Medford, Massachusetts

I

THEORETICAL
FOUNDATIONS

How Theories of Speech Affect Research in Reading and Writing

Alvin M. Liberman
Haskins Laboratories

> *When we remember that words are sounds merely, we shall conclude that the idea of representing those sounds by marks, so that whoever should, at any time after, see the marks would understand what sounds they meant, was a bold and ingenious conception, not likely to occur to one man of a million in the run of a thousand years. . . . That it was difficult of conception and execution is apparent, as well by the foregoing reflections as by the fact that so many tribes of men have come down from Adam's time to ours without ever having possessed it.*
>
> —Abraham Lincoln

My aim is to promote two notions about the relation between reading/writing and speech: The right theory of speech is essential to a coherent account of reading/writing, and the conventional theory of speech is the wrong theory. To say, as I do, that the conventional theory has therefore made it hard for researchers to see how reading/writing differ from speech is not to deny progress in the field; indeed, I believe, to the contrary, that research of the last few decades has brought insights that are both new and important. I would only suggest that the researchers who are responsible for those insights have either worked from the right theory or else managed somehow to ignore the wrong one. Naturally, I believe about the "right" theory, not that it is perfectly and forever true, only that it is, by comparison with its more conventional competitor, more nearly right, and more likely, therefore, to head the reading/writing researcher in the right direction.

I should say that the conventional theory I consider wrong and the unconventional theory I consider right are only about speech in the narrow sense, by which I mean the component of the broader language faculty that comprises the production and perception of consonants and vowels. Though one of the virtues of the unconventional theory is that it makes speech an organic part of language instead of the biologically arbitrary appendage that the conventional theory portrays, it is nonetheless possible for our purposes to deal with speech in isolation. However, I reserve the right to suggest at a later point that the biologically based fit of speech to the other components of language is an important reason why appreciation of the alphabetic principle is hard to come by.

To advance the two notions that are the point of this chapter, I rely almost entirely on facts that are in plain sight, requiring only to be thought about if their implications for speech and reading are to be seen. Because I had not myself thought about those facts, I would therefore emphasize I was long ago taken in by the conventional view. Specifically, I was led by it to suppose that speech is an acoustic alphabet, with segments of sound as discrete as the letters that convey them, and that I could, therefore, contrive an acoustic alternative for use in a reading machine for the blind (Liberman, 1996). Only after I had failed miserably to produce that alternative, and had then done a lot of research to find out why, did I begin to see that I might have known better before I started had I simply gone beyond surface appearances to take account of the somewhat deeper, if still visible, considerations I invite you to think about. (A reading machine for the blind is now a reality, but it produces speech, not an acoustic alphabet.) I claim that the conventional view fails the reading/writing researcher for much the same reason it failed me. If that failure has gone largely unnoticed, it is not because the conventional speech researchers have been unable or unwilling to understand what might seem plain, but only because they have not been concerned with the relevance of their theory to research on reading/writing or reading machines, and have therefore not had occasion to measure its implications against the hard realities of those enterprises.

In addition to the facts about language that are apparent to everyone, I refer to just a few that have come from research on speech, but those are easily understood without a technical background in acoustic phonetics; moreover, they are not in dispute. All this is to say that the matter is not difficult at all, except, perhaps, in the telling.

THE RELEVANCE OF A THEORY OF SPEECH

As for the first notion—that a proper theory of speech is essential to an understanding of how people read—the most relevant consideration arises out of the deep biological gulf that separates the two processes. Speech, on the one side, is a product of biological evolution, standing as the most obvious, and arguably the most important, of our species-typical behaviors. Reading/writing, on the other, did not evolve biologically, but rather developed (in some cultures) as a secondary response to that which evolution had already produced. A consequence is that we are biologically destined to speak, not to read or write. Accordingly, we are all good at speech, but disabled as readers and writers; the difference among us in reading/writing is simply that some are fairly easy to cure and some are not.

Viewing the matter from a slightly different angle, we see that, being at least as old as our species, speech has been around for 200,000 years or more, although the idea that it could be rendered alphabetically was born no more than 4,000 years ago. Subtracting the latter number from the former, we conclude that it took our ancestors at least 196,000 years just to discover how to describe what it was they did when they spoke. Why did it take so long? Why was it so hard for our prealphabetic ancestors to make the momentous discovery, and why is it so hard for our preliterate children to understand it? Why has an alphabet been developed only once in all of human history? Surely, questions like those cry out for a theory of speech that explains in the same breath why an alphabetic description of speech is not immediately apparent to everyone, and why it should be almost wholly beyond the reach of some. Nothing less will do if we are to know how to teach children who are somehow ready to cope, while also helping those who are not.

CONTRASTING VIEWS OF THE BIOLOGY OF SPEECH

There is a question that goes to the heart of the difference between the conventional and unconventional views of speech: Does the specialization for language extend to the motor and perceptual processes underlying the consonants and vowels that speech and reading/writing use in common? The guiding assumption of the conventional view is that it does not (Crowder, 1983; Diehl & Kluender, 1986a, 1986b, 1986c; Fujisaki & Kawashima, 1970; Kuhl, 1981; Lindblom, 1991; Massaro, 1987a, 1987b; Stevens & Blumstein, 1978; Sussman, 1989; Warren, 1993). On that view, language simply appropriated modes of motor control and auditory perception that had already evolved in connection with nonlinguistic functions. Having been adopted by language for its purposes, those plain vanilla processes are now seen on the conventional view to work horizontally, serving linguistic and nonlinguistic behaviors alike.

According to the unconventional view, the specialization for language extends much farther, embracing even the very low level where the primary motor and perceptual representations of speech are to be found (Liberman & Mattingly, 1985, 1989; Mann & Liberman, 1983; Mattingly & Liberman, 1990; Remez, Rubin, Berns, Pardo, & Lang, 1994; Whalen & Liberman, 1987). In other words, there are distinctly linguistic representations, not in the higher reaches of the cognitive machinery, but down among the structures of action and perception. Thus, language is seen as a vertically organized system in which linguistically specialized structures (and processes) are as central to phonetics as they are to syntax.

Among the more particular assumptions of the two views, perhaps the most fundamental concerns the nature of the ultimate constituents of speech (and, for that matter, language). On the conventional view, they are sounds. Just about everybody (including Lincoln, as the otherwise insightful epigraph makes clear) simply takes that for granted. And just about everybody holds that the sounds of speech are serviceable as consonants and vowels to the extent that they evoke distinctive auditory percepts.

The unconventional theorist, on the other hand, takes the ultimate constituents to be, not sounds, but articulatory gestures. Thus, the consonant we write as *b* is a closure of the vocal tract at the lips, *d* a closure at the alveolar ridge, and so forth. This notion came originally from research on speech that revealed vast context-conditioned variations in the sound as a result of the coarticulation of seemingly invariant gestures. Among the unconventional investigators who take such gestures to be the primitives of the phonetic system, there is some question about exactly how they should be defined, but little of what I mean to say here turns on the answer. What is most important for our purposes are just two considerations: one is that the gesture-as-primitive view permits us to see a system in which the defining gestures can be overlapped and merged (i.e., coarticulated) so as to produce phonetic strings at the high rates that are, in fact, achieved; the other, that the phonetically relevant gestures were presumably selected (and refined) in evolution because they lent themselves to just those articulatory and coarticulatory maneuvers that were appropriate to their specifically phonetic function. Accordingly, they form a natural class, a phonetic modality, as it were, that has a linguistic purpose and no other.

As for speech production, the conventional view is that it is controlled by mechanisms of a general motor sort, mechanisms that are constrained to produce exactly the sounds that define the consonants and vowels. According to the unconventional view, on the other hand, the mechanisms of articulation and coarticulation are not instances of some more general mechanism of motor control, but rather the workings of a biological specialization—a phonetic module—that is no less distinctly linguistic than the specialized gestures it manages. The aim of its specialized gestures is not to achieve particular acoustic targets, but to represent consonants and vowels invariantly in rapidly produced strings, allowing the resulting sounds to go wherever the acoustically complex effects of coarticulation happen to take them. That the articulation of consonants and vowels is, in fact, a biological specialization is plainly shown by the inability of nonhuman primates to learn to produce even the simplest syllables. They can't do it, not because they are not smart enough, or because they lack the appropriate pieces of anatomy, but because, being other than human, they are not endowed with a phonetic module.

Turning now to perception, we see, on the conventional view, only the most general processes of the auditory modality, which is to say that perception of consonants and vowels is supposed to be no different from perception of other sounds. All use the same mode of signal analysis, and evoke in the same perceptual register the same set of auditory primitives. Thus, the difference in perception between a consonant and some non-speech sound is only in the particular mix of auditory primitives they comprise. They are made of the same perceptual stuff.

According to the unconventional theorist, on the other hand, the phonetic gestures are recovered in perception by the specialized phonetic module that controlled their production. Such a specialized process is necessary in order that proper account be taken of the specifically phonetic complications that coarticulation introduces into the relation between acoustic signal and the gestural message it conveys. Given that the message and the process that recovers it are both specific to phonetic communication, the resulting representation is specific to that kind of communication, too, which is to say that its modality is distinctly phonetic, not auditory.

There is one more important assumption of the conventional view, this one made necessary by the prior assumption that speech rests on motor and perceptual representations of some general sort. For it falls to anyone who holds that speech is supported in that way to explain how its initially nonphonetic representations are invested with phonetic significance, and so made appropriate for linguistic communication. The conventional explanation is that this is done at a cognitive stage, beyond action and perception, where the very ordinary motor and auditory representations are translated into units of a linguistic sort. There are various notions among the conventional theorists about exactly how that is done, but those seem to be distinctions without a difference, for they all come, necessarily, to the same thing: Speaker and listener must, in effect, attach phonetic labels to their respective nonphonetic acts and percepts; neither party can experience phonetic representations at the level of action and perception, because phonetic representations are not supposed to exist there.

The unconventional theory needs no such assumption as the one just described, because it takes the primary representations of speaker and listener to be immediately phonetic; they are precognitive acts and percepts, not cognitive afterthoughts.

THE IMPLICATIONS FOR READING AND WRITING

From what has so far been said about the two theories, it is clear that they see the relation of speech to reading/writing in drastically different ways. They must, of course, agree that reading/writing are not supported by a biological specialization at the level of act or percept—that is, in production or perception of the letters of the alphabet—and, accordingly, that the letters can take on linguistic significance only by virtue of being named after the consonants and vowels to which they have been arbitrarily assigned. Given that area of agreement between the theories, the critical difference hinges, then, on the clear implication of the more conventional theory that what is true of the link between signal and language in reading/writing must be true in speech, too: The primary acts and percepts of speech can be no more linguistic than those of reading/writing, and no less arbitrarily connected to language. Thus, the conventional view reduces the difference between speech and reading/writing to a matter of making or hearing sounds, in the one case, and drawing or seeing print, in the other.

On the unconventional theory, however, the difference between speech and reading/writing is profound. In contrast to the letters of the alphabet, the gestural representations that are the input to the phonetic module in production and its output in perception are, by their very nature, pieces of language, not arbitrary stand-ins. Accordingly, speaker and listener are immediately engaged in the language business in a way that writer and reader are not; the difference between making or hearing sounds, on the one hand, and drawing or seeing print, on the other—the only difference the conventional view allows—has precious little to do with the matter.

Consider, now, the implications of the contrasting views of speech for the questions we should answer if we would understand the reading process and the difficulties that some have with it.

ARE WRITING/READING HARD?

The answer given by the conventional view of speech is "not really"; no harder, certainly, than speech. That is, of course, exactly what the avatars of Whole Language take as their most fundamental premise (Goodman,

1986). Indeed, it may very well be the conventional theory of speech that initially emboldened them to promote a proposition that is so at odds with the most obvious facts, and so harmful to an understanding of how we ought to teach children to read. But then, if they had really thought hard about the implications of the conventional theory, they would have been led to the even worse conclusion, if that were possible, that reading and writing must be, not just as easy as speech, but significantly easier. For if, as the conventional view would have it, the difference is only that between sound-tongue-ear for speech and print-finger-eye for reading/writing, then reading/writing has the advantage on all counts.

Taking, first, the nature of the signal, one quickly sees the superiority of print. Typically, the printed characters are crisp and clear; the signal-to-noise ratio could hardly be better. The speech signal, on the other hand, leaves much to be desired from a physical point of view, if only because much of the acoustic information that is most important for phonologic purposes is least prominent acoustically. As for the effectors—fingers versus tongue—the fingers win, and by a wide margin. The moving finger writes, and having written, moves on to play Bach's Goldberg Variations or do brain surgery; in contrast, the moving tongue speaks, and having spoken, lapses into inactivity, except as it is occasionally called on to lick the lips or help in swallowing. Imagine fixing a stylus to your tongue and trying then to write your name. Turning finally to the receptors—the ear versus the eye—I simply note that, as a channel for transmission of information, the eye is better than the ear by several orders of magnitude. How, then, are we to understand why it is that speech is, by every conceivable measure, the easier? Indeed, if linguistic communication were as the conventional view of speech says it is, then our concerns would be the exact reverse of what they are: Having taken it for granted that reading and writing are dead easy, the members of this conference would be exchanging ideas about how to teach would-be speakers to overcome the difficulties caused by the evident limitations of tongue and ear, and what to do for those who can't manage. The unconventional view does not blink those shortcomings, but rather shows how speech, in a triumph of evolution over engineering, found ways around them. Special exertions by speaker and listener are not called for. What that means becomes clearer next, when we consider the requirements of phonological communication and how they are met.

WHAT IS HARD ABOUT WRITING AND READING?

Surely, we can't know how to teach children to read or write except as we understand what they have to learn and why the learning might not be easy. But, as we have seen, the conventional view of speech tells us that reading/writing should be even easier than speecn, which we already know to be quite easy, so the conventional view is not likely to be helpful at this very earliest stage of our inquiry. Let us, however, overlook that most unfortunate implication of the conventional view, and put our attention instead on what it reveals about the well-documented difficulty of grasping the alphabetic principle. For that purpose, we must digress a bit to consider the nature of phonological communication and the requirements it imposes.

Everyone understands that the function of the phonologic mode of communication is to generate an uncountably large number of words by variously combining and permuting the small number of meaningless segments we call consonants and vowels. That is the combinatorial principle that allows to language its property of openness or generativity, a property that is unique among natural communication systems; not surprisingly, then, it is the design feature that characterizes language at all levels. But if the principle is to work at the level of phonology, two requirements must be met. The more obvious is that the segments be commutable, which is to say discrete, invariant, and categorical. The possibly less obvious requirement derives from the fact that, if all utterances are to be formed by a small number of segments, then, inevitably, those segments will run to long strings, so it becomes essential that their production and perception be expeditious.

Now, on the conventional view, it is sounds and the ordinary auditory percepts they evoke that must have those critical properties, from which it follows that speech could only be an acoustic alphabet, offering a discrete, invariant, and categorical sound (and auditory percept) for each phonetic segment. Of course, the sounds would presumably be smoothed and connected at the places where they join, much as the shapes of cursive writing are, but, one way or another, there would have to be, for each segment, a commutable piece of sound. To produce such sounds, speakers would necessarily make a discrete articulatory gesture for each one, in which case they could not produce a syllable like "bag," but only the three syllables, "buh ah guh." If speech had to be like that, it would come nowhere near meeting the requirements for commutability and speed, so a communication system that was generative at the level of word formation would not be possible.

Nor would things be much better if a means could somehow be found to deliver the alphabetic sounds more rapidly, for that would surely defeat the ear. The point is that speakers normally produce phonetic segments at rates that average about 10 or 12 per second and, for short periods, run up to 20 or 25. Now, if each of those segments were represented by a discrete sound, as the conventional view says they must be, then rates that high would strain the temporal resolving power of the ear, and also overreach its ability to keep the order of the segments straight (Warren, 1993).

But even if we put all of the foregoing considerations aside, and assume that speech as portrayed by the conventional view could somehow be made to work, we are still not at all enlightened about why the alphabetic principle should not have been almost immediately apparent to those who lived before it was discovered, and why it is not equally apparent now to every normal child. All would have mastered a language that was conveyed, presumably, by an acoustic alphabet. Why, then, would they not already understand the alphabetic principle, and quickly learn to apply it in the visual modality simply by substituting the alphabetic letters for the correspondingly alphabetic sounds?

If the conventional view leaves us puzzled about why it is hard to be aware that words come apart, it does suggest why some teachers might misunderstand how they are put together. The misunderstanding manifests itself, and also begins to take its toll, when, having taught a child the "spelling-to-sound rules," the teacher urges the child to "blend"—that is, to form the alphabetic sounds, "buh, ah, and guh," for example, into the proper word *bag*. I cannot presume to know what is in the mind of teachers who try to get children to do that, but I suspect it is a resolution of the apparent conflict between what they believe about speech and what their ears tell them about how it sounds. With encouragement from the conventional view, they presumably believe that there are three sounds in *bag*, and that these are represented by the letters *b*, *a*, and *g*. However, I should think that these teachers would find it unsettling that they can't really hear three sounds, but rather something that is, from a purely auditory point of view, all of a piece. Perhaps, then, they suppose that the auditory appearances are deceiving, that the three sounds have been so thoroughly blended as to hide their individual identities. If so, then they are using the word *blend* in its correct sense to mean a combination in which the constituent parts are indistinguishable; but they are imagining a most unfortunate contingency, for blending would cause language to lose its vital phonologic core, with the result that the combinatorial principle would no longer be available to produce vocabularies that are large and expandable. In any case, it is physically and physiologically impossible to produce a word by blending, or otherwise combining, the discrete sounds that are taken to be its individual phonetic constituents. So while *blend* is the right word, it is the wrong idea.

I do not mean to suggest that implying to a child that *bag* is a blend of three sounds is necessarily to court failure in reading and writing. It is rather to tell a white lie, and is better by far than characterizing the printed word as a picture, or advising the child to guess what the print says. Learning letter-to-sound correspondences and trying, on that basis, to "sound out" words is likely, at least, to help bring the child to the correct understanding that words come apart, and that the alphabet has something to do with the parts. The error is in the belief that the parts are sounds. Most, but obviously not all, children who are taught that error manage somehow to rise above it, and so learn to read and write. Still, things would almost certainly go better if they were acquainted with the true state of affairs.

In contrast to the conventional theory, the unconventional account of these matters shows how phonological communication is possible, and, by the same token, why the alphabetic principle is hard to grasp. Remember that speakers are able to produce strings of phonetic segments at high rates, but only because the segments are gestures that are efficiently overlapped and merged. By that means, the speaker succeeds in producing phonologic structures that effectively "spell" the words they convey. But there are several reasons why the illiterate or preliterate speaker nevertheless does not know how to spell, or even that words have a spelling. Perhaps the most obvious is that the phonetic module spells for the speakers. Once they have thought of the word, whatever that means, the phonetic module takes over, automatically selecting and coordinating the appropriate gestures. The speaker cannot know how the module did what it did, because it is true of all biological modules that their processes are not available to conscious inspection. On the other hand, speakers *can* be aware of the representations the phonetic module deals with; but there is no reason they should be, because being inherently phonetic, the motor structures that are represented do not require translation, so they do not invite attention. And, finally, it is probably relevant that the mechanisms of articulation and coarticulation produce smoothed and context-sensitive movements at the surface, and so obscure the exact nature of the distal motor structures that are the actual phonetic units.

The relevant considerations are much the same in perception. There, coarticulation has allowed information about several successive segments to be conveyed simultaneously in the acoustic signal, and so relaxed the constraint on rate of perception imposed by the temporal resolving power of the ear. Listeners can, therefore, keep up with the speaker, but only because their phonetic modules are specialized to process the acoustic signal so as to extract the coarticulated gestures that produced its uniquely phonetic complications. A consequence is that the listener is likely to lack phonologic awareness for much the same reasons that keep a speaker in the dark. Although the signal is, in fact, parsed into its phonetic constituents, the listener is none the wiser, because the module runs on automatic in perception just as it does in production. Deliberate, cognitive procedures are never necessary to do the job. Indeed, the job cannot be done cognitively, because the complexities of the speech code are apparently too great, too special to language, and too deep in our biology; certainly, no one has succeeded yet, though, given the intense and long-continued efforts to build an automatic speech recognizer, we know it is not for want of trying.

As for the representations that are the result of the module's efforts, they are already phonetic, as I've said so many times, hence perfectly appropriate for all further linguistic processing. Therefore, the listener does not have to give them the attention they would require if, like the letters of the alphabet, they had to be translated into pieces of language. Finally, coarticulation has destroyed anything that remotely resembles a straightforward relation between the segments of the phonetic message and such segments as can be found in the acoustic signal. A consequence is that the consonants, at least, have never in the listener's experience been isolated and pointed to, as words, for example, commonly are. Surely, that is one reason why preliterate children are more likely to be aware of words than of the phonologic segments that form them. None of this is to say that listeners cannot be aware of the phonologic constituents of words—indeed, if they could not, the use of alphabetic transcriptions would be impossible—only that the unconventional view shows us why such awareness does not come for free with mastery of speech.

WHAT LINKS WRITING TO READING AND SPEAKING TO LISTENING?

In linguistic communication, where every sender is a receiver and every receiver a sender, the processes of production and perception must somehow be linked. Mattingly and I called this the "requirement for parity," and wondered how it is met (Liberman, 1996; Liberman & Mattingly, 1989).

In reading/writing, parity cannot be said to rest on a primary biological base, but must rather have been established by agreement. Somehow, those who developed an alphabet arrived at a compact that specified which optical shapes were relevant to language, and which piece of language each was relevant to. A result is that learning to read and write is largely a matter of mastering the arbitrary terms of that compact, and, for all the reasons the unconventional view has revealed, that is rather hard, and commonly requires help from a tutor.

In the matter of parity, as in all things, the conventional view of speech implies that as it is in reading/writing, so must it be in speech, in which case learning speech has got to be just like learning to read and write. Thus here again we find in the conventional view of speech full justification for one of the fundamental, and fundamentally wrong, assumptions of Whole Language—namely, that children should learn to read as they learned to speak, which is to say that the educational process should be geared to provide conditions just like those under which speech was acquired; children need not, and should not, be taught to analyze the language as linguists do (Goodman, 1986).

The unconventional view, on the other hand, claims that parity in speech does not derive from a compact of some kind, but rather reflects a fundamental aspect of our biology. Parity is exactly what evolved: The necessary link between production and perception is given immediately by the genetically determined phonetic module, which provides that the specifically phonetic motor structure in the mind of the speaker is reproduced in the mind of the listener; there is no need for the two parties to connect grossly dissimilar but equally nonphonetic acts and percepts that were, like the letters of the alphabet, selected by earlier generations and then arbitrarily assigned to phonetic categories. Thus, the phonetic module makes for a deep and immediate intimacy between speaker and listener, an intimacy as necessary for linguistic communication as that which sex affords is necessary for reproduction. An important difference, of course, is that the one proceeds from parity, whereas it is disparity that lies at the root of the other. But an equally important similarity is that both kinds of intimacy are the products of co-evolution, since the two sides of the connection had, in each case, to develop in step, change for change, else neither system could ever have become functional.

Although parity in speech is part of its underlying biology, it does not follow that speech is not learned, only that it need not be taught. For surely, the necessary and sufficient conditions for learning speech are but two: membership in the human race, and exposure to a mother tongue. To get an idea of the nature of that kind of learning, it is helpful, I think, to see the phonetic module as one of a class of modules that have certain characteristics in common (Liberman, & Mattingly, 1989). One of those is plasticity over periods of time during which the module is shaped by environmental conditions. An example is the module for sound localization, which responds to interaural differences of time and intensity, using them as a basis for computing and then representing location in azimuth. Of course, those interaural differences change considerably as the head grows, and the distance between the ears increases, so the module must be continuously recalibrated. One might reasonably suppose that, in a somewhat similar way, the biologically coherent phonetic module is calibrated over several years by the phonetic environment in which it finds itself. In that case, the obvious effect of experience on speech would be to shape or hone a genetically determined system, not, as in the case of reading/writing, to provide the basis for acquiring arbitrary connections by processes of a cognitive sort. Given a normal environment, speech "emerges," in the terminology of Whole Language, but reading and writing most certainly do not. Thus, the unconventional view permits us to see that learning to speak and learning to read or write are fundamentally different processes.

IMPLICATIONS FOR READING DISABILITY

Accepting the conventional view of speech, the reading/writer researchers must believe, as I earlier said, that the phonologic segments are plainly displayed on the auditory surface, there for all to hear. Accordingly, such researchers have no way to see why it should be hard to be aware of those segments, and so to grasp the alphabetic principle. They can hardly be expected, then, to look to that difficulty for the causes of reading/writing disability, and indeed, they do not. Rather, they look where the conventional view most directly tells them to, which is at some aspect of the visual system. That system is the seemingly most promising target, because the substitution of eye for ear is virtually the only important difference between speech and reading/writing that the conventional view allows. So if reading proves to be hard, then it must be that some aspect of vision is at fault. Small wonder, then, that one or another aspect of visual function is the place where many of the theories of disability locate the problem (Geiger & Lettvin, 1988; Orton, 1937; Pavlides, 1985; Stein, Riddell, & Fowler, 1988).

At the same time, the conventional view permits, if it does not actually encourage, the belief that the problem might be with the ear. That belief begins with the conventional assumption that speech is a string of brief sounds that follow each other in rapid succession. The problem, then, is that the auditory system of some children can't keep up. As a consequence, they have language problems, from which reading problems follow (Tallal, 1980). Now, if speech were a string of acoustic segments, one for each phonologic segment, then it would be true that the relevant sounds would, indeed, be very brief, and would follow each other in rapid succession—so brief and in such rapid succession that, as I earlier pointed out, sound segments would come along at rates between 10 and 25 per second. It is also true, as I said in the same context, that rates that high would strain the ability of everybody's auditory system, not just those of some unfortunate children. Fortunately, speech does not require people to do what their ears do poorly, which takes us now to the unconventional view and its radically different implications for how we might see disability in reading/writing.

Let us consider first the theory about disability to which I just alluded. On the unconventional view of speech, the known limitation on ability to perceive the order of brief sounds presented rapidly and in series is irrelevant to speech perception, because phonetic segments are not sounds, and speech is not a string of them. The unconventional view tells us that the true phonetic elements are gestures, and that their coarticulation smears the information for each one over a considerable stretch of the acoustic signal, overlapping it grossly with information for other segments. One important consequence is that ordinal position is marked, not by the temporal order of the sounds, but by their acoustic shapes. Thus, the syllables *ba* and *ab*, when pronounced briefly, have acoustic patterns in which information about consonant and vowel are completely overlapped. Accordingly, there are not two acoustic segments—one for each phoneme—hence no way to perceive which came first by paying attention to the way sounds succeed each other in time. Nevertheless, the listener infallibly knows which came first and which second because the acoustic shapes of the two syllables are very different. In that case, indeed they are exact mirror images. Given the services of the phonetic module, which are always at the disposal of the listener, the one shape is perceived as an opening gesture (consonant first, vowel second), the other as a closing gesture (vowel first, consonant second).

Having just seen what the unconventional view says is not true of speech, and therefore of a theory that locates the cause of reading/writing disability in the ear, I turn now to what it says is true, and how that gives us an entirely different slant on the probable causes of failure. We earlier saw how the unconventional view shows that learning to speak, however fluently, will not be sufficient to produce awareness of phonologic structure. Acting on precisely that consideration, Isabelle Liberman, Donald Shankweiler, Ignatius Mattingly, and their colleagues began the line of thought that led them to find that phonologic awareness is, in fact, largely absent in preliterate children (Liberman, 1973; Liberman, Shankweiler, Fischer, & Carter, 1974; Mattingly, 1972a, 1972b). Subsequent research by them and others amply confirmed that finding, while also establishing that the extent to which awareness is present counts as one of the best predictors of success in reading/writing (for reviews, see Blachman, 1989; Routh & Fox, 1984), and that training in awareness has generally happy consequences for those who get it (Ball & Blachman, 1988; Bradley & Bryant, 1983; Content, Kolinsky, Morais, & Bertelson, 1986; Lundberg, Frost, & Peterson, 1988; Olofsson & Lundberg, 1983; Vellutino & Scanlon, 1987).

Proceeding further with the implications of the unconventional view, researchers picked up on its assumption that there is a distinct phonological faculty—I have here called it a *phonetic module*—that is independent of cognition and, indeed, of all other-than-linguistic modes of production and perception. They found it reasonable to suppose that if such a faculty exists—though the conventional view provides no place for it—then it might work more or less well among otherwise normal children, with the result that there would be differences in the ease with which they would learn to read and write (Brady, 1991; Liberman, 1992; Liberman & Liberman, 1990; Liberman, Shankweiler, & Liberman, 1989). Most obviously, the effect would be on the general quality or clarity of the phonologic representations, which would, in turn, affect the child's ability to become aware of them, and so to comprehend and apply the alphabetic principle. One would expect, too, an effect on the phonologic basis of the working memory that is an integral part of syntactic processing, and therefore on the child's ability to comprehend at the level of the sentence. Indeed, everything about language or reading/writing that depends on phonologic structures and processes would presumably be affected in some way. Exactly how, and with what consequences, are questions that motivate the research our colleagues are now actively pursuing. What is reasonably clear at this point is only that the leads afforded by the unconventional view are promising, and that the relevant research on the role of specifically phonologic processes is nearer its beginning than its end. It is very hard, I think, to see how we should ever have arrived at that beginning if researchers had remained true to the conventional view of speech. On the other hand, the hypothesis that phonologic factors deserve careful attention is now common enough that researchers may have lost sight of what the unconventional view of speech had to do with it.

REFERENCES

Ball, E. W., & Blachman, B. A. (1988). Phoneme segmentation training: Effect on reading readiness. *Annals of Dyslexia, 38,* 208–225.

Blachman, B. A. (1989). Phonological awareness and word recognition: Assessment and intervention. In A. G. Kamhi and H. W. Catts (Eds.), *Reading disorder: A developmental language perspective* (pp. 133–158). San Diego: College-Hill Press.

Bradley, L., & Bryant, P. E. (1983). Categorizing sounds and learning to read: A causal connection. *Nature, 301,* 419–421.

Brady, S. A. (1991). The role of working memory in reading disability. In S. A. Brady & D. P. Shankweiler (Eds.), *Phonological processes in literacy: A tribute to Isabelle Y. Liberman* (pp. 129–151). Hillsdale, NJ: Lawrence Erlbaum Associates.

Content, A., Kolinsky, R., Morais, J., & Bertelson, P. (1986). Phonetic segmentation in pre-readers: Effects of corrective information. *Journal of Experimental Child Psychology, 42,* 49–72.

Crowder, R. G. (1983). The purity of auditory memory. *Philosophical Transactions of the Royal Society of London, B302,* 251–265.

Diehl, R. L., & Kluender, K. R. (1989a). On the categorization of speech sounds. In S. Harnad (Ed.), *Categorical perception* (pp. 226–253). Cambridge, England: Cambridge University Press.

Diehl, R. L., & Kluender, K. R. (1989b). On the objects of speech perception. *Ecological Psychology, 1,* 121–144.

Diehl, R. L., & Kluender, K. R. (1989c). Reply to commentators. *Ecological Psychology, 1*(2), 195–225.

Fujisaki, H., & Kawashima, T. (1970). Some experiments on speech perception and a model for the perceptual mechanism. In *Annual Report of the Engineering Research Institute* (Vol. 29, pp. 207–214). Tokyo: Faculty of Engineering, University of Tokyo.

Geiger, G., & Lettvin, J. Y. (1988). Dyslexia and reading as examples of alternative visual strategies. In C. von Euler, I. Lundberg, & G. Lennerstrand (Eds.), *Brain and reading (Wenner-Gren Symposium Series 54)* . New York: Macmillan.

Goodman, K. S. (1986). *What's whole in whole language: A parent–teacher guide.* Portsmouth, NH: Heinemann.

Kuhl, P. K. (1981). Discrimination of speech by nonhuman animals: Basic auditory sensitivities conducive to the perception of speech-sound categories. *Journal of the Acoustical Society of America, 70*, 340–349.

Liberman, A. M. (1992). The relation of speech to reading and writing. In R. Frost & L. Katz (Eds.), *Orthography, phonology, morphology, and meaning* (pp. 167–178). Amsterdam: Elsevier Science Publishers B.V.

Liberman, A. M. (1996). *Speech: A special code.* Cambridge, MA: MIT Press.

Liberman, A. M., & Mattingly, I. G. (1985). The motor theory of speech perception revised. *Cognition, 21*, 1–36.

Liberman, A. M., & Mattingly, I. G. (1989). A specialization for speech perception. *Science, 243*, 489–494.

Liberman, I. Y. (1973). Segmentation of the spoken word and reading acquisition. *Haskins Laboratories Status Report on Speech Research, SR33*, 157–166.

Liberman, I. Y., & Liberman, A. M. (1990). Whole language vs. code emphasis: Underlying assumptions and their implications for reading instruction. *Annals of Dyslexia, 40*, 51–76.

Liberman, I. Y., Shankweiler, D. P., Fischer, F. W., & Carter, B. J. (1974). Explicit syllable and phoneme segmentation in the young child. *Journal of Experimental Child Psychology, 18*, 201–212.

Liberman, I. Y., Shankweiler, D., & Liberman, A. M. (1989). The alphabetic principle and learning to read. In D. Shankweiler & I. Y. Liberman (Eds.), *Phonology and reading disability: Solving the reading puzzle* (IARLD Research Monograph Series). Ann Arbor: University of Michigan Press.

Lindblom, B. (1991). The status of phonetic gestures. In I. G. Mattingly & M. Studdert-Kennedy (Eds.), *Modularity and the Motor Theory of speech perception* (pp. 7–24). Hillsdale, NJ: Lawrence Erlbaum Associates.

Lundberg, I., Frost, J., & Peterson, O.-P. (1988). Effects of an extensive program for stimulating phonological awareness in preschool children. *Reading Research Quarterly, 23*, 263–284.

Mann, V. A., & Liberman, A. M. (1983). Some differences between phonetic and auditory modes of perception. *Cognition, 14*, 211–235.

Massaro, D. W. (1987a). Psychophysics versus specialized processes in speech perception: An alternative perspective. In M. E. H. Schouten (Ed.), *The psychophysics of speech perception* (pp. 46–65). Boston: Nijhoff.

Massaro, D. W. (1987b). *Speech perception by ear and eye: A paradigm for psychological inquiry.* Hillsdale, NJ: Lawrence Erlbaum Associates.

Mattingly, I. G. (1972a). *Reading, the linguistic process, and linguistic awareness.* Cambridge, MA: MIT Press.

Mattingly, I. G. (1972b). Speech cues and sign stimuli: An ethological view of speech perception and the origin of language. *Amer Scientist, 60*(3), 327–337.

Mattingly, I. G., & Liberman, A. M. (1990). Speech and other auditory modules. In G. M. Edelman, W. E. Gall, & W. M. Cowan (Eds.), *Signal and sense: Local and global order in perceptual maps* (pp. 501–519). New York: Wiley.

Olofsson, A., & Lundberg, I. (1983). Can phonemic awareness be trained in kindergarten? *Scandinavian Journal of Psychology, 24*, 35–44.

Orton, S. T. (1937). *Reading, writing and speech problems in children.* New York: Norton.

Pavlides, G. T. (1985). Eye movement differences between dyslexics, normal, and retarded readers while sequentially fixating digits. *American Journal of Opto and Physiological Optics, 62*, 820–832.

Remez, R. E., Rubin, P. E., Berns, S. M., Pardo, J. S., & Lang, J. M. (1994). On the perceptual organization of speech. *Psychological Review, 101*, 129–156.

Routh, P. K., & Fox, B. (1984). M . . . m is a little bit of May: Phonemes, reading and spelling. In N. D. Gadow & P. Bralen (Eds.), *Advances in learning and behavioral disabilities .* Greenwich, CT: JAI Press.

Stein, J., Riddell, P., & Fowler, S. (1988). Disordered right hemisphere function in developmental dyslexia. In C. v. Euler, I. Lundberg & G. Lennerstrand (Eds.), *Brain and Reading.* New York: Macmillan.

Stevens, K. N., & Blumstein, S. E. (1978). Invariant cues for place of articulation in stop consonants. *Journal of the Acoustical Society of America, 64*, 1358–1368.

Sussman, H. (1989). Neural coding of relational invariance in speech perception: Human language analogs to the barn owl. *Psychological Review, 96*, 631–42.

Tallal, P. (1980). Auditory temporal perception, phonics, and reading disabilities in children. *Brain and Language, 9*, 182–198.

Vellutino, F. R., & Scanlon, D. (1987). Phonological coding, phonological awareness, and reading ability: Evidence from a longitudinal and experimental study. *Merrill-Palmer Quarterly, 33*, 321–363.

Warren, R. M. (1993). Perception of acoustic sequences: Global integration versus temporal resolution. In S. McAdams & E. Bigand (Eds.), *Thinking in sound.* Oxford, England: Oxford University Press.

Whalen, D. H., & Liberman, A. M. (1987). Speech perception takes precedence over nonspeech perception. *Science, 237*, 169–171.

2

Ability to Encode Phonological Representations: An Underlying Difficulty of Poor Readers

Susan Amanda Brady
University of Rhode Island and Haskins Laboratories

Numerous phonological deficits are associated with reading disability. As the literature attests, poor readers have been documented to have difficulties on measures of metaphonological awareness and on several other phonological processes, such as verbal short-term memory and rapid naming (e.g., Brady & Shankweiler, 1991; Gough, Ehri, & Treiman, 1992; Wagner & Torgesen, 1987). This chapter entertains the possibility that many of these language weaknesses stem from deficits in a more basic phonological process—ability to encode phonological representations. In the first section, two relevant experimental procedures are discussed: categorical perception, because it fairly directly assesses phonological encoding, and pseudorepetition, because it incorporates many phonological processes, including encoding, and emerges as a powerful correlate of reading ability. Here the evidence linking each of these to individual differences in reading skill are reviewed, and the argument is made that the common demands of speech perception contribute to the difficulties poor readers encounter on both.

The second portion of the chapter critiques, and rejects, a hypothesis that a more general auditory problem causes the phonological deficits of poor readers. In the final section of the chapter, I discuss one of the mechanisms by which speech perception can exert influence on early reading; namely, through phoneme awareness.

RESEARCH ON SPEECH PERCEPTION
AND READING ABILITY

The phonological basis of skilled reading, and the associated phonological deficits seen in disabled readers, have prompted theorists to posit a core phonological process that could account for a variety of commonly observed correlates with reading performance (Brady, 1991; Fowler & Liberman, 1995; Liberman & Shankweiler, 1979; Shankweiler & Crain, 1986). There are a number of reasons to consider speech perception, the initial encoding of linguistic input, as a plausible candidate. For example, the range of success children experience in acquiring phoneme awareness could derive from the quality of perception of speech sounds: If the phonemic categories are less well defined or are broader for children having difficulty learning to read than for the better readers, discovery of the phonemic elements in words might be more elusive (e.g., Fowler, 1991). Second, the host of associated phonological deficits experienced by less skilled readers on measures of verbal short-term memory, vocabulary acquisition, and confrontation naming also could be viewed as compatible with problems encoding speech stimuli. In verbal memory, inefficient or inaccurate formation of phonological representations might limit resources available for recall or might result in a less durable memory trace. This, in turn, could impede reading by disrupting decoding and comprehension of text (for discussion see Perfetti, 1985; Shankweiler, 1989). For learning new words, if the phonological form of new items tends to be imprecise or unstable, more extensive exposure might be necessary to retain accurate representations of lexical items (Aguiar & Brady, 1991; Kamhi, Catts, & Mauer, 1990). Likewise, the problems reported on productive naming tasks for poor readers could be a by-product of the same difficulty establishing fully specified phonemic representations of words: If the input for the word is faulty in some way, subsequent production of that lexical item could in turn be hampered by the quality of the representation (Elbro, in press). In brief, deficits at the level of phonological encoding could have repercussions throughout the language system, contributing to the range of language weaknesses documented for less skilled readers.

Categorical Perception

When interest in the speech perception abilities of poor readers emerged, categorical perception tasks were thought to be an ideal way to examine whether deficits were present. In this paradigm, a speech continuum is constructed, changing in equal acoustic steps from one phoneme to another (e.g., a nine-step continuum from /ba/ to /pa/). Identification and discrimination measures are conducted, using stimuli from the continuum. In the identification portion, subjects are asked to identify randomized items from the continuum with each stimulus presented multiple times throughout the task. The stereotypic identification function has identification perfect within categories and sharply switching at the phoneme boundary. In the discrimination measure, pairs of stimuli are presented, usually at a fixed distance on the continuum (e.g., Items 1 and 3, 2 and 4, 3 and 5), and listeners are asked to judge whether they are the same or different. Discrimination in categorical perception shows an inverse pattern to identification performance: Subjects are very poor at noting the differences between variants within a phoneme category, but quite sensitive to comparable acoustic differences across a phoneme boundary. This phenomenon, first studied with normal adults, contrasted with the typical observation of continuous perception[1] with nonspeech stimuli, and was initially thought to be unique to speech processing (Liberman, Cooper, Shankweiler, & Studdert-Kennedy, 1967; Studdert-Kennedy, Liberman, Harris, & Cooper, 1970). Although subsequent research on perception of nonlinguistic stimuli has undermined that claim, nonetheless categorical perception is characteristic of speech, and categorical perception tasks have been useful for studying processes of speech perception (see Repp, 1984, for a review).

The nature of the categorical perception task seemed a promising technique to explore whether poor readers have differences in their phoneme categories: For example, would the phoneme boundaries of poor readers suggest broader, less well-defined categories? The relative normalcy of poor readers in ordinary speaking and listening suggested that, if present, deficits in speech perception would necessarily be slight. In the first study to examine this question, Brandt and Rosen (1980) tested dyslexic children, and normal children and adults, on /ba/–/da/ and /da/–/ga/ continua. Focusing mainly on the phoneme boundaries on the identification tasks, Brandt and Rosen reported that the groups performed comparably. They concluded that dyslexic children have normal consonant categories and were inclined to discount the potential importance of speech perception in reading ability. A number of subsequent researchers investigating this same question disagreed with Brandt and Rosen's conclusion, although they did not dispute the results discussed in Brandt and Rosen's paper. A second study by Godfrey, Syrdal-Lasky, Millay, and Knox (1981) confirmed a lack of difference in phoneme boundaries for stimuli from /ba/–/da/ and /da/–/ga/ continua and a predictable correspondence between identification and

---

[1]For example, given a color spectrum with fine gradations of shade, subjects may divide the series reliably into discrete categories (e.g., purple, blue, green), but still be able to distinguish items within a category (e.g., a more purplish blue from a greener blue).

discrimination tasks (i.e., discrimination peaks at the identification boundaries). Nonetheless, these authors suggested that dyslexic and normal children do differ in important aspects of their speech perform-ance. In particular, they reported a significant difference in consistency of labeling of the stimuli, even for the best exemplars (i.e., the endpoint stimuli in the continua), resulting in a more gradual slope near the phoneme boundary. In addition, significant effects were obtained on the discrimination measures, with the dyslexic subjects not only discriminat-ing true variation between the stimuli more poorly than the controls, but also reporting identical stimuli to be different more often. Although Brandt and Rosen didn't make statistical comparisons of these aspects of identification and discrimination performance, Godfrey et al. and later Werker and Tees (1987) both commented that the descriptive data from Brandt and Rosen's report looked similar to the (significant) outcomes in their experiments.

Subsequent studies have confirmed that less skilled readers apply normal category boundaries when labeling speech stimuli. Only occa-sional reports of differences in phoneme boundaries were noted by Steffens, Eilers, Gross-Glenn, and Jallad (1992) on one of three speech continua given to dyslexic adults, and by deWierdt (1988) with a group of prereaders who later emerged as poor readers. At the same time, several studies also found that the identification and/or discrimination of speech tends to be less accurate among poor readers (de Weirdt, 1988; Hurford, Gilliland, & Ginavan, 1992; Hurford & Sanders, 1990; Lieberman, Meskill, Chatillon, & Schupack, 1985; Manis, McBride, Seidenberg, Doi, & Custodio, 1993; Mody, Studdert-Kennedy, & Brady, in press; Pallay, 1986; Reed, 1989; Steffens et al., 1992; Werker & Tees, 1987).[2] However, the particular task or stimulus characteristics yielding these differences are not always consistent. For example, whereas Godfrey et al. (1981) obtained significant reading group effects on both identification and discrimination tasks, poor readers studied by Werker and Tees (1987) were less accurate only on discrimination.

Although reading group differences in speech perception have most frequently been studied and obtained using synthetic stop contrasts such as /ba/–/da/ or /da/–/ga/, significant group effects are not restricted to this class of phonemes. Extending the affected stimuli beyond stop

---

[2]To pinpoint reading-group differences in speech perception, it is important to note that, even for apparently simple speech perception tasks, accuracy may be influenced by the nature of the response required. In an interesting within-subjects comparison of 10 adult dyslexics, Lieberman et al. (1985) reported that the error rate went from 26.5% to 42.5% when, instead of saying which stop consonant they had heard, subjects were asked to write down their responses. This outcome raises concerns about the interpretation of studies that have relied on orthographic skills for subjects' identification responses (Manis et al., 1993; McBride-Chang, 1995).

contrasts, Lieberman et al. (1985) documented that dyslexic adults differed significantly on perception of phonetically similar, synthetic steady-state vowels (but see Steffens et al., 1992). Other synthetic speech contrasts such as /sa/–/sta/ (Steffens et al., 1992) have also yielded reading ability effects on identification or discrimination tasks (however, see Mody et al., in press, for lack of effect for /seI/–/steI/ ("say/stay")). Even with natural speech stimuli that convey more of the redundant acoustic information specifying phonemic identity, reading-group differences in speech perception are often evident when close phonetic distinctions differentiate a phonological contrast, especially under somewhat demanding speech recognition conditions. For example, using natural speech, deficits in discrimination performance by reading-disabled children were found on both stop consonant (/di/–/gi/) and on liquid (/ri/–/li/) pairs of stimuli (Hurford et al., 1992). Lieberman et al. (1985) also found less skilled readers to be less able to recognize consonant-vowel-consonant utterances excised from the presumably crude speech of 1½-year-old children.

The fact that reading-disabled individuals find close phonetic judgments difficult across such a variety of contrasts suggests that there is not a particular aspect of the acoustic requirements of speech signal processing that is the source of difficulty. Poor readers have been stymied for diverse kinds of stimuli manipulations: when the direction of the second and third formant transitions was altered for voiced stop consonant stimuli (e.g., Godfrey et al., 1981), when presented with vowel stimuli using different steady-state frequency levels for the first and second formants (Lieberman et al., 1985), and when a /sa/–/sta/ continuum was achieved by changing the amount of silence inserted between the offset of the /s/ and the onset of the /a/ (Steffens et al., 1992). It appears that the only common requirement for detecting subtle reading-group differences in perceptual ability is the need to use phonetically similar stimuli, and poor readers are hindered more if the stimuli are composed of minimal or degraded cues. Some authors, using multiple sets of speech stimuli, commented that if one of the contrasts were harder overall, then reading-group differences in perception between good and poor readers were more apparent for that contrast (e.g., Godfrey et al., 1981).

However, it does not seem that the large numbers of trials presented in the usual categorical perception study are always essential. Categorical perception studies, as described previously, routinely use multiple tokens of each item or pair in the continuum resulting in a task that, particularly for young children, is no doubt tedious. For example, Godfrey et al. (1981) administered 96 identification trials and 120 discrimination trials. The fact that reading group differences are evident on the endpoint stimuli, as discussed, rather than at the crossover point, suggests that future studies of speech perception might rely on endpoint stimuli, as long as a close phonetic contrast with demanding stimuli (e.g., synthetic stimuli, infant speech) is employed. This conclusion is supported by occasional reports of group differences in how long children take to reach criterion on an introductory task using only endpoint stimuli (in order to ensure that the children understand the procedure and can reliably perceive the phonetic contrast under study). For example, in the Godfrey et al. (1981) study, all of the control participants were able to pass the initial criterion tests, whereas 47% of the dyslexic children required more practice to label the stimuli appropriately or were unable to reach a satisfactory level of performance to go on to the remainder of the experiment. Likewise, Mody et al. (in press) reported that their less skilled readers performed significantly worse on the training tasks for both the discrimination and identification training. In the study by deWierdt (1988), younger children (first graders) also had more difficulty on the training component. Such observations underscore that the problems with perception are not restricted to perceiving ambiguous stimuli near a phoneme boundary; they also occur for unambiguous but phonetically similar items.

Finally, the issue of top-down effects on speech perception needs to be considered. When reading-disabled children experience uncertainty about the identity of speech stimuli, they may draw more heavily on lexical information. Most of the studies on categorical perception have used nonsense syllable contrasts, thereby minimizing this issue. To examine whether reading-group differences in lexical effects might be present, Reed (1989) designed a pair of stimuli continua. The two continua both went from /b/ to /d/. In one, the /b/-end of the series was a real word (*bop*) and the /d/-end was not (*dop*). In the second, the /b/-end was nonsense (*bodge*) and the /d/-end was a real word (*dodge*). If top-down effects were influencing perception of these CVC stimuli, the phoneme boundary would differ in the two series. That is, the lexical attribute of the real words would compensate for ambiguous acoustic input near the crossover point, leading to more stimuli being identified as the real word in each continuum. By comparing differences in the phoneme boundaries for the two continua, Reed calculated an estimate of the potential top-down effects on speech perception. The good readers, like normal adults (Ganong, 1980), were not influenced by the presence of lexical anchors in the stimuli series. In contrast, significant shifts in the phoneme boundaries were seen for the poor readers. These results are similar to those of Perfetti and Roth (1981) in research examining the reading strategies of good and poor readers: Poor readers, when struggling to decode words, compensated for weak bottom-up ability to analyze the phonetic representation of written words by guessing based on the context. Good readers, although in fact better at contextual prediction, were so accurate and fast at decoding that contextual information made little difference in their reading performance. The Reed results indicate that such compensatory reliance on world (and word) knowledge may also be a factor in ordinary speech perception for childen with reading difficulties.

In sum, the categorical perception procedure has had mixed results. The initial hypothesis that the boundaries of the phonetic space of good and poor readers would reveal differences has not been supported: By and large, poor readers appear to have comparable boundaries and normal phonemic categories. However, other differences in performance on speech perception tasks have been documented for poor readers ranging in age from elementary years (e.g., Godfrey et al., 1981; Werker & Tees, 1987) to adulthood (e.g., Lieberman et al., 1985). Specifically, a number of studies have found that poor readers perform less accurately on perception measures when phonetically similar stimuli are presented, particularly if the phonetic specifications for the stimuli are somewhat impoverished. Although the reading group differences don't appear to be distinct enough to be useful for diagnostic purposes, the collective pattern of these studies points to less precise identification and discrimination of speech by individuals with reading disability.

Speech Repetition

The second major means of examining the ability to encode phonetic stimuli is speech repetition. For this task the participant is asked to repeat speech stimuli immediately after each item is heard. Both real-word and pseudoword stimuli have been used. Those studies using words have generally not obtained reading group differences when high-frequency, one-syllable words were used (e.g., Lieberman et al., 1985). Presenting such items in noise has sometimes lowered the performance of poor readers significantly more than it has that of better readers (Brady, Shankweiler, & Mann, 1983; Watson & Miller, 1993), although this pattern does not appear to be reliable (Cornelissen, Hansen, Bradley, & Stein, 1996; Kamhi, Catts, Mauer, Apel, & Gentry, 1988; Pennington, Van Orden, Smith, Green, & Haith, 1990; Snowling, Goulandris, Bowlby, & Howell, 1986). On the other hand, manipulating the phonological demands by increasing the length of the words (e.g., *agriculture*) or the phonemic similarity of short phrases to be repeated (e.g., *blue plaid pants*) does result in significantly less accurate repetition by less skilled readers (e.g., Brady, Poggie, & Rapala, 1989; Catts, 1986, 1989; Rapala & Brady, 1990), mirroring clinical observations that individuals with reading difficulty are more apt to misproduce long, phonologically complex words such as *statistical* or *preliminary* (Johnson, 1980; Miles, 1974; Taylor, Fletcher, & Satz, 1982).

Reading-group differences have been more robust when pseudoword stimuli (e.g., *ponverlation*) have been used. Pseudowords, also referred to as nonwords,[3] generally have been constructed by taking real words and substituting one or more phonemes to produce a nonword that has a phonological sequence and intonation pattern that conforms with English phonology. Snowling (1981) was among the first to emphasize the greater difficulty that poor readers have with nonlexical stimuli. Similarly, Brady et al. (1989) reported that 21% of the variance between their groups of good and poor readers was accounted for by performance on a monosyllabic pseudoword repetition task, whereas only 14% was accounted for by the multisyllabic real-word task. In recent years the evidence for reading-group differences on pseudoword repetition has been mounting. In several additional studies of elementary school children, those with reading difficulty have been documented to do less well than same-age peers for repetition of pseudowords or of lexical items with which they were not familiar (Aguiar, 1993; Futransky, 1992; Hansen & Bowey, 1994; Kamhi et al., 1988; Rapala & Brady, 1990; Snowling et al., 1986; Stone & Brady, 1995; Taylor, Lean, & Schwartz, 1989). Weaknesses in pseudoword repetition also characterized 4-year-old children who subsequently were making slower progress in learning to read (Gathercole, 1995). Likewise, inner-city kindergarten children (Robertson, 1997) had less accurate pseudoword repetition both in kindergarten and in first grade, and were also doing less well at reading acquisition, than were middle-class children. The reading group differences hold up in older subjects as well, although in order to avoid ceiling effects both for skilled and less skilled readers it appears the stimuli need to be made increasingly long and complex. For example, using polysyllabic pseudowords that were three to eight syllables long, a study with college students also reported significantly worse accuracy on a repetition task by a group of learning-disabled students, the majority of whom had reading or spelling difficulty (Apthorp, 1995).

Even more convincing, a number of studies have reported that less skilled readers are less accurate at pseudoword repetition than younger, reading-age-matched children (Stone & Brady, 1995; Taylor, Lean, & Schwartz, 1989; see also discussion of Snowling et al., 1986, later in this chapter). Furthermore, various statistical analyses indicate a noteworthy association with reading performance. In Stone and Brady (1995), pseudoword repetition was one of several other basic phonological measures, including verbal memory span, verbal working memory, multiple productions of words and of tongue twisters (e.g., saying "bublu" 10

---

[3]Although the label "nonword" is shorter and correct in that the constructed stimuli are not actual words, the scope and construction of what a nonword is seems too open-ended. For example, environmental stimuli might potentially be designated as nonword items. In contrast, "pseudoword" reflects the phonological constraints generally adhered to in designing the stimuli. For the sake of clarity, the term "pseudoword" is used in this chapter.

times), and an object naming task. The individual variable most strongly associated with performance on reading measures was the pseudoword repetition task. A similar finding with a slightly different set of measures was reported by Taylor et al. (1989). The study by Hansen and Bowey (1994), using a correlational strategy rather than reading-level-matched groups, likewise included a number of basic phonological measures, but in addition assessed children's performance on odd-one-out meta-phonological tasks in which the "odd one" in sets of three differed in terms of the onset, the rime, or an individual phoneme in medial or final position. Using multiple regression techniques, Hansen and Bowey found that the pseudoword repetition task and the phoneme awareness measures shared a considerable amount of the variance in reading measures (i.e., decoding, word recognition, and comprehension). But, when pseudoword repetition scores were entered after the 11% to 14% accounted for by performance IQ and vocabulary scores, and after the 22% to 34% accounted by for phoneme awareness measures, repetition accounted for an additional 5% to 6% of the variance. These findings and the growing number of supportive findings from studies with reading-age controls, plus the relative ease of administering a repetition task, have led to rising interest in why pseudoword repetition reliably separates reading groups.

Factors Relevant to Pseudoword Repetition Performance. Researchers have been quick to point out that pseudoword repetiton has multiple cognitive requirements: First, the stimulus must be perceived and encoded; second, there is a very brief memory requirement; third, despite the lack of meaning for the stimuli, there may nonetheless be top-down effects from similar lexical items; and fourth, in almost all procedures the response is organized for a response and is articulated (see Corneliesen et al., 1996, for an exception). The separability of these cognitive steps is difficult to achieve, but it is widely appreciated that the efficacy of pseudoword measures may arise from the multiple demands such a task makes (see Gathercole, 1995; Gathercole, Willis, Emslie, & Baddeley, 1991; Snowling, Chiat, & Hulme, 1991 for discussion of phonological memory and output factors in repetition performance). Evaluating what factors influence performance on pseudoword repetition in the general population may help shed light on sources of difficulty for poor readers.

One issue that has drawn particular attention in investigations of performance factors influencing pseudoword repetition is the role of prior vocabulary knowledge. Because significant correlations between pseudoword repetition and vocabulary knowledge have been reported numerous times (e.g., Gathercole & Baddeley, 1989, 1990), the potential for top-down effects on repetition performance has been considered. Two aspects of current models of speech perception provide a basis for such effects.

Proposals that pseudowords may be processed element by element, with long-term representations being activated whenever a sequence matching a portion of an existing lexical item is encoded (Frauenfelder, Baayen, Hellwig, & Schreuder, 1993; Marslen-Wilson, 1987; McClelland & Elman, 1986), together with arguments that the lexicon may be organized in terms of phonological neighbors (e.g., Cluff & Luce, 1990), provide a rationale for the interface of pseudowords with phonologically similar real words. Evidence of priming effects of pseudowords on semantic associates of real words has added to the evidence that there may not be a sharp distinction between the processing of lexical and nonlexical items (Connine, Blasko, & Titone, 1993).

The implication for pseudoword repetition, of course, is that the extent of one's vocabulary would influence the likelihood of potential facilitory effects of vocabulary knowledge on repetition tasks. Such benefits have been documented in samples of young children. Gathercole et al. (1991) focused on lexical factors in a study of the repetition abilities of more than 100 children in a longitudinal study extending from ages 4 through 6. For the 40 pseudowords used, a group of adults was asked to rate the "wordlikeness" on a 5-point scale of each of the 30 polysyllabic pseudowords in the set. The rated wordlikeness accounted for 10% to 18% of the variance in repetition scores for the three age groups even after length (i.e., number of syllables) was controlled. This association between wordlikeness and repetition accuracy was replicated in an independent longitudinal study conducted by Gathercole (1995). In addition, in the former study the stimuli were assessed for the presence of derivational/inflectional morphemes and/or root morphemes. In contrast to the first outcome described, the influence of the number of constituent morphemes, adjusted for confounding effects of nonword length, was not significant, although the particular morpheme counting procedure employed has been questioned (Dollaghan, Biber, & Campbell, 1995). Two additional studies have documented lexical influences on pseudoword repetition for normally achieving school-age children (Dollaghan, Biber, & Campbell, 1993, 1995). Both used pseudoword pairs in which one item included a syllable that was a familiar monosyllabic word (e.g., BATHesis), whereas the other did not (e.g., FATHesis). Repetition for the word-including items was significantly more accurate, even for the matching unstressed portion of the pseudowords. An analysis of the errors also suggests the impact of long-term lexical knowledge on pseudoword repetition: The vast majority of repetition errors consisted of transformations of pseudowords into real words (e.g., *spad* → *spell*). However, although lexicalization was prevalent, the authors pointed out that many of the errors, consisting of a single feature error (e.g., *flig* → *flick*), could also be interpreted as stemming in part from perceptual or articulatory factors.

Although vocabulary influences on pseudoword repetition appear to be considerable, other linguistic attributes also exert noteworthy effects. Several studies have now established that longer pseudowords, generally measured in terms of the number of syllables, tend to be harder to repeat accurately than shorter stimuli (Apthorp, 1995; Gathercole, 1995; Snowling, 1981). Countering the vocabulary effects, Gathercole (1995) reported that the effect of the number of syllables on repetition accuracy remained significant even when wordlikeness ratings were covaried out. At this point, two broad factors appear to effect repetition performance: lexical mediation and bottom-up phonological processing. Returning to the focus on the link between speech repetition and reading ability, the next question is whether one or both factors accounts for less accurate repetition by disabled readers.

Exploring the Basis of Inaccurate Speech Repetition by Poor Readers. The clear association of stronger vocabulary knowledge with better reading ability (e.g., Kail & Leonard, 1986; Vellutino & Scanlon, 1987), particularly as children get older, raises the obvious question as to whether reading-group differences in pseudoword repetition are simply the consequence of greater top-down influence on performance for skilled readers. However, a number of studies indicate that such an account is not sufficient. Some studies have statistically controlled for vocabulary size and have still obtained reading group differences in performance (e.g., Apthorp, 1995; Bowers, 1989; Taylor et al., 1989; see also Hansen & Bowey, 1994). In a further check of the role of vocabulary knowlege, Brady et al. (1989) reorganized the subjects from two reading groups with overlapping vocabulary scores into two groups of subjects with lower and higher vocabulary scores, regardless of reading status. Whereas the reading groups had significantly differed in repetition accuracy, the two vocabulary groups did not. More recently, Stone and Brady (1995) chose to handle the vocabulary issue by selecting chronological groups matched on vocabulary knowledge, and younger reading-age controls with less vocabulary knowledge than the older poor readers, but comparable IQ equivalent scores. As noted previously, the less skilled readers were nonetheless worse at pseudoword repetition than were both control groups, indicating that lexical mediation accounts are not sufficient to explain the difficulties encountered by individuals with reading problems. Similarly, Snowling et al. (1986) found that although reading-disabled children were comparable on a lexical decision task to reading-age control subjects who were an average of two years younger, thus confirming vocabulary weaknesses, their repetition for these words they did not know (in essence, pseudowords) was significantly worse.

These outcomes indicate that vocabulary differences probably contribute to reading-group differences in repetition performance, but are not the whole explanation. In the Gathercole (1995) longitudinal study mentioned earlier, the pseudoword stimuli were divided into two lists, low and high wordlikeness, and the correspondence of performance on these two types of stimuli with other variables was examined. At both age 4 and age 5, better repetition was obtained for the high-wordlike set, and greater developmental improvement was seen on the high-wordlike set, as one would anticipate if vocabulary growth were a factor. Beginning reading scores, however, were not correlated significantly with scores on high-wordlike set, but with performance on the low-wordlike set at age 4. The lack of a significant association at age 5 suggests that these findings need to be replicated to ensure their reliability, yet they may indicate the importance of early phonological representation in reading acquisition.

Other studies likewise point to an association between phonological factors in repetition performance and reading ability. Paralleling the results with real words, increasing the length and the complexity of pseudoword stimuli also has been documented to widen the gap between skilled and less skilled readers. For example, Apthorp (1995) found that her learning-disabled group showed a steeper decline in accuracy for the longer stimuli than did the control group, even when covarying for vocabulary and memory span scores. Snowling (1981) likewise showed significant effects of pseudoword length on repetition of four-syllable stimuli, even though the reading-matched control subjects were several years younger in age.

In sum, speech repetition measures, and particularly pseudoword repetition tasks, genuinely seem to be harder for impaired readers. The contrast in reading-group performance appears to be reliable enough to suggest that repetition measures may have clinical value, provided that the appropriate level of stimulus difficulty is used to avoid ceiling effects. In addition, the evidence that reading-group differences cannot merely be attributed to extent of vocabulary knowledge heightens the theoretical interest of this kind of measure. Preliminary results that the deficits of poor readers pertain to the phonological attributes of pseudowords (e.g., syllable length and phonological complexity) indicate it would be worthwhile to further explore the role of phonological factors. To advance our understanding, it would be beneficial to attempt to clarify the respective roles on pseudoword performance of encoding, phonological memory, and output components of the task. The evidence for encoding difficulties for poor readers on simple phoneme identification tasks, as reviewed earlier, provides a rationale that the perceptual requirements for pseudoword repetition contribute to inaccurate performance by disabled readers on this task as well. Likewise, the fact that reading-group effects are more pronounced with novel stimuli, which necessarily have greater encoding demands, than for real words also is compatible with the proposal that encoding processes figure in the pseudoword repetition deficits of poor readers.

DO SPEECH PERCEPTION DEFICITS STEM FROM A MORE GENERAL AUDITORY TEMPORAL PROCESSING PROBLEM?

In contrast to the growing consensus that a specific deficit in phonological processes is the basis of reading disability and associated language problems, for a number of years Tallal has championed an alternative explanation. She proposed that a more general auditory temporal processing difficulty accounts for the deficits of individuals with reading problems (Tallal, 1980, 1984; Tallal, Miller, & Fitch, 1993), as well as those of language-impaired children (Tallal, 1990; Tallal & Piercy, 1973, 1974, 1975; Tallal & Stark, 1981) and adult aphasics (Tallal & Newcombe, 1978). Although this position recently has been carefully critiqued in two publications (Mody, Studdert-Kennedy, & Brady, 1997; Studdert-Kennedy & Mody, 1995), because the issues are central to a discussion of speech perception and reading ability a brief overview of the claims regarding reading-disabled children are summarized here.

The core of the temporal processing hypothesis with respect to children with reading problems is that auditory limitations in processing brief and/or rapidly changing acoustic events cause the deficits observed on language measures. That is, the inaccuracies that poor readers demonstrate on tasks such as stop consonant identification are thought to arise from a nonlinguistic difficulty processing the brief formant transitions in consonant stimuli (Tallal, 1980). Thus, although not disagreeing about the prevalence of language problems for poor readers, the auditory temporal processing position ascribes the basis to a nonlinguistic origin. If true, diagnosis and treatment of reading disability conceivably would hinge on assessing and remediating the more general auditory deficit, rather than targeting language skills (cf., Tallal et al., 1996).

A key argument in this line of reasoning is that deficits should be present not only on speech tasks, but also on measures using nonspeech sounds. Accordingly, a procedure used with both speech stimuli and tones, referred to as temporal order judgment (TOJ), has played a central role in the research examining this question. In a TOJ task, designed to assess rate of auditory processing, the subject is asked to judge the identity and order of two stimuli (i.e., was the order 1-1, 2-2, 2-1, or 1-2). Two dimensions are typically manipulated, the length of the interval between the stimuli and the duration of the stimuli themselves. In the initial study with reading-impaired children using this paradigm, Tallal (1980) reported that 9 of the 20 subjects performed less well on discrimination and on TOJ for brief, rapidly presented tones (75 ms in duration) than did a group of control subjects from a previous study. Despite the lack of uniformity in this outcome, a significant correlation was obtained between tone TOJ and decoding scores for the reading-impaired subjects. Three subsequent studies also found an association between reading attainment and performance on TOJ for brief tones (Bedi, 1994; Reed, 1989; Watson & Miller, 1993). In addition, one of these (Reed, 1989) demonstrated TOJ difficulty by reading-disabled subjects with stop consonant stimuli (i.e., /ba/–/da/ tokens consisting of formant transitions for the first 35 ms to 40 ms followed by steady-state vowel patterns for a total of 250 ms), but not for steady-state vowels (i.e., /ɛ/–/ae/, each 250 ms in duration). This pattern of results, similar to that observed by Tallal with the other language impaired groups noted previously, has been interpreted as an indication of a general auditory deficit, not one specific to speech. The rationale has been that the deficit results in difficulty processing rapidly changing stimuli (e.g., consonant transitions) or brief stimuli (e.g., tones), but not longer, steady-state items such as vowels. Likewise other perception studies reporting a lack of significant reading-group problems on other perceptual tasks with vowel stimuli such as discrimination measures (e.g., deWierdt, 1988) have been seen as compatible with this interpretation.

Recall, however, that correct performance of the TOJ task requires both identification and ordering of the stimuli. As discussed in the reviews cited previously (Mody et al., 1997; Studdert-Kennedy & Mody, 1995), errors on this kind of task could either arise from faulty identification (e.g., in a 1-2 trial, erroneously classifying the first item as "2" and hence labeling the sequence as 2-2) or from difficulty ordering the stimuli (e.g., misjudging 1-2 for 2-1). Although both Tallal and Reed acknowledged identification problems as a potential source of difficulty, the temporal processing explanation has been favored by Tallal, as noted earlier. Yet, for some time the appropriate control conditions to evaluate these alternatives had not been conducted. Recent experiments attempting to resolve the ambiguity of TOJ performance by poor readers fail to support the temporal processing explanation.

Mody et al. (1997), in keeping with the categorical perception results for poor readers described earlier in this chapter, proposed that difficulties in identifying /ba/ and /da/ at rapid rates of presentation occur because of their close phonetic similarity rather than from a deficit in judgments of temporal order itself. By this account, children who are less skilled readers should find TOJ for /ba/–/da/ to be more difficult than TOJ for less phonetically similar pairs of speech sounds (i.e., /ba/–/sa/ and /da/–/ʃa/). That is, if perception of speech is somewhat impaired, discriminating or identifying phonemes that differ on a single phonetic feature should be more difficult, particularly with short intervals between the stimuli, than for stimuli contrasting in three features, thus leading to less accurate performance on the TOJ task. In contrast, to support a temporal order explanation, all of these pairs of stimuli should be comparably difficult for poor readers. The results supported the former account: Whereas significant reading-group differences occurred for discrimination and TOJ for the /ba/–/da/ condition, a minimal number of errors were made by poor readers on the other pairs and no group differences were present. Thus, poor readers can judge the temporal order of two items, even if they are presented rapidly, provided that they can identify the items to be ordered.

Although the Mody et al. (1997) findings just described indicate that difficulty on /ba/–/da/ TOJ doesn't reflect a general weakness with temporal order analysis, a second experiment was conducted to test whether the difficulty arises because this particular contrast entails close analysis of brief formant transitions. A nonspeech task was administered, using sine wave stimuli that mirrored the frequencies of the second and third formants from the /ba/ and /da/ stimuli. Consequently, these stimuli had the rapidly changing acoustic properties of their speech equivalents, but did not sound like speech. The children were given identification training (labeling them as a rising or a falling sound) and discrimination training at long intervals (400 ms). Unlike the speech results, no reading-group difference was obtained on a subsequent discrimination task with reduced intervals. Indeed, the less skilled readers were not affected by the differences in the rate of presentation for the nonspeech pairs. These results support the conclusion that the problems experienced by poor readers with speech stimuli pertain to the phonological requirements, not the acoustic demands (also see Pallay, 1986).

A last experiment by Mody et al. (1997) likewise confirmed that poor readers are adept at processing the acoustic aspects of signals conveying speech, even if such information requires phonetic processing of brief formant transitions. The logic for this experiment hinges on characteristics of the speech cues in syllables with a fricative stop cluster such as /steI/. Such syllables have initial frication noise, followed by a silent gap, and then a vocalic portion. Two cues specify the stop consonant: the silence after the fricative, indicating that the vocal tract has closed; and the rising formant transition after the silence at the beginning of the vocalic portion, indicating that the tract is reopening. These two cues, the duration of the silence and the extent of the first formant (F1) frequency rise, are usually reciprocally related and can be synthesized to "trade": In other studies, the presence of a stop has been specified either by a short silence and a sharp F1 rise in frequency, or by a longer silence and a more gradual

F1 frequency rise (e.g., Best, Morrongiello, & Robson, 1981). In recent years, an interesting finding has emerged that adults and children differ somewhat in which cue is more salient. These age effects have been reflected in differences for younger and older subjects in the category boundaries (e.g., in a /seI/–/steI/ continuum) for stimuli incorporating "trading cues." Young children (3–5 years old) have been interpreted to rely more on subtle differences in formant transitions than do adults, who give more weight to the duration of the silence (Morrogiello, Robson, Best, & Clifton, 1984; Nittrouer, 1992). Note that the age pattern demonstrates that adults, who presumably have mature perceptual skills, were *less* sensitive to rapid intrasyllabic formant transitions (i.e., the transition information was weighted less heavily in categorizing stimuli). This is contrary to the prediction the temporal processing position has made; indeed, a study by Tallal and Stark (1978) with language-impaired children and one by Steffens et al. (1992) with adult dyslexics both reported that the impaired subjects were less sensitive to the extent of the F1 transition.

Returning to the Mody et al. (1997) experiment, the goal was to examine whether skilled and less skilled readers would differ in perception of stimuli from a /seI/–/steI/ continuum in terms of how much of an F1 transition is necessary to cue the presence of /t/. They did not: The phoneme boundaries were the same for the two groups. Thus, not only are the skilled and less skilled readers comparable on the nonspeech sine wave task, but even in the context of a speech task, perception of brief formant transitions does not appear to be the locus of difficulty for children with reading problems. Instead, this set of experiments clarifies that poor readers are at a disadvantage when phonetically similar stimuli must be distinguished. Rather than temporal ordering presenting a problem for less skilled readers on speech TOJ tasks, the underlying weakness entails identification of phonemes.

Although the converging evidence indicates that the basis of language difficulties for poor readers is phonological, the question of why poor readers have been documented on occasion to perform less well on the nonverbal tone versions of the TOJ remains to be resolved. One important issue concerns the construct tapped by this task. Recent work by Watson and Miller (1993) raised questions about whether tone TOJ even should be viewed as an optimal measure of temporal processing per se. In their study, a sample of 94 undergraduates that included 24 reading-disabled individuals were given a battery of 35 tests designed to assess nine factors possibly relevant to reading skill. The latent variable of auditory temporal processing was assessed by three tasks in addition to one for temporal order of tones. These three were: (a) single-tone duration, in which subjects were asked to discriminate whether the duration of a test tone is the same or different from the duration of a target tone; (b) pulse-train discrimination, in which subjects judged whether a sequence of six short tones differs in the temporal separation of the tones from a comparison sequence; and (c) embedded test-tone loudness, in which subjects were instructed to detect an extra tone varying in duration (and perceived loudness) in a sequence of nine tones. All clearly call for evaluation of a temporal dimension (duration), whereas tone TOJ requires identification of the frequency of the tone (not a temporal property), and only secondarily an evaluation of the order. Reading-group differences, as noted earlier, were obtained for tone TOJ, but not for the three auditory temporal measures. Furthermore, using a structural equation approach, nonverbal temporal processing was *not* found to be related to phonological or to reading variables.

These findings add to the reservations about the relevance of tone TOJ to reading performance: Although less skilled readers do sometimes perform less well on this measure, the Mody et al. (1997) and Watson & Miller (1993) studies demonstrated that a common problem does not appear to underlie difficulty on tone TOJ and on phonological measures, nor is tone TOJ clearly a measure of temporal processing (see Mody et al., 1997, for further discussion of this point). Furthermore, performance on tone TOJ does not bear a consistent association with reading disability. Rather, just as attention deficits often co-occur with reading disability but have an independent cause (Shaywitz, Fletcher, & Shaywitz, 1994), so too might tone TOJ have a spurious link with reading. The practical implication of this conclusion, of course, is that reading remediation strategies targeting performance on nonverbal skills such as tone TOJ are not justified (cf. Tallal et al., 1996).[4]

CONSEQUENCES OF SPEECH PERCEPTION ON EARLY READING: THE MECHANISM OF PHONEME AWARENESS

Given the apparent link between speech perception and reading problems, by what mechanism does speech perception bear on reading acquisition? In this final section, current evidence regarding the association between speech perception and phoneme awareness is considered.

Phoneme awareness refers to the ability to segment the consonants and vowels in words, and to be able to categorize words on the basis of these

---

[4]See Brady, Scarborough, and Shankweiler (1996) for a critique of other methodological limitations of the training studies by Merzenich, Jenkins, Miller, Schreiner, and Tallal (1996) and Tallal et al. (1996), and for a discussion of the validity for the treatment of dyslexia.

individual phonemic segments (e,g., Brady, Fowler, Stone, & Winbury, 1994). The necessity of accurate phoneme identification in phoneme awareness implicates the relevance of speech perception. It has long been known that certain phonemes (e.g., fricatives) are easier to discover because of their perceptual salience (e.g., Marsh & Mineo, 1977; Treiman & Baron, 1981). Even for less advanced awareness measures such as rhyme oddity (i.e., picking out which of three words does not rhyme with the others), children make more errors if the odd word is phonetically similar to the other words than if the contrast is more extreme (e.g., Snowling, Hulme, Smith, & Thomas, 1994). These findings again point to the importance of perceptual factors in ability to analyze the phonological structure of words. Accordingly, the variance shared by phoneme awareness and pseudorepetition measures (e.g., Hansen & Bowey, 1994) may be because both depend on accurate speech perception.

If speech perception abilities indeed play an underlying role in the development of phoneme awareness, one would anticipate that the quality of a poor reader's phonological representations for words somehow differs from that of a good reader's. Two hypotheses, not incompatible, have been articulated in recent years about how the representations of less skilled readers may differ. First, as Fowler (1991) discussed, the child's phonological system may initially represent lexical items in terms of more global phonological attributes (i.e., gestures) that extend through the word. Shifting to a fully phonemic representation for words may be a gradual process that takes place over a number of years. Consequently, Fowler proposed, the emergence of phoneme awareness may be constrained for some children, not only by metaphonological demands but also by a poor fit between the phonemic targets and a child's internal phonological representations. Thus, Fowler's hypothesis, echoed in similar terms in related articles (e.g., Treiman, Zukowski, & Richmond-Welty, 1995; Walley, 1993), is that the phonology of children changes from larger structures to more segmental phonemic elements, and that the nature of a child's representations will influence both perception and retrieval of speech, and related literacy skills. The usual progression of awareness from larger to smaller phonological segments, as well as the nature of spelling errors (e.g., difficulty accurately representing clusters), are seen as compatible with this position.

The second argument is that the phonological representations of poor readers are "faulty or impoverished" (e.g., Snowling et al., 1988). Variations on this concept have been introduced for a number of years by researchers referring to the speech perception, verbal working memory, or confrontation naming difficulties of poor readers (e.g., Brady, 1991; Katz, 1986). Recently, Elbro (in press) proposed a "distinctness hypothesis," suggesting that the errors evident on various tasks occur because the lexical representations of poor readers are less distinctly or less completely specified. According to this position, the phonemic structure is essentially the same for poor readers, but the robustness of the phonemic details differs. Although there might be sufficient detail to allow poor readers usually to identify words or to remember them and pronounce them, the reduced quality would tend to make performance of these tasks slightly less accurate. Supporting this view, Elbro, Nielsen, and Petersen (1994) found some indications of less distinct phonological representations by adult dyslexics on word recognition and word production tasks. For example, given phonologically similar alternatives on a vocabulary measure (e.g., "is capital punishment the same as *excursion, exclusion,* or *execution*"), the dyslexic subjects were more often incorrect, although this group difference was not evident when semantic vocabulary alternatives were presented. Likewise, taking advantage of a frequent characteristic of Danish that phonological variants of words are permissible, Elbro et al. (1994) documented that adult dyslexics more often produced the reduced forms that preserve less of the distinctness of the words (for an example of an English equivalent: "scuse me" versus "excuse me"). Elbro (in press) left open whether the problem originates with the encoding of words, or from other processing requirements such as lexical accessibility.

Some empirical support for an association between phoneme awareness and speech perception has accrued (e.g., Hansen & Bowey, 1994; Hurford, 1991). Four recent studies have focused on this question with children or adults beyond the beginning stages of reading. McBride-Chang (1995), using structural equation modeling on a data set from regular third- and fourth-grade children, found that a speech perception factor based on three identification tasks contributed unique variance to a phonological awareness construct. A second, unpublished study of somewhat older school-age dyslexic and normal readers also reported an interesting association between phoneme awareness and speech perception (Manis et al., 1993). For a subgroup of dyslexic children who were particularly low in phoneme awareness skill, their scores on identification of stimuli from a bath–path continuum were correspondingly poorer, especially for the endpoints. The interpretation of both of these studies is qualified by the fact that subjects had to respond by pointing to written versions of the stimuli they heard, which may have amplified the group differences, but a third study likewise found an association between speech perception and awareness. Watson and Miller (1993), as mentioned earlier, tested 94 college undergraduates, including 24 reading-disabled students, on a variety of phonological and cognitive constructs. Using a structural equation approach, they found a substantial relationship between speech perception and phoneme awareness. Interestingly, speech perception was not related directly to reading ability, but was identified as an underlying factor for phonological awareness, as mentioned, and for other constructs for verbal short-term memory and for long-term verbal memory (although see McBride-Chang, 1995, for a different association between perception and short-term memory). Last, a study using a training strategy (Hurford, 1990) provided intriguing evidence on this issue. Reading-disabled children from second and third grades were trained for a total of 2 to 3 hours on phoneme discrimination for a number of phoneme pairs, proceeding from a vowel pair to a liquid pair and finally to a pair of stop consonants. Subsequently, performance on phoneme awareness for the experimental group was found to have improved significantly, although this had not been the target of the training procedures.

In light of the association between speech perception and phoneme awareness in older readers, one might project that those prereaders with good speech perception skills would be particularly adept at discovering the sounds in words and at learning to read. However, a small number of predictive studies with more typical samples of young children failed to obtain noteworthy correlations between early speech perception and later reading success (e.g., Mann & DiTunno, 1994; see Scarborough, 1996, for a review). Three explanations for these results can be considered. First, speech perception ability may indeed be a negligible factor in becoming a reader, despite the apparent correspondence later on. The training study by Hurford (1990) stands alone as contrary evidence; the other studies with older subjects described previously don't address the question of causality. On the other hand, the measures used with young children, often simple discrimination or identification tasks with high-frequency monosyllabic words, may not be sufficiently sensitive to tap individual differences. Earlier, the study by Gathercole (1995) was discussed, noting that performance on the pseudoword repetition task at age 4 did correspond significantly with beginning reading measures taken in following years.

A third explanation may be that variations in early speech perception skills are overshadowed by changes in phonology induced by the development of awareness. Recent work by Fowler and her colleagues (Fowler, Brady, & Eisen, 1995) demonstrated sharp differences in speech perception for 5-year-old children who had attained phoneme awareness versus those (normal) children who still were naive about phonemic segments. Fully 100% of the children who were phonemically aware could identify unambiguous end point stimuli on "s(vowel)" and "sh(vowel)" contrasts, whereas only one third of those lacking awareness of phonemes could identify to 90% criterion which syllable had been presented. This pattern suggests a close tie between perception and awareness; although accurate phonemic perception was sometimes observed to be present without awareness, the reverse never occurred.

A subsequent phonemic awareness training study (Fowler, Brady, & Yehuda, 1995) was designed to examine whether perceptual accuracy precedes phoneme awareness or if phoneme awareness sharpens perceptual accuracy. Following a total of approximately 90 minutes of awareness training on /s/ and /∫/ phonemes with children who were initially perceptually inaccurate, effects were seen on perception as well. The perceptual identity functions for these phonemes now reflected systematic categorization of the endpoints, suggesting that acquiring awareness sharpens differentiation of phonemic categories. Whether the discovery of some phonemes cascades to improved perception of other phonemes remains to be studied, and whether such changes would take place in children at risk for reading problems also should be explored, but the results indicate that it may be fruitful to take a close developmental perspective on the link between perception and awareness.

In conjunction with the Hurford (1990) results cited previously, Fowler, Brady, and Yehuda (1995) proposed a reciprocal relationship between perception and awareness: Not only is perception evidently a central element of phoneme awareness, and enhancing perception can facilitate awareness, but heightening phonemic awareness in turn impacts on perception of close phonemic contrasts. The importance of fostering the connection between perception and awareness is compatible with the efficacy for reading-disabled children of the Lindamood program (Lindamood & Lindamood, 1969; see, e.g., Alexander, Anderson, Heilman, Voeller, & Torgesen, 1991). For children struggling to apprehend the presence of phonemes in spoken words, Lindamood's focus on how speech sounds are articulated may provide a way to identify phonemic segments, and perforce to attain awareness of them.

CONCLUDING REMARKS

In closing, the role of speech perception in reading development and reading disabilities is complex. The results of categorical perception studies reveal a persistent pattern of difficulty on identification and discrimination by poor readers, suggesting that they are less accurate in their ability to form phonological representations. The subtleness of this phenomenon makes categorical perception less than ideal as a diagnostic tool, yet it may be helpful in reaching an understanding of the various phonological deficits that poor readers experience. The evidence that poor readers are also consistently less accurate on pseudorepetition measures appears to have better potential for applied purposes, but is harder to explain theoretically because of the numerous factors affecting pseudoword performance. Here it is proposed that inferior pseudoword repetition by disabled readers results in part from difficulty establishing speech representations.

Recent studies (e.g., Mody et al., 1997; Watson & Miller, 1993) failed to support the hypothesis that a general auditory temporal processing deficit is the basis of language and reading problems. Instead, several findings added to the impetus to focus on the quality of phonological representations of disabled readers: the evidence reviewed here of less accurate speech perception by poor readers, and of an association between perceptual performance and phoneme awareness, and the indications of less phonemically accurate entries in the lexicons of less skilled readers (e.g., Elbro et al., 1994; Katz, 1986). Understanding how the phonological representations of poor readers differ, whether less segmentally (Fowler, 1991), less distinctly (Elbro, in press), or both, stands as an important challange. Attaining this knowledge may be central to fully explaining, and addressing, the phonological deficits of disabled readers.

ACKNOWLEDGMENT

The author gratefully acknowledges the helpful comments of Anne Fowler on an earlier draft. The preparation of this chapter was supported by a grant to Haskins Laboratories from the National Institutes of Health and Human Development (HD-01994).

REFERENCES

Aguiar, L. (1993). *Reading ability, vocabulary acquisiton, and phonological processes: An investigation of vocabulary acquisition by skilled and less-skilled readers.* Unpublished dissertation, University of Rhode Island, Kingston.

Aguiar, L., & Brady, S. (1991). Vocabulary acquisition and reading ability. *Reading and Writing: An Interdisciplinary Journal, 3,* 413–425.

Alexander, A. W., Anderson, H. G., Heilman, P. C., Voeller, K. K., & Torgesen, J. K. (1991). Phonological awareness training and remediation of analytic decoding deficits in a group of severe dyslexics. *Annals of Dyslexia, 41,* 193–206.

Apthorp, H. (1995). Phonetic coding and reading in college students with and without learning disabilities. *Journal of Learning Disabilities, 28,* 342–352.

Bedi, G. C. (1994). *Low-level visual and auditory processing in dyslexic readers.* Unpublished doctoral dissertation, City University of New York.

Best, C., Morrogiello, B., & Robson, R. (1981). Perceptual equivalence of acoustic cues in speech and non-speech perception. *Perception and Psychophysics, 29,* 191–211.

Bowers, P. (1989). Naming speed and phonological awareness: Independent contributors to reading disabilities. In S. McCormack, J. Zutell, P. Scharer, & P. O'Keefe (Eds.), *Cognitive and social perspectives for literacy research and instruction* (pp. 165–173). Chicago: National Reading Conference.

Brady, S. (1991). The role of working memory in reading disability. In S. Brady & D. Shankweiler (Eds.), *Phonological processes in literacy: A tribute to Isabelle Y. Liberman* (pp. 129–152). Hillsdale, NJ: Lawrence Erlbaum Associates.

Brady, S., Fowler, A., Stone, B., & Winbury, N. (1994). Training phonological awareness: A study with inner-city kindergarten children. *Annals of Dyslexia, 44,* 26–59.

Brady, S., Poggie, E., & Rapala, M. (1989). An investigation of speech perception abilities in children who differ in reading skill. *Language and Speech, 32,* 109–122.

Brady, S., Scarborough, H., & Shankweiler, D. (1996). A perspective on two recent research reports. *Perspectives, 22*(3), 5–8.

Brady, S., & Shankweiler, D. (Eds.). (1991). *Phonological processes in literacy: A tribute to Isabelle Y. Liberman.* Hillsdale, NJ: Lawrence Erlbaum Associates.

Brady, S., Shankweiler, D., & Mann, V. A. (1983). Speech perception and memory coding in relation to reading ability. *Journal of Experimental Child Psychology, 35,* 345–367.

Brandt, J., & Rosen, J. J. (1980). Auditory phonemic perception in dyslexia: Categorical identification and discrimination of stop consonants. *Brain & Language, 9,* 324–337.

Catts, H. (1986). Speech production/phonological deficits in reading-disordered children. *Journal of Learning Disabilities, 19,* 504–508.

Catts, H. (1989). Speech production deficits in developmental dyslexia. *Journal of Speech and Hearing Disorders, 54,* 422–428.

Cluff, M., & Luce, P. (1990). Similarity neighborhoods of spoken two-syllable words: Retroactive effects on multiple activation. *Journal of Experimental Psychology: Human Perception and Performance, 16,* 551–563.

Connine, C., Blasko, D., & Titone, D. (1993). Do the beginnings of spoken words have a special status in auditory word recognition? *Journal of Memory and Language, 32,* 193–210.

Cornelissen, P. L., Hansen, P. C., Bradley, L., & Stein, J. F. (1996). Analysis of perceptual confusions between nine sets of consonant-vowel sounds in normal and dyslexic adults. *Cognition, 59,* 275–306.

deWeirdt, W. (1988). Speech perception and frequency discrimination in good and poor readers. *Applied Psycholinguistics, 16,* 163–183.

Dollaghan, C., Biber, M., & Campbell, T. F. (1993). Constituent syllable effects in a nonsense word repetition task. *Journal of Speech and Hearing Research, 36,* 1051–1054.

Dollaghan, C., Biber, M., & Campbell, T. F. (1995). Lexical influences on nonword repetition. *Applied Psycholinguistics, 16,* 211–222.

Elbro, C. (in press). Early linguistic abilities and reading development: A review and a hypothesis about underlying differences in distinctness of phonological representations of lexical items. *Reading and Writing: An Interdisciplinary Journal,*

Elbro, C., Nielsen, I., & Petersen, D. (1994). Dyslexia in adults: Evidence for deficits in non-word reading and in the phonological representation of lexical items. *Annals of Dyslexia, 44,* 205–226.

Fowler, A. (1991). How early phonological development might set the stage for phoneme awareness. In S. Brady & D. Shankweiler (Eds.), *Phonological processes in literacy: A tribute to Isabelle Y. Liberman* (pp. 97–117). Hillsdale, NJ: Lawrence Erlbaum Associates.

Fowler, A., Brady, S., & Eisen, A. (1995). *The perception and awareness of phonemes in young five-year olds.* Paper presented at the Society for Research in Child Development, Indianapolis, IN.

Fowler, A., Brady, S., & Yehuda, N. (1995, November). *On the perceptual basis of phoneme awareness.* Paper read at the 46th Annual Conferences of the Orton Dyslexia Society, Houston, TX.

Fowler, A., & Liberman, I. (1995). Morphological awareness as related to reading and spelling ability. In L. Feldman (Ed.), *Morphological aspects of language processing* (pp. 157–188). Hillsdale, NJ: Lawrence Erlbaum Associates.

Frauenfelder, U., Baayen, R. H., Hellwig, F. M., & Schreuder, R. (1993). Neighborhood density and frequency scores across languages and modalities. *Journal of Memory and Language, 32,* 781–804.

Futransky, J. (1992). *Relations among verbal working memory, listening comprehension, and reading skills.* Unpublished doctoral dissertation, University of Rhode Island, Kingston.

Ganong, W. F. (1980). Phonemic categorization in auditory word perception. *Journal of Experimental Psychology: Human Perception and Performance, 6,* 110–125.

Gathercole, S. (1995). Is nonword repetition a test of phonological memory or long-term knowledge? It all depends on the nonwords. *Memory and Cognition, 23,* 83–94.

Gathercole, S. E., & Baddeley, A. D. (1989). Evaluation of the role of phonological STM in the development of vocabulary in children: A longitudinal study. *Journal of Memory and Language, 28,* 200–213.

Gathercole, S., & Baddeley, A. (1990). The role of phonological memory in vocabulary acquisition: A study of young children learning arbitrary names of toys. *British Journal of Psychology, 81,* 439–454.

Gathercole, S., Willis, C., Emslie, H., & Baddeley, A. (1991). The influences of the number of syllables and wordlikeness on children's repetition of nonwords. *Applied Psycholinguistics, 12,* 349–367.

Godfrey, J. J., Syrdal-Lasky, A. K., Millay, K. K., & Knox, C. M. (1981). Performance of dyslexic children on speech perception tests. *Journal of Experimental Child Psychology, 32,* 401–424.

Gough, P., Ehri, L., & Treiman, R. (1992). *Reading acquisition.* Hillsdale, NJ: Lawrence Erlbaum Associates.

Hansen, J., & Bowey, J. (1994). Phonological analysis skills, verbal working memory, and reading ability in second-grade children. *Child Development, 65,* 938–950.

Hurford, D. (1990). Training phonemic segmentation ability with a phonemic discrimination intervention in second- and third-grade children with reading disabilities. *Journal of Learning Disabilities, 23,* 564–569.

Hurford, D. (1991). The possible use of IBM-compatible computers and digital-to-analog conversion to assess children for reading disabilities and to increase their phonemic awareness. *Behavior Research Methods, Instruments, and Computers, 23*(2), 319–323.

Hurford, D. P., Gilliland, C., & Ginavan, S. (1992). Examination of the intrasyllabic phonemic discrimination deficit in children with reading disabilities. *Contemporary Eductional Psychology, 17,* 83–88.

Hurford, D. P., & Sanders, R. E. (1990). Assessment and remediation of a phonemic discrimination deficit in reading disabled second and fourth graders. *Journal of Experimental Child Psychology and Psychiatry, 50,* 396–415.

Johnson, D. J. (1980). Persistent auditory disorders in young dyslexic adults. *Bulletin of the Orton Society, 30,* 268–276.

Kail, R., & Leonard, L. (1986). Word-finding abilities in language impaired children. *ASHA Monographs, 25.*

Kamhi, A. G., Catts, H. W., & Mauer, D. (1990). Explaining speech production deficits in poor readers. *Journal of Learning Disabilities, 23,* 632–636.

Kamhi, A., Catts, H., Mauer, D., Apel, K., & Gentry, B. (1988). Phonological and spatial processing abilities in language- and reading-impaired children. *Journal of Speech and Hearing Disorders, 53,* 316–327.

Katz, R. B. (1986). Phonological deficiencies in children with reading disability: Evidence from an object-naming task. *Cognition, 22,* 250–257.

Liberman, A. M., Cooper, F. S., Shankweiler, D. P., & Studdert-Kennedy, M. (1967). Perception of the speech code. *Psychological Review, 74,* 431–461.

Liberman, I. Y., & Shankweiler, D. P. (1979). Speech, the alphabet, and teaching to read. In L. B. Resnick & P. A. Weaver (Eds.), *Theory and practice of early reading* (Vol. 2, pp. 109–134). Hillsdale, NJ: Lawrence Erlbaum Associates.

Lieberman, P., Meskill, R. H., Chatillon, M., & Schupack, H. (1985). Phonetic speech perception deficits in dyslexia. *Journal of Speech and Hearing Research, 28,* 448–486.

Lindamood, C. H., & Lindamood, P. C. (1969). *The A.D.D. program: Auditory discrimination in depth.* Boston: Teaching Resources Corporation.

Manis, F., McBride, C., Seidenberg, M., Doi, L., & Custodio, R. (1993, April). *Speech perception and phonological awareness in normal and disabled readers.* Poster presented at the biennial meeting of the Society for Research in Child Development, New Orleans, LA.

Mann, V. A., & Ditunno, P. (1990). Phonological deficiencies: Effective predictors of future reading problems. In G. Pavlides (Ed.), *Perspectives on dyslexia* (Vol. 2, pp. 105–131). New York: Wiley.

Marslen-Wilson, W. (1987). Functional parallelism in spoken word recognition. *Cognition, 25,* 71–102.

Marsh, G., & Mineo, R. (1977). Training preschool children to recognize phonemes in words. *Journal of Educational Psychology, 69,* 748–753.

McBride-Chang, C. (1995). What is phonological awareness? *Journal of Educational Psychology, 87,* 179–192.

McClelland, J., & Elman, J. (1986). The Trace model of speech perception. *Cognitive Psychology, 18,* 1–86.

Merzenich, M. M., Jenkins, W. M., Miller, S. L., Schreiner, C., & Tallal, P. (1996). Temporal processing deficits of language-learning impaired children ameliorated by training. *Science, 271,* 77–81.

Miles, T. R. (1974). *The dyslexic child.* Hove, England: Priory Press.

Mody, M., Studdert-Kennedy, M., & Brady, S. (1997). Speech perception deficits in poor readers: Auditory processing or phonological coding? *Journal of Experimental Child Psychology, 64,* 199–231.

Morrogiello, B. A., Robson, R. C., Best, C. T., & Clifton, R. K. (1984). Trading relations in the perception of speech by 5-year-old children. *Journal of Experimental Child Psychology, 37,* 231–250.

Nittrouer, S. (1992). Age-related differences in perceptual effects of formant transitions within syllables and across syllable boundaries. *Journal of Phonetics, 20,* 351–382.

Pallay, S. L. (1986). *Speech perception in dyslexic children.* Unpublished doctoral dissertation, City University of New York.

Pennington, B. F., Van Orden, G., Smith, S., Green, P., & Haith, M. (1990). Phonological processing skills and deficits in adult dyslexics. *Child Development, 61,* 1753–1778.

Perfetti, C. A. (1985). *Reading ability.* New York: Oxford University Press.

Perfetti, C. A., & Roth, S. (1981). Some of the interactive processes in reading and their role in reading skill. In A. M. Lesgold & C. Perfetti (Eds.), *Interactive processes in reading* (pp. 269–297). Hillsdale, NJ: Lawrence Erlbaum Associates.

Rapala, M. M., & Brady, S. A. (1990). Reading ability and short-term memory: The role of phonological processing. *Reading & Writing: An Interdisciplinary Journal, 2,* 1–25.

Reed, M. A. (1989). Speech perception and the discrimination of brief auditory cues in reading disabled children. *Journal of Experimental Child Psychology, 48,* 270–292.

Repp, B. (1984). Categorical perception: Issues, methods, findings. In N. J. Lass (Ed.), *Speech and language: Advances in research and practice* (Vol. 10, pp. 243–335). New York: Academic Press.

Robertson, K. (1997). *Phonological awareness in socially disadvantaged and advantaged children.* Unpublished doctoral dissertation, University of Rhode Island, Kingston.

Scarborough, H. (1996, April). *Phonological awareness: Some other pieces of the puzzle.* Paper presented at the Conference on the Spectrum of Developmental Disorders XVIII, Baltimore, MD.

Shankweiler, D. P. (1989). How problems of comprehension are related to difficulties in decoding. In D. Shankweiler & I. Y. Liberman (Eds.), *Phonology and reading disability* (pp. 1–33). Ann Arbor: University of Michigan Press.

Shankweiler, D., & Crain, S. (1986). Language mechanisms and reading disorders: A modular approach. *Cognition, 24,* 139–168.

Shaywitz, S. E., Fletcher, J. M., & Shaywitz, B. E. (1994). A conceptual framework for learning disabilities and attention deficit-hyperactivity disorder. *Canadian Journal of Special Education, 9,* 1–32.

Snowling, M. (1981). Phonemic deficits in developmental dyslexia. *Psychological Research, 43,* 219–234.

Snowling, M., Chiat, S., & Hulme, C. (1991). Words, nonwords, and phonological processes: Some comments on Gathercole, Willis, Emslie, and Baddeley. *Applied Psycholinguistics, 12,* 369–373.

Snowling, M., Goulandris, N., Bowlby, M., & Howell, P. (1986). Segmentation and speech perception in relation to reading skill: A developmental analysis. *Journal of Experimental Child Psychology, 41,* 489–507.

Snowling, M., Hulme, C., Smith, A., & Thomas, J. (1994). The effects of phonetic similarity and list length on children's sound categorization performance. *Journal of Experimental Child Psychology, 58,* 160–180.

Snowling, M., Van Wagtendonk, B., & Stafford, C. (1988). Object-naming deficits in developmental dyslexia. *Journal of Research in Reading, 11,* 67–85.

Steffens, M. L., Eilers, R., Gross-Glenn, K., & Jallad, B. (1992). Speech perception deficits in adult subjects with familial dyslexia. *Journal of Speech and Hearing Research, 35,* 192–200.

Stone, B. H., & Brady, S. A. (1995). Evidence for phonological processing deficits in less-skilled readers. *Annals of Dyslexia, 45,* 51–78.

Studdert-Kennedy, M., Liberman, A. M., Harris, K. S., & Cooper, F. S. (1970). Motor theory of speech perception: A reply to Lane's critical review. *Psychological Review, 77,* 234–249.

Studdert-Kennedy, M., & Mody, M. (1995). Auditory temporal perception deficits in the reading-impaired: A critical review of the evidence. *Psychonomic Bulletin & Review, 2,* 508–514.

Tallal, P. (1980). Auditory temporal perception, phonics and reading disabilities in children. *Brain and Language, 9,* 182–198.

Tallal, P. (1984). Temporal or phonetic processing deficit in dyslexia? That is the question. *Applied Psycholinguistics, 5,* 13–24.

Tallal, P. (1990). Fine-grained discrimination deficits in language-learning impaired children are specific neither to auditory modality nor to speech perception. *Journal of Speech and Hearing Research, 33,* 616–617.

Tallal, P., Miller, S. L. Bedi, G., Byma, G., Wang, X. Nagarajan, S., Schreiner, C., Jenkins, W. M., & Merzenich, M. M. (1996). Language comprehension in language-learning impaired children improved with acoustically modified speech. *Science, 272,* 81–84.

Tallal, P., Miller, S., & Fitch, R. H. (1993). Neurobiological basis of speech: A case of preeminence of temporal processing. In P. Tallal, A. M. Galburda, R. R. Llinas, & C. von Euler (Eds.), *Temporal processing in the nervous system* (Vol. 682, pp. 27–47). New York: Annals of the New York Academy of Sciences.

Tallal, P., & Newcombe, F. (1978). Impairment of auditory perception and language comprehension in dysphasia. *Brain and Language, 5,* 13–24.

Tallal, P., & Piercy, M. (1973). Developmental aphasia: Impaired rate of nonverbal processing as a function of sensory modality. *Neuropsychologia, 11,* 389–398.

Tallal, P., & Piercy, M. (1974). Developmental aphasia: Rate of auditory processing and selective impairment of consonant perception. *Neuropsychologia, 12,* 83–93.

Tallal, P., & Piercy, M. (1975). Developmental aphasia: The perception of brief vowels and extended stop consonants. *Neuropsychologia, 13,* 69–74.

Tallal, P., & Stark, R.E. (1978). Identification of a /sa/–/sta/ continuum by normally developing and language-delayed children. *Journal of the Acoustical Society of America, 64,* 50.

Tallal, P., & Stark, R. E. (1981). Speech acoustic cue discrimination abilities of normally developing and language impaired children. *Journal of the Acoustical Society of America, 69,* 568–574.

Taylor, H. G., Fletcher, J. M., & Satz, P. (1982). Component processes in reading disabilities: Neuropsychological investigation of distinct reading subskill deficits. In R. N. Malatesha & P. G. Aaron (Eds.), *Reading disorders: Varieties and treatments* (pp. 121–147). New York: Academic Press.

Taylor, H. G., Lean, D., & Schwartz, S. (1989). Pseudoword repetition ability in learning-disabled children. *Applied Psycholinguistics, 10,* 203–219.

Treiman, R., & Baron, J. (1981). Segmental analysis ability: Development and relation to reading ability. In G. MacKinnon and T. Waller (Eds.), *Reading research: Advances in theory and practice* (Vol. 3, pp. 159–198). New York: Academic Press.

Treiman, R., Zukowski, A., & Richmond-Welty, E. D. (1995). What happened to the "n" of *sink*? Children's spellings of final consonant clusters. *Cognition, 55,* 1–38.

Vellutino, F. R., & Scanlon, D. M. (1987). Linguistic coding and reading ability. In S. Rosenberg (Ed.), *Advances in psycholinguistics* (pp. 1–69). New York: Cambridge University Press.

Wagner, R. K., & Torgesen, J. (1987). The nature of phonological processing and its causal role in the acquisition of reading skills. *Psychological Bulletin, 101,* 192–212.

Walley, A. C. (1993). The role of vocabulary development in children's spoken word recognition and segmentation ability. *Developmental Review, 13,* 286–350.

Watson, B. U., & Miller, T. K. (1993). Auditory perception, phonological processing and reading ability/disability. *Journal of Speech and Hearing Research, 36,* 850–863.

Werker, J., & Tees, R. (1987). Speech perception in severely disabled and average reading children. *Canadian Journal of Psychology, 41,* 48–61.

3

The Role of Temporal Processing in Developmental Language-Based Learning Disorders: Research and Clinical Implications

Paula Tallal
Rutgers University, Newark, New Jersey

Steven L. Miller
Rutgers University, Newark, New Jersey

William M. Jenkins
University of California, San Francisco

Michael M. Merzenich
University of California, San Francisco

It is estimated that approximately 8% of children with normal peripheral hearing, motor abilities, and nonverbal intelligence nonetheless fail to develop speech and language at or near the expected age (Tomblin, 1996). These children are diagnosed as specifically language impaired (SLI). Longitudinal research studies that have followed the development of SLI children from preschool through elementary school have shown a striking relationship between early language impairment and subsequent academic achievement disorders, specifically reading impairments (developmental dyslexia; see Aram, Ekelman, & Nation, 1984; Aram & Hall, 1989; Catts, 1993; Rissman, Curtiss, & Tallal, 1990; Silva, Williams, & McGee, 1987; Stark et al., 1984). Over the past 20 years, Tallal and colleagues have focused on understanding the etiology of early language impairment and the relationship between SLI and dyslexia.

The primary tenant of our research program is that higher cognitive functions are built upon more basic underlying neurobiological processes. Thus, if we are to understand speech, language, and reading, we must understand the basic component neural mechanisms upon which these higher cognitive functions depend. Several decades of research with both SLI and dyslexic children have demonstrated commonalties between these populations in the area of deficient phonological processing (Brady, 1986; Bruck, 1992; Farmer & Klein, 1995; Gowasmi & Bryant, 1990; Liberman, Shankweiler, Fischer, & Carter, 1974; Tallal, Miller, & Fitch, 1993; Wagner & Torgeson, 1987). In order to better understand phonological processing disorders, it is important to understand which component acoustic processes are critical to analyzing the complex acoustic wave form of speech.

A large series of studies has demonstrated that language-learning-impaired children (both SLI and some dyslexics) are characterized by severe deficits in higher order auditory processing, specifically rapid temporal integration of acoustically varying signals and serial memory (Cowan, 1992; Farmer & Klein, 1995; Hari & Kielsila 1996; Stark & Tallal, 1988; Tallal et al., 1993). These deficits occur for both nonspeech as well as speech stimuli, and specifically impact central auditory processing in the tens of millisecond (msec) time range. For example, the syllables /bae/, /dae/, and /gae/ differ from each other only in approximately the first 40 msecs, during which time the articulators move rapidly from the initial place of articulation for each consonant into the vowel. These movements of the articulators produce very rapid frequency changes within ongoing, fluent speech that are known as *formant transitions*. SLI and dyslexic individuals have particular difficulty in both perceiving intrasyllabic acoustic differences between speech contrasts that incorporate brief, rapidly changing and/or transient acoustic cues, such as formant transitions or voice onset time, as well as controlling the temporal motor production of these speech sounds (Reed, 1989; Stark, Bernstein, Condino, Bender, & Tallal, 1984; Steffens, Eilers, Gross-Glenn, & Jallad, 1992; Tallal & Piercy, 1974). The specificity of this deficit has been linked directly to the rate of intrasyllabic acoustic change within speech syllables. Using computer-generated synthetic speech, Tallal and Piercy (1975) demonstrated that the ability of SLI children to discriminate between isolated syllables incorporating rapidly changing formant transitions significantly improved when the duration of the formant transitions was extended.

Another series of studies found that this basic processing deficit was highly correlated with many of the most severe aspects of these children's language and reading deficits. Specifically, highly significant correlations have been demonstrated between elevated temporal integration thresholds for nonverbal tone sequences and speech perception deficits, speech production deficits, receptive language deficits, and reading decoding deficits (Stark & Tallal, 1979; see Stark & Tallal, 1988, for review).

It is of considerable interest that similar transient processing deficits have been reported to occur in the visual modality (see Farmer & Klein,

1995, for review). That is, SLI children also need significantly more time between two visual stimuli to discriminate and/or sequence them correctly. Recently, a potential neurobiological substrate for these temporal processing deficits was proposed. Galaburda and Livingstone (1993), studying the brains of dyslexics, found selective deficits in the magnocellular layers of both the visual (lateral geniculate nucleus) and auditory (medial geniculate nucleus) regions of the thalamus—an important way station in the brain for transient (rapidly changing) sensory information transmission. However, there were no deficits in the parvocellular regions of the thalamus—the regions known to transmit static aspects of sensory stimuli (such as form or color in the visual system). Taken together, these behavioral as well as neurobiological data suggest that a pervasive transient processing deficit may characterize individuals with developmental language learning impairments. Given the growing body of evidence demonstrating basic temporal processing deficits, it is important to investigate further the precise relationship between these deficits and developmental speech, language, and reading disorders.

There appears to be considerable overlap at the neuroanatomical, neurophysiological, and neuropsychological levels between the pattern of deficits found in language-impaired and reading-impaired children. Longitudinal studies also demonstrate considerable continuity between early language impairment and subsequent learning deficits (especially reading). Thus, to emphasize the changing characteristics of these children throughout development, we refer to them as *language learning impaired* (LLI).

One approach to further evaluating the interrelationship of temporal processing disorders and language learning impairments (LLI) is to investigate whether LLI children would benefit from training aimed at specifically ameliorating their temporal processing disorder. We recently undertook a series of studies aimed at investigating this hypothesis. Specifically, we predicted that (a) if the critical acoustic cues within the context of fluent, ongoing speech could be altered to be emphasized and extended in time and (b) the rate of temporal integration of LLI children could be speeded up so they could better access the rapidly changing acoustic cues within speech, then the temporal processing as well as phonological processing and language comprehension abilities of these children should commensurately improve. We conducted two studies to date to test these predictions, and the results were presented in two back-to-back papers in *Science* (Merzenich et al., 1996; Tallal et al., 1996). In both studies, two basic methodologies were employed: computer "games" designed to adaptively change temporal integration rates for acoustic cues within both nonspeech and speech stimuli, and listening exercises designed to explicitly train online phonological discrimination and language comprehension using acoustically modified speech.

COMPUTER "GAMES"

Four computer games were developed, one using nonverbal stimuli and three using verbal stimuli. Two of the games were adaptive; by *adaptive* we mean that the simulus sets and series of trials were controlled by each subject's trial-by-trial performance. Both of the adaptive computer games were developed with the aim of first establishing the precise acoustic parameters within stimulus sets required for each subject to maintain 80% correct performance on that stimulus set. Once that threshold point was determined for each subject, the subject's own performance determined the acoustic parameters of each subsequent trial. The goal of the training was to first determine the threshold for specific temporal variables and then, for subjects with elevated thresholds, attempt to drive them to process closer and closer to a more normal threshold.

For example, in the nonverbal computer training game, the subjects were first trained to touch an upward-going arrow on the computer screen whenever they heard a frequency sweep tone that went from a low to higher frequency, and a downward-going arrow for a frequency sweep tone going from a high to lower frequency. Once the association was trained for single stimuli, then two stimulus pairs were presented in sequence and the subject was trained to touch the arrows representing the two stimuli they heard in the correct order. The duration of the sweep tones and interstimulus interval (ISI) between tones was increased until the subject performed the task consistently at 80% correct. Once this threshold was determined, the program adaptively decreased the ISI and stimulus duration millisecond by millisecond, trial by trial, according to the ability of the subject to continue to maintain 80% correct performance. Feedback (thumbs up or down) and points won or lost were given for each trial. Bonus points and brief video animations were given for 10 trials correct. The game was designed to be fun for the subject and to maintain ongoing attention to the task for 20 minutes. After 20 minutes the total number of points won on that game was recorded and the subject moved to a different computer to play a different computer game. There were two games used in the first study (summer 1994) and four in the second study (summer 1995).

SPEECH AND LANGUAGE TRAINING
WITH ACOUSTICALLY MODIFIED SPEECH

A two-stage processing algorithm was developed to alter those aspects of the acoustic waveform that previous research had shown to be most problematic for LLI children to identify and discriminate. In the first stage, the duration of the speech signal was prolonged by 50% while preserving its spectral content and natural quality. In the second processing stage, fast (3 to 30 Hz) transitional elements of speech were differentially amplitude enhanced (made louder) by as much as 20 dB. This two-step acoustic modification process was applied to speech and listening exercises that were recorded on audiotapes, as well as to the speech tracks of children's stories. Subjects rotated through four 20-minute training exercises presented with this acoustically modified speech per day. The exercises were designed as games (i.e., "Simon Says") to train explicit aspects of phonology, semantics, grammatical morphology, and syntax. For homework, children listened to a child's "book on tape" recorded with acoustically modified speech.

Study 1

In the first study conducted in the summer of 1994, seven LLI children without other primary sensory, motor, cognitive, emotional, or neurological impairments participated as subjects The children were between the ages of 5 and 9 years at the onset of the study, had a nonverbal IQ of 80 or above, and were at least 1 SD from the mean of normal for their age in receptive and expressive language development. All subjects that met these criteria also showed severe auditory rate processing deficits as assessed with the Tallal Repetition Test. The elementary-school-aged children were also experiencing severe difficulty learning to read and spell, an expected outcome of developmental language impairment.

The children participated in the study for 6 weeks. Each child participated 3 hours per day, 5 days a week. In Weeks 1 (pretraining) and 6 (posttraining), benchmark testing was done using a series of standardized speech, language, and auditory temporal processing measures (see Tallal et al., 1996, for testing details). These standardized benchmark tests were given with natural, unmodified speech both at pre- and posttraining.

Results of Study 1. The effects of training with temporally modified speech, and nonspeech temporal integration training, on speech and language skills in LLI children can be evaluated by comparing pre- and posttraining test scores (see Fig. 3.1). A repeated measures analysis of variance comparing pre- and posttest performance of each child across all standardized speech and language measure shows that performance significantly improved [$F(1,6) = 200.1, p < .001$] by approximately 1.5 to 2 years, with the LLI children as a group approaching normal limits for their age in speech discrimination and language comprehension. Figure 3.2 shows that the duration as well as temporal integration thresholds of these children were also significantly decreased. Furthermore, the extent to which temporal thresholds decreased proved to be significantly correlated with posttraining receptive language outcomes ($r = .81, p < .05$).

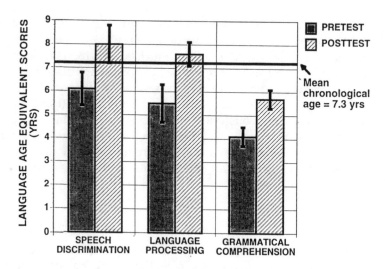

FIG. 3.1. Pretraining and posttraining language equivalent scores are shown for the language impaired children who participated in Study 1 (*N* = 7). Pretraining scores demonstrate that these children performed below expectation for their chronological age (mean indicated by solid line) on standardized speech and language tests. Posttraining scores show that after 4 weeks of acoustic modification training, these children's performance improved on the average of 2 years, with scores on the speech discrimination and online language processing tests reaching age-appropriate levels.

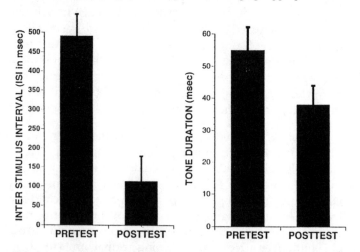

FIG. 3.2. Pretest and posttest thresholds shown for two-tone sequencing ability on the Tallal Repetition Test. Both the mean duration of the silent gap (interstimulus interval) between the tones and the duration of the tones significantly decreased after 4 weeks of adaptive computer training.

These results were dramatic and highly supportive of the Tallal temporal processing hypothesis. That is, improvement in temporal processing coupled with training with temporally modified speech resulted in significant improvement in speech and language. From a clinical perspective these exciting results clearly held promise for a new and highly effective therapy for LLI children. However, from a theoretical, research perspective many questions remained: Could these results be replicated in a larger, independent sample? How specific are these results to the temporal acoustic manipulations that are the basis of the therapy? How much of the improvement resulted from placebo or other generalized training effects? How does this new therapy compare to more conventional speech/language therapy?

Study 2

To address these issues, a second, larger study was undertaken in the summer of 1995. In addition to replicating the results of Study 1, the purpose of the second study was to add a *treatment* control group in order to assess the *specificity* of the temporally based treatment effects.

Twenty-two children participated in Study 2 (mean age 7.4 years; mean language age 4.9 years). They were selected based on the same criteria used in Study 1. The design of Study 1 was replicated, except that four computer games instead of two were used. The children were divided into two matched groups on the basis of their pretraining test measures of nonverbal IQ, receptive language abilities, gender, and age. Both groups performed the same training exercises used in Study 1. However, to assess the specificity as well as efficacy of the acoustically modified speech and temporal training, we presented half of the children with the computer games that adaptively trained temporal processing *and* the language exercises recorded with acoustically modified speech (modified speech group). The other LLI children received essentially the same training, but with computer games that were *not* temporally adaptive, and with precisely the *same* language exercises, but with natural, unmodified speech (natural speech group). The children in the two groups participated together so that they received equal reinforcement, encouragement, speech therapy, and computer training. Thus, more general effects of attention, motivation, reinforcement, and exposure in the laboratory to daily, rigorous speech therapy were equal for both groups. There was no "placebo" control group in the usual sense; rather, both groups received *treatment*; one with and one without temporal modification.

Results of Study 2. A comparison of the two treatment groups is shown in Fig. 3.3. A repeated measures ANOVA comparing performance on pretraining and posttraining measures showed that performance improved

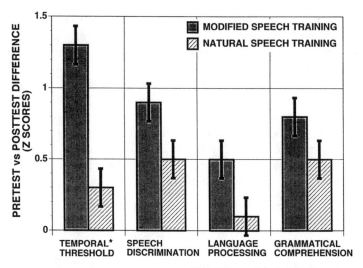

FIG. 3.3. Pretest versus posttest differences (Z scores) are shown on each measure for the modified speech training (N = 11) as compared to the natural speech training (N = 11) groups who participated in Study 2. Although both groups received essentially the same 4-week training program, the performance of the group that received the training with acoustically modified speech improved significantly more on outcome measures of temporal, speech and language processing.

significantly [$F(1, 20) = 34.18$, $p < .001$], replicating the results of Study 1. However, as predicted, improvement made by the modified speech training group was significantly greater than that made by the group that received essentially the same training, but with natural, unmodified speech [$F(1, 20) = 5.44$, $p < .015$]. Again, as was the case in Study 1, there was a significant correlation between improvement in a child's threshold for correctly sequencing and segmenting successive rapidly presented nonverbal auditory sweep tones and that child's posttraining receptive language outcomes ($r = .89$, $p < .01$).

CONCLUSION FROM TRAINING STUDIES

It has been demonstrated that children with LLI need significantly more time than normally developing children to integrate two different brief, rapidly presented (within tens of milliseconds) sensory events or produce rapid sequential motor movements in this same time window. Tallal and colleagues have hypothesized that this basic temporal integration deficit may underlie developmental phonological disorders, resulting in a cascade of negative effects on subsequent receptive and expressive language development and ultimately reading and spelling acquisition (dyslexia). Although previous research has shown high correlations between severity of nonverbal temporal processing deficits and various components of language and reading, specifically phonologically based skills, correlations cannot address issues of causality or etiology.

In these studies we addressed the question of whether direct manipulation of the temporal components within the ongoing acoustic waveform of speech, coupled with training aimed at reducing temporal integration thresholds, will result in improved perception of speech and language. To address this question we developed (a) a computer algorithm that enhances (amplifies and extends) those aspects of the acoustic signal (rapid changes) that have been demonstrated to be deficiently processed by LLI children, and (b) computer "games" designed to adaptively drive reductions in temporal integration thresholds in nonspeech as well as phonological stimuli. We modified ongoing speech in real time in the form of a series of speech and language training exercises, and provided extensive exposure to this modified speech signal over the course of 4 weeks. Results demonstrated significant reductions in temporal integration thresholds coupled with dramatic improvement in all areas of receptive speech and language assessed. Furthermore, changes in temporal threshold were highly correlated with language improvements.

The results of Study 1 were replicated in an independent study. In the replication study the specificity of the improvement in speech and language was demonstrated by comparison with a treatment control group that received the same therapy, but without temporal modification. The group receiving the temporally based therapy improved significantly more than did the group receiving essentially the same treatment but without temporal modification.

Two other important findings from this study deserve discussion. Significant improvement was demonstrated not only for acoustically modified speech but also *unmodified*, natural speech after one month of intensive receptive language training with temporally modified speech. Furthermore, a significant amount of the gains made from the training were maintained at 12-weeks follow-up, suggesting that the processing skills of these children may have been permanently modified. Physiological studies of neural plasticity in animals and humans have shown dramatic remapping of cortical neurons as a result of intensive training (Recanzone, Schreiner, & Merzenich, 1993). Although physiological change was not addressed directly in the current study, the behavioral results led us to hypothesize that cortical remapping for rapidly changing temporal events may have occurred in these children, thus rendering them better equipped to process the rapid acoustic changes occurring in natural speech.

Finally, the degree of change in receptive language processing, including receptive phonology, morphology, and syntax, suggests that the symptomatology of LLI children may mainly reflect bottom-up processing constraints rather than a defect in language competence per se. It seems unlikely that these children learned the equivalent of two years of language in one month. Rather, it appears that they actually had developed considerably more language than they were able to demonstrate or use "online" under normal listening and speaking conditions. However, access to an acoustic signal that they could adequately process for a period of time appears to have significantly improved their subsequent processing of natural online speech.

DISCUSSION

Since the publication of these studies in *Science* there has been considerable discussion concerning the theoretical implications of the research, as well as the generalizability of the demonstrated clinical improvements to other populations. We address some of the most frequently asked questions next.

1. What Is the Hypothesized Relationship Between Temporal Processing Deficits, Phonological Deficits, Phonological Awareness Deficits, and Dyslexia?

Farmer and Klein (1995) recently reviewed the literature pertaining to temporal processing deficits in dyslexics. (See also the series of critiques accompanying this review.) They cited considerable evidence supporting the case for a temporal processing deficit in some dyslexics. Because these authors did such a complete recent review of the literature, there is no need to detail each study here. In summary, the Farmer and Klein review concluded that: Like SLIs, dyslexic children need more time to discriminate, sequence, and remember nonverbal auditory, visual, and tactile information; like SLIs, dyslexics identify and discriminate speech sounds that incorporate rapid acoustic changes less well than do nondyslexic children; and like SLIs, dyslexics' motor sequencing abilities (oral and manual) are slower than those of nondyslexic controls.

There is striking similarity between data derived from studies with SLI children and those derived from dyslexic children, with two notable exceptions: In the few studies that have explicitly selected dyslexic subjects that do not have concomitant oral language deficits, it was found that this subgroup also fails to show temporal processing deficits. Importantly, this same subgroup *also fails to show any phonological decoding deficits as measured by nonsense word reading* (see Stark & Tallal, 1988, for review). These results apply consistently for children, but not always for adult dyslexics. Thus, only that subgroup of dyslexic children that exhibit phonological decoding deficits also show similar temporal processing deficits to SLIs.

Unfortunately, few studies on dyslexia include standardized measures of oral language abilities in selecting their populations, and thus phonological and other language processing deficits often go unnoticed or unreported. However, when aspects of oral language have been explicitly assessed (phonological perception, speech production, rapid word naming, receptive morphology), in each instance they have been reported to be impaired in dyslexics (Brady, 1986; Scarborough, 1990; Stark & Tallal, 1988; Stone & Brady, 1995; Wolf, 1986).

These data suggest that at least a large subgroup of dyslexics may be on a continuum with early SLI. As reported previously, longitudinal studies following language-impaired children from the preschool years through elementary school provide strong evidence that early language disorders place a child at very high risk for subsequent dyslexia. This is especially the case for those language-impaired children who have receptive as well as expressive deficits (Rissman et al., 1990). These cumulative data suggest that there is considerable overlap between early developmental language disorders, especially those including processing deficits, and subsequent reading disorders, especially those characterized by phonological processing and awareness disorders. The exact percentage of dyslexic children that have either previous or concomitant oral language processing disorders (including phonological processing deficits) has not been established empirically. However, given the evidence from longitudinal studies that a large percentage of SLI children become dyslexic, coupled with findings that a large percentage of dyslexic children have phonologically based problems similar to those known to also occur in younger SLI children, it seems likely that there is considerable overlap between SLI and dyslexia. It may be more the age of the child when first assessed, and the nature of his or her processing problems at that age, that determines whether a child will be classified as SLI or dyslexic. Clarifying differences within subgroups of dyslexics, particularly pertaining to oral language abilities (especially phonological processing), remains an area for fruitful research.

2. How Generalizable Are These Results to Less Severely Language Impaired Children?

Two studies have been completed, both with children selected to meet our research criteria as SLI. How restrictive was that criteria? We selected children aged 5 to 10 years old who were already receiving speech, language, and/or reading services. We scanned school or clinic records to determine if a child had a nonverbal IQ of 80 or above and scored 1 SD or more below the mean of normal for their age on a battery of standardized receptive and expressive language measures. Children who had diagnoses of hearing loss, PDD, autism, or frank neurological deficits were excluded. The parents of all children meeting these basic criteria were contacted for participation in the training studies. All children whose parents agreed to bring them to Rutgers "camp" for 6 weeks were further tested to ensure that they still currently meet the study criteria based on current test scores. All of the children meeting these criteria were included as subjects.

It has been suggested that the children we included in these training studies represent only a small percentage of the most severe language-impaired cases. However, this is not the case. We have used a similar criteria for selecting our LLI subjects as Tomblin is using in a current epidemiological study of SLI. Tomblin's preliminary estimate is that approximately 8% of children in the United States meet this criteria as SLI (Bruce Tomblin, personal communication, 1996). Based on these epidemiological estimates, we anticipate that our training results will generalize to approximately 8% of the population, and it is this population that may benefit most from these new temporally based therapies.

3. What Was the Focus of Training and Which Outcomes of Interest Were Assessed?

The first study was designed to improve speech discrimination (phonological discrimination), online processing and memory for language, receptive grammar, and temporal integration rates in LLI children. Reading skills were neither trained nor assessed pre- or posttraining. As reported previously, the results demonstrated that highly significant improvements in each of the targeted speech and language areas were achieved after only one month of training with acoustically modified speech, coupled with adaptive temporal integration training.

The first question to address was whether these results would be replicated on an independent group of LLI children selected using the same criteria. The answer to that question is yes. The results of the first 6-week training study ($N = 7$) was replicated in a second, independent study ($N = 11$). Both the pattern and magnitude of improvement in speech and language skills were comparable across the two studies. The second question is whether the documented improvement resulted from general features of the 6-week program we offered these children (i.e., increased attention, reinforcement, improved self-esteem, intensive daily speech therapy) or was specific to the acoustic manipulations around which this new training program was designed. We demonstrated the specificity of the result by comparing two groups of LLI children matched at the onset of the study on age, nonverbal IQ, gender, and receptive language abilities. One group got the new temporally based training ($N = 11$). The other group ($N = 11$) got the identical training experience, but without acoustic modification. The children participated together so they received the same attention, reinforcement, directed intensive speech therapy, and so on. However, one group heard acoustically modified speech over their headphones, whereas the other received the exact same speech training, but in natural unmodified speech. Both groups played computer games for the same amount of time and received the same attention, reinforcement, and training. However, the modified speech group played temporally adaptive computer games presented auditorily, whereas the natural speech group worked for the same period of time on memory and attention games presented visually.

Significant group differences demonstrated that the group receiving modified speech and adaptive acoustic training improved more in each area of speech and language assessed as compared to the group that received the same training program but with natural unmodified speech. Clearly, the acoustic manipulations within the speech and nonspeech training exercises were selectively better at driving rapid improvement in speech, language, and temporal processing in LLI children. Given the stringency applied in the treatment control condition (i.e., virtually identical training except for the acoustic modifications), it is very difficult to attribute the marked gains in speech and language performance to other, more general training or placebo effects.

4. What Is the Role of Acoustic Modification of Speech as Compared to Adaptive Temporal Integration Training?

Two factors were manipulated simultaneously in these studies. Therefore, we cannot separate out the effectiveness of one as compared to the other at this point. However, patterns within the data suggest that temporal integration training and language training with acoustically modified speech contributed synergistically to the significant improvements achieved by these LLI children. Both the number of trials completed by an individual subject as well as the change in temporal threshold achieved throughout the training correlated significantly with language processing outcomes. This suggests that these variables were working in concert to drive improvements. Whereas we clearly need further studies to determine the precise role each approach played in achieving the overall outcome of language improvements, what we know at this point is that the total program works very effectively to improve speech and language processing in LLI children.

OUR WORKING HYPOTHESIS

1. Etiology

Our research has shown that LLI children process information chunked in hundreds of milliseconds rather than tens of milliseconds. This allows them to process larger chunks within language (syllables and whole words) but not make discriminations at the rate required to discriminate individual phonemes within syllables or words (especially those characterized by acoustic changes occurring in tens of milliseconds). We hypothesize that this basic deficit in processing brief, transient sensory information initially leads to a failure by the infant to set up distinctive phonological representations for the sounds of its native language. This phonological deficit, in turn, delays the overall acquisition of language. Specific deficits may be observed in acquiring morphological and syntactic structures that are weak or unstressed in the native language. As such, the exact structures affected may be different across different languages. Indeed, cross-linguistic studies of SLI children have shown that they have most difficulty with whichever grammatical structures are weak or unstressed in that native language (Leonard, Sabbadini, Leonard, & Volterra, 1987). However, we propose that over time, and if linked with explicit speech and language therapy, these children may use other top-down aspects of the language signal (at the syllable or word level), coupled with redundancies and explicit rules of grammar (within phrases and sentences), to learn to compensate for their bottom-up processing deficits. That is, they show slow but steady improvement in speech and language acquisition, despite their temporal processing constraints. Thus, by the time they reach kindergarten many of these children may have compensated (learned to talk in simple phrases and sentences) and, thus, may or may not overtly be identified as speech or language impaired. Instead, they come to their teachers' attention because they are failing to acquire appropriate prereading skills. By the time they enter elementary school, the focus of these children's difficulties has shifted from language to reading acquisition. However, upon assessment, their problems remain phonologically based.

Schools are in the business of teaching reading, not speech. Unless a child has an obvious speech articulation problem or a severe expressive language deficit, he or she is unlikely to be brought to the attention of a speech language pathologist upon reaching school age. Receptive language deficits are particularly difficult to notice or diagnose. They have been referred to as the "silent deficit," and due to this many children with receptive language processing deficits may never be clinically diagnosed.

Once a child enters school and is having difficulty learning, the most likely school assessment the child will get in the early grades will focus on reading, not language. Longitudinal data cited earlier suggest that the majority of children with receptive language deficits will have difficulty learning to read for similar reasons that they had earlier difficulty learning to talk. Having great difficulty from infancy processing information in the tens of millisecond time range, they have learned to chunk speech only into larger units (syllables, words). This processing strategy may eventually lead to developing adequate (although not good) language skills—at least well enough to get the gist of most conversations and to learn to talk in short phrases and sentences. However, it does not work adequately for learning to read. Specifically, children who cannot process the acoustic cues that are required to discriminate individual phonemes within words cannot become aware that words are made up of smaller units (phonemes); that is, these children have phonological awareness deficits, as so well documented by most dyslexia research. Furthermore, detailed study shows that these now-identified "poor readers" have a myriad of accompanying oral speech and language problems that range from having difficulty producing tongue twisters (Stone & Brady, 1995), to discriminating speech sounds that differ by only brief rapidly changing acoustic cues (Reed, 1989), to grammatical deficits (Scarborough, 1990), to naming words rapidly (Wolf, 1986), to remembering strings of digits (Cowan, 1992). This is similar to the constellation of deficits observed in younger SLI children. Furthermore, like SLI children, reading-impaired individuals also have temporal processing deficits for nonverbal, rapidly presented sensory stimuli. Temporal processing deficits have now been well documented in dyslexics through the lifespan (see most recently Hari & Kiesila, 1996, for review).

2. Implications for Remediation

How do we think this new therapeutic program works? First, the adaptive computer game training was shown to be highly effective in significantly speeding up temporal integration rates. Indeed, as a group, thresholds went from 400 msec pretraining to 100 msec posttraining. For some LLI children, thresholds posttraining approached the normal tens of millisecond range. This alone is a striking result.[1] We anticipate that with longer training times and more trials these new therapies may continue to drive these children's processing rates into the normal range. The data from our first two studies demonstrate that faster processing rates correlated

---

[1]Recall that basic sensory thresholds have been thought to be relatively fixed in an individual. For example, the amplitude of sound that an individual requires to detect a stimulus of a specific duration and frequency is relatively constant. We would not expect training to change this threshold in any significant way; that is, by allowing a person to hear much softer sounds by training them on a hearing test.

significantly with improved ability to process the individual sounds within words—a fundamental goal of both speech and language therapy for SLI children, as well as phonological awareness training for reading-impaired (dyslexic) children. In addition to increasing temporal integration processing rates, we also altered the acoustic aspects of ongoing speech that previous research has shown to be most problematic for LLI children. We then used this acoustically modified speech to intensively train those aspects of language processing that previous research has shown to be most impaired (phonology, morphology, syntax). With vastly increased sensory processing rates coupled with intensive language training with acoustically modified speech, these studies show that LLI children clearly are able to better process speech and language. After training, these children appear to have been able to set up distinct (not "fuzzy") phonological representations for each phoneme in their language. Furthermore, the results of our follow-up studies demonstrate that these improvements are enduring. That means that such a child is now able to approach speech, language, and reading with a neural processing system more attuned to adequate online processing; that is, more like that of children who are learning to read normally.

Any new approach raises as many new questions as it answers. This is certainly the case with these studies. In proceeding it will be very important to differentiate questions pertaining to theoretical considerations (e.g., Is speech "special"?, What is the role of nonverbal acoustic processing in speech perception? Did improved phonological processing lead to improved phonological awareness, or vice versa?) from those addressing primarily clinical considerations of efficacy and generalizability. The data to date, albeit on only a limited number of subjects, show that dramatic, replicable, ongoing improvements in speech and language skills can be achieved in a relatively short but intensive program using these new therapies. From a theoretical perspective, we are aware of the vast amount of research that still remains to be done before the many questions raised by this new line of research are finally answered. We are currently undertaking efficacy trials in three dozen clinical and school sites with both language-impaired and reading-impaired children in an attempt to begin to address some of these questions. However, from a clinical perspective, we are guided by a statement given by Reid Lyon to *Science*: "Let the adults argue theory, but in the meantime, if the games work let the children play them" (Barinaga, 1996).

ACKNOWLEDGMENT

The work reported in this chapter was supported through funding by the National Institutes of Health, Charles A. Dana Foundation, and the March of Dimes.

REFERENCES

Aram, D. M., Ekelman, B. L., & Nation, J. E. (1984). Preschoolers with language disorders: 10 years later. *Journal of Speech Hearing Research, 27,* 232–244.

Aram, D., & Hall. N. (1989). Longitudinal follow-up of children with preschool communication disorders: Treatment implications. *School Psychology Review, 18,* 487–501.

Barinaga, M. (1996). Research news: Giving language skills a boost. *Science, 271*(5), 27–28.

Brady, S. (1986). Short-term memory, phonological processing and reading ability. *American Dyslexia, 36,* 138–153.

Bruck, M. (1992). Persistence of dyslexics' phonological awareness deficits. *Developmental Psychology, 28,* 874–886.

Catts, H. W. (1993). The relationship between speech-language impairments and reading disabilities. *Journal of Speech Hearing Research, 36*(5), 948–958.

Cowan, N. (1992). Verbal memory span and the timing of spoken recall. *Journal of Memory and Language, 31*(5), 668–684.

Farmer, M. E., & Klein, R. (1995). The evidence for a temporal processing deficit linked to dyslexia: A review. *Psychonomic Bulletin and Review, 2*(4), 460–493.

Galaburda, A., & Livingstone, M. (1993). Evidence for a magnocellular defect in developmental dyslexia. In P. Tallal, A. M. Galaburda, R. R. Llinas, & C. von Euler (Eds.), *Temporal information processing in the nervous system: Special reference to dyslexia and dysphasia* (pp. 70–82). New York: The New York Academy of Sciences.

Gowasmi, U., & Bryant, P. (1990). *Phonological skills and learning to read.* Hillsdale, NJ: Lawrence Erlbaum Associates.

Hari, R., & Kiesila, P. (1996). Deficit of temporal auditory processing in dyslexic adults. *Neuroscience Letters, 205,* 138–140.

Leonard, L. B., Sabbadini, L., Leonard, J. S., & Volterra, V. (1987). Specific language impairment in children: A cross-linguistic study. *Brain and Language, 32,* 233–252.

Liberman, I., Shankweiler, D., Fischer, F. W., & Carter, B. (1974). Explicit syllable and phoneme segmentation in the young child. *Journal of Experimental Child Psychology, 18,* 201–212.

Merzenich, M., Jenkins, W., Johnston, P. S., Schreiner, C., Miller, S. L., & Tallal, P. (1996). Temporal processing deficits of language-learning impaired children ameliorated by training. *Science, 271,* 77–80.

Recanzone, G. H., Schreiner, C. E., & Merzenich, M. M. (1993). Plasticity in the frequency representation of primary auditory cortex following discrimination training in adult owl monkey. *Journal of Neuroscience, 13*(1), 87–103.

Reed, M. A. (1989). Speech perception and the discrimination of brief auditory cues in reading disabled children. *Journal of Experimental Child Psychology, 48,* 270–292.

Rissman, M., Curtiss, S., & Tallal, P. (1990). School placement outcomes of young language impaired children. *Journal of Speech-Language Pathology & Audiology, 14*(2), 49–58.

Scarborough, H. S. (1990). Very early language deficits in dyslexic children. *Child Development, 61,* 1728–1743.

Silva, P. A., Williams, S., & McGee, R. (1987). A longitudinal study of children with developmental language delay at age three: Later intelligence, reading and behaviour problems. *Developmental Medical Child Neurology, 29,* 630–640.

Stark, R., & Tallal, P. (1979). Analysis of stop consonant production errors in developmentally dysphasic children. *Journal of the Acoustical Society of America, 66,* 1703–1712.

Stark R., & Tallal, P. (1988). *Language, speech and reading disorders in children: Neuropsychological studies.* Boston: College-Hill Press.

Stark, R. E., Bernstein, L. E., Condino, R., Bender, M., & Tallal, P. (1984). Four-year follow-up study of language impaired children. *Annals of Dyslexia, 34,* 49–68.

Steffens, B., Eilers, R. E., Gross-Glenn, K., & Jallad, B. (1992). Speech perception in adults subjects with familial dyslexia. *Journal of Speech and Hearing Research, 35*(1), 192–200.

Stone, B., & Brady, S. (1995). Evidence for phonological processing deficits in less-skilled readers. *Annals of Dyslexia, 45*, 51–78.

Tallal, P., Miller, S. L., Bedi, G., Byma, G., Wang, X., Nagarajan, S. S., Schreiner, C., Jenkins, W. M., & Merzenich, M. M. (1996). Language comprehension in language-learning impaired children improved with acoustically modified speech. *Science, 271*, 81–84.

Tallal, P., Miller, S., & Fitch, R. (1993). Neurobiological basis of speech: A case for the preeminence of temporal processing. In P. Tallal, A. M. Galaburda, R. R. Llinas, & C. von Euler (Eds.), *Temporal information processing in the nervous system: Special reference to dyslexia and dysphasia. Annals of the New York Academy of Sciences, 682*, 27–47.

Tallal, P., & Piercy, M. (1974). Developmental aphasia: Rate of auditory processing and selective impairment of consonant perception. *Neuropsychologia, 12*, 83–93.

Tallal, P., & Piercy, M. (1975). Developmental aphasia: The perception of brief vowels and extended stop consonants. *Neuropsychologia, 13*, 69–74.

Tomblin, J. B. (1996, May). *The big picture of SLI: Results of an epidemiological study of SLI among kindergarten children.* Paper presented at the 17th Annual Symposium on Research in Child Language Disorders, Madison, WI.

Wagner, R. K., & Torgeson, J. K. (1987). The nature of phonological processing and its causal role in the acquisition of reading skills. *Psychological Bulletin, 101*, 192–212.

Wolf, M. (1986). Rapid alternating stimulus naming in the developmental dyslexias. *Brain and Language, 27*, 360–379.

A Provisional, Integrative Account of Phonological and Naming-Speed Deficits in Dyslexia: Implications for Diagnosis and Intervention

Maryanne Wolf
Eliot-Pearson Department of Child Study
Tufts University

> *I have a difficult time seeing scientific results, especially in neurobiology, as anything but provisional approximations, to be enjoyed for a while and discarded as better accounts become available. But skepticism about the current reach of science, especially as it concerns the mind, does not imply diminished enthusiasm for the attempt to improve provisional approximations.*
>
> —Damasio (1994, p. xviii)

Research in developmental dyslexia began with a cognitive mystery, as an opthamologist and a neurologist tried to unravel why an otherwise well-functioning human being with normal vision, intelligence, and education could not read. Since that time the field has had more than its expected share of large and small mysteries and contradicting observations to resolve. This chapter is about a middle-sized mystery that captured my imagination years ago through the work of the late neurologist Norman Geschwind: What explains the almost, but-not-quite, ubiquitous presence of naming-speed problems in dyslexic persons from prereading ages across the life span? In Damasio's terms, this chapter represents a *provisional approximation* of naming-speed deficits in the dyslexias. I emphasize within this account how these deficits distinguish dyslexic readers from other persons, and what their presence may be telling us about an extraordinarily critical but less understood property of oral and written language: the precise requirements of time.

The question of naming speed's role in helping to understand reading loss cannot, however, be resolved in a vacuum. It is important to place naming-speed deficits in three research contexts: their relationship to well-explicated core deficits in phonology that are known to be a primary source of developmental dyslexia; their relationship to less explicated, psychophysical deficits in several sensory and motor systems among many dyslexic readers; and their relationship to the hypothesized neuro-physiological underpinnings of developmental dyslexia. This chapter is based largely upon the first context. Links to the psychophysical and neurophysiological data are begun here, but represent the next step in the research program (see Wolf, 1995).

The central tenet of the best developed theory of reading disabilities is that core deficits in phonological processes impede the acquisition of word recognition skills (Brady, 1995; Perfetti, 1985; Shankweiler & Liberman, 1972; Stanovich, 1986, 1992; Vellutino & Scanlon, 1987; Wagner, Torgesen, & Rashotte, 1994). The primary assumptions of this position are incorporated in this chapter.

A parallel body of evidence, based historically on research in the neurosciences, indicates that deficits in naming speed represent a major, prevalent characteristic of severely impaired readers (Bowers, Steffy, & Tate, 1988; Denckla & Rudel, 1976a, 1976b; Lovett, 1992; Spring & Capps, 1974; Spring & Davis, 1988; Wolf, 1982, 1991a, 1991b). Current practice among many researchers (including myself at one time) is to subsume naming-speed deficits under phonological processes. The goal of this chapter is to describe an alternative, integrative account—the Double-Deficit Hypothesis—in which naming-speed and phonological deficits are depicted as separable sources of reading dysfunction whose *combined* presence leads to the most profound forms of reading impairment in children (Bowers & Wolf, 1993a, 1993b; Wolf & Bowers, 1995).

The implications of this hypothesis, worked out in collaboration with Patricia Bowers, are significant for diagnosis and treatment. If the two deficits are to some important degree independent, then two dissociated, single-deficit subgroups and one combined deficit subgroup would be hypothesized. Single phonological-deficit readers would be appropriately treated by current practice. The single naming-speed-deficit readers, however, would be either classified as having phonological deficits and given inappropriate intervention, or missed altogether because these readers have impaired comprehension but adequate phonological decoding skills (as assessed on nonsense word decoding). Furthermore, readers with double deficits would typically receive treatment related to only one deficit, with insufficient attention to issues related to fluency and automaticity.

To present a case for the independent roles of naming-speed and phonological deficits in reading failure, this chapter begins with a brief background in the cognitive neurosciences on naming-speed deficits. We then move quickly into a longer look at a systematic set of questions about naming-speed that underlie my research program. The implications of the Double-Deficit Hypothesis for diagnosis, teaching methods, and intervention are discussed within that framework.

The final section in this chapter is the briefest and most speculative, in which I begin to link naming-speed research to several hypothesized neurophysiological mechanisms. I use this literature to conjecture that the processes underlying naming-speed provide us with a small behavioral window on the brain's ability to activate and integrate designated ensembles of neurons within a very small temporal window.

BACKGROUND

The systematic use of the naming process to study other language processes began with early work in behavioral neurology and aphasiology. Goodglass, Kaplan, and their colleagues (1972) demonstrated that the word-retrieval or naming process is a complex, multicomponent set of subprocesses that are relatively easily probed and highly susceptible to disruption (Goodglass, 1980). In other words, what we call *naming* is only the surface of a system of interconnecting perceptual, cognitive, and linguistic subprocesses, each of which is necessary for the normal retrieval of words to occur.

Geschwind, one of the most influential neurologists of the latter half of this century, was the first to conjecture about connections between the underlying requirements of naming and developing reading. Geschwind (1965) hypothesized that the best predictor of reading readiness would be the young child's ability to name colors. The principle was that color naming, like reading, requires all the cognitive, linguistic, and perceptual processes underlying the retrieval of a verbal label for an abstract visual symbol, yet does not require that the child know letters.

Denckla (1972) and Rudel (Denckla & Rudel, 1974, 1976a, 1976b) pursued this hypothesis in a series of studies with average and dyslexic readers. They found that color-naming speed, rather than color-naming accuracy, differentiated dyslexic reading groups from other children. Based on this finding, they designed rapid automatized naming (RAN) tasks, in which the child names 50 stimuli as rapidly as possible (e.g., 5 common letters, or 5 digits, or 5 colors, or 5 pictured objects, repeated randomly 10 times on a board). They found that basic-symbol-naming speed differentiated dyslexic children from average readers, as well as other learning-disabled children (Denckla & Rudel, 1976b), a conclusion also reached by Spring and Capps (1974).

A RESEARCH PROGRAM ON WORD RETRIEVAL
AND NAMING SPEED

My work on naming speed began in the late 1970s as the direct result of the previously cited work and psycholinguistic research on the word-retrieval process. Goodglass had used various naming measures to study language breakdown with aphasic adults. I wondered whether the systematic study of naming in children could teach us about the development of oral and written language. My goal was ultimately to find an earlier, more precise means of identifying at-risk readers.

A provocative statement by Andrew Ellis, a British neuropsychologist, was instrumental. Evoking evolutionary principles, Ellis stated that, "Whatever dyslexia may ultimately turn out to be, it is not a reading disorder" (Ellis, 1985, p. 170). He enjoined cognitive scientists to try to find an early developing cognitive system that used many of the same components as reading, but that developed before reading was acquired. Like Geschwind, Ellis sought to find a system that could become an early window on the development of processes to be used later in reading. Connecting Geschwind, Ellis, and Goodglass, my originating hypothesis was that the word-retrieval system would provide an extraordinary potential match for a reading-precursor system: It represents the activation and integration of many of the important components utilized by reading (e.g., visual, phonological, semantic, memory, and articulatory systems); it possesses the critical characteristics of an automatic system (LaBerge & Samuels, 1974; Logan, 1988; Stanovich, 1990); and it is relatively independent from IQ (Bowers, Steffy, & Tate, 1988).

For the last 15 years I have studied the naming system in general, and naming speed in particular, and what they can teach us about reading development and failure. The rest of the chapter describes some of the major conclusions reached by members of my lab and myself in a program that has proceeded through seven phases. Each phase represents a kind of small mystery, with its own set of questions and clues, that has led me to study different groups of children, different languages, and ultimately, the human brain.

Phase I: A Working Model of the Word-Retrieval System

Question: Can we use information from the neurosciences on the loss of word-retrieval abilities to construct a heuristic model of the normal word-retrieval system?

Based on research studies in experimental psychology and neurological case reports of anomia over the last hundred years, I began the construction of a fairly simple model of all processes whose damage or malfunctioning has been reported to result in word-finding loss. The result was a description of key components of word-retrieval. Briefly, according to this model, naming requires at a basic level: (a) attention to the stimulus; (b) modality-specific information and its cumulative integration (e.g., information from both visual and auditory perception); (c) working memory and stored knowledge of the stimulus; (d) integration of conceptual information with stored lexical (i.e., phonological and semantic) information; (e) access and retrieval of the phonological label; (f) motoric activation leading to the articulation of the stimulus label; and (g) rapid rates of processing within and across all the individual subprocesses. External factors such as stimulus clarity, rate of presentation, word frequency, and familiarity level were also included as influences on speed and accuracy of retrieval, as was age of the subjects.

The components of the basic model were used as the basis for the selection of a battery of psychometric measures. The specific instruments were chosen or designed based on the tasks' ability to probe disruption in the major components. (For a detailed description, see Wolf, 1982, 1991a.)

Phase II: Validation of the Word-Retrieval Battery With Average and Dyslexic Readers

Question: Will a battery of word-finding tasks be capable of differentiating average from dyslexic children in the early reading stages? Will particular aspects of retrieval prove capable of distinguishing reader groups (e.g., receptive versus expressive aspects of the process)?

Phase II investigated the results of the selected battery with a cross-sectional study of 64 children aged from 6 to 11 (32 average readers, 32 severely impaired readers). The findings indicated: (a) a strong, general relationship between all word-retrieval and reading measures ($r^2 = .74$; $p < .001$); (b) the robust ability of all expressive word-retrieval tasks to differentiate average from severely impaired readers (Wolf, 1982); and (c) the lack of ability of receptive vocabulary measures and a visually distorted perceptual measure (see Bisiach, 1966) to differentiate reading groups. A fourth conclusion was the powerful ability of naming-speed tasks to differentiate average from impaired readers at every age. The rapid automatized naming (RAN) tasks first used by Denckla and Rudel (1974, 1976a, 1976b) were by far the best predictor of dyslexic group membership.

Phase III: Longitudinal Investigation of Naming and Naming-Speed Processes in Early Reading Development

Questions: Given the powerful ability of the naming and naming-speed measures to differentiate reader groups, would naming tasks be equally powerful predictors of later reading performance? Would specific aspects of word retrieval be differen-

tially predictive of particular aspects of later reading (e.g., word identification, comprehension)? Do naming and naming-speed problems persist over time for dyslexic readers? Do they continue to differentiate average from dyslexic readers? Will they differentiate dyslexic from garden-variety poor readers and reading-age-matched children?

Phase III comprised an 8-year longitudinal effort to chart the development of carefully defined word-retrieval processes, and to study the predictive relationships between these processes and specific reading operations. Subjects included 115 children from three schools (of varying socioeconomic status) who were tested from Kindergarten to grade 4 and again in grade 7 (Wolf, Bally, & Morris, 1986). After excluding subjects who were missing any year of data, 8 children were classified as dyslexic readers, 24 as garden-variety poor readers, and 43 as average-to-able readers (Wolf & Obregón, 1989). The grade 2 performance of 17 average subjects was used as a reading-age-matched comparison.

First, longitudinal analyses indicated clear developmental patterns of reading prediction according to age and the type of reading and naming (Wolf, 1991a). For example, early naming speed is most predictive of later word recognition (i.e., regular and irregular words; nonsense words); whereas early confrontation naming, which places heavy emphasis on semantic processes and expressive vocabulary development, is more highly predictive of later reading comprehension. Regression analyses indicate the entire battery in Kindergarten is highly predictive of each form of grade 4 reading. After grade 2, however, two cognitive developmental changes are occurring that change specific naming-to-reading predictions: Rapid processing (or automaticity) emerges, and the underlying requirements involved in naming and reading become more differentiated. From this time on, naming-speed tasks predict word recognition and oral reading, but predict comprehension only through the shared variance with word recognition.

This pattern of developmental differentiation helps reconcile earlier results by Perfetti, Finger, and Hogaboam (1978), who found no relationship between grade 3 discrete-trial naming speed and grade 3 reading comprehension. That is, no or little relation between these particular tasks would be expected by grade 3, because naming speed predicts word recognition rather than comprehension (see also Bowers & Swanson, 1991; Spring & Davis, 1988). The data strongly reinforce Stanovich's (1986) conclusions about the changing relationships among individual cognitive tasks over development.

A second provocative finding is the sustained deficit in general word-retrieval (i.e., confrontation naming and semantic fluency) that appears among all impaired readers, but potentially for different reasons between the dyslexic and garden-variety reader groups. Dyslexic subjects appear to have depressed naming performance based on faulty retrieval of known words, whereas the garden-variety poor readers have the same depressed naming performance, but based on less vocabulary knowledge (Wolf & Obregón, 1992). In recent work by Haynes (1994) with a different sample of impaired and garden-variety readers, this pattern was not found for the same confrontation naming test, the Boston Naming Test (Kaplan, Goodglass, & Weintraub, 1983). Dyslexic readers differed significantly from average readers, but *not* garden-variety readers. However, in a study by Goswami and Swan (1994) using a more carefully controlled confrontation naming task, dyslexic readers differed from both average and garden-variety readers. We interpret these somewhat equivocal findings as evidence that there is less universality for confrontation-naming deficits than for naming speed, a finding also shown by Berninger and her colleagues (Berninger et al., 1995). Nevertheless, as discussed by Felton, Naylor, and Wood (1990), severe word-retrieval problems often characterize some of the most impaired dyslexic readers into adulthood.

Third, based on comparisons with average readers, the naming-speed deficits in dyslexic readers appear persistent and severe, extending from prereading stages through early adolescence. Consistent, significant differences in naming speed were found between dyslexic and both average readers and garden-variety poor readers. Stanovich (1995, personal communication, 1995) recently suggested that this finding helps reconcile his earlier differing conclusions, because his sample had consisted primarily of less impaired, garden-variety poor readers.

Importantly, there appeared significant differences between grade 4 dyslexic readers and grade 2 reading-age-matched average readers (Biddle, 1995; Segal & Wolf, 1993; Wolf & Obregón, 1989). This latter finding, also replicated in a fifth through seventh grade sample (Wolf & Segal, 1995), helps eliminate reading exposure as a primary factor in group differences. The principal conclusions that emerged from this longitudinal study are that naming-speed deficits are a powerful, predictive, and diagnostic indicator of severe reading disabilities and that they should be considered a specific core deficit in the dyslexias.

Phase IV: Intervention in Naming and Naming Speed

Questions: If naming and naming-speed processes are related to reading development and breakdown and potentially constitute a separate core deficit in dyslexia, can they be changed through intervention? If change can be effected in retrieval processes, will there be generalization to reading behavior in dyslexic readers?

Phase IV (Segal & Wolf, 1993; Wolf & Segal, 1995), the most applied phase in our research, holds particular interest for practitioners and particular trepidation for theorists. As Vellutino (Vellutino, Steger, Moyers, Harding, & Niles, 1977) pointed out long ago, the remediation of underlying process deficits has simply not proven a promising method in reading intervention. Furthermore, few studies have ever attempted to intervene in the retrieval problems of poor readers (Bowers, 1993; Levy & Hinchley, 1990), although good studies exist with language-impaired populations (German, 1992; Lahey & Edwards, 1995; McGregor & Leonard, 1989). Clearly, as Blachman (1994) stated with tongue in cheek, we weren't about to train the rapid naming of digits and expect to improve reading!

Two pilot training studies with older dyslexic readers were conducted by Denise Segal, a psycholinguist and researcher in semantic development, and myself. The goal of the first study was to investigate whether targeted word-retrieval skills can be changed. If successful, the second study was to test for possible generalization to reading. At the core of each training study was an approach that emphasized the interconnectedness (Curtis, 1987) of reading skills with retrieval rate and accuracy, and vocabulary elaboration (RAVE). Our basic notion was that fast, accurate retrieval—whether for oral or written language—occurs best for words that are highly familiar and that possess rich associations for the reader, whether able or impaired.

We incorporated in both pilot studies a notion of a developmental continuum of word knowledge, based on Beck, Perfetti, and McKeown's (1982) work in vocabulary intervention, as well as work by Kameenui, Dixon, and Carnine (1987). They described levels of lexical access as moving from unknown to acquainted, and then to highly familiar or established. Furthermore, they proposed that in order to understand the meaning of a word in depth that children must be aware of "commonly accessed meaning components" and the way a word changes in diverse contexts (Beck, Perfetti, & McKeown, 1982, p. 507). We integrated these concepts in our approach to vocabulary development (see Segal & Wolf, 1993) and integrated it with general and specific strategies for rapid, accurate word retrieval. For example, for some words, visual mnemonic strategies (see Wing, 1990) were used (e.g., to retrieve the word *barometer*, the students were taught to visualize a "tall Baron Meter," carrying numerous measurement devices!).

We did not include an emphasis on phonology for two reasons, one practical and one theoretical. First, our subjects at Landmark School had been given years of phonological-based intervention. Second, although a number of superb programs have demonstrated the effectiveness of phonological training, there have been few studies concerning naming-fluency skills. We wished to understand in our pilot work whether retrieval skills in and of themselves are amenable to treatment in dyslexic children.

In the first pilot study, RAVE-I (Retrieval-rate, Accuracy, and Vocabulary Elaboration, Study I), 28 dyslexic readers (ages 12 to 14 years) were selected from Landmark School, a residential school for dyslexic children. They received an 8-week intensive program of language games and exercises aimed at both increasing the breadth and depth of their knowledge of a specific corpus of target words and improving their ability to retrieve these and related words rapidly and accurately. Very importantly, both word-specific and general strategies were designed to aid flexibility during word-finding problems.

Findings from the pre- and posttest battery comparisons indicated substantial improvement in both quantitative measures of expressive vocabulary and qualitative measures of depth of vocabulary knowledge for the trained words, the ability to give semantic associations, and the ability to use diverse linguistic contexts. Perhaps of most importance, improved naming rate on an untrained specific, continuous naming-speed task, the Rapid Alternating Stimulus (RAS) task (Wolf, 1986), was demonstrated.[1] These preliminary results indicate that some aspects of word-retrieval problems in dyslexic readers are amenable to treatment and that gains in retrieval rate may be generalizable to other naming-speed tasks (see Wolf & Segal, 1995).

In the second pilot study (RAVE-II), an elaborated intervention program emphasized this same approach with a less intensive, daily time allotment (10 minutes per day) over a longer period of time (6 months). For this study, 31 adolescent dyslexic readers were selected from the same residential school on the basis of school-identified word-retrieval problems or the absence of these problems and on similar performance on school-administered reading measures. We specifically investigated whether (a) greater gains in retrieval speed and vocabulary would be found in dyslexics with prominent retrieval and naming-speed deficits; and (b) whether retrieval intervention generalized to reading gains in these subjects. In other words, in RAVE-II, if improvements in word-retrieval processes resulted in improved reading skills for this retrieval-deficit subgroup of poor readers but not for the nonretrieval-deficit, poor reader group, we would have some additional evidence for the core-deficit role of naming-speed processes.

Posttest data have been analyzed and indicate several interesting and, to us, exciting results (Feinberg, 1995). First, there appear to be, as in RAVE I, clear qualitative gains in vocabulary knowledge, for trained groups (e.g., depth of knowledge, quality of definitions). Second, however,

---

[1]The original sample included six control dyslexic readers, but only four were able to be tested in posttesting. Thus, there was no statistically valid comparison possible in this pilot study.

unlike RAVE I, there was no generalization to rate of retrieval gains on untrained tasks. This may or may not have been due to the brief daily time given. Third, and most importantly, there were differential gains in reading comprehension for the trained, retrieval-deficit group. No other group showed significant posttreatment gains on any reading measure, although the no-retrieval-deficit, trained group showed gains that approached significance. These results can only be suggestive until replicated. Nevertheless, they are our first indications that some changes in retrieval can be trained in older dyslexic students and, very importantly, that some generalization to reading comprehension can occur.

Very essential questions remain unanswered: whether these results can be replicated in other populations, whether such intervention programs for younger at-risk populations would show similar or greater treatment effects, and whether similar programs in conjunction with phonologically based programs would prove more beneficial to a wider group of impaired children. In future studies, we (Morris, Lovett, & Wolf, 1995) hope to explore a more elaborated version of the RAVE II program with the addition of an orthographic fluency component (based on Bowers' work; see Bowers, Golden, Kennedy, & Young, 1994). Using a population of young, at-risk readers, we hope to examine and compare the effectiveness of Lovett's elegant phonological programs with and without the RAVE retrieval and fluency emphases. In so doing, we hope to address some of the field's concerns about "treatment resisters" (Blachman, 1994; Torgesen, 1995) and some of the described limits of phonological awareness programs (Torgesen, Wagner, & Rashotte, 1994).

Transition Phase and an Emerging Reconceptualization

These data, when combined with the extensive similar results by my colleague, Patricia Bowers (e.g., Bowers et al. 1988; Bowers & Swanson, 1991), and other colleagues (Ackerman & Dykman, 1993; Ackerman, Dykman, & Gardner, 1990; Berninger et al.,1995; Blachman, 1984, 1994; Fawcett & Nicolson, 1994; Felton & Brown, 1990; Lovett, 1995; Nicolson & Fawcett, 1995; Scarborough, 1990; Spring & Davis, 1988), indicate the presence of a second specific core deficit in visual naming speed among many dyslexic readers. A question emerges: How do these deficits fit within the context of the field's more coherent story of phonological-core deficits? My colleagues and I believe phonological processes play a central role in reading and are a major source of reading disabilities (Wagner, Torgesen, Laughon, Simmons, & Rashotte, 1993). Where we differ is in the characterization of the disabled reader and in the theoretical depiction of naming speed. First, we have come to believe that explanations of reading failure based solely on phonology are necessary, but insufficient to describe the heterogeneity of impaired readers. Second, we believe that phonological and naming-speed processes represent two independent deficits, whose conflation has obscured some of this heterogeneity with important implications for intervention.

As discussed earlier, it has been common practice among researchers of reading to explain the phenomenon of naming speed as another manifestation of phonological problems; and, indeed, naming speed has been variously described. For example, it has been described as phonological encoding (Näslund & Schneider, 1991) and retrieval from long-term phonological memory (Blachman, 1994; Wagner & Torgesen, 1987). Bowers and Wolf (1993b; Wolf & Bowers, 1995) argued strongly for the separation of the two deficits within a broader model for prediction, assessment and intervention. They based their arguments on several types of evidence: (a) the underlying cognitive requirements of naming speed, (b) the independent contribution of naming speed beyond phonology to various word-recognition processes in reading, (c) the relative lack of correlations between naming speed and performance on conventional phonological awareness measures, (d) data from other language systems, and (e) a reanalysis of longitudinal samples in the United States and Canada according to performance on phonological decoding tasks, naming-speed tasks, or both. A summary of the former types of evidence is the topic of a recent review by myself and Bowers (Wolf & Bowers, 1995). For this chapter, I restrict myself to the latter meta-analysis of subtypes (Phase V), which best represents our efforts to integrate psycholinguistic and neurosciences traditions in reading disabilities research.

Phase V: The Double-Deficit Hypothesis

Questions: Do phonological and naming-speed deficits represent independent core deficits in developmental dyslexia? If so, what patterns in performance accompany single-deficit subgroups and combined-deficit subgroups?

On the basis of the cumulative data on independent deficits and on early subtype research by Lovett (1987), Bowers and Wolf (1993a, 1993b; Wolf & Bowers, 1995) developed an alternative conceptualization of reading disabilities, the Double-Deficit Hypothesis. According to this hypothesis, four groups are predicted: a no-deficit, average reading group; a visual naming-speed-deficit-only group (VNS), with intact phonological skills; a phonological-deficit group (PD) with intact naming-speed skills; and a double-deficit group (DD) (see Fig. 4.1). To test this hypothesis, Bowers and I (Bowers & Wolf, 1993a, 1993b; Wolf & Bowers, 1995) simply conducted a reanalysis of our longitudinal samples of good and poor readers in Canada and the United States along two dimensions: the presence or

Average Group	**Rate Group**
No Deficits	Naming-Speed Deficit
Average Reading	Intact Phonological Decoding
	Impaired Comprehension

Phonology	**Double-Deficit**
Intact Naming Speed	Naming-Speed Deficit
Phonological-Decoding Deficit	Phonological-Decoding Deficit
Impaired Comprehension	Severe Comprehension Deficit

FIG. 4.1.   Double-Deficit Hypothesis.

absence of naming-speed deficits and phonological-decoding deficits for nonsense words.

A quick review of the implications of this hypothesis for diagnosis and treatment are important to repeat. Under the current practice of subsuming naming speed under phonology, the phonological-deficit readers would be appropriately treated, but the VNS readers would either be classified as having phonological deficits and given inappropriate intervention, or missed altogether because of these readers' intact phonological-decoding skills. Most pertinently, readers with double deficits would typically receive treatment related to only one deficit, with insufficient attention to issues related to fluency and automaticity (see discussion in Adams, 1990).

Using the grade 4 performance of my longitudinal sample on RAN letters and nonsense word decoding, 61 readers fell into the average, no-deficit group, 7 into VNS, 8 into PD, and 6 into DD. Results from repeated measures MANOVA and regression analyses indicated the following. First, the PD group resembled average readers on letter naming speed, whereas the VNS and DD groups differed significantly from the other two. This pattern was found for RAN numbers, RAN objects, and RAN colors, and both rapid alternating stimulus tasks (RAS). Second, the converse was found on nonsense word decoding. The VNS and average readers were similar in performance, and the PD and DD readers were significantly different from the other two. These data clearly indicate the presence of two independent core deficits in impaired readers.

The subgroups' performance on reading measures is equally important to understand. First, the double-deficit readers were the most impaired group on each of the eight reading measures. Bowers and Wolf (1993a) interpreted this finding as an indication that when both deficits co-occur, there are few compensatory mechanisms available. This is supported by an examination of the two single-deficit subgroups, who were generally less impaired in reading (although more so than average readers) and significantly different from each other only on nonsense word decoding and the reading rate variables. We would argue, however, that the similar-appearing impairment levels in comprehension and oral reading of the two single-deficit subgroups were based on dissimilar patterns of process strengths and weaknesses.

More specific work is clearly needed to understand these subtypes. In order to eliminate, at least in part, the possible role of IQ-related factors in subgroup membership, the PPVT scores were analyzed with no significant between-group differences found in my sample.

Regression analyses were also used to test the independent contributions of the naming speed and phonological decoding to reading performance. There were significant independent contributions by both variables to each reading outcome with two exceptions: The phonological factor made no significant contribution to reading rate, and the naming-speed factor made no significant contribution to comprehension.

After the new conceptualization of a problem, the task of accumulating supportive evidence begins. What constitutes appropriate evidence in the present case? First, *replication* is essential, particularly in larger clinical samples of children with profound reading impairments. Second, if the Double-Deficit Hypothesis is correct, *differential treatment outcomes* would be predicted for various subgroups. Third, replication of these findings in *other language systems*, particularly in orthographies with greater regularity, would buttress our conclusions. The principle here is that if we can replicate our results in an orthography whose regularity places fewer demands on phonological requirements for the developing reader (see Cossu, Shankweiler, Liberman, Katz, & Tola, 1988), we might see the naming-speed deficits playing a more visible role in identification. Finally, we asked whether evidence at the neurophysiological level could be demonstrated for members of the various subgroups (e.g., in brain electrical activity). If so, we would have a whole new level of evidence for the independence of the subgroups (see complex issues in subtyping research in Doehring, Trites, Patel, & Fiedorowicz, 1981).

Phase VI: Other Levels of Evidence

Question: Will the subgroups predicted by the Double-Deficit Hypothesis characterize severely impaired readers in the most severely impaired clinical populations?

At a recent Society for Research in Child Development meeting (1995), Bowers and I asked two admittedly agnostic colleagues in the field, Maureen Lovett and Frank Manis, if they would be willing to reanalyze their data according to the criteria and predictions in the Double-Deficit Hypothesis. This section represents their findings.

Lovett's (1995) clinical intervention sample consisted of 76 very severely impaired readers in Toronto. Each individual was at least two standard deviations below in various reading measures, and most were below the first percentage in reading for their age. Thus, Lovett's subjects were more impaired than most of Wolf's and Bowers' previous samples. Using naming-speed and nonsense-word-decoding measures as criteria variables, Lovett's (1995) analysis indicated that 79% of her readers could be characterized by our subtypes with the majority (41) falling in the double-deficit category; 17 in the phonological deficit group; and 18 in the visual naming-speed group. The breakdown of performance on reading measures closely followed trends in our data, with the double-deficit group significantly more impaired than the single-deficit groups on every measure. Lovett's phonological group was more impaired than the VNS group on most reading measures (except for word-identification latencies), whereas the VNS group was significantly more impaired than PD, but not DD. (See new data by Krug, 1995, that replicates these results in a grade 5 sample with important information about the cognitivie profiles of each group.)

Manis and Doi (1995) also found that the majority of their subjects could be characterized by our subtypes. To test further the independence of the deficit predictor variables (word naming speed and nonsense word decoding), they conducted regression analyses with all reading measures as outcome variables. For each reading variable, both word naming speed and nonsense word decoding contributed significant independent variance. Manis and Doi interpreted these results as clear support for the differential roles of word naming speed and phonological decoding processes as separate core deficits.

Question: Are differential treatment effects found for members of different subgroups?

According to the Double-Deficit Hypothesis, phonological-deficit readers will clearly benefit from current phonological-based intervention, but children with VNS deficits and double deficits will be less successfully remediated. Lovett's highly successful intervention programs with their explicit, systematic emphases on phonological treatments offer a superb test of this prediction (Lovett et al., 1994). By reanalyzing her treatment outcome data on the specified subgroups, Lovett found both significant differences in the effectiveness of her program for every subgroup and differential outcomes for individual subgroups that followed our predictions. More specifically, the phonological-deficit-only group exhibited significantly greater gains in every posttreatment measure than either the naming-speed or double-deficit groups (i.e., greater generalized gains in phonological processing, in nonword and word identification skill, and on standardized reading measures). In other words, systematic phonological intervention makes a powerful contribution to all reading-disabled children, but some groups of readers have deficit patterns that may benefit from additional or different emphases in intervention.

These data underscore the importance of an integrative account of phonological and naming-speed deficits in our conceptualization of reading disabilities. Such an account helps us understand why, as pointed out by Torgesen, Wagner, and Rashotte (1994), some of our impaired readers may remain impervious to our best efforts. Equally importantly, these data point us in new directions for intervention that may complement current intervention, or, for some children, change it substantively, a point made eloquently by Blachman (1994).

Question: Will naming-speed deficits be more visible in a more regular orthography? Will the double-deficit subgroups characterize readers in a different language?

Significant naming-speed deficits have been demonstrated in German-speaking children (Schneider & Näslund, 1992; Wimmer, 1993; Wimmer & Hummer, 1990; Wolf, Pfeil, Lotz, & Biddle, 1994), Dutch-speaking children (Yap & van der Leij, 1993, 1994), Finnish-speaking children (Korhonen, 1995), and Spanish-speaking children (Novoa, 1988; Novoa & Wolf, 1984). The orthographic regularity of these writing systems (see Valtin, 1989) provides researchers with an opportunity to test the relationship between naming speed and reading in languages where phonological coding presents fewer problems. For example, Wimmer (1993) showed that young German dyslexic readers (in grades 2 and 4) have less pronounced difficulties in standard phonemic segmentation tasks, scoring "high in absolute terms" on these tests and on tests of recognition accuracy for words and pseudowords. By contrast, they have significant problems in naming-speed measures and a "pervasive speed deficit for all types of reading tasks" (1993, p. 2). Further, digit naming speed was the best predictor of reading differences among German normally achieving and dyslexic children.

Wolf et al. (1994) replicated and extended those findings with a larger sample of German children in grades 2 and 4 and with a more extensive battery of naming-speed and phonological measures. They found significant differences between good and poor readers on all naming-speed and reading measures. The phonological awareness deficits of German readers were less pronounced, and decoding of nonsense words was less impeded in average and poor German readers than would be expected in comparable English-speaking groups. The clear exception was the most impaired reading group, who were the equivalent of double-deficit readers and exhibited naming-speed and phonological deficits. Like the Bowers and Wolf findings (1993a), a fair number of German children have solely visual naming speed or solely phonologically based problems.

Perhaps the most unexpected finding in the German data was the result of a fortuitous, unplanned comparison between the grade 2 classes. The first class was taught by traditional German reading methods, which emphasize structured, phonic rules in German. The second class was taught with methods modeled after whole-language principles. The children from the code-structure emphasis were significantly faster on every measure pertaining to the development of automaticity, as measured by six naming-speed and six reading-speed tasks and a unitization comparison similar to Byrne and Fielding-Barnsley (in press). A second analysis was conducted for grade 4 students who had similar curricular methods in grade 2. No significant differences were found on these measures by grade 4. Foorman (1994) suggested that although no differences in automaticity were found in grade 4, differences in comprehension and other untested aspects of fluency might appear later for these children. A longitudinal follow-up is being conducted by Lotz.

These cross-linguistic data suggest that when the phonological demands placed on young readers are reduced, the naming-speed deficit becomes a dominant diagnostic indicator for at-risk readers. In contrast to English-speaking children, many at-risk German prereaders who possess limited phonological skills may be able to master the less stringent demands for phonemic analysis and synthesis imposed by the regular German orthography, and in turn increase their phonological skills. However, our data indicate that these adequate phonological skills do not result in improved reading speed and fluency, if a naming-speed problem is also present (a conclusion also reached by Wood, 1995). The naming-speed-deficit children have continued difficulty mastering reading in German, as do the small group of DD children with both deficits.

Question: Are there electrophysiological differences among Double-Deficit subgroups during the processing of written language?

Brian McPherson (1995), in a dissertation study with Holcomb, Ackerman, Dykman (neuropsychologists specializing in evoked potential research), and myself, conducted an evoked potential study of phonological and orthographic priming among adolescent average readers and two groups of dyslexic readers, divided according to performance on phonological decoding. Sixteen impaired readers had phonological problems; 14 had no phonological problems but did have naming-speed problems.

The results were a fascinating first glimpse at the potentially underlying differences that exist between these impaired reader subgroups. Unlike average readers, who exhibit a strong left hemisphere parietal lobe phonological-priming effect, the phonological-deficit group showed a virtual *absence* of phonological priming in the left hemisphere for visually presented rhymed words (e.g., best–rest). In contrast, the naming-speed deficit subgroup showed what McPherson characterized as an *overabundance* of phonological priming over the left hemisphere TCP site, as well as greater amplitude than controls. The priming effect for the nonphonological, naming-speed deficit group was larger and endured longer than even the controls, especially in parietal regions. In other words, the naming-speed group demonstrated a priming effect where it should be, but seemed less prepared to move on to the next stages of processing (see also results by Ackerman, Dykman, & Oglesby, 1994; Wood, 1995). We return to possible explanations of this inability to proceed in our last phase.

These results are the first attempt to look at possible differences in the underlying brain electrical activity of dyslexic readers characterized by patterns in two subgroups. The dramatic differences in location, duration, and amplitude found between these groups in a phonological task represent a significant step in our ability to prove the existence of separate subgroups of readers.

Phase VII: The Nature of Naming-Speed Deficits

Question: What aspect(s) in the naming-speed requirements is responsible for break-down in naming-speed performance? If these loci can be isolated, will they inform us about this potential source of reading failure?

Mateo Obregón (1994), in a master's thesis, explored these questions by designing an elegant computer program for parsing the speech stream during naming-speed performance on the RAN. In so doing, he was attempting to investigate and isolate three suggested sources of break-down: differences at the level of articulation, end-of-line scanning problems, and interstimulus intervals between stimulus responses. There were no differences in either the speed of articulation for individual verbal labels or the line-to-line scanning by dyslexic readers. Rather, there were large significant differences across all categories of the RAN stimuli during the interstimulus intervals, or the *gap* in time it takes to process each stimulus and move on to the next (Obregón & Wolf, 1995).

I have come to believe that it is what happens *within* that temporal gap that ultimately connects naming-speed findings to the increasing psychophysical evidence regarding rapid processing in visual, auditory, and motoric domains within dyslexic children. (See, for example, Breit-meyer, 1993; Chase & Jenner, 1993; Fawcett & Nicolson, 1994; Lovegrove, 1993; Tallal, Miller, & Fitch, 1993; Tallal, Miller, Jenkins, & Merzenich, chap. 3, this volume; Wolff, 1993). Nicolson & Fawcett (1995) addressed the question whether there exists a basic reaction time (RT) deficit across several modalities and investigated the level of complexity at which RT differences appear or disappear for dyslexics. Their results indicated no RT differences for basic level, unimodal tasks; *quantitative* rate deficits in each modality when the complexity of choice was introduced; and the largest, qualitative difference, on lexical decision tasks. They concluded that there may be two deficits at work in dyslexics: a phonological deficit and a nonphonological deficit in stimulus-classification speed. The sever-ity of lexical decision tasks would reflect both deficits in operation.

I would suggest that it is not so much a stimulus classification-time deficit, but rather what occurs when dyslexic readers are required to *"assemble component* units of behavior into temporally ordered larger en-sembles" (Wolff, 1993, p. 101). Under these conditions they need more time. Thus they take longer on serial tasks, and do better with elongated ISIs in various modalities (see Tallal, Miller, & Fitch, 1993). With more time available, both anticipatory and inhibitory processes would receive more time for preparing for the next behaviors.

FUTURE DIRECTIONS

How do we explain some of the psychophysical findings and naming-speed deficits in terms of neurophysiological mechanisms? There are several promising directions. At the neuronal level, Galaburda's cytoar-chitectonic studies are particularly compelling because they isolate cellular differences in size, structure, myelination, and organization in the mag-nocellular systems in thalamic regions responsible for vision and audition (Galaburda, Menard, & Rosen, 1994; Livingstone, Rosen, Drislane, & Galaburda, 1991). The magnocellular systems have critical roles in rapid processing and in *inhibiting* previous information. Whether or not these anomalies in the magnocellular system will be found across many dyslexic persons and whether they are ultimately responsible for the visual and auditory deficits noted remains an unproven, but enormously attractive possibility.

Two earlier lines of investigation that are less known but equally important to note are Ojemann's work on a cortical precise timing mecha-nism and Furster's (1989) studies of the prefrontal cortex's role in the temporal organization of behavior. Ojemann (1983, 1990) found, through electrical stimulation mapping techniques, that there are common brain mechanisms in the thalamus and left peri-sylvian cortex for some language and motor functions. He contended that in the cortical areas responsible for both sequential motor movements and speech sound identification (critical to phonology), there may be a *precise timing mechanism* that operates for both production and decoding. A deficit in Ojemann's concept of a precise timing mechanism offers one explanation for the conjunction of naming speed and motoric deficits noted in dyslexic populations (see Wolf, 1991a).

Llinas (1993) developed a unique hypothesis for the "binding problem" in theories of human consciousness, with implications for timing deficits in dyslexic children. Like a growing number of researchers, Llinas believed that a perceptual image is constructed from all the cells that are firing in a particular *rhythm* (or rate of oscillation) at a particular instant. Thalamic mechanisms are believed responsible for setting this rhythm within various sensory regions in the cortex. In addition, Llinas posited a general mechanism, the intraluminar nucleus in the thalamus, that sends and receives axons from the entire cortex. The intraluminar nucleus, Llinas hypothesized, has a radar-wavelike scanning system that sweeps across the cortex every 12.5 thousandths of a second and *makes an image* of all that is firing at that instant. This thalamic-cortical dialogue of sampled activity is the basis of consciousness and the perceived image. If, as Llinas (1993) in part speculated, such a precise rhythm is lost in (a) particular neuronal ensembles, (b) in the inhibitory interneurons that are intrinsic to coordination, or (c) in the thalamic system, this "dyschronicity" might cause a timing deficit that looks as general and sweeping as the increasing psychophysical evidence about particular visual, auditory, and motoric deficits.

Summary

There are, to be sure, many loose ends in this last stage of conceptualizing. For example, what connects all the psychophysical data to naming-speed deficits? It is my view that naming speed is connected to the growing psychophysical evidence because it makes use of many of the same processes (i.e., vision, auditory, and motor processes)—just as reading does at a far more complex level of amalgamation (Ehri, 1992). Naming speed is neither a primarily visual (Wood, 1995) or primarily phonological activity (Wagner & Torgesen, 1987). Rather, it is more appropriately depicted as a complex, rapid integration of many cognitive, perceptual, and linguistic processes.

Within this view, both naming and reading represent two levels of rapid, precise integration of cognitive systems, a basic level and a more complex level. Early fissures in the basic system alert us to future weaknesses in the later developing system, and they may even cause them to happen (see Bowers et al., 1994; Wolf & Bowers, 1995). Thus, naming speed provides us with a deceptively simple, extraordinarily useful, early window on some developing disabilities in the reading systems.

In sum, I am convinced that naming-speed deficits are a second core deficit in reading disabilities and that their conjunction with phonological deficits represents a formula for the most impaired readers. The Double-Deficit Hypothesis is ultimately not about two or three subtypes patterns; the complexity of the reading process mitigates against such tidy categories. Rather, this hypothesis is an effort to understand more of the heterogeneity of our disabled readers than is currently modeled. Its most important contribution is the potential for new directions it gives to intervention efforts. By directing our attention to dual emphases on phonological processes and automaticity/fluency skills, we may well increase our effectiveness for a greater number of our at-risk children.

ACKNOWLEDGMENTS

I wish first to thank my colleague Patricia Greig Bowers for her intellectual companionship out of which the Double-Deficit Hypothesis emerged. Second, I thank all past and present members of the Tufts Developmental Neurolinguistic Lab for Dyslexia Research, particularly Heidi Bally, Kathleen Biddle, Charles Borden, Kathy Feinberg, Jennifer Keates, Cynthia Krug, Cory Lewkowicz, Ruth Lotz, Mateo Obregón, Claudia Pfeil, Haleh Rakni, and Denise Segal. I am grateful to Colleen Cunningham, Muriel Goodridge, and Priya Mammen for work on this chapter. Finally, I wish to acknowledge the support of the Stratford Foundation, Educational Foundation of America, and Biomedical Support Grants for the first phases of this work, and the Fulbright Research Fellowship and Tufts Eliot-Pearson Department of Child Study Fund for Faculty Support for research conducted in Germany. Finally, I wish to acknowledge the NICHHD Shannon Award for funding for this chapter.

REFERENCES

Ackerman, P. T., & Dykman, R. A. (1993). Phonological processes, confrontation naming, and immediate memory in dyslexia. *Journal of Learning Disabilities, 26,* 597–609.

Ackerman, P. T., Dykman, R. A., & Gardner, M. Y. (1990). Counting rate, naming rate, phonological sensitivity, and memory span: Major factors in dyslexia. *Journal of Learning Disabilities, 23,* 325–337.

Ackerman, P. T., Dykman, R. A., & Oglesby, D. (1994). Visual event-related potentials of dyslexic children to rhyming and nonrhyming stimuli. *Journal of Clinical and Experimental Neuropsychology, 16*(1), 138–154.

Adams, M. (1990). *Beginning to read*. Cambridge, MA: MIT Press.

Beck, I. L., Perfetti, C. A., & McKeown, M. G. (1982). Effects of long-term vocabulary instruction of lexical access and reading comprehension. *Journal of Educational Psychology, 74*, 506–521.

Berninger, V., Abbot, S. P., Greep, K., Reed, E., Hooven, C., & Abbot, R. D. (1995, March). *Single, double, and triple deficits in impaired readers at the end of first grade: Individual differences in learner characteristics and response to intervention*. Paper presented at the Society for Research in Child Development, Indianapolis, IN.

Biddle, K. R. (1995). *The development of visual naming speed and verbal fluency in average and impaired readers: The implications for assessment, intervention, and theory*. Unpublished doctoral dissertation, Tufts University, Boston.

Bisiach, E. (1966). Perceptual factors in pathogenesis of anomia. *Cortex, 2*, 90–95.

Blachman, B. A. (1984). Relationship of rapid naming ability and language analysis skills to Kindergarten and first-grade reading achievement. *Journal of Educational Psychology, 76*, 610–622.

Blachman, B. A. (1994). What we have learned from longitudinal studies of phonological processing and reading, *and* some unanswered questions: A response to Torgesen, Wagner, and Rashotte. *Journal of Learning Disabilities, 27*, 287–291.

Bowers, P. G. (1993). Text reading and rereading: Predictors of fluency beyond word recognition. *Journal of Reading Behavior, 25*, 133–153.

Bowers, P. G., Golden, J., Kennedy, A., & Young, A. (1994). Limits upon orthographic knowledge due to processes indexed by naming-speed. In V. W. Berninger (Ed.), *The varieties of orthographic knowledge, Vol. I: Theoretical and developmental issues* (pp. 173–218). Dordrecht, The Netherlands: Kluwer.

Bowers, P. G., Steffy, R., & Tate, E. (1988). Comparison of the effects of IQ control methods on memory and naming speed predictors of reading disability. *Reading Research Quarterly, 23*, 304–309.

Bowers, P. G., & Swanson, L. B. (1991). Naming speed deficits in reading disability: Multiple measures of a singular process. *Journal of Experimental Child Psychology, 51*, 195–219.

Bowers, P. G., & Wolf, M. (1993a). Theoretical links among naming speed, precise timing mechanisms and orthographic skill in dyslexia. *Reading and Writing: An Interdisciplinary Journal, 5*(1), 69–85.

Bowers, P. G., & Wolf, M. (1993b, April). *A "Double-Deficit Hypothesis" for developmental reading disorders*. Paper presented at the Society for Research in Child Development, New Orleans, LA.

Brady, S. (1995, May). *Current thoughts on the association between speech perception and reading ability*. Paper presented at Extraordinary Brain III Conference, Kauai, Hawaii.

Breitmeyer, B. (1993). Sustained (P) and transient (M) channels in vision: A review and implications for reading. In D. M. Willows, R. S. Kruk, & E. Corco (Eds.), *Visual processes in reading and reading disabilities* (pp. 95–110). Hillsdale, NJ: Lawrence Erlbaum Associates.

Byrne, B., & Fielding-Barnsley, R. (in press). Evaluation of a program to teach phonological awareness to young children: A 2- and 3-year follow-up, and a new preschool trial. *Journal of Educational Psychology*.

Chase, C., & Jenner, A. R. (1993). Magnocellular visual deficits affect temporal processing of dyslexics. *Annals of the New York Academy of Sciences, 682*, 326–329.

Cossu, G., Shankweiler, D., Liberman, I., Katz, L., & Tola, G. (1988). Awareness of phonological segments and reading ability in Italian children. *Applied Psycholinguistics, 9*, 1–16.

Curtis, M. E. (1987). Vocabulary testing and vocabulary instruction. In M. G. McKeown & M. E. Curtis (Eds.), *The nature of vocabulary acquisition* (pp. 37–51). Hillsdale, NJ: Lawrence Erlbaum Associates.

Damasio, A. R. (1994). *Descartes' error*. New York: Putnam.

Denckla, M. B. (1972). Color-naming defects in dyslexic boys. *Cortex, 8*, 164–176.

Denckla, M. B., & Rudel, R. G. (1974). "Rapid automatized naming" of pictured objects, colors, letters and numbers by normal children. *Cortex, 10*, 186–202.

Denckla, M. B., & Rudel, R. G. (1976a). Naming of objects by dyslexic and other learning-disabled children. *Brain and Language, 3*, 1–15.

Denckla, M. B., & Rudel, R. G. (1976b). Rapid automatized naming (R.A.N.): Dyslexia differentiated from other learning disabilities. *Neuropsychologia, 14*, 471–479.

Doehring, D., Trites, R., Patel, P., & Fiedorwicz, A. (1981). *Reading disabilities: The interaction of reading, language, and neuropsychological deficits.* New York: Academic Press.

Ehri, L. C. (1992). Reconceptualizing the development of sight word reading and its relationship to recoding. In P. B. Gough, L. C. Ehri, & R. Treiman (Eds.), *Reading acquisition* (pp. 107–143). Hillsdale, NJ: Lawrence Erlbaum Associates.

Ellis, A. W. (1985). The cognitive neuropsychology of developmental (and acquired) dyslexia: A critical survey. *Cognitive Neuropsychology, 2*, 169–205.

Fawcett, A., & Nicolson, R. (1994). Naming speed in children with dyslexia. *Journal of Learning Disabilities, 27*, 641–646.

Feinberg, K. (1995). *Vocabulary knowledge and word-retrieval ability of adolescents with dyslexia.* Unpublished master's thesis, Tufts University, Boston.

Felton, R. H., & Brown, I. S. (1990). Phonological processes as predictors of specific reading skills in children at risk for reading failure. *Reading and Writing: An Interdisciplinary Journal, 2*, 39–59.

Felton, R. H., Naylor, C., & Wood, F. B. (1990). Neuropsychological profile of adult dyslexics. *Brain and Language, 39*, 485–497.

Foorman, B. R. (1994). Phonological and orthographic processing: Separate but equal? In V. W. Berninger (Ed.), *The varieties of orthographic knowledge I: Theoretical and developmental issues* (pp. 319–355). Dordrecht, The Netherlands: Kluwer.

Furster, J. (1989). A theory of prefrontal cortex and the temporal organization of behavior. In J. Furster (Ed.), *The prefrontal cortex* (pp. 157–196). New York: Raven.

Galaburda, A. M., Menard, M. T., & Rosen, G. D. (1994). Evidence for aberrant auditory anatomy in developmental dyslexia. *Proceedings of the National Academy of Sciences, 91*, 8010–8013.

German, D. J. (1992). Word-finding intervention for children and adolescents. *Topics in Language Disorders, 13*(1), 33–50.

Geschwind, N. (1965). Disconnection syndrome in animals and man (Parts I, II). *Brain, 88*, 237–294, 585–644.

Goodglass, H. (1980). Disorders of naming following brain injury. *American Scientist, 68*, 647–655.

Goodglass, H., & Kaplan, E. (1972). *The assessment of aphasia and related disorders.* Philadelphia: Lea & Febiger.

Goswami, U., & Swan, D. (1994, April). *Confrontation naming in dyslexic and garden-variety poor readers.* Paper presented at the Society for Scientific Study of Reading, New Orleans, LA.

Haynes, C. (1994). *Differences between name recognition and name retrieval abilities in relationship to reading performance.* Unpublished doctoral dissertation, Harvard University, Cambridge, MA.

Kameenui, E. J., Dixon, R. C., & Carnine, D. W. (1987). Issues in the design of vocabulary instructions. In M. G. McKeown & M. Curtis (Eds.), *The nature of vocabulary acquisition* (pp. 129–145). Hillsdale, NJ: Lawrence Erlbaum Associates.

Kaplan, E., Goodglass, H., & Weintraub, S. (1983). *The Boston Naming Test.* Philadelphia: Lea & Febiger.

Korhonen, T. (1995). The persistence of rapid naming problems in children with reading disabilities: A nine-year follow-up. *Journal of Learning Disabilities, 28,* 232–239.

Krug, C. (1995). *The diagnostic implications of the "Double-Deficit Hypothesis": An investigation of fifth grade readers classified by decoding skill and visual naming-speed.* Unpublished doctoral dissertation, Tufts University, Boston.

LaBerge, D., & Samuels, S. J. (1974). Toward a theory of automatic information processing in reading. *Cognitive Psychology, 6,* 293–323.

Lahey, M., & Edwards, J. (1995). *Why are specifically language-impaired children slower than their peers in naming pictures?* Submitted manuscript.

Levy, B. A., & Hinchley, J. (1990). Individual and developmental differences in acquisition of reading skills. In T. H. Carr & B. A. Levy (Eds.), *Reading and its development: Component skills approaches.* New York: Academic Press.

Livingstone, M. S., Rosen, G. D., Drislane, F. W., & Galaburda, A. M. (1991). Physiological and anatomical evidence for a magnocellular defect in developmental dyslexia. *Neurobiology, 88,* 7943–7947.

Llinas, R. (1993). Is dyslexia a dyschronia? In P. Tallal, A. Galaburda, R. Llinas, & C. von Euler (Eds.), *Temporal information processing in the nervous system* (pp. 48–62). *Annals of the New York Academy of Sciences, 682.*

Logan, G. D. (1988). Toward an instant theory of automatization. *Psychological Review, 95,* 492–527.

Lovegrove, W. (1993). Weakness in the transient visual system: A causal factor in dyslexia? In P. Tallal, A. Galaburda, R. Llinas, & C. von Euler (Eds.), *Temporal information processing in the nervous system: Special reference to dyslexia and dysphasia* (pp. 57–69). *Annals of the New York Academy of Sciences, 682.*

Lovett, M. (1987). A developmental approach to reading disability: Accuracy and speed criteria of normal and deficient reading skill. *Child Development, 58,* 234–260.

Lovett, M. (1992). Developmental dyslexia. In F. Boller & J. Grafman (Eds.), *Handbook of neuropsychology* (Vol. 7, pp. 163–185). Amsterdam: Elsevier.

Lovett, M. (1995, March). *Remediating dyslexic children's word identification deficits: Are the core deficits of developmental dyslexia amenable to treatment?* Symposium paper presented at Society for Research in Child Development, Indianapolis, IN.

Lovett, M., Borden, S., DeLuca, T., Lacerenza, L., Benson, N., & Brackstone, D. (1994). Treating the core deficits of developmental dyslexia: Evidence of transfer of learning after phonologically- and strategy-based reading training programs. *Developmental Psychology, 30,* 805–822.

Manis, F., & Doi, L. (1995, March). *Word naming speed, phonological coding and orthographic knowledge in dyslexic and normal readers.* Symposium paper presented at the Society for Research in Child Development, Indianapolis, IN.

McGregor, K., & Leonard, L. B. (1989). Facilitating word-finding skills of language-impaired children. *Journal of Speech and Hearing Disorders, 54,* 141–147.

McPherson, W. B. (1995). *A comparison of normal and disabled readers' event-related brain potentials elicited during phonological processing.* Unpublished doctoral dissertation, Tufts University, Boston.

Morris, R., Lovett, M., & Wolf, M. (1995). Treatment of developmental reading disabilities (NICHHD Grant #1 R55 HD/OD30970-01A1).

Näslund, J. C., & Schneider, W. (1991). Longitudinal effects of verbal ability, memory capacity, and phonological awareness on reading performance. *European Journal of Psychology of Education, 4,* 375–392.

Nicolson, R. I., & Fawcett, A. J. (1995). Reaction times and dyslexia. *Quarterly Journal of Experimental Psychology, 47,* 29–48.

Novoa, L. (1988). *Word-retrieval process and reading acquisition and development in bilingual and monolingual children*. Unpublished doctoral dissertation, Harvard University, Cambridge, MA.

Novoa, L., & Wolf, M. (1984, October). *Word-retrieval and reading in bilingual children*. Paper presented at Boston University Language Conference, Boston.

Obregón, M. (1994). *Exploring naming timing patterns by dyslexic and normal readers on the serial RAN task*. Unpublished master's thesis, Tufts University, Boston.

Obregón, M., & Wolf, M. (1995, April). *A fine-grained analysis of serial naming duration patterns in developmental dyslexia*. Poster presented at the Society for Research in Child Development, Indianapolis, IN.

Ojemann, G. A. (1983). Brain organization for language from the perspective of electrical stimulation mapping. *Behavioral Brain Science, 6*, 189–230.

Ojemann, G. A. (1990). Organization of language derived from investigations during neurosurgery. *Neuroscience, 2*, 297–305.

Perfetti, C. A. (1985). *Reading ability*. New York: Oxford University Press.

Perfetti, C. A., Finger, E., & Hogaboam, T. (1978). Sources of vocalization latency differences between skilled and less skilled young readers. *Journal of Educational Psychology, 70*, 730–739.

Scarborough, H. S. (1990). Very early language deficits in dyslexic children. *Child Development, 61*(6), 1728–1743.

Schneider, W., & Näslund, J. C. (1992). Cognitive prerequisites of reading and spelling: A longitudinal approach. In A. Demetriou, M. Shayer, & A. Efklides (Eds.), *Neo-Piagetian theories of cognitive development: Implications and applications for educators* (pp. 256–274). London: Routledge.

Segal, D., & Wolf, M. (1993). Automaticity, word retrieval, and vocabulary development in children with reading disabilities. In L. Meltzer (Ed.), *Cognitive, linguistic, and developmental perspectives on learning disorders* (pp. 141–165). Boston: Little, Brown.

Shankweiler, D., & Liberman, I. Y. (1972). Misreading: A search for causes. In J. F. Kavanagh & I. Y. Liberman (Eds.), *Language by ear and by eye* (pp. 293–317). Cambridge, MA: MIT Press.

Spring, C., & Capps, C. (1974). Encoding speed, rehearsal, and probed recall of dyslexic boys. *Journal of Educational Psychology, 66*, 780–786.

Spring, C., & Davis, J. (1988). Relations of digit naming speed with three components of reading. *Applied Psycholinguistics, 9*, 315–334.

Stanovich, K. E. (1986). "Matthew effects" in reading: Some consequences of individual differences in acquisition of literacy. *Reading Research Quarterly, 4*, 360–407.

Stanovich, K. E. (1990). Concepts in developmental theories of reading skill: Cognitive resources, automaticity and modularity. *Developmental Review, 10*, 72–100.

Stanovich, K. E. (1992). Speculations on the causes and consequences of individual differences in early reading acquisition. In P. B. Gough, L. C. Ehri, & R. Treiman (Eds.), *Reading acquisition* (pp. 307–342). Hillsdale, NJ: Lawrence Erlbaum Associates.

Stanovich, K. E. (1995, May). *Processing models and definitional issues in dyslexia*. Paper presented at Extraordinary Brain III Conference, Kauai, Hawaii.

Tallal, P., Miller, S., & Fitch, R. (1993). Neurological basis of speech: A case for the prominence of temporal processing. In P. Tallal, A. Galaburda, R. Llinas, & C. von Euler (Eds.), *Temporal information processing in the nervous system* (pp. 27–37). *Annals of the New York Academy of Sciences, 682*.

Torgesen, J. K. (1995, May). *Instructional alternatives for children with severe reading disabilities*. Paper presented at Extraordinary Brain III Conference, Kauai, Hawaii.

Torgesen, J. K., Wagner, R. K., & Rashotte, C. A. (1994). Longitudinal studies of phonological processing and reading. *Journal of Learning Disabilities, 27*(10), 276–286.

Valtin, R. (1989). Awareness of features and functions of language. In F. Downing & R. Valtin (Eds.), *Language awareness and learning to read* (pp. 227–260). New York: Springer-Verlag.

Vellutino, F., & Scanlon, D. (1987). Phonological coding, phonological awareness, and reading ability: Evidence from a longitudinal and experimental study. *Merrill Palmer Quarterly, 33,* 321–363.

Vellutino, F., Steger, B., Moyers, S., Harding, C., & Niles, J. (1977). Has the perceptual deficit hypothesis led us astray? *Journal of Learning Disabilities, 10,* 375–384.

Wagner, R. K., & Torgesen, J. K. (1987). The nature of phonological processing and its causal role in the acquisition of reading skills. *Psychological Bulletin, 101,* 192–212.

Wagner, R. K., Torgesen, J. K., Laughon, P. L., Simmons, K., & Rashotte, C. A. (1993). Development of young readers' phonological processing abilities. *Journal of Educational Psychology, 85*(1), 83–103.

Wagner, R. K., Torgesen, J. K., & Rashotte, C. A. (1994). The development of reading-related phonological processing abilities: New evidence of bidirectional causality from a latent variable longitudinal study. *Developmental Psychology, 30,* 73–87.

Wimmer, H. (1993). Characteristics of developmental dyslexia in a regular writing system. *Applied Psycholinguistics, 14,* 1–34.

Wimmer, H., & Hummer, P. (1990). How German-speaking first graders read and spell: Doubts on the importance of the logographic stage. *Applied Psycholinguistics, 11,* 349–368.

Wing, C. S. (1990). A preliminary investigation of generalization to untrained words following two treatments of children's word-finding problems. *Language, Speech, and Hearing Services in Schools, 21,* 151–156.

Wolf, M. (1982). The word-retrieval process and reading in children and aphasics. In K. Nelson (Ed.), *Children's language* (pp. 437–493). Hillsdale, NJ: Lawrence Erlbaum Associates.

Wolf, M. (1986). Rapid alternating stimulus naming in the developmental dyslexias. *Brain and Language, 27,* 360–379.

Wolf, M. (1991a). Naming speed and reading. The contribution of the cognitive neurosciences. *Reading Research Quarterly, 26*(2), 123–141.

Wolf, M. (1991b, April). *Word-wraiths: The unique contribution of the naming system to reading prediction and intervention in developmental dyslexia.* Paper presented at the Society for Research in Child Development, Seattle, WA.

Wolf, M. (1995, March). *The "Double-Deficit Hypothesis" in developmental reading disorders.* Symposium paper at Society for Research in Child Development, Indianapolis, IN.

Wolf, M., Bally, H., & Morris, R. (1986). Automaticity, retrieval processes, and reading: A longitudinal study in average and impaired readers. *Child Development, 57,* 988–1000.

Wolf, M., & Bowers, P. (1995). *The "Double-Deficit Hypothesis" for the developmental dyslexias.* Paper in preparation.

Wolf, M., & Obregón, M. (1989, April). *88 children in search of a name: A five year investigation of rate, word-retrieval, and vocabulary in reading development and dyslexia.* Paper presented at Society for Research in Child Development, Kansas City, MO.

Wolf, M., & Obregón, M. (1992). Early naming deficits, developmental dyslexia, and a specific deficit hypothesis. *Brain and Language, 42,* 219–247.

Wolf, M., Pfeil, C., Lotz, R., & Biddle, K. (1994). Towards a more universal understanding of the developmental dyslexias: The contribution of orthographic factors. In V. W. Berninger (Ed.), *The varieties of orthographic knowledge I: Theoretical and developmental issues* (pp. 137–171). Dordrecht, The Netherlands: Kluwer.

Wolf, M., & Segal, D. (1995). *Retrieval-rate, accuracy and vocabulary elaboration (RAVE) in reading-impaired children: A pilot intervention program.* Submitted manuscript.

Wolff, P. (1993). Impaired temporal resolution in developmental dyslexia. In P. Tallal, A. Galaburda, R. Llinas, & C. von Euler (Eds.), *Temporal information processing in the nervous system* (pp. 87–103). *Annals of the New York Academy of Sciences, 682,* 87–103.

Wood, F. (1995, March). *Naming speed deficits in dyslexia.* Poster presented at meetings of Society for Research in Child Development, Indianapolis, IN.

Yap, R. L., & van der Leij, A. (1993). Word processing in dyslexics: An automatic decoding deficit? *Reading and Writing: An Interdisciplinary Journal, 5*(3), 261–279.

Yap, R. L., & van der Leij, A. (1994). Testing the automatization deficit hypothesis of dyslexia via a dual-task paradigm. *Journal of Learning Disabilities, 27*(10), 660–665.

II

SUBTYPES OF DYSLEXIA

5

Subtypes of Dyslexia:
An Old Problem Revisited

Jack M. Fletcher
University of Texas—Houston Medical School

Robin Morris
Georgia State University

G. Reid Lyon
National Institute of Child Health and Human Development, Bethesda, MD

Karla K. Stuebing
University of Texas—Houston Medical School

Sally E. Shaywitz
Yale University School of Medicine

Donald P. Shankweiler and Len Katz
University of Connecticut
Haskins Laboratories

Bennett A. Shaywitz
Yale University School of Medicine

From the earliest observations of unexpected reading failure, investigators have puzzled over the apparent heterogeneity of children with dyslexia. These observations have led to speculative hypotheses as well as empirical investigations of the possibility that dyslexia represents different subtypes that vary in phenotypic characteristics, neurobiological correlates, and response to intervention.

The interest in this apparent heterogeneity has multiple sources, including: (a) epidemiological studies suggesting multiple distributions of reading skills (Rutter & Yule, 1975); (b) clinic-based studies suggesting that children identified as dyslexic have problems with a variety of cognitive and neuropsychological skills (Rourke, 1985); and (c) comorbidity of reading disability with attention deficit hyperactivity disorder (ADHD) and other academic skill disorders (arithmetic, spelling). These sources led to a search for possible subtypes of dyslexia and learning disability, often giving rise to findings that were difficult to interpret according to hypothetical models of the relationship of cognitive skills and reading.

A major factor in these interpretative difficulties reflects two competing interests underlying research on dyslexia. One set of investigations has been oriented toward understanding the cognitive basis of reading failure in children. These investigations, conducted primarily by cognitive psychologists, have produced important findings on the relationship of key linguistic skills and reading (Liberman, Shankweiler, & Liberman, 1989; Vellutino, 1991). The second set of investigations, conducted largely by neuropsychologists and behavioral neurologists, viewed the reading problem as one of many characteristics of children with dyslexia (Benton, 1975). Of particular interest to the latter investigations was the possibility that variations in neuropsychological functioning would shed light on the neurobiological basis of dyslexia (Rourke, 1985).

The question of subtypes is critical to both sets of investigations. However, like many studies of children with learning disabilities, the search for subtypes has been hampered by a number of problems, of which three are primary. First, there has been a failure to examine definitional issues that influence which children are identified as dyslexic (Fletcher & Morris, 1986). Second, most investigations have not selected variables for classification according to a contemporary framework relating cognitive skills and reading. Third, clinical and statistical approaches to subtype analysis have not devoted sufficient attention to reliability and validity issues (Morris & Fletcher, 1988). All three of these problems led to a variety of subtypes that varied across laboratories and methods. Not surprisingly, the subtype research has had little impact on neurobiological and intervention studies of children who have reading disabilities.

The purpose of this chapter is to evaluate the possibility that dyslexia may represent multiple subtypes. This evaluation occurs in the context of a general discussion of classification issues in disorders such as dyslexia. We provide a brief historical review of the evolution of the concept of dyslexia and the hypothesis that dyslexia may represent different subtypes. Three specific attempts to derive subtypes are reviewed, including studies from the Florida Longitudinal Project (Satz & Morris, 1981), Lyon and associates (Lyon, 1985a, 1985b), and a recent study from the Yale Center for the Study of Learning and Attention Disorders (Morris et al., 1997). The purpose of reviewing the first two sets of studies is to elaborate on methodological issues in subtype studies, which are exemplified by these studies. The Morris et al. study expanded on previous investigations because variable selection was based on a theoretically motivated model of language and reading developed by Haskins Laboratories (Liberman et al., 1989). As such, this study avoided a major limitation of most previous subtype studies because the classification variables were consistent with current hypotheses concerning the cognitive basis of reading disability. However, variables were also selected to permit broader specifications of the phenotypic variability possibly associated with dyslexia, thus attempting to bridge the gap between neuropsychological approaches to subtypes (reviewed in Hooper & Willis, 1989; Rourke, 1985) and cognitive approaches to reading disability (Liberman et al., 1989).

CLASSIFICATION OF DYSLEXIA

The need for better definitions and classifications of dyslexia has been frequently emphasized (see Fletcher & Morris, 1986). A general framework for approaching classification issues in disorders such as dyslexia was provided by Morris and Fletcher (1988). The literature on subtyping learning disabilities was reviewed by Rourke (1985) and Hooper and Willis (1989). In the next sections, we briefly review issues concerning the nature of classification and the application of classification approaches to dyslexia.

What Is Classification?

Implicit within any conceptualization of a set of phenomena as an entity is a classification. If we decide to set off reading failure as an entity, disorder, diagnosis, or any partition of individuals who read poorly from those who read less poorly, a classification hypothesis has been developed. Classification hypotheses can occur at the level of the individual or the group. The hypotheses can be tested, but the test is at the level of the independent variable—not the way that psychological research is typically conceptualized, which is at the level of the dependent variable. What is often not recognized is that the results of any experiment are a test not only of the hypotheses leading to the selection of the dependent variables, but also of the hypotheses leading to the selection of the independent variable—in most of the research considered in this volume, a test of the classification that led to identification of individuals as impaired or not impaired in reading. If the results of a study are null, the problem could reside at the level of the dependent variable, but another possibility is always that the classification that led to the use of an independent variable was not valid (Morris & Fletcher, 1988).

Classification—the testing of hypotheses about the validity of independent variables—is an enterprise unto itself. In classification, the questions about the independent variables are made explicit. Studies can be designed to explicitly evaluate the validity of the classifications that led the investigator to set aside, subdivide, or otherwise identify a set of observations as an entity.

Classification is not identification. Classification leads to a set of criteria that permit the identification of individuals into the subsets of the classification. It is always possible that although the classification is valid, the procedures whereby the classification is operationalized are not valid. It is also possible to have classifications that have limited validity, but which validly identify individuals with the characteristics of interest.

The use of IQ discrepancy definitions for dyslexia is a case in point, exemplifying the relationship of classification, definition, and identification. Individuals with dyslexia are validly *identified* with IQ discrepancy definitions, but the underlying *classification* is not valid because of poor coverage and lack of discriminative validity. In other words, IQ discrepancy *definitions* succeed in separating normal and disabled readers, but fail to separate subgroups of poor readers (Fletcher et al., 1994; Stanovich & Siegel, 1994).

Early Classifications of Dyslexia

The notion that subgroups of poor readers may exist has been apparent since the earliest observations of unexpected reading failure (see Doris, 1993). These early descriptions separated cases of reading failure into an acquired type—alexia, where word blindness was complete—and a congenital type—dyslexia, or partial word blindness (Hinschelwood, 1896). Both types were conceptualized as visual agnosias for words and were viewed as severe perceptual disorders. Implicit in these early descriptions was the notion that whereas the cause of alexia was known brain damage, the cause of dyslexia was only suspected brain damage. To understand the cause of dyslexia required a classification that separated alexia and dyslexia on the basis of their association with known brain damage, representing an early exclusionary criterion. Consequently, to understand the cause of dyslexia, cases had to be selected where there was no evidence of injury to the brain. At the time, it was important to understand the cause in order to develop effective treatments.

Particularly puzzling to early investigators was the presence of reading failure in children who were not mentally deficient, socially underprivileged, and who seemed to have received adequate instruction (see Fletcher et al., 1996). These early observations ultimately evolved into the World Federation of Neurology definition of dyslexia in 1968 (Critchley, 1970). This definition formed the basis for Rutter and Yule's (1975) specification of specific reading retardation as a disorder distinguished from general backward reading in prevalence, gender, neurologic characteristics, and change over time—marked by the presence of IQ discrepancy in specific reading retardation and not general reading backwardness. Here it is important to recognize that the Isle of Wight studies by Rutter and Yule (1975) were based on an epidemiological design in which no exclusionary criteria were applied, such that the backward reading group included children with mental deficiency and actual brain injury—13% had cerebral palsy. As such, Rutter and Yule (1975) actually provided strong support for the two-factor theory of mental retardation (Zigler & Hodapp, 1988), not the two-group classification of reading underachievement as it is commonly employed to separate discrepant from nondiscrepant low achievement (Fletcher et al., 1994).

The consequences of discrepancy-based classifications for interventions are most alarming. Such classifications are not stable over time (S. E. Shaywitz, Escobar, B. A. Shaywitz, Fletcher, & Makuch, 1992). Identifying a child as dyslexic because of a discrepancy between reading and IQ in grade 1 is not reliable by grade 3. Because of random variation, children will move around the cutpoint. Discrepancy definitions are also influenced by regression to the mean. If children are defined into discrepancy and low achievement groups, and then not randomly assigned to treatments, the discrepancy group will show improvement over time solely because of regression to the mean (B. A. Shaywitz, Fletcher, Holahan, & S. E. Shaywitz, 1992). Finally, because of problems with the floors of achievement tests and the need for children to fail at reading in order to obtain a discrepancy, the use of IQ discrepancies makes it difficult to intervene with poor readers prior to grade 2. This is unfortunate, because early intervention approaches have been effective with poor readers (see Foorman, Francis, S. E. Shaywitz, B. A. Shaywitz, & Fletcher, chap. 11, this volume).

It is not surprising that the major findings of the Isle of Wight studies are largely unreplicated, given that most subsequent studies excluded children with mental deficiency and brain injury. Thus, we are left with a heterogeneous group with no obvious proxy for isolating the "unexpected" cases so that we might identify the cause of dyslexia and develop effective treatments (Stanovich & Siegel, 1994).

Why Subtypes?

The search for subtypes that would lead to the identification of the neurobiological causes of dyslexia and, subsequently, to effective treatment pervaded much of dyslexia research for many years. One consequence of this approach was a focus on dyslexia as more than a disorder of reading. Investigators puzzled over the relationship of dyslexia with deficits in finger recognition, spatial orientation, right–left orientation, perceptual motor skills, and other processes with no obvious relationship to normal reading (Benton, 1975; Satz & van Nostrand, 1973). In fact, these findings tended to drive theories of reading, such as the notion of reading disability as a parietal lobe disorder epitomized by color naming deficits (Benton, 1975). Reading was therefore viewed as a heavily visual process. Nonetheless, it was common up into the 1980s to focus on these characteristics as the phenomenon of interest. Here, investigators were frustrated because of the heterogeneity of the phenotypic presentation of these disorders. This was repeatedly emphasized in the 1970s, culminating in the 1976 NIMH conference published in Benton and Pearl (1978). From this conference, investigators left determined to address the heterogeneity problem by identifying subtypes of dyslexia. There were many studies that used either rational or statistical approaches—seldom both—to search archival databases for subtypes. This research was a complete and utter failure and seems to have largely disappeared at this point in time.

There are several factors underlying the failure of these studies. First, there was no coherent theory to guide the selection of classification attributes. Second, there was no overarching model of classification to guide the investigation. Third, there was insufficient attention to fundamental methodological issues involving reliability and validity. And fourth, there was insufficient attention to sampling issues and related methodological issues.

In the past 10 years, matters have shifted. There is now a coherent theoretical framework for classification models that can be articulated for dyslexia (Morris & Fletcher, 1988). The sources of variability can be addressed. Finally, the goals have changed. There is less emphasis on discovering the cause of dyslexia; rather, the interest is the development of treatments, reflecting development of theories of reading. The problem of heterogeneity remains. It is not clear how to link treatment with classifications when subjects vary on multiple dimensions. For example, treatment investigations must consider the presence of ADHD. If the outcome measure is sensitive to compliance or attention, the effect of intervention may be on processes not specific to the reading disorder. Similarly, other cognitive problems may influence response to treatment. People with dyslexia do not have problems restricted to the phonological domain.

Groups differ on virtually every cognitive dimension, reflecting the heterogeneity associated with the disorder (Fletcher et al., 1994).

Given these complexities, it is not surprising that subtype investigations seem to have lost their one-time prominence in the literature. However, important advances have occurred that may revive this approach to dyslexia research. There are two important assumptions about dyslexia that must be recognized in order to appreciate the value of subtype research. First, dyslexia is clearly more than a reading disorder. We have a good understanding of the cognitive basis of single-word decoding skills. However, many individuals with dyslexia have other language problems. Word decoding problems occur at all levels of IQ and socioeconomic status (Siegel, 1992). Individual children with dyslexia also have problems with visual–spatial skills, finger agnosia, and other nonlinguistic skills. The question is whether this phenotypic variation is relevant, which is fundamentally a classification issue. Second, dyslexia can only be appreciated in a multivariate context. It is difficult to imagine a skill that, when appropriately measured in a sufficiently large sample, will not yield statistically significant differences between dyslexic and normal readers. This problem, clearly outlined in the Benton and Pearl (1978) proceedings by Doehring (1978), shows that all of the reported differences between dyslexics and normals are real. Indeed, each of these univariate differences can be turned into a theory. The question is whether such univariate differences are meaningful, which can only be pursued in the context of other phenotypic differences. Such variation may not be important for understanding the reading problem, but may be important for understanding response to treatment interventions or the neurobiology of dyslexia. Investigating subtypes is one approach to addressing these issues, which the following three sets of studies demonstrate.

FLORIDA STUDIES

The Florida study applied cluster analysis to neuropsychological test scores obtained on 89 children selected according to a cluster analysis of the Reading, Spelling, and Arithmetic subtests of the Wide Range Achievement Test (Morris, Blashfield, & Satz, 1981; Satz & Morris, 1981). These children were selected from a larger group of 236 children in the Florida Longitudinal Project (Satz, Taylor, Friel, & Fletcher, 1978) who were evaluated in the fifth grade (about 10.5 years of age). The 89 children selected for the cluster analysis of cognitive variables represented subgroups with the lowest WRAT scores in the sample, performing about one standard deviation below the sample mean.

The cluster analyses were performed using four variables: Beery Test of Visual-Motor Integration, a measure of visual-motor copying (Beery &

Buktenica, 1967); Recognition-Discrimination, a measure of geometric shape matching (Satz & Fletcher, 1982); the Similarities subtest of the WISC-R (Wechsler, 1974); and a verbal fluency measure requiring the child to retrieve words that began with specific letters (Spreen & Benton, 1969). These measures were selected because they were highly reliable and represented the underlying dimensions of the overall test battery administered in grade 5.

The cluster analysis was performed using an average-linkage, hierarchical agglomerative technique, followed by K-means iterative partitioning to group individuals most similar to each other on the four variables. Hierarchical agglomerative techniques work by combining pairs of observations into nonoverlapping clusters on the basis of profile similarity, beginning with a set of clusters equal to the number of subjects and recomputing successive combinations of subjects into cluster solutions.

A major problem in cluster analysis is determining the optimal number of clusters. Hence, different clustering solutions were followed with an iterative partitioning method, in which subjects were reassigned to alternative clusters to determine whether the assigned subtype was the most appropriate classification for each subject. The similarity coefficient was squared Euclidean distance, which compares profiles based on shape, scatter, and elevation. From this analysis, six clusters (subgroups) emerged, representing five subtypes and one cluster of outliers ($n = 3$). The profiles of the five subtypes are presented in Fig. 5.1, along with scores on the Peabody Picture Vocabulary Test.

As Fig. 5.1 shows, Subtype 1 ($n = 27$) was relatively lower on the verbal tasks, with a lower PPVT score. Performance on the visual–spatial tests was in the average range, so that this subtype represented a "general verbal" group. Subtype 2 ($n = 14$) was impaired on only the Verbal Fluency test, and thus represented a "specific verbal" (naming) group. Subtype 3 ($n = 10$) was impaired on all of the cognitive tests (verbal and visual–spatial) and was labeled a "mixed-global" subtype. Subtype 4 ($n = 23$) was impaired primarily on the nonverbal perceptual tests, and was defined as a "visual–spatial" subtype. Subtype 5 ($n = 12$) showed no impairment on any of the neuropsychological tests, and was labeled an "unexpected" subtype.

In order to assess the adequacy and stability of the six-cluster solution, a variety of internal validity studies were conducted (Morris et al., 1981). These results, which showed that the subtypes were reliable, were also replicated by van der Vlugt and Satz (1985) in Holland and in a separate study in Pittsburgh (Johnston, 1985). The five subgroups also differed on a variety of variables not used for clustering, including family history, neurological status, and developmental patterns (Morris et al., 1981).

Although the clusters were reliable and replicable, they have not had much impact on research on reading disabilities. This most likely reflects

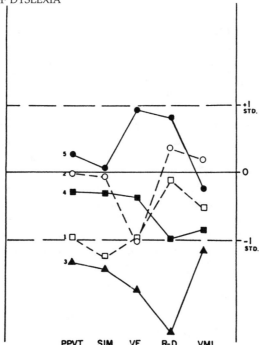

FIG. 5.1. Standardized z-scores for children with reading disabilities representing five subtypes produced by cluster analysis of the WISC-R Similarities (SIM) subtest, Verbal Fluency (VF), Recognition-Discrimination (RD), and the Beery Test of Visual-Motor Integration (VMI). The Peabody Picture Vocabulary Test (PPVT) mean for each cluster is also included. Adapted from "Neuropsychology and Cluster Analysis: Problems and Pitfalls," by R. Morris, R. Blashfield, and P. Satz, 1981, *Journal of Clinical Neuropsychology*, *3*, 79–99. Used with permission.

the nature of the classification variables. The measures used do not have great theoretical relevance to current theories of reading, which emphasize various language skills, particularly in the phonological domain. In addition, the external validity component was atheoretical, using available variables that weren't designed for explicit external validity studies. This latter problem was addressed in the next study.

LYON STUDIES

Lyon and his associates (Lyon, 1983, 1985a, 1985b; Lyon, Stewart, & Freedman, 1982; Lyon & Watson, 1981) questioned the appropriateness of a single-deficit classification model for reading disability, and hypothesized that children with reading disability constitute a heterogeneous population composed of a number of subtypes. Specifically, Lyon (1983) proposed that reading development is a complex process that requires the concerted participation of cognitive, linguistic, and perceptual subskills. As such, deficiencies in any one subskill can limit the acquisition of fluent decoding and/or reading comprehension abilities.

Within this theoretical context, two series of investigations were conducted: one series with older LD readers, the second with younger LD readers. In the first series (Lyon & Watson, 1981), a battery of tasks designed to assess linguistic and perceptual skills related to reading development were administered to 100 LD readers and 50 normal readers matched for age (11 and 12 years of age) and IQ (Mean Full Scale IQ = 105.7). The data were submitted to a number of cluster analyses to test the hypothesis that subtypes could be identified. Six subtypes were identified and characterized by significantly different patterns of linguistic and perceptual deficits (Fig. 5.2). The six-subtype solution remained stable across internal validation studies employing different variable subsets and clustering algorithms. Furthermore, 94% of the subjects were recovered into similar subtypes in a cross-validation study using a new subject sample (Lyon, 1983).

The unique feature of this study was in Lyon's attempt to externally validate the six-subtype solution through the application of an educational

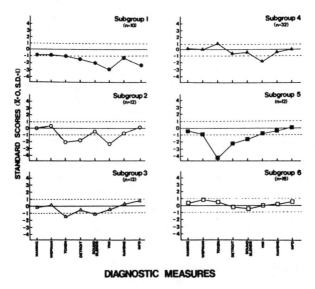

FIG. 5.2. Standardized z-scores for six subtypes of reading disability produced by cluster analysis of eight variables. VMI = Beery Test of Visual-Motor Integration. From "Empirically Derived Subgroups of Learning Disabled Readers: Diagnostic Characteristics," by R. Lyon and B. Watson, 1981, *Journal of Learning Disabilities*, 14(5), 256–261. Copyright © 1981 by PRO-ED, Inc. Reprinted by permission.

intervention study (Lyon, 1985a, 1985b). Because of the small sample size available, a standard aptitude-by-treatment design where subtypes were crossed with a number of different interventions could not be employed. Instead, a pilot investigation was conducted to determine whether members from each subtype would respond differently to one teaching condition. Because the children for this study had to be matched for preintervention achievement levels and other relevant variables (age, gender, IQ, SES), the initial subject pool from the subtype identification study was reduced from 100 to 30. Five subjects were selected from each of the six subtypes and matched on their ability to read single words, age, gender, and SES. The subjects were reading below the 8th percentile on the Reading Recognition subtest of the Peabody Individual Achievement Test (PIAT) (Dunn & Markwardt, 1970) and received 26 hours of specific reading intervention using a well-sequenced synthetic phonics program designed by Traub and Bloom (1975).

Following the 26-hour intervention, a posttest using the PIAT indicated significant gains for only two of the six subtypes. Subjects from Subtype 6 in Fig. 5.2 increased reading scores by an average of 18 percentile rank points, and members of Subtype 4 in Fig. 5.2 gained an average of 8 points. Slight increases were apparent for Subtypes 2 and 3, but were not significant. Members of Subtypes 1 and 5 showed no change.

The data show that those children with either unitary linguistic deficits or mixed visual-memory and linguistic deficits (Subtypes 1, 2, 3, 5) did not respond favorably to the particular alphabetic phonics approach used. Conversely, children in subtypes characterized by adequate performance on all measures (Subtype 6) or by low scores on only visual memory and visual spatial tasks (Subtype 4) responded positively to the intervention.

In the second series of subtype studies with younger LD readers (ages 6.5 to 9.0 years), Lyon et al. (1982) identified five subtypes based on cluster analyses of scores on linguistic, perceptual, and memory tasks obtained by 75 reading disabled and 42 normal control children. Following the subtype identification phase, an educational intervention study was conducted in which the members of one subtype characterized by severe deficits in word recognition, deficits on phonological memory span tasks, and intact visual–perceptual, motor, and visual memory abilities, were randomly divided into two groups and provided two distinctly different types of reading intervention for 30 hours. One group received the Traub and Bloom (1975) synthetic phonics program. The second group was initially taught to recognize phonetically predictable whole words via orthographic patterns and then to identify sound–symbol relationships using an analytic phonics method, rather than a synthetic phonics method. Posttest data indicated a strong superiority for the orthographic/analytic phonics condition as compared to synthetic phonics training alone, suggesting that orthographic context might serve as an effective strategy to enhance phonics skills for readers with severe deficits in memory for linguistic units (related and unrelated words and sentences). These studies supported the hypothesis of subtype by treatment interactions for children with reading disability.

YALE CENTER STUDY

The dyslexia classification project from the Yale Center for the Study of Disorders of Learning and Attention (B. A. Shaywitz, S. E. Shaywitz, & Fletcher, 1992) was designed in part to test hypotheses concerning the definition and classification of dyslexia. Although components of the project addressed both the neurobiology and the cognitive/linguistic basis of dyslexia, these studies were also conceptualized as examinations of the external validity of any resultant classifications of reading disability. These studies also provided the theoretical basis for selecting variables for classification and external validity studies. Consistent with the framework for classification studies outlined by Skinner (1981) and applied to dyslexia by Morris and Fletcher (1988), the classification studies of the dyslexia project included three components: theory formulation, internal validity, and external validity.

The theory formulation component included an approach to sampling that avoided as much as possible a priori conceptualizations of dyslexia, but also provided a manageable framework for selecting subjects. Described by Fletcher et al. (1994), the sampling strategy resulted in 378 children aged 7.5 to 9.5 years. These children were identified into nine groups representing children who met either low achievement or discrepancy definitions of reading disability, math disability, or both reading and math disability, along with contrast groups of non-LD children with ADHD, below average IQ, and normal children. Subsequent examinations of the external validity of this hypothetical nine-group classification of learning disability using cognitive measures revealed: no basis for separating children according to low achievement and discrepancy definitions (Fletcher et al., 1994), no basis for separating children with reading and both reading and math disability, and no basis for separating the math disability and ADHD groups. As expected, the latter groups can be separated on measures of behavioral functioning. Based on the cognitive measures, four primary groups were apparent: reading disability, ADHD/ math disability, below average IQ, and no disability.

The cognitive measures were selected according to a hypothetical model of the relationship of language and reading skills, including measures of phonological awareness, naming skills, vocabulary/lexical skills, morpho-syntactic ability, speech production and perception, and verbal memory. In addition, nonverbal measures hypothesized to be weakly related to reading ability were included, including measures of nonverbal memory, nonverbal contrasts of phonological deletion tasks, visual–spatial skills, and visual attention. Additional measures included a thorough assessment of reading, spelling, and math abilities, a neuromaturational assessment of motor and sensory skills (i.e., "soft signs"), motor speed and dexterity, parent and teacher behavior rating scales, and developmental history. These latter measures were conceptualized as the basis for external validity studies, whereas the cognitive measures were conceptualized as yielding the variables to classify dyslexia subtypes.

Selection of the cognitive variables for classification was based on the results of a series of confirmatory factor analyses of the cognitive test battery (Fletcher et al., 1996). Variable selection is essential, because subtyping efforts are enhanced when the redundancy across measurement domains is reduced and the number of classification attributes is minimized. The results of the confirmatory factor analysis yield a solution with eight specific factors and one general factor. For the purposes of the cluster analysis, the variables with the highest loading on the eight specific factors were selected as classification attributes. All variables were adjusted to z-scores based on the within-sample variation in age. This placed the measures on a common metric essential for any examination of profile differences, such as cluster analysis.

The internal validity studies assessed the reliability and internal consistency of the subtypes. These studies are critically important. With an established database, an investigator can run a canned statistical package (e.g., SAS Proc Cluster) and obtain a set of subtypes in a matter of seconds. Based on the output, a case can be made for the adequacy of a particular solution. Visual inspection of the profiles suggest that the results are meaningful. The literature is full of studies that stop at this point. However, cluster analysis, like other exploratory techniques (e.g., common factor analysis) is a *heuristic* method. The goal is to use the statistical methods to identify latent structure inherent in the data that is masked by group averages. The problem is that the methods can be method dependent. Simple changes in the variables clustered, number of clusters, sample, and methods for clustering will yield entirely different results. There are no confirmatory methods for cluster analysis that indicate the best resolution of the structure of the data. Of utmost importance is the ability to demonstrate that the results are not method driven but are largely impervious to variations in methods, variables, and sampling decisions.

To implement this rigorous approach to internal validity, we used methods similar to those that demonstrated success for the Florida Longitudinal Project (Morris et al., 1981). Of utmost consideration was the importance of demonstrating that the results were not simply the product of the methods. Hence, three primary clustering algorithms were employed, including Ward's method, average linkage, and complete centroid. Each of these methods makes different decisions concerning the partitioning of subjects into types. Similarity coefficients, which indicate the proximity of individual subjects to the centroid of the subtype, included both squared Euclidean distance and a correlation coefficient. The former weights the elevation and shape of the subtype profile, whereas the latter evaluates similarity only according to the shape of the profile. Multiple decisions were used for estimating the number of clusters, including 17 starting and stopping points. Each decision was empirically evaluated by comparing overlap across the three primary methods and visually evaluating subtype profiles. These decisions were also evaluated by using the K-means relocation procedure, which attempts to place each subject in a different cluster to ensure that the best choice has been made. If the appropriate decision has been made concerning the number of clusters, relocation moves relatively few subjects to a different cluster.

The external validity studies compared the resultant subtypes on multiple dimensions, including: other cognitive measures, other achievement measures, IQ scores, family history of LD, parent and teacher rating skills of behavior and academic performance, and neuromaturational measures.

The three methods of clustering were applied to 232 children, including those subjects who met criteria for reading and both reading and math disability, along with the below average IQ and nondisabled subjects. The normal and below average group should cluster separately from the reading-disabled children if the cutpoints established for reading disability and IQ are meaningful relative to the cognitive profiles associated with dyslexia subtypes.

Figure 5.3 summarizes the results of these cluster analyses. Nine subtypes emerged from this extensive approach to analysis, which placed 208 of the 232 subjects into clusters (i.e., coverage of 90%). This solution had good stability and replicated across the different methods and decisions employed for the study.

As Fig. 5.3 shows, the subtypes include two groups of children (upper panel, $n = 25$), 90% of whom are not disabled in reading. There are also two subtypes (lower panel) with largely flat profiles well below the sample mean. One subtype, labeled Global Deficit ($n = 35$), has a clearly flat profile. These children include virtually all (15/17) of the below average IQ children, along with other reading-disabled children (71% of this cluster), and no nondisabled children. The other subtype (Global Language; $n = 21$) tends to show better performance on visual processing measures relative to language measures. This cluster includes one child in the below average/mentally deficient group, with the rest disabled in reading.

The middle panel includes five "specific" subtypes of predominantly reading disabled children. Figure 5.4 shows the individual profiles of these subtypes. The groups labeled Phonology-VSTM(Verbal Short-Term Mem-

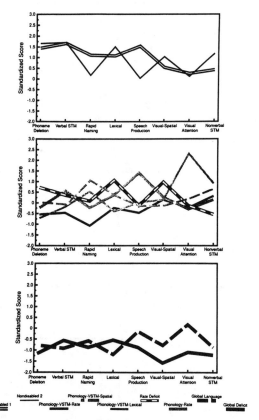

FIG. 5.3. Standardized z-scores for nine subtypes produced by cluster analysis of eight variables. The two subtypes in the upper panel are largely nondisabled, whereas the subtypes in the lower panel tend to be lower in overall level of function. The five subtypes in the middle panel are largely children with reading disabilities who show variable profile configurations (Morris et al., 1997). V = Verbal, STM = Short-Term Memory. Figure copyright © J. M. Fletcher. Reprinted by permission.

ory)-Rate (n = 43), Phonology-Rate (n = 18) and Phonology-VSTM-Lexical (n = 15) include only 6% nondisabled and 2% below average IQ children. The group labeled Phonology-VSTM-Nonverbal (n = 31) includes 20 reading disabled children and 11 nondisabled children. It is characterized by a relative strength in rapid automatized naming (i.e., Rate), but relative weaknesses in phonological awareness, verbal short-term memory, and spatial skills. Hence, four of the five subtypes are impaired on the measure of phonological awareness, basically varying in whether they are impaired in rapid automatized naming and verbal short-term memory.

The fifth specific subtype, labeled Rate Deficit (n = 15), is not impaired on the phonological awareness measure, but is impaired on a variety of

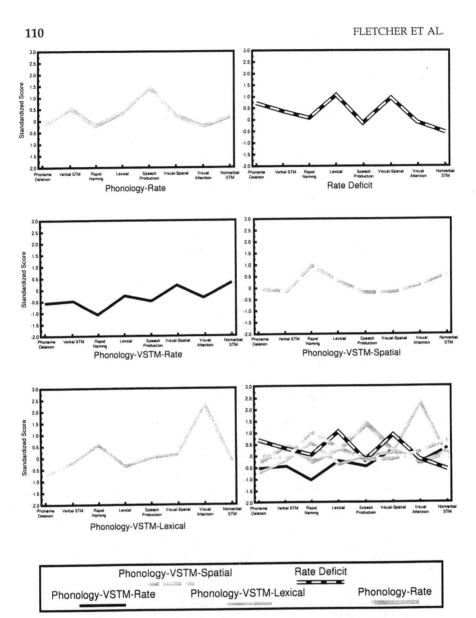

FIG. 5.4. Standardized z-scores for the five subtypes of children largely
disabled in reading plotted separately for each subtype (Morris et al., 1997).
V = Verbal; STM = Short-Term Memory. Figure copyright © J. M. Fletcher.
Reprinted by permission.

measures associated with requirements for rapid and/or sequential responses, including rapid automated naming, speech production, Corsi
blocks, and visual attention. This subtype includes eight disabled and
seven nondisabled readers.

In an extensive series of external validity studies, the two nondisabled groups (upper panel of Fig. 5.3) were not distinguishable. Of the two lower profile subtypes (lower panel of Fig. 5.3), the Global Language subtype had a higher Performance IQ and better math scores than did the Global Deficit group, but otherwise these groups were not different.

The Phonology-VSTM-Rate subtype clearly differed from the other four "specific" subtypes in the middle panel of Fig. 5.3. This subtype had lower Verbal IQ scores that were nonetheless well within the average range, poorer academic skills in all areas, poorer language skills, and poorer motor coordination. They were also more likely to have a family history of reading problems involving both parents, and were identified with reading and language problems earlier in their development. Except for higher IQ and math scores, this subtype was similar to the two "global" subtypes, functioning largely at a higher level.

In contrast, the other four "specific" subtypes differed from the Phonology-VSTM-Rate and global subtypes. The Rate deficit group had higher Verbal IQ and reading decoding and comprehension scores than the other specific subtypes. However, they were moderately impaired on measures of fluency and automaticity of oral reading, and also showed motor incoordination comparable to the Phonology-VSTM-Rate subtype. The Phonology-Rate group tended to be somewhat less impaired than the Phonology-VSTM-Spatial and Phonology-VSTM-Lexical subtypes, but tended to have more children with ADHD. The latter two subtypes were hard to distinguish except that the Phonology-VSTM-Lexical subtype had lower Verbal IQ scores and semantic language scores, but better perceptual motor skills than the Phonology-VSTM-Nonverbal subtype.

CONCLUSIONS

The Yale subtyping study, building upon previous efforts, demonstrated the validity of two of the assumptions of subtyping research. The first is that dyslexia is more than a reading disorder per se. Even the five "specific" subtypes show varying degrees of impairment in other cognitive and academic skills. Second, a multivariate context is essential to appreciating the complexity of cognitive functioning in children with dyslexia.

The presence of two lower-functioning (global) and five specific subtypes generally supports the two-group classification of reading disability commonly represented as "specific" and "garden-variety" poor readers. The results are also consistent with the phonological core-variable difference model set forth by Stanovich (1988), with six of the seven subtypes showing impairment in phonological awareness skills. The subtypes are not captured by variation in IQ scores. Even the low-functioning or garden-variety groups have many children (71%) with Performance IQ scores ≥ 90, and represent children who tend to have severe language impairments. None of the subtypes are captured by an approach based on IQ discrepancy. The need for a multivariate context is clearly apparent when the effect of including several of the low-functioning children with average IQ scores is considered. The effect on mean performance on any single variable, which usually correlates at least moderately with IQ, would surely lead to a significant difference on that variable. The limitations of this approach were highlighted by Doehring's (1978) critique of the "single syndrome" paradigm and by Satz and Fletcher (1980) of the "contrasting groups" approach. Even if phonological awareness skills are strongly associated with reading failure, the strength of this association can only be appreciated in the context of other cognitive skills. Indeed, this study, like those of Fletcher et al. (1994) and Stanovich and Siegel (1994), stands out because it shows that measures of phonological awareness skills yield larger and more consistent differences (relative to normals) than other measures used for subtyping.

The implications of these subtypes await further external validity studies. Particularly important is the possibility that these subtypes will respond differently to various reading interventions. For example, will the three subtypes that show more impairment in verbal short-term memory show better response to an intervention that emphasizes drill and repetition? Similarly, do the other two subtypes who don't have short-term memory problems need as much drill and repetition? These questions await further research, but highlight the importance of understanding individual differences in response to intervention. It is possible that a treatment *on the average* looks ineffective, but actually works well with some subjects and not others. Combining this approach to subtypes with an individual growth curves approach to assessing the effects of intervention would elucidate this possibility.

ACKNOWLEDGMENTS

Supported in part by NICHD grants P0121889, Psycholinguistic and Biological Mechanisms of Dyslexia, and P50 25802, Center for the Study of Learning and Attention Disorders. The assistance of Rita Taylor for manuscript preparation and Christy Brandenburg for graphic presentations is gratefully acknowledged.

REFERENCES

Beery, K., & Buktenica, E. (1967). *Developmental test of visual-motor integration.* Chicago: Follett.
Benton, A. L. (1975). Developmental dyslexia: Neurological aspects. In W. J. Friedlander (Ed.), *Advances in neurology* (Vol. 7, pp. 2–44). New York: Raven Press.

Benton, A. L., & Pearl, D. (Eds.). (1978). *Dyslexia: An appraisal of current knowledge.* New York: Oxford University Press.

Critchley, M. (1970). *The dyslexic child.* Springfield, IL: Charles C. Thomas.

Doehring, D. G. (1978). The tangled web of behavioral research on developmental dyslexia. In A. L. Benton & D. Pearl (Eds.), *Dyslexia: An appraisal of current knowledge* (pp. 123–138). New York: Oxford University Press.

Doris, J. (1993). Defining learning disabilities: A history of the search for consensus. In G. R. Lyon, D. B. Gray, J. F. Kavanagh, & N. A. Krasnegor (Eds), *Better understanding learning disabilities* (pp. 97–116). Baltimore: Paul H. Brookes.

Dunn, M., & Markwardt, F. D. (1970). *Peabody Individual Achievement Test.* Circle Pines, MN: American Guidance Associates.

Fletcher, J. M., Francis, D. J., Stuebing, K. K., Shaywitz, B. A., Shaywitz, S. E., Shankweiler, D. P., Katz, L., & Morris, R. (1996). Conceptual and methodological issues in construct definition. In G. R. Lyon (Ed.), *Attention, memory, and executive functions* (pp. 17–42). Baltimore: Paul H. Brookes.

Fletcher, J. M., & Morris, R. D. (1986). Classification of disabled learners: Beyond exclusionary definitions. In S. Ceci (Ed.), *Handbook of cognitive, social, and neuropsychological aspects of learning disabilities* (Vol. 1, pp. 55–80). Hillsdale, NJ: Lawrence Erlbaum Associates.

Fletcher, J. M., Shaywitz, S. E., Shankweiler, D. P., Katz, L., Liberman, I. Y., Fowler, A., Francis, D. J., Stuebing, K. K., & Shaywitz, B. A. (1994). Cognitive profiles of reading disability: Comparisons of discrepancy and low achievement definitions. *Journal of Educational Psychology, 85,* 1–18.

Hinschelwood, J. (1896). A case of dyslexia: A peculiar form of word-blindness. *Lancet, 101,* 1451–1454.

Hooper, S. R., & Willis, W. G. (1989). *Learning disability subtyping: Neuropsychological foundations, conceptual models, and issues in clinical differentiation.* New York: Springer-Verlag.

Johnston, C. (1985). *Learning disability subtypes: A cross-validation.* Unpublished doctoral dissertation, University of Florida, Gainesville.

Liberman, I. Y., Shankweiler, D. P., & Liberman, A. M. (1989). The alphabetic principle and learning to read. In D. P. Shankweiler & I. Y. Liberman (Eds.), *Phonology and reading disability: Solving the reading puzzle* (IARLD Monograph Series, pp. 1–33). Ann Arbor: University of Michigan Press.

Lyon, G. R. (1983). Learning disabled readers: Identification of subgroups. In H. R. Myklebust (Ed.), *Progress in learning disabilities* (Vol. 5, pp. 103–133). New York: Grune & Stratton.

Lyon, G. R. (1985a). Educational validation of learning disability subtypes. In B. P. Rourke (Ed.), *Neuropsychology of learning disabilities: Essentials of subtype analysis* (pp. 228–256). New York: Guilford.

Lyon, G. R. (1985b). Identification and remediation of learning disability subtypes: Preliminary findings. *Learning Disability Focus, 1,* 21–35.

Lyon, G. R., Stewart, N., & Freedman, D. (1982). Neuropsychological characteristics of empirically derived subgroups of learning disabled readers. *Journal of Clinical Neuropsychology, 4,* 343–365.

Lyon, G. R., & Watson, B. (1981). Empirically derived subgroups of learning disabled readers: Diagnostic characteristics. *Journal of Learning Disabilities, 14,* 256–261.

Morris, R., Blashfield, R., & Satz, P. (1981). Neuropsychology and cluster analysis: Problems and pitfalls. *Journal of Clinical Neuropsychology, 3,* 79–99.

Morris, R., & Fletcher, J. M. (1988). Classification in neuropsychology: A theoretical framework and research paradigm. *Journal of Clinical and Experimental Neuropsychology, 10,* 640–658.

Morris, R., Stuebing, K. K., Fletcher, J. M., Shaywitz, S. E., Shankweiler, D., Katz, L., Francis, D. J., & Shaywitz, B. A. (1997). *Subtypes of phonologically based reading disabilities: An evaluation.* Manuscript submitted for publication.

Rourke, B. P. (Ed.). (1985). *Neuropsychology of learning disabilities: Essentials of subtype analysis.* New York: Guilford.

Rutter, M., & Yule, W. (1975). The concept of specific reading retardation. *Journal of Child Psychology and Psychiatry, 16,* 181–197.

Satz, P., & Fletcher, J. M. (1980). Minimal brain dysfunctions: An appraisal of research concepts and methods. In H. Rie & E. Rie (Eds.), *Handbook of minimal brain dysfunctions: A critical view* (pp. 669–714). New York: Wiley.

Satz, P., & Fletcher, J. M. (1982). *Florida Kindergarten Screening Battery.* Odessa, FL: Psychological Assessment Resources.

Satz, P., Taylor, H. G., Friel, J., & Fletcher, J. M. (1978). Some developmental and predictive precursors of reading disabilities: A six year follow-up. In A. L. Benton & D. Pearl (Eds.), *Dyslexia: An appraisal of current knowledge* (pp. 313–348). New York: Oxford University Press.

Satz, P., & Morris, R. (1981). Learning disability subtypes: A review. In F. J. Pirozzolo & M. C. Wittrock (Eds.), *Neuropsychological and cognitive processes in reading* (pp. 109–141). New York: Academic Press.

Satz, P., & van Nostrand, G. (1973). Developmental dyslexia: An evaluation of a theory. In P. Satz & J. Ross (Eds.), *The disabled learner: Early detection and intervention* (pp. 121–148). Rotterdam: Rotterdam University Press.

Shaywitz, B. A., Fletcher, J. M., Holahan, J., & Shaywitz, S. E. (1992). Discrepancy compared to low achievement definitions of reading disability: Results from the Connecticut Longitudinal Study. *Journal of Learning Disabilities, 25,* 639–648.

Shaywitz, B. A., Shaywitz, S. E., & Fletcher, J. M. (1992). The Yale Center for the Study of Learning and Attention Disorders. *Learning Disabilities, 3,* 1–12.

Shaywitz, S. E., Escobar, M. D., Shaywitz, B. A., Fletcher, J. M., & Makuch, R. (1992). Distribution and temporal stability of dyslexia in an epidemiological sample of 414 children followed longitudinally. *New England Journal of Medicine, 326,* 145–150.

Siegel, L. S. (1992). Dyslexic vs. poor readers: Is there a difference? *Journal of Learning Disabilities, 25,* 618–629.

Skinner, H. A. (1981). Toward the integration of classification theory and methods. *Journal of Abnormal Psychology, 90,* 68–87.

Spreen, O., & Benton, A. L. (1969). *Spreen-Benton Language Examination Profile.* Iowa City: University of Iowa.

Stanovich, K. E. (1988). Explaining the differences between the dyslexic and garden-variety poor reader: The phonological core-variable differences model. *Journal of Learning Disabilities, 21,* 590–604.

Stanovich, K. E., & Siegel, L. S. (1994). Phenotypic performance profiles of children with reading disabilities: A regression-based test of the phonological-core variable differences model. *Journal of Educational Psychology, 86,* 24–53.

Traub, M., & Bloom, F. (1975). *Recipe for reading.* Cambridge, MA: Educators Publishing Service.

van der Vlugt, H., & Satz, P. (1985). Subgroups and subtypes of learning-disabled and normal children: A cross cultural replication. In B. P. Rourke (Ed.), *Neuropsychology of learning disabilities: Essentials of subtype analysis* (pp. 212–227). New York: Guilford.

Vellutino, F. R. (1991). Introduction to three studies on reading acquisition: Convergent findings on theoretical foundations of code-oriented versus whole language approaches to reading instruction. *Journal of Educational Psychology, 83,* 437–443.

Wechsler, D. (1974). *Manual for the Wechsler Intelligence Scale for Children—Revised.* San Antonio, TX: Psychological Corp.

Zigler, E., & Hodapp, R. M. (1986). *Understanding mental retardation.* New York: Cambridge University Press.

6

Subtypes of Developmental Dyslexia: Differences in Phonological and Orthographic Coding

Keith E. Stanovich
Linda S. Siegel
Alexandra Gottardo
Penny Chiappe
Robindra Sidhu
University of Toronto

The quest to define subtypes of poor readers has been an enticing one for the field of reading. There is enormous face validity to the idea that reading-disabled individuals differ among themselves in the way that they have become poor readers and in the cognitive underpinnings of their disability. Yet the field has made very little progress toward defining separable groups of disabled readers—that is, subgroups who are behaviorally, genetically, and physiologically different from each other. However, the field *has* made what might be termed "negative progress." We are here referring to the early history of the field in which the definition of reading disability or dyslexia was tied to the notion of aptitude/achievement discrepancy (Ceci, 1986; Reynolds, 1985; Shepard, 1980; Siegel, 1989; Stanovich, 1991, 1993b, 1994). From the very beginning of research on reading disability, it was assumed that poor readers who were of high intelligence formed a group who were cognitively and neurologically different. Investigators who pioneered the study of the condition then known as *congenital word-blindness* (e.g., Hinshelwood, 1917) were at pains to differentiate reading-disabled children with high intelligence from other poor readers.

Recent data—some from our own laboratory—have indicated that, contrary to some of the foundational beliefs in the reading disabilities field, the phenotypic indicators of poor reading (difficulties in phonological coding and weak phonological sensitivity) seem not to be correlated in any reliable way with degree of discrepancy between intelligence and reading achievement; nor do reading-disabled children with high and low IQs seem to differ greatly in other information processing operations that support word recognition (Felton & Wood, 1992; Fletcher, 1992; Fletcher et al., 1994; Fletcher, Francis, Rourke, Shaywitz, & Shaywitz, 1992; Francis, Shaywitz, Stuebing, Shaywitz, & Fletcher, 1996; Fredman & Stevenson, 1988; Hurford et al., 1994; Maughan, Hagell, Rutter, & Yule, 1994; Pennington, Gilger, Olson, & DeFries, 1992; Rispens, van Yeren, & van Duijn, 1991; Schuerholz et al., 1995; Share, McGee, McKenzie, Williams, & Silva, 1987; Shaywitz, Fletcher, Holahan, & Shaywitz, 1992; Siegel, 1988, 1989, 1992; Stanovich & Siegel, 1994; Taylor, Satz, & Friel, 1979). Recent evidence thus suggests that if there is a special group of reading-disabled children who are behaviorally, cognitively, genetically, and/or neurologically "different," it is becoming increasingly unlikely that they can be easily identified by examining achievement/IQ discrepancies.

Are there other, more promising cognitive tools for partitioning the space of poor readers? The classic subtyping literature in our field is not encouraging on this score (see Fletcher & Morris, 1986; Lyon, 1987; McKinney, 1984; Morris & Satz, 1984; Satz, Morris, & Fletcher, 1985; Speece & Cooper, 1991; Torgesen, 1991). This older subtyping work is, in retrospect, disappointing, because much of it was purely empirical and not grounded in extant theory, and some of it was grounded in theory but the theories have become dated and do not reflect the latest work in human information processing or cognitive psychology.

SUBTYPES BASED ON THE COGNITIVE NEUROPSYCHOLOGY OF WORD RECOGNITION

There is, however, a body of subtyping work that is not subject to either of these criticisms. It is the body of work that has grown up around the study of the acquired dyslexias and the attempt to conceptualize them within the framework of theories of adult word recognition. In the early 1980s, researchers (e.g., Coltheart, Masterson, Byng, Prior, & Riddoch, 1983; Temple & Marshall, 1983) began to present cases of developmental dyslexics whose performance patterns mirrored those of certain classic acquired dyslexic cases (Beauvois & Derouesne, 1979; Coltheart, Patterson, & Marshall, 1980; Marshall & Newcombe, 1973; Patterson, Marshall, & Coltheart, 1985) and to interpret these cases of developmental dyslexia within the functional cognitive architecture assumed by dual-route[1] theory (Carr & Pollatsek, 1985; Coltheart, 1978; Humphreys & Evett, 1985).

---

[1]Although current theorizing in this field has been immensely influenced by connectionist models of word recognition (Hinton & Shallice, 1991; Manis et al., 1996; Metsala & Brown, in press; Plaut, McClelland, Seidenberg, & Patterson, 1996; Plaut & Shallice, 1994; Seidenberg,

The extrapolation from the acquired dyslexia literature to the interpretation of the performance patterns of developmental cases proved controversial, however (see Ellis, 1979, 1984; Frith, 1985; Snowling, 1983). For example, Bryant and Impey (1986) criticized the authors of the developmental case studies for not including control groups of nondisabled readers to form a context for their case descriptions. Recently, Castles and Coltheart (1993) tried to answer these criticisms—first by demonstrating that their dual-route subtypes can be defined by reference to the performance of normal controls, and then by showing that the subtypes so defined are not at all rare in the dyslexic population.

Castles and Coltheart (1993) analyzed the exception word and nonword reading performance of 53 dyslexic individuals and 56 nondyslexic chronological-age controls. They were motivated by a desire to distill subgroups that were relatively skilled at sublexical processing (indexed by the reading of pseudowords) relative to lexical processing (indexed by the reading of exception words) and vice versa or, to use the terms popularized in Olson's (e.g., Olson, Wise, Connors, Rack, & Fulker, 1989) influential studies, subgroups characterized by relatively unique deficits in phonological coding and orthographic coding. Castles and Coltheart (1993) regressed the controls' pseudoword performance on their ages and determined 90% confidence intervals around the regression line in the normal sample. They found that fully 38 dyslexics fell outside of the 90% confidence limits for this regression. Similarly, the dyslexics were markedly below performance expectations when exception word performance was plotted against age. Castles and Coltheart (1993) found that 40 of the 53 dyslexics fell below the 90% confidence intervals around the regression line based on the sample of nondyslexics.

Castles and Coltheart (1993) next used these same criteria to define the dissociations that would identify the phonological and surface dyslexia subtypes, and found that 18 of the 53 subjects fulfilled one or the other of the dissociation criteria. Specifically, 10 of the subjects fit the surface dyslexia pattern: They were below the normal range in exception word

---

1993, 1994; Seidenberg & McClelland, 1989), we will retain dual-route nomenclature throughout this discussion. However, our adherence to this nomenclature is largely driven by explicative convenience and historical precedent rather than by a desire on our part to advance a strong position on particular micro-debates in the dual-route versus connectionist literature (see Besner, Twilley, McCann, & Seergobin, 1990; Coltheart et al., 1993; Plaut & Shallice, 1994; Seidenberg, 1993, 1994). Instead, from the standpoint of the reading disability theorist standing outside of these debates, it seems quite possible that many of these disputes arise from attempts to characterize performance at different levels of analysis (Fodor & Pylyshyn, 1988; McCloskey, 1991; Smolensky, 1988, 1989). The data patterns described remain of importance to theories of reading disability whether verbally characterized in the representational language of dual-route theory or the sub-symbolic language of connectionist theory.

reading but were within the normal range on pseudoword reading. Eight subjects fit the phonological dyslexia pattern: They were below the normal range in pseudoword word reading but were within the normal range on exception reading. These 18 cases might be termed the "hard" subtypes. They fit the classic dissociation definitions: normal on one subprocess (at least by these particular operational criteria), and subnormal on the other.

However, Castles and Coltheart (1993) argued that additional cases of subtypes could be identified based not on abnormal performance on one measure and normal performance on the other, but instead by *relative* imbalances on the two tasks among children who might well show depressed performance on both. Castles and Coltheart (1993) argued that a principled way of operationalizing this imbalance was, again, by reference to the performance of the normal control group. We might term cases defined in this way the "soft" subtypes. They of course will be more numerous than the hard subtypes, because they form a superset of the hard subtypes—most children qualifying for one of the hard subtypes will also qualify for one of the soft subtypes.

The soft subtypes are defined by running a regression line with 90% confidence intervals through the exception word by pseudoword plot for the control children. This regression line and confidence intervals are then superimposed upon the scatterplot of the performance of the dyslexic sample. Subjects falling below the lower confidence interval in this plot and not its converse qualify for the soft surface dyslexia subtype: They are unusually impaired on exception word reading relative to their performance on pseudowords when the relationship among these two subskills in the normal population is used as the benchmark. An analogous regression defines the soft phonological dyslexia subtype.

Using this procedure, Castles and Coltheart (1993) defined 16 surface dyslexics and 29 phonological dyslexics. They thus argued that the vast majority of dyslexics in their sample (45 out of 53) displayed some type of dissociation, and they concluded that

> developmental dyslexics do not form a homogeneous population. The results reported here support the notion that a clear double dissociation exists between surface and phonological dyslexic reading patterns, with some children displaying a specific difficulty reading via the lexical procedure in the absence of any difficulty with the sublexical procedure and others showing precisely the reverse pattern. . . . It would seem that these reading patterns are not rare phenomena, but are quite prevalent in the developmental dyslexic population. (p. 174)

In the remainder of this chapter, we attempt to explore some of the implications of the procedure introduced by Castles and Coltheart (1993) and to more closely examine the data patterns they obtained in light of the results from some parallel investigations.

PROBLEMS WITH THE CASTLES AND COLTHEART (1993) ANALYSES

To begin with, conceptual and statistical interpretation of the Castles and Coltheart (1993) data is problematic for a reason argued by Bryant and Impey (1986) a decade ago: the lack of reading-level controls. If the processing trade-offs involving the lexical and sublexical procedures are specifically bound up with the overall level that the reader has attained, then extrapolating from the reading patterns of children at a higher reading level is an inappropriate way of defining abnormal patterns of processing skills at a lower reading level.

A reanalysis of the Castles and Coltheart (1993) data (Anne Castles is thanked for providing the raw data from their study, which allowed us to conduct a series of replots and reanalyses) serves to confirm these fears. When the performance of the CA controls on exception words is plotted against reading age and the performance on pseudowords is plotted against reading age, both variables display statistically significant quadratic trends ($p < .001$ in the case of pseudowords). In precisely the range of reading ages where the reading-disabled sample resides, the slope relating performance to reading age is steeper.

Another way of viewing this problem is to note that when the entire sample is considered, the slope of the function relating exception word performance to reading age (in months) is steeper for the reading-disabled sample than for the CA controls (.260 versus .128). However, when the range of reading ages is restricted to the lower range (< 117 months) where there is overlap between the CA controls and reading-disabled sample, there is no difference in slopes (.260 versus .310).

Similarly, when the entire sample is considered, the slope of the function relating pseudoword performance to reading age (in months) is steeper for the reading-disabled sample than for the CA controls (.305 versus .114). However, when the range of reading ages is restricted to the lower range (< 117 months) where there is overlap between the CA controls and reading-disabled sample, there is no difference in slopes (.305 versus .378).

In short, the difference in the growth functions when the entire sample of CA controls is compared with the sample of dyslexics is simply a function of the differing distributions of the two samples across the reading age continuum. The steeper slope displayed by the dyslexics is not a function of being dyslexic—it is simply a property of these particular pseudowords and exception words being given to children of these particular reading levels. When reading at the same level, control children display exactly the same slope (this, of course, is a variant of the arguments for reading-level controls that have appeared in the literature before; see Bryant & Goswami, 1986; Bryant & Impey, 1986). In fact, we can easily see that a regression line dominated by high reading-age control children is an inappropriate one for the dyslexic children by simply pondering the fact that it is equally inappropriate for *normal* children of reading ages similar to the dyslexics.

The moral here is that if the processing trade-offs involving the lexical and sublexical procedures are specifically bound up with the overall level that the reader has attained, then extrapolating from the reading patterns of children at a higher reading level is an inappropriate way of defining abnormal patterns of processing skills at a lower reading level. This admonition applies equally to the procedures used to define the soft subtypes as it does the hard subtypes. If Fig. 5 and Fig. 6 in the Castles and Coltheart (1993) paper—the plots of exception word reading by pseudoword reading for the nondyslexics and dyslexics, respectively—are superimposed upon each other, the dyslexic subjects are virtually outside of the normal space.

SUBTYPES DERIVED FROM COMPARISONS
WITH READING-LEVEL CONTROLS:
MANIS ET AL. (1996)

In a recent study, Manis, Seidenberg, Doi, McBride-Chang, and Peterson (1996) added an important context for the Castles and Coltheart type of analysis—a reading-level control. First, they replicated the Castles and Coltheart procedures with chronological age controls, as in the original investigation. Out of their 51 dyslexics they found only half as many hard subtype cases as did Castles and Coltheart: 5 surface dyslexics and 5 phonological dyslexics (they found, as did Castles and Coltheart, that most dyslexics were significantly depressed on their use of *both* the sublexical and lexical procedures; in our search for subtypes we should not lose sight of the fact that *most* dyslexics are low on *both*). However, they found, as did Castles and Coltheart, that large numbers of soft subtypes could be defined by using the exception word/pseudoword regression criteria derived from CA controls: 17 subjects were soft phonological dyslexics and 15 were soft surface dyslexics.

Manis et al. (1996) next did a soft subtype analysis using a regression line based on the performance of reading-level controls rather than CA controls. Twelve of the 17 phonological dyslexics also qualified for that subtype based on the RL analysis. In contrast, five children defined as phonological dyslexics based on the CA analysis were no longer so when an RL control group was employed. However, an even more striking outcome was obtained when the performance of the surface dyslexics was examined. Only 1 out of 15 surface dyslexics qualified for this subtype label when an RL control group was employed. As a result of these findings, Manis et al. (1996) concluded that "the phonological dyslexic profile represents a specific deficit in phonological processing, whereas the surface dyslexic profile represents a more general delay in word recognition" (p. 179).

RETROSPECTIVE ANALYSIS OF READING-LEVEL COMPARISONS IN CASTLES AND COLTHEART (1993) AND STANOVICH AND SIEGEL (1994)

In the remainder of this chapter, we present further comparisons involving reading-level control groups—some derived from our own data, and one from the original Castles and Coltheart (1993) study itself. Given that the latter study was a CA match investigation, it might be wondered how this was possible. It was possible because the Castles and Coltheart (1993) study shares a characteristic of many other studies in our literature: Even when subjects are reported to be matched at a particular chronological age or reading age or IQ or whatever other variable, there is often enormous variability around the point of the match (as identified by a statistic such as the mean). This is certainly true in the Castles and Coltheart study. The CAs in their study spanned 7½ years (90 months to 179 months) and the reading ages spanned 7 years (78 months to 163 months). More important, however, at the lower reading ages there is overlap between the groups. We thus formed matched reading-level groups of 17 nondyslexic children and 40 dyslexic children from the Castles and Coltheart data—a comparison not examined in their original paper.

Table 6.1 indicates that although the match was less than perfect (there was an almost 3-month difference in reading age), the difference was not statistically significant. The reading-level controls outperformed the dyslexics on all three stimulus types. The difference was much larger on pseudowords, and the interaction between stimulus type and subject group was highly significant ($p < .001$). The dyslexics named about the same number of pseudowords as exception words, whereas the RL controls named about six more pseudowords than exception words—a very large difference. Thus, the reading-level match from the Castles and Coltheart data replicates the classic finding of a dyslexic pseudoword reading deficit in an RL match (Rack, Snowling, & Olson, 1992; Stanovich & Siegel, 1994).

TABLE 6.1
Mean Differences Between the Reading-Level-Matched
Dyslexics ($N = 40$) and the Nondyslexics ($N = 17$)
in the Castles & Coltheart (1993) Study

Variable	Dyslexics	Controls	t Value
Reading age	101.0	103.9	1.34
Exception words	13.0	14.9	2.17*
Pseudowords	13.8	20.6	3.61***
Regular words	22.5	26.0	2.80**

*$p < .05$. **$p < .01$. ***$p < .001$, all two-tailed.

Figure 6.1 illustrates one of the plots that identifies the soft subtypes, but this time using only the RL control group as a benchmark rather than the full CA-matched control group. The number of pseudowords read correctly is plotted against the number of exception words read correctly. The performance of the reading-disabled children is represented by Xs and the performance of the nondisabled RL-matched group is represented by squares. The regression line and confidence intervals displayed in the figure are based on the data from the 17 RL controls (the squares). This plot in part identifies the soft phonological subtype (children low on pseudoword reading relative to exception word reading). There are 15 phonological dyslexics according to this criterion. Figure 6.2 displays the performance of the dyslexics plotted so as to identify surface dyslexics (children low on exception word reading relative to pseudoword reading). The number of exception words read correctly is plotted against the number of pseudowords read correctly. The performance of the reading-disabled children is again represented by Xs, and the performance of the nondisabled RL-matched group is represented by squares. The regression line and confidence intervals displayed in the figure are again based on the data from the 17 RL controls (the squares). Figure 6.2 indicates that the Coltheart and Castles (1993) data patterns themselves converge with the findings of Manis et al. (1996): Most surface dyslexics disappear when a reading-age control is employed—only two are left in Castles and Coltheart sample. Thus, a reanalysis of the original Castles and Coltheart (1993) data replicates the trend demonstrated by Manis et al. (1996). When an RL control group is used, surface dyslexics defined by a CA-match are disproportionately eliminated.

We also retrospectively analyzed data previously reported by Stanovich and Siegel (1994) in terms of the Castles and Coltheart subtypes, and examined the effects of changing to reading-level controls in the definitions of the subtypes. We matched 47 dyslexic subjects who had

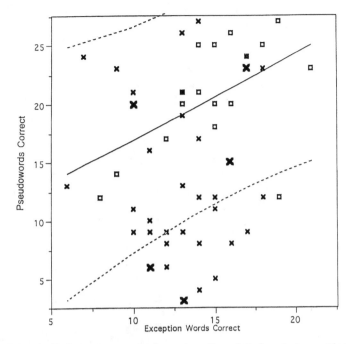

FIG. 6.1. Performance on pseudoword reading plotted against exception word reading for the reading-disabled children (Xs) and RL controls (squares) in the Castles and Coltheart (1993) data. The regression line and confidence intervals were derived from the data of the RL controls. Larger Xs indicate two individuals with reading disability with the same scores, and filled squares indicate that two individuals, one from each group, have the same scores.

been given the exception words studied by Baron (1979) with a group of 146 CA controls. The mean age of the dyslexics (138.1 months) was similar to that in the Castles and Coltheart (1993) study (137.9 months) and in the Manis et al. (1996) study (149.2 months). All of these children had been administered the Reading of Symbols subtest of the Goldman/Fristoe/Woodcock Sound Symbol Test (Goldman, Fristoe, & Woodcock, 1974), which involves the reading of pronounceable nonwords. Using the regression lines derived from the performance of the CA controls on this test and on the Baron (1979) exception words, 10 phonological dyslexics and 9 surface dyslexics were defined in our sample. However, when regression lines were derived from 87 reading-level controls with a mean age of 102 months, 7 phonological dyslexics were defined but *no* surface dyslexics were identified. Thus, in fairly extreme form we replicated the tendency—observed by Manis et al. (1996) and demonstrated in our reanalysis of the Castles and Coltheart (1993) data—for surface dyslexia to be very infrequent when defined by reference to reading-level controls.

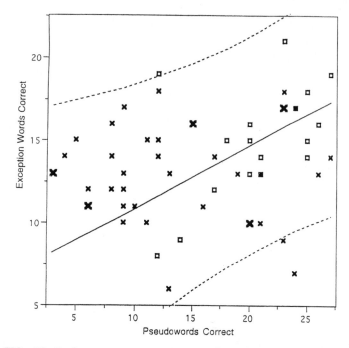

FIG. 6.2. Performance on exception word reading plotted against pseudoword reading for the reading-disabled children (Xs) and RL controls (squares) in the Castles and Coltheart (1993) data. The regression line and confidence intervals were derived from the data of the RL controls. Larger Xs indicate two individuals with reading disability with the same scores, and filled squares indicate that two individuals, one from each group, have the same scores.

PHONOLOGICAL AND SURFACE SUBTYPES
IN A YOUNGER SAMPLE

We have conducted a subtype analysis of the Castles and Coltheart type on a sample of children who were considerably younger than those studied by Manis et al. (1996) and those examined in the post hoc analyses of the Castles and Coltheart (1993) and Stanovich and Siegel (1994) studies. Our study extended beyond their findings in three ways. As Table 6.2 indicates, our dyslexics and RL controls were considerably younger than the children in the other studies. Thus, we examined whether the results generalize to earlier reading levels and how early the subtypes can be reliably identified. Second, both the Castles and Coltheart and the Manis et al. (1996) studies examined samples that *varied* widely in age. In contrast, our dyslexics, as well as their CA controls, were all third graders and our RL controls were all first and second graders. Finally, in our

TABLE 6.2
Mean Age Differences (in Months) Among the Three Studies

Variable	Dyslexics	RL Controls
Post-hoc analysis of Castles & Coltheart (1993)	137.9	102.0
Manis et al. (1996)	149.2	102.0
Post-hoc analysis of Stanovich & Siegel (1994)	138.1	102.0
The present investigation	107.5	88.9

battery, unlike in the Castles and Coltheart (1993) study, we had a variety of other tasks that can provide some converging validation for the subtypes (see also Manis et al., 1996).

Recall that the soft dyslexia subtypes are defined by plotting pseudoword performance against exception word performance (and vice versa) and examining the 90% confidence intervals around the regression line determined from the CA control group. A phonological dyslexic is a child who is an outlier when pseudowords are plotted against exception words but is within the normal range when exception words are plotted against pseudowords. Surface dyslexics are defined conversely. Figure 6.3 displays the data from our 68 third-grade reading-disabled children, and plots experimental exception word performance against experimental pseudoword performance. The regression line and confidence intervals from the 44 CA controls in our sample is also displayed. All four groups that are defined by conjoining the results of this with the converse plot not shown (pseudoword performance against exception word performance) are indicated. Specifically, the points labeled with Ys are the surface dyslexics (low in the exception word by pseudoword plot and in the normal range on the converse plot), the triangles are the phonological dyslexics (low in the pseudoword by exception word plot and in the normal range on the converse plot), the Xs are subjects who are low on both measures, and the crosses represent individuals who are low on neither.

One interesting difference between our results and those involving the CA controls in the Castles and Coltheart (1993) and Manis et al. (1996) investigations concerns the fact that Manis et al. (1996) found that only 9.8% of their sample were outside the regression criterion on both measures, and Castles and Coltheart (1993) found only 5.7% of their sample low on both. In contrast, in our younger sample, 27.9% of the dyslexics (19 out of 68 children) were low on both types of stimuli. Perhaps these findings indicate that, with development, there is increasing dissociation between lexical and sublexical processes in dyslexics. The proportion of surface dyslexics was fairly similar across the three studies (30.2% in the Castles & Coltheart study, 29.4% in Manis et al., and 22.1% in our sample).

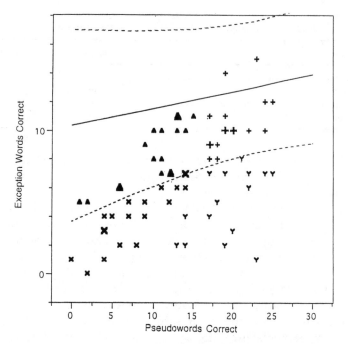

FIG. 6.3. Performance on exception word reading plotted against pseudoword reading for the reading-disabled children in the present study. The regression line and confidence intervals were derived from the data of the CA controls. **Y** = surface dyslexics, **▲** = phonological dyslexics, × = low on both, + = low on neither. Larger points indicate two individuals with the same scores.

In contrast, the proportion of phonological dyslexics in the Castles and Coltheart (1993) study (54.7%) was higher than that observed in the other two investigations (33.3% in Manis et al., and 25.0% in our sample).[2]

Table 6.3 displays the comparisons between the 23 reading-level controls and the 68 dyslexics in our sample. The groups were matched closely on their WRAT reading raw scores. The dyslexics scored somewhat higher on the WRAT spelling subtest and on the Woodcock Word Identification subtest, perhaps indicating some degree of regression in the matched groups. The sample can be more closely matched on these variables at a cost in sample size, but it does not materially affect the results. The older dyslexics were superior in arithmetic performance, a common finding in an RL match (see Stanovich & Siegel, 1994). On two measures of pseudoword reading (the Woodcock Word Attack and some experimental

---

[2]A 90% confidence interval was used in the present study and in the Castles and Coltheart (1993) study. Manis et al. (1996) employed a 95% confidence interval.

TABLE 6.3
Mean Differences Between the Dyslexics ($N = 68$)
and the Reading-Level Controls ($N = 23$)

Variable	Dyslexics	RL Controls	t Value
WRAT Reading (raw)	51.2	51.0	0.12
WRAT Spelling (raw)	33.1	31.4	1.86
Woodcock Word Ident (raw)	46.8	42.6	1.83
WRAT Arithmetic	23.5	20.3	5.72**
Woodcock Word Attack (raw)	12.1	15.5	−2.25*
Rosner AAT	16.8	21.1	−2.16*
Wordlikeness choice	11.8	11.8	0.01
Exception words	6.9	6.4	0.52
Regular words	8.4	9.2	−0.73
Pseudowords	13.9	16.8	−2.05*

*$p < .05$. **$p < .001$, all two-tailed.

pseudowords of the type used by Coltheart & Leahy, 1992) we replicated the finding of a dyslexic deficit in an RL match. On a measure of phonological sensitivity (the Rosner Auditory Analysis Test), the dyslexics displayed a significant deficit, consistent with other research in the literature (Bowey, Cain, & Ryan, 1992; Bradley & Bryant, 1978; Bruck, 1992; Bruck & Treiman, 1990; Olson, Wise, Conners, & Rack, 1990). On a measure of orthographic processing (a wordlikeness choice task; see Siegel, Share, & Geva, 1995) the two groups displayed no difference; nor were any differences displayed on a set of exception and a set of regular words. These exception words and the experimental pseudowords were used to define the dyslexic subgroups in our study.

Figure 6.4 displays the performance of the dyslexics plotted so as to identify phonological dyslexics (children low on pseudoword reading relative to exception word reading). The number of pseudowords read correctly is plotted against the number of exception words read correctly. The performance of the reading-disabled children is represented by Xs, and the performance of the nondisabled RL-matched group is represented by squares. The regression line and confidence intervals displayed in the figure are based on the data from the 23 RL controls (the squares in Fig. 6.4).

Figure 6.5 shows the performance plotted so as to identify surface dyslexics (children low on exception word reading relative to pseudoword reading). The number of exception words read correctly is plotted against the number of pseudowords read correctly. The performance of the reading-disabled children is again represented by Xs, and the performance of the nondisabled RL-matched group is represented by squares. The regression line and confidence intervals displayed in the figure are again based on the data from the 23 RL controls (the squares).

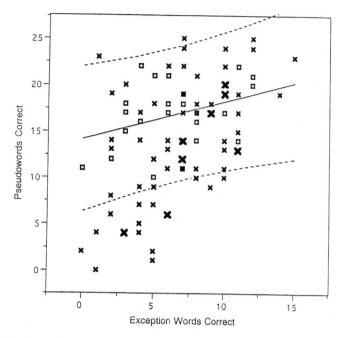

FIG. 6.4. Performance on pseudoword reading plotted against exception word reading for the reading-disabled children (Xs) and RL controls (squares) in the present study. The regression line and confidence intervals were derived from the data of the RL controls. Larger Xs indicate two individuals with reading disability with the same scores, and filled squares indicate that two individuals, one from each group, have the same scores.

Seventeen children were identified as phonological dyslexics by employing these two scatterplots and regressions (not all of these were identical to those identified from the CA regression lines; due to differing slopes and intercepts, some CA phonological dyslexics were low on neither measure in the RL analysis and some children who were low on both in the CA analysis were phonological dyslexics in the RL analysis). Figure 6.5 indicates that, consistent with the findings from the older sample of Manis et al. (1996) and our reanalysis of the Castles and Coltheart data presented previously, surface dyslexics virtually disappear when a reading-age control is employed—only one is left in our sample. This is consistent with the two found in the Castles and Coltheart sample, none found in the reanalysis of the Stanovich and Siegel data, and one found in the Manis et al. sample. In contrast, substantial numbers of phonological dyslexics in RL control comparisons were identified in all the samples.

In light of the similarity in the data patterns of the RL comparisons in all four of these studies, it is interesting to note that the original Bryant

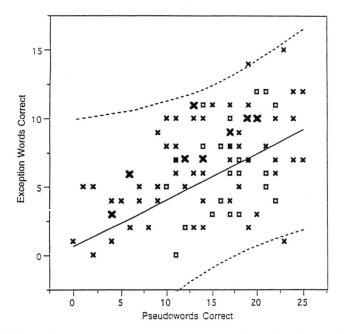

FIG. 6.5. Performance on exception word reading plotted against pseudoword reading for the reading-disabled children (Xs) and RL controls (squares) in the present study. The regression line and confidence intervals were derived from the data of the RL controls. Larger Xs indicate two individuals with reading disability with the same scores, and filled squares indicate that two individuals, one from each group, have the same scores.

and Impey (1986) study—the first to analyze the patterns revealed in the surface and phonological dyslexic case studies in the context of reading level controls—obtained a converging outcome. The one pattern of HM, the phonological dyslexic of Temple and Marshall (1983), that Bryant and Impey could not match to a child in their RL control group was HM's nonword reading. HM read considerably fewer nonwords than the worst nonword reader in Bryant and Impey's control group. This contrasts with the performance of CD, Coltheart et al.'s (1983) surface dyslexic. Bryant and Impey were able to find a match in their RL control group for every pattern displayed by CD. The performance of CD, as did that of most of the surface dyslexics in our study, disappeared into the distribution of RL controls. Likewise, the four acquired surface dyslexia cases studied by Birnboim (1995) displayed many performance similarities to second-grade reading-level controls. In short, the results from case studies of developmental phonological and surface dyslexia are entirely consistent with the patterns displayed in three studies with larger-scale sampling of reading-disabled children.

The results of all of these analyses suggest that the surface dyslexics defined by CA comparisons appear to be children with a type of reading disability that could be characterized as a developmental lag. The performance of surface dyslexics is in no way unusual, at least in comparison to other normal readers at the same level of overall ability (see Beech & Harding, 1984; Stanovich, Nathan, & Zolman, 1988; Stanovich & Siegel, 1994). In contrast, phonological dyslexia defined by comparison with a CA control group seems to reflect true developmental deviance. This conclusion is reinforced by examining performance comparisons between the surface dyslexics and RL controls on the other variables contained in our performance battery (see also Manis et al., 1996). Table 6.4 presents these comparisons and it is apparent that on only one variable (WRAT Spelling) were the two groups significantly different. The two groups of children performed similarly on several tasks not used to define the dyslexic subtypes (Rosner AAT, wordlikeness choice task, two subtests of the Woodcock), as well as measures of syntactic processing and verbal working memory that were included in this study. The latter two measures add to the picture of developmental lag that seems to characterize the surface subtype: These children had syntactic processing skills and verbal memory skills commensurate with their reading-level controls.

Comparisons of the phonological dyslexics (from the CA match, in order to be comparable with the surface dyslexia results) to RL controls are in marked contrast to those involving the surface dyslexics. Table 6.5 indicates that here, there were several significant differences between the groups. The phonological dyslexics were markedly inferior not only on the experimental pseudowords that in part defined the group, but also on the Woodcock Word Attack subtest (not used to define the groups).

TABLE 6.4
Mean Differences Between the Surface Dyslexics ($N = 15$)
and the RL Controls ($N = 23$)

Variable	Dyslexics	Controls	t Value
WRAT Reading (raw)	53.1	51.0	0.96
WRAT Spelling (raw)	33.7	31.4	2.09*
Woodcock Word Ident (raw)	46.4	42.6	1.09
Woodcock Word Attack (raw)	15.4	15.5	−0.04
Exception words	4.8	6.4	−1.66
Regular words	11.3	9.2	1.45
Pseudowords	19.2	16.8	1.96
Rosner AAT	21.5	21.1	0.17
Wordlikeness choice	11.2	11.8	−0.69
Syntactic Proc (z score)	.256	.235	0.12
Working Mem (z score)	.090	.310	−1.03

*$p < .05$.

TABLE 6.5
Mean Differences Between the Phonological Dyslexics ($N = 17$)
and the RL Controls ($N = 23$)

Variable	Dyslexics	Controls	t Value
WRAT Reading (raw)	49.9	51.0	−0.58
WRAT Spelling (raw)	32.0	31.4	0.50
Woodcock Word Ident (raw)	46.8	42.6	1.28
Woodcock Word Attack (raw)	7.9	15.5	−5.07***
Exception words	8.3	6.4	2.04*
Regular words	7.2	9.2	−1.68
Pseudowords	9.9	16.8	−5.71***
Rosner AAT	13.9	21.1	−3.16**
Wordlikeness choice	12.2	11.8	0.51
Syntactic Proc (z score)	−.473	.235	−3.15**
Working Mem (z score)	−.172	.310	−2.30*

*$p < .05$. **$p < .01$. ***$p < .001$, all two-tailed.

Their phonological problems were further indicated by a significant deficit in phonological sensitivity as indicated by their performance on the Rosner Auditory Analysis Test. They were significantly *better* at reading exception words. One very interesting finding that serves to confirm the developmental deviancy of this group in the phonological/language domain was that phonological dyslexics performed significantly worse than these younger controls on the measures of syntactic processing skill and verbal working memory, perhaps indicating that these tasks are in part tapping their core phonological deficit (Bruck, 1992; Goswami & Bryant, 1990; Gottardo, Stanovich, & Siegel, 1996; Olson, 1994; Perfetti, 1994; Shankweiler, Crain, Brady, & Macaruso, 1992; Shankweiler et al., 1995; Share, 1995; Siegel & Ryan, 1988; Stanovich, 1988, 1991; Stanovich & Siegel, 1994; Wagner, Torgesen, & Rashotte, 1994).

These results, taken in conjunction with the results on the convergence of the subtypes by Manis et al. (1996), present a consistent picture of developmental deviancy and developmental lag that appears to characterize the phonological and surface subtypes, respectively. In our thinking about subtypes, it is also important not to ignore the "deviant on both" group—the children below the CA control group confidence intervals for *both* pseudowords and exception words. As noted previously, this group was much larger in our sample of younger subjects (27.9% of the dyslexics) than in the Manis et al. and Castles and Coltheart samples who were 2½ to 3½ years older. We conjecture that members of this "deviant on both" group are perhaps phonological dyslexics of the future, a hypothesis supported by the results displayed in Table 6.6, which compares the performance of the phonological dyslexics to that of the deviant on both

TABLE 6.6
Mean Differences Between the Phonological Dyslexics ($N = 17$)
and the "Deviant on Both" Group ($N = 19$)

Variable	Phonological	Both	t Value
WRAT Reading (raw)	49.9	47.1	1.69
WRAT Spelling (raw)	32.0	30.7	1.18
Woodcock Word Ident (raw)	46.8	40.6	2.43*
Woodcock Word Attack (raw)	7.9	8.0	0.08
Exception words	8.3	3.9	6.23***
Regular words	7.2	4.4	2.85**
Pseudowords	9.9	7.7	1.58
Rosner AAT	13.9	13.3	0.32
Wordlikeness choice	12.2	10.7	1.86
Syntactic Proc (z score)	−.473	−.308	0.61
Working Mem (z score)	−.172	−.352	0.76

$*p < .05.$ $**p < .01.$ $***p < .001$, all two-tailed.

groups. Here we see that the both deviant group shares *all* of the phonological deficits of the phonological dyslexics—they are equally impaired at reading pseudowords and in phonological sensitivity. They share the syntactic processing problems and verbal working memory deficits—deficits that may well arise from processing problems at the phonological level (see Gottardo, Stanovich, & Siegel, 1996; Shankweiler, Crain, Brady, & Macaruso, 1992). The *differences* between the groups arise because the phonological dyslexics are better at reading words, particularly exception words.

SUBTYPE PROPERTIES ARE PREDICTABLE FROM TRENDS IN READING-LEVEL INVESTIGATIONS

One final point that needs to be emphasized is that the patterns and trends in the samples of dyslexics that have been considered here are, in some sense, a necessary consequence of the well-known finding that dyslexics show a pseudoword reading deficit in an RL match and simultaneously show no deficit in reading exception words (or in other tasks that rely heavily on orthographic coding; see Olson et al., 1989; Siegel et al., 1995; Stanovich & Siegel, 1994). When these empirical trends are put together with the innovative Castles and Coltheart (1993) procedure for defining subtypes, then it is almost *necessarily* the case that the trends that we have outlined will be found. That is, the conclusions about these different subtypes have actually been implicit in the findings of many studies using an RL match and examining pseudoword and exception word processing but have remained implicit until the Castles and Coltheart (1993) procedures revealed a way of drawing this implicit pattern to our attention. We demonstrated this point by running simulations based on data extrapolated from our RL controls.

For example, in one simulation, the data from the 44 CA controls and 23 RL controls in our sample were utilized without change. However, the data from the 68 dyslexics was simulated based on the data from the RL controls. Dyslexic pseudosubjects were created by randomly assigning exception word values from a distribution with the same mean and variance as the RL controls. They were simultaneously assigned pseudoword values from a distribution with the same variance as the RL controls but with a mean three points lower (simulating the RL deficit on pseudowords). The correlation between pseudowords and exception words in the simulated data was slightly lower (.40) than that in the actual data (.53), but this does not materially affect the results.

Using the regression lines from the CA controls (i.e., the Castles and Coltheart procedure), substantial numbers of phonological and surface dyslexics were identified in the simulated data set. When the RL controls are used to construct the regression lines, just as in the four actual empirical studies discussed here, there are still 11 phonological dyslexics identified. In contrast, just as in the actual empirical data, surface dyslexia disappears when confidence intervals are derived from an RL rather than CA control group (no surface dyslexics were identified in the simulated data). This, then, is the sense in which we mean that these subtype patterns have been implicit in the statistical relationships among word recognition variables that have been known for some time. Virtually any data set that displays this pattern of relationships (a group pseudoword RL deficit but no exception word deficit) will reveal subtypes of poor readers with the characteristics that have been described by Castles and Coltheart (1993), Manis et al. (1996), and in the investigation reported here.

CONCLUSIONS

Given that IQ-based discrepancies have been shown to have low returns for the field as mechanisms for demarcating conceptually interesting subtypes (Fletcher et al., 1994; Francis et al., 1996; Siegel, 1988, 1989, 1992; Stanovich, 1991, 1993b, 1994; Stanovich & Siegel, 1994), it appears that Castles and Coltheart (1993) were correct in maintaining that the search for subtypes should proceed from psychological mechanisms that closely underpin the word recognition process (see Baron & Strawson, 1976; Byrne, Freebody, & Gates, 1992; Murphy & Pollatsek, 1994). In this chapter, we have explored the implications of reading disability subtypes so defined.

What we have demonstrated is that there appear to be marked conceptual differences between the subtypes that have been identified. Phonological dyslexia appears to reflect true developmental deviancy—that is, the pattern of linguistic and information processing strengths and weaknesses displayed do not match those found in reading-level controls. In contrast, surface dyslexia has consistently—from the original analysis of Bryant and Impey (1986) to the samples analyzed here—resembled a form of developmental delay. Interestingly, when trying to simulate surface dyslexia with a connectionist network, Plaut and Shallice (1994) reported that damaging the network did not work as well as simply examining the undamaged network at an earlier point in its learning curve. They found that "a much better match to fluent surface dyslexia is found in the behavior of the *undamaged* network earlier in learning, before it has mastered the entire training corpus" (p. 24).

We would conjecture that the two subtypes might separate when other methods of differentiating subtypes are employed—for example, response to treatment, genetic analyses, and neurological investigation. That is, it is hypothesized that phonological dyslexia will be more refractory to treatment than surface dyslexia (see Vellutino et al., in press), will have a higher heritability, and will more clearly display brain anomalies. Based on the data from our investigation, it is also conjectured that the "deviant on both" subtype will be more similar to phonological dyslexia than to surface dyslexia in these characteristics.

How might a younger child deviant on both stimulus types develop into a phonological dyslexic? Some children in the both-deviant group might continue to practice reading and to receive considerable exposure to print (Stanovich, 1993a; Stanovich & Cunningham, 1993; Stanovich, West, & Harrison, 1995). This print exposure may result in these children having relatively less seriously impaired orthographic processing mechanisms (Siegel et al., 1995; Stanovich & Siegel, 1994; Zivian & Samuels, 1986). It may also result in these children building exception word recognition abilities (which depend on orthographic representations in the mental lexicon; see Ehri, 1992; Perfetti, 1992, 1994; Stanovich, 1990; Stanovich & West, 1989). However, their more seriously impaired phonological processing abilities will likely not develop at the same rate (Manis, Custodio, & Szeszulski, 1993; Olson, 1994; Snowling, 1980), thus resulting in greater dissociation between phonological coding ability and exception word fluency at more advanced stages of development (see also Manis et al., 1996).

Consider how the two subtypes might also arise through different combinations of relative phonological impairment and experience with print. Individuals who are matched on their level of phonological skill may vary greatly in their level of print exposure (Cipielewski & Stanovich, 1992; Cunningham & Stanovich, 1990; Stanovich & West, 1989). Low print exposure might not have very dire consequences for a reader with high levels of phonological coding skill. When such a reader does open a book, phonological coding enables the reading process—irrespective of the inadequately developed orthographic lexicon. However, the situation is probably different for a reader with somewhat depressed phonological skills (and we must never forget that even the surface dyslexics have phonological processing problems to some degree). Without efficiently functioning phonological coding processes, a system designed for compensatory processing would actually draw more on orthographic knowledge—but in the case of the surface dyslexic, that orthographic knowledge may be lacking in part due to inadequate exposure to print.

Thus, surface dyslexia may arise from a milder form of phonological deficit than that of the phonological dyslexic, but one conjoined with exceptionally inadequate reading experience. This is a somewhat different interpretation of surface dyslexia (see also Manis et al., 1996) than the common one of differential impairment in a dual-route architecture (Castles & Coltheart, 1993). As Snowling, Bryant, and Hulme (1995) noted: "Many poor readers have low levels of exposure to print (Stanovich, 1993a)—lack of reading experience may cause dyslexic children to resemble surface dyslexic patients. Arguably, what such children lack is the word-specific knowledge that is normally acquired by reading. In our view, it is misleading to describe such children as having an aberrant 'lexical' but intact 'sub-lexical' mechanism" (p. 6).

In contrast, the phonological dyslexic pattern might become more apparent when a more severe pathology underlying the functional architecture of phonological coding (Castles & Coltheart, 1993; Coltheart, Curtis, Atkins, & Haller, 1993; Coltheart et al., 1980, 1983; Patterson et al., 1985; Plaut & Shallice, 1994) is conjoined with relatively high levels of exposure to print. The latter would hasten the development of the orthographic lexicon (which is critical for the processing of exception words) but the former would be relatively refractory to direct remediation efforts (Lovett et al., 1994; Lovett, Warren-Chaplin, Ransby, & Borden, 1990; Vellutino et al., in press) and result in relatively slow growth in the ability to read pseudowords (Manis et al., 1993; Olson, 1994; Snowling, 1980).

ACKNOWLEDGMENTS

This research was supported by grant #0GP0001607 from the Natural Sciences and Engineering Research Council of Canada to Keith E. Stanovich. The authors wish to thank Mae Burgess, Norman Himel, Margaret

Lesperance, Sharon Smith, Ron Stringer, and Christine Wasson for help in data collection.

REFERENCES

Baron J. (1979). Orthographic and word-specific mechanisms in children's reading of words. *Child Development, 50,* 60–72.

Baron, J., & Strawson, C. (1976). Use of orthographic and word-specific knowledge in reading words aloud. *Journal of Experimental Psychology: Human Perception and Performance, 2,* 386–393.

Beauvois, M. F., & Derouesne, J. (1979). Phonological alexia: Three dissociations. *Journal of Neurology, Neurosurgery, and Psychiatry, 42,* 1115–1124.

Beech, J., & Harding, L. (1984). Phonemic processing and the poor reader from a developmental lag viewpoint. *Reading Research Quarterly, 19,* 357–366.

Besner, D., Twilley, L., McCann, R., & Seergobin, K. (1990). On the association between connectionism and data: Are a few words necessary? *Psychological Review, 97,* 432–446.

Birnboim, S. (1995). Acquired surface dyslexia: The evidence from Hebrew. *Applied Psycholinguistics, 16,* 83–102.

Bowey, J. A., Cain, M. T., & Ryan, S. M. (1992). A reading-level design study of phonological skills underlying fourth-grade children's word reading difficulties. *Child Development, 63,* 999–1011.

Bradley, L., & Bryant, P. E. (1978). Difficulties in auditory organization as a possible cause of reading backwardness. *Nature, 271,* 746–747.

Bruck, M. (1992). Persistence of dyslexics' phonological awareness deficits. *Developmental Psychology, 28,* 874–886.

Bruck, M., & Treiman, R. (1990). Phonological awareness and spelling in normal children and dyslexics: The case of initial consonant clusters. *Journal of Experimental Child Psychology, 50,* 156–178.

Bryant, P. E., & Goswami, U. (1986). Strengths and weaknesses of the reading level design: A comment on Backman, Mamen, and Ferguson. *Psychological Bulletin, 100,* 101–103.

Bryant, P., & Impey, L. (1986). The similarities between normal readers and developmental and acquired dyslexics. *Cognition, 24,* 121–137.

Byrne, B., Freebody, P., & Gates, A. (1992). Longitudinal data on the relations of word-reading strategies to comprehension, reading time, and phonemic awareness. *Reading Research Quarterly, 27,* 141–151.

Carr, T. H., & Pollatsek, A. (1985). Recognizing printed words: A look at current models. In D. Besner, T. G. Waller, & G. E. MacKinnon (Eds.), *Reading research: Advances in theory and practice* (Vol. 5, pp. 1–82). Orlando, FL: Academic Press.

Castles, A., & Coltheart, M. (1993). Varieties of developmental dyslexia. *Cognition, 47,* 149–180.

Ceci, S. J. (1986). *Handbook of cognitive, social, and neuropsychological aspects of learning disabilities* (Vol. 1). Hillsdale, NJ: Lawrence Erlbaum Associates.

Cipielewski, J., & Stanovich, K. E. (1992). Predicting growth in reading ability from children's exposure to print. *Journal of Experimental Child Psychology, 54,* 74–89.

Coltheart, M. (1978). Lexical access in simple reading tasks. In G. Underwood (Ed.), *Strategies of information processing* (pp. 151–216). London: Academic Press.

Coltheart, M., Curtis, B., Atkins, P., & Haller, M. (1993). Models of reading aloud: Dual-route and parallel-distributed-processing approaches. *Psychological Review, 100,* 589–608.

Coltheart, V., & Leahy, J. (1992). Children's and adult's reading of nonwords: Effects of regularity and consistency. *Journal of Experimental Psychology: Learning, Memory, and Cognition, 18,* 718–729.

Coltheart, M., Masterson, J., Byng, S., Prior, M., & Riddoch, J. (1983). Surface dyslexia. *Quarterly Journal of Experimental Psychology, 35A,* 469–496.

Coltheart, M., Patterson, K., & Marshall, J. C. (1980). *Deep dyslexia.* London: Routledge & Kegan Paul.

Cunningham, A. E., & Stanovich, K. E. (1990). Assessing print exposure and orthographic processing skill in children: A quick measure of reading experience. *Journal of Educational Psychology, 82,* 733–740.

Ehri, L. C. (1992). Reconceptualizing the development of sight word reading and its relationship to recoding. In P. B. Gough, L. C. Ehri, & R. Treiman (Eds.), *Reading acquisition* (pp. 107–143). Hillsdale, NJ: Lawrence Erlbaum Associates.

Ellis, A. W. (1979). Developmental and acquired dyslexia: Some observations on Jorm. *Cognition, 7,* 413–420.

Ellis, A. W. (1984). The cognitive neuropsychology of developmental (and acquired) dyslexia: A critical survey. *Cognitive Neuropsychology, 2,* 169–205.

Felton, R. H., & Wood, F. B. (1992). A reading level match study of nonword reading skills in poor readers with varying IQ. *Journal of Learning Disabilities, 25,* 318–326.

Fletcher, J. M. (1992). The validity of distinguishing children with language and learning disabilities according to discrepancies with IQ: Introduction to the Special Series. *Journal of Learning Disabilities, 25,* 546–548.

Fletcher, J. M., Francis, D. J., Rourke, B. P., Shaywitz, B. A., & Shaywitz, S. E. (1992). The validity of discrepancy-based definitions of reading disabilities. *Journal of Learning Disabilities, 25,* 555–561.

Fletcher, J. M., & Morris, R. (1986). Classification of disabled learners: Beyond exclusionary definitions. In S. J. Ceci (Ed.), *Handbook of social, and neuropsychological aspects of learning disabilities* (Vol. 2, pp. 55–80). Hillsdale, NJ: Lawrence Erlbaum Associates.

Fletcher, J. M., Shaywitz, S. E., Shankweiler, D., Katz, L., Liberman, I., Stuebing, K., Francis, D. J., Fowler, A., & Shaywitz, B. A. (1994). Cognitive profiles of reading disability: Comparisons of discrepancy and low achievement definitions. *Journal of Educational Psychology, 86,* 6–23.

Fodor, J. A., & Pylyshyn, Z. W. (1988). Connectionism and cognitive architecture: A critical analysis. *Cognition, 28,* 3–71.

Francis, D. J., Shaywitz, S. E., Stuebing, K., Shaywitz, B. A., & Fletcher, J. M. (1996). Developmental lag versus deficit models of reading disability: A longitudinal, individual growth curves analysis. *Journal of Educational Psychology, 88,* 3–17.

Fredman, G., & Stevenson, J. (1988). Reading processes in specific reading retarded and reading backward 13-year-olds. *British Journal of Developmental Psychology, 6,* 97–108.

Frith, U. (1985). Beneath the surface of developmental dyslexia. In K. Patterson, J. Marshall, & M. Coltheart (Eds.), *Surface dyslexia* (pp. 301–330). Hove, England: Lawrence Erlbaum Associates.

Goldman, R., Fristoe, M., & Woodcock, R. (1974). *GFW Sound-Symbol Tests.* Circle Pines, MN: American Guidance Service.

Goswami, U., & Bryant, P. (1990). *Phonological skills and learning to read.* Hove, England: Lawrence Erlbaum Associates.

Gottardo, A., Stanovich, K. E., & Siegel, L. S. (1996). The relationships between phonological sensitivity, syntactic processing, and verbal working memory in the reading performance of third-grade children. *Journal of Experimental Child Psychology, 63,* 563–582.

Hinshelwood, J. (1917). *Congenital word-blindness.* London: Lewis.

Hinton, G., & Shallice, T. (1991). Lesioning an attractor network: Investigations of acquired dyslexia. *Psychological Review, 98,* 74–95.

Humphreys, G. W., & Evett, L. J. (1985). Are there independent lexical and nonlexical routes in word processing? An evaluation of the dual-route theory of reading. *Behavioral and Brain Sciences, 8,* 689–740.

Hurford, D. P., Johnston, M., Nepote, P., Hampton, S., Moore, S., Neal, J., Mueller, A., McGeorge, K., Huff, L., Awad, A., Tatro, C., Juliano, C., & Huffman, D. (1994). Early identification and remediation of phonological-processing deficits in first-grade children at risk for reading disabilities. *Journal of Learning Disabilities, 27,* 647–659.

Lovett, M., Warren-Chaplin, P., Ransby, M., & Borden, S. (1990). Training the word recognition skills of reading disabled children: Treatment and transfer effects. *Journal of Educational Psychology, 82,* 769–780.

Lovett, M. W., Borden, S., DeLuca, T., Lacerenza, L., Benson, N., & Brackstone, D. (1994). Treating the core deficits of developmental dyslexia: Evidence of transfer of learning after phonologically- and strategy-based reading training programs. *Developmental Psychology, 30,* 805–822.

Lyon, G. R. (1987). Learning disabilities research: False starts and broken promises. In S. Vaughn & C. S. Bos (Eds.), *Research in learning disabilities* (pp. 69–85). Boston: College-Hill Press.

Manis, F. R., Custodio, R., & Szeszulski, P. A. (1993). Development of phonological and orthographic skill: A 2-year longitudinal study of dyslexic children. *Journal of Experimental Child Psychology, 56,* 64–86.

Manis, F. R., Seidenberg, M. S., Doi, L. M., McBride-Chang, C., & Peterson, A. (1996). On the bases of two subtypes of developmental dyslexia. *Cognition, 58,* 157–195.

Marshall, J. C., & Newcombe, F. (1973). Patterns of paralexia: A psycholinguistic approach. *Journal of Psycholinguistic Research, 2,* 175–199.

Maughan, B., Hagell, A., Rutter, M., & Yule, W. (1994). Poor readers in secondary school. *Reading and Writing: An Interdisciplinary Journal, 6,* 125–150.

McCloskey, M. (1991). Networks and theories: The place of connectionism in cognitive science. *Psychological Science, 2,* 387–395.

McKinney, J. (1984). The search for subtypes of specific learning disability. *Journal of Learning Disabilities, 17,* 43–50.

Metsala, J. L., & Brown, G. D. A. (in press). Normal and dyslexic reading development: The role of formal models. In C. K. Leong & C. Hulme (Eds.), *Cognitive and linguistic bases of reading and spelling.* Mahwah, NJ: Lawrence Erlbaum Associates.

Morris, R., & Satz, P. (1984). Classification issues in subtype research: An application of some methods and concepts. In R. Malatesha & H. Whitaker (Eds.), *Dyslexia: A global issue* (pp. 59–82). The Hague: Martinus Nijhoff.

Murphy, L., & Pollatsek, A. (1994). Developmental dyslexia: Heterogeneity without discrete subgroups. *Annals of Dyslexia, 44,* 120–146.

Olson, R. K. (1994). Language deficits in "specific" reading disability. In M. Gernsbacher (Ed.), *Handbook of psycholinguistics* (pp. 895–916). San Diego: Academic Press.

Olson, R. K., Wise, B., Conners, F., & Rack, J. (1990). Organization, heritability, and remediation of component word recognition and language skills in disabled readers. In T. Carr & B. A. Levy (Eds.), *Reading and its development: Component skills approaches* (pp. 261–322). New York: Academic Press.

Olson, R. K, Wise, B., Conners, F., Rack, J., & Fulker, D. (1989). Specific deficits in component reading and language skills: Genetic and environmental influences. *Journal of Learning Disabilities, 22,* 339–348.

Patterson, K., Marshall, J. C., & Coltheart, M. (1985). *Surface dyslexia.* Hove, England: Lawrence Erlbaum Associates.

Pennington, B. F., Gilger, J., Olson, R. K., & DeFries, J. C. (1992). The external validity of age- versus IQ-discrepancy definitions of reading disability: Lessons from a twin study. *Journal of Learning Disabilities, 25,* 562–573.

Perfetti, C. A. (1992). The representation problem in reading acquisition. In P. B. Gough, L. C. Ehri, & R. Treiman (Eds.), *Reading acquisition* (pp. 145–174). Hillsdale, NJ: Lawrence Erlbaum Associates.

Perfetti, C. A. (1994). Psycholinguistics and reading ability. In M. Gernsbacher (Ed.), *Handbook of psycholinguistics* (pp. 849–894). San Diego: Academic Press.

Plaut, D. C., McClelland, J. L., Seidenberg, M. S., & Patterson, K. (1996). Understanding normal and impaired word reading: Computational principles in quasi-regular domains. *Psychological Review, 103*, 56–115.

Plaut, D., & Shallice, T. (1994). *Connectionist modelling in cognitive neuropsychology: A case study.* Hove, England: Lawrence Erlbaum Associates.

Rack, J. P., Snowling, M. J., & Olson, R. K. (1992). The nonword reading deficit in developmental dyslexia: A review. *Reading Research Quarterly, 27*, 28–53.

Reynolds, C. R. (1985). Measuring the aptitude-achievement discrepancy in learning disability diagnosis. *Remedial and Special Education, 6*, 37–55.

Rispens, J., van Yeren, T., & van Duijn, G. (1991). The irrelevance of IQ to the definition of learning disabilities: Some empirical evidence. *Journal of Learning Disabilities, 24*, 434–438.

Satz, P., Morris, R., & Fletcher, J. M. (1985). Hypotheses, subtypes, and individual differences in dyslexia: Some reflections. In D. B. Gray & J. F. Kavanagh (Eds.), *Biobehavioral measures of dyslexia* (pp. 25–40). Parkton, MD: New York Press.

Schuerholz, L. J., Harris, E., Baumgardner, T., Reiss, A., Freund, L., Church, R., Mohr, J., & Denckla, M. B. (1995). An analysis of two discrepancy-based models and a processing-deficit approach in identifying learning disabilities. *Journal of Learning Disabilities, 28*, 18–29.

Seidenberg, M. S. (1993). A connectionist modeling approach to word recognition and dyslexia. *Psychological Science, 4*, 299–304.

Seidenberg, M. S. (1994). Language and connectionism: The developing interface. *Cognition, 50*, 385–401.

Seidenberg, M. S., & McClelland, J. L. (1989). Visual word recognition and pronunciation: A computational model of acquisition, skilled performance, and dyslexia. In A. M. Galaburda (Ed.), *From reading to neurons* (pp. 256–305). Cambridge, MA: MIT Press.

Shankweiler, D., Crain, S., Brady, S., & Macaruso, P. (1992). Identifying the causes of reading disability. In P. B. Gough, L. C. Ehri, & R. Treiman (Eds.), *Reading acquisition* (pp. 275–305). Hillsdale, NJ: Lawrence Erlbaum Associates.

Shankweiler, D., Crain, S., Katz, L., Fowler, A., Liberman, A., Brady, S., Thornton, R., Lundquist, E., Dreyer, L., Fletcher, J., Stuebing, K., Shaywitz, S., & Shaywitz, B. (1995). Cognitive profiles of reading-disabled children: Comparison of language skills in phonology, morphology, and syntax. *Psychological Science, 6*, 149–156.

Share, D. L. (1995). Phonological recoding and self-teaching: Sine qua non of reading acquisition. *Cognition, 55*, 151–218.

Share, D. L., McGee, R., McKenzie, D., Williams, S., & Silva, P. A. (1987). Further evidence relating to the distinction between specific reading retardation and general reading backwardness. *British Journal of Developmental Psychology, 5*, 35–44.

Shaywitz, B. A., Fletcher, J. M., Holahan, J. M., & Shaywitz, S. E. (1992). Discrepancy compared to low achievement definitions of reading disability: Results from the Connecticut Longitudinal Study. *Journal of Learning Disabilities, 25*, 639–648.

Shepard, L. (1980). An evaluation of the regression discrepancy method for identifying children with learning disabilities. *The Journal of Special Education, 14*, 79–91.

Siegel, L. S. (1988). Evidence that IQ scores are irrelevant to the definition and analysis of reading disability. *Canadian Journal of Psychology, 42*, 201–215.

Siegel, L. S. (1989). IQ is irrelevant to the definition of learning disabilities. *Journal of Learning Disabilities, 22*, 469–479.

Siegel, L. S. (1992). An evaluation of the discrepancy definition of dyslexia. *Journal of Learning Disabilities, 25,* 618–629.

Siegel, L. S., & Ryan, E. B. (1988). Development of grammatical-sensitivity, phonological, and short-term memory skills in normally achieving and learning disabled children. *Developmental Psychology, 24,* 28–37.

Siegel, L. S., Share, D., & Geva, E. (1995). Evidence for superior orthographic skills in dyslexics. *Psychological Science, 6,* 250–254.

Smolensky, P. (1988). On the proper treatment of connectionism. *Behavioral and Brain Sciences, 11,* 1–74.

Smolensky, P. (1989). Connectionist modeling: Neural computation/mental connections. In L. Nadel, L. A. Cooper, P. Culicover, & P. M. Harnish (Eds.), *Neural connections, mental computation* (pp. 49–67). Cambridge, MA: MIT Press.

Snowling, M. (1980). The development of grapheme–phoneme correspondence in normal and dyslexic readers. *Journal of Experimental Child Psychology, 29,* 294–305.

Snowling, M. (1983). The comparison of acquired and developmental disorders of reading—A discussion. *Cognition, 14,* 105–118.

Snowling, M. J., Bryant, P. E., & Hulme, C. (1995). *Theoretical and methodological pitfalls in making comparisons between developmental and acquired dyslexia: Some comments on Castles and Coltheart (1993).* Unpublished manuscript.

Speece, D., & Cooper, D. (1991). Retreat, regroup, or advance? An agenda for empirical classification research in learning disabilities. In L. Feagans, E. Short, & L. Meltzer (Eds.), *Subtypes of learning disabilities* (pp. 33–49). Hillsdale, NJ: Lawrence Erlbaum Associates.

Stanovich, K. E. (1988). Explaining the differences between the dyslexic and the garden-variety poor reader: The phonological-core variable-difference model. *Journal of Learning Disabilities, 21,* 590–612.

Stanovich, K. E. (1990). Concepts in developmental theories of reading skill: Cognitive resources, automaticity, and modularity. *Developmental Review, 10,* 72–100.

Stanovich, K. E. (1991). Discrepancy definitions of reading disability: Has intelligence led us astray? *Reading Research Quarterly, 26,* 7–29.

Stanovich, K. E. (1993a). Does reading make you smarter? Literacy and the development of verbal intelligence. In H. Reese (Ed.), *Advances in child development and behavior* (Vol. 24, pp. 133–180). San Diego: Academic Press.

Stanovich, K. E. (1993b). Dysrationalia: A new specific learning disability. *Journal of Learning Disabilities, 26,* 501–515.

Stanovich, K. E. (1994). Does dyslexia exist? *Journal of Child Psychology and Psychiatry, 35,* 579–595.

Stanovich, K. E., & Cunningham, A. E. (1993). Where does knowledge come from? Specific associations between print exposure and information acquisition. *Journal of Educational Psychology, 85,* 211–229.

Stanovich, K. E., Nathan, R. G., & Zolman, J. E. (1988). The developmental lag hypothesis in reading: Longitudinal and matched reading-level comparisons. *Child Development, 59,* 71–86.

Stanovich, K. E., & Siegel, L. S. (1994). The phenotypic performance profile of reading-disabled children: A regression-based test of the phonological-core variable-difference model. *Journal of Educational Psychology, 86,* 24–53.

Stanovich, K. E., & West, R. F. (1989). Exposure to print and orthographic processing. *Reading Research Quarterly, 24,* 402–433.

Stanovich, K. E., West, R. F., & Harrison, M. (1995). Knowledge growth and maintenance across the life span: The role of print exposure. *Developmental Psychology, 31,* 811–826.

Taylor, H. G., Satz, P., & Friel, J. (1979). Developmental dyslexia in relation to other childhood reading disorders: Significance and clinical utility. *Reading Research Quarterly, 15,* 84–101.

Temple, C. M., & Marshall, J. C. (1983). A case study of developmental phonological dyslexia. *British Journal of Psychology, 74,* 517–533.

Torgesen, J. K. (1991). Subtypes as prototypes: Extended studies of rationally defined extreme groups. In L. Feagans, E. Short, & L. Meltzer (Eds.), *Subtypes of learning disabilities* (pp. 229–246). Hillsdale, NJ: Lawrence Erlbaum Associates.

Vellutino, F. R., Scanlon, D. M., Sipay, E., Small, S., Pratt, A., Chen, R., & Denckla, M. (in press). Cognitive profiles of difficult to remediate and readily remediated poor readers: Toward distinguishing between constitutionally and experientially based causes of reading disability. *Journal of Educational Psychology,*

Wagner, R. K., Torgesen, J. K., & Rashotte, C. A. (1994). The development of reading-related phonological processing abilities: New evidence of bi-directional causality from a latent variable longitudinal study. *Developmental Psychology, 30,* 73–87.

Zivian, M. T., & Samuels, M. T. (1986). Performance on a word-likeness task by normal readers and reading-disabled children. *Reading Research Quarterly, 21,* 150–160.

III

*BEGINNING TO READ
AND SPELL*

A Cross-Linguistic Study
of Early Literacy Acquisition

Maggie Bruck
Fred Genesee
Markéta Caravolas
McGill University

Over the past two decades, much progress has been made in delineating the predictors of early reading acquisition in alphabetic languages (e.g., Adams, 1990; Brady & Shankweiler, 1991; Gough, Ehri, & Treiman, 1992). This literature has highlighted some of the early skills that underlie the successful acquisition of word recognition skills, or, conversely, the early warning signs of risk factors involved in reading disabilities or dyslexia. Although the conclusions are based on a large number of different studies, most of the work and therefore most of the models of early reading acquisition are based on studies of native English-speaking children learning to read English. Although it is true that there are some studies of children learning different alphabetic languages (e.g., French, Italian, Danish, Swedish), there are few if any studies that directly compare the development of English children with children learning other alphabetic languages. Therefore, it is important to determine the degree to which current models generalize to children learning other alphabetic languages. The results of a study described in this chapter represent a first step in addressing this issue. The study directly compares the early reading acquisition of French- and English-speaking children.

Based on our review of the literature in 1987, when we began the study, we selected four sets of predictor variables to investigate: phonological awareness, knowledge of letter names, parent–child reading habits, and nonverbal cognitive ability. The rationale behind inclusion of these variables follows.

There is converging evidence from a large number of studies of English–speaking children that phonological awareness skills of kindergarten children is the best predictor of grade 1 reading and spelling ability (Adams, 1990; Brady & Shankweiler, 1991; Gough, Ehri, & Treiman, 1992). It is also clear, however, that phonological awareness is not a unitary skill. Current linguistic descriptions of the phonological units of words include at least three hierarchical levels, the largest being the syllable and the smallest being the phoneme. At an intermediate level, syllables are divided into onset and rime units (e.g., the word *stop* can be segmented into its onset "st" and rime "op"). Developmental research supports the psycholinguistic validity of these distinctions for English speakers; children first develop awareness of syllables, then onsets and rimes and, finally, phonemes (Treiman & Zukowski, 1991). At present, although there is some disagreement about whether phonemes or onset-rime units are the most important predictors of literacy in English-speaking children, it is clear that syllable awareness does not play a major role.

A second factor that has consistently predicted early reading skills in English-speaking children is letter name knowledge. This relationship has been well documented over a number of decades (e.g., Adams, 1990; Gates, 1940), although it is not clear whether letter name knowledge is important because it provides children with a nameable referent to associate with phonemes (e.g., Ehri, 1984) or because it reflects accuracy in the representations and discrimination of individual letters (e.g., Adams, 1990), skills that are all necessary for accurate word recognition.

Next, most models of early reading acquisition include (if only implicitly) factors related to exposure to print and literacy in school and the home. Children who come from print-rich environments are more likely to become good readers than children raised in less rich environments (see Adams, 1990, for a review). In a recent review of this literature, Scarborough and Dobrich (1994) argued that although there are indeed correlations between early reading skills and print exposure, the size of the relationship is relatively small.

Finally, a measure of nonverbal cognitive ability was included. Generally, kindergarten measures of cognitive functioning (in addition to verbal measures of cognitive functioning) account for little unique variance in the prediction of later reading skills for English-speaking children (e.g., Share, Jorm, Maclean, & Matthews, 1984), especially after phonological awareness variables and letter knowledge variables have been accounted for. Nevertheless, we included a nonverbal cognitive measure to determine the comparability of our English and French samples.

There are several reasons to question whether the same patterns of relationships would be obtained for children learning to speak and read other languages. First, the phonological structures of languages differ, and these linguistic differences might be expected to influence the development of certain types of skills, including phonological awareness skills. For example, French is a syllable-timed language, whereas English is stress-timed. Previous work on the perceptual units used for online speech processing suggests that French speakers rely on a syllabic routine to a greater extent than do English speakers, who show greater reliance on phonemic routines for segmentation (Cutler, Mehler, Norris, & Segui, 1986). Another difference between the two languages concerns the structure of monosyllabic words. Our own analyses indicate that there are relatively more open syllable words (CV) in French, whereas there are relatively more closed syllable words (CVC, CVCC) in English. If these differences are also reflected at the level of explicit segmentation (i.e., awareness), then French-speaking children might be expected to show higher syllable but lower phoneme and rime awareness than English-speaking children. Also, one might predict that if the syllable is the most salient unit in processing spoken French (or if French-speaking children have superior awareness of syllables), then syllable awareness may be the best predictor of early reading skills for French-speaking children, whereas onset-rime or phoneme awareness may be the best predictor for English-speaking children.

Differences in the consistency or transparency of written language is a second factor that could lead to cross-linguistic differences in patterns of reading acquisition. Although all alphabetic languages reflect the spoken language at the level of phonology, some do this more consistently and, thus, more transparently, than others. Languages such as Finnish or Serbo-Croation are considered transparent because they are highly consistent and regular, whereas English is considered much less transparent—the same letters can be associated with different sounds, the same sounds are associated with different spellings, and there is inconsistency among the associations. Although French is not considered one of the most transparent languages, compared to English it is considered more consistent and more regular, at least in terms of reading. One would predict that it would be easier for a child to learn to read a more transparent language; thus, French-speaking children might be expected to learn more quickly than English-speaking children once reading instruction has begun. It is also possible that the precursor skills, such as phonological awareness, are more important for children learning to read a less transparent language on the assumption that they need a large array of skills to help them "crack a code" that is replete with irregularities, inconsistencies, and ambiguities inherent in the spelling-sound system.

The final group of factors that might lead to cross-linguistic differences in reading acquisition concerns cultural differences in early literacy exposure. Children who come from backgrounds where reading is taught informally through games and songs or through extensive exposure to environmental print might acquire better precursor skills than children not exposed to these forms of literacy. Such differences might, in turn, affect the early acquisition of reading skills. There were differences in the early reading experiences of the two language communities in which we conducted our research. First, the English-speaking children received explicit teaching in letter names during kindergarten as well as much indirect tuition in reading through educational materials and the media, such as *Sesame Street*. The French-speaking children, in comparison, attended kindergarten classes in which there was no direct training in preliteracy skills. Our analysis of curriculum materials indicated to us that this was standard practice and was dictated by the Ministry of Education in Quebec. In a related vein, there is no analogous program to *Sesame Street* on French television in Quebec. Television programming for French-speaking children is oriented toward social and emotional development. Based on these cultural differences, one would predict that the English-speaking kindergarten children would have better preliteracy skills (particularly as indicated by letter knowledge) than their French-speaking peers.

METHOD

Design

The subjects were French- and English-speaking children attending schools in their native language in the Montreal area. They were tested in February through March of their kindergarten year, with a battery of tests that assessed phonological awareness, letter knowledge, and nonverbal ability. The amount that parents read to their kindergarten children was also determined by means of a parent questionnaire. Approximately 14 months later, at the end of grade 1, their word and nonword reading skills were assessed.

There were two major methodological hurdles involved in this project. The first concerned curriculum differences between the French and English school systems. There are separate French-medium and English-medium schools in Montreal. They are administratively and pedagogically distinct. The English schools that the English-speaking children attended emphasized a "whole language" approach. In kindergarten, there was a great deal of environmental print in their classrooms; they were encouraged to write stories relating personal experiences and using invented spellings; and they were read to extensively. The French kindergarten classrooms were quite different; although the children were read to, their classrooms contained little print and they did not engage in the kinds of preliteracy activities that are characteristic of whole language classrooms. The reading curricula in grade 1 were also different. The grade 1 English-speaking children received little if any explicit instruction in phonics.[1] In contrast, the French-speaking children were taught reading using a phonics-based approach.

We were unable to control for this confounding variable because we were unable to find English-medium schools in the Montreal area that based reading instruction on a phonics approach and, conversely, we were unable to find French-medium schools that practiced whole language in the way that was characteristic of the English-medium schools. It may be that languages, such as French, that are relatively transparent with respect to spelling-sound correspondences, lend themselves naturally to a systematic phonics-based approach—it is the easiest and fastest way to teach the written language; whereas for English, a strict phonics approach may be less likely because of the irregularities and inconsistencies in the writing system. Generally speaking, identifying schools in which this confound between language and teaching approach could be clarified may be difficult.

A second methodological hurdle concerned the development of equivalent tests to assess phonological awareness and reading achievement in French and English. This difficulty undoubtedly accounts for the dearth of cross-linguistic studies. We employed a number of methodological techniques to overcome this hurdle; these are described in this chapter. As can be seen, the results of this study confirm our efforts to develop tests that were equivalent in English and French.

Subjects

Two groups of children were tested: English-speaking children who were attending English-medium schools and French-speaking children who were attending French-medium schools (hereafter these groups are simply referred to as the English children and the French children). The English and French children lived in different although comparable neighborhoods that could be classified as predominantly upwardly mobile and middle class.

In order to qualify for participation, the children had to be nonreaders, as indicated by parental information provided on a background question-

---

[1]It was impossible for us to determine exactly how the English children were taught. The teachers told us that they did not teach any structured phonics, although when necessary they attempted to provide children with strategies for sounding out unfamiliar words. However, we suspect that there was some structured phonics provided by some of the more experienced teachers who were unwilling to disclose these practices because of the political and educational incorrectness of these practices.

naire (discussed later) and by their performance on a reading screening test. In this test, the children were shown six high-frequency words, and any child who could read more than two of these words was excluded. Including only nonreaders allowed us to make more precise estimates of the relationship between preliteracy skills in kindergarten and reading achievement 1 year later, in grade 1 (e.g., Wagner & Torgeson, 1987).

In order to ensure adequate sample sizes, three cohorts of children were tested over a period of 3 years. In total, there were 105 English children and 94 French kindergarten children who met the entry criteria and who were tested in their kindergarten year. The English children were sampled from six schools, and the French children were sampled from two schools. When the children were retested in grade 1, there were 90 children remaining in the English sample and 85 in the French sample. The results for only those children who were tested in both their kindergarten and grade 1 years are presented here.

Demographic data were obtained from questionnaires that were filled out by parents when they gave permission for their children to participate in the kindergarten testing. The parents were asked for information about their language background, their education, how well their children could read in English or French, and how often they read to their children; the latter information was provided on a 5-point scale, ranging from 1 (every day) to 5 (never).

Kindergarten Test Battery

In February/March of their kindergarten year, the children were given eight phonological awareness tasks, a test of letter knowledge, and a test of nonverbal cognitive abilities.

Phonological Awareness Tasks. The phonological awareness tasks were selected to satisfy three broad criteria. First, the memory and other cognitive demands of the tasks were minimized so that they would be suitable for children at the kindergarten level (Stanovich, Cunningham, & Cramer, 1984; Yopp, 1988). Second, the tasks were constructed to assess children's awareness of specific phonological units. Two tasks assessed children's ability to manipulate syllables (syllable counting, final syllable the same); four assessed onset-rime awareness (onset deletion, cluster onsets the same, singleton onsets the same, rimes the same); and two assessed awareness of single phonemes (first phoneme of the cluster the same, final phoneme the same). Finally, in order to control for frequency effects, all items in all tasks were phonologically legal nonwords.

A French battery and an English battery were constructed. We used a number of procedures to ensure that the tests were equated across the two languages. First, the number of syllables and phonemes per item were equated across test forms (e.g., the items on the French deletion task contained the same number of phonemes and syllables as the items on the English deletion task). The phonological structure (CVC) of the items was similar across test forms. The use of nonwords controlled for frequency (lexicality) effects across the forms. Finally, the items were phonologically legal in the respective language. A brief description of each task is provided in this section (for full details, see Bruck & Genesee, 1995).

There were six same-different tasks; all had the same format. Each task started with 3 demonstration trials. The experimenter said a pair of nonwords and then told the child why they sounded the same. She explicitly told the child the shared elements of the pairs (e.g., In the English version: "I am going to say two funny made-up words, *fest–dest*.[2] They both sound the same at the end. They both have *est* at the end."). One of the demonstration trials was an example of a pair that did not share sounds, and here the experimenter explicitly pointed out how the two relevant units were not the same (e.g., "I am going to say two funny made-up words: *nast–verp*. They do not sound the same at the end. One has *ast* and one has *erp*.") This demonstration was followed by 6 practice trials with feedback. There were 14 experimental trials (7 same-trials and 7 different-trials); no feedback was given. To minimize fatigue and increase concentration, there was a short break halfway through these trials. Each child was then reminded what part of the word to monitor. A description of the items in each of the six tasks is now provided with examples from the English battery.

1. *Syllable-end.* All items contained two syllables with primary stress on the second syllable (e.g., *tan'kay–bir'kay*). The same items shared all phonemes in the second syllable. The different items shared no phonemes in the second syllable (e.g., *dis'per–ves'tick*).

2. *Cluster onsets.* All items had a CCVC structure. Same items contained the same cluster onset, but did not share any other phonemes (e.g., *plam–plack*). Different items had no phonemes in common (e.g., *plid–dree*).

3. *Singleton onsets.* The stimuli were CVC items. The same items shared the initial consonant (onset) only (e.g., *foik–fev*). The different items did not share any common phonemes (e.g., *gad–rell*).

4. *Rimes.* The stimuli were CVCC items. The same items shared rimes (e.g., *pisk–nisk*). The different items did not share any common phonemes (e.g., *lisk–farp*).

---

[2]All examples of stimuli are taken from the English test form and are given their conventional English spelling.

5. *First phoneme of the cluster.* The stimuli were CCVC items. Same items shared the initial consonant only (e.g., *blit–brive*). Different items did not share any common phonemes (e.g., *smat–brile*).

6. *Last phoneme.* The stimuli were CVC items. Same items shared the final consonant (e.g., *tig–mag*). Different items did not share any common phonemes (e.g., *dib–veck*).

Two additional tasks with a different format were also administered. These measured syllable segmentation and onset-rime segmentation, respectively.

7. *Syllable counting.* The experimenter said a nonword and asked the child to tell how many syllables were in the "word" by giving the experimenter the correct number of poker chips. After a series of practice trials with feedback, there were 15 experimental trials with equal numbers of one-, two-, and three-syllable items; no feedback was given.

8. *Onset deletion.* The experimenter said a CVC nonword. The child was told to repeat the word and then to take off the first part and to say what was left. After a series of demonstration and practice trials (with feedback), the child was given 10 experimental trials without feedback.

Raven's Progressive Matrices (Colored Version). In this 36-item test, the child was presented with a series of geometric patterns with a portion missing and was told to complete the pattern by selecting the appropriate missing portion from among six alternatives. This test measures the ability to form comparisons, to reason by analogy, and to organize spatial perceptions into systematically related wholes (Raven & Summers, 1986; Sattler, 1988). It was used in the present study to assess nonverbal reasoning ability.

Letter Knowledge. The children were randomly shown each of the 26 uppercase letters and asked for the name of each.

Procedures for Kindergarten Battery. The French children were tested in French by a native speaker of French and the English children were tested in English by a native speaker of English. All children were tested individually during three sessions, each approximately 30 minutes long, that were separated by at least 1 day. In the first session, the children were first given the reading screening test, and if they could read two or fewer of the six high-frequency words, testing proceeded. The phonological awareness and cognitive tests were divided into three blocks and presented in a counterbalanced order across sessions.

Grade 1 Test Battery

Although there are a number of standardized word recognition and nonword reading tests in English, such tests do not exist in French. Therefore, we attempted to construct equivalent word and nonword reading tests in English and in French. The word recognition task in each language consisted of 27 monosyllabic words. These items were selected in the following manner. First, based on reviews of several English and French early reading programs, spelling patterns that are commonly taught to grade 1 children were identified. Words were then selected as exemplars of each of these patterns. All items were high-frequency words: These items were found on lists of words that are common to grade 1 and grade 2 readers, or they were among the most frequent words in the Kucera and Francis *Word Frequency Count*, which is available in English (Kucera & Francis, 1967) as well as French (Baudot, 1992). All the words were also "regular" in that they could be pronounced correctly using spelling-sound knowledge. The French and English items were equated in terms of number of grapheme–phoneme correspondences and also in terms of number of letters.

A nonword list was constructed by changing the first letter of each item on the word recognition task, so that it formed a nonword.

Pilot testing with French and English subjects revealed that there were no ceiling effects with grade 1 readers. Furthermore, there were no floor effects for any of the items.

The word and nonword tests were administered to the project children in May of their grade 1 year. The word and nonword tests were administered on different days.

RESULTS

Demographic Characteristics of Kindergarten Children

As shown in Table 7.1, the French and English children were of similar age at the time of the kindergarten testing. Similar proportions of both groups had attended preschool, as indicated by parent questionnaires. Although there were no differences in the educational levels of the French and English fathers, the French mothers had more education than the English mothers, $X^2(2) = 9.65$, $p < .01$.

There were also differences in how frequently the parents read to their children: The English parents were more likely to read to their children daily, whereas the French parents were more likely to read to their children two or fewer times a week, $X^2(3) = 35.24$, $p < .01$. These differences do not reflect social class factors, which did not differ between the groups,

TABLE 7.1
Background Characteristics of Kindergarten Samples

	English (n = 90)	French (n = 85)
Age at kindergarten testing	5,9	6,0
Attended preschool (%)	80	80
Mother's highest level of education (%)		
High school	50	36
College	35	58
Graduate school	15	6
Father's highest level of education (%)		
High school	31	29
College	43	50
Graduate school	27	21
Amount of parent–child reading (%)		
Daily	52	18
3–4 times/week	37	35
1–2 times/week	4	27
"Now and then"/never	7	20

but rather cultural factors. Differences in French and English children's exposure to preliteracy activities are evidenced in the school, the media, and the home.

Kindergarten Test Battery Performance

The children's performance on this test battery is summarized in Table 7.2. One-way analyses of variance with language group (English, French) as the independent variable were carried out on each measure. (Asterisks in the table indicate significant differences between the English and French children.)

The English children performed significantly better than the French children on three of the four onset-rime tasks and on both phoneme tasks. The French children outperformed the English children on one task only—syllable counting. Also, as expected, the English children had better letter knowledge than their French peers. Between-group differences on the phonological awareness test battery and on the letter knowledge tests are not due to differences in nonverbal cognitive skills, because both groups performed comparably on Raven's Colored Progressive Matrices.

Although the pattern of results on the phonological awareness tasks supports our initial hypothesis that the phonological structure of a language can influence metaphonological development, we nevertheless carefully examined the possibility that these differences could be due to

TABLE 7.2
Kindergarten Phonological Awareness Scores (% Correct Items)

Measure	English (n = 90)	French (n = 85)
Syllable tasks		
Syllable counting (%)	74	80**
Syllable-end (%)	83	83
Onset-rime tasks		
Onset cluster (%)	77	67**
Onset simple (%)	77	64**
Rime same (%)	79	74
Onset deletion (%)	27	18*
Phoneme tasks		
Phoneme cluster (%)	72	56**
Last phoneme (%)	70	56**
Letter name (%)	92	49**
Raven's (raw score)	18	19

*Significant main effects for language group, $p < .05$. **Significant main effects for language group, $p < .01$.

differences in the levels of difficulty of the tests in the two languages; for example, it is possible that the French syllable counting task was easier than the English syllable counting task. In order to address the issue, we adapted a paradigm that Cutler and her colleagues developed to examine differences in the online speech segmentation of English and French speakers (Cutler et al., 1986).

The French tasks were given to a group of English children, and the English tasks to a group of French children. If our primary findings of between-group differences on phonological awareness measures reflect the greater salience of a particular processing unit in each language, then the same pattern of between-group differences should be found regardless of the language of the test battery. On the other hand, if these between-group differences merely reflect the fact that the test items were not equated for difficulty across the languages, then one would expect that the same pattern of between-group differences would not be obtained when children were given the tests in their nonnative language.

Eighteen English children and 19 French children were given portions of the original phonological awareness test battery. Because of time constraints, the children were given only those tests that produced significant between-group differences for the project children; the deletion task was not administered because the project children found it very difficult. The new groups of English and French children met the same criteria for inclusion as the project children (i.e., they were nonreaders and were educated in their native language). They were selected from the same schools as the project children, they were tested at the same time of year as the project children, and they were of the same age as the project children. Although these "test validation" subjects were given the tests in an unfamiliar language, the instructions were given in their native language.

Two-way analyses of variance were carried out on the data. The independent variables were language group of the children (English/French) and language of the test (English/French). As can be seen in Table 7.3, there were main effects of language group for all the tests that had been significant in the primary analyses. That is, the French children performed better than the English children on the syllable counting task, regardless of the language of the test; and the English children performed better than the French children on the onset-rime and phoneme items, regardless of the language of the test. Importantly, there were no significant interaction effects. These results suggest that the test forms were parallel and that between-group differences in the primary analyses reflect language processing routines idiosyncratic to the language.

To summarize to this point, the French children were superior on syllable segmentation, whereas the English children were superior on onset-rime and phoneme segmentation. The English children also knew more letter names than did their French peers, and they were read to more at home than were the French children.

These differences cannot be attributed to background factors such as age, preschool attendance, or nonverbal abilities; the groups were equivalent on these measures. Furthermore, socioeconomic status, as measured

TABLE 7.3
Cross-Language Kindergarten Test Comparisons on Selected
Phonological Awareness Tasks (% Correct Items)

	Native English Speakers		Native French Speakers	
	English test (n = 90)	French test (n = 18)	French test (n = 85)	English test (n = 19)
Syllable tasks				
Syllable counting	74	71	80	85*
Onset-rime tasks				
Onset cluster same	77	81	67	71**
Onset simple same	77	83	64	61**
Phoneme tasks				
Phoneme cluster same	72	78	56	68**
Last phoneme same	70	72	56	62**

*Significant main effects for language group, $p < .05$. **Significant main effects for language group, $p < .01$.

by maternal and paternal education, is not an explanatory factor; that is, although the French mothers were more educated than the English mothers, this difference did not coincide with an overall superiority for the French children.

Two other factors can explain these differences. The first is language specific: The patterns of performance on the phonological awareness tasks are consistent with the phonological structures of these languages. The second factor is cultural: The finding that the French parents read less to their children and that preliteracy skills are less emphasized in the French curriculum and in French children's media could account for the fact that the French children did poorly, particularly on the letter knowledge task. This conclusion is supported by a significant correlation between parent–child reading and alphabet knowledge in the French sample ($r = .34$).

Grade 1 Reading Test Performance

At the end of grade 1, the English children obtained poorer reading scores than their French agemates—they made twice as many errors as the French children on both the word recognition task (English 48% errors vs. French 24% errors) and on the nonword task (English 64% errors vs. French 37% errors). There are two likely explanations for these results. First, it may be easier to learn a more consistent (and more transparent) orthography compared to a less consistent (and less transparent) orthography. Second, direct phonics instruction may produce better early reading skills than whole language instruction. Of course, these two explanations are not mutually exclusive because, as was noted, the language with the less transparent orthography (English) was taught using whole language.

Predicting Grade 1 Reading Levels From Kindergarten Variables

In these analyses, we asked whether the same kindergarten variables would predict reading achievement in grade 1 for both groups of children. In order to address this issue, two stepwise regression analyses were conducted for each language group. In the first analysis, the grade 1 word reading scores served as the dependent variable. In the second analysis, the grade 1 nonword reading scores served as the dependent variable. For all analyses, the independent variables were the same kindergarten measures. These were the eight phonological awareness tasks, letter knowledge, frequency of parent–child reading, and Raven's Colored Progressive Matrices scores.

These results are presented in Table 7.4. Several interesting patterns of results emerged. First, the onset-rime measures were the most important predictors of reading success for the English children, whereas syllable

TABLE 7.4
Stepwise Regression Analyses—Kindergarten
Predictors of Grade 1 Reading Ability

English (n = 90)			French (n = 85)		
(a) Predicting Grade 1 Word Reading					
Step Entered	R	Increase in R^2	Step Entered	R	Increase in R^2
1. Simple onset	.57		1. Syllable end	.54	
2. Letter names	.68	.14*	2. Letter names	.63	.09*
3. Rimes	.71	.04*	3. Reads at home	.65	.04*
(b) Predicting Grade 1 Nonword Reading					
Step Entered	R	Increase in R^2	Step Entered	R	Increase in R^2
1. Simple onset	.58		1. Syllable end	.47	
2. Rimes	.66	.09*	2. Letter names	.54	.08*
3. Letter names	.68	.03*	3. Syllable count	.57	.02*

*Significant increase in R^2.

segmentation was the most important predictor for the French children. Second, letter naming was an important predictor in all cases. Third, frequency of home reading accounted for a small but unique portion of the variance in the French children's grade 1 word reading scores. Simple correlations between the two French reading scores (word, nonword) and amount of parent home reading were significant ($r = .25$, $r = .24$, respectively). These correlations were not significant for the English children ($r = -.09$, $r = -.13$). Differences in the French and English results probably reflect the fact that there was little variability in the English home reading scores (most of the children were read to frequently), whereas there was a wide variation for the French sample (from reads daily to reads infrequently). Thus, when there is variability on measures of parent–child reading, this variable can be a significant predictor of grade 1 reading results.

The major conclusions of these analyses is that the same predictor variables—namely, phonological awareness and letter knowledge—contributed significantly to predictions of grade 1 achievement in the case of both the English and French children. The specific phonological awareness measures varied as a function of language, but the general construct itself was still important. These results were obtained despite the fact that the children showed significantly different levels of performance on a number of these tasks in both kindergarten and grade 1.

In the next and final set of analyses, we asked whether the same predictor variables identify good and poor readers equally well in English and French. In other words, is kindergarten performance an equally good predictor of both reading failure and reading success for French and English children? It is possible, for example, that kindergarten performance is a better indicator of reading success for French children, whereas it is a better indicator of reading failure for English children? To our knowledge this issue has not been addressed in the literature, even for English-speaking children.

In order to address these issues, we carried out a series of discriminant function analyses using the following procedures. Two analyses were carried out for each language group. In the first, a subset of the children were classified as good or poor readers on the basis of their grade 1 *word* recognition scores. Children who scored at the mean or higher were selected as good readers, and children who scored in the bottom 20% (or the closest raw score to that centile) were selected as poor readers. This procedure eliminated 24 children from the English sample and 18 children from the French sample. The predictor variables were those that had significantly entered the stepwise multiple regressions described previously. In the second analysis, the same procedures were repeated, except children were selected as good or poor readers based on their *nonword* performance—this procedure eliminated 25 children from the English sample and 19 from the French sample.

The results are presented in Table 7.5. As can be seen, although it seems that the hit rate for accurate classification rate was similar across language groups, there was a slight difference in the pattern of classifications. For the English children, classification was slightly better for good readers; whereas for the French children, classification was slightly better for poor readers. Nevertheless, it is clear that kindergarten predictions of grade 1 reading occur because of success in identifying both successful and unsuccessful readers, and this pattern occurs in English and in French.

DISCUSSION AND SUMMARY

The major goal of this study was to examine whether current models of early reading acquisition that have been developed primarily from English populations also hold for children learning to speak and read other languages. Our results indicate that the answer is primarily yes, at least in the case of French. The broad strokes of current models of early reading acquisition seem to hold up, although some of the precise details may vary as a function of language-specific and orthographic factors.

Our results also indicate that although the overall relationship between early reading acquisition and preliteracy skills was similar for both our

TABLE 7.5
Discriminant Function Analyses
Classification Accuracy for Grade 1 Good and Poor Readers

	English (n = 90)				French (n = 85)		
				Classification Variable: Word Recognition			
		Predicted Group				*Predicted Group*	
Actual Group	*N*	*Good*	*Poor*	*Actual Group*	*N*	*Good*	*Poor*
Good	46	89%	11%	Good	53	81%	19%
Poor	20	20%	80%	Poor	14	14%	86%
	Cases correctly classified: 86%				Cases correctly classified: 82%		
				Classification Variable: Nonword Reading			
		Predicted Group				*Predicted Group*	
Actual Group	*N*	*Good*	*Poor*	*Actual Group*	*N*	*Good*	*Poor*
Good	46	91%	9%	Good	45	87%	13%
Poor	19	21%	79%	Poor	15	13%	87%
	Cases correctly classified: 86%				Cases correctly classified: 80%		

French-speaking and English-speaking subject groups, there were substantial differences in these children's development of preliteracy skills.
We attribute some of these differences to culture-specific factors. More
specifically, French schools, homes, and media provide French-speaking
children with relatively fewer preliteracy opportunities than is the case
for their English-speaking peers. Interestingly, however, although the
French-speaking children had fewer such experiences and, in fact, lower
levels of preliteracy skills in kindergarten, this did not seem to have major
repercussions for their development of word recognition skills in grade
1. It may be that preliteracy skills are deemphasized in language communities that learn a relatively transparent orthography because it is
assumed that reading acquisition is relatively straightforward. Conversely, English-speaking communities may place a great deal of emphasis
on preliteracy skills because it is difficult for children to learn English,
one of the more inconsistent and less transparent alphabetic languages.
In order to be successful, English-speaking children may need to come
to the reading classroom equipped with all the skills and help they can
get. These differing expectations may become part of the culture of literacy
in these communities.

Having said this, however, the same markers of early reading acquisition that were identified for English-speaking children also held for

French-speaking children; namely, knowledge of letter names and phonological awareness. The nature of the specific metaphonological skills that were important differed and, we believe, reflect the particular phonological characteristics of each language. It also appears to be the case that preliteracy development of these skills and knowledge predicts both reading success as well as difficulty for both French- and English-speaking children. We did not find, as might have been expected, that, for example, lack of these skills put English-speaking children at risk, whereas excellence in these skills protected French-speaking children from reading failure.

There were clear differences in the rates at which the two groups of children developed early reading skills: Notwithstanding poorly developed preliteracy skills and no reading instruction in kindergarten, by the end of grade 1 the French children demonstrated better reading ability than their English peers, who were advantaged in these two domains. Because of unavoidable sampling problems, it is not possible to determine from the present study whether this difference reflects instructional factors or language-specific/orthographic factors or, alternatively, a combination of the two. In any case, the results of the predictive analyses are not changed by this confound.

The present results support the following conclusions. Current models of early reading acquisition that emphasize the importance of knowledge of the sublexical structures of language apply to children acquiring languages with different phonological structures. The most significant predictors of early reading acquisition are the same for children acquiring different languages; namely, knowledge of letter names and phonological awareness. Phonological awareness is a significant predictor of both early success and early difficulty in learning to read, and this is true for children acquiring languages with different phonological characteristics. Notwithstanding such cross-linguistic similarities, the development of phonological awareness in preliterate children is susceptible to language-specific phonological characteristics. In other words, the precise sublexical units of language that assume importance in children's phonological awareness are linked to the salient phonological structures of the language they are learning. Early levels of development of phonological awareness can also be influenced by culture-specific factors and, in particular, preliterate exposure to and experiences with literacy.

ACKNOWLEDGMENTS

We are grateful to the many principals, teachers, students, and parents who were so highly cooperative in this research project. This research was supported by Grants 0GP000A1181 from the Natural Sciences and

Engineering Research Council to M. Bruck, 410-91-1936 from the Social Sciences and Humanities Research Council to F. Genesee, and 94-ER-2015 from Fonds pour la Formation de Chercheurs et l'Aide à la Recherche to M. Bruck and F. Genesee.

REFERENCES

Adams, M. J. (1990). *Beginning to read: Thinking and learning about print*. Cambridge, MA: MIT Press.

Baudot, J. (1992). *Fréquences d'utilisation des mots en français écrit contemporain*. Montréal: Les Presses de L'Université de Montréal.

Brady, S., & Shankweiler, D. (Eds.). (1991). *Phonological processes in literacy*. Hillsdale, NJ: Lawrence Erlbaum Associates.

Bruck, M., & Genesee, F. (1995). Phonological awareness in young second language learners. *Journal of Child Language, 22*, 307–324.

Cutler, A., Mehler, J., Norris, D., & Segui, J. (1986). The syllable's differing role in the segmentation of French and English. *Journal of Memory and Language, 25*, 385–400.

Ehri, L. (1984). Summaries and a critique of five studies related to letter-name knowledge and learning to read. In L. Gentile, M. Kamil, & J. Blanchard (Eds.), *Reading research revisited* (pp. 131–153). Columbus, OH: Merrill.

Gates, A. I. (1940). A further evaluation of reading readiness. *Elementary School Journal, 40*, 577–591.

Gough, P., Ehri, L., & Treiman, R. (Eds.). (1992). *Reading acquisition*. Hillsdale, NJ: Lawrence Erlbaum Associates.

Kucera, H., & Francis, W. (1967). *Computational analysis of present-day American English*. Providence, RI: Brown University Press.

Raven, J. C., & Summers, B. (1986). *Manual for Raven's Progressive Matrices and Vocabulary Scales* (Research Suppl. No. 3). London: Lewis.

Sattler, J. M. (1988). *Assessment of children* (3rd ed.). San Diego: Author.

Scarborough, H., & Dobrich, W. (1994). On the efficacy of reading to preschoolers. *Developmental Review, 14*, 245–302.

Share, D. L., Jorm, A. F., Maclean, R., & Matthews, R. (1984). Sources of individual differences in reading acquisition. *Journal of Educational Psychology, 76*, 1309–1324.

Stanovich, K. E., Cunningham, A. E., & Cramer, B. (1984). Assessing phonological awareness in kindergarten children: Issues of task comparability. *Journal of Experimental Child Psychology, 38*, 175–190.

Treiman, R., & Zukowski, A. (1991). Children's awareness of syllables, onsets, rimes and phonemes. In S. Brady & D. Shankweiler (Eds.), *Phonological processes in literacy* (pp. 67–83). Hillsdale, NJ: Lawrence Erlbaum Associates.

Wagner, R., & Torgeson, J. (1987). The nature of phonological processing and its causal role in the acquisition of reading skills. *Psychological Bulletin, 101*, 192–212.

Yopp, H. K. (1988). The validity and reliability of phonemic awareness tests. *Reading Research Quarterly, 23*, 159–177.

8

Sight Word Learning in Normal Readers and Dyslexics

Linnea C. Ehri
City University of New York Graduate School

Learning to read words by sight is a central part of developing skill as a reader. In this chapter, I cite theory and evidence drawn from my research and that of others to explain what sight word learning involves and its course of development in normal readers (Ehri, 1980, 1984, 1987, 1991, 1992, 1994, in press). Then, I consider whether sight word learning in dyslexic readers develops normally or is impaired. Finally, I provide a glimpse of an instructional approach that is consistent with my theory of sight word learning and may hold promise in treating sight word reading difficulties in dyslexics.

READING PROCESSES VERSUS METHODS OF INSTRUCTION

A presentation on how children learn to read can go in one of two directions. It can focus on methods of teaching reading, or it can focus on processes that develop as beginners learn to read. My focus is on processes rather than on methods. It is important to be clear about this. I see too many instances in which processes are confused with methods and an argument erupts that is unresolvable because the parties are talking about two different things.

Let me supply an example. What does the term *sight word learning* mean to you? What kind of mental image does this term evoke? Teachers who say, "I object to it" or "I support it" or "I do it everyday with my students" are referring to a method of instruction. They probably envision students speeding through a set of flash cards practicing how to read single words.

A very different reaction to this term is to think of sight word learning as a process, as something that all beginners go through to attain skill in reading. Holding this meaning, one envisions the mind of the reader and perhaps imagines a mental dictionary lodged somewhere in the left hemisphere. The dictionary holds all the written and spoken words that are familiar to the reader. The dictionary is linked to the reader's eyes such that when the eyes light on words that exist in the dictionary, the pronunciations and meanings of the words are immediately activated in memory.

It is important to realize that reading processes can be described separately from reading methods and that no particular instructional method is entailed by any process. When I talk about sight word learning as a process, I am not suggesting anything about the activities that teachers should use to help students learn sight words. Many different activities might do the job.

Also it is important to realize that, by singling out processes and talking about their development, I am not suggesting that the processes should be taught in isolation. Likewise, I am not arguing against teaching them in context. The point is that I am not making any declarations about how to teach the processes.

What I want to do is set aside questions about instruction temporarily and focus on reading processes. Understanding how processes develop will place us in a better position to design and evaluate instruction that teaches students these processes.

VARIOUS WAYS TO READ WORDS

The basic unit of written English is the word. Written words are invariant when they recur in text. Their spellings are prescribed in dictionaries. Readers and spellers come to rely on this constancy as they acquire proficiency. It is important to explain how readers and spellers process and remember the written forms of words. At least five different ways of reading words can be distinguished (Ehri, 1991, 1994):

1. By sounding out and blending letters, referred to as *decoding* or *phonological recoding*.
2. By pronouncing common spelling patterns, a more advanced form of decoding.

3. By retrieving sight words from memory.
4. By analogizing to words already known by sight.
5. By using context to predict words.

In each case, the processes differ. As readers attain skill, they become capable of reading words in all five ways.

One way to read words is to *transform graphemes into phonemes and blend them into pronunciations that approximate real words.* Readers use a decoding strategy mainly to read words they have never seen before. This is a slower way of reading words than sight word reading. In English, this strategy works sometimes but not always, because the relationship between spellings and pronunciations is often variable or irregular.

Whereas beginning readers decode words by attacking individual letters, more advanced readers process chunks of letters when they decode words. They learn how these letter chunks are pronounced from their experiences reading different words that share common letter patterns. When they see new words containing these chunks, they can pronounce the whole chunk without sounding letter by letter. Treiman, Goswami, and Bruck (1990), among others, have shown that words having common chunks are easier to decode by readers who are familiar with the letter patterns. Table 8.1 includes a list of common spelling patterns found at the ends of single-syllable words in English. These 37 chunks are found in nearly 500 primary grade words (Stahl, Osborn, & Lehr, 1990). Also, Table 8.1 contains a list of common affixes occurring in words (Becker, Dixon, & Anderson-Inman, 1980).

TABLE 8.1
Common Spelling Patterns in Words

Common Endings (Rhyme Spellings) of Single Syllable Words						
-ack	-all	-ain	-ake	-ale	-ame	-an
-ank	-ap	-ash	-at	-ate	-aw	-ay
-eat	-ell	-est				
-ice	-ick	-ide	-ight	-ill	-in	-ine
-ing	-ink	-ip	-ir			
-ock	-oke	-op	-ore	-or		
-uck	-ug	-ump	-unk			

Common Affixes						
-al	-able	-ate	-ant			
-ed	-en	-er	-ent			
-ize	-ist	-ing	-ive	-ite	-ion	-ic
-ful	-ly	-less	-ment	-ness	-ous	
com-	con-	de-	dis-	ex-	im-	in-
or-	pre-	pro-	re-	un-		

A very different way to read words is *by sight*. Consider the list of words in Table 8.2, taken from Adams and Huggins' (1985) test of sight word reading. These words cannot be phonologically recoded because they contain letters that deviate from the conventional spelling system. Despite this, you can read the words easily because you have stored them as sight words in memory. This is considered a test of sight word reading, because other ways of reading the words have been precluded by the fact that the words are spelled irregularly. However, the process of sight word reading is not limited to irregular words. All words that are practiced enough become sight words.

When readers read words by sight, they access information stored in memory from previous experiences reading the words. Sight of the word activates its spelling, pronunciation, and meaning immediately in memory, without any sounding out or blending required. Reitsma (1983) found that first graders required a minimum of four experiences reading words to read them by sight.

You can tell when readers are reading words by sight because they read the words as whole units, with no pauses between sounds, and they read the words within one second of seeing them. When sight words are known well enough, readers can recognize their pronunciations and meanings *automatically*, without expending any attention or effort decoding the words (LaBerge & Samuels, 1974). This allows word reading to operate unconsciously.

You can experience automatic word recognition by naming the pictures in Fig. 8.1. Move across the rows from left to right and say the name of each picture as quickly as you can. Ignore the words printed on the pictures. Most people find it impossible to ignore the words. This is evidence that your mind is processing the words automatically despite your intention to ignore them (Ehri, 1977; Golinkoff & Rosinski, 1976; Guttentag & Haith, 1978; Rosinski, Golinkoff, & Kukish, 1975).

Another way to read words is by *analogy* (Baron, 1977; Bowey & Hansen, 1994; Bruck & Treiman, 1992; Cunningham, 1976; Gaskins et al., 1988; Glushko, 1979, 1981; Goswami, 1986, 1990; Laxon, Coltheart, & Keating, 1988; Marsh, Freidman, Welch, & Desberg, 1981). Readers may read a new word by recognizing how its spelling is similar to a word they already know as a sight word. They access the similar sight word in memory and then

TABLE 8.2
Words from Adams and Huggins' (1985) Test of Sight Word Reading

none	island	busy	bouquet	rhythm
calf	depot	yacht	fiance	heights
break	react	suede	guitar	
prove	sugar	tongue	chauffeur	

FIG. 8.1. Picture naming task to demonstrate that words are processed automatically despite the reader's intention to ignore them. *Source*: From "Learning to Read and Spell Words" by L. C. Ehri, *Journal of Reading Behavior, 19,* 5–11. Copyright © 1987 by National Reading Conference. Reprinted by permission.

adjust the pronunciation to accommodate the new word; for example, reading *fountain* by analogy to *mountain*, or *brother* by analogy to *mother*. Goswami (1986, 1990) found that beginning readers can use their knowledge of rhyming words to read new words by analogy. However, Ehri and Robbins (1992) showed that having some decoding skill is required for beginners to analogize by accessing sight words in memory.

You can experience various ways to read words by pronouncing the following list of pseudowords: *jone, dalf, greak, brove, disland, nepot, heact, tugar, fusy, bacht, tuede, fongue, souquet, riance, nuitar, mauffeur, phythm, beights.* As you do this, reflect on the processes you are using. You may sound out and blend some words letter by letter, but you may read chunks of letters in other words. You may decode some of the words, but you may read other words by analogy to sight words you already know. To see how the pseudowords might be read by analogy, compare them to the columns of words in Table 8.2.

One final way to read words is *by using context such as pictures and the preceding text to make predictions about upcoming words* (Biemiller, 1970; Clay, 1968, 1969; Goodman, 1976; Stanovich, 1980; Weber, 1970). Readers have various knowledge sources available to support word prediction: their knowledge about language, their knowledge of the world, and their memory for the text already read (Rumelhart, 1977). However, predicting words based on context does not account for the way that readers read most words in text, because most of the words cannot be guessed accurately, particularly important content words (Gough & Walsh, 1991). To read these words accurately, a reader must use processes other than pure contextual guessing.

Now that I have distinguished various ways to read words, let us consider which way is most efficient for reading text. If readers know words by sight and can recognize them automatically as they read text, then word reading operates unconsciously. In contrast, each of the other ways of reading words requires conscious attention, however slight. If readers attempt to decode words, or to find analogous words in memory, or to predict words from context, their attention is shifted at least momentarily from the text to the word itself to resolve the word's identity, regardless of how easy it is to decode the word or to guess it. This suggests that being able to read words automatically by sight is the most efficient, unobtrusive way to read words in text (Perfetti, 1985; Stanovich, 1980). Thus, building a sight vocabulary is essential for achieving text reading skill.

Although sight word reading is the primary way that words are identified when text is read, the other ways to read words may not lie dormant. According to interactive models that portray text reading processes, there are multiple sources of information that are activated in parallel to create redundancy (Rumelhart, 1977). With regard to word reading processes in these models, sight word reading is *supported* by the other ways of reading words. Sight word reading is a fast-acting process, faster than the other forms of word reading, so this is how the pronunciations and meanings of words are identified. The other word reading processes contribute by confirming the identities already determined. Confirmatory processes are thought to happen automatically as well. Knowledge of the grapho-phonic system confirms that the word's pronunciation fits the spelling on the page. Knowledge of syntax confirms that the word fits into the structure of the sentence. World knowledge and text memory confirm that the meaning of the word is consistent with the text's meaning up to that point. Having confirmation from multiple sources (i.e., redundancy) operating during text reading serves to maintain highly accurate reading, to make the reader sensitive to errors, and to provide a means of self-correction when errors disrupt comprehension.

SIGHT WORD LEARNING

Now let us consider the matter of sight word learning. As I have said, sight words are words that readers read by remembering how they read them before. The term *sight* indicates that sight of the word activates that word in memory, including information about its spelling, pronunciation, typical role in sentences, and meaning. How might this capability be explained? The kind of process I proposed to be at the heart of sight word learning is a *connection-forming* process (Ehri, 1980, 1984, 1987, 1992; Ehri & Wilce, 1979, 1980, 1985, 1986, 1987a, 1987b). Connections are formed that link the written forms of words to their pronunciations and meanings in memory.

What kinds of connections are formed to store sight words in memory? According to the traditional view, readers memorize associations between visual features of words and their meanings (Haber & Haber, 1981). For example, consider the following words:

dog   *green*   *tent*   *on*   *ate*

Each has a shape that distinguishes it from the others, as revealed in outlines of their borders. Also, they have distinctive sequences of letters. However, an explanation involving connections between visual features and meanings is inadequate.

Consider the feat that skilled readers perform when they read words by sight. They are able to recognize in an instant any one of many thousands of words. They recognize one unique word and bypass other similarly spelled, similarly shaped words. For example, consider all the words that must be overlooked to read the word *stick* accurately: not only *stink*, *slick*, and *slink*, which have similar shapes as well as letters, but also *sting*, *sling*, and *string*, as well as *sick*, *sing*, and *sink*. Distinctive shapes are not sufficiently rich to support these discriminations; sight word reading must involve remembering letters in the words. These are the distinctive cues that make one word different from all the others. However, remembering links between letter sequences and meanings is not how the letters are retained in memory by readers.

Skilled readers can learn to read new sight words with very little practice (Reitsma, 1983). This rules out associations between letter sequences and meanings, because they are arbitrary and hence would require more learning time than this. A mnemonically powerful system is needed to account for learning this rapid. Also, if meanings were the anchors for words in memory, we would expect many more synonymous misreadings of words; for example, misreading *huge* as *immense* or *gigantic*. In actuality, these are rare. Skilled readers do not misread words very often, and when they do, the misreadings resemble closely the spellings of the words.

Findings of my research indicate that another type of connection explains the links formed to store sight words in memory. Readers form connections between graphemes seen in the spellings of specific words and phonemes detected in their pronunciations. The connections are formed out of readers' knowledge of grapheme–phoneme relations. Readers look at the spelling, they pronounce the word, they apply their grapho-phonic knowledge to analyze how the graphemes symbolize the phonemes in that word. Doing this a few times secures the sight word in memory.

In Fig. 8.2, I have depicted how readers might form connections to learn several sight words. I have used capital letters to designate the spellings of words, phonetic symbols between slashes to indicate phonemes, and lines linking graphemes to phonemes to indicate connections. Notice that in some spellings, digraphs rather than individual letters are linked to a phoneme. Notice that when sounds involving the vocalic phonemes /l/ and /r/ occur alone in an unstressed syllable, they may be treated as one phoneme, as Treiman (1993) found. Alternatively, they might be analyzed as two phonemes, schwa plus /r/ or schwa plus /l/, to adhere to the principle that every syllable has a vowel. Notice that although the grapheme G has the potential for symbolizing /j/ or /g/,

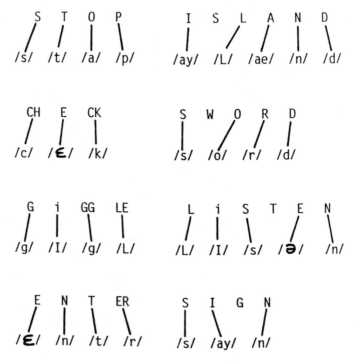

FIG. 8.2. Illustration of the connections formed between graphemes in the spellings of words and phonemes detected in their pronunciations when readers store sight words in memory.

in the word *giggle,* the letter G is remembered as symbolizing the phoneme /g/, not /j/, because the pronunciation of the word specifies /g/.

This connection-forming process is the way that the spellings of words are bonded to their pronunciations along with their meanings. The bonded unit is stored in memory as that word. The next time the reader sees the word, he or she can retrieve the word from memory to read it. Perfetti (1992) described a similar process for representing words in memory.

Note what readers need to know about the grapho-phonic spelling system to secure complete representations of sight words in memory. Readers need sufficient familiarity with letter shapes. They need to know which phonemes these letters typically symbolize in words. They need to know how to segment pronunciations into phonemes. They need to be able to group letters into the functional graphemic units that match up to the phonemes they detect. This is consistent with research showing that the two best predictors of first-grade reading achievement, when the predictors are measured at entry to kindergarten, are letter knowledge and phonemic segmentation skill (Share, Jorm, Maclean, & Matthews, 1984).

This process of forming connections allows readers to remember how to read not only words containing conventional grapheme–phoneme correspondences, such as *stop,* but also words that are spelled irregularly. Connections that might be formed to remember irregular words are illustrated in Fig. 8.2. Note that the same types of connections are evident. It turns out that most of the letters in irregular words conform to grapheme–phoneme conventions, for example, all but S in *island,* all but W in *sword,* all but T in *listen,* and all but G in *sign.* For letters that do not have sounds, readers may remember them as extra visual forms, or they may flag them as silent in memory, or they may remember a special spelling pronunciation that includes the silent letter—for example, remembering *listen* as "lis-ten" or *chocolate* as "choc-o-late" (Drake & Ehri, 1984; Ehri & Wilce, 1982).

Beginning readers need to learn to regard spellings of words as phonemic maps that lay out the pronunciations of words visually. They need to become skilled at computing these mappping relations spontaneously when they see unfamiliar words and pronounce them. This process needs to be activated during text reading when new words are encountered. Readers may phonologically recode new words, or analogize, or perhaps they may combine context cues with some of the letters they see to predict the word (Tunmer & Chapman, 1996). Regardless of how they identify the word's pronunciation and meaning, the event that is critical for sight word learning is that, when they say the word, they need to look at the spelling and compute connections between graphemes and phonemes in order to retain the written form as a sight word in memory. Knowledge of grapheme–phoneme relations provides a powerful mnemonic system that bonds the written forms of specific words to their pronunciations in memory. Once readers know the grapho-phonic spelling system, they can learn to read words and build a lexicon of sight words easily.

PHASES OF DEVELOPMENT

I have explained how sight words are remembered by readers who have full knowledge of the grapho-phonic spelling system. Now let us turn to the question of development: Do beginners learn sight words any differently from more mature readers? The answer is yes. In our studies of the development of sight word learning, we have found that different types of connections predominate at different points in development. To capture these changes, I have distinguished four phases of development labeled to reflect how the alphabetic system is involved in the connections that are formed at each phase (Ehri, 1995).

When I talk about the alphabetic or grapho-phonic system, I am referring to the spelling regularities that underlie the written forms of English words (Venezky, 1970). Earlier I argued that all learners must internalize this system so that they can use it to build a sight vocabulary. The term *alphabetic* indicates that, in English, written words consist of fixed sequences of letters symbolizing the pronunciations of specific words, that individual letters and combinations of letters function as symbols for the phonemes and phoneme blends in these words, and that letters combine in consistent patterns across words to symbolize larger syllabic and sub-syllabic units as well (Becker et al., 1980; Treiman, 1992; Wylie & Durrell, 1970).

The four phases of sight word learning are: pre-alphabetic, partial alphabetic, full alphabetic, and consolidated alphabetic. Each phase is labeled to reflect the *predominant* type of connection that links the written forms of sight words to their pronunciations and meanings in memory. There are some parallels between these phases and the three stages proposed by Frith (1985)—logographic, alphabetic, and orthographic. However, I have changed the labels to be more precise. My labels reflect the fact that the alphabetic system provides the basis for the development of sight word reading. My labels avoid the impression that word reading processes during the first phase are like those used by mature readers of logographic orthographies—for example, readers of Chinese who process written words as fully analyzed Gestalts. My label for the final phase, consolidated alphabetic, captures more precisely the type of connections formed than the label "orthographic," which has multiple meanings (Wagner & Barker, 1994).

PRE-ALPHABETIC PHASE

The pre-alphabetic phase characterizes sight word learning at the earliest period, before children know much about the alphabetic system and, of course, long before they can read independently. This phase is called *pre-alphabetic* because, unlike the phases that come later, readers do not use letter-sound relations in their reading. In this phase, children remember how to read sight words by forming connections between selected visual attributes in or around words and their pronunciations or meanings (Ehri & Wilce, 1985; Gough & Hillinger, 1980; Gough, Juel, & Roper/Schneider, 1983). For example, they might remember *yellow* by the tall posts in the middle. We have called this *visual cue reading*. The idea is that readers select single salient visual cues to remember how to read words. In a study by Gough, Juel, and Griffith (1992), a thumbprint appearing next to a word was found to be the salient cue used by beginners.

When pre-alphabetic readers read print in their environment, they select salient visual cues that may or may not involve the written words themselves. In one study, we identified children between the ages of 3 and 5 who could read many signs and labels in their environment (Masonheimer, Drum, & Ehri, 1984). We showed the children each label with one letter altered, for example, *Pepsi* changed to *Xepsi*. Children persisted in reading the label as "Pepsi" and failed to notice the change even when we drew their attention to the possibility of an error. This occurred because the children had not used any letter cues to remember how to read the labels.

Because pre-alphabetic readers do not use letter-sound connections to remember sight words, they are not held to one pronunciation of the written word. They may remember the concept rather than the pronunciation. Harste, Burke, and Woodward (1982) observed that children sometimes used variable rather than exact wordings when they read labels. For example, one child read *Crest* as "brush teeth" one time and as "toothpaste" another time. This lack of correspondence at the letter-sound level but consistency at the semantic level indicates that the connections formed are between salient visual cues and meanings. This contrasts with later phases when children form connections between spellings and pronunciations, and this restricts their reading of print to one word.

The pre-alphabetic phase is really a phase that occurs by default, as Byrne (1992) pointed out. Young children have a desire to remember how to read words, but they cannot take advantage of systematic relations between letters and sounds. By default, they resort to visually salient cues. However, in most cases, these cues are unreliable because they recur in several words. Also, they are hard to remember because the connections they provide are arbitrary and unsystematic; for example, the thumbprint, or the tall posts in "yellow" (Mason, 1980).

PARTIAL ALPHABETIC

The next phase of sight word learning is called the *partial alphabetic phase.* Partial alphabetic readers remember how to read sight words by forming connections between only some of the letters in written words and sounds detected in their pronunciations. Because the first and final letters and sounds in words are the easiest to pick out, these may become the connections that are remembered. We have called this *phonetic cue reading* (Ehri, 1987; Ehri & Wilce, 1985, 1987a, 1987b; Rack, Hulme, Snowling, & Wightman, 1994; Scott & Ehri, 1989).

To learn sight words in this way, partial alphabetic readers must be able to distinguish some sounds in words, and they must recognize which letters in the words are related to those sounds. They may use their knowledge of letter-sound or letter-name relations to form connections. For example, to remember how to read *spoon*, partial alphabetic readers might look at the word while saying it and recognize some of its parts. They might detect initial /s/ and final /n/ in speech and recognize that the letters they see, *s* and *n*, symbolize these sounds. Recognizing these connections is facilitated by the fact that the *names* of these letters contain the relevant sounds. These partial connections are held in memory and enable the readers to remember how to read *spoon* the next time they see it.

One reason why the connections are partial rather than complete is that readers are unable to segment the word's pronunciation into all of its sounds. Another reason is that they lack full knowledge of the spelling system, particularly vowels. In addition, they may not know how to group letters into graphemes.

In one study, we selected children in the first year of school (Ehri & Wilce, 1985). We gave them tests to distinguish pre-alphabetic readers from partial alphabetic readers. None of the children could decode unfamiliar words, so they had not reached the full alphabetic phase. The only way that these children could read words was by remembering them by sight. We taught the children to read six words by sight, those listed in Fig. 8.3. Some beginners learned to read written forms containing visually distinctive letters. Words in the visual set all had different shapes but the letters bore no relationship to sounds (see the actual shapes and letters reproduced in Fig. 8.3). Other beginners learned to read words having simplified letter-sound spellings. Words in the letter-sound set had letters

Spellings Read

Words Learned	Visual Cues	Letter-Sound Cues
"giraffe"	W BC	J R F
"balloon"	X G S T	B L U N
"mask"	u H E	M S K
"knee"	F o	N E
"scissors"	Q D j K	S Z R S
"turtle"	Y M P	T R D L

FIG. 8.3. Appearance of visually distinctive spellings and simplified letter-sound spellings that beginners were taught to read.

that could be linked to sounds in the words, but their shapes were not distinctive.

Results of this study are shown in Fig. 8.4, which depicts the mean number of visual spellings and phonetic spellings that were read correctly per trial over five trials of practice. Pre-alphabetic readers learned to read the visually distinctive spellings easier than the letter-sound spellings. In contrast, partial alphabetic readers learned to read the letter-sound spellings easier than the visual spellings.

Readers who can form connections out of partial phonetic cues have an advantage over readers who are limited to visual cues in building a sight vocabulary. This is because phonetic cue readers have a system they can use to remember words. In contrast, visual cue readers have to remember arbitrary, ideosyncratic connections. This makes the words much harder to remember.

One limitation of sight word reading based on partial letter-sound cues is that words with similar letters are often mistaken for each other. For example, *want* and *what*, *look* and *like*, *house* and *horse* may be mixed up. Readers are much better off if they can form complete connections between all the letters they see in a word and sounds in its pronunciation. This greatly reduces such errors.

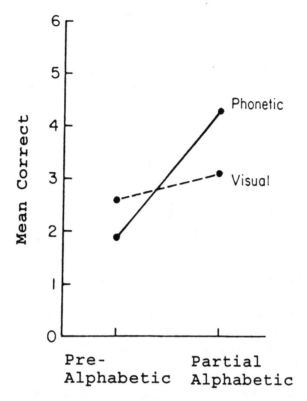

FIG. 8.4. Mean number of visual and phonetic spellings that were read by readers at the pre-alphabetic phase and by readers at the partial alphabetic phase of development.

FULL ALPHABETIC PHASE

The next phase is referred to as the *full alphabetic phase*. Beginners remember sight words by forming complete connections between letters seen in written words and phonemes detected in their pronunciations. This is possible because readers know how graphemes symbolize phonemes in the conventional spelling system, and because they can segment pronunciations of words into phonemes. When readers apply this knowledge to form connections for specific sight words, spellings become fully bonded to pronunciations in memory. Several examples of words analyzed in this way were shown in Fig. 8.2.

One advantage of representing sight words completely in memory is that word reading becomes much more accurate. Whereas partial alphabetic readers' memory for initial and final letters may cause them to confuse similarly spelled words, full alphabetic readers' representations eliminate confusion because their representations are sufficiently complete to distinguish easily among similarly spelled words.

In one of our experiments (Ehri & Wilce, 1987a), we selected children who were partial alphabetic readers. We trained half of them to use full alphabetic cues to read words. We did this not by teaching sounding out and blending skills, but rather by teaching them to read many spellings that differed in only one letter, for example, *sap, sam, sad,* and *sat.* The other children were given letter-sound practice, so they remained partial cue readers. Following training, we gave students several practice trials to learn to read a set of 15 similarly spelled words by sight, for example, *spin, stab, stamp,* and *stand.* Results are presented in Fig. 8.5. The full cue readers learned to read many more words than the partial cue readers did. In fact, full cue readers learned to read the sight words perfectly after only a few practice trials, whereas partial cue readers never learned to read the words perfectly. These differences show the enormous advantage provided when students know how to connect spellings fully to pronunciations in their sight word learning.

One characteristic that distinguishes full alphabetic from partial alphabetic readers is the ability to decode words never read before. In our study (Ehri & Wilce, 1987a), we also assessed students' ability to decode nonwords following training. As evident from performances on the decoding task in Fig. 8.5, full cue readers read many more nonwords than partial cue readers. It is this ability that helps full alphabetic readers compute all the connections and store sight words in memory.

Although full alphabetic readers can decode words, when they practice reading specific words often enough, the words become known by sight.

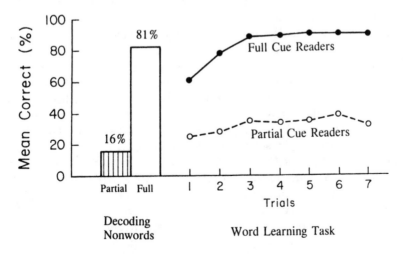

FIG. 8.5. Mean performances of full cue readers and partial cue readers on a decoding task and a word learning task.

The advantage of sight word reading over decoding is that sight word reading operates much faster. In one study (Ehri & Wilce, 1983), we had skilled readers in first, second, and fourth grades read familiar sight words (e.g., *man, car, hat,* and *dog*) and unfamiliar but simply spelled nonwords (*baf, jad, kiv,* and *fup*). We found that they read the familiar sight words much faster than the nonwords. In fact, they read the sight words as rapidly as they named digits (e.g., 2, 3, 5, 8), indicating that the words were read as single units rather than as letters processed sequentially.

In this same study, we tested disabled readers in grades 1, 2, and 4 as well. They were very slow and inaccurate in reading the nonwords. Although they read the sight words more accurately, they did not read them as rapidly as single digits until 4th grade. This is consistent with results of other studies indicating that disabled readers have weak decoding skills and are slow in learning to read words by sight (Rack, Snowling, & Olson, 1992).

CONSOLIDATED ALPHABETIC PHASE

Full alphabetic readers are able to remember complete information about the spellings of a rapidly growing number of sight words. As fully connected spellings of more and more words are retained in memory, letter patterns that recur across different words become familiar. Repeated experience reading a letter sequence that symbolizes the same phoneme blend across different words yields a consolidated unit in which several graphemes become bonded to a blend of phonemes. Consolidation allows readers to operate with multiletter units that may be morphemes, syllables, or parts of syllables. These letter patterns become part of a reader's generalized knowledge of the spelling system (Bowey & Hansen, 1994; Ehri, 1991, 1994; Henry, 1988, 1989; Laxon, Coltheart, & Keating, 1988; Marsh et al., 1981; Templeton, 1992; Treiman, Goswami, & Bruck, 1990).

Larger letter units are valuable for sight word learning because they reduce the number of connections that are needed to secure words in memory. For example, *-est* might become known as a consolidated unit from its occurrence in several sight words known by the reader, for example, *nest, best, rest, test,* and *west*. When a new word is encountered, such as *chest*, a reader in the consolidated phase needs to form only two separate connections linking *ch* to /č/ and *est* to /ɛst/. In contrast, a full alphabetic reader would need to form four separate connections linking *ch, e, s,* and *t,* to /č/, /ɛ/, /s/, and /t/, respectively.

Knowing letter chunks is particularly valuable for learning multisyllabic words. For example, knowing the following spelling patterns as consolidated units—*in, er, est,* and *ing*—makes learning longer sight words such as *interesting* much easier, because it reduces the number of connections required to secure the word in memory, from an impossibly large number if segmented into graphemes (i.e., 10 with *ng* as one grapheme), to a more manageable number (i.e., 4) if segmented into syllables.

A number of studies have shown that older readers are sensitive to commonly occurring letter sequences whereas beginning readers are not. Results suggest that second grade is when children's sight vocabularies grow large enough for consolidated units to begin emerging (Bowey & Hansen, 1994; Juel, 1983; Leslie & Thimke, 1986; Treiman, Goswami, & Bruck, 1990).

BUILDING A SIGHT VOCABULARY

The four phases I have outlined portray the connection-forming mechanism for storing sight words in memory and how it changes during development. Instruction is especially important for helping students reach the full alphabetic phase in their sight word learning, when they are able to analyze and connect all the graphemes in spellings to all of the phonemes in pronunciations of words (Carnine, 1977; Chall, 1967, 1983).

Building a sight vocabulary also requires that readers practice reading text so that they are exposed to the written forms of unfamiliar words often enough for the words to be added to their lexicons. Stanovich and his colleagues (Cunningham & Stanovich, 1990; Stanovich & West, 1989; Stanovich, West, & Cunningham, 1991) showed the importance of exposure to text for lexical development. Because this is where students encounter the written forms of most words, it is important for sight word learning mechanisms to be active during text reading.

SIGHT WORD LEARNING IN DYSLEXICS

Now let us turn our attention to evidence regarding the sight word learning of disabled readers. From many studies, we know that dyslexics are particularly deficient in their phonological processing (Bruck & Waters, 1990; Ehri, 1986, 1989; Frith, 1985; Rack et al., 1992; Stanovich, 1986; Wagner & Torgeson, 1987). They have trouble segmenting words into phonemes. They have trouble reading pseudowords. They have trouble spelling words. Spelling difficulties may persist even when reading has been remediated. In light of these problems, if my theory of sight word learning is correct, we would expect the sight word learning of dyslexics to be deficient. They should have difficulty advancing from the partial alphabetic phase to the full alphabetic phase, and the consolidated phase may be out of reach.

I performed a study with Jill Saltmarsh to compare sight word learning processes in normal beginning readers and disabled readers to see whether both groups would acquire fully analyzed representations of words in memory (Ehri & Saltmarsh, 1995). Findings of a Dutch study by Reitsma (1983) had indicated that beginning readers remember letter details about sight words but disabled readers do not. Our study was intended to replicate and extend Reitsma's study using English-speaking beginning and disabled readers.

The approach we used was to have subjects read a set of words enough times so that the words became known by sight. Then we assessed subjects' sensitivity to single letter alterations in the words. The testing schedule was as follows:

1. Subjects practiced reading 16 target words for 12 trials. If they erred, they were told how to read them correctly. The words were simplified phonetic spellings of real words; for example, *cradle* spelled *kradl*, *messenger* spelled *mesnjr*.
2. Subjects waited 3 days.
3. Subjects read again the words they had learned. This time original spellings were mixed in with altered versions in which one letter was changed. For example, subjects read not only *kradl* and *mesnjr* but also *cradl* and *mesngr*. Reading accuracy and latency were measured for each word.

Of interest was whether subjects would read original spellings of the words *faster* than altered spellings. If they sensed the alterations, as reflected by longer latencies, this would indicate that they had stored the original letters in memory. For example, if subjects had learned to read *kradl* as the original spelling, then in the reaction time (RT) task they should read this spelling faster than *cradl*, even though the two words are phonetically equivalent. Reitsma (1983) observed Dutch beginners read original words faster than altered spellings if they had practiced reading the words a minimum of four times.

According to my theory (Ehri, 1992), readers learn to read sight words by forming connections between graphemes and phonemes. Readers in the full alphabetic phase should bond all of the letters to all of the phonemes in pronunciations. In the case of *kradl*, the bonds would consist of each letter connected to one of the five phonemes. In contrast, beginning readers and disabled readers have only limited knowedge of grapheme–phoneme relations and limited phonemic segmentation skill. As a result, they should form partial rather than complete connections when they store sight words in memory. Only the more salient letters and sounds may be bonded; for example, those in initial and final positions of words. Medial letters and sounds should be overlooked.

The present study was performed to seek evidence consistent with this view. Subjects were taught to read 16 words having simplified phonetic spellings that conformed to basic grapheme–phoneme correspondences. Some additional examples of words that were taught are:

jenral (general)	*stupd (stupid)*	*latr (lantern)*
satsfy (satisfy)	*rlax (relax)*	
dusen (dozen)	*perfum (perfume)*	

After subjects learned to read the words, their reaction times to read original words and altered spellings were measured. Several types of alterations were examined:

1. Phonetically equivalent letters were substituted, at the beginning, middle, or end of words (e.g., *genral, satsfi, duzen*; compare to original spellings listed previously).
2. Letters were added or deleted in various positions of words (e.g., *latrn, stup*).
3. Phonetically nonequivalent letters were substituted (e.g., *rlaz, pervum*).

We designed our spellings to resemble those typically produced by beginners who spell words phonetically or semiphonetically but not correctly. In this way, we were able to modify original spellings in ways that made them plausible to beginners, even though they were phonetically dubious.

The subjects in our study were 30 first-grade, normal readers and 15 older disabled readers in grades 2 to 4. All disabled readers read at least one grade level below their expected level on the Boder word reading test (Boder & Jarrico, 1982). The first graders were divided into high and low reader groups based on Boder test scores. Mean scores placed the high first-grade readers at the second-grade reading level, the disabled readers at the first-grade reading level, and the low readers at the pre-primer reading level.

Recall that readers were taught to read the target words and then were tested three days later. We found that readers did remember how to read most of the original spellings. We only analyzed latencies when a subject read both original and altered versions as the target word.

We expected that the three reader groups would be influenced differently when they read altered versions of the words in the reaction time task. High beginning readers were expected to read original words faster than all types of altered versions, indicating that their lexical representations were sufficiently complete to be sensitive to these alterations. In contrast, low and disabled readers were expected to be sensitive to initial and final letter changes but not medial letter changes.

The results were very interesting. To extract the relevant comparisons, we distinguished 13 types of spelling alterations. Some of the spelling changes did not affect the words phonetically; for example, *kradl* changed to *cradl*. Other changes did. For each type, we compared subjects' RTs to read original and altered versions of the words. For present purposes, I want to focus on the overall pattern of differences characterizing each reader group rather than focus on each type of spelling alteration.

In Fig. 8.6 are plotted differences in mean RTs to read original and altered versions of the words divided by the standard deviation. If the black horizontal bar extends to the right, subjects read original versions faster than altered versions. If the bar extends to the left, subjects read

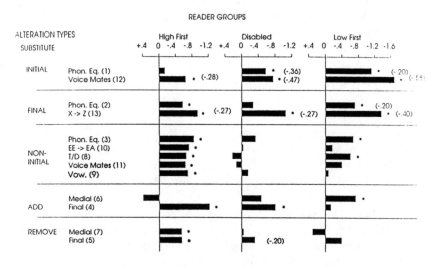

FIG. 8.6. Differences in response latencies between mean RTs to read original words and mean RTs to read altered spellings of words as a function of reader ability group and type of spelling alteration. RT to altered spelling was subtracted from RT to original spelling and the difference was divided by the standard deviation. Asterisks indicate which differences were statistically significant at $p < .05$. *Source*: From "Beginning Readers Outperform Older Disabled Readers in Learning to Read Words by Sight" by L. Ehri and J. Saltmarsh, in *Reading and Writing: An Interdisciplinary Journal*, 7, Figure 3, p. 311. Copyright © 1995, reprinted with kind permission from Kluwer Academic Publishers.

original versions slower than altered versions. An asterisk indicates that a difference is statistically significant. The various types of alterations are listed on the left. Single letters were substituted, added, or removed in initial, noninitial, medial, or final positions. The letter changes involved substituting phonetically equivalent letters (Phon. Eq.) or voicing mates of letters (e.g., *v* for *f* in *perfum*), or *z* for *x* in *relax*, or *ea* for *ee* in *freez*, or *d* for *t* (e.g., *sadsfy*), or a vowel (Vow.) letter (e.g., *o* for *a* in *latrn*). Performances of the three reader groups are presented vertically.

Most important to notice in Fig. 8.6 is the number of statistically significant differences for each reader group. High first graders were sensitive to most of the spelling changes, 11 out of 13 types. Low first graders were sensitive to over half of the changes, 7 out of 13 types. In contrast, disabled readers were sensitive to only a few changes, 4 out of 13 types.

The only types of letter alterations that influenced disabled readers were those involving changes in initial or final letters of words. Medial changes had no impact. In contrast, low first-grade readers were sensitive not only to initial and final changes, but also to three medial changes.

The tendency to process only partial letter information in words was evident in disabled readers' misreadings during the reaction time task. When they erred in reading words, they tended to produce other words on the list having similar initial letters. High readers did this much less often.

These findings support our hypotheses. They indicate that disabled readers retain less complete representations of sight words in memory than do normal readers. Disabled readers are sensitive to boundary letters but lack sensitivity to medial letters. This fits the pattern of a phonetic cue reader and indicates that disabled readers have not progressed beyond the partial alphabetic stage in their sight word learning.

In this same study we compared the three reader groups on some other alphabetic capabilities: spelling words, reading nonwords, and learning to read sight words. We were interested in whether their performances on these tasks were developmentally consistent with their level of word reading. We conducted analyses of covariance with the number of words read on the Boder test as the covariate. Essentially, this equated the three groups for word reading ability. If differences remained significant favoring both normal groups over the disabled group, this would suggest the presence of deficits rather than slow growth in the disabled readers.

A main effect of reader group was detected in one of the three analyses, that involving the sight word learning measure. The dependent measure was the number of trials taken to learn to read the words perfectly. Results revealed that disabled readers required significantly more trials than did the two normal groups who did not differ:

Actual means = 4.4 trials (high first) vs. 9.3 (disabled) vs. 9.1 (low first).

Means adjusted for covariate = 6.8 trials (high) vs. 9.2 (disabled) vs. 6.8 (low).

This points to a deficit rather than a delay in sight word learning ability among disabled readers.

Our explanation for disabled readers' sight word learning deficit is that they lacked sufficient grapho-phonic knowledge to analyze grapheme–phoneme matches in order to store complete representations of sight words in memory. They processed salient letters at word boundaries, but they failed to compute the connections between graphemes and phonemes in the interior of words. This yielded lexical representations that lacked the letter detail needed to detect spelling alterations.

FUTURE DIRECTIONS

In this chapter, I have put together theory and research to construct a coherent view of sight word reading and its development in normal and disabled readers. In considering future directions that this research might take, I see several possibilities.

One direction involves the conduct of more basic research to test the adequacy of the theory about sight word learning processes and how they change during development. My portrayal of sight word learning may prove to be oversimplified. It may even prove to be wrong. Researchers need to take a critical view of these claims and devise ways to disprove hypotheses. We know less about sight word learning during the consolidated phase, so there is a need for more research to study how knowledge of larger units is formed and used to store sight words in memory. We need to understand more about how learning to spell contributes to sight word learning, because memory for the spellings of words is thought to underlie effective sight word learning (Ehri, in press; Ehri & Wilce, 1987b).

Another direction involves exploring the implications of sight word learning processes for improving instruction aimed at both beginning readers and disabled readers. We need research to examine the impact of instructional programs, both existing and new, on students' success in learning to read words by sight. Such efforts should focus not only on overall reading achievement scores at the end of a grade, but also on specific word learning processes as they are affected by instruction.

One example of an attempt to translate theory and evidence about sight word learning into instructional practice was provided by teachers at Benchmark School who have made adjustments in their reading program to address these processes (Gaskins, Ehri, Cress, O'Hara, & Donnelly, 1996). Benchmark is a school for bright reading-disabled children. Students have been taught decoding skills through an analogy approach that involves learning how to use a set of key words to read new words. Because some students were having trouble retaining the key words in memory as sight words, the teachers decided to change the way they teach the key words. They developed exercises to help students form complete connections between graphemes and phonemes within each key word.

For example, students are taught to segment the word into its sounds by holding up fingers as they articulate each sound, then to look at the word's spelling and reconcile spellings and pronunciations by matching up letters to the sounds. Students practice writing as well as reading the key words to acquire completely connected representations of words in lexical memory. Enriching this analogy-based approach to reading instruction with an approach that teaches phonemic awareness, grapheme–phoneme relations, and how to use this knowledge to build a sight vocabulary appears to hold much potential. The instructional procedures are consistent with my theory about sight word learning. The next step is to investigate whether the approach helps disabled readers acquire decoding and spelling skills more effectively than the analogy approach without this addition.

A third direction for the future involves research on teacher understandings about sight word learning as well as other literacy acquisition processes in students, and how teachers' understandings drive what they do when they teach reading. I believe that in order for teachers to teach reading effectively, they need to understand what impact their methods have on learners (Ehri & Williams, 1996). This requires having working knowledge of three ingredients: (a) reader processes and their course of development; (b) how specific methods of instruction contribute to the development of these processes in readers, particularly the methods employed by the teacher him- or herself; and (c) measuring devices that inform teachers whether students are acquiring the targeted processes. We need research that examines how to convey knowledge about reading acquisition processes to teachers in a form that proves useful in their teaching.

The job of teaching beginners to read is not easy, but it is one of the most important challenges facing educators. It is my greatest hope that my research and the research of my colleagues will serve to improve teachers' success in teaching students to read.

REFERENCES

Adams, M., & Huggins, A. (1985). The growth of children's sight vocabulary: A quick test with educational and theoretical implications. *Reading Research Quarterly, 20,* 262–281.

Baron, J. (1977). Mechanisms for pronouncing printed words: Use and acquisition. In D. LaBerge & S. Samuels (Eds.), *Basic processes in reading: Perception and comprehension* (pp. 175–216). Hillsdale, NJ: Lawrence Erlbaum Associates.

Becker, W., Dixon, R., & Anderson-Inman, L. (1980). *Morphographic and root word analysis of 26,000 high frequency words.* Eugene, OR: University of Oregon College of Education.

Biemiller, A. (1970). The development of the use of graphic and contextual information as children learn to read. *Reading Research Quarterly, 6,* 75–96.

Boder, E., & Jarrico, S. (1982). *The Boder test of reading–spelling patterns.* New York: Grune & Stratton.

Bowey, J., & Hansen, J. (1994). The development of orthographic rimes as units of word recognition. *Journal of Experimental Child Psychology, 58,* 465–488.

Bruck, M., & Treiman, R. (1992). Learning to pronounce words: The limitations of analogies. *Reading Research Quarterly, 27,* 374–388.

Bruck, M., & Waters, G. (1990). An analysis of the component spelling and reading skills of good readers–good spellers, good readers–poor spellers, and poor readers–poor spellers. In T. Carr & B. Levy (Eds.), *Reading and its development* (pp. 161–206). San Diego: Academic Press.

Byrne, B. (1992). Studies in the acquisition procedure for reading: Rationale, hypotheses and data. In P. Gough, L. Ehri, & R. Treiman (Eds.), *Reading acquisition* (pp. 1–34). Hillsdale, NJ: Lawrence Erlbaum Associates.

Carnine, D. (1977). Phonics versus look-say: Transfer to new words. *The Reading Teacher, 30,* 636–640.

Chall, J. S. (1967). *Learning to read: The great debate.* New York: McGraw-Hill.

Chall, J. S. (1983). *Stages of reading development.* New York: McGraw-Hill.

Clay, M. (1968). A syntactic analysis of reading errors. *Journal of Verbal Learning and Verbal Behavior, 7,* 434–438.

Clay, M. (1969). Reading errors and self-correction behavior. *British Journal of Educational Psychology, 39,* 47–56.

Cunningham, P. (1976). Investigating a synthesized theory of mediated word identification. *Reading Research Quarterly, 11,* 127–143.

Cunningham, A., & Stanovich, K. (1990). Assessing print exposure and orthographic processing skill in children: A quick measure of reading experience. *Journal of Educational Psychology, 82,* 733–740.

Drake, D., & Ehri, L. (1984). Spelling acquisition: Effects of pronouncing words on memory for their spellings. *Cognition and Instruction, 1,* 297–320.

Ehri, L. (1977). Do adjectives and functors interfere as much as nouns in naming pictures? *Child Development, 48,* 697–701.

Ehri, L. (1980). The development of orthographic images. In U. Frith (Ed.), *Cognitive processes in spelling* (pp. 311–338). London: Academic Press.

Ehri, L. (1984). How orthography alters spoken language competencies in children learning to read and spell. In J. Downing & R. Valtin (Eds.), *Language awareness and learning to read* (pp. 119–147). New York: Springer-Verlag.

Ehri, L. (1986). Sources of difficulty in learning to spell and read. In M. Wolraich & D. Routh (Eds.), *Advances in developmental and behavioral pediatrics* (pp. 121–195). Greenwich, CT: JAI Press.

Ehri, L. (1987). Learning to read and spell words. *Journal of Reading Behavior, 19,* 5–31.

Ehri, L. C. (1989). The development of spelling knowledge and its role in reading acquisition and reading disability. *Journal of Learning Disabilities, 22,* 356–365.

Ehri, L. (1991). Development of the ability to read words. In R. Barr, M. Kamil, P. Mosenthal, & P. Pearson (Eds.), *Handbook of reading research volume II* (pp. 383–417). New York: Longman.

Ehri, L. (1992). Reconceptualizing the development of sight word reading and its relationship to recoding. In P. Gough, L. Ehri, & R. Treiman (Eds.), *Reading acquisition* (pp. 107–143). Hillsdale, NJ: Lawrence Erlbaum Associates.

Ehri, L. (1994). Development of the ability to read words: Update. In R. Ruddell, M. Ruddell, & H. Singer (Eds.), *Theoretical models and processes of reading* (4th ed., pp. 323–358). Newark, DE: International Reading Association.

Ehri, L. (1995). Phases of development in learning to read words by sight. *Journal of Research in Reading, 18,* 116–125.

Ehri, L. (in press). Learning to read and learning to spell are one and the same, almost. In L. Rieben, C. Perfetti, & M. Fayol (Eds.), *Learning to spell.* Mahwah, NJ: Lawrence Erlbaum Associates.

Ehri, L., & Robbins, C. (1992). Beginners need some decoding skill to read words by analogy. *Reading Research Quarterly, 27,* 12–26.

Ehri, L., & Saltmarsh, J. (1995). Beginning readers outperform older disabled readers in learning to read words by sight. *Reading and Writing: An Interdisciplinary Journal, 7,* 295–326.

Ehri, L., & Wilce, L. (1979). The mnemonic value of orthography among beginning readers. *Journal of Educational Psychology, 71,* 26–40.

Ehri, L., & Wilce, L. (1980). The influence of orthography on readers' conceptualization of the phonemic structure of words. *Applied Psycholinguistics, 1,* 371–385.

Ehri, L., & Wilce, L. (1982). The salience of silent letters in children's memory for word spellings. *Memory and Cognition, 10,* 155–166.

Ehri, L. C., & Wilce, L. S. (1983). Development of word identification speed in skilled and less skilled beginning readers. *Journal of Educational Psychology, 75,* 3–18.

Ehri, L., & Wilce, L. (1985). Movement into reading: Is the first stage of printed word learning visual or phonetic? *Reading Research Quarterly, 20,* 163–179.

Ehri, L., & Wilce, L. (1986). The influence of spellings on speech: Are alveolar flaps /d/ or /t/? In D. Yaden & S. Templeton (Eds.), *Metalinguistic awareness and beginning literacy* (pp. 101–114). Portsmouth, NH: Heinemann.

Ehri, L., & Wilce, L. (1987a). Cipher versus cue reading: An experiment in decoding acquisition. *Journal of Educational Psychology, 79,* 3–13.

Ehri, L., & Wilce, L. (1987b). Does learning to spell help beginners learn to read words? *Reading Research Quarterly, 22,* 47–65.

Ehri, L., & Williams, J. (1996). Learning to read and learning to teach reading. In F. Murray (Ed.), *The teacher educator's handbook: Building a knowledge base for the preparation of teachers* (pp. 231–244). San Francisco: Jossey-Bass.

Frith, U. (1985). Beneath the surface of developmental dyslexia. In K. Patterson, J. Marshall, & M. Coltheart (Eds.), *Surface dyslexia: Neuropsychological and cognitive studies of phonological reading* (pp. 301–330). Hove, England: Lawrence Erlbaum Associates.

Gaskins, I., Downer, M., Anderson, R., Cunningham, P., Gaskins, R., Schommer, M., & The Teachers of Benchmark School. (1988). A metacognitive approach to phonics: Using what you know to decode what you don't know. *Remedial and Special Education, 9,* 36–41.

Gaskins, I., Ehri, L., Cress, C., O'Hara, C., & Donnelly, K. (1996). Procedures for word learning: Making discoveries about words. *The Reading Teacher, 50,* 312–327.

Glushko, R. J. (1979). The organization and activation of orthographic knowledge in reading aloud. *Journal of Experimental Psychology: Human Perception and Performance, 5,* 674–691.

Glushko, R. J. (1981). Principles for pronouncing print: The psychology of phonography. In A. M. Lesgold & C. A. Perfetti (Eds.), *Interactive processes in reading* (pp. 61–84). Hillsdale, NJ: Lawrence Erlbaum Associates.

Golinkoff, R., & Rosinski, R. (1976). Decoding, semantic processing and reading comprehension skill. *Child Development, 47,* 252–258.

Goodman, K. (1976). Reading: A psycholinguistic guessing game. In H. Singer & R. Ruddell (Eds.), *Theoretical models and processes of reading* (2nd ed., pp. 497–508). Newark, DE: International Reading Association.

Goswami, U. (1986). Children's use of analogy in learning to read: A developmental study. *Journal of Experimental Child Psychology, 42,* 73–83.

Goswami, U. (1990). A special link between rhyming skill and the use of orthographic analogies by beginning readers. *Journal of Child Psychology and Psychiatry, 31,* 301–311.

Gough, P., & Hillinger, M. (1980). Learning to read: An unnatural act. *Bulletin of the Orton Society, 30,* 180–196.

Gough, P., Juel, C., & Griffith, P. (1992). Reading, spelling and the orthographic cipher. In P. Gough, L. Ehri, & R. Treiman (Eds.), *Reading acquisition* (pp. 35–48). Hillsdale, NJ: Lawrence Erlbaum Associates.

Gough, P., Juel, C., & Roper/Schneider, D. (1983). Code and cipher: A two-stage conception of initial reading acquisition. In J. A. Niles & L. A. Harris (Eds.), *Searches for meaning in reading/language processing and instruction* (32nd Yearbook of the National Reading Conference, pp. 207–211). Rochester, NY: National Reading Conference.

Gough, P., & Walsh, S. (1991). Chinese, Phoenicians, and the orthographic cipher of English. In S. Brady & D. Shankweiler (Eds.), *Phonological processes in literacy: A tribute to Isabelle Y. Liberman* (pp. 199–209). Hillsdale, NJ: Lawrence Erlbaum Associates.

Guttentag, R., & Haith, M. (1978). Automatic processing as a function of age and reading ability. *Child Develoment, 49,* 707–716.

Haber, R., & Haber, L. (1981). The shape of a word can specify its meaning. *Reading Research Quarterly, 16,* 334–345.

Harste, J., Burke, C., & Woodward, V. (1982). Children's language and world: Initial encounters with print. In J. Langer & M. Smith-Burke (Eds.), *Bridging the gap: Reader meets author* (pp. 105–131). Newark, DE: International Reading Association.

Henry, M. (1988). Beyond phonics: Integrated decoding and spelling instruction based on word origin and structure. *Annals of Dyslexia, 38,* 258–275.

Henry, M. K. (1989). Children's word structure knowledge: Implications for decoding and spelling instruction. *Reading and Writing: An Interdisciplinary Journal, 2,* 135–152.

Juel, C. (1983). The development and use of mediated word identification. *Reading Research Quarterly, 18,* 306–327.

LaBerge, D., & Samuels, J. (1974). Toward a theory of automatic information processing in reading. *Cognitive Psychology, 6,* 293–323.

Laxon, V., Coltheart, V., & Keating, C. (1988). Children find friendly words friendly too: Words with many orthographic neighbours are easier to read and spell. *British Journal of Educational Psychology, 58,* 103–119.

Leslie, L., & Thimke, B. (1986). The use of orthographic knowledge in beginning reading. *Journal of Reading Behavior, 18,* 229–241.

Marsh, G., Freidman, M., Welch, V., & Desberg, P. (1981). A cognitive-developmental theory of reading acquisition. In G. Mackinnon & T. G. Waller (Eds.), *Reading research: Advances in theory and practice* (Vol. 3, pp. 199–221). New York: Academic Press.

Mason, J. (1980). When do children begin to read: An exploration of four-year-old children's letter and word reading competencies. *Reading Research Quarterly, 15,* 203–227.

Masonheimer, P., Drum, P., & Ehri, L. (1984). Does environmental print identification lead children into word reading? *Journal of Reading Behavior, 16,* 257–272.

Perfetti, C. (1985). *Reading ability.* New York: Oxford University Press.

Perfetti, C. (1992). The representation problem in reading acquisition. In P. Gough, L. Ehri, & R. Treiman (Eds.), *Reading acquisition* (pp. 107–143). Hillsdale, NJ: Lawrence Erlbaum Associates.

Rack, J., Hulme, C., Snowling, M., & Wightman, J. (1994). The role of phonology in young children learning to read words: The direct-mapping hypothesis. *Journal of Experimental Child Psychology, 57,* 42–71.

Rack, J., Snowling, M., & Olson, R. (1992). The nonword reading deficit in developmental dyslexia: A review. *Reading Research Quarterly, 27,* 28–53.

Reitsma, P. (1983). Printed word learning in beginning readers. *Journal of Experimental Child Psychology, 75,* 321–339.

Rosinski, R., Golinkoff, R., & Kukish, K. (1975). Automatic semantic processing in a picture–word interference task. *Child Development, 46,* 243–253.

Rumelhart, D. (1977). Toward an interactive model of reading. In S. Dornic (Ed.), *Attention and performance VI* (pp. 573–603). Hillsdale, NJ: Lawrence Erlbaum Associates.

Scott, J., & Ehri, L. (1989). Sight word reading in prereaders: Use of logographic vs. alphabetic access routes. *Journal of Reading Behavior, 22,* 149–166.

Share, D., Jorm, A., Maclean, R., & Matthews, R. (1984). Sources of individual differences in reading acquisition. *Journal of Educational Psychology, 76,* 1309–1324.

Stahl, S., Osborn, J., & Lehr, F. (1990). *Beginning to read: Thinking and learning about print by Marilyn Jager Adams: A Summary.* Urbana-Champaign, IL: Center for the Study of Reading.

Stanovich, K. (1980). Toward an interactive-compensatory model of individual differences in the development of reading fluency. *Reading Research Quarterly, 16,* 32–71.

Stanovich, K. E. (1986). Matthew effects in reading: Some consequences of individual differences in the acquisition of literacy. *Reading Research Quarterly, 21,* 360–406.

Stanovich, K., & West, R. (1989). Exposure to print and orthographic processing. *Reading Research Quarterly, 24,* 402–433.

Stanovich, K., West, R., & Cunningham, A. (1991). Beyond phonological processes: Print exposure and orthographic processing. In S. Brady & D. Shankweiler (Eds.), *Phonological processes in literacy* (pp. 219–235). Hillsdale, NJ: Lawrence Erlbaum Associates.

Templeton, S. (1992). Theory, nature and pedagogy of higher-order orthographic development in older students. In S. Templeton, & D. Bear (Eds.), *Development of orthographic knowledge: The foundations of literacy* (pp. 253–277). Hillsdale, NJ: Lawrence Erlbaum Associates.

Treiman, R. (1992). The role of intrasyllabic units in learning to read and spell. In P. Gough, L. Ehri, & R. Treiman (Eds.), *Reading acquisition* (pp. 65–106). Hillsdale, NJ: Lawrence Erlbaum Associates.

Treiman, R. (1993). *Beginning to spell.* New York: Oxford University Press.

Treiman, R., Goswami, U., & Bruck, M. (1990). Not all nonwords are alike: Implications for reading development and theory. *Memory and Cognition, 18,* 559–567.

Tunmer, W., & Chapman, J. (1996). Language prediction skill, phonological recoding ability, and beginning reading. In C. Hulme & R. M. Joshi (Eds.), *Reading and spelling: Development and disorder.* Mahwah, NJ: Lawrence Erlbaum Associates.

Venezky, R. (1970). *The structure of English orthography.* The Hague: Mouton.

Wagner, R., & Barker, T. (1994). The development of orthographic processing ability. In V. Berninger (Ed.), *The varieties of orthographic knowledge I: Theoretical and developmental issues* (pp. 243–276). Dordrecht, The Netherlands: Kluwer.

Wagner, R., & Torgeson, J. (1987). The nature of phonological processing and its causal role in the acquisition of reading skills. *Psychological Bulletin, 101,* 192–212.

Weber, R. (1970). A linguistic analysis of first grade reading errors. *Reading Research Quarterly, 5,* 427–451.

Wylie, R., & Durrell, D. (1970). Teaching vowels through phonograms. *Elementary English, 47,* 787–791.

9

Spelling in Normal Children and Dyslexics

Rebecca Treiman
Wayne State University, Detroit, Michigan

Developmental dyslexia is typically defined on the basis of reading problems. *Dyslexia* is a disorder in learning to read that sometimes exists in children who have adequate learning opportunities, no known brain damage, and no serious emotional or personality disorders. Although the definition of dyslexia focuses on reading, dyslexics also have serious problems with spelling. Indeed, dyslexics' spelling levels are typically below their reading levels, and spelling problems persist even among dyslexics who have apparently "caught up" in reading (Boder, 1973; Critchley, 1975). Despite the severity of spelling problems in dyslexics, much less is known about dyslexics' spelling than about their reading. The chapters in the present volume are no exception to the general trend, because most of them focus on reading as opposed to writing.

To understand the spelling problems of dyslexics, one must first know something about how normal children learn to spell and the kinds of errors they make. Without such a background, one may label dyslexics' errors as "bizarre," not knowing that such errors are common among young children who are progressing normally in learning to spell and read. The first part of this chapter, therefore, provides an overview of the development of spelling in normal children. In the second part of the chapter, I review the research that has been done with dyslexics. The focus is on studies that have compared dyslexics with normally developing younger children. I ask whether dyslexics show the same patterns of performance as do normal younger children or whether they make qualitatively different types of spelling errors. That is, do dyslexics learn to spell in much the same way as do normal children, only more slowly, or do they show unusual patterns of development?

THE DEVELOPMENT OF SPELLING IN NORMAL CHILDREN

The Precursors of Alphabetic Writing

For most children in a literate society, writing does not emerge all at once in kindergarten or first grade. Typically, a long period of development precedes the first independent readable spellings. Thus, preschoolers may "write" by making marks with a crayon or pencil before they know the conventional letters. Their writing, unconventional as it is, differs noticeably from their drawing. For example, children's writings tend to be smaller than their drawings and often consist of linearly arranged strings of symbols (Ferreiro & Teberosky, 1982; Tolchinsky-Landsmann & Levin, 1985). Although children as young as 3 or 4 years old know that writing looks different than drawing, they do not yet understand that alphabetic writing represents the sounds of language. Instead, young children seem to believe that the written forms of words should reflect their meanings. For example, they think that the names of large objects, such as *whale*, should be spelled with more letters than the names of small objects, such as *mosquito* (Ferreiro & Teberosky, 1982; Levin & Korat, 1993; Levin & Tolchinsky Landsmann, 1989; Lundberg & Tornéus, 1978).

The hypothesis that the physical features of words are analogous to the physical features of the corresponding objects becomes untenable as children learn more about print. For example, a child named Jessie might learn to spell her own name and the word *Dad*. She observes that the word *Dad* has fewer letters than the word *Jessie*, even though Dad is bigger and older than Jessie. Thus, the child is forced to give up the idea that printed words are direct representations of meaning and to entertain the possibility that print might represent speech.

According to some investigators (e.g., Ferriero & Teberosky, 1982), children first believe that the correspondence between writing and speech is at the level of the syllable. Only later do children learn that, for English and other alphabetic systems, the link between print and speech is primarily at the level of individual sounds or phonemes. Bobby, the 5-year-old kindergartener whose writing is reproduced in Fig. 9.1, seems to relate print and speech mainly at the syllabic level. Bobby writes the monosyllabic words *should* and *be* with one letter each. The use of *b* for *be* reflects the letter's name; the use of *c* for *should* may reflect the similarity between

FIG. 9.1. Message written by Bobby, a kindergartener. Message reads, "Why should I be warm enough?" This message was produced when Bobby's mother told him that he must wear a jacket or sweater when he went outside so that he would be warm.

the name of the letter *c*, /si/, and the first sound in the spoken form of *should*, /ʃ/. Bobby's spellings of *why* as "ye" and *I* as "ie" reflect a syllabic hypothesis overlaid with the effects of experience. Bobby's older brother had told him that an *e* should be added to the end of the word when a letter says its name. Thus, Bobby included an *e* after his *y* spelling of *why* and his *i* spelling of *I*. The syllabic hypothesis also surfaces in Bobby's two-letter spelling of *enough*. Had Bobby not written *warm* as he did, one might have concluded that he linked print and speech solely at the level of syllables. However, Bobby's "wom" spelling of *warm* reveals a beginning ability to divide syllables into smaller units of sound and to represent these units with letters. Bobby seems to have segmented the spoken word *warm* into three parts, writing *w* for the initial /w/, *o* for the middle /ɔr/, and *m* for the final /m/. His failure to treat /r/ as a separate unit is typical of beginning spellers and is discussed later. Bobby's case forms a bridge between what I have called the *precursors of alphabetic writing* and the emergence of the alphabetic principle.

The Alphabetic Principle Emerges

Trevor, the first grader whose writing is depicted in Fig. 9.2, is a year older than Bobby and has a stronger grasp of the alphabetic principle. In the two entries from his writing journal that appear in Fig. 9.2, Trevor uses the alphabetic principle more or less consistently instead of only sporadically, as Bobby does. For example, the spoken word *eat* contains two phonemes, /i/ and /t/, and Trevor uses one letter to symbolize each phoneme. *Pop* has three phonemes, /p/, /ɑ/, and /p/, and Trevor spells it with three letters. Trevor seems to fall back on a syllabic strategy when he writes *like* as "l" on the second line of his October 6 journal entry. On

October 5

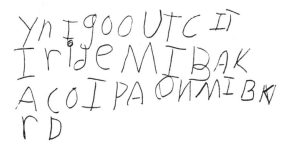

October 6

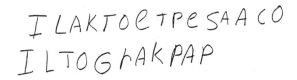

FIG. 9.2. Journal entries of Trevor, a first grader. October 5 entry reads, "When I go outside I ride my bike and I play on my bike ride." October 6 entry reads, "I like to eat pizza and I like to drink pop."

the first line, though, he writes this word as "lak," using one letter for each of its three sounds. Jillian, a classmate of Trevor's whose journal entry from late March appears in Fig. 9.3, has an even better grasp of the alphabetic principle than Trevor does.

Much of the research on children's early spelling has focused on children whose spellings are similar to Trevor's and Jillian's. The pioneering research in this area was carried out by Read (1975). He analyzed over 2,500 spellings produced by 32 children who began to write as preschoolers, generally between about 2½ and 4 years old. Although these children were younger than Trevor and Jillian, their spellings were similar. Read suggested that children spell primarily by trying to symbolize the sounds in words rather than by trying to reproduce memorized strings of letters. However, because the children in Read's study began to write much earlier than usual, Gibson and Levin (1975) suggested that the findings might not generalize to children who learn to write and read at school.

Following up on Read's (1975) research, I analyzed a large collection of first graders' writings (Treiman, 1993). My study differed from Read's in that the children were not precocious or advanced. They were learning to read and write at school rather than at home. The children's teacher

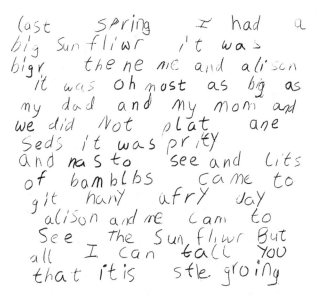

FIG. 9.3. Story written by Jillian, a first grader, in late March. Story reads, "Last spring I had a big sunflower. It was bigger than me and Alison. It was almost as big as my dad and my mom. And we did not plant any seeds. It was pretty and nice to see and lots of bumblebees came to get honey. Every day Alison and me came to see the sunflower. But all I can tell you that it is still growing."

was a strong believer in the whole-language approach. Although school policy dictated that the children receive some phonics instruction, the teacher stressed independent writing. She felt that children should figure out the spellings of words on their own, and thus did not tell them how to spell a word even if they asked. I collected 5,617 spellings that were produced by 43 children who were in this same teacher's first-grade class during two successive school years.

Data like mine (Treiman, 1993) and Read's (1975) reveal the kinds of spellings that are produced by children engaged in meaningful writing. To complement such naturalistic data, a number of experimental studies have been conducted. In the following sections, I discuss four conclusions about early spelling development in normal children that are suggested by the results of the naturalistic and experimental research.

Children May Use Groups of Sounds That Are Larger Than Single Phonemes. When children first begin to relate print and speech, they seem to do so at the level of syllables (Ferreiro & Teberosky, 1982). English-speaking children may realize that this syllabic hypothesis is untenable when they learn to write or recognize their name and try to understand why their name is spelled as it is (Ferreiro & Teberosky, 1982). At 3½, for example, Bobby knew the spelling of his name. He seemed to understand the function of the *b*s because he could hear the syllable /bi/ in the spoken form of his name. However, he was puzzled about the *o* and *y*, because there was no /o/ or /wai/ in his name's spoken form. Having heard his parents and older brother discuss the silent *k* of *knife* and other peculiarities of English, Bobby concluded that the *o* and *y* in his name were silent letters. Solutions such as these, creative as they are, cannot last forever. As children learn the conventional spellings of words, they see that the number of letters in a word's spelling does not usually match the number of syllables in its spoken form. Children are forced to go beyond the syllabic hypothesis and to relate print and speech at a more fine-grained level. But what level of analysis is appropriate? Children's analyses of spoken words do not always reach the level of single phonemes, and they may therefore spell groups of phonemes with single letters.

One example of this grouping phenomenon involves final consonant clusters. Children sometimes fail to spell the first consonants of these clusters. For example, Trevor did not represent the /ŋ/ of *drink*, writing "grak" (Fig. 9.2), and Bobby failed to spell the /r/ of *warm*, writing "wom" (Fig. 9.1). These omissions occur for a variety of phonemes, including *nasals* like the /ŋ/ of *drink* and the *liquids* /r/ and /l/ as in *warm* and *cold* (Read, 1975, 1986; Snowling, 1994; Treiman, 1993; Treiman, Zukowski, & Richmond-Welty, 1995). Children may produce errors like "wom" for *warm* because they consider *warm* to contain three units of sound—initial /w/ followed by /ɔr/ followed by /m/. For children, /ɔ/ and /r/ form a single unit rather than a sequence of two phonemes. Children may use a single vowel letter to represent this unit, producing "wom." Consistent with this interpretation, first graders who were asked to pronounce the individual sounds of syllables while putting down one token for each sound often used three tokens for a nonword such as /pɪlt/ (*pilt*), saying that its three sounds were /p/, /ɪl/, and /t/ (Treiman et al., 1995).

Another case in which children seem to group together what for adults are separate phonemes is that of initial consonant clusters. Young children sometimes fail to spell the second and third consonants of these clusters. For example, Trevor spelled *play* as "pa" (Fig. 9.2) and another first grader spelled *street* as "set" (Treiman, 1993; see also Bruck & Treiman, 1990; Miller & Limber, 1985; Treiman, 1985b, 1991). Children's omissions of consonants in initial clusters, like their omissions of consonants in final clusters, may reflect their groupings of sounds. Syllable-initial consonant clusters, or *onsets*, appear to form cohesive units for both children and adults (Bowey & Francis, 1991; Fowler, Treiman, & Gross, 1993; Kirtley, Bryant, Maclean, & Bradley, 1989; Treiman, 1985a, 1989, 1992). Children may consider the spoken word *play* to contain the initial consonant unit /pl/ followed by the vowel /e/. They may symbolize the onset with a single letter rather than analyzing it into two phonemes and symbolizing each phoneme with a separate letter.

A final example of children's tendency to use units larger than single phonemes in relating print and speech is their use of a consonant letter to represent all of the phonemes in the letter's name. Examples include "frmmr" for *farmer*, "lefit" for *elephant*, and Jillian's "bamblbs" for *bumblebees* (Fig. 9.3). The first *r* of "frmmr" apparently stands for both /ɑ/ and /r/, which together constitute the name of the letter *r*. In "lefit," *l* represents /ɛl/, the name of the letter *l*. In "bamblbs," the last *b* seems to symbolize both /b/ and /i/. Several researchers have observed such letter-name spellings among young children (Chomsky, 1979; Ehri, 1986; Gentry, 1982; Read, 1975; Treiman, 1993, 1994). The errors appear to be more common for some consonants than for others (Treiman, 1993, 1994). Errors such as "frmmr" for *farmer* and "lefit" for *elephant*, which involve letter-name spellings of *r* and *l*, are more frequent than errors such as "bamblbs" for *bumblebees* and "ms" for *mess*, which involve letter-name spellings of *b* and *s*. Children most often group /ɑr/ and /ɛl/—the two English letters whose names consist of a vowel phoneme followed by a liquid phoneme. Because of the close bond between vowels and liquids (Derwing & Nearey, 1990, 1991; Treiman, 1984; Treiman et al., 1995), children are likely to use a familiar letter-name spelling for a vowel-liquid sequence, such as *r* for /ɑr/.

Misspellings such as "wom" for *warm*, "pa" for *play*, and "cr" for *car* suggest that children do not suddenly grasp the idea that print represents the level of phonemes. For some period of time, normally developing children may be unable to carry out full phonemic analyses of spoken words. They divide *warm* into /w/ + /ɔr/ + /m/, *play* into /pl/ + /e/, and *car* into /k/ + /ɑr/. During this time, children symbolize speech at a level that is intermediate between syllables and phonemes rather than dividing words into individual phonemes and representing each phoneme with a letter.

Children's Errors May Represent Aspects of Words' Sounds That Are Not Obvious to Adults. Even when children succeed in fully dividing spoken words into phonemes, their analyses may not always match those assumed by conventional English. For example, the children in Read's (1975) study sometimes spelled /d/ before /r/ as *g* or *j*, writing *dreidel* as "gradl" or *dragon* as "jragin." Trevor makes the same sort of error in "grak" for *drink* (Fig. 9.2). Also, the children studied by Read sometimes symbolized /t/ before /r/ as *ch*, spelling *try* as "chrie" or *truck* as "chrac." These errors, which also appear in other studies (Treiman, 1985c, 1993), are not as bizarre as they might first seem. The use of *j* or *g* for /d/ before /r/ makes sense given that /d/ in this context is pronounced similarly to the initial sound of *Jim*, /ʤ/, which is typically spelled as *j* (*Jim*) or *g* (*gym*). When /d/ occurs before /r/, the contact between the tongue and the top of the mouth is made further back in the mouth than when /d/ occurs before a vowel. Also, the closure is released more slowly than when /d/ precedes a vowel. This gives /d/ before /r/ a degree of frication or turbulence that is similar to (although not as marked as) the frication that occurs in /ʤ/. Likewise, /t/ becomes similar to the /tʃ/ of *Chuck* when it occurs before /r/. Errors such as "gradl" for *dreidel* and "chrie" for *try* are thus reasonable spellings that reflect the words' sounds. The errors suggest that children have analyzed spoken words into phonemes but that their phonemic classifications do not match those assumed by the conventional writing system.

Errors such as "hr" for *her* and Jillian's "bigr" for *bigger* and "sunfliwr" for *sunflower* (Fig. 9.3) may also reflect phonemic analyses that do not match those embodied in the standard English writing system. *Her* is conventionally spelled as if it contained three phonemes—an initial consonant followed by a vowel followed by /r/. In most varieties of American English, however, *her* does not contain a separate vowel. Rather, /r/ takes the place of the vowel and is said to be syllabic. The spoken word *her* contains two units of sound rather than three. American children may analyze *her* into /h/ followed by syllabic /r/ and may therefore spell it without a vowel (Read, 1975; Treiman, 1993; Treiman, Berch, Tincoff, & Weatherston, 1993; Treiman, Goswami, Tincoff, & Leevers, 1997). Thus, even when children do analyze speech at a fine-grained level, their analyses may not always match those assumed by the conventional writing system.

Children's Misorderings of Letters Are Often Linguistically Based. We have seen that omission errors as in "bow" for *blow* and substitution errors as in "chruck" for *truck* are phonologically based. For example, the latter error does not reflect any visual similarity between *t* and *ch*, but instead reflects the similarity in sound between /t/ before /r/ and /tʃ/. It is widely assumed that errors that involve the misordering of letters from the conventional spelling of a word have a visual rather than a phonological basis. A child who misspells *her* as "hre" is thought to have reversed the *e* and the *r* in the memorized spelling of the word. However, if reversal errors always reflected the misordering of letters in memory, one could not explain why errors such as "hre" for *her* are more common than errors such as "hme" for *hem* (Treiman, 1993; Treiman et al., 1993). To explain this difference, one must consider the linguistic structures of the two words. The spoken form of *hem* consists of a consonant followed by a vowel and another consonant. The linguistic structure of the spoken word helps children sequence the vowel and the *m* in spelling. For children, however, the spoken form of *her* contains an initial consonant followed by a syllabic /r/. Young children frequently omit the vowel altogether when spelling such words, as discussed earlier. In other cases, a child may remember having seen an *e* in the printed form of *her* or may realize that this word, like all other English words, must contain a vowel. Because the spoken form of the word does not indicate where the vowel should go, the child may misspell the word as "hre." Errors that include a final *e* may be particularly common because many words, like *came* and *hope*, end with a "silent" *e*. Thus, an error such as "hre" for *her* may be an invention that reflects both phonology—the syllabic /r/ in the word's sound—and orthographic knowledge—the knowledge that all English words must contain a vowel letter. It may be largely a coincidence that this error contains all of the letters of the conventional spelling.

Children's Spellings Reflect the Orthographic Patterns to Which They Have Been Exposed. The words of English or of any other language are not random strings of letters. Instead, the letters follow predictable patterns. Some of the patterns reflect the sound patterns of the spoken language. For example, printed English words do not begin with *bw* because spoken words do not begin with /bw/. Other constraints on the arrangements of letters in printed words are purely orthographic. For example, *ck* may occur in the middles and at the ends of English words, as in *packet* and *pack*, but may not occur at the beginnings of words.

The first graders in my naturalistic study (Treiman, 1993) appeared to appreciate these orthographic patterns, for they made more errors like "kack" for *cake*, which conform to the positional constraints on *ck*, than "ckak" for *cake*, which violate the constraints. Apparently, the children had begun to pick up the restriction against initial *ck*. The restriction was not formally taught at school. The children probably discovered it on their own from seeing words like *sick* and *package* but not words like *ckan*. The children appeared to follow other orthographic patterns of English as well. Further evidence of children's knowledge of orthographic patterns comes from experimental findings. In one study, children were shown pairs of pronounceable nonwords such as *ckun* and *nuck* and judged which one looked more like a real word (Treiman, 1993). The correct answer, of course, is *nuck*. Middle-class kindergartners performed significantly above chance when tested near the end of the school year and performance improved in first and second grades. The results of this and other studies (Cassar & Treiman, in press; Niles, Grunder, & Wimmer, 1977; Pick, Unze, Brownell, Drozdal, & Hopmann, 1978; Rosinski & Wheeler, 1972) indicate that children learn which letter sequences may and may not occur in English words.

Young children's spelling errors are not always orthographically legal. This is especially true when there are strong counteracting factors involving phonology. For example, as discussed previously, children may misspell *her* as "hr," using a single consonant letter for the syllabic /r/. This error is phonologically reasonable but orthographically odd, in that it does not include a vowel. Orthographic correctness is one of several factors that are involved in children's spelling. For young children, it is a weaker force than phonological correctness. Still, many of children's errors reveal a surprisingly good knowledge of the letter patterns that do and do not occur in print.

Toward More Sophisticated Spelling

As children progress, their knowledge of the spelling system grows and deepens and they become better and better spellers. At least four kinds of changes occur with increasing spelling skill.

Children Internalize the Classifications of Sounds That Are Embodied in the Conventional Orthography. As children learn to read, they see how sounds are classified by the conventional writing system. For example, the first sound of *dry* is classified as /d/ rather than /dʒ/, *her* is considered to contain a vowel, and *warm* is considered to contain /r/. Before children learn to read, their choices in cases such as these may not match those of the conventional writing system. For example, some children may classify the first sound of *dry* as a type of /dʒ/ rather than a type of /d/. As children see that this sound is always spelled with *d*, their classifications gradually change. Learning to read and write may thus shape children's conceptions of speech, changing their classifications of certain potentially ambiguous sounds (Derwing, 1992; Fowler, 1991). Orthography, originally learned as a representation of speech, takes on a life of its own and begins to influence children's views about the language itself.

Children Rely More on Conventional Spellings. When children first start to write, they may know the conventional spellings of only a few words. For example, when Bobby wrote the message in Fig. 9.1 he knew how to spell his own name, the names of other family members, and a few common words like *no*. If children do not ask an adult how to spell sounds (like Bobby, who wanted to write the message on his own) or if the adult will not provide such information (like the teacher in the classroom studied by Treiman, 1993), children must come up with spellings on their own. Given their limited knowledge, it is not surprising that children's choices are sometimes unconventional. As children learn to read and spell more and more words, they acquire a broader base of knowledge from which to induce conventional phoneme–grapheme correspondences. In addition, many children are explicitly taught these correspondences as part of phonics instruction. As a result, unconventional spellings become less common. Errors increasingly involve possible spellings of sounds that are used in the wrong contexts. For example, a child may misspell *plaid* as "plad," using the typical *a* rather than the atypical *ai* to represent the /æ/ phoneme.

Children Rapidly Learn About the Letter Patterns in Printed Words. As discussed earlier, even young children know a good deal about the letter patterns that may appear in printed words. Orthographic knowledge increases rapidly across the early school years as children learn more and more words and make generalizations about the kinds of letter sequences that do and do not occur (Cassar & Treiman, in press; Niles et al., 1977; Pick et al., 1978; Rosinski & Wheeler, 1972; Treiman, 1993). Thus, even when older children's spellings are wrong, the errors often "look right."

Children Come to Understand That Morphemes Are Often Spelled in a Consistent Fashion. The English writing system is typically considered an alphabet, albeit irregular. However, English often deviates systematically from the alphabetic principle in the case of words that contain more than one morpheme or unit of meaning. For example, one would expect *health* to be spelled as *helth* based on the phonemes that it contains. The *a* in the conventional spelling shows that the word is morphologically related to *heal*. As another example, *jumped* and *hemmed* end with different phonemes—/t/ for *jumped* and /d/ for *hemmed*. However, because the final sounds both represent the past tense marker, the words are both spelled with final *ed*.

It takes time for children to learn about the morphological consistencies in English spelling (Carlisle, 1987; Ehri, 1986; Gentry, 1982; Henderson, 1985; Templeton, 1992; Waters, Bruck, & Malus-Abramowitz, 1988). Indeed, poor adult spellers may never fully master this aspect of the system (Fischer, Shankweiler, & Liberman, 1985). Errors such as "finaly" for *finally* or "sine" for *sign* may arise because children do not know that *finally* is related to *final* or that *sign* is related to *signal*. A word such as *signal* may not even be in a young child's vocabulary. In addition, children may not have mastered the often complex rules by which suffixes and prefixes are added to spoken words. For example, the changes that take place between *magic* and *magician* or *original* and *originality* involve variations in pronunciation and stress.

With simple suffixes and relatively common words, even young children have some ability to represent morphological relationships among words in spelling. Treiman, Cassar, and Zukowski (1994) examined children's spellings of words like *dirty* and *attic*. Both words contain a *flap*—a quick tap of the tongue against the upper part of the mouth. Flaps, being voiced, are similar to /d/ and children often misspell them as *d* (Read, 1975). If children use the root word *dirt* to aid their spelling of *dirty*, they should be unlikely to misspell the flap of *dirty* with a *d*. Such errors should be more common on *attic*, which is not related to *at*. Supporting these predictions, even kindergartners produced more correct spellings of flaps when there was a stem that could help them, as with *dirty*, than when there was no such stem, as with *attic*. However, young children did not use their knowledge of the stem to the maximum extent possible. They were not as likely to spell *dirty* with a *t* as to spell *dirt* with a *t*. Children's ability to use morphological relations to aid their spelling improves across the school years (see also Treiman & Cassar, 1996).

SPELLING IN DEVELOPMENTAL DYSLEXIA

Given the overview of spelling development in normal children, I now turn to the case of dyslexics. As mentioned previously, dyslexics have serious problems with spelling, often more serious problems than they do with reading. The dyslexics who wrote the jokes in Fig. 9.4 were

> Two guys in the desert oone guy has a car
> door. So the other guy says why do you have
> a car doo? becose if im hot il open the
> window.
>
> Haw do you stop a dull frum crcing
> -tak a away his credicrd
>
> What do yuo get when you sros a mink and a
> kagroo
> -a fer cote with pocits
>
> Noc noc hos wer
> Bow how
> Don't criy its oley a joke

FIG. 9.4. Jokes written by dyslexic children aged 8 to 11. First joke reads, "Two guys in the desert. One guy has a car door. So the other guy says why do you have a car door? Because if I'm hot I'll open the window." Second joke reads, "How do you stop a bull from charging? Take away his credit card." Third joke reads, "What do you get when you cross a mink and a kangaroo? A fur coat with pockets." Fourth joke reads, "Knock knock who's there? Boo hoo. Don't cry, it's only a joke."

between 8 and 11 years old. They had at least average IQs and were receiving individualized treatment using a phonics approach. Although these children were at least two years older than the first graders Trevor and Jillian, their spelling is not much better.

As compared to normal children of the same age, dyslexics perform poorly on any type of spelling test. A more interesting and theoretically important comparison involves older dyslexics and younger normal children. If dyslexics learn to spell in much the same way as normal children, but at a slower rate, they should be indistinguishable from younger normal children of the same spelling level. However, if dyslexics approach the task of spelling in a qualitatively different way than normal children, then the two groups may show very different patterns of performance. Such differences, if they exist, would provide valuable clues to the nature and causes of dyslexics' spelling and reading problems. In the following review, I therefore concentrate on studies that have used a *spelling-level match* design, in which dyslexics are compared with younger normal children who perform at the same level on some particular spelling test. The studies reviewed here examine individuals who have been identified as dyslexic or as having specific learning disabilities in the area of written language. I do not consider studies of children who are identified as generally learning disabled. These children's difficulties extend to academic areas other than reading and spelling, and their spelling problems might differ from those of dyslexic children.

Because most research on dyslexia has focused on reading, many studies have used a reading-level-match design in which dyslexics are compared with younger normal children of the same reading level. The problem with this design, if used to investigate spelling skills, is that dyslexics are typically more delayed in spelling than in reading. Dyslexics who are matched with younger normal children in reading ability may spell more poorly than the normals. If the dyslexics are worse than the reading-level-matched normals on spelling or some related skill, the difference could reflect the lack of matching of the two groups for spelling level. However, if the dyslexics are not worse than the normals, their performance becomes more impressive.

In the following sections, I discuss studies that have attributed dyslexics' spelling problems to difficulties with serial order, difficulties in grasping the alphabetic nature of English writing, and difficulties in understanding the morphological basis of the English writing system.

Dyslexia as a Problem With Serial Ordering

Early researchers suggested that dyslexics have a general difficulty with serial ordering in language that shows up in the misordering of letters in spelling as well as in the misordering of words in speech (Critchley, 1975;

Lecours, 1966; Orton, 1931). In addition to misordering letters in words, dyslexics may also rotate individual letters, for example writing *b* as *d*. The dyslexics who produced the spellings depicted in Fig. 9.4 made some sequencing errors, as in *yuo* for *you*, and some letter reversal errors, as in *dull* for *bull*.

Several researchers have asked whether dyslexics are more likely than younger normal children to make errors that involve the misordering of letters in words. Nelson (1980) tested 30 children who had been diagnosed as dyslexic by a hospital clinic. The dyslexic children, who averaged 11.1 years old, were compared with 30 normally achieving children with a mean age of 7.7 years. The two groups of children performed at the same level on a single-word spelling test that Nelson developed. Examining the dyslexics' first 20 errors on this test, Nelson found that 8% involved misorderings of letters from the conventional spelling of the word. The figure was 9% for the control children, not a significant difference. Moats (1983) studied 27 dyslexic children in the fourth through eighth grades, the majority of whom attended a private school for dyslexics. The dyslexic children scored at a second- or third-grade level on a standardized single-word spelling test. The dyslexics were compared with 27 second graders who performed at the same level on the spelling test. Moats found that 2% of the dyslexics' errors on the spelling test involved serial order. The figure for the normal second graders was 4%, a nonsignificant difference. Pennington et al. (1986) compared 24 dyslexic adults with family histories of dyslexia to 17 normally achieving children with an average age of 11.6 years. Both groups had a mean grade equivalent of about 6.6 on a standardized spelling test. Pennington et al. found that sequencing errors were uncommon (less than 8%) in both groups. Neither the adult dyslexics nor the normal control group made any reversal errors, such as *b* for *d*.

Although there are gaps in the research—for example, a lack of studies that have used a spelling-level-match design to examine reversal errors in dyslexic children—the results do not support the idea that dyslexics are especially prone to serial ordering errors or letter reversal errors in spelling. In fact, the research on normal children's spelling reviewed earlier suggests that errors involving the misordering of letters from the conventional spelling of a word do not necessarily reflect problems in visual memory. "Hre" for *her* may be an invention that reflects the syllabic /r/ in the word's spoken form and the writer's knowledge that all English words must contain a vowel letter. It may be little more than a coincidence that the error contains the same letters as the conventional spelling but in the wrong order. Research is needed to determine whether the misordering errors of dyslexics are influenced by the same factors that operate for normal children.

Dyslexia as a Problem in Grasping the Alphabetic Basis of English Spelling

As the idea that dyslexia reflects a general problem with serial ordering waned in popularity, dyslexics' problems came to be seen as primarily linguistic in nature. Specifically, dyslexics were thought to have difficulty in learning and using the alphabetic principle. Dyslexics may progress normally through the precursors of alphabet writing (although this has not been investigated, to my knowledge). However, because of underlying phonological difficulties, dyslexics stumble when it comes to grasping the alphabetic principle. Dyslexics try to compensate for this problem by relying heavily on visual memorization. The alphabetic principle hypothesis has been put forward by many investigators (e.g., Frith, 1985; Goswami & Bryant, 1990; Liberman, Rubin, Duques, & Carlisle, 1985; Shankweiler et al., 1995; Stanovich, 1992). Even those who argue that there are different subtypes of dyslexia typically claim that the majority of dyslexics have trouble with phonological processing (e.g., Boder, 1973).

The idea that most developmental dyslexics have difficulty learning and using the alphabetic principle leads to several predictions. First, dyslexics' spelling errors should differ from those of younger normal children of the same spelling level. Dyslexics should be more likely to produce bizarre spellings that have little or no phonological connection to the target word. Second, dyslexics should perform relatively well on common words whose spellings they have been able to memorize. However, they should have great difficulty constructing plausible spellings for unfamiliar words and nonsense words. Third, because dyslexics tend to rely heavily on memorization, their knowledge of orthographic patterns may actually be better than that of younger normal children of the same spelling level. Finally, dyslexics' phonological skills should be worse than those of spelling-level-matched controls. These predictions are explored in turn in the following sections.

"Phonetic" and "Nonphonetic" Errors. A number of researchers have tested the hypothesis that dyslexics have trouble learning and using the alphabetic principle by examining their spelling errors. To find out whether dyslexics' errors show less understanding of the alphabetic principle than do the errors of normally progressing younger children, researchers have typically divided errors into "phonetic" and "nonphonetic" categories. Phonetic errors, such as "plad" for *plaid*, are those in which each phoneme is represented with a letter or letter group that may be used to symbolize that sound in conventional English. Some investigators use a strict criterion for phonetic errors, counting an error as phonetic only if it sounds like the target word when read aloud. "Plad" for *plaid* is a phonetic error by the strict criterion. "Tak" for *take* is not

phonetically correct by a strict criterion because the rules of English call for a final *e* in this context. Other investigators use a lax criterion for phonetic errors. They count an error as phonetic if each phoneme is symbolized with a letter that is used in some English word to represent that sound, even if not in the same context. By this criterion, "tak" for *take* is phonetic, because /e/ is spelled with single *a* in words such as *bacon*. Nonphonetic errors include "pad" for *plaid*, "wom" for *warm*, and "doo" for *door*, in which a phoneme is not represented. Also, "plag" for *plaid* and "jry" for *dry* are counted as nonphonetic because some phoneme is symbolized with a letter that is never used to represent that phoneme in conventional English. Researchers have assumed that children who make a preponderance of phonetic errors understand the alphabetic principle. Children who make many nonphonetic errors are believed to lack an appreciation of the alphabetic principle. They are thought to spell words via rote visual memorization rather than via a sound-based process. As I discuss later, these assumptions are problematic. Before discussing these problems, however, I review the studies that have employed a phonetic/nonphonetic classification.

Four studies have found that dyslexics do not produce a higher percentage of nonphonetic errors than do younger normal children of the same spelling age. Nelson (1980), in the study described earlier, used a lax criterion to distinguish between phonetic and nonphonetic errors. The percentage of errors that were nonphonetic was 35% for dyslexics and 36% for younger normal children, a nonsignificant difference. In some of the analyses reported by Moats (1983), a lax criterion was used to classify errors as phonetic or nonphonetic by reference to the conventional spelling system. For dyslexic children in the fourth through eighth grades, 39% of the errors were nonphonetic. The figure was 44% for normal second graders. The difference was not significant. Pennington et al. (1986) used both lax and strict scoring systems in their study of dyslexic adults and normally achieving children. Using a lax criterion, 35% of the dyslexic adults' errors were phonetically inaccurate, as compared to 33% of the normal children's errors. Using a strict criterion, 75% of the adults' errors were inaccurate, as were 71% of the normal children's. The differences were not significant. Finally, Bradley and Bryant (1979) studied 62 dyslexic children with a mean age of 10 years, 4 months, and 30 younger normal children. The two groups performed similarly on a standardized spelling test, with spelling ages of about 7 years. For both dyslexics and normals, at least one phoneme was spelled correctly in at least 90% of the errors. Errors in which none of the phonemes were correct were no more common among the dyslexics (3%) than among the normals (5%). These results suggest that dyslexics' errors do not differ from those of younger normal readers and spellers in phonetic accuracy.

However, other studies have found nonphonetic errors to be more frequent among dyslexics than among normal children of the same spelling level. Bruck (1988) compared 17 dyslexic children who attended a remedial reading and spelling program at a reading disabilities clinic with 17 normal children. The dyslexics had a mean age of 10.7 years and the normals a mean age of 7.6 years. Both groups had a grade equivalent of about 3.6 on a standardized spelling test. The children spelled real words and nonwords, and Bruck used a strict criterion to score the children's errors as phonetic or nonphonetic. For dyslexics, 59% of the errors were nonphonetic. The figure was 41% for the normal children, a significant difference. A potential problem with this study is that the dyslexics produced somewhat fewer correct spellings of real words than the normals did, although the difference was not significant. Even though the dyslexic and control groups performed similarly on the standardized spelling test, the dyslexics' true level of performance may have been overestimated by this test. Because of measurement error, two samples that have the same mean score on a test may differ when tested again, the means reverting closer to the true population means. This problem of regression to the mean frequently arises in studies using a spelling-level- or reading-level-match design (Jackson & Butterfield, 1989). If the dyslexics in Bruck's study were poorer spellers than the controls, it would not be surprising that their errors were less phonetic. The errors of poorer spellers tend to be less phonetic than the errors of better spellers according to either strict or lax classification schemes (Finucci, Isaacs, Whitehouse, & Childs, 1983; Lennox & Siegel, 1993; Nelson, 1980).

A similar problem may arise in the study by Olson (1985). He compared a group of dyslexics (mean age 15.3 years) with younger normal children (mean age 10.1 years). The two groups performed similarly on a standardized single-word reading test. When the children's spellings were rated for phonetic similarity to the target word, the dyslexics' errors were significantly less phonetic than were the normal children's errors. However, if the dyslexics were poorer spellers than the control children, this is not surprising.

Stronger support for the idea that dyslexics' spelling errors are less phonetic than those of normal children comes from two studies in which children spelled many items containing consonant clusters. Bruck and Treiman (1990) tested 23 dyslexics (mean age 10 years, 2 months) and 23 normal first and second graders who performed at the same level on a standardized spelling test. Using a lax criterion for phonetic legality, the dyslexics produced 36% nonphonetic errors as compared to 21% for the normal children. The difference was statistically reliable. Kibel and Miles (1994) studied 21 dyslexic children between 9 and 15 years old and 21 normal children aged 7 to 11. The children were matched on a pairwise basis for their performance on a standardized spelling test. When given words that contained many consonant clusters, the dyslexics were significantly more likely than the normals to produce errors in which phonemes were omitted or incorrectly represented. Both Bruck and Treiman and Kibel and Miles found that dyslexics often failed to spell consonants in clusters, as in "bot" for *blot*. As discussed earlier, such errors are nonphonetic according to traditional classification schemes but are common among young normal children. It appears that dyslexics make cluster omission errors even more frequently than do younger normal children of the same spelling level.

A serious problem with all the studies that have classified errors as phonetic or nonphonetic from the viewpoint of the conventional system involves the classification scheme itself. Researchers have typically assumed that children who make many nonphonetic errors fail to represent the sounds of words in their spelling and instead spell on a visual basis. This assumption is probably incorrect. As I have shown, errors such as "bot" for *blot*, "wom" for *warm*, and "jry" for *dry*—errors that are nonphonetic by either a strict or a lax criterion—are common among normal beginners. They reflect children's tendency to treat /bl/ and /ɔr/ as units and their classification of /d/ before /r/ as a type of /ʤ/. The errors are very much phonologically based. If dyslexics make many "nonphonetic" errors, we can say that their spellings are not conventional but we cannot claim that they fail to appreciate the role of phonology in spelling.

Moats (1983) attempted to go beyond traditional phonetic/nonphonetic classification schemes in some of her analyses by determining whether dyslexics' errors were phonetically accurate from the perspective of normal beginning spelling. Thus, "wed" for *wind* and "chran" for *train* were classified as preconventional phonetically accurate errors. There are some problems with Moats' classification scheme. "Stuck" for *struck* was considered phonetically inaccurate, even though research discussed earlier shows that omissions of the second and/or third consonants of initial clusters are common among normal beginners. As another example, "wom" for *warm* was counted as phonetically inaccurate, even though such liquid omissions are common among young children. Such problems would lead Moats to overestimate the percentage of errors that were phonetically inaccurate from both the viewpoint of the conventional system and the viewpoint of normal children's early spellings. It is striking, then, that only 16% of dyslexics' errors fell into this phonetically inaccurate category. This percentage is lower than the percentages of nonphonetic errors reported for dyslexic children by Bruck (1988), Bruck and Treiman (1990), and Nelson (1980), and for dyslexic adults by Pennington et al. (1986). It was also lower than the percentage of nonphonetic errors that Moats obtained when she used traditional scoring criteria.

Thus, many of dyslexics' errors that are "nonphonetic" with regard to the conventional English writing system are indeed phonologically based. Dyslexics' "nonphonetic" errors are more likely to be reasonable errors, such as "stuck" for *struck* and "wet" for *went*, than bizarre errors, such as "foz" for *past* (Bruck & Treiman, 1990; Kibel & Miles, 1994; Moats, 1983). Dyslexics' spelling errors are qualitatively similar to those of normal younger children. It is still unclear whether dyslexics' tendency to make relatively primitive phonologically based spellings such as "stuck" for *struck* and "wet" for *went* is higher than would be expected given their scores on standardized spelling tests. The results of Moats (1983) suggest that it is not, whereas the results of Bruck and Treiman (1990) and Kibel and Miles (1994) suggest that it is. What is clear is that dyslexics attempt to represent the sounds of words in their spelling, even if they do not necessarily do so in a conventional manner.

Spelling of Nonwords. If dyslexics have trouble grasping the alphabetic principle and instead rely on visual memorization, they should have special difficulty spelling nonwords. Dyslexics should perform as well on common real words as do younger normal children of the same spelling level. However, dyslexics should do significantly more poorly on nonwords. Put another way, the difference between real words and nonwords should be larger for dyslexics than for younger normal children of the same spelling level. Although many investigators have tested this hypothesis for reading (see Rack, Snowling, & Olson, 1992), only a few have done so for spelling.

In Bruck's (1988) study, described earlier, children's spellings of nonwords were scored as correct or incorrect using a strict criterion. The spelling had to be pronounced like the target word using conventional spelling-sound rules in order to count as correct. The difference between real words and nonwords was not significantly larger for the dyslexics than for the normal children. Siegel and Ryan (1988) used a reading-level-match design. They compared groups of reading-disabled children who scored at the second through sixth grade levels on a standardized reading test ($n = 43$) and groups of normally achieving children who scored at the same levels ($n = 67$). When the children's spellings of nonwords were classified as correct or incorrect, the dyslexics produced significantly fewer correct spellings than the normals. A problem with this study is that no data on the children's spelling of real words are reported. As compared to the normal children, the dyslexics may have been poorer spellers of real words as well as poorer spellers of nonwords. Finally, Martlew (1992) compared 12 dyslexic children with a mean age of 10 years and 3 months to 12 normal children about 2 years younger. The two groups performed similarly on a standardized spelling test. The children were asked to spell eight words and three nonwords. The dyslexics made significantly more errors on the nonwords than did the younger normal children, but did not make significantly more errors on the words. These results suggest that dyslexics have particular difficulties with nonwords. However, the small number of stimuli and the small number of participants make it difficult to draw strong conclusions.

Based on the results of these few studies, it is not clear whether dyslexics have more trouble spelling nonwords than would be expected given their level of performance on real words. An important issue that has not been addressed in the research concerns the scoring of nonword spellings. The same issues arise here as in scoring errors on real words. For example, most researchers would consider "pit" for /pɪlt/ (*pilt*) an error. However, the error is not bizarre but is of a type common among normal beginners. Even if dyslexics could be shown to have more difficulty using conventional phoneme–grapheme correspondences to spell nonwords than expected given their level of performance on real words, I suspect that their errors are more like "pit" for /pɪlt/ than like "gam" for /pɪlt/.

Orthographic Knowledge. As discussed earlier, normal children quickly learn which letter sequences may and may not occur in printed words. Their spellings, even when incorrect, often reveal a knowledge of orthographic patterns. For example, first graders are more likely to misspell *cake* as "cack" than as "ckak" (Treiman, 1993).

Given their level of performance on standardized spelling tests, dyslexics' knowledge of orthographic patterns appears to be as good as or even better than normals'. Nelson (1980), in the study described earlier, classified dyslexics' and normals' spelling errors as orthographically legal (e.g., "cack" for *cake*) or illegal (e.g., "ckak" for *cake*). For dyslexics, 82% of the errors were orthographically legal. The figure was 87% for normal children, not a significant difference. In the study by Pennington et al. (1986), both the dyslexic adults and the normal children produced 95% or more orthographically legal errors. Perhaps because of their greater exposure to print, the dyslexics were significantly better than the younger normal children on a measure of complex orthographic accuracy that assessed such things as correct doubling of the *p* in *opportunity* and use of *phys* in *physician*.

In two other studies, dyslexics and normals were matched on reading ability rather than spelling ability. In Olson's (1985) study, described earlier, the spelling errors of dyslexic and normal children were rated for visual similarity to the target word. No reliable differences were found between the dyslexics and the normals. As mentioned earlier, however, the dyslexics' errors were rated as less phonetically accurate than the normals'. Siegel, Share, and Geva (1995) compared groups of dyslexics performing at the first-grade through eighth-grade levels on a standardized single-word reading test ($n = 255$) with groups of normal children performing at each of these levels ($n = 340$). The children were shown pairs of nonwords such as *moke* and *moje* and were asked which one looked more like a word. The correct answer, of course, is *moke*. The dyslexics did significantly better than the normal children. Given that the dyslexics studied by Olson and Siegel et al. may have been poorer spellers than the normal controls, it is striking that they did as well as or better than the normals on the orthographic measures.

Thus, dyslexics' orthographic skills are at least commensurate with their overall level of spelling (and reading) development. Indeed, the results of Pennington et al. (1986) and Siegel et al. (1995) suggest that dyslexics may actually know more than younger normal children about the orthographic sequences that may and may not occur in English words.

Phonological Awareness. The results of Bruck and Treiman (1990) suggest that dyslexics' phonological awareness skills are lower than expected given their performance on standardized spelling tests. The dyslexic children in this study performed significantly worse than did the younger normal children in phoneme deletion tasks, for example, deleting the /p/ of /ploi/ to yield /loi/. Children in both groups often responded /oi/ rather than /loi/, but the dyslexics did so even more often than the normals. The dyslexics were also poorer than the spelling-level-matched normal children in phoneme recognition tasks such as detecting the /l/ in /ploi/. These difficulties, it appeared, were linked to children's tendency to omit the *l* when spelling syllables such as /ploi/. These results support the idea that dyslexics have a special tendency to treat onset clusters in spoken words as units. To my knowledge, no other studies have used a spelling-level-match design to compare the phonological skills of older dyslexics and younger normals.

Conclusions About the View of Dyslexia as a Problem in Grasping the Alphabetic Principle. The idea that dyslexia reflects a difficulty learning and using the alphabetic principle has been widely accepted by reading researchers. For example, the results reviewed by Rack et al. (1992) suggest that dyslexics have more difficulty pronouncing nonwords than would be expected given their level of performance on real words, especially if the nonwords are phonologically complex (e.g., *molsmit*) or if they have not been preceded by similar real words. Spelling is thought to involve phonology to a greater extent than reading (e.g., Bradley & Bryant, 1979; Goswami & Bryant, 1990). One would therefore expect phonological difficulties to manifest themselves even more clearly in spelling than in reading. Surprisingly, the studies reviewed here yield mixed results. Some studies find dyslexics' spelling to be indistinguishable from that of normal younger children, whereas other studies find differences.

Dyslexics' spelling errors are qualitatively similar to those of younger normal children. Far from being bizarre or unmotivated, dyslexics' misspellings usually have a linguistic basis. Dyslexics do not predominantly make errors like "foz" for *past* that reflect total ignorance of alphabetic principle. Rather, they tend to produce spellings like "wid" for *wind*, "bot" for *blot*, and "crd" for *card*—spellings that are similar to those produced by normal beginners. These errors may appear "nonphonetic" when judged against the conventional English writing system. However, the errors have a reasonable linguistic explanation.

Some of the studies point to quantitative differences between dyslexics and normal younger children. Specifically, dyslexics may make a larger number of primitive phonologically based spellings such as "bot" for *blot* and "crd" for *card* than do normal children of the same spelling age. Dyslexics' phonological skills may be somewhat lower than expected given their level of performance on standardized spelling tests, and their orthographic skills may be somewhat better. Dyslexics' errors, to a greater degree than normals', may reflect the use of units larger than single phonemes. Thus, dyslexics may be especially likely to write /ɑr/ with a single *r* or /bl/ with a single *b*. However, other studies have not found quantitative or qualitative differences between dyslexics and younger normal children.

The evidence does not support the strong claim that dyslexics are unable to link speech and print in their spelling. However, dyslexics may have more difficulty doing this at a fine-grained level than would be expected given their ability to spell real words. Moats (1983) and Nelson (1980) may not have found differences between dyslexics and spelling-level-matched controls because they analyzed children's errors on standardized spelling tests. These tests include words with a variety of linguistic structures; they do not permit an in-depth investigation of particular word types. To determine whether dyslexics and younger normal children show different patterns of spelling errors, we must look in detail at their performance on specific kinds of words and nonwords and must go beyond simple phonetic/nonphonetic classification schemes.

Dyslexia as a Problem in Grasping the Morphological Basis of English Spelling

In normal children, the development of spelling does not stop with the acquisition of the alphabetic principle. As discussed earlier, children learn that alphabetic spelling is sometimes overridden by morphological considerations. Thus, *health* is not spelled as *helth*, as it sounds, but with an *a* that shows its link to *heal*. Do dyslexics grasp the morphological basis of English spelling or does development stop, for them, with the acquisition of the alphabetic principle? Few studies have addressed this issue.

Carlisle (1987) studied 17 ninth graders who were identified as having specific learning disabilities in reading and written language skills. The ninth graders performed at the same level as a group of fourth graders on a standardized spelling test. They were comparable to the fourth graders on a spelling test involving base words such as *magic* and derived forms such as *magician*. However, the learning-disabled ninth graders were significantly better than the fourth graders on an oral test tapping knowledge of derivational morphology. They seemed to know more about derivational morphology than they could reveal in print. The learning-disabled students appeared to spell derived words as wholes to a greater degree than did the fourth graders. For instance, they might spell *magic* correctly but be unable to spell *magician*, or vice versa. Thus, Carlisle's dyslexics seemed to have difficulty going beyond the alphabetic principle to grasp the morphological basis of English spelling.

Bruck (1993) found a different pattern of results in a study of 15 college students with childhood diagnoses of dyslexia. The dyslexics were compared with 15 sixth graders who performed at a similar level (eighth to ninth grade) on a standardized spelling test. The dyslexics performed worse than the sixth graders on most of the experimental spelling tests, except for tests involving knowledge and use of morphological information. Here, the college dyslexics did as well as the sixth graders. Bruck suggested that use of morphological information was less of a problem for her adult dyslexics than might be expected, perhaps because these students were reading complex materials on a daily basis.

CONCLUSIONS

Developmental dyslexia has typically been defined by exclusion. Dyslexics are individuals who fail to develop literacy skills commensurate with their age and general level of intellectual functioning, and whose difficulties cannot be explained by lack of educational opportunity, known brain damage, or emotional or personality disorder. Researchers have long sought symptoms that would positively identify dyslexics and distinguish them from those with other types of reading and spelling problems. Spelling errors, it was thought, might be markers of dyslexia. Thus, individuals who make large numbers of misordering errors such as "trial" for *trail*, reversal errors such as "dull" for *bull*, or "nonphonetic" errors such as "fegr" for *finger* might be positively identified as dyslexic. The errors would shed light on the underlying causes for their disability.

These hopes have not materialized in any simple form. Dyslexics' spelling certainly looks more primitive than that of normal children of the same age. However, dyslexics' spelling does not look all that different from the spelling of younger children. According to some studies, in fact, dyslexics are indistinguishable from younger normal children in terms of misordering errors, reversal errors, and ability to spell words and non-words in a "phonetic" manner. Such results lead to the sobering sugges-tion that spelling errors may not provide markers of dyslexia and may not shed light on the underlying causes of the disability. In this view, dyslexics learn to spell much as normal children do, only much more slowly. The reasons for the slowness remain a mystery.

However, other studies have found subtle differences between the spellings of dyslexics and younger normal children. These differences lie not in misordering errors and reversal errors, long thought to be the hallmark of dyslexia, but in phonologically based errors. Dyslexics, even more than younger normal children, may have difficulty carrying out fine-grained analyses of spoken words. They may be more apt to produce errors such as "bot" for *blot* or "crd" for *card*, in which sequences of phonemes are spelled as units. These errors are not markers of dyslexia in any simple sense, because young normal children make them as well. However, the errors may be especially persistent in dyslexics. What may turn out to distinguish dyslexics from normals may be a profile of performance in which primitive phonologically based errors coexist with relatively high levels of knowledge about the orthographic structure of printed words. In this view, dyslexics understand that print is a representation of spoken language. However, their difficulty in analyzing spoken syllables into small units makes it hard for them to learn conventional phoneme–grapheme correspondences.

Although there has been much less research on spelling than on reading, the situation is starting to change (see Brown & Ellis, 1994; Perfetti, Fayol, & Rieben, in press; Moats, 1995; Templeton & Bear, 1992; Treiman, 1993). We now understand that research on abnormal develop-ment cannot proceed in the absence of detailed knowledge of normal development. Without this background, one may label certain dyslexic misspellings as "bizarre," not knowing that these errors are common among normally developing younger children and that they have a reasonable linguistic basis. The stage is set for more sophisticated research on the spelling development of dyslexic children. The findings, it is hoped, will help to clear up the many questions and ambiguities that have arisen in the research reviewed here.

ACKNOWLEDGMENTS

Preparation of this chapter was supported by NSF Grant SBR-9408456. I thank Ruth Tincoff and Marie Cassar for their comments on a draft of the manuscript, and Maggie Bruck for sharing the dyslexics' writings.

REFERENCES

Boder, E. (1973). Developmental dyslexia: A diagnostic approach based on three atypical reading–spelling patterns. *Developmental Medicine and Child Neurology, 15,* 663–687.

Bowey, J. A., & Francis, J. (1991). Phonological analysis as a function of age and exposure to reading instruction. *Applied Psycholinguistics, 12,* 91–121.

Bradley, L., & Bryant, P. E. (1979). Independence of reading and spelling in backward and normal readers. *Developmental Medicine and Child Neurology, 21,* 504–514.

Brown, G. D. A., & Ellis, N. C. (Eds.). (1994). *Handbook of normal and disturbed spelling: Theory, process and intervention.* Chichester, England: Wiley.

Bruck, M. (1988). The word recognition and spelling of dyslexic children. *Reading Research Quarterly, 23,* 51–69.

Bruck, M. (1993). Component spelling skills of college students with childhood diagnoses of dyslexia. *Learning Disability Quarterly, 16,* 171–184.

Bruck, M., & Treiman, R. (1990). Phonological awareness and spelling in normal children and dyslexics: The case of initial consonant clusters. *Journal of Experimental Child Psychology, 50,* 156–178.

Carlisle, J. F. (1987). The use of morphological knowledge in spelling derived forms by learning-disabled and normal students. *Annals of Dyslexia, 27,* 90–108.

Cassar, M., & Treiman, R. (in press). The beginnings of orthographic knowledge: Children's understanding of simple letter patterns. *Journal of Educational Psychology.*

Chomsky, C. (1979). Approaching reading through invented spelling. In L. B. Resnick & P. A. Weaver (Eds.), *Theory and practice of early reading* (Vol. 2, pp. 43–65). Hillsdale, NJ: Lawrence Erlbaum Associates.

Critchley, M. (1975). Specific developmental dyslexia. In E. H. Lenneberg & E. Lenneberg (Eds.), *Foundations of language development: A multidisciplinary approach* (Vol. 2, pp. 361–366). New York: Academic Press.

Derwing, B. L. (1992). Orthographic aspects of linguistic competence. In P. Downing, S. D. Lima, & M. Noonan (Eds.), *The linguistics of literacy* (pp. 193–211). Amsterdam/Philadelphia: John Benjamins.

Derwing, B. L., & Nearey, T. M. (1990, November). *Real-time effects of some intrasyllabic collocational constraints in English.* Paper presented at the International Conference on Spoken Language Processing, Kobe, Japan.

Derwing, B. L., & Nearey, T. M. (1991, August). *The "vowel-stickiness" phenomenon: Three experimental sources of evidence.* Paper presented at the Twelfth International Congress of Phonetic Sciences, Aix-en-Provence, France.

Ehri, L. C. (1986). Sources of difficulty in learning to spell and read. In M. L. Wolraich & D. Routh (Eds.), *Advances in developmental and behavioral pediatrics* (Vol. 7, pp. 121–195). Greenwich, CT: JAI Press.

Ferreiro, E., & Teberosky, A. (1982). *Literacy before schooling.* New York: Heinemann.

Finucci, J. M., Isaacs, S. D., Whitehouse, C. C., & Childs, B. (1983). Classification of spelling errors and their relationship to reading ability, sex, grade placement, and intelligence. *Brain and Language, 20,* 340–355.

Fischer, F. W., Shankweiler, D., & Liberman, I. Y. (1985). Spelling proficiency and sensitivity to word structure. *Journal of Memory and Language, 24,* 423–441.

Fowler, A. E. (1991). How early phonological development might set the stage for phoneme awareness. In S. A. Brady & D. P. Shankweiler (Eds.), *Phonological processes in literacy: A tribute to Isabelle Y. Liberman* (pp. 97–117). Hillsdale, NJ: Lawrence Erlbaum Associates.

Fowler, C. A., Treiman, R., & Gross, J. (1993). The structure of English syllables and polysyllables. *Journal of Memory and Language, 32,* 115–140.

Frith, U. (1985). Beneath the surface of developmental dyslexia. In K. E. Patterson, J. C. Marshall, & M. Coltheart (Eds.), *Surface dyslexia: Neuropsychological and cognitive studies of phonological reading* (pp. 301–330). Hillsdale, NJ: Lawrence Erlbaum Associates.

Gentry, J. R. (1982). An analysis of developmental spelling in GNYS AT WRK. *The Reading Teacher, 36*, 192–200.

Gibson, E. J., & Levin, J. (1975). *The psychology of reading*. Cambridge MA: MIT Press.

Goswami, U., & Bryant, P. E. (1990). *Phonological skills and learning to read*. Hove, England: Lawrence Erlbaum Associates.

Henderson, E. (1985). *Teaching spelling*. Boston: Houghton Mifflin.

Jackson, N. E., & Butterfield, E. C. (1989). Reading-level-matched designs: Myths and realities. *Journal of Reading Behavior, 21*, 387–412.

Kibel, M., & Miles, T. R. (1994). Phonological errors in the spelling of taught dyslexic children. In C. Hulme & M. Snowling (Eds.), *Reading development and dyslexia* (pp. 105–127). London: Whurr.

Kirtley, C., Bryant, P., Maclean, M., & Bradley, L. (1989). Rhyme, rime, and the onset of reading. *Journal of Experimental Child Psychology, 48*, 224–245.

Lecours, A.-R. (1966). Serial order in writing—A study of misspelled words in "developmental dysgraphia." *Neuropsychologia, 4*, 221–241.

Lennox, D., & Siegel, L. S. (1993). Visual and phonological spelling errors in subtypes of children with learning disabilities. *Applied Psycholinguistics, 14*, 473–488.

Levin, I., & Korat, O. (1993). Sensitivity to phonological, morphological, and semantic cues in early reading and writing in Hebrew. *Merrill-Palmer Quarterly, 39*, 213–232.

Levin, I., & Tolchinsky Landsmann, L. (1989). Becoming literate: Referential and phonetic strategies in early reading and writing. *International Journal of Behavioural Development, 12*, 369–384.

Liberman, I. Y., Rubin, H., Duques, S., & Carlisle, J. (1985). Linguistic abilities and spelling proficiency in kindergarteners and adult poor spellers. In D. B. Gray & J. F. Kavanagh (Eds.), *Biobehavioral measures of dyslexia* (pp. 163–176). Parkton, MD: New York Press.

Lundberg, I., & Tornéus, M. (1978). Nonreaders' awareness of the basic relationship between spoken and written words. *Journal of Experimental Child Psychology, 25*, 404–412.

Martlew, M. (1992). Handwriting and spelling: Dyslexic children's abilities compared with children of the same chronological age and younger children of the same spelling level. *British Journal of Educational Psychology, 62*, 375–390.

Miller, P., & Limber, J. (1985, October). *The acquisition of consonant clusters: A paradigm problem.* Paper presented at the Boston University Conference on Language Development, Boston, MA.

Moats, L. C. (1983). A comparison of the spelling errors of older dyslexic and second-grade normal children. *Annals of Dyslexia, 33*, 121–139.

Moats, L. C. (1995). *Spelling: Development, disabilities and instruction*. Baltimore: York Press.

Nelson, H. E. (1980). Analysis of spelling errors in normal and dyslexic children. In U. Frith (Ed.), *Cognitive processes in spelling* (pp. 475–493). London: Academic Press.

Niles, J. A., Grunder, A., & Wimmer, C. (1977). The effects of grade level and school setting on the development of sensitivity to orthographic structure. In P. D. Pearson & J. Hansen (Eds.), *Reading: Theory, research, and practice* (pp. 183–186). Clemson, SC: National Reading Conference.

Olson, R. K. (1985). Disabled reading processes and cognitive profiles. In D. Gray & J. Kavanagh (Eds.), *Biobehavioral measures of dyslexia* (pp. 215–243) Parkton, MD: York Press.

Orton, S. T. (1931). Special disability in spelling. *Bulletin of the Neurological Institute of New York, 1*, 159–192.

Pennington, B. F., McCabe, L. L., Smith, S. D., Lefly, D. L., Bookman, M. O., Kimberling, W. J., & Lubs, H. A. (1986). Spelling errors in adults with a form of familial dyslexia. *Child Development, 57*, 1001–1013.

Perfetti, C. A., Fayol, M., & Rieben, L. (Eds.). (in press). *Learning to spell: Research, theory, and practice across languages.* Mahwah, NJ: Lawrence Erlbaum Associates.

Pick, A. D., Unze, M. G., Brownell, C. A., Drozdal, D. G., & Hopmann, M. R. (1978). Young children's knowledge of word structure. *Child Development, 49,* 669–680.

Rack, J. P., Snowling, M. J., & Olson, R. K. (1992). The nonword reading deficit in developmental dyslexia: A review. *Reading Research Quarterly, 27,* 29–53.

Read, C. (1975). *Children's categorization of speech sounds in English* (NCTE Research Report No. 17). Urbana, IL: National Council of Teachers of English.

Read, C. (1986). *Children's creative spelling.* London: Routledge and Kegan Paul.

Rosinski, R. R., & Wheeler, K. E. (1972). Children's use of orthographic structure in word discrimination. *Psychonomic Science, 26,* 97–98.

Shankweiler, D., Crain, S., Katz, L., Fowler, A. E., Liberman, A. M., Brady, S. A., Thornton, R., Lundquist, E., Dreyer, L., Fletcher, J. M., Stuebing, K. K., Shaywitz, S. E., & Shaywitz, B. A. (1995). Cognitive profiles of reading-disabled children: Comparison of language skills in phonology, morphology, and syntax. *Psychological Science, 6,* 149–156.

Siegel, L. S., & Ryan, E. B. (1988). Development of grammatical-sensitivity, phonological, and short-term memory skills in normally achieving and learning disabled children. *Developmental Psychology, 24,* 28–37.

Siegel, L. S., Share, D., & Geva, E. (1995). Evidence for superior orthographic skills in dyslexics. *Psychological Science, 6,* 250–254.

Snowling, M. J. (1994). Towards a model of spelling acquisition: The development of some component skills. In G. D. A. Brown & N. C. Ellis (Eds.), *Handbook of spelling: Theory, process and intervention* (pp. 111–128). Chicester, England: Wiley.

Stanovich, K. E. (1992). Speculations on the causes and consequences of individual differences in early reading acquisition. In P. B. Gough, L. Ehri, & R. Treiman (Eds.), *Reading acquisition* (pp. 307–342). Hillsdale, NJ: Lawrence Erlbaum Associates.

Templeton, S. (1992). Theory, nature, and pedagogy of high-order orthographic development in older students. In S. Templeton & D. R. Bear (Eds.), *Development of orthographic knowledge and the foundations of literacy* (pp. 253–277). Hillsdale, NJ: Lawrence Erlbaum Associates.

Templeton, S., & Bear, D. (1992). *Development of orthographic knowledge and the foundations of literacy.* Hillsdale, NJ: Lawrence Erlbaum Associates.

Tolchinsky-Landsmann, L., & Levin, I. (1985). Writing in preschoolers: An age related analysis. *Applied Psycholinguistics, 6,* 319–339.

Treiman, R. (1984). On the status of final consonant clusters in English syllables. *Journal of Verbal Learning and Verbal Behavior, 23,* 343–356.

Treiman, R. (1985a). Onsets and rimes as units of spoken syllables: Evidence from children. *Journal of Experimental Child Psychology, 39,* 161–181.

Treiman, R. (1985b). Phonemic analysis, spelling, and reading. In T. Carr (Ed.), *New directions for child development: The development of reading skills* (Vol. 27, pp. 5–18). San Francisco: Jossey-Bass.

Treiman, R. (1985c). Phonemic awareness and spelling: Children's judgments do not always agree with adults'. *Journal of Experimental Child Psychology, 39,* 182–201.

Treiman, R. (1989). The internal structure of the syllable. In G. Carlson & M. Tanenhaus (Eds.), *Linguistic structure in language processing* (pp. 27–52). Dordrecht, The Netherlands: Kluwer.

Treiman, R. (1991). Children's spelling errors on syllable-initial consonant clusters. *Journal of Educational Psychology, 83,* 346–360.

Treiman, R. (1992). The role of intrasyllabic units in learning to read and spell. In P. B. Gough, L. Ehri, & R. Treiman (Eds.), *Reading acquisition* (pp. 65–106). Hillsdale, NJ: Lawrence Erlbaum Associates.

Treiman, R. (1993). *Beginning to spell: A study of first-grade children.* New York: Oxford University Press.

Treiman, R. (1994). Use of consonant letter names in beginning spelling. *Developmental Psychology, 30,* 567–580.

Treiman, R., Berch, D., Tincoff, R., & Weatherston, S. (1993). Phonology and spelling: The case of syllabic consonants. *Journal of Experimental Child Psychology, 56,* 267–290.

Treiman, R., & Cassar, M. (1996). Effects of morphology on children's spelling of final consonant clusters. *Journal of Experimental Child Psychology, 63,* 141–170.

Treiman, R., Cassar, M., & Zukowski, A. (1994). What types of linguistic information do children use in spelling? The case of flaps. *Child Development, 65,* 1310–1329.

Treiman, R., Goswami, U., Tincoff, R., & Leevers, H. (1997). Effects of dialect on American and British children's spelling. *Child Development, 68,* 211–227.

Treiman, R., Zukowski, A., & Richmond-Welty, E. D. (1995). What happened to the "n" of *sink*? Children's spellings of final consonant clusters. *Cognition, 55,* 1–38.

Waters, G. S., Bruck, M., & Malus-Abramowitz, M. (1988). The role of linguistic and visual information in spelling: A developmental study. *Journal of Experimental Child Psychology, 45,* 400–421.

Children's Understanding of the Connection Between Grammar and Spelling

Peter E. Bryant
University of Oxford

Terezinha Nunes
University of London

Miriam Bindman
University of London

When psychologists and teachers talk about regularities and irregularities in written language, they are usually referring to rules for representing sounds by alphabetic letters. They call a written word "regular" if its spelling conforms to accepted letter-sound correspondences, and "irregular" if it does not. However, there are strong lexical and grammatical regularities in English spelling, and in the spelling of most other European languages as well. Words such as *heal* and *health* or *muscle* and *muscular* share a lexical root that is represented by the same spelling sequence, despite the fact that these sequences actually represent different sounds. The final phonemes in the three words *waited, killed,* and *kissed* are different in each case, but they are spelled in the same way in all three words for syntactic reasons: All three words are past verbs, and "-ed" is the conventional spelling for the past tense morpheme. Much the same point can be made about the opening phonemes in the words *where* and *who*. These are pronounced differently but spelled the same, and the common spelling reflects their common grammatical status: Both are interrogatives.

No one disputes the existence of these regularities, and several people have drawn attention to their importance in learning to read (Beers & Beers, 1992; Frith, 1985; Marsh & Desberg, 1983; Marsh, Friedman, Desberg, & Saterdahl, 1981; Marsh, Friedman, Welch, & Desberg, 1980; Smith,

Baker, & Groat, 1982; Sterling, 1983). Children must learn about them if they are to read and to spell correctly, and it follows that some of the difficulties that children have in learning to read and write might take the form of a failure to appreciate or to understand the links among semantics, syntax, and spelling. In this chapter we consider the way in which children learn about the connections between syntax and spelling, and the problems that this learning sometimes causes them.

THE CONNECTIONS BETWEEN CHILDREN'S AWARENESS OF SPOKEN LANGUAGE AND THEIR LEARNING ABOUT WRITTEN LANGUAGE—PHONOLOGY AND SYNTAX

One potent reason for distinguishing learning about simple letter-sound rules from learning about syntactic regularities in spelling is that these two forms of learning may well take place at different times. Young children blithely ignore many of the syntactic regularities in spelling when they begin to write words, and yet at the same time show a considerable respect for and knowledge of the basic letter-sound rules. Spellings—often called "invented spellings"—like *haplt* for *helped*, *watid* for *waited*, and *wrx* for *works* are common enough in the writing of children up to the age of 7 or 8 years (Read, 1986; Treiman, 1993), and they demonstrate both a considerable ingenuity in applying letter-sound rules and also a striking disregard for the conventional spelling of morphemes. In all three words the child's spelling is a decent representation of the word's sounds, but the child shows no sign of knowing that these words include a morpheme that marks the verb's tense and that has a distinctive, conventional spelling.

Children's initial approach to spelling suggests that their first major task in learning to write, and probably to read as well, is to understand what kind of a script they are learning and to master the system of letter-sound correspondences. There is considerable evidence that, in order to do so, they draw on their phonological knowledge (Goswami & Bryant, 1990). The evidence for a link between children's reading in the early stages and their awareness that words and syllables can be broken up into smaller segments of sound is overwhelming. The greater the child's phonological awareness, as it has come to be called, the quicker he or she learns to read and to write. Furthermore, the possibility that there is a causal link between phonological awareness and learning to read is bolstered by several studies showing that teaching children about sounds in words speeds their progress in learning to read and write (Adams, 1990; Goswami & Bryant, 1990).

The connection makes perfect sense. In order to learn about the alphabet and letter-sound correspondences, the child has to understand that words and syllables consist of sounds that are represented by letters (/c/ by *c*, /a/ by *a*) or by sequences of letters (/at/ by *at*), and thus the child's phonological awareness plays a considerable role in this first essential step in learning to read and write.

However, this phonological connection, as we call it, has very little to do with grammar. A child's phonological sensitivities will not tell him or her why the same sequence of sounds is spelled differently in *kissed* and *fist* or in *when* and *went*. Nor will they tell the child why *the boy's cut* and *the boys cut* have entirely different meanings. These distinctions in spelling depend on grammar, and it is hard to resist the conclusion that children must draw on their grammatical knowledge to understand which spelling to adopt. In particular, they must understand that particular morphemes, such as the morpheme that signals the past tense, may be spelled in a specific and distinctive way. Thus, there may well be another connection for children to make between spoken and written language: We call this the *syntactic connection*.

THE DEVELOPMENT OF SPELLING AND THE SYNTACTIC CONNECTION: EVIDENCE FROM A LONGITUDINAL STUDY

The Predictions

There is an implicit developmental claim in the argument that we have developed so far: Children begin to form what we call the phonological connection some time before they learn about the syntactic connection. At first they wrestle with letter-sound correspondences, and then later they turn their attention to the regularities in written language that are based on grammar.

Our hypothesis makes two predictions. One is that there is a developmental shift from concentrating primarily on letter-sound correspondences to learning how to represent grammatical distinctions in spelling. The other is that this second form of learning is based on children's awareness of grammatical distinctions.

The most stringent tests of predictions about developmental sequences are longitudinal studies. These show not just whether older children behave differently from younger children, but also whether such differences are to be found in the development of individual children. Longitudinal research demonstrates that individual children progress from one way of behaving to another. Longitudinal research also provides a plausible test of causal ideas, and hence of our idea that children base their learning how to spell morphemes on their morpho-syntactic awareness.

If this is true, measures of this awareness taken on one occasion should predict the subsequent progress that children make in spelling morphemes.

The Measures

We have carried out a 3-year longitudinal study to look at both children's spelling of morphemes and their morpho-syntactic awareness, and to trace the relation between the two. The children—363 in number at the outset of the project—were 6, 7, or 8 years old when we first saw them. We confine ourselves here to describing the results in two different sessions, 6 months apart, in the first year of the project.

In the spelling tasks that we gave the children in these two sessions, we concentrated on past verbs and interrogatives. We asked the children to write for us the words that are presented in Table 10.1. We gave them regular past verbs with the *-ed* spelling (e.g., *kissed*), and irregular past verbs whose endings are spelled phonetically (e.g., *felt*). Half of each of these types ended in a *d* sound, and the other half in a *t* sound, in their spoken form. We also included words that are not past verbs but end with a sound similar to the past verbs in our list.

This made six categories of verbs and nonverbs: We predicted that there would be markedly different patterns in the way that children spelled these six kinds of words at different ages. At first, they would spell them phonetically, later they would introduce the conventional *-ed* spelling (particularly with past verbs), and finally they would learn that there are some exceptions to the rule that past verbs end with an *-ed* spelling.

In addition, we asked the children to write some interrogatives, because these provide another instance in which the spelling of a sound depends on the grammatical status of the word that the sound is in. Most of these interrogatives began with a "w" sound (the exceptions were *who* and *how*) when spoken, and most in their written form started with the *wh–* spelling (the exception is *how*).

We wanted to relate the spelling of these words to their morpho-syntactic awareness, and thus we devised three morpho-syntactic tasks. Our hypothesis was that children's spelling of these morphemes depends on their awareness of differences in parts of speech (past verbs vs. nonverbs, and interrogatives vs. noninterrogatives). Our tasks were designed as specific measures of this kind of awareness, which we have called *morpho-syntactic awareness*. Two of these tasks were quite new, and the third was based on a pseudoword technique originally devised by Jean Berko (1958).

TABLE 10.1
The Words in Our Spelling List

Regular Past Verbs	
/d/ Sound Ending	*/t/ Sound Ending*
Called	Dressed
Covered	Kissed
Filled	Laughed
Killed	Learned
Opened	Stopped

Irregular Past Verbs	
/d/ Sound Ending	*/t/ Sound Ending*
Found	Felt
Heard	Left
Held	Lost
Sold	Sent
Told	Slept

Nonverbs	
/d/ Sound ending	*/t/ Sound Ending*
Bird	Belt
Cold	Except
Field	Next
Gold	Paint
Ground	Soft

Interrogatives
How
What
When
Where
Which
Who
Why

The three tasks are presented in Table 10.2. Our two new tasks took the form of a series of analogies. In the sentence analogy task we spoke a sentence, and then spoke exactly the same sentence except that this time the tense of the verb was changed. The change was either from present to past tense or from past to present. Then we spoke another sentence in which the tense of the verb was the same as the first of the original two sentences, and asked the child to carry out exactly the same transformation on this new sentence. We wanted to see if the child could make the same change in tenses as we had. In some of the trials we used regular past verbs and in others irregular ones. The word analogy task took a similar form, except that we used single words and the range of grammatical

TABLE 10.2
Sample Questions From the Three Morpho-Syntactic Tasks

The Sentence Analogy Task

---

1. Tom helps Mary   Tom helped Mary
   Tom sees Mary
2. Jane threw the ball   Jane throws the ball
   Jane kicked the ball   _____

The Word Analogy Task

---

1. anger	angry		2. teacher	taught
strength	_____		writer	_____
3. walk	walked		4. cried	cry
shake	_____		drew	_____

The Pseudoword Task

---

1. This is a person who knows how to snig. He is snigging onto his chair. He did the same thing yesterday. What did he do yesterday?
2. Ever since he learned how to do it, this man has been seeping the iron bar into a knot. Yesterday he sept it into a knot. Today he will do the same thing. What will he do today?

---

transformations was greater. Some involved past verbs, and others different aspects of grammar.

The third test of children's morpho-syntactic awareness was an adaptation of Berko's (1958) pseudoword task, which is a direct and simple way of measuring awareness of grammatical distinctions. We gave the children pictures and, in describing these pictures, we introduced pseudowords. Then we asked children questions that required them to transform these new nonverbs by adding a morpheme. Two trials dealt with singular to plural transformations ("This is a picture of a *zug*. Here is another picture and there are two of them in it. There are two _____."). In five of the trials the transformation involved present and past tenses ("This is a picture of a man who knows how to *mab*. Here he is *mabbing* along the street. Yesterday he did it too. Yesterday he _____.").

The Results

We had two questions to answer. The first was whether children first spell phonetically and later learn the conventional spelling of grammatical morphemes. The second was the causal question: Is learning how to spell morphemes based on children's morpho-syntactic awareness?

To answer the developmental question we looked at the children's spellings of the endings of past verbs. If children begin by spelling phonetically and by paying little attention to grammatical distinctions, they should at first produce a large number of phonetic spellings (*kist* for *kissed*). We also predicted incorrect generalizations, although in slightly older children. When children initially learn that past verb endings are spelled as -*ed*, they should apply this liberally to irregular past verbs as well as to regular ones.

Table 10.3 shows that the children frequently made both kinds of mistakes. The data in this table are from Time 1, and they also support our developmental prediction: The phonetic transcriptions declined between 7 and 8 years, but the generalization of the -*ed* sequence to irregular past verbs actually increased during the same period.

We also found another, much more striking, kind of error, which we called *overgeneralizations*. As Table 10.3 shows, some of the time the children wrote the conventional spelling for the endings of past verbs at the ends of words that are not verbs at all. They spelled the endings of some nonverbs as -*ed* (*sofed* for *soft*, *necsed* for *next*, and *grouned* for *ground*). This kind of mistake was less frequent than the other two kinds, but its occurrence was common enough, widespread enough, and surprising enough to merit a great deal of attention.

These overgeneralizations increased and then decreased with age, as Table 10.3 shows. Our explanation for them is that when children have

TABLE 10.3
Mean Number (out of 10) of Correct Spellings, and of
Phonetic Errors, Generalizations, and Overgeneralizations at Time 1*

A. Correct Spellings			
	6-Year-Olds	7-Year-Olds	8-Year-Olds
Regular verbs:	2.28	3.37	5.68
the correct -*ed* ending	(3.42)	(3.59)	(3.34)
Irregular verbs:	5.98	7.19	7.90
the correct *d* or *t* ending	(3.15)	(2.55)	(2.33)
Nonverbs:	6.04	7.49	8.25
the correct *d* or *t* ending	(3.46)	(2.58)	(2.66)

B. Incorrect Spellings			
	6-Year-Olds	7-Year-Olds	8-Year-Olds
Regular verbs:	3.29	3.75	2.53
phonetic endings (e.g., *dresst*)	(2.81)	(2.86)	(2.26)
Irregular verbs:	0.50	0.78	0.83
generalization of -*ed* ending (e.g., *sleped*)	(1.13)	(1.29)	(1.24)
Nonverbs:	0.33	0.57	0.44
overgeneralization of -*ed* ending (e.g., *sofed*)	(0.69)	(1.01)	(0.81)

*The figures in parentheses are standard deviations.

learned to use letter-sound correspondences reasonably well, they begin to realize that there are exceptions to these correspondences. One of these is that some words, which end in the /d/ or /t/ sound, end with an -*ed* spelling in their written form. However, at first they do not understand the grammatical basis for the -*ed* sequence. They attach it to nonverbs as well as to past verbs because, although they now know about this spelling sequence, they have not yet made the syntactic connection.

The Spelling Stage Model

Given our results, it seemed to us extremely likely that children go through a sequence of qualitatively distinct stages when learning to spell. Our final developmental model contained five such stages, which we outline in Table 10.4.

The first is prephonetic: Many of the children, particularly the younger ones, failed to represent the endings of the words that they were given in any consistent or comprehensible way.

The second stage is the phonetic stage, in which children tend to spell all the endings, past verbs included, phonetically.

In the third stage children make generalizations and overgeneralizations: They write *slept* as *sleped*, for example, but also *soft* as *sofed*. Their use of the -*ed* ending shows that they realize that there is more to spelling than just the use of letter-sound correspondences, but they have not yet grasped the syntactic connection.

In the fourth stage, which is the stage of generalizations only, the children realize that there is a grammatical basis to the -*ed* ending, and put it only at the ending of past verbs, although they generalize this

TABLE 10.4
The Five Developmental Stages and the
Characteristics of the Children Assigned to Them

	Characteristics of the Children's Spelling at This Stage	Typical Spelling
Stage 1	Unsystematic spelling of word endings	
Stage 2	Frequent inappropriate phonetic transcriptions of endings; failure to produce conventional spellings of morphemes	kist, slept, soft
Stage 3	Some -*ed* endings, but generalizations to irregular verbs and nonverbs (i.e., failure to confine this sequence to past verbs)	kissed, sleped, sofed
Stage 4	-*ed* spellings confined to past verbs, with generalizations to irregular verbs	kissed, sleped, soft
Stage 5	-*ed* spellings confined to regular past verbs; no generalizations	kissed, slept, soft

TABLE 10.5
Mean Ages and Mean Number of Words Read in a
Standardized Single-Word Reading Test in the
First Session by the Children in the Different Stages

	Stage 1 at Time 1 N = 58	Stage 2 at Time 1 N = 78	Stage 3 at Time 1 N = 86	Stage 4 at Time 1 N = 52	Stage 5 at Time 1 N = 63
Mean age at Time 1	7y 0m	7y 3m	7y 9m	8y 0m	8y 2m
Mean score in reading test	9.28	17.46	37.88	42.55	50.90

ending to irregular verbs as well. The children in this stage are much more consistent in using the -ed spelling with past verbs.

In the fifth and final stage they write the -ed ending at the end of regular past verbs only, and now return to writing the end of irregular verbs phonetically as they used to in the second stage.

If our model is right, it should be possible to assign each child to one of the five stages on the basis of their spelling in each session, but there is also a more stringent way to test the hypothesis. When children change from one stage to another over time, the change should be upward on our developmental scale and not downward. When we assign the children to stages in two different sessions that we are reporting in this chapter (the first session and a following one 6 months later), the children should be either at the same stage in both sessions or at a higher stage in the later session than in the first one. Our developmental hypothesis demands that individual changes over time should be in one direction but not in the other, and our longitudinal data allow us to test this prediction by plotting each individual child's position in our sequence of stages in both sessions.

We found that 92.8% of the children (337 out of 363) in the first session, and 95% (307 out of 323) in the next, fell unambiguously into one of the five stages in our sequence of stages.[1] Our notion that these stages are developmental was supported by the fact that, as Table 10.5 shows, there was a direct relationship between the stage to which the children were assigned according to our scheme and their ages as well as their scores on a standardized reading test. The higher the stage, the older the children were and the more advanced their reading was on the whole.

---

[1]Most of the 26 children who could not be classified in our stages tended to spell the endings of regular verbs that we had designated as ending in /t/ (e.g., *learned*) as *d* (e.g., *learnd*). In another analysis we categorized all *d* or *t* spellings at the ends of regular past verbs as phonetic transcriptions. Sixteen of the 26 excluded children now fell into the phonetic stage. However, for our main analysis we decided to stick to a strict criterion for phonetic spellings (i.e., only *ts* for words ending in /t/ sounds and only *ds* for words ending in /d/ sounds).

Our second prediction also received a great deal of support. The vast majority of the children conformed to our developmental hypothesis over time. We found that 87.37% of them either stayed at the same stage over the two sessions or went to a higher stage in the second session than in the first: 52.98% of the total number of children stayed at the same stage in the two sessions, whereas 34.39% changed in the direction that was right according to our hypothesis. Only 12.63% changed in the wrong direction.

We also found that the scores for spelling the *wh–* sequence at the beginning of interrogatives were very strongly related ($r = 0.74$) to success in writing the *-ed* sequence at the end of the regular past verbs. We concluded that the same factor or factors probably determine children's progress in learning about both spelling sequences.

Morpho-Syntactic Awareness and Our Stage Model

In Table 10.6 we present the scores for the three morpho-syntactic awareness tasks. The table shows that the children's scores in all three of these tasks increased with age, and that these scores were also strongly related to the stage assigned to the children in our developmental model. The connection between morpho-syntactic awareness and our sequence of stages could just have been a function of age, but the differences between stage groups were still significant when age differences were controlled in analyses of covariance.

We turn now to relationships across time, because these are a more powerful test of our causal hypothesis. We predicted that the children's performance in the morpho-syntactic awareness tests in the first session should predict who would go to a more advanced developmental stage by the following session and who would not. Those who moved to a higher stage subsequently should have started with higher scores in the morpho-syntactic tasks than those who stayed where they were.

TABLE 10.6
Mean Correct Scores in the Three Morpho-Syntactic Awareness Tasks in
Terms of the Children's Spelling Stages in the First Session*

	Stage 1 at Time 1	Stage 2 at Time 1	Stage 3 at Time 1	Stage 4 at Time 1	Stage 5 at Time 1
Sentence analogy task	1.67	2.83	3.84	4.65	5.07
(out of 8)	(1.75)	(2.13)	(2.15)	(2.22)	(2.04)
Word analogy task	1.04	1.44	2.27	2.61	3.08
(out of 8)	(1.31)	(1.47)	(1.55)	(1.64)	(1.62)
Pseudoword task	3.78	4.41	4.97	5.15	6.30
(out of 10)	(1.82)	(1.81)	(1.96)	(2.49)	(2.23)

*The figures in parentheses are standard deviations.

TABLE 10.7

The Mean Morpho-Syntactic Awareness Scores of Those Children in the
Pregrammatical Stages (Stages 1, 2, or 3) at Time 1 in Terms of Whether
They Advanced to a Grammatical Stage (Stage 4 or 5) at Time 2*

Task	Those Who Remained in Pregrammatical Stage at Time 2 (N = 138)	Those Who Advanced to a Grammatical Stage at Time 2 (N = 52)
Sentence analogy task at Time 1	2.45	4.02
(out of 8)	(2.13)	(2.03)
Word analogy task at Time 1	1.48	2.14
(out of 8)	(1.46)	(1.63)
Pseudoword task at Time 1	4.23	5.02
(out of 10)	(1.88)	(1.82)

*The figures in parentheses are standard deviations.

The first three stages in our scheme are essentially pregrammatical and the last two are grammatical: In Stages 1, 2, and 3 the children do not base their spelling on grammatical distinctions; in Stages 4 and 5 they do. Thus, we concentrated on the children who were at one of the pregrammatical stages in the first session, and we divided them into those who made the shift from Stage 1, 2, or 3 (pregrammatical) to Stage 4 or 5 (grammatical), and those who did not manage to make this shift. We argued that the ones who made the jump from pregrammatical to grammatical should have scored more highly on the morpho-syntactic awareness tasks in Session 1 than those who remained in the pregrammatical stages.

In all three tests, as Table 10.7 shows, the children who advanced from a pregrammatical stage at Time 1 to a grammatical stage at Time 2 had better scores in the morpho-syntactic awareness task at Time 1 than did those who remained at a pregrammatical level. These differences were significant in analyses of covariance in which the children's initial stage in the first session was entered as a covariate. Thus, these tests predict who later on will make progress to a higher level of spelling and who will not.

THE IMPACT OF INDIVIDUAL DIFFERENCES
IN MORPHO-SYNTACTIC AWARENESS
ON SPELLING MORPHEMES

There is another way to test the hypothesis that the child's awareness of morphemes in spoken language has a significant impact on the progress that he or she makes in learning how to spell these morphemes. Children's scores in the initial morpho-syntactic awareness tasks should predict the number of times that they write these morphemes correctly in the following session 6 months later.

In fact, two of the morpho-syntactic awareness tasks do this quite well. We ran three fixed-order multiple regressions in which the outcome measure was the number of times the children spelled the ending of the 10 regular past verbs correctly with an -ed at Time 2. We entered three steps into these multiple regressions, always in the same order. First we entered age, then IQ,[2] and finally the children's scores in each of the morpho-syntactic tasks. Thus, we had controlled for the influence of differences in age and IQ by the time that we came to consider the connection between the children's performance in the morpho-syntactic tasks and their success with the -ed sequence 6 months later.

Table 10.8 shows that there was a significant relationship between the children's scores in the two analogy tasks in the first session and their -ed spellings 6 months later, even after controlling for age and IQ differences. The pseudoword task, in contrast, did not produce a significant prediction of the children's success with regular past verbs in this analysis. We do not know the reason for the difference between tasks, but the considerable success of the two analogy tasks establishes a strong connection between children's progress in mastering the spelling of this particular morpheme and the extent of their grammatical awareness.

These two variables are connected, but that does not tell us anything about cause and effect. A child's morpho-syntactic awareness may have an effect on his or her spelling, but it is just as likely that the causal relationships work the other way round. Many of the children had made considerable progress with learning how to spell the -ed morpheme in the first session, and thus these children may also have done well in the morpho-syntactic tasks in that session just because the experience of learning how to spell this morpheme may have made them generally more aware of its grammatical basis. Of course, for the most part these same children would have continued to do well in spelling -eds in the second of the two sessions; thus, the fact that there was a connection between two of the morpho-syntactic awareness scores in the first session and spelling the -ed morpheme in the second could simply mean that experience with spelling affects morpho-syntactic awareness and not the other way round.

The solution is to run multiple regressions that control for initial differences in -ed spelling. If the children's morpho-syntactic scores in the first session were to predict their -ed spelling scores in the second session even after controlling for differences in -ed spelling scores in the first

---

[2]In the first session we also gave all the children a shortened version of the WISC-R test, and a standardized reading (Schonell) and spelling (Schonell) test.

TABLE 10.8

The Results of Three Three-Step Fixed-Order Multiple Regressions
That Measure the Relation Between Performance in the
Morpho-Syntactic Awareness Tasks at Time 1 and Correct -ed
Spelling in the Second Session 6 Months Later; the Outcome
Measure in All Three Analyses Is the Number of Correct -ed Spellings at
Time 2 (the Three Analyses All Shared the Same First Two
Steps but Contained a Different Third and Final Step)

Step	Name of Variable	R^2 Change	F	P
First step	Age in the second session	0.142	50.58	<.001
Second step	IQ (WISC-R)	0.112	45.94	<.001
Final step	Word analogy task	0.057	25.65	<.001
Final step	Sentence analogy task	0.036	15.11	<.001
Final step	Pseudoword task	0.009	3.73	N.S.*

*N.S. = Not significant.

session, one could justly claim strong support for the idea that the children's initial morpho-syntactic awareness had influenced the progress that they had made with spelling this morpheme.

We carried out two further fixed-order multiple regressions. The outcome measure was again the children's -ed spelling in the second session, but this time there were four independent variables. First we entered the children's age and next their IQ, as in the earlier multiple regressions. The third step, a new one, was the number of times that they had correctly spelled the endings of past regular verbs with -ed in the first session. The final step, as before, was one of the two morpho-syntactic awareness scores that were successful predictors in the earlier analyses—word analogy scores task in one regression and sentence analogy scores in the other.

In these two regressions, which are presented in Table 10.9, the bulk of the variance in the children's spelling scores in the later session was accounted for by their spelling scores in the first session. Neither of the two morpho-syntactic awareness tasks accounted for much extra variance. Nevertheless, there was a highly significant relationship between children's performance in the word analogy task in the first session and their correct -ed spelling in the second, even after all the variance due to their spelling-eds in the earlier session had been controlled.

This positive result is impressive, because the control that we put in for the child's earlier spelling scores was a very stringent one. The fact that morpho-syntactic awareness, as measured by one of our tasks, still makes a significant contribution to the children's -ed spelling 6 months later after differences in the children's earlier -ed spelling had been controlled for suggests that this awareness did contribute to the progress that the children made in learning about spelling morphemes in the interven-

TABLE 10.9
The Results of Three Four-Step Fixed-Order Multiple Regressions That
Measure the Relation Between Performance in the Morpho-Syntactic
Awareness Tasks in the First Session and Correct -ed Spelling in the
Second Session 6 Months Later, With Controls for Differences in -ed
Spellings in the First Session (the Third Step in Each Analysis);
the Outcome Measure in All Three Analyses Is the Number of
Correct -ed Spellings in the Second Session (the Two Analyses
Shared the Same First Three Steps but Contained
a Different Fourth and Final Step)

Step	Name of Variable	R^2 Change	F	P
First step	Age in the second session	0.142	50.58	<.001
Second step	IQ (WISC-R)	0.112	45.94	<.001
Third step	Number of correct -ed spellings in the first session	0.439	435.24	<.001
Final step	Word analogy task	0.018	12.58	<.001
Final step	Sentence analogy task	0.004	2.28	N.S.*

*N.S. = Not significant.

ing 6 months. The result supports our hypothesis that morpho-syntactic awareness does have a significant impact on children's progress in learning how to spell grammatical morphemes.

Nevertheless, we did have to face a possible objection to this conclusion. Our hypothesis is a specific one: Morpho-syntactic awareness helps children to distinguish, and thus to learn, the conventional spelling for morphemes. Thus this awareness, according to our ideas, should be related to spelling morphemes and not to other aspects of spelling. It should not be related to success in spelling the final phoneme in our nonverb list: the /d/ at the end of *ground* and the /t/ at the end of *soft*. These sounds do not represent single morphemes, and there is no reason, according to our hypothesis, why the extent of the children's morpho-syntactic awareness should affect how well they spell these /d/s and /t/s.

Hence we also looked at the relationship between children's word and sentence analogy scores in the first session and their success in spelling the endings of nonverbs in the second. We carried out exactly the same kind of four-step multiple regression with this spelling score as we had with the -ed spelling in regular past verbs. We controlled not only for differences in age and IQ, but also for their spelling of the endings of nonverbs in the initial session.

Thus, the outcome measure in these new regressions was the children's scores for nonverb endings in the second session. There were four independent variables: we entered the children's age and IQ as the first two steps; as the third step we entered their scores for spelling nonverb endings in the first session; and the fourth and final step was the children's performance in the initial word analogy task in one analysis and the sentence analogy score in the other.

There was no sign of a significant connection between the children's word or sentence analogy scores and their success in spelling the endings of nonverbs in these two multiple regressions. We concluded from this that the significant connection between the children's word analogy scores and their spelling of the -ed morpheme is a specific one. Children's awareness of morphemes in spoken language, as measured by our word analogy task, does have an effect on the progress that they make in learning how to spell these morphemes.

We should like to add that we do not wish to eliminate the opposite causal hypothesis that learning the conventional spelling for morphemes actually increases the children's morpho-syntactic awareness, which was suggested by Derwing, Smith, and Wiebe (1995), or another possible hypothesis that there is an interaction between these two variables. Because our 3-year longitudinal study contains measures of both variables over time, we shall be able, after further analysis, to examine and compare all three possibilities.

Reading and Spelling Difficulties

A review of some of the results that we have presented so far suggests that they might also tell us something new about reading and spelling difficulties. The aim of most studies of backwardness in reading is to identify the stumbling blocks that impede the progress of children who fall seriously behind. Our work certainly suggests that we may have found a serious source of their difficulties. We have shown that it is initially quite difficult for children to learn the conventional spelling for morphemes, that some children evidently find this learning harder than do others, and that the difficulties with this spelling tend to be particularly formidable for those children who are relatively insensitive to morphemes in spoken language.

But we cannot say that this obstacle and the reasons for it are an important factor in backwardness in reading. To make that claim we would have to show, for example, that children who have fallen seriously behind in learning to read have a particularly low level of morpho-syntactic awareness, in just the same way that many studies have shown that such children are at a particular disadvantage in tests of phonological awareness (Hulme & Snowling, 1994).

We decided to find out whether backward readers are at a particular disadvantage in morpho-syntactic tasks. We looked at the older children in our sample whose reading was at a very low level for their age. We assigned anyone in the 8-year-old group whose reading score was one standard deviation below the average for that age group to the group of backward readers. (We looked only at 8-year-old backward readers because the reading scores of the 6- and 7-year-olds were too low to allow us to form proper control groups for the backward readers at those age levels.) Using this criterion we identified 22 (out of 133) 8-year-old backward readers, and we then looked at how well they did in the three morpho-syntactic tasks in comparison to two control groups.

One control group (the chronological age match) consisted of the other 111 8-year-old children—the ones whose reading scores were not particularly low.[3] The other (the reading-age-match) contained a group of 6-year-olds whose absolute reading levels were much the same as those of the backward readers. In fact, it was quite difficult to form this reading-age-match group because the average reading score for the 8-year-old backward readers was below the average reading score for the 6-year-old group—our youngest age group. We had to eliminate those 6-year-old children who had unusually high reading scores. That meant that the average reading score of the remaining 6-year-olds, although roughly the same as that of the 8-year-old backward readers, was rather below the average for the age group. However, their reading age on this standardized test was in line with their chronological age (in fact, it was slightly higher) as Table 10.10 shows, and thus they deserved the title of normal readers.

These two kinds of comparison produced very different results. The backward readers were at a disadvantage when compared to the other children in their age group (the chronological-age match) in all three morpho-syntactic tests. The differences between the two groups in the word and sentence analogy tasks were significant even when IQ differences were controlled in analyses of covariance. However, the difference fell short of significance in the pseudoword task, which was due to a particularly close relationship between IQ and this task: Putting in IQ as a covariate had the effect of wiping out the difference between groups in this task.

Thus, in comparison to their agemates, backward readers do rather poorly in morpho-syntactic awareness tasks, as measured by our two analogy tasks. However, one cannot set much store by these chronological-age comparisons on their own, because they do not tell us whether we are dealing with a cause or an effect of the reading backwardness. One cannot ignore the possibility that children learn a lot about grammar

---

[3]The relatively high reading age of the chronological-age-match group (see Table 10.10) is due to the fact that the group did not contain the 8-year-olds who had low reading ages, because these children were in the backward readers' group.

TABLE 10.10
Mean Scores of the Backward Readers and of the Chronological-Age-
and Reading-Level-Match Groups: Basic Characteristics of the Three
Groups and Their Relative Scores in the Three Morpho-Syntactic Tasks*

	Eight-Year-Old Backward Readers N = 22	Eight-Year-Old Chronological Age-Match Group N = 111	Six-Year-Old Reading-Level-Match Group N = 77
Mean age in Session 1	8 yrs, 5 mos	8 yrs, 6 mos	6 yrs, 5 mos
Mean IQ	92.72	107.60	102.76
Mean reading level (number of words read)	12.68	46.26	12.55
Mean reading age	6 yrs, 10 mos	9 yrs, 2 mos	6 yrs, 10 mos
Mean word analogy score (out of 8)	1.91 (1.48)	2.86 (1.69)	1.20 (1.36)
Mean sentence analogy score (out of 8)	3.45 (2.13)	4.82 (2.03)	2.15 (1.96)
Mean pseudoword score (out of 10)	4.32 (1.59)	5.60 (2.42)	4.44 (1.77)

*The figures in parentheses are standard deviations.

through the experiences that they have in reading and writing. It is quite possible that the backward readers fared worse in the morpho-syntactic tasks because they had fallen behind in reading and hence had missed some essential experiences that would have helped them to learn about grammar. Their reading difficulties may have held back their morpho-syntactic awareness rather than the other way round.

The reading-level match is a step toward eliminating this problem. Because the two groups involved in this type of comparison are at the same reading level, it is impossible to explain a disadvantage on the part of the backward readers in the outcome measure as the result of the backward readers' low reading level. However, this point is an academic one as far as our own results are concerned because, as Table 10.10 shows, the backward readers' performance was better than that of the reading-level-match group in the word and sentence analogy tasks, and the two groups were at roughly the same level in the pseudoword task.

The pattern of backward readers being worse than the children in the chronological-age-match group, but no worse than those in the reading-level group, is quite a common one. Unfortunately, it is impossible to interpret (Bryant & Goswami, 1986). For our purposes, it is enough at this stage to say that we cannot claim that backward readers have any more difficulties in making morpho-syntactic judgments than one would expect from their reading level.

CONCLUSIONS

Learning to read and write is as much a syntactic problem as a phonological one. No one is properly literate unless he or she has a reasonable understanding of the orthographic patterns that are based on syntactic regularities. Until a child has learned about the conventional spelling for past verb endings and for interrogatives and knows how to mark possessives with apostrophes, for example, he or she does not really know how to spell.

The results that we have reported in this chapter allow us to propose a tentative hypothesis about children's learning of the grammatical basis for particular spelling sequences. This hypothesis is a developmental one, and it rests on two discoveries. The first is of a clear developmental sequence in learning about the -ed sequence, and the second is of a link between children's progress through this developmental sequence and their awareness of syntactic distinctions.

When we began our project we were confident that there would be a developmental pattern in which children would spell word endings phonetically at first and then, when they were older, would begin to apply the conventional -ed ending to regular past verbs. However, the developmental sequence, which we found in the children aged between 6 and 9 years and which we eventually described in a five-stage model, turned out to be more complex and a great deal more interesting than that.[4]

We found good evidence for an intermediate stage between the times when children spell word endings phonetically and when they adopt the conventional spelling for these endings. In this intermediate stage, children begin to use the conventional, nonphonetic -ed pattern but they do not confine their use of it to past verbs. When children write *sofed* and *coled* they show that they have learned that words ending in /t/ or /d/ are often spelled with an -ed ending, but that they do not know that this spelling sequence has a grammatical basis.

Another interesting new point that we learned about the developmental sequence was of a definite developmental change in slightly older children who have passed this intermediate stage and who confine the -ed ending to past verbs. At first these children, who have mastered the basic grammatical connection between past verbs and the -ed sequence, do not

---

[4]We have reported data on children's spelling and not on their reading. It is possible that the stages of development that we have reported apply to spelling only, and not to reading. Our own view is that such a separation between reading and spelling is unlikely. We have also collected data on children's awareness of the conventional spelling of morphemes in a reading task, which we have not analyzed yet, and this should tell us whether reading and spelling are alike from the point of view of the importance of learning about the conventional spelling of morphemes.

distinguish regular and irregular past verbs: Not only do they write *killed*, they also write *heared*. But when they are a bit older they begin to confine the *-ed* spelling to regular past verbs and no longer produce generalizations like *heared* and *sleped*.

This last developmental change poses an extraordinarily interesting question. What exactly are they learning when they finally manage to confine the conventional *-ed* spelling to regular past verbs and to spell the endings of irregular past verbs phonetically? The data that we have presented in this chapter do not answer the question, but we can at least suggest two alternative answers. One is that the children learn about the exceptions to the *-ed* rule on a rote basis: They simply learn that many past verbs are spelled with an *-ed* ending but that several are not and are spelled phonetically. The other possibility is that the children actually learn a deeper and altogether more subtle rule.

The verbs that we have called regular past verbs are regular in two senses: In their written form they are spelled with the conventional *-ed* ending, and in their spoken form they share exactly the same stem in the past tense as in the present tense (*kill–killed*, *kiss–kissed*). Irregular past verbs are also irregular in two senses: In their written form they are not spelled with the conventional *-ed* ending, and in their spoken form the stem changes from the present to the past tense (*tell–told*, *lose–lost*). This means that a child could form a rule for deciding which past verbs are spelled with the conventional *-ed* ending and which must be spelled phonetically. The *-ed* words are those whose stems are the same in the present and past tenses, whereas the words with phonetic spellings are those whose stems change from the present to the past tense.

As far as we can discern, this last rule is not taught in schools, or at any rate in schools in England. However, it is still possible that children learn it for themselves, and some preliminary results of ours with 8- to 10-year-old children suggest that they do indeed do so. In spoken sentences we introduced pseudoverbs in their present and past form. Some of these were regular in formation (/feach/–/feacht/) and others irregular (/feep/–/fept/). We found that many of the children put the *-ed* at the end of the past pseudoverbs in the regular pairs more often than in the irregular pairs. In the example just given, they tended to write "feached" rather than "feacht" and "fept" rather than "feped."

All in all, our developmental data show that children treat the spelling of word endings as a problem to be solved and that they form their own hypotheses about the solutions to this problem. Although these hypotheses are at first incorrect (first "Some words ending in /d/ or /t/ have *-ed* endings" and later "All past verbs end with an *-ed*"), each one is a step closer to the correct pattern. We have also shown that this whole developmental process lasts for around 3 years.

This last point, however, needs some qualification. We base it on one highly specific instance—the understanding of the *-ed* spelling pattern. However, there are many other examples in English of direct connections between grammar and orthography that also deserve attention, and some take much longer for the children to understand. Our data suggest that children conquer the *wh–* sequence that we have mentioned briefly at roughly the same time as the *-ed* pattern, and in much the same way. However, learning about the use of apostrophes to signify possessives, which is another striking instance of spelling indicating a grammatical relation, takes a great deal longer. We have data from our longitudinal project and from two pilot studies about children's learning of the use of apostrophes. These data show that many 12-year-old children are completely unaware of the grammatical basis for apostrophes in spelling. Learning about the grammatical basis of spelling English takes a long time.

The second part of our hypothesis concerns the causes that underlie this developmental sequence. We have proposed that the developmental changes that we have just described are based on the children's knowledge of grammar, and we claim that the evidence for this idea is very strong. Some previous studies have already established a relationship between children's awareness of morphemes and the progress that they make in reading (Carlisle, 1995; Fowler & Liberman, 1995). In our own study, the more advanced children in our project certainly did use some grammatical knowledge: The fact that the children at Stage 4 in our developmental sequence spelled irregular past verbs with an *-ed* ending is sufficient evidence for that. A child who writes "heared" has almost certainly never seen this sequence of letters before. When children spell past verbs, regular or irregular, but not other words in this way, it is clear that they have understood the grammatical significance of the *-ed* ending.

Our tests of morpho-syntactic awareness add considerable empirical support to the case for the grammatical connection. There was a strong relationship between these three tasks and the sequence of developmental stages that we have outlined, and the three tests also predicted children's subsequent progress from pregrammatical to grammatical stages. Thus, there is a connection between the children's spelling and their morpho-syntactic awareness.

Our results also suggest that this connection is a causal one. The scores in one of the three morpho-syntactic tasks—the word analogy task—predicted the children's correct use of the *-ed* spelling sequence 6 months later, even after stringent controls for differences between them in spelling *-ed*s correctly at the time that they were given the morpho-syntactic tests. Thus, the fact that the children's word analogy scores are related to spelling *-ed*s 6 months later cannot be explained as an artifact due to these morpho-syntactic scores and the -*ed* spelling being related from the start. The relationship suggests that those who make good progress in learning about this spelling pattern do so because they have a relatively high level of morpho-syntactic awareness. The specificity of this relationship is also encouraging: In an exactly similar analysis, the word analogy tasks did not predict the children's spelling of nonverb endings.

However, predictive studies on their own are not enough to answer the question about causes. We also need intervention studies. We need to find ways of improving children's grammatical awareness and then to measure the consequences of this improvement on their spelling. It would be wise at the same time to answer the opposite question: Will interventions that improve children's spelling also affect their morpho-syntactic awareness? Our prediction is that training in morpho-syntactic awareness will improve spelling, but that training just in spelling will not improve morpho-syntactic awareness.

Any discussion of causes in the development of reading and spelling takes one directly to the question of backwardness in reading. Because children's learning how to spell morphemes depends partly on their morpho-syntactic awareness, it seems possible that those children who are generally backward in reading may also be particularly insensitive to syntactic distinctions. Our own results do not allow us to claim that they are. However, it is worth noting that our selection of the group of backward readers depended entirely on the standardized reading test that we used in our project, and this test, being a single-word test in which the words were mainly singular nouns and present tense verbs, is not really relevant to the syntactic issues that we have discussed in this chapter.

Standardized reading and spelling tests come in several different forms but, as far as we know, none of them includes any systematic attempt to gauge children's understanding of the conventional spelling for morphemes. Because we have established that the development of this understanding is an important part of children's learning about written language, we would also like to propose that reading and spelling tests that are used, among other things, to identify children with reading difficulties should take this orthographic development into account.

REFERENCES

Adams, M. J. (1990). *Beginning to read*. Boston: MIT Press.

Beers, C. S., & Beers, J. W. (1992). Children's spelling of English inflectional morphology. In S. Templeton & D. R. Bear (Eds.), *Development of orthographic knowledge and the foundations of literacy* (pp. 231–251). Hillsdale, NJ: Lawrence Erlbaum Associates.

Berko, J. (1958). The child's learning of English morphology. *Word, 14*, 150–177.

Bryant, P. E., & Goswami, U. (1986). The strengths and weaknesses of the reading level design—comment on Backman, Mamen and Ferguson. *Psychological Bulletin, 100,* 101–103.

Carlisle, J. F. (1995). Morphological awareness and early reading achievement. In L. B. Feldman (Ed.), *Morphological aspects of language processing* (pp. 189–210). Hillsdale, NJ: Lawrence Erlbaum Associates.

Derwing, B. L., Smith, M. L., & Wiebe, G. E. (1995). On the role of spelling in morpheme recognition: Experimental studies with children and adults. In L. B. Feldman (Ed.), *Morphological aspects of language processing* (pp. 3–28). Hillsdale, NJ: Lawrence Erlbaum Associates.

Fowler, A. E., & Liberman, I. Y. (1995). The role of phonology and orthography in morphological awareness. In L. B. Feldman (Ed.), *Morphological aspects of language processing* (pp. 157–188). Hillsdale, NJ: Lawrence Erlbaum Associates.

Frith, U. (1985). Beneath the surface of developmental dyslexia. In K. Patterson, M. Coltheart, & J. Marshall (Eds.), *Surface dyslexia* (pp. 301–330). Hove, England: Lawrence Erlbaum Associates.

Goswami, U., & Bryant, P. (1990). *Phonological skills and learning to read.* Hove, England: Lawrence Erlbaum Associates.

Hulme, C., & Snowling, M. (1994). *Reading development and dyslexia.* London: Whurr.

Marsh, G., & Desberg, P. (1983). The development of strategies in the acquisition of symbolic skills. In D. R. Rogers & J. A. Sloboda (Eds.), *The acquisition of symbolic skills* (pp. 149–154). New York: Plenum.

Marsh, G., Friedman, M. P., Desberg, P., & Saterdahl, K. (1981). Comparison of reading and spelling strategies in normal and reading disabled children. In M. Friedman, J. P. Das, & N. O'Connor (Eds.), *Intelligence and learning* (pp. 363–367). New York: Plenum.

Marsh, G., Friedman, M. P., Welch, V., & Desberg, P. (1980). The development of strategies in spelling. In U. Frith (Ed.), *Cognitive processes in spelling* (pp. 121–147). London: Academic Press.

Read, C. (1986). *Children's creative spelling.* London: Routledge & Kegan Paul.

Smith, P. T., Baker, R. G., & Groat, A. (1982). Spelling as a source of information about children's linguistic knowledge. *British Journal of Psychology, 73,* 339–350.

Sterling, C. M. (1983). Spelling errors in context. *British Journal of Psychology, 74,* 353–364.

Treiman, R. (1993). *Beginning to spell.* New York: Oxford University Press.

IV

*IMPLICATIONS FOR
INTERVENTION*

11

The Case for Early Reading Intervention

Barbara R. Foorman
University of Houston

David J. Francis
University of Houston

Sally E. Shaywitz
Yale University, Medical School

Bennett A. Shaywitz
Yale University, Medical School

Jack M. Fletcher
University of Texas—Houston, Medical School

We argue that children who fail to grow in literacy-related skills exhibit deficits rather than developmental lags in these skills and, therefore, deserve early intervention. In short, the adage "Just wait, they'll catch up" does not hold up to the empirical data. In this chapter, we explain why this adage does not hold and also provide empirical support for the kinds of early reading interventions that work.

INSTITUTIONALIZED NOTIONS OF DEVELOPMENTAL LAG

Imagine the following directive to regular education teachers:

> Teach to the children performing at the mean of the class and those that fall below this mean shall be given a few years to catch up and if they continue to fail they shall be delivered to special services for diagnostic

243

testing and treatment. (And, P.S., if their conduct is so disruptive that you must get them out of your classroom earlier, try referral for the emotionally disturbed—ED—label.)

We hope this directive sounds implausible to you. However, we find that the directive characterizes classroom practice and administrative policy in the United States (and with respect to the use of the ED label, see Singer, Palfrey, Butler, & Walker, 1989). Children with an obvious sensory impairment (e.g., mental retardation, speech and language) will qualify for special services early on. Children whose native language is not English will be placed in English as a second language (ESL) classes or bilingual classes. Children who are in schools where the majority of children participate in the federal lunch program and who are in the bottom of their class in reading achievement may receive early remediation through Title 1 funding. However, for many low achievers, the belief that their low achievement is due to a developmental lag is reflected in educational policies that encourage retention without intervention. That is, children are asked to repeat a grade with the belief that an additional year will give them time to "catch up."

Why are children retained in the early grades without focused intervention when research clearly shows that retention only works when coupled with intervention in targeted areas (see Mantzicopoulos & Morrison, 1992, for a review)? There are two main reasons, both emerging out of the cognitive revolution in the 1960s that supplanted behavorism in the United States. One reason for the institutionalization of the developmental lag explanation for low achievement is the influence of constructivist educational ideas. The other reason has to do with the emergence of psychometric definitions of learning disabilities that focus on the discrepancy between IQ and achievement. Next we show how constructivist practices and a discrepancy-based definition of learning disabilities have reinforced a "wait-and-see" or "wait-for-failure" response to low achievement in the early grades. The result is that many children are not receiving the early intervention they need.

The Constructivist Philosophy

According to the constructivist view, development unfolds in an ever purposeful fashion, with appropriate environmental stimulation, toward more reasoned problem solving. As the title of Piaget's only collection of educational essays—*To Understand Is to Invent*—implies, learning is a process of knowledge construction: "Remember also that each time one prematurely teaches a child something he could have discovered for himself, that child is kept from inventing it and consequently from understanding it completely. This obviously does not mean the teacher should not devise experimental situations to facilitate the pupil's invention" (Piaget, 1970, p. 715).

The first wave of constructivist curricula in the 1960s in the United States produced preschool programs strongly tied to their founders' interpretation of Piagetian theory (e.g., Weikart's Perry Preschool Project in Ypsilanti, Michigan; Kamii & DeVries' curriculum, and Lavatelli's curriculum). In the 1970s, the constructivist movement came to be known as Discovery Learning or Open Concept education. Unfortunately, many of the educational innovations during this period eventually were reduced to architectural interpretations of "open" as meaning "no walls."

Behaviorism in the guise of the Back to Basics Movement in the late 1970s wiped out Discovery Learning, but constructivism became rejuvenated during the 1980s with the translation of Vygotsky's *Mind in Society* into English in 1978. Vygotsky's emphasis on the individual mind being constructed within a societal context appealed to the increasingly multicultural context of American education, and provided a theoretical framework for promotions of mixed-ability groupings such as Cooperative Learning. Vygotsky's zone of proximal development also provided a role for the teacher. The Piagetian teacher had been a facilitator of developmental processes underlying readiness to learn. The Vygotskian teacher played a more directive role, enabling learning to proceed in advance of development by introducing psychological tools. The use of tools such as counting on fingers or using a calculator first emerges in interpersonal communication, then becomes internalized as intrapersonal communication. Bruner described the nature of tutorial learning as "scaffolding," where the teacher provides a mental framework upon which the child's competence can be realized (e.g., Wood, Bruner, & Ross, 1976). "Scaffolding" came to describe the learning in the zone of proximal development (see Wertsch & Rogoff, 1984). However, for Bruner, scaffolding involved *joint* consciousness between the tutor and the tutored, whereas the Marxist–Leninist ideology of Vygotsky placed consciousness within the tutor, only to be displaced in the tutored as instruction became complete. Evidently the Russian verb describing this instruction in the zone of proximal development has both the connotation of "instruct" as "instill" and "educate" as "to draw out." The latter would be more in tune with the Socratic tradition influencing constructivist education.

Thus, Bruner's metaphor of scaffolding as a description of the dyadic interaction in the zone of proximal development helped to democratize Vygotsky's views and make them palatable to constructivists. Somewhat later, Rogoff (1990) coined another metaphor for the interaction in the zone of proximal development—*cognitive apprenticeship*, which captured the emphasis on socially relevant activities that Vygotsky's colleagues attributed to the zone of proximal development after Vygotsky's death. But the picture of apprenticeship that emerged was, again, imbued with Socratic ideology: The all-knowing master became the compassionate mentor who brings to birth the intelligence within; the ignorant apprentice became the potential prodigy. Apprenticeship in the zone of proximal development was not to require any of the repetitive skill-building work of apprenticeships in the business world.

The interventionist interpretation of Vygotsky's ideas are alive and well today in Moscow's Institute of Defectology and Feuerstein's center in Israel. The emphasis is on a tutor's guided instruction with special education children. In New Zealand and the United States, Clay and Cazden (1992) described the Reading Recovery tutorial in Vygotskian terms. Reading Recovery is a reading intervention designed by Clay (1985) in New Zealand for beginning readers who are falling behind. The children receive 30 minutes of daily tutorial for 12 to 20 weeks, at which point they are either on grade level and, therefore, "recovered," or candidates for special education. The format for the Reading Recovery lessons was clearly a product of Clay's constructivist leanings: After an initial period of "roaming around the known" the child is introduced to new learning. However, Socratic principles characterize this new learning in a manner inconsistent with Vygotskian instruction in the zone of proximal development. Elements of Goodman's (1970) and Smith's (1971) psycho-linguistic guessing game approach to reading seem to permeate the Reading Recovery sessions in the United States, as tutors are trained to encourage children to draw upon their natural facility in oral language to construct meaning from print. Unfortunately, this idea that literacy emerges naturally out of children's oral language faculties is blatantly wrong, as Vygotsky (1962, pp. 180–181) himself pointed out: "Written speech is a separate linguistic function, differing from oral speech in both structure and mode of functioning." Yet, the term *emergent literacy* has been extended beyond Clay's (1966) original meaning of "partly formed" to include a sequence of "literacy events" that supposedly evolve naturally within a literate culture. Such a perspective reinforces the wait-until-ready mode of Piagetian constructivism and perpetuates the notion of developmental lag, rather than focusing on the diagnostic skills valued by Vygotsky's interventionist pedagogy.

The Discrepancy Approach to Classification and Labeling

In addition to constructivism, another central reason for institutionalized notions of developmental lag is the discrepancy approach to the diagnosis of learning disabilities and, more specifically, reading disabilities. According to this approach, children are classified as learning disabled if there is a significant discrepancy between their aptitude, usually measured by an IQ test, and their achievement. The two most common methods for calculating this discrepancy involve comparisons of standard scores from tests of IQ and achievement, and regression formulas that adjust for the correlation of the IQ and achievement tests (see Fletcher et al., 1994; Frankenberger & Fronzaglio, 1991).

The idea that subgroups of poor readers exist based on relationships of IQ and reading had its impetus with the Isle of Wight studies summarized in Rutter and Yule (1975). Using this epidemiological sample, Rutter and Yule (1975) noted that the distribution of reading skills in this population was bimodal. The bimodality represented two different groups of poor readers who had deficient reading abilities below levels that would be expected based on their IQ score (specific reading retardates), or at levels consistent with IQ (general reading backwardness). Rutter and Yule (1975) observed a number of differences between these two subgroups, including differences in the developmental course of reading skills over time. More recent studies have not supported either the presence of bimodality in the distribution of reading skills (S. E. Shaywitz, Escobar, B. A. Shaywitz, Fletcher, & Makuch, 1992) or the existence of cognitive skill differences between poor readers with poor reading skills being discrepant or not discrepant with IQ (Fletcher et al., 1994; Stanovich & Siegel, 1994). However, these studies have not evaluated the hypothesis of variations in the developmental course of reading disabilities (see Fletcher, Francis, Shaywitz, Foorman, & S. E. Shaywitz, in press, for a review). Showing that the developmental course was different for IQ-discrepant readers and low achievement readers, as demonstrated by Rutter and Yule (1975), would support the two-group classification of discrepancy and low achievement groups.

The important point for purposes of this chapter is that the reliance on a discrepancy approach to the diagnosis of reading disabilities, and the larger problem of learning disabilities, reinforces a "wait-for-failure" attitude with regard to intervention. If a child's discrepancy between IQ and achievement is not yet great enough (according to whatever formula is being used), the child is not considered eligible for services. This approach provides an excuse for "waiting-for-failure" before providing intervention.

EMPIRICAL STUDIES OF LAG VERSUS DEFICIT IN READING DISABILITIES

Central to research on intervention is the question of when to intervene. Common sense tells us that we should intervene at the point when the child begins to fall behind. In the previous section we examined why a wait-and-see, or, more precisely, a wait-for-failure, view pervails in decisions regard-

ing classification of reading disabilities. In this section we examine empirical evidence of whether, compared to normal children, the cognitive
processes of children with learning difficulties go through the same sequence of stages at a slower rate (i.e., a developmental lag) or a different
sequence, with certain processing strengths compensating for deficits.

Epidemiological Data

First, let us dispell the myth of developmental lag with the only data able
to do so in a conclusive manner—long-term, longitudinal data. Such data
are available in the United States from the Connecticut Longitudinal Study
(CLS), a study based on an epidemiological sample of 407 children (S. E.
Shaywitz, B. A. Shaywitz, Fletcher, & Escobar, 1990; S. E. Shaywitz et al.,
1992). Growth in reading achievement from age 7 through 14 is plotted in
Fig. 11.1 for 340 of the children, divided into three reading groups: those
without reading disability, those with only low reading achievement, and
those with a discrepancy between IQ and reading achievement (Francis,
S. E. Shaywitz, Stuebing, B. A. Shaywitz, & Fletcher, 1994). The curves of
all three groups fit a quadratic model of growth to a plateau. Reading
groups did not differ in age at which scores reached a plateau, but they did
differ in the level at which the scores reached a plateau. Francis et al. (1994)
interpreted these results as supporting a deficit model of reading disabilities. If children with reading disabilities were merely delayed in their
reading development, they would differ from normals only in the age at
which scores plateau. However, the fact that reading scores of both groups

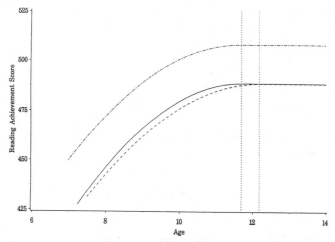

FIG. 11.1. Mean achievement curves of the three reading groups: children
without reading disabilities (· - ·), those in the low achievement (LA) group
(—), and those in the FSIQ-achievement-discrepant (RD) group (---).
(Reprinted with permission of Paul H. Brookes Publishing Co.)

TABLE 11.1
Correlations Between Decoding and Comprehension
in the Connecticut Longitudinal Study

Comprehension	Decoding								
	Gr. 1	Gr. 2	Gr. 3	Gr. 4	Gr. 5	Gr. 6	Gr. 7	Gr. 8	Gr. 9
Grade 1	.89								
Grade 2	.75	.83							
Grade 3	.70	.74	.77						
Grade 4	.64	.71	.74	.73					
Grade 5	.58	.63	.68	.67	.70				
Grade 6	.59	.65	.67	.68	.66	.69			
Grade 7	.53	.61	.65	.65	.67	.68	.69		
Grade 8	.49	.58	.62	.62	.64	.65	.65	.63	
Grade 9	.52	.58	.60	.62	.60	.63	.63	.61	.63

Note. All correlations are significant at $p < .001$, and sample sizes range from 390 to 403.

of poor readers plateaued at a lower level than did those of normals indicates a deficit in reading skill rather than a developmental lag.

To understand the nature of this deficit, it is interesting to examine the relation between decoding and comprehension in the CLS data. Decoding was measured by a composite of the averages of the word identification and word attack subtests of the Woodcock Johnson Psycho-Educational Test Battery (WJ; Woodcock & Johnson, 1977). Comprehension was measured by the WJ passage comprehension score. As can be seen from Table 11.1, correlations between these decoding and comprehension scores ranged from .89 in grade 1 to .63 in grade 9. Moreover, the correlation between grade 1 decoding and grade 9 comprehension was .52, and the correlation between grade 2 decoding and grade 9 comprehension was .58. Thus, the relation between decoding and comprehension was highly stable over time and early decoding correlated highly with later comprehension. The fact that between 25% and 36% of the variability in grade 9 comprehension was accounted for by early decoding skills is a remarkably large amount, given that comprehension places demands on processes such as memory that are clearly outside the word recognition module.

Predictors of Decoding Success

As illustrated in the CLS data just described, decoding skills in first and second grades are highly predictive of comprehension skills in ninth grade, 7 years later. This suggests, at the least, that early intervention should target these skills; we say more about that later in the chapter. But first, an obvious question is: What predicts successful early decoding? Two decades of research provide a clear answer to this question: sensi-

tivity to the sound structure of words (*phonological awareness*), and familiarity with the written symbols—letters—that represent these speech sounds
(*orthographic awareness*). For example, a 5- or 6-year-old's success in saying
"mask" without /m/ and identifying the printed letter *m* indicates insight
into the *alphabetic principle* that is the hallmark of a good decoder. In short,
a good decoder understands the *code* or, more accurately, the *cipher* that
explains the mapping of print to speech and this cipher must be taught.
In Spanish, the task of deciphering print is easier than in English because
Spanish orthography is highly predictable—usually one sound per letter
unit. English has the reputation for being very unpredictable, but, in fact,
about 50% of English words are predictable, that is, regular in their
pronunciation (Hanna, Hanna, Hodges, & Rudorf, 1966). Before assuming
that the other 50% need to be memorized as unanalyzable wholes, appreciate the fact that approximately another 37% of words are predictable
in all but one sound (Hanna et al., 1966). These are the words in which
phonics rules help to draw attention to combinations of letters that make
a single sound (e.g., *oa* in *boat*; *kn* in *knit*; *eigh* in *neigh*) or new sound (e.g.,
oi in *boil*). That means that only 13% of words need to be learned by sight.
Many of these irregular words occur so frequently that they may be learned
very early (e.g., *the, of*). Others will simply have to be memorized (e.g., *ocean*).

In sum, we conclude that orthographic awareness, or familiarity with the
written symbols that represent speech sounds, must indeed be instructed—
in the Vygotskian sense, rather than constructed in the Piagetian sense. An
orthography is an artificial system for representing speech. The English
orthography has a different cipher for mapping the Roman alphabet onto
speech than does, for example, Spanish orthography, but the point is that
both ciphers are arbitrary and must be taught. However, what about the
other prerequisite to good decoding—phonological awareness? Must these
skills also be taught?

At first we may be tempted to give in to the constructivists on this
one. After all, phonology is part of linguistics, and Chomsky criticized
Skinner on this very point: Language acquisition is largely an innate rather
than a learned phenomenon. With respect to phonology, the natural
categories for speech production and recognition are the articulatory
gestures we call consonants and vowels. But what about the category of
speech represented by alphabetic orthographies—the phoneme? Is the
phoneme a natural category whose awareness emerges without instruction? The phoneme *is* a natural category, but awareness of the phoneme
typically does not emerge without explicit instruction. Because of coarticulation, information about each of the phonemes is widely spread
through the acoustic signal. As a consequence, the segmented nature of
the phonemic structure is not apparent at the acoustic level. It follows
further that the acoustic syllable (e.g., /c/ /a/ /t/) cannot be divided

into three sounds in such a way that each sound corresponds to one of the three phonemes. Nevertheless, the phonemes are there, albeit as articulatory gestures (see Liberman, chap. 1, this volume). We can refer to a child's "phonemic awareness" as sensitivity to these smallest units of sound, and measure it by the kind of segmentation task described earlier (i.e., "say 'mask' without /m/"). Using data from the Yale University Center for Learning and Attention Disorders, Fletcher et al. (1994) found phonemic awareness to be a common deficit in children with reading disabilities, with or without discrepancies in IQ.

Trade-Offs in Phonological and Orthographic Processing

In fact, the centrality of phonemic awareness deficits in children with reading disabilities has been demonstrated by many researchers (for reviews, see Adams, 1990; Goswami & Bryant, 1990; Vellutino, 1991). Stanovich (1988) captured this centrality in the name of his hypothesized model of reading disability: phonological-core variable-difference model. Recently, Stanovich and Siegel (1994) validated this model in a cross-sectional study of 907 subjects ages 7 to 16. Using regression-based logic to match these subjects on reading age (in contrast to chronological age), Stanovich and Siegel showed that children with reading disabilities, with or without discrepancies with IQ, had a deficit in phonological processing that was to some extent compensated for by orthographic skill (see Siegel, Share, & Geva, 1995, for a stronger interpretation of this database). The cognitive differences between the two groups of children with reading disabilities all resided outside the word recognition module.

We replicated Stanovich and Siegel's (1994) study with a younger sample—5- through 8-year-olds. We used both the reading-age match based on age/grade standardized scores used by Stanovich and Siegel (1994) and a reading-performance match using w-scores, which are Rasch-scaled scores based on a common metric regardless of age or grade (Foorman, Francis, Fletcher, & Lynn, 1996). This more statistically reliable performance-based match did not result in the cognitive trade-offs in phonological and orthographic processing seen in the performance of the older children with reading disabilities in the Stanovich and Siegel study who were matched on reading age. The deficit in phonological processing was still there; in fact, it was more obvious with the performance-based match. But, significantly, the compensatory role of orthographic processing was not apparent. In fact, at lower levels of decoding, differences between normal and disabled readers on orthographic processing were reduced, rather than increased to favor disabled readers as the reading-age match suggested. For the first and second graders with reading disabilities in our study, orthographic processing did not compensate for deficiencies in phonological processing. It was not until decoding was in the normal range that skill in orthographic processing became predictive of decoding and could be described as a compensatory mechanism.

Is it possible that, over time, orthographic skills may develop sufficiently well to compensate for phonological deficiencies? Stanovich and Siegel's (1994) study cannot answer this question, because their data are cross-sectional rather than longitudinal. Our design provided for longitudinal data in three cohorts: a kindergarten–grade 1 cohort, a grade 1–grade 2 cohort, and a grade 2 cohort. Each year we assessed phonological and orthographic processing in four assessments—during the beginning of October, December, February, and April. By analyzing the data for growth in phonological and orthographic processing, we were able to provide preliminary answers to the question of cognitive trade-offs.

Our analysis of phonological skill was based on Wagner, Torgesen, and Rashotte's (1994) phonological synthesis and analysis tasks. Synthesis tasks consisted of:

1. Blending onset-rhyme units into words (e.g., "m-ouse"; "ch-ild").
2. Blending phonemes into words (e.g., "i-f"; "w-a-sh").
3. Blending phonemes into nonwords (e.g., "i-th" to rhyme with *with*; "y-a-s" to rhyme with *gas*).

Phonological analysis tasks consisted of:

1. First sound comparison (e.g., "Which of these pictures—drum, tie, and cup—start with the same sound as this picture, tool?").
2. Phoneme elision (e.g., "Say 'meat.' Now tell me what word would be left if I said 'meat' without saying /t/").
3. Sound categorization (e.g., "Which word does not sound like the other ones in 'hop-tap-lop'?")
4. Phoneme segmentation (e.g., "Tell me each sound in the word *ate* in the order that you hear it").

Scores were based on the total number correct out of the 15 items on each task. Scores were factor analyzed and found to support the two-factor structure of analysis and synthesis found by Wagner et al. (1994).

Preliminary individual growth curve analyses were performed on phonological synthesis and analysis factor scores, with contrasts formed to compare normal controls and disabled readers, and subgroups of disabled readers—those whose low achievement coincided with a discrepancy in IQ (reading discrepant—RD) and those for whom it did not (low achieving— LA). Low achievement was based on a Basic Reading (age standardized) score below the 25th percentile on the WJ-R and WISC-R (Wechsler, 1974)

Verbal (VIQ) or Performance IQ (PIQ) above 79. The discrepancy identification was based on a regression discrepancy of 1.5 standard errors between the WJ-R Basic Reading score and the WISC-R FSIQ. Normal readers had WJ-R Basic Reading scores above the 25th percentile, VIQ and PIQ scores above 79, and no discrepancy between these scores. Children in each of the three cohorts were identified as late as possible—at the end of first or second grade.

Results of growth curve analyses were similar for phonological synthesis and analysis across the 12 time points from kindergarten through second grade. There were significant interactions of the first contrast between normal controls and the two groups of disabled readers (RD and LA) with a quadratic trend, $t(1, 3152) = -9.25$, $p < .01$ for synthesis and $t(1, 3152) = -7.88$, $p < .01$ for analysis. There was also a significant effect of that first contrast with a cubic trend, $t(1, 3152) = 5.24$ and 3.74, $p < .01$, for synthesis and analysis, respectively. There were no significant effects or interactions for the second contrast between the two groups of disabled readers. The patterns of significant interactions for the first contrast are portrayed in Fig. 11.2 for phonological synthesis (panel A) and phonological analysis (panel B).

The cubic component refers to the rate of acceleration of the rate of change. The fact that the normal controls differed from the two groups of disabled readers in this acceleration rate is apparent from Fig. 11.2. Both RD and LA groups made little progress in phonological processing during kindergarten (i.e., at age 5). In contrast, the control group made rapid gains during kindergarten. The quadratic component refers to the rate of deceleration. The controls reached their maximum point of acceleration at the middle of second grade (i.e., around age 8). Then their learning rate tapered off at the end of second grade. In contrast, the two groups of poor readers continued the rate of acceleration in phonological analysis and synthesis during second grade. Interpretation of the second grade pattern must be made cautiously, however, because controls were close to the ceiling of the test, particularly phonological synthesis (panel A).

Thus, a deficit model of phonological processing is supported by these preliminary analyses of growth curves because disabled readers—whether their poor reading was discrepant or not with their IQ—had nonintersecting trajectories of growth in phonological processing skill, with normal readers' performance exceeding that of poor readers' at every age. Exactly when these groups of poor readers will plateau on phonological processing is impossible to say, given the restricted age range of our sample and the limited range of this version of the test (but see Francis, Shaywitz, Stuebing, Shaywitz, & Fletcher, 1996; Shaywitz et al., 1995, for confirmation of the deficit hypothesis in the CLS data through grade 9). However, it is clear that the relative lack of development of phonological analysis skill during

Change in Mean Phonological Processing (Synthesis) Over Time for Three Reading Groups

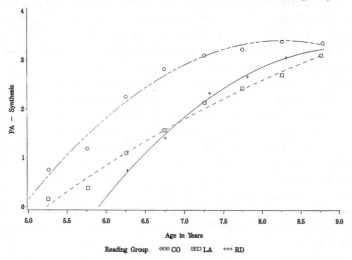

Change in Mean Phonological Processing (Analysis) Over Time for Three Reading Groups

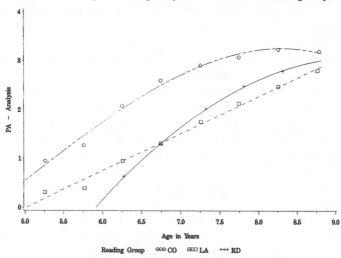

FIG. 11.2. A. Change in mean phonological processing (synthesis) over time for three reading groups. B. Change in mean phonological processing (analysis) over time for three reading groups.

kindergarten suggests the need for early intervention, because this is the skill most predictive of success in early reading (Wagner et al., 1994).

The hope that poor readers can compensate for deficient phonological skills with orthographic skills is diminished when results of growth curve analyses on first and second graders' orthographic processing are examined. We measured orthographic processing with a composite score derived from standardizing and then averaging the percent correct on a spelling recognition test and a spelling dictation test where we used only the words with exceptional spelling patterns (e.g., *comb*). The recognition test was Olson, Kliegl, Davidson, and Foltz's (1985) pseudohomophone choice test (e.g., *rane rain*). Although phonological processing is involved in both of these tests of orthographic processing, in neither case is it sufficient for accuracy. What is sufficient is word-specific information about letter sequences, that is, orthographic knowledge (see Foorman, 1994, 1995, for a review).

Results of growth curve analyses on orthographic processing revealed a significant interaction of the first contrast between normal controls and the two groups of disabled readers with time, $t(1, 2527) = 7.50$, $p < .01$. There was also a significant main effect for the quadratic trend, $t(1, 2527) = 3.54$, $p < .01$. There were no significant main effects or interactions for the second contrast of the two groups of disabled readers (RD and LA). The significant difference in slope for the first contrast is clearly portrayed in Fig. 11.3. The normals' strong, linear rate of improvement in ortho-

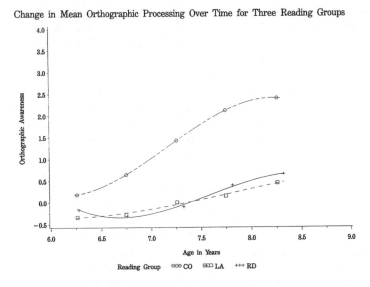

Change in Mean Orthographic Processing Over Time for Three Reading Groups

FIG. 11.3. Change in mean orthographic processing over time for three reading groups.

graphic processing was apparent across first and second grades (i.e., ages 6.25 to 8.25). However, the pattern for the two groups of poor readers was much flatter. Moreover, the RD group actually declined in performance across the first three assessments and exhibited little improvement during the first three assessments in second grade (means not shown). Thus, based on Fig. 11.3, the prospect of skill in orthographic processing turning into a compensatory mechanism any time soon for these children with reading disabilities appears poor indeed. A better prospect for preventing reading difficulties would seem to be to intervene early to ensure growth in phonological processing skill.

THE PROMISE OF EARLY READING INTERVENTIONS

What evidence do we have that early interventions in phonological processing promote success in beginning literacy? Our description of the evidence is divided into two sections: Prevention of reading disabilities, and early interventions for children with identified reading disabilities.

Prevention of Reading Disabilities

Several curricula exist for developing phonological awareness in kindergarteners that have been empirically validated in classroom studies with teachers delivering the instruction. These curricula have been developed by Lundberg, Frost, and Petersen (1988); Byrne and Fielding-Barnsley (1991); and Blachman, Ball, Black, and Tangel (1994). The Lundberg et al. (1988) curriculum was first developed in Swedish and then translated into Danish for use with Danish children. It has recently been translated into English by Adams and Huggins (1993), and consists of approximately 20 minutes of daily phonological awareness activities spread out over 8 months. We selected the Lundberg et al. curriculum as our experimental program for preventing reading disabilities because it incorporated the initial and final sounds activities of Byrne and Fielding-Barnsley and the phonemic segmentation activities of Blachman et al., and led up to these activities with more general activities in the areas of listening, rhyming, identifying sentences and words, and manipulating syllables. The activities involving syllables, initial sounds, and phonemes consist of analyzing words into the relevant constituent parts as well as synthesizing (i.e., blending) the parts back into the whole word. For example, in an exercise on initial sounds, the child might analyze *sand* into *s-and*, then synthesize it into *sand* again. At the phoneme level, the analysis into *s-a-n-d* is made more concrete with the aid of colored blocks.

We trained seven public school kindergarten teachers to deliver the Lundberg et al. phonological awareness activities as part of their kindergarten curriculum. These teachers taught 14 morning and afternoon kindergarten classes at two schools designated as eligible for participation in the Chapter 1 program, based on percent participation in the federal lunch program. Our project director provided one week of in-service training (about 30 hours) on phonological awareness during the summer. Also, during that week the manual of activities was distributed and initial activities were discussed. During the year the project director initially made weekly and then biweekly observations of each teacher, and met with the teachers during their weekly team meetings to discuss lesson plans. Four kindergarten teachers at a neighboring school that did not qualify for Chapter 1 services provided control classrooms. These control teachers participated in the usual inservice provided by the school district.

We randomly selected 100 children from the experimental classrooms and 81 children from the control classrooms to evaluate for development in phonological and orthographic processing, serial naming, and visual–spatial ability. Phonological processing was measured with the Wagner et al. (1994) synthesis and analysis tasks described earlier. We measured orthographic processing with the percent of alphabetic letter names and sounds correctly identified. Serial naming was measured by seconds per object correctly identified on a test of rapid automatized naming (RAN). Visual–spatial ability was measured by averaging the percent correct on a test of visual–motor integration (Beery, 1989) and a test of visual–spatial recognition (Satz & Fletcher, 1982). All of these tests were administered four times during the kindergarten year, in October, December, February, and April. We also measured baseline expressive and receptive syntax by administering in October the Recalling Sentences and Sentence Structure subtests of the Clinical Evaluation of Language Functions–Revised (CELF-R; Semel, Wiig, & Secord, 1987).

Individual growth curve methodology was used to examine individual as well as group differences in the rate of change in phonological and orthographic processing, rapid naming, and visual–spatial ability (see Francis et al., 1994, for a description of this methodology). Age was centered at the mean age during the April wave of data collection. Initially, we examined effects of time (i.e., the linear effects of age), quadratic trend, treatment (i.e., experimental versus control groups), and the interactions of treatment with time and with quadratic trend. Then, we adjusted treatment for the effects of language (by covarying the mean standard score for the CELF-R subtests) and demographics. Demographics included gender and ethnicity contrasts. The only two outcome measures that had significant effects in the initial model were phonological analysis and rapid naming. As can be seen in Table 11.2, there were significant interactions of time ×

TABLE 11.2
Individual Growth Curve Results (t-Tests) for
Outcome Measures in the Kindergarten Study

Variable	Phonological Processing		Orthographic Processing (1,505)	Serial Naming (1,682)	Visual–Spatial (1,678)
	Synthesis (1,504)	Analysis (1,504)			
Intercept	9.42	10.16	20.44	9.70	44.41
Time	7.14	4.29	14.13	-1.16^{NS}	5.75
Quadratic	$-.07^{NS}$	$-.67^{NS}$	$.37^{NS}$	3.08	-1.03^{NS}
Treatment	$-.54^{NS}$	1.10^{NS}	$.16^{NS}$	$.92^{NS}$	$.89^{NS}$
Time × treat	1.08^{NS}	4.13	-1.21^{NS}	-2.15	$.69^{NS}$
Quad × treat	1.85^{NS}	2.68	-1.39^{NS}	-1.90^{NS}	$-.03^{NS}$
Treat adjusted for:					
Language	$.63^{NS}$	2.43*	1.01^{NS}	$.01^{NS}$	1.47^{NS}
Demographics	$-.20^{NS}$	1.01^{NS}	$.43^{NS}$	$.68^{NS}$	$.65^{NS}$
Lang & demo	$.61^{NS}$	2.33*	—	$.00^{NS}$	1.47^{NS}

Note. Degrees of freedom are provided parenthetically for the model without covariates. Treat = treatment; Quad = quadratic; Lang = language; Demo = demographics. All t-values are significant at $p < .05$, unless indicated by NS (for nonsignificant).
*Includes interaction of time × language.

treatment for both phonological analysis and rapid naming. Additionally, for phonological analysis there was a significant interaction of quadratic × treatment. When treatment was controlled for group differences in language and demographics, only phonological analysis had significant effects. The central role played by expressive and receptive syntax in phonological analysis is underscored by the fact that in the final model, with all covariates included, the only significant covariates were language and the interaction of time × language.

The significant treatment effect in phonological analysis skills, controlled for group differences in language and the interaction of time × language, is portrayed in Fig. 11.4. The control group's gradual improvement in these skills across the kindergarten year probably reflects effects of maturation. The experimental group's lower performance in the first half of the year is not surprising, given their lower socioeconomic status (as indicated by their schools' Chapter 1 status). The experimental group's accelerated learning relative to the control group during the second half of the year fits with the shift in the Lundberg et al. curriculum from sentence- and word-level activities to sublexical activities based on syllables and phonemes.

Our finding that 20 minutes daily of rhyming, alliterating, or segmenting in kindergarten can accelerate the development of phonological analysis skills relative to controls is encouraging in light of Wagner et al.'s (1994) results that phonological analysis was the single reliable cause of

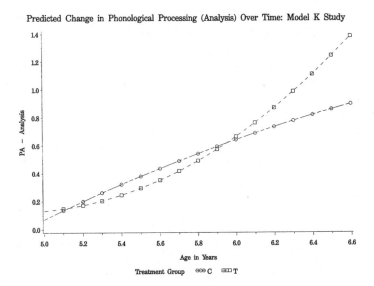

FIG. 11.4. Predicted change in phonological processing (analysis) over time: kindergarten study.

first-grade decoding (compared to phonological synthesis, memory, and serial and isolated naming). They found that phonological synthesis was the single reliable cause of second-grade decoding. We await our follow-up data to test the predictive validity of kindergarten growth in phonological synthesis and analysis on success in beginning reading.

Early Interventions for Children With Identified Reading Disabilities

In the area of learning disabilities there are no empirically validated answers to the question of what intervention(s) work best for which children in what setting(s) for what duration and for what reason (Farnham-Diggory, 1986; Lyon & Moats, 1988; Schonhaut & Satz, 1983; Spreen, 1988; Taylor, 1989). In fact, at this point it is apparent that severe reading disabilities diagnosed after age 8 are refractory to treatment. Surveys reported by Keeney and Keeney (1968) in Strag (1972) found that:

> When the diagnosis of dyslexia was made in the first two grades of school nearly 82 percent of the students could be brought up to their normal classroom work, while only 46 percent of the dyslexic problems identified in the third grade were remediated and only 10 to 15 percent of those observed in grades five to seven could be helped when the diagnosis of learning problems was made at those grade levels. (p. 52)

The youngest grade at which our participating school district identified children as learning disabled was second grade. Therefore, in our study of early interventions for children with identified reading disabilities, we included all 146 second and third graders with reading disabilities in 13 elementary schools. We assessed the students' literacy-related skill development as they received 60 minutes a day of either a synthetic phonics program called Alphabetic Phonics (Cox, 1991), a synthetic/analytic phonics program based on our revision of Recipe for Reading (Traub & Bloom, 1992) that used onset-rime segments of words as the units for analysis and synthesis, or a sight-word program called Edmark (Edmark, 1984), delivered by their special education teacher in the resource room. The 14 participating teachers received 30 hours of training during the summer, bimonthly monitoring by our project director, and quarterly discussions with teachers delivering the same intervention. As in the kindergarten study described previously, individual growth curve methodology was used to examine skill development in phonological and orthographic processing, rapid naming, and visual–spatial ability. Orthographic processing was measured with spelling recognition and dictation of exception words, as was done in our replication of Stanovich and Siegel's (1994) study described earlier. In this study of reading disabilities we also examined growth in word reading and end-of-year achievement in reading and spelling.

Because a detailed description of the results of this study is available elsewhere (Foorman, Francis, Fletcher, Winikates, & Mehta, in press), only a summary is provided here. We evaluated literacy-related skill development in 114 of the original 146 students in our study who had received at least 6 months of treatment. Students receiving a synthetic phonics program attained greater skill in phonological analysis and synthesis than did their peers in a combined synthetic and analytic phonics program or a sight word program, controlling for group differences in memory and demographic variables. This advantage of synthetic phonics relative to a combination of synthetic and analytic phonics in the phonological domain transferred to greater accuracy in orthographic processing and word reading, as well as to baseline models of May achievement in spelling, decoding, and comprehension. On May achievement tests, the synthetic phonics group did not outperform the sight-word group when group differences in memory and demographics were controlled. However, the sight-word group did attain greater skill in orthographic processing and word reading in the growth curve analyses, and did have higher spelling achievement than the synthetic/analytic phonics group, even after controlling for group differences in memory and demographics. In sum, the synthetic phonics group and the sight-word group were not different from each other on most measures, but both groups were better than the synthetic/analytic (i.e., onset-rime) group.

Further research on the viability of a sight word approach with minority students is suggested by the fact that inclusion in the model of memory and ethnic contrasts reduced the significance level of the phonics treatment effect. Furthermore, the poor transfer of onset-rime instruction (used with the synthetic/analytic phonics group) to reading and spelling growth and achievement raises questions about the viability of "word family" approaches to teaching students with reading disabilities, although the notable decoding gains of some students suggests large teacher effects in the ability to execute effective onset-rime instruction. Some teachers were successful at engendering reflective knowledge of rimes so that their students could analogize target rime patterns to new words (see Lovett et al., 1994, for similar success). Also, these teachers emphasized the onsets of target words and how knowledge of these phonemes could be used strategically to decode new words.

CONCLUSION

In this chapter we have shown that institutionalized notions of developmental lag persist in school settings because of misconstrued theories of constructivism that promote a wait-and-see attitude, and the IQ-achievement discrepancy approach to classification of learning disabilities that requires a wait-for-failure process of identification. Empirical studies of children with reading disabilities do not support the belief that reading disabilities are due to a developmental lag; rather, they support a deficit model whereby deficiencies in phonological processing retard development of reading and spelling. Contrary to claims by Siegel et al. (1995), our growth curves analyses do not suggest that orthographic knowledge can compensate for phonological deficiencies unless decoding skills are normal. To prevent and treat phonological deficiencies, we argue for early intervention. Empirical support for early intervention is offered with results from an English version of the Lundberg et al. (1988) phonological awareness program, and a comparison of a synthetic phonics, a synthetic/analytic phonics, and a sight-word program for second and third graders with reading disabilities.

ACKNOWLEDGMENTS

This research was supported by Grants HD28171 and HD30995 from the National Institute of Child Health and Human Development. We thank teachers and administrators in Alief, ISD for their participation and sup-

port for this research. We also thank Drs. Terri Beeler and Debbie Winikates for their excellent work as project directors.

REFERENCES

Adams, M. J. (1990). *Beginning to read*. Cambridge, MA: MIT Press.
Adams, M. J., & Huggins, A. (1993). Lundberg, Frost, & Petersen's program for stimulating
    phonological awareness among kindergarten, first-grade, and special education students.
    Unpublished manuscript, BBN Labs, Cambridge, MA.
Beery, K. (1989). *Developmental Test of Visual-motor Integration*. Chicago: Follett.
Blachman, B. A., Ball, E. W., Black, R. S., & Tangel, D. M. (1994). Kindergarten teachers
    develop phoneme awareness in low-income, inner-city classrooms: Does it make a
    difference? *Reading and Writing, 6,* 1–18.
Byrne, B., & Fielding-Barnsley, R. (1991). Evaluation of a program to teach phonemic
    awareness to young children. *Journal of Educational Psychology, 83,* 451–455.
Clay, M. (1966). *Emergent reading behavior*. Unpublished doctoral dissertation, University of
    Auckland Library, New Zealand.
Clay, M. (1985). *The early detection of reading difficulties*. Portsmouth, NH: Heinemann.
Clay, M., & Cazden, C. B. (1992). A Vygotskian interpretation of Reading Recovery. In C. B.
    Cazden (Ed.), *Whole language plus* (pp. 114–135). New York: Teachers College Press.
Cox, A. R. (1991). *Structures and techniques: Multisensory teaching of basic language skills*.
    Cambridge, MA: Educators Publishing Service.
Edmark Corporation. (1984). *Edmark Reading Program*. Redmond, WA: Author.
Farnham-Diggory, S. (1986). Time now, for a little serious complexity. In S. J. Ceci (Ed.),
    Handbook of cognitive, social and neuropsychological aspects of learning disabilities (Vol. 1, pp.
    123–158). Hillsdale, NJ: Lawrence Erlbaum Associates.
Fletcher, J. M., Francis, D. J., Shaywitz, B. A., Foorman, B. R., & Shaywitz, S. E. (in press).
    Diagnostic utility of intelligence testing and the descrepancy model for children with
    learning disabilities: Historical perspectives and current research. In National Research
    Council (Ed.), *IQ testing and educational decision making*. Washington, DC: National
    Academy of Sciences.
Fletcher, J. M., Shaywitz, S. E., Shankweiler, D. P., Katz, L., Liberman, I. Y., Stuebing, K. K.,
    Francis, D. J., Fowler, A. E., & Shaywitz, B. A. (1994). Cognitive profiles of reading
    disability: Comparisons of discrepancy and low achievement definitions. *Journal of
    Educational Psychology, 86,* 6–23.
Foorman, B. R. (1994). Phonological and orthographic processing: Separate but equal? In
    V. W. Berninger (Ed.), *The varieties of orthographic knowledge I: Theoretical and developmental
    issues* (pp. 319–355). Dordrecht, The Netherlands: Kluwer.
Foorman, B. R. (1995). Practiced connections of orthographic and phonological processing.
    In V. W. Berninger (Ed.), *The varieties of orthographic knowledge II: Relationships to phonology,
    reading, and writing* (pp. 377–419). Dordrecht, The Netherlands: Kluwer.
Foorman, B. R., Francis, D. J., Fletcher, J. M., & Lynn, A. (1996). Relation of phonological
    and orthographic processing to early reading: Comparing two approaches to regression-
    based, reading-level-match designs. *Journal of Educational Psychology, 88*(4), 639–652.
Foorman, B. R., Francis, D. J., Fletcher, J. M., Winikates, D., & Mehta, P. (in press). Early
    interventions for children with reading disabilities. *Scientific Studies of Reading*.
Francis, D. J., Shaywitz, S. E., Stuebing, K. K., Shaywitz, B. A., & Fletcher, J. M. (1994). The
    measurement of change: Assessing behavior over time and within a developmental

context. In G. R. Lyon (Ed.), *Frames of reference for the assessment of learning disabilities* (pp. 29–58). Baltimore, MD: Brookes.

Francis, D. J., Shaywitz, S. E., Stuebing, K. K., Shaywitz, B. A., & Fletcher, J. M. (1996). Developmental lag versus deficit models of reading disability: A longitudinal, individual growth curves analysis. *Journal of Educational Psychology, 88,* 3–17.

Frankenberger, W., & Fronzaglio, K. (1991). A review of states' criteria and procedures for identifying children with learning disabilities. *Journal of Learning Disabilities, 24,* 495–500.

Goodman, K. S. (1970). Reading: A psycholinguistic guessing game. In H. Singer & R. B. Ruddell (Eds.), *Theoretical models and processes of reading* (pp. 259–272). Newark, DE: International Reading Association.

Goswami, U., & Bryant, P. E. (1990). *Phonological skills and learning to read.* Hillsdale, NJ: Lawrence Erlbaum Associates.

Hanna, P. R., Hanna, J. S., Hodges, R. E., & Rudorf, E. H. (1966). *Phoneme–grapheme correspondences as cues to spelling improvement.* Washington, DC: U.S. Government Printing Office.

Keeney, A. H., & Keeney, V. T. (1968). *Dyslexia: Diagnosis and treatment of reading disorders.* St. Louis, MO: Mosby.

Lovett, M. W., Borden, S. L., DeLuca, T., Lacerenza, L., Benson, N. J., & Brackstone, D. (1994). Treating the core deficits of developmental dyslexia: Evidence of transfer of learning after phonologically- and strategy-based reading raining programs. *Developmental Psychology, 30,* 805–822.

Lundberg, I., Frost, J., & Petersen, O. (1988). Effects of an extensive program for stimulating phonological awareness in preschool children. *Reading Research Quarterly, 23,* 263–284.

Lyon, G. R., & Moats, L. C. (1988). Critical issues in the instruction of the learning disabled. *Journal of Consulting and Clinical Psychology, 56,* 830–835.

Mantzicopoulos, P., & Morrison, D. (1992). Kindergarten retention: Academic and behavioral outcomes through the end of second grade. *American Education Research Journal, 29,* 182–198.

Olson, R. K., Kliegl, R., Davidson, B. J., & Foltz, G. (1985). Individual and developmental differences in reading disability. In G. E. MacKinnon & T. G. Waller (Eds.), *Reading research: Advances in theory and practice* (Vol. 4, pp. 1–64). New York: Academic Press.

Piaget, J. (1970). Piaget's theory. In P. Mussen (Ed.), *Manual of child psychology* (3rd ed., pp. 703–732). New York: Wiley.

Rogoff, B. (1990). *Apprenticeship in thinking.* New York: Oxford University Press.

Rutter, M., & Yule, W. (1975). The concept of specific reading retardation. *Journal of Child Psychology and Psychiatry, 16,* 181–197.

Satz, P., & Fletcher, J. M. (1982). *The Florida Kindergarten Screening Battery.* Odessa, FL: Psychological Assessment Resources.

Schonhaut, S., & Satz, P. (1983). Prognosis for children with learning disabilities: A review of follow-up studies. In M. Rutter (Ed.), *Developmental neuropsychiatry* (pp. 542–563). New York: Guilford.

Semel, L., Wiig, E., & Secord, W. (1987). *Clinical evaluation of language fundamentals—revised.* New York: Psychological Corporation.

Shaywitz, B. A., Holford, T. R., Holahan, J. M., Fletcher, J. M., Stuebing, K. K., Francis, D. J., & Shaywitz, S. E. (1995). A Matthew effect for IQ but not for reading: Results from a longitudinal study. *Reading Research Quarterly, 30,* 894–906.

Shaywitz, S. E., Escobar, M. D., Shaywitz, B. A., Fletcher, J. M., & Makuch, R. (1992). Distribution and temporal stability of dyslexia in an epidemiological sample of 414 children followed longitudinally. *New England Journal of Medicine, 326,* 145–150.

Shaywitz, S. E., Shaywitz, B. A., Fletcher, J. M., & Escobar, M. D. (1990). Prevalence of reading disability in boys and girls: Results of the Connecticut Longitudinal Study. *Journal of the American Medical Association, 264,* 998–1002.

Siegel, L. S., Share, D., & Geva, E. (1995). Evidence for superior orthographic skills in dyslexics. *Psychological Science, 6,* 250–254.

Singer, J. D., Palfrey, J. S., Butler, J. A., & Walker, D. K. (1989). Variations in special education classification across school districts: How does where you live affect what you are labeled? *American Educational Research Journal, 26,* 261–282.

Smith, F. (1971). *Understanding reading.* New York: Holt, Rinehart & Winston.

Spreen, O. (1988). Prognosis of learning disability. *Journal of Consulting and Clinical Psychology, 56,* 836–842.

Stanovich, K. E. (1988). Explaining the differences between the dyslexic and the garden-variety poor reader: The phonological-core variable-difference model. *Journal of Learning Disabilities, 21,* 590–612.

Stanovich, K. E., & Siegel, L. (1994). Phenotypic performance profile of children with reading disabilities: A regression-based test of the phonological-core variable-difference model. *Journal of Educational Psychology, 86,* 24–53.

Strag, G. A. (1972). Comparative behavioral ratings of parents with severe mentally retarded, special learning disability, and normal children. *Journal of Learning Disabilities, 5,* 52–56.

Taylor, H. G. (1989). Learning disabilities. In E. J. Mash & R. A. Barkley (Eds.), *Treatment of childhood disorders* (pp. 347–380). New York: Guilford.

Traub, N., & Bloom, F. (1992). *Recipe for reading* (3rd ed.). Cambridge, MA: Educators Publishing Service.

Vellutino, F. R. (1991). Introduction to three studies on reading acquisition: Convergent findings on theoretical foundations of code-oriented versus whole-language approaches to reading instruction. *Journal of Educational Psychology, 83,* 437–443.

Vygotsky, L. S. (1962). *Thought and language.* Cambridge, MA: MIT Press.

Vygotsky, L. S. (1978). *Mind in society: The development of higher psychological processes.* Cambridge, MA: Harvard University Press.

Wagner, R., Torgesen, J. K., & Rashotte, C. A. (1994). Development of reading-related phonological processing abilities: New evidence of bidirectional causality from a latent variable longitudinal study. *Developmental Psychology, 30,* 73–87.

Wechsler, D. (1974). *Wechsler Intelligence Scale for Children—Revised.* San Antonio, TX: Psychological Corporation.

Wertsch, J. V., & Rogoff, B. (1984). Editors notes. In B. Rogoff & J. Wertsch (Eds.), *Children's learning in the "zone of proximal development"* (pp. 1–6). San: Francisco: Jossey-Bass Inc., Publishers.

Wood, D., Bruner, J. S., & Ross, G. (1976). The role of tutoring in problem solving. *Journal of Child Psycyology and Psychiatry, 17,* 89–100.

Woodcock, R. W., & Johnson, M. B. (1977). *Woodcock-Johnson Psychoeducational Test Battery.* Boston: Teaching Resources.

12

Assessing the Child's and the Environment's Contribution to Reading Acquisition: What We Know and What We Don't Know

Brian Byrne
Ruth Fielding-Barnsley
Luise Ashley
Kim Larsen
University of New England

OVERVIEW

The work we describe in this chapter is concerned with or has consequences for intervention in reading acquisition. Each of the research studies has told us something about the process of reading acquisition, but in each case there are still unanswered questions. Here we try to summarize what we have learned in each case, and what we have yet to learn. Some of the data have been in print for several years, and some are new.

As well as having implications for intervention, the research we describe is united by being related to the theme captured by the chapter title, namely the relative contributions of the child and the environment to the development of reading skill. By contribution of the child we mean the assumptions, powers of induction, and learning mechanisms that the child brings to the task of mastering an alphabetic writing system. By contribution of the environment we mean instruction, formal and informal, that is needed for mastery to occur. Figure 12.1 expresses the issue as we see it.

As illustrated in Fig. 12.1, acquisition of different aspects of human skill and knowledge depends in different proportions on learner-internal capacities and learner-external information. For instance, learning to talk

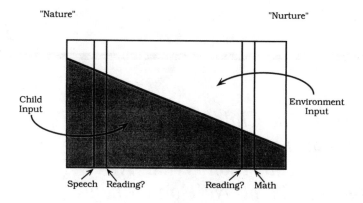

FIG. 12.1. Schematic representation of how different abilities depend on different mixes of the learner's and the environment's contributions during acquisition. The central point is the relative position of abilities on the "nature–nurture" dimension rather than any attempt to locate an ability in absolute terms.

is generally seen as requiring less direct instruction than learning to do mathematics, and hence it could be inferred that these two abilities would be located at different places on a diagram representing the relative mix of internal processes and external support. Theorists who consider that learning to read and learning to talk employ the same mechanisms (e.g., Goodman, 1986) implicitly position literacy acquisition at the "nature" end. This is based on the assumption that they, too, subscribe to the view that there is a substantial biological endowment supporting the acquisition of spoken language and that the child makes considerable progress on the basis of minimal input (see Crain, 1991, for such a viewpoint about spoken language). Theorists who consider that learning written language is less natural than learning spoken language (e.g., Liberman & Liberman, 1992) would tend to locate literacy acquisition further toward the "nurture" end, along with other culturally determined bodies of knowledge like, say, mathematics.

We find compelling the arguments of Liberman and Liberman (1992) for locating literacy acquisition closer to mathematics than speech. Space prohibits a full rehearsal of these arguments, but they include the uncontroversial observations that spoken language is universal, whereas written language is not, and that children can hardly be prevented from learning to talk despite the absence of lessons, whereas many children fail to learn to read well despite intensive instruction. But even if everyone agreed that learning to read requires relatively more environmental support than learning to talk, there would still be work to do to specify what it is that children bring to the task of learning to read and what they need to garner from the environment, because no act of knowledge acquisition occurs without contributions from both the learner and the environment. Information on the specifics of the child's and the environment's contributions is required if we are to devise good teaching strategies and remediation programs. The research that we describe has as its major goal the identification of the child's contribution to reading acquisition and, by subtraction, what the environment must supply.

The research is very far from exhaustive; it is better to think of it as a sample of the questions that arise in attempting to delineate the child's contribution to literacy acquisition. The first of these questions concerns the hypotheses that preliterate children form during their initial systematic contacts with print. If they readily assume that the elements of alphabetic print represent the phonemic elements of speech, then they can be seen as needing minimal input—just enough examples of print to detect the representative function of alphabetic orthography. If, in contrast, their initial hypotheses do not include phonemic representation, their instructional needs will be greater—they will presumably need to be told that letters represent phonemes. The second question is closely related to the first: If children do not readily assume that print represents sound, does telling them that this is so enhance their progress in reading? We present evidence that this is indeed the case, and that the advantages of direct instruction for preschoolers carry through for at least 3 years at school. Third, we turn to the question of whether all children can be thought of as occupying the same location on the diagram or, in contrast, whether some need more instructional input than others. We present evidence that children from families with histories of reading difficulties do apparently need more environmental support than other children. Finally, we consider how children who lack efficient knowledge of the alphabetic principle can nevertheless continue to make progress in reading. In particular, we present evidence that they are more than ordinarily dependent on input, in the form of print exposure, than are children with well-established decoding skills.

Question 1: Children's Initial Hypotheses
About How Print Represents Speech

It is argued that in the course of learning to talk, children make a good deal of progress on the basis of a small amount of information. Evidence that children can begin to fix the meaning of a new word after just one encounter with it exemplifies this claim (Carey, 1982). More generally, the fact that children master the extraordinarily complex rules and principles of syntax at the young age that they do (Crain, 1991), and the fact that their vocabularies expand at such an extraordinary rate (Miller, 1977), attest to the efficiency with which they benefit from linguistic input. If learning to read is anything like as natural as learning to talk, we might expect similar rapid progress. For instance, in the beginning stages of reading acquisition a child exposed to systematic pairings of print and speech in an alphabetic script might quickly realize that the elements of print represent elements of phonology, in particular phonemes. Once the child understands this basic principle of alphabetic orthography, he or she might then go on to quickly absorb the vast array of detailed mappings between letters and letter groups on the one hand and phonemes and phoneme groups on the other. The research we describe next was directed at the first of these possibilities, that initial insights into the alphabetic principle can be triggered by limited acquaintance with systematic print–speech pairings.

By *systematic*, we mean pairings which could potentially reveal the fundamental mapping of print onto speech. Learning to recognize McDonalds and Burger King is not systematic in that sense, because there are too many mismatches between the print sequences and the sounds they stand for. However, learning to read the couplet *dog* and *den* is systematic. An understanding of the segmental structure of speech might be triggered by the fact that each word has three letters—and hence three phonemes— and insight into phoneme invariance might be triggered by the fact that both words start with the same letter—and hence the same phoneme

The research we have conducted at the University of New England has generally not favored the proposition that insights into the alphabetic principle come easily to children (see Byrne, 1992, for earlier work). In recent research (Byrne, 1996), we approached the question by teaching preliterate 4-year-olds to read the pair of words *hat* and *hats*. When they had learned them, with the aid of pictures, they were taught a second pair, *book* and *books*, also with the help of pictures. We were interested to know what they learned about the letter *s*. In these words, it represents both a morpheme and a phoneme. If the idea that the fundamental secrets of alphabetic orthography will rapidly reveal themselves once children acquire systematic print–speech pairings, our young subjects should have understood that *s* stands for /s/. If, on the other hand, children's initial hypotheses are that print represents aspects of the morphology and/or the semantics of language, as Ferreiro (1986) and others suggested, then they may have detected the morphological or semantic function of *s*, but not its phonological function.

To find out, we conducted a series of transfer tests. In the first, the aim was simply to see if these children could transfer their newfound knowledge to novel situations. We showed the children pairs of words like *bike* and *bikes*, and *cup* and *cups*, one pair at a time, and invited them to specify which one in each printed pair said the corresponding spoken word ("one says 'bike' and one says 'bikes'; which one says 'bikes?'"). The children performed very well on this task, confirming that transfer was possible. Then we presented them with a choice in which it was necessary to have induced the phonemic value of *s* to perform well. They were shown a pair like *bus* and *bug*, and asked which was which. In another version of the experiment with different children, we used transfer pairs like *pur* ("purr") and *purs* ("purse"), which preserve the *print sequence + s* structure of the singular-plural pairs. On these tasks, the majority of children failed (i.e., they performed at chance level). We conducted a third transfer test, this time using plurals that did not have the same phonetic value as the training items, namely pairs like *dog* and *dogs*. Here the morpheme assumes the voiced /z/ form. Nevertheless, all children readily made the transfer, evidence perhaps that it was the morphemic value of *s* and not its phonemic value that they had acquired. We add that another group of children who knew the sound of the letter *s* prior to the experiment handled all transfer tasks easily.

In a second experiment, we shifted attention to another level of phonology, the syllable. We taught a new group of children to read the words *small* and *smaller*, and *fat* and *fater* ("fatter"), again using pictures as aids. The first transfer test comprised other comparatives, like *mean* and *meaner*, and performance was at an above-chance level. However, the children as a group failed on a transfer test that relied on them having detected the phonological value of *er*, with items like *corn* and *corner*, and *post* and *poster*.

One further feature of the results is that, in each of these experiments except the first one (and including some control experiments not described here), there were 2 or 3 out of the 12 participants who did succeed in inducing the phonological values of the discriminating print elements.

It is worth mentioning here that in a much longer series of experiments (Byrne, 1992) we have shown that children will not induce letter–phoneme correspondences from systematic encounters with written words, even when morphological inflections are not possible distracters. For instance, preliterate children taught to read *sat* and *mat* are not capable of deciding between "sow" and "mow" as pronunciations for *sow*. Even a learning set consisting of four words—*fat, bat, fin,* and *bin*—which is quite challenging for a preschool child to acquire, did not provoke a grasp of letter–phoneme relations.

The conclusion that we wish to defend is that children's initial hypotheses about the level of language that print represents when they have their first systematic encounters with print do not typically include phonology. It is not perfectly clear what level of representation they do detect under the circumstances of the experiments we have outlined, but one possibility is that they focus on the morphemic values of print elements. If correct, this means that even before children are confronted with the problem of "phonemic awareness" they need to abandon a purely morphemic hypothesis; they need to realize that, at bottom, alphabets represent the meaningless phonological elements of language. Even syllabic writing systems would prove elusive for a morphemically oriented learner (unless by happy coincidence the language was constructed entirely from monosyllabic morphemes).

We also wish to defend the idea that, for some, the seeds of reading disability may be sown in these early stages as a result of hypotheses about the representational function of print that do not include phonology. Here is a self-description, collected by Johnston (1985), from an adult nonreader: "I had learned symbols . . . 1 and 2 and 3 . . . so I wanted that for five-letter words. . . . I had this idea that . . . I was going to know just by looking. . . . But there's no way you could possibly take all the words in the dictionary and just learn them by sight . . ." (p. 157). This reads like a persistent nonsegmental hypothesis about the nature of orthography, one that finally undermined this man's prospects for becoming a competent reader.

Question 1: What We Know. We know that most children do not detect the phonological values of print upon their first systematic contacts with written language, even when such values are potentially available in the input. The notion that most children will make rapid strides in achieving alphabetic literacy on the basis of rather minimal input appears to be erroneous. We also know that a minority of children do appear to induce phonological representation from systematic encounters with print.

Question 1: What We Don't Know. We don't know what it takes for a learner to focus on the phonological level of representation, and conversely why some learners seem unable to do so. Also, we don't know what the characteristics are of the minority of children who appear spontaneously to discover that letters represent phonology from minimal encounters such as those in our experiment. Is it something in the child, in a constitutional sense, or something in the child's experience that supports the inductive process?

Question 2: The Roles of Phonemic Awareness and Letter Knowledge in Literacy Acquisition

We have listed as a point of ignorance how children come to understand that print represents phonological structures as well as, say, morphological ones. It seems that they cannot be relied on to realize this fact all by themselves after minimal exposure to written language. Thus, one's best guess might be to directly tell them about these structures and how letters represent them. In this section we report evidence on that straightforward idea. The essential point emerging from the data is that in order to enjoy a smooth entry into the world of reading and writing, a child needs two things: an understanding of the principle of phonemic segmentation of speech, and knowledge of which letters represent which phonemes. The data come from a longitudinal intervention study that began when the participants were in preschool and is now in its sixth year (Byrne & Fielding-Barnsley, 1991, 1993a, 1995).

We began with 128 preschoolers, 64 of whom were introduced to phonology via the principle of phoneme identity. The aim was to teach the children that words could begin and end with the same sound (e.g., *sun, sailor, sea, spider; bus, horse, octopus, dress*) using pictures and games. We were successful in doing so with 61 of the 64 children (see Byrne & Fielding-Barnsley, 1991). The measure of phoneme identity was a 48-item test in which the children were asked to indicate which of 3 pictured items (e.g., *seal, key, book*) started the same as a pictured target (*sun*), or which item ended the same as a target (e.g., *kite; sock, nose, boat*). The children in the control group were exposed to the same posters and games, but were invited to categorize the contents in formal and semantic terms (color, shape, edibility, etc.). At the end of the 12 weeks of instruction, only a minority of the control children understood the principle of phoneme identity.

We administered a structured decoding test to all the children. We challenged them with a 12-item test in which we presented a word like *sat* and asked whether it said "sat" or "mat," or *pal*, with "pal" and "pam" as the choices. The letters in these items were all ones whose sounds were part of the intervention program. The experimental group children scored 8.1 out of a possible 12, significantly ahead of the controls' score of 6.1 (which, in turn, was not significantly above the chance score of 6).

As well as assessing the children's knowledge of phoneme identity, we tested for knowledge of the sounds of these critical letters independently of the decoding test. The data make a strong case for the combination of phonemic awareness and letter knowledge being necessary but not sufficient for successful decoding. In Table 3 of Byrne and Fielding-Barnsley (1991) there is an analysis of these data as a set of pass/fail contingencies. For the sake of consistency in the present report, the same data are analyzed here in continuous form, and expressed as regression analyses in the first section of Table 12.1. Together, letter knowledge and phonemic awareness account for 54% of the variance in decoding, with both making separate and substantial contributions. The fact that the variance accounted for was *only* 54% reflects, in part, the fact

TABLE 12.1
Regression Analyses Predicting Decoding From
Letter Knowledge and Phonemic Awareness

Grade	Step	R^2 Change	F Change
Preschool	Letter knowledge	.43	130.74*
	Phonemic awareness	.11	29.75*
	Total	.54	
Kindergarten	Letter knowledge	.24	36.47*
	Phonemic awareness	.16	30.03*
	Total	.40	
First	Letter knowledge	.08	9.80*
	Phonemic awareness	.17	24.40*
	Total	.25	
Second	Letter knowledge	.08	9.35*
	Phonemic awareness	.12	16.65*
	Total	.20	

*$p < .01$.

that 9 of the 45 children who were secure in phonemic awareness and letter knowledge performed poorly on the decoding test. (In contrast, there is a good case for saying that no children could decode unless they *were* secure in phonemic awareness and letter knowledge—see Byrne & Fielding-Barnsley, 1991).

The separate contributions of phonemic awareness and letter knowledge to decoding is confirmed for each of the first 3 school years starting with kindergarten, as the other regression analyses in Table 12.1 show. In each case after preschool, the decoding performance is based on pseudoword reading, and phonemic awareness and alphabet knowledge are either assessed in the same year as decoding or are the latest available measures. We stopped assessing alphabet knowledge after grade 1 because most children had reached ceiling on it, which in turn accounts for its declining contribution to decoding as schooling progresses. The main points in the present context are that the child's grasp of the phonological organization of the speech stream continues to contribute to the ability to read novel print sequences, but that variance in decoding still remains unexplained after phonemic awareness and letter knowledge have made their contributions. In confirmation of this last point, one of us (Fielding-Barnsley, 1997) has observed that kindergarten children who are very high in phonemic awareness and letter knowledge still benefit from having had explicit instruction in decoding and blending when they are asked to read novel words created from the letters in word lists that they have been taught to read (see also Cunningham, 1990).

At the end of grade 2, a full 3 years after the intervention program, there was a small but significant difference in favor of the trained children in reading comprehension as well as in pseudoword reading (Byrne & Fielding-Barnsley, 1995). (When only the least-frequent regularly spelled real words are considered, a significant difference in word identification is also in evidence.) These data, then, confirm what several research groups have documented, namely the efficacy of early intervention in phonemic awareness (e.g., Blachman, Ball, Black, & Tangel, 1994; Bradley & Bryant, 1983; Hatcher, Hulme, & Ellis, 1994; Torgesen, Morgan, & Davis, 1992). We think that the present results may be the first to record an experimentally induced decoding advantage over such a long time span (3 years), and perhaps the first to note an advantage for an experimental group in reading comprehension.

Question 2: What We Know. We know that the combination of phonemic awareness and letter knowledge is necessary for a grasp of the alphabetic principle and for the development of decoding skills. We also know that this combination is not sufficient for the development of secure decoding skills.

Question 2: What We Don't Know. We don't know why phonemic awareness and letter knowledge are not sufficient to guarantee the acquisition of decoding. On a narrow interpretation of the Connectionist position, one might expect a smooth passage into decoding by children with the right "grain" of phonemic awareness once they had acquired a reasonable corpus of sight words (Seidenberg, 1992). Yet for some children this progression does not seem to occur. Seidenberg suggested several sources of further difficulties that children might encounter in reading acquisition, including problems with the orthographic processor and resource limitations. A major research question is which of these and/or other factors might undermine reading development after phonemic awareness is firmly in place.

Question 3: Individual Differences in the Child–Environment Mix in Reading Acquisition

Figure 12.2 represents this third question within the conceptual framework that links our various studies: Does every apprentice reader fall at the same spot on the nature–nurture diagram, or is it more like the situation portrayed in Fig. 12.2?

In pursuing this question, we took note of evidence from the Colorado twin study that reading disability has a significant inherited component (Cardon et al., 1994; Olson, Gillis, Rack, DeFries, & Fulker, 1991), and of work of Scarborough (1989, 1991) and others (e.g., Gilger, Pennington, & DeFries, 1991) that tells us that children who have a parent or sibling with

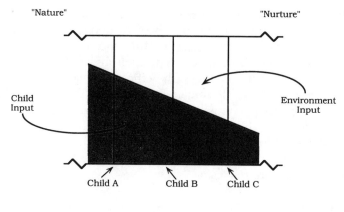

FIG. 12.2. Schematic representation of how different children might require different mixes of internal and external input when learning to read. Child A might be one who, for example, induces the representational function of print at the phonological level after minimal experience with systematic print–speech pairings (see Question 1). Child C might be one who, perhaps for genetic reasons, needs very intensive teaching in order to achieve even minimal levels of phonemic awareness (see Question 3).

a marked reading problem have themselves an elevated chance of developing similar problems. Whether these two observations are linked remains to be determined, but it is plausible to conceive of a genetically determined deficit that compromises internal processes and thus forces greater dependence on external support. For "at-risk" preschool children (those with a family history of reading problems) we instituted an intervention program very similar to the one described in the previous section. (Here we acknowledge the collaboration of Donald Shankweiler in designing this study and in writing the grant application for this project). This is a preliminary report on the project in which we compare those children with the ones from our longitudinal intervention study described earlier. The comparison must be tentative because, in some respects, the longitudinal group provides only an approximate basis for comparison. In the following discussion, we identify the points where caution is in order.

We identified preschoolers as being at risk if a parent reported a significant reading problem in him- or herself or in an older sibling of the child. The existence of reading disability was confirmed, in the case of an adult, with norm-based testing on word identification, decoding, reading comprehension, and reading speed. Reading disability was declared to be present if the person scored one standard error or more below the performance that would be expected on the basis of age and years of schooling, the two variables that made significant contributions to explaining the variance in a composite measure based on the tests. The normative data were collected on a local sample of 200 adults, selected to represent a cross-section of employment levels and schooling histories (we gratefully acknowledge the contribution of Barbara Hindson to this data collection). In the case of a sibling, we were satisfied that reading disability was present if the child had been selected for remedial treatment in school. In some cases, test results were available and provided by the school, and in other cases the referral had been on teachers' recommendations.

Table 12.2 presents details of the sample of 34 boys and 20 girls. At the time of writing, 40 of these have been through the intervention program, and the outcome data are based on this subsample. Verbal IQ was estimated using the Revised Peabody Picture Vocabulary Test (PPVT; Dunn & Dunn, 1981). Phonemic awareness was assessed on the same principles as the children in the longitudinal study described previously had been, namely the principle of phoneme identity. The test format varied somewhat (as discussed later in this section). The test of rhyme awareness involved the children identifying which of three words sounded most like a target (e.g., *cat; hat, clock, bed*). Print awareness was measured using Clay's (1975) Concepts About Print Test (CAP).

The children in the at-risk sample, selected because they had an immediate relative with a reading problem, themselves had a profile characteristic of reading-disabled children—a verbal IQ about 5 points below normal, lower levels of phonological awareness and alphabet knowledge, and less familiarity with the world of print and books. The measure of phonemic awareness for both groups involved identifying which word started the same as a target word, but there was just one foil (two

TABLE 12.2
Pretest Means for At-Risk and Normal Preschool Children
(SDs in Parentheses)

Variable	At-Risk Sample (N = 54)	Normal Sample (N = 128)
Age (months)	55.7 (4.9)	55.2 (3.5)
Verbal IQ (PPVT)*	95.6 (13.8)	100.8 (13.5)
Phonemic awareness (see text for explanation)	10.8 (2.3)	11.6 (5.4)
Rhyme awareness (max = 10)*	5.5 (2.6)	7.2 (2.8)
Letter names[†]	9.1 (5.0)	12.8 (8.1)
Print awareness (CAP)*	3.6 (2.5)	5.4 (3.1)

*Denotes significant difference for that measure between groups.
[†]The letter name tests employed a forced-choice technique, with chance levels of 6.5 (at-risk sample) and 4.5 (normal sample). Direct statistical comparison is complicated by the different test formats, but the absolute difference in favor of the normal sample should be seen against the lower chance score for that sample, emphasizing the superiority of the normal sample.

alternatives) in the 20-item test for the at-risk group, whereas for the longitudinal group there were two foils (three alternatives) in a 24-item test. In addition, the at-risk children's test incorporated features that may have made it marginally more difficult. The correct answer and the foil were matched in global similarity relative to the target. For instance, the target "beak" had "bowl" as the correct response and "pig" as the foil; "beak" and "pig" are similar in phonetic feature configuration (e.g., both begin with bilabial stops, both vowels are high front, and both end with velar stops). This global similarity had to be ignored by the child (see Byrne & Fielding-Barnsley, 1993b, for a fuller description of this test). As a result of this difference between the tests, direct comparison of the means is not possible. What can be said is that the at-risk sample was only just above chance as a group (the difference between the mean and chance was significant), whereas the normal sample was quite safely above chance as a group. When we classify the children as passing or failing on their respective tests, we have figures of 8% passing for the at-risk children against 29% passing for the others, a significant difference ($p < .01$). Passing was defined as 14 out of 20 for the at-risk children and 16 out of 24 for the longitudinal group. Both pass scores corresponded to the upper end of distributions centred on the chance values for the two tests. Given these observations and the fact that the structure of the rhyme awareness test was identical for the two groups, it appears that phonological awareness in general is lower in the at-risk sample.

Not included in Table 12.2 is a confrontation naming test, the Hundred Pictures Naming test (Fisher & Glenister, 1992). Children were presented with line drawings of common objects and asked to name them. The scores are not in Table 12.2 because there are no adequate norms for children as young as the ones in this study, and the test was not given to the normal sample. The mean score was 75.8, S.D. = 12.7. We mention this test again later in the chapter.

The intervention had three main facets: the phonemic awareness program used in the longitudinal training study documented previously, intensive training in the letters representing the phonemes used, and shared book reading. The book reading was modeled on a program pioneered and researched by Whitehurst and his colleagues at Stony Brook (Whitehurst et al., 1988), and involves structured activities designed to engage the child and to promote knowledge of print and of language skills. It is entitled *dialogic reading*. The children were taught in groups ranging from one to six subjects, depending for the most part on patterns of attendance at preschool. The number of weeks of instruction, at about 40 minutes per week in a single session, ranged from 16 to 20.

Posttests included phonological awareness, alphabet knowledge, concepts about print, and the structured decoding test used in the longitudinal

TABLE 12.3
Preintervention and Postintervention Means (and Standard Deviations)
for At-Risk Preschoolers Who Have Completed Intervention ($N = 40$)

Test	Preintervention	Postintervention
Phonemic awareness	10.7 (2.3)	14.1 (2.6)
Rhyme awareness	5.8 (2.7)	7.5 (2.2)
Letter names	9.7 (5.4)	13.1 (7.0)
Print awareness	3.4 (2.4)	7.9 (3.5)

study (does *sat* say "sat" or "mat," etc.). There were significant improvements in phonemic and rhyme awareness, in alphabet knowledge, and in print awareness (see Table 12.3). The decoding test score, 8.0, was significantly above the chance value of 6, $t(39) = 5.26$, $p < .001$.

The improvement is not surprising given the intensiveness of the teaching. What is more instructive is comparing these children with the longitudinal sample at the same stage, and with that comparison things look less rosy (even though the intervention was more extensive for the at-risk children, including as it did the shared book reading and letter training). Only 5% of the "normal" sample showed no growth in phonemic awareness across the period of instruction, compared with 32% of the at-risk children. The respective figures for substantial improvement (to substantially above-chance values) were 93% and 48%. Just 2% of the longitudinal sample could be classed as showing partial improvement, compared with 20% of the at-risk children. In summary, close to a third of the at-risk children did not benefit from instruction that helped nearly all of an unselected sample of preschoolers, and another one fifth showed only marginal improvement compared to just 1 in 50 of the normal sample.

Interestingly, on the test of decoding the at-risk children performed as well as the normal intervention group, with means of 8.0 out of 12 and 8.1 out of 12, respectively. Their strong showing, despite lower mean levels of phonemic awareness, can be attributed to the more intensive letter instruction given to the at-risk children than to the comparison sample. Only 28% (11 out of 40) did not have secure knowledge of the critical letters, compared with 44% of the less intensively trained normal sample.

Although the training regimens for the at-risk and normal children were not the same in all respects (more attention was paid to letter knowledge for the at-risk sample, plus they received dialogic reading), the relative contributions to decoding from letter knowledge and phonemic awareness were virtually identical across the two groups. Recall that for our control children the contributions to decoding from knowledge of the letters involved in the decoding test and phonemic awareness were 43% and 11%, respectively (Table 12.1). The analogous figures for the at-risk group were 41% and 13%, to the same total of 54%. Thus it appears that at-risk children utilize their basic understanding of phonological structure and knowledge of letter-sound correspondences to underpin print decoding in the same kind of way as normal children do. Just like the normals, they rely on the combination of phonemic awareness and alphabet to support decoding. We find this encouraging in that it suggests to us that once basic knowledge is available to at-risk children, their progress in the early stages of reading acquisition proceeds as normal. This, in turn, suggests that the first place to focus in intervention is on these foundation insights and knowledge—phonemic awareness and letter-sound correspondences. Of course, the possibility of continuing difficulties that are due to processes entering reading mastery at later stages is not ruled out by this analysis.

Table 12.4 presents correlations between pretest variables and the two main outcome measures, phonemic awareness and decoding (the structured word choice test). The only variable in our pretest battery that correlated significantly with posttest phonemic awareness was confrontation naming, the 100 Pictures Test. Interestingly, the PPVT, a recognition naming test, did not correlate with phonemic awareness. This finding is reminiscent of the observation of Katz (1986) that older children with identified reading problems have difficulties in accurate name recall, even when they are familiar with the objects and their names as recognition vocabulary items. It is also consistent with the accounts of naming deficits in reading-disabled children (see Bowers & Wolf, 1993, for a review).

In predicting decoding, note that the naming task is again a significant correlate, but this time probably because of its association with phonemic awareness (the naming test does not increase the variance accounted for in decoding above the 54% accounted for by critical letter knowledge and phoneme identity). Pretest letter knowledge also correlates significantly, probably through its association with knowledge of the six letters critical

TABLE 12.4
Correlations Between Pretest Measures and Postintervention Phonemic
Awareness and Decoding for At-Risk Children

Postintervention Measure	Verbal IQ (PPVT)	Phonemic Awareness	Rhyme Awareness	Naming (100 Pictures Test)	Letter Names	Print Awareness (CAP)
			Pretest Measures			
Phonemic awareness	.13	.07	.23	.44*	.19	.22
Decoding	.01	−.08	.26	.44*	.38*	.20

*p < .01.

to the decoding task (pretest letter knowledge does not increase variance accounted for in decoding above the 54% mentioned previously).

The pretest measure of phonemic awareness did not correlate significantly with either posttest phonemic awareness or decoding. This is probably due to the chance-level performance of all but 3 of the 40 children. That is, most of the variance in pretest scores did not signify variance in embryonic levels of phonemic awareness.

We next summarize this preliminary report of the at-risk intervention study in the framework of what we know and what we don't.

Question 3: What We Know. We do know several things. First, we know that preschool children selected on the basis of a family history of reading difficulties show a profile characteristic of older children with reading problems. Second, we know that a smaller proportion of these children than normal respond to an intervention program that advances the phonemic awareness of an unselected sample of preschool children. Third, we know that of the pretests that we ran, only naming correlated significantly with improvements in phonemic awareness under the intervention. And fourth, we know that at-risk children move into decoding on the same combination of phonemic awareness and letter knowledge on which normal children depend.

Question 3: What We Don't Know. We don't know two things: If genetic factors are at work within this sample of children, how do they influence how much children profit from the intervention? What do we do about the children who resist acquiring insights into phonological structure?

At this point, we venture some impressions gained in observing these children, particularly the ones who make little progress. In watching these children struggle even with ideas like rhyme ("do plane and train sound like each other?" "Sure, you can go places in both"), the very distinct impression was of modularity at work, at least the cognitive impenetrability aspect of modularity. The speech code was simply not available as an object of contemplation to these children—it was just an access route to meaning. Despite our best efforts, they glazed over when invited to think about the constituent sounds of the words in vocabularies. The invitation meant nothing to them.

We believe that resistant children need one-to-one tutoring, but this should be delivered sensitively. There is always the danger that continued failure in the face of intensive tutoring will induce negative attitudes in such children, and there may be cases where leaving intervention until the child is older would be wise. We have yet to gather data on how being in the at-risk category, being a treatment resistor, and being young might interact to undermine literacy devlopment. Until we do, we do not feel confident to make recommendations about how to handle these difficult cases. It is hoped that future research, by us and others, will result in worthwhile guidelines.

Question 4: Later Progress in Reading

The final selection of studies from our group addresses the relative contributions of print exposure and the child's pseudoword decoding ability to the development of word-specific knowledge in older readers. Treating print exposure as environmental input and decoding skill now as the child's contribution to further development of orthographic knowledge, we can consider this question within the general framework that encompasses these various research projects.

It is known that better decoders, on the average, are quicker to learn irregularly spelled English words than are poor decoders, quite possibly because they can exploit whatever regularities exist in "irregular" words to help create high-quality orthographic representations, tied at multiple levels to the word's phonology (Ehri, 1992; Gough & Walsh, 1991). The data we present examine relative contributions of decoding and print exposure to orthographic knowledge across school grades and between normally achieving and disabled readers (more complete details are in Larsen, 1994).

We developed a title recognition test (Cunningham & Stanovich, 1990) for Australian children's literature, and administered it to second-, third-, and fourth-grade good and poor readers. In addition, we assessed word-specific knowledge using irregularly spelled words like *height, plough,* and *chalk,* and decoding using nonwords like *fidot, peb,* and *yentop.* Irregular word reading, the criterion variable, was treated as an index of orthographic knowledge. Decoding and the title recognition score were entered in that order as predictors. Table 12.5 contains the results. There was an increasing contribution from print exposure as children progressed through the school grades.

In the context of the present volume, however, we are more interested in the pattern for disabled readers (also shown in Table 12.5). We have data for 33 grade 3 and 28 grade 4 children classified as 18 months or more behind grade level on the Neale Analysis of Reading (Neale, 1988). These children were administered the same reading and title recognition tests as were the normal children. As expected, they scored significantly lower than the normal children on each of the reading lists, and lower on the title recognition test, too. Important for the regression analysis, however, the disabled readers' variances on the predictor measures of decoding and print exposure were as large or larger than the normal children's. Thus,

TABLE 12.5
Regression Analyses Predicting Word-Specific Knowledge
(Irregular Word Reading) From Decoding (Pseudoword Reading)
and Print Exposure (Title Recognition Test); Normal
and Reading-Disabled Children by Grades

Grade	Step	Normal Children R^2 Change	Reading-Disabled Children R^2 Change
2	Decoding	.66**	(Not tested)
	Print exposure	.00	
3	Decoding	.34**	.05
	Print exposure	.04*	.14**
4	Decoding	.27**	.06
	Print exposure	.16**	.25**

*$p < .05$. **$p < .01$.

there is no question of restriction of range explaining the different patterns in the regression analyses, which are presented in Table 12.5

In contrast to the normal readers, the ability of the disabled readers to decode pseudowords did not contribute significantly to explaining the variance in word-specific knowledge, and the contributions of print exposure were higher. Thus, it appears that for the reading-disabled children the growth of word-specific knowledge is unaffected by whatever decoding skills they use to read nonwords, and is inordinately dependent on having seen the words in print. In that sense, they appear to constitute a special population. It is not just that the fourth-grade poor readers, for example, are behaving like second-grade normal children—second graders show very heavy reliance on decoding in the acquisition of a sight-word vocabulary. For retarded readers in our samples, there was a clear dissociation between decoding of pseudowords and irregular word reading, something that is quite uncharacteristic of normal readers. The ability to decode pseudowords can be treated as a proxy for the ability to decode previously unencountered real words. Conceivably, therefore, the (low) levels of pseudoword reading that the poor readers in our samples exhibited may be insufficient to help them find and fix in memory the pronunciations of real words, including irregular ones, almost all of which benefit to some degree from regular letter-sound relationships.

On the basis of these observations, we would expect disabled readers to continue to make very slow progress in developing high-quality orthographic representations—it would seem that about the only way they can compensate for their low and underutilized decoding skills is to read copiously, and this is precisely what their problems, and maybe their social settings, discourage them from doing.

Question 4: What We Know. We know that print exposure makes an increasing contribution to children's orthographic knowledge as they advance through the school system. Also, we know that poor readers do not appear to be able to employ the decoding skills they possess in supporting the development of orthographic knowledge.

Question 4: What We Don't Know. We don't know why there appears to be a functional dissociation between nonword and irregular reading in disabled readers. Is it because disabled readers have levels of decoding that are below some threshold for assisting in the deciphering and fixing of irregular words, or is there some constitutional deficit that inhibits the development of a link between pseudoword decoding and knowledge of exception words? Additionally, we don't know how a functional link might be established between these two subskills in disabled readers.

CONCLUSION

We think that the answer to the question of whether the acquisition of reading needs substantial amounts of environmental support must be in the affirmative. From children's earliest ideas about print through their understanding of the alphabetic principle to the setting up of high-quality orthographic representations for speech, they need to be directly instructed and given many opportunities to experience print. Some children appear to require more external input than do others, right from the beginning.

If there is another uniting theme in this collection of research studies it is the importance of ensuring that children have a firm grip on the alphabetic principle and on the derived skill of deciphering novel print sequences. The consequences of failing to do so are serious. It appears that we cannot rely on children figuring out these things for themselves, but we are beginning to get a clearer understanding of how to help children gain the insights and master the skills.

As far as future directions in research are concerned, our *what we don't know* lists provide some specific research questions. In general, we need to identify those points at which children "fall between the cracks" in reading acquisition, and to develop effective intervention techniques that prevent them from doing so. If we can, in addition, identify in advance those children who are at risk of going astray, so much the better. But as Vellutino, Scanlon, and Sipay (chap. 16, this volume) argue, learning disabilities only truly become apparent when children try to learn, and fail. To emphasise prior identification at the expense of careful assessment while children are actually learning to read risks missing children who really need help. In this regard, as in most others concerning the acquisition of literacy, it is important not to believe that we know more than we do.

ACKNOWLEDGMENTS

Ruth Fielding-Barnsley made a special contribution to the research described as Questions 2 and 3, Luise Ashley to Question 3, and Kim Larsen to Question 4. We are indebted to Ken Brookman, Fiona King, Sarah Lawrence, and Amanda White, who taught many of the preschool children described in Queston 3. The research has been substantially supported by grants from the Australian Research Council, to whom we express gratitude. We also thank the very many children who participated in the studies, the parents who gave us permission to work with their children, and the staffs of the schools and preschools who have supported and encouraged the research.

REFERENCES

Blachman, B. A., Ball, E. W., Black, R. S., & Tangel, D. M. (1994). Kindergarten teachers develop phoneme awareness in low-income, inner-city classrooms: Does it make a difference? *Reading and Writing, 6,* 1–18.

Bowers, P. G., & Wolf, M. (1993). Theoretical links among naming speed, precise timing mechanisms and orthographic skill in dyslexia. *Reading and Writing, 5,* 69–86.

Bradley, L., & Bryant, P. E. (1983). Categorizing sounds and learning to read—a causal connection. *Nature, 301,* 419–421.

Byrne, B. (1992). Studies in the acquisition procedure for reading: Rationale, hypotheses, and data. In P. B. Gough, L. C. Ehri, & R. Treiman (Eds.), *Reading acquisition* (pp. 1–34). Hillsdale, NJ: Lawrence Erlbaum Associates.

Byrne, B. (1996). The learnability of the alphabetic principle: Children's initial hypotheses about how print represents spoken language. *Applied Psycholinguistics, 17,* 401–426.

Byrne, B., & Fielding-Barnsley, R. (1991). Evaluation of a program to teach phonemic awareness to young children. *Journal of Educational Psychology, 83,* 451–455.

Byrne, B., & Fielding-Barnsley, R. (1993a). Evaluation of a program to teach phonemic awareness to young children: A 1-year follow-up. *Journal of Educational Psychology, 85,* 104–111.

Byrne, B., & Fielding-Barnsley, R. (1993b). Recognition of phoneme invariance by beginning readers: Confounding effects of global similarity. *Reading and Writing, 6,* 315–324.

Byrne, B., & Fielding-Barnsley, R. (1995). Evaluation of a program to teach phonemic awareness to young children: A 2- and 3-year follow-up and a new preschool trial. *Journal of Educational Psychology, 87,* 488–503.

Cardon, L. R., Smith, S. D., Fulker, D. W., Kimberling, W. J., Pennington, B. F., & DeFries, J. C. (1994). Quantitative trait locus for reading disability on Chromosome 6. *Science, 266,* 276–279.

Carey, S. (1982). Semantic development: The state of the art. In E. Wanner & L. R. Gleitman (Eds.), *Language acquisition: The state of the art* (pp. 347–389). Cambridge, England: Cambridge University Press.

Clay, M. (1975). *The early detection of reading difficulties: A diagnostic survey.* Auckland, New Zealand: Heinemann.

Crain, S. (1991). Language acquisition in the absence of experience. *Behavioral and Brain Sciences, 14,* 597–650.

Cunningham, A. E. (1990). Explicit versus implicit instruction in phonemic awareness. *Journal of Experimental Child Psychology, 50,* 429–444.

Cunningham, A. E., & Stanovich, K. E. (1990). Assessing print exposure and orthographic skill in children: A quick measure of reading experience. *Journal of Educational Psychology, 82,* 733–740.

Dunn, L. M., & Dunn, L. M. (1981). *Peabody picture vocabulary test—revised.* Circle Pines, MN: American Guidance Service.

Ehri, L. C. (1992). Reconceptualizing the development of sight word reading and its relationship to recoding. In P. B. Gough, L. C. Ehri, & R. Treiman (Eds.), *Reading acquisition* (pp. 107–143). Hillsdale, NJ: Lawrence Erlbaum Associates.

Ferreiro, E. (1986). The interplay between information and assimilation in beginning literacy. In W. H. Teale & E. Sulzby (Eds.), *Emergent literacy: Writing and reading* (pp. 15–49). Norwood, New Jersey: Ablex.

Fielding-Barnsley, R. (1997). Explicit instruction in decoding benefits children high in phonemic awareness and alphabet knowledge. *Scientific Studies of Reading, 1,* 82–95.

Fisher, J. P., & Glenister, J. M. (1992). *The hundred pictures naming test.* Hawthorn, Australia: Australian Council for Educational Research.

Gilger, J. W., Pennington, B. F., & DeFries, J. C. (1991). Risk for reading disability as a function of parental history in three family studies. *Reading and Writing, 3,* 205–218.

Goodman, K. S. (1986). *What's whole about whole language: A parent–teacher guide.* Portsmouth, NH: Heinemann.

Gough, P. B., & Walsh, M. A. (1991). Chinese, Phoenicians, and the orthographic cipher of English. In S. Brady & D. Shankweiler (Eds.), *Phonological processes in literacy: A tribute to Isabelle Y. Liberman* (pp. 199–209). Hillsdale, NJ: Lawrence Erlbaum Associates.

Hatcher, P., Hulme, C., & Ellis, A. W. (1994). Ameliorating early reading failure by integrating the teaching of reading and phonological skills: The phonological linkage hypothesis. *Child Development, 65,* 41–57.

Johnston, P. H. (1985). Understanding reading disability. *Harvard Educational Review, 55,* 153–177.

Katz, R. B. (1986). Phonological deficiencies in children with reading disability: Evidence from an object-naming task. *Cognition, 22,* 250–257.

Larsen, K. P. (1994). *Irregular word reading, nonword reading, and print exposure.* Unpublished master's thesis, University of New England, Armidale, New South Wales, Australia.

Liberman, I. Y., & Liberman, A. M. (1992). Whole language versus code emphasis: Underlying assumptions and their implications for reading instruction. In P. B. Gough, L. C. Ehri, & R. Treiman (Eds.), *Reading acquisition* (pp. 343–366). Hillsdale, NJ: Lawrence Erlbaum Associates.

Miller, G. A. (1977). *Spontaneous apprentices.* New York: Seabury.

Neale, M. D. (1988). *Neale analysis of reading ability—revised.* Hawthorn, Australia: Australian Council for Educational Research.

Olson, R. K., Gillis, J. J., Rack, J. P., DeFries, J. C., & Fulker, D. W. (1991). Confirmatory factor analysis of word recognition and process measures in the Colorado reading project. *Reading and Writing, 3,* 235–248.

Scarborough, H. S. (1989). Prediction of reading disability from familial and individual differences. *Journal of Educational Psychology, 81,* 101–108.

Scarborough, H. S. (1991). Antecedents to reading disability: Preschool language development and literacy experiences of children from dyslexic families. *Reading and Writing, 3,* 219–234.

Seidenberg, M. S. (1992). Dyslexia in a computational model of word recognition in reading. In P. B. Gough, L. C. Ehri, & R. Treiman (Eds.), *Reading acquisition* (pp. 243–273). Hillsdale, NJ: Lawrence Erlbaum Associates.

Torgesen, J. K., Morgan, S. T., & Davis, C. (1992). Effects of two types of phonological awareness training on word learning in kindergarten children. *Journal of Educational Psychology, 84,* 364–370.

Whitehurst, G. J., Falco, F., Lonigan, C. J., Fischel, J. E., Valdez-Manchaca, M. C., & Caulfield, M. (1988). Accelerating language development through picture-book reading. *Developmental Psychology, 24,* 552–558.

Approaches to the Prevention
and Remediation of Phonologically
Based Reading Disabilities

Joseph K. Torgesen
Richard K. Wagner
Carol A. Rashotte
Florida State University

There are few topics in education that have been the subject of as much heated discussion and controversy as the issue of how best to help children learn to read. Although research on this topic has a long history (Adams, 1990; Clark, 1988), it is still a topic about which there is enormous diversity of opinion among both researchers and teachers. Part of the problem, of course, is that the question of how best to teach children to read is too broadly focused to be addressed by a single answer. Answers to this question are likely to be conditional upon many different factors, such as the abilities and motivations that children bring with them to school; the abilities, knowledge, personality, and motivation of their teachers; and the support for the child available in the home and neighborhood. With these factors, and others, providing contextual constraints on effectiveness of various instructional methods, it is not surprising that we currently have so little consensus about instructional methods for children who experience special difficulties learning to read.

Although there is no denying the difficulties of obtaining clear, research-based answers to instructional questions for children with reading disabilities, recent scientific advances in several areas do make it possible now to conduct studies that may lead to more definitive answers than have been available in the past. In this chapter, our goal is to provide an overview of a recently initiated program of research to study both the prevention and remediation of a specific type of reading disabilities. The chapter is divided into three sections. First, we briefly describe the scientific advances upon which the research is built. Second, we discuss assumptions and rationale for specific aspects of our research approach. Third, the chapter concludes with a presentation of preliminary findings from a prevention study that is currently under way.

A SCIENTIFIC CONTEXT FOR INTERVENTION RESEARCH ON READING DISABILITIES

The last 20 years have been a very productive period in the study of reading and reading disabilities. For example, we now have a much improved understanding of the nature and developmental course of specific developmental reading disability (dyslexia), and we also know a great deal more about the reading acquisition process per se. Improvements in knowledge in both of these areas provide a useful starting place for modern intervention research on reading disabilities. In addition, there have also been important developments in methods of measurement and analysis of growth patterns in individual children that make it possible to obtain a more complete picture of variability in response to different instructional approaches than has been possible in the past. Each of these developments is now briefly reviewed.

The Nature of Developmental Reading Disabilities

Systematic research on reading disabilities over the last 2 decades has produced a strong consensus that the fundamental reading problem for most dyslexic children involves difficulties acquiring accurate and fluent word identification skills (Morrison, 1987; Stanovich, 1988). More specifically, most reading-disabled children have great difficulty learning to utilize regularities in correspondence between graphemes and phonemes in translating written to oral language (Rack, Snowling, & Olson, 1992; Vellutino & Scanlon, 1991). Children with reading disabilities are often unable to attain fully alphabetic or phonological reading skills. Not only does this limit their early independence in reading, but it probably also interferes with subsequent development of orthographic word reading strategies that are the basis for fluent reading (Share & Stanovich, 1995).

The most widely accepted current explanation for the difficulties of dyslexic children in acquiring accurate word reading skills involves a dysfunction "in the phonological component of their natural capacity for language" (Liberman, Shankweiler, & Liberman, 1989, p. 1). This dysfunction limits the performance of dyslexic individuals on a variety of non-reading tasks, such as those that assess awareness of the phonological structure of words, those that require rapid access to phonological information in long-term memory, and those that involve representation of phonological information in short-term memory (Shankweiler & Liberman, 1989; Wagner & Torgesen, 1987). These intrinsic limitations in ability to process phonological information not only interfere with dyslexic children's understanding of how letters represent the sounds in words, but also limit the efficiency with which they can apply whatever understanding they are able to attain. Although there may be more than one subtype of specific developmental dyslexia (Castles & Coltheart, 1993), the best-described and most common subtype is phonologically based reading disability.

The Reading Acquisition Process

We now have a relatively clear understanding of the cognitive disabilities associated with the most common form of reading disabilities. However, before instructional implications can be derived from this information about the nature of dyslexia, the role of phonology, or phonological processes, in learning to read must also be well understood. Without such understanding, we run the risk of focusing or sequencing instruction inefficiently, or in the worst case, of missing critical instructional activities altogether.

There is, in fact, a very solid empirical and theoretical foundation supporting a critical role for phonological knowledge and skills in the development of reading ability. Two types of empirical studies have established a causal link between variation in phonological ability and progress in learning to read. First, training studies have shown that specific training in phonological awareness can have a positive impact on success in early reading (Ball & Blachman, 1991; Bradley & Bryant, 1985; Brady, Fowler, Stone, & Winbury, 1994; Cunningham, 1990; Lundberg, Frost, & Peterson, 1988; Torgesen, Morgan, & Davis, 1992). A few studies have shown that training in phonological awareness as an oral language skill, by itself, can positively influence rate of reading acquisition. However, most studies show that combining phonological awareness training with training in letter-sound correspondences is most effective in accelerating the rate of growth in reading skills.

The second method for studying causal relationships between phonological abilities and reading growth has involved the use of path analysis and structural equation models of longitudinal data. For example, we have recently reported (Torgesen, Wagner, & Rashotte, 1994; Wagner, Torgesen, & Rashotte, 1994; Wagner et al., in press) very strong evidence from a large randomly selected sample that variation in phonological skills among kindergarten, first-, and second-grade children are critically important in determining the subsequent growth of their ability to read

words accurately. Both individual differences in awareness of the phonological structure of words and ability to rapidly access phonological
information in long-term memory (Bowers, Golden, Kennedy, & Young,
1994) are causally related to children's ability to acquire effective word
reading skills.

Share and his colleagues (Share & Jorm, 1987; Share & Stanovitch, 1995)
recently proposed the self-teaching model of reading acquisition, which
proposes a central role for phonological skill in reading growth. This
model integrates a vast amount of data to show that phonological abilities
and alphabetic reading skills are critical to both early independence in
reading and to growth of fully specified orthographic representations for
words that are the basis of accurate and fluent reading in mature readers.

In this model, emergent skills in phonological decoding, which consist
of letter-sound knowledge and a basic level of phonological awareness,
provide the basis for acquiring accurate orthographic representations of
words from the very beginning of the learning process. A basic proposition of the model is that if children use partial or complete phonological
cues to derive an approximate pronunciation for a word in text, and
combine this approximate pronunciation with contextual constraints to
identify the fully correct pronunciation, the prior attention to individual
letters that is involved in alphabetic decoding provides a solid basis for
acquisition or refinement of an orthographic representation for the word.
As children's increasingly developed alphabetic reading skills lead to
more detailed analysis of the internal structure of words in print, they
begin to acquire increasingly explicit and more fully specified orthographic representations. However, according to the self-teaching model,
if children's alphabetic reading skills do not develop, their orthographic
representations are likely to remain incompletely specified, and they will
be inaccurate readers and poor spellers.

Measurement of Growth and Change

The third major scientific advance mentioned at the beginning of this
section, involving methods for the analysis of change and growth, provides an important new way to describe the impact of interventions on
individual children. Whereas traditional measures for analysis of treatment effects allowed tests of hypotheses about change in groups, new
methods, involving the estimation of individual growth curves for each
subject within groups, allow an examination of factors associated with
variation in children's response to specific instructional methods (Francis,
Fletcher, Stuebing, Davidson, & Thompson, 1991; Willett, 1988).

This latter capability provides an important new tool for dealing with
the inevitable heterogeneity within any sample of reading-disabled chil-

dren, no matter how carefully selected. For example, even though our research focuses on children with phonologically based reading disabilities, our samples are heterogeneous with regard to other variables important to learning. Children in our samples vary in general intelligence, other language skills, socioeconomic background, race, gender, and level of symptoms of attention deficit disorder. The advantage of using individual growth curves to describe the changes occurring as a result of treatment is that we can study the way these additional factors influenced response to treatment without having to depend upon an a priori typology for classifying the children into more homogeneous subgroups. Furthermore, we can use all the information present in our independent variables, because these techniques allow the use of continuously distributed variables, rather than just categorical variables, in examining the correlates of change (Ragosa, 1988).

Summary of Recent Advances as a Context for Intervention Research

The material reviewed briefly in this section documents recent advances that may help intervention research to provide clearer answers to questions about instructional methods for reading-disabled children than have been available in the past. We now understand that the primary locus of reading difficulty for dyslexic children involves problems in acquiring accurate and fluent word reading skills. Furthermore, we have solid evidence that the primary basis of these word reading difficulties involves inefficiency in processing the phonological features of language. We also have both data and theory showing how phonological abilities and alphabetic reading skills are critically important in general models of reading acquisition. Finally, we have available new data analytic techniques that allow a much more complete description of the factors that influence individual differences in response to specific instructional methods.

GUIDING ASSUMPTIONS OF OUR INTERVENTION RESEARCH

Based on the scientific advances outlined previously, both our prevention research and remediation research are guided by four principles:

1. *The research should be focused on children with phonologically based reading disabilities.* We chose this focus because of the evidence that this is the most common form of reading disability, and because it is possible to identify children at risk for this type of disability before reading

instruction begins. Evidence on this latter point is presented in the next section.

2. *If preventive and remedial approaches to reading instruction are to be successful, they* must *lead to the development of accurate and fluent text-based word reading skills.* Because of the consensus that difficulties with word identification processes are the primary bottleneck to reading growth in dyslexic children, instructional approaches must effectively address this component skill. Although many of these children may also require special instruction to support comprehension processes, the first instructional goal should be enhancement of growth in word reading ability.

3. *As the basis for early independence in word identification and gradual development of fully specified orthographic representations, the early growth of alphabetic reading skills* must *be fostered.* In other words, the path to accurate and fluent text-based word reading ability starts with the early development of alphabetic reading skills. This may be our most controversial principle, because of the difficulties in previous research in teaching generalizable alphabetic reading skills to children with phonologically based reading disabilities (Lovett, Warren-Chaplin, Ransby, & Borden, 1990; Lyon, 1985; Snowling & Hulme, 1989). However, given the importance of alphabetic, or phonological, reading skills in most scientific accounts of reading growth (Adams, 1990; Share & Stanovich, 1995; Vellutino, 1991), it seems essential to address this issue in effective instruction for children with reading disabilities.

4. *As a basis for the acquisition of the alphabetic principle, instruction* must *stimulate the growth of phonological awareness.* This principle is based on evidence that individual differences in phonological awareness are causally related to the acquisition of effective word reading skills.

Although the instructional directions contained in the last three principles seem relatively clear, there are many important questions that remain open for research. For example, should instruction in alphabetic reading skills utilize traditional synthetic phonics methods that provide intensive, decontextualized practice in "sounding out" both words and nonwords, or should phonics instruction be embedded within the context of whole word reading and intertwined with the use of context? There is a possibility, for example, that the former type of instruction may overload the weak phonological abilities of many children, whereas the latter approach may not provide enough systematic instruction and practice in alphabetic reading strategies to establish an analytic approach when confronted with new words in text. Second, there may be important instructional options in stimulating phonological awareness in children with phonological weaknesses. Phonological awareness can be stimulated directly through oral language activities that do not involve letters, or it can be stimulated through writing and spelling activities that are embedded within the context of reading instruction. Which of these approaches, or what kind of balance between them, will prove most effective for children with phonological reading disabilities is an unresolved question. Finally, it is clear that children must be taught to use whatever alphabetic reading skills they acquire in the service of getting meaning from text. Whether to focus relatively more time on building autonomous alphabetic decoding skills or to work toward earlier integration of phonics and context based skills to decipher meaningful text is an important question that also remains open.

In the research reported in the next section, we hope to be able to provide beginning answers to some of these questions by contrasting instructional methods that vary along some of the dimensions already outlined.

A Program of Research to Study Preventive and Remedial Interventions

We are presently engaged in a 5-year project funded by the National Institute of Child Health and Human Development to conduct both prevention and remediation studies with children who have phonologically based reading disabilities. Each of these studies has two major goals: to determine which type of instructional program has the largest immediate impact on word level reading skills, and long-term impact on fluency and comprehension skills; and to determine the individual characteristics (cognitive, family background, behavioral) that are most strongly predictive of individual differences in both immediate and long-term response to the instructional programs examined. Although a total of four studies (two prevention, two remediation) will be conducted, in this section we focus only on the first prevention study that is currently in progress.

Until recently, an important impediment to research on the prevention of reading disabilities has been the lack of means to identify theoretically coherent groups of at-risk children before reading instruction begins. With development of knowledge about the role of phonological processes in early reading growth, this is no longer the obstacle it once was. For example, in a longitudinal sample of randomly selected children we have been studying for several years, we used logistic regression procedures to identify the children most likely to be in the bottom 10% of readers in second grade (244 children remained in the sample at second grade, after excluding four children with estimated verbal IQ below 75). The predictive measures, which included letter name knowledge, phonological awareness, and rapid naming ability for digits, were administered in the first semester of kindergarten. These procedures identified 23 children as at risk to show serious, phonologically based reading disabilities by second grade. Of these 23 at-risk children, 14 actually obtained reading scores in the bottom 10% in second grade. Of the nine "false positives" in this group, five were in the bottom 20%, two in the bottom 30%, and two were slightly above-average readers. A comparison of the the at-risk group with the entire sample on measures taken at mid-second grade is provided in Table 13.1.

The SES score is the combined parental score on the Hollingshead Four Factor Index of Social Status (Hollingshead, 1975). The Word Attack and Word Identification subtests are from the *Woodcock Reading Mastery Test—Revised* (Woodcock, 1987), and Verbal Intelligence was estimated from the Vocabulary subtest of the *Stanford Binet Intelligence Scale: Fourth Edition* (Thorndike, Hagen, & Sattler, 1986). Scores on these latter three tests are standard scores derived from the test standardization sample. All phonological scores are unit-weighted composites of the several tests associated with each phonological variable in the measurement model from our longitudinal study (Wagner et al., 1994), and they have been standardized on our sample (Mean = 100, S.D. = 15). It is clear from this table that our procedures can be used to identify a group of children seriously impaired in both word-level reading skills and phonological processing in the second grade. The at-risk group is significantly different from the sample as a whole on all measures except verbal intelligence, with the difference between groups being particularly large for word-level reading skills and some of the phonological variables. Within the at-risk group, estimated verbal intelligence ranged from 82 to 128.

TABLE 13.1
Comparison of At-Risk Children With Total Sample
on Selected Variables at Mid-Second Grade

Variable	At-Risk (n = 23)		Rest of Sample (n = 221)	
	Mean	S.D.	Mean	S.D.
SES	36.2	(13.5)	43.8	(12.3)
Word attack	79.0	(13.9)	93.6	(15.3)
Word identification	77.4	(15.8)	99.5	(17.7)
Letter-sound naming	89.2	(16.1)	101.1	(15.0)
Phonological analysis	88.5	(17.2)	101.2	(13.4)
Phonological synthesis	87.7	(17.8)	101.3	(13.4)
Phonological memory	92.2	(14.4)	100.8	(13.3)
Rapid automatic naming of digits and letters	82.1	(17.0)	101.9	(14.3)
Verbal intelligence (SB-Voc)	95.1	(11.7)	100.7	(15.6)
Gender	12F	11M	118F	103M
Race	13W	10B	170W	51B

In selecting the sample for our current prevention study, we first screened 1,436 kindergarten children from 13 elementary schools in the first month of school using a test of letter-name knowledge. From this initial sample, 382 children were selected for further screening using a phoneme elision task (deletion of a phoneme in a word), serial naming for numbers (naming a series of 36 single digits as rapidly as possible), and the Stanford-Binet Vocabulary subtest (Thorndike et al., 1986). Because so few of these children were able to identify number names correctly, this task was not used in the final selection criteria. Two hundred children were selected because of extremely low scores on the letter naming and phoneme elision tasks, along with performance on the vocabulary subtest indicating an estimated verbal IQ above 75.

Subjects in the final sample were randomly assigned to four treatment conditions: a group receiving explicit oral and phonological awareness training plus synthetic phonics instruction (PASP), a group receiving implicit phonological awareness training plus phonics instruction embedded within real-word reading and spelling activities (EP), a regular classroom support group receiving individual instruction to support the goals of the regular classroom reading program (RCS), and a no-treatment control group.

Although the subjects in our study were selected to be relatively homogeneous with regard to their level of phonological development in kindergarten, they are heterogeneous on a number of other important variables. For example, estimated verbal intelligence ranges from 78 to 126, and the children vary broadly in socioeconomic status and home literacy environment. We also expect children in the sample to vary in the extent they show attentional problems, because of the results of recent epidemiological studies (Wood, Felton, & Flowers, & Naylor, 1992) that suggest extensive comorbidity of phonologically based reading disabilities and attention deficit disorder (ADD). Finally, the sample is composed of 54% minorities (largely African American).

Children in each treatment condition are provided with 80 minutes of one-on-one supplemental instruction in reading each week that will go on for 2½ years, beginning in the second half of kindergarten. Two 20-minute instructional sessions are led by certified teachers, and two of the sessions are led by instructional aides who follow the teacher's instructions to reinforce what the children learned in the previous teacher-led session. We are assessing regular classroom reading instruction through the use of teacher surveys and direct observation in each classroom in which our subjects receive the bulk of their reading instruction.

This study contrasts the effectiveness of three different approaches to providing supplemental reading instruction for the at-risk children in our sample. The two experimental approaches contain relatively explicit instruction in phonics provided in two different ways. One of these approaches (PASP) is a multisensory synthetic phonics program containing intensive training in phonological and articulatory awareness, whereas the other approach (EP) provides less intensive, but still systematic, phonics training in the context of early and meaningful experiences in reading and writing text. Both approaches recognize that the children being treated have special difficulties processing phonological information. However, the PASP program attempts to ameliorate these difficulties through an intensive program of oral and phonological awareness training, whereas the EP program seeks to reduce the demands on these skills by using an approach to phonics instruction that does not require full phonological decoding, but instead emphasizes the early integration of partial phonological decodings with context clues to identify unknown words. The progress of children in these groups will be contrasted with each other and with a third regular classroom support group (RCS) that receives individual tutoring in the activities and skills being taught in the regular classroom reading program. Although this condition does not involve an experimental curriculum per se, a potential advantage of this group over the other two is that its instructional activities will be closely coordinated with the instructional activities taking place in the child's regular classroom. It is also included as a control against the possibility that the effectiveness of the experimental curriculums is primarily the result of intensity (one-on-one) of instruction rather than content or method. The curriculum in each of the three treatment conditions will now be briefly described.

The Phonological Awareness Plus Synthetic Phonics (PASP) Program. This group is receiving the Auditory Discrimination in Depth Program as outlined by Lindamood and Lindamood (1984) through kindergarten, first grade, and perhaps some of second grade. It will be followed by reading instruction and practice designed to consolidate and build on the phonological reading skills imparted by the early part of the program.

The program begins with instruction designed to make children aware of the specific mouth movements required to produce each phoneme. As part of this instruction, the children also learn labels for each phoneme that are descriptive of these mouth movements and positions (i.e., the label "lip popper" is used for the phonemes /b/ and /p/, the label "tip tapper" is assigned to the phonemes /t/ and /d/, and the phonemes /k/ and /g/ are labeled "scrapers"). Once the children attain a high criterion of knowledge in oral awareness, they engage in an extensive series of problem-solving exercises that involve representing sequences of phonemes with either mouth-form pictures or colored blocks. This training focuses on helping them acquire sensitivity to the sequences of sounds in syllables, and it also enables them to learn to represent these sequences with concrete visual objects. Throughout the program, instructional interactions consist primarily of questions that the teacher asks in order to help the child "discover" that he or she can "think about" the sounds in words by both feeling what happens in the mouth and hearing the sounds with the ear. The object of the teacher's questions is to help the children learn to verify the nature and order of the phonemes in words from their own sensory experience. As they learn to label each phoneme with a descriptive name, they are also taught to associate specific letters with each phoneme. Thus, once they become facile at representing sequences of sound with concrete objects, it is a natural transition to begin to represent them with letters.

All work in spelling and reading begins with nonword syllables first, in order to reinforce the habit of feeling and hearing the individual sounds in words. As students begin to experience success in spelling simple-syllable (CVC) patterns, they are introduced to reading similar patterns. Once children can accurately decode simple CVC words, they are explicitly introduced to the way some words deviate from regular pronunciation patterns. They are encouraged to notice the parts of irregular words that "do not play fair," and they are taught to rapidly recognize lists of high-frequency words, some of which are regular and others irregular. During this period in which alphabetic reading skills are being firmly established, the children also read short books in which the vocabulary is phonetically consistent with their decoding skills. After they have had some beginning practice reading multisyllable words, they begin to read stories from trade books, and they engage in the same activities with these books as the students in the "embedded phonics" program. During oral reading activities they are encouraged to rely on their skills in phonological decoding, but they are also encouraged to ask whether the pronunciation of an unfamiliar word "makes sense" in the context of the story. During second grade, most of the students also will write summaries of the stories they read, as well as engage in free writing activities.

The Embedded Phonics (EP) Program. In its early phases, the instructional periods in this program consist of four main activities: (a) acquiring a useful vocabulary of fluently recognized sight words by using word level drill and word games, (b) instruction in letter-sound correspondences in the context of the sight words being learned, (c) writing the words individually and in sentences, and (d) reading the sentences that are written. Some letter sounds (short vowel, *r*-controlled vowels) are taught through memorization of picture-word cards, but most grapheme–phoneme correspondences are taught in the context of writing activities. The children also receive direct instruction in a small number of highly useful phonics generalizations.

The words the children learn are taken from a basal series that contains short stories. The stories are read orally after the words in them are learned, and the primary emphasis during the entire basal phase is on acquiring word-level reading skills (sight vocabulary and supportive alphabetic decoding skills). After the children finish the first-grade reader in the basal series, the emphasis of the program shifts from learning to read by writing to learning to read by reading. Less time is spent on individual word drills, and more time is spent on reading stories from trade book series. Discussion focuses more on constructing the meaning of the stories that are read. Writing activities during this phase of instruction continue to include generation of sentences containing specific words, but more free writing and writing summaries of stories that are read are also included. During this later period, which will continue to the end of second grade, specific spelling instruction and practice will be provided not only on lists of words from the regular class, but also on a larger corpus of commonly occurring words.

The Regular Classroom Support (RCS) Group. The goal of the instruction and practice activities provided to this group is to support the reading instruction being provided in the regular classroom. The instruction provided to children in this group necessarily varies somewhat across the different schools in the study, but we had expected it to contain a preponderance of activities consistent with the whole-language approach to reading instruction.

The three most common instructional activities designated by the regular classroom teachers during the second semester of kindergarten involved learning the names of letters, learning to print letters, and child dictation of sentences followed by teacher-supported reading of the sentences. Although the classrooms from which our sample was taken employ a primarily whole-language approach to reading instruction, the regular classroom teachers apparently recognize the word reading difficulties of the children in our project. Thus, in first grade, they have consistently tended to ask our teachers to engage in a variety of activities to strengthen alphabetic reading skills and sight word vocabulary. This has tended to make the RCS condition more similar to the EP condition than we had anticipated when we began the study.

Throughout the instructional period, and for two years afterward, we will monitor the growth of children in the study on a variety of reading and other cognitive skills. Thus far, we have conducted four assessments of their word-level reading skills and phonological awareness. Although we have not yet conducted analyses of individual growth patterns, Figure 13.1 provides a picture of growth in real-word reading ability and alphabetic reading skills (as measured by ability to read phonetically regular

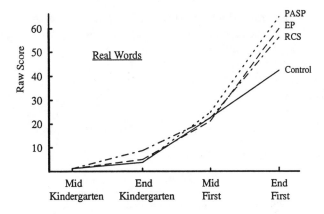

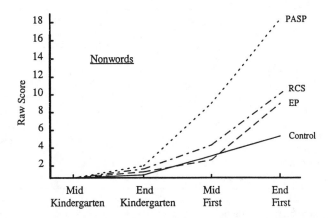

FIG. 13.1. Growth of word and nonword reading skills from mid-kindergarten to end of first grade. (Note: *Real Words* was an experimental test designed to be maximally sensitive to growth in word reading ability in young children. It consisted of 128 high-frequency, one- to three-syllable words, which were read from a list under untimed conditions. *Nonwords* was an experimental test designed to be maximally sensitive to the growth of alphabetic reading skills in young children. It was composed of 58 nonwords that gradually increased in difficulty from 2 to 7 phoneme words.)

nonwords) at the group level. The control group was assessed only at pretest, end of kindergarten, and end of first grade. At the end of first grade, all the treatment groups are reading real words equally well, and, as a group, they are reading significantly better than the no treatment control children. With regard to alphabetic reading skills, the PASP group is significantly ahead of all other groups, whereas the two other treatment groups are doing better than the no-treatment control group.

Table 13.2 provides data on some additional measures of reading, phonological awareness, and spelling taken at the end of first grade for the three treatment groups as well as children in the no-treatment control group. Similar to the experimental measure of alphabetic reading skills reported in Fig. 13.1, the largest differences among the groups occurred on the Word Attack subtest, which is also a measure of nonword reading. On this measure, the PASP group again performed significantly better than did the other treatment groups, whereas all the treatment groups performed better than the control group.

TABLE 13.2
Reading, Phonological Awareness, and Spelling
Scores for All Groups at the End of First Grade*

	Group							
	Control (N = 29)		RCS (N = 34)		PASP (N = 35)		EP (N = 33)	
Measure	X	S.D.	X	S.D.	X	S.D.	X	S.D.
Blend phonemes[1]	11.4	5.4	13.0	5.5	14.9	3.6	13.1	4.0
Phoneme elision[2]	8.8	2.9	10.2	4.8	11.6	4.1	9.5	4.0
Phoneme segmentation[3]	5.1	3.3	6.7	8.0	8.0	3.1	5.4	3.2
Word attack[4]	2.6	3.5	5.8	6.7	9.6	7.8	5.4	5.1
Word identification[5]	17.7	13.4	25.3	13.9	25.5	15.5	23.0	11.9
Passage comprehension[6]	7.3	6.7	11.4	7.1	10.7	7.5	9.6	6.5
Letter-sound knowledge[7]	21.5	6.6	26.9	4.2	29.1	3.3	26.4	4.0
Spelling[8]	17.3	6.7	19.1	6.4	20.8	4.8	19.2	5.0

*This table contains raw score data for children in the study who were promoted to first grade from kindergarten. Numbers in original sample not promoted to first grade in the Control, RCS, PASP, and EP groups were 7, 7, 2, and 7, respectively. We are continuing to train the children that were not promoted, but because their classroom experience is so different, their data are not included here.

[1]*Blending phonemes test*—a measure of phonological awareness that requires children to recognize spoken words from separately presented phonemes (e.g., /k/–/a/–/t/ = *cat*).

[2]*Phoneme elision*—a measure of phonological awareness that requires children to form a new word by deleting a specific sound from a target word (e.g., delete /d/ from *card* = *car*).

[3]*Phoneme segmentation*—a measure of phonological awareness that requires children to pronounce the phonemes in words separately (e.g., *cat* = /k/–/a/–/t/).

[4]*Word Attack* subtest from the Woodcock Reading Mastery Test—Revised (Woodcock, 1987).

[5]*Word Identification* subtest from the Woodcock Reading Mastery Test—Revised.

[6]*Passage Comprehension* subtest from the Woodcock Reading Mastery Test—Revised.

[7]*Letter-sound knowledge*—children are required to give all the sounds represented by individual letters. In cases where a letter typically represents more than one phoneme, the children are asked to give all the sounds the letter represents.

[8]*Spelling* subtest from the Wide Range Achievement Test—Revised (Jastak & Wilkinson, 1984).

Overall group differences on the phonological awareness measures were also significant, but the only group comparisons that were significant were between the PASP and the no-treatment control group. Overall group differences on the Word Identification and Passage Comprehension tests were not significant, although when the treatment groups are compared as a group with the no-treatment control group, the differences are statistically reliable. The overall group differences in knowledge of letter-sound correspondences were also reliable, with the PASP group attaining the highest score, and each of the other treatment groups scoring higher than the control group. Finally, the treatment groups performed better than did the control group on the spelling subtest of the Wide Range Achievement Test—Revised (Jastak & Wilkenson, 1984), although there were no differences among treatment groups.

At this point, we are encouraged by the fact that we have a strong manipulation of alphabetic reading skills among our groups. We are not surprised that this difference is not yet reflected in greater real-word reading skill on measures like the Word Identification subtest. There are both psychometric and experiential reasons why the PASP group's newly acquired alphabetic reading skills are not reflected in a more generalized reading advantage. However, if differential growth in alphabetic reading skills continues to characterize the groups through second grade, we would expect differences in this skill to have a more generalized impact on reading as the children progress through the early elementary grades. We want to stress at this time, however, that these results are far too preliminary to make conclusions about the relative effectiveness of the different methods. Not only are there no reliable differences among treatment groups in reading vocabulary or reading comprehension, but also it is very possible that the other groups may catch up in alphabetic reading skill during second grade. Alternatively, the EP group in particular may remain behind in alphabetic reading skills but nevertheless maintain equivalent growth in real-word reading and reading comprehension because of their emerging skill in integrating the use of partial phonics cues and context while reading text.

In addition to acceleration of growth at the group level, the special instruction has also had the effect of increasing variability of performance on measures of alphabetic reading skills. For example, in the PASP group, five children attained scores above the 2.6 grade level, whereas six children (17%) still attained a score of zero or one on the task. In contrast, in the no-treatment control group, 57% of the children attained a score of zero or one, whereas the highest score was at the 1.2 grade level, and only one child attained that score. Variability in performance on the other two treatment groups fell between these two extremes.

Although many of the children in our sample are clearly responding well to the opportunity for extra instruction provided in each of the treatment groups, is also clear that we have a substantial number of children who would, at this point, be classified as treatment resisters in each of our instructional conditions. Because we are planning to examine ways that various child characteristics (home and family background, behavioral characteristics both in the regular classroom and in our instructional sessions, and various cognitive and language abilities) predict individual growth in reading, we hope to acquire new understanding about the conditions under which children respond well or poorly to each instructional method. Of course, these analyses will be particularly interesting if different child characteristics are associated with good and poor performance for different instructional methods.

We recognize that the ultimate test of effectiveness for the preventive interventions we are studying will come in the years following the conclusion of the intervention. If our inteventions are not sufficient to build the capacity for continued growth in reading once they are finished, then, at least in one important sense, we will not have succeeded at the "prevention" task. At this point, it seems reasonable to expect that there will be significant diversity in children's continued growth following the intervention, and we are hoping that our examination of individual growth trajectories will provide useful information about the characteristics of children who may require additional instructional support. In this and other studies, our ultimate goal is to understand more about the instructional conditions that must be in place for *all children* to acquire during their elementary school years the foundation for useful adult reading skills.

ACKNOWLEDGMENTS

The research reported in this chapter was supported by grants number HD23340 and HD30988 from the National Institute of Child Health and Human Development, and by grants from the National Center for Learning Disabilities, and the Donald D. Hammill Foundation.

REFERENCES

Adams, M. J. (1990). *Beginning to read: Thinking and learning about print*. Cambridge, MA: MIT Press.

Ball, E. W., & Blachman, B. A. (1991). Does phoneme awareness trainng in kindergarten make a difference in early word recognition and developmental spelling? *Reading Research Quarterly, 26*, 49–66.

Bowers, P., Golden, J., Kennedy, A., & Young, A. (1994). Limits upon orthographic knowledge due to processes indexed by naming speed. In V. W. Berninger (Ed.) *The varieties of orthographic knowledge I: Theoretical and developmental issues* (pp. 173–216). Dordrecht, The Netherlands: Kluwer.

Bradley, L., & Bryant, P. (1985). *Rhyme and reason in reading and spelling.* Ann Arbor: University of Michigan Press.

Brady, S., Fowler, A., Stone, B., & Winbury, N. (1994). Training phonological awareness: A study with inner-city kindergarten children. *Annals of Dyslexia, 44,* 26–59.

Castles, A., & Coltheart, M. (1993). Varieties of developmental dyslexia. *Cognition, 47,* 149–180.

Clark, D. B. (1988). *Dyslexia: Theory and practice of remedial instruction.* Parkton, MD: York.

Cunningham, A. E. (1990). Explicit versis implicit instruction in phonemic awareness. *Journal of Experimental Child Psychology, 50,* 429–444.

Francis, D. J., Fletcher, J. M., Stuebing, K. K., Davidson, K. C., & Thompson, N. M. (1991). Analysis of change: Modeling individual growth. *Journal of Consulting and Clinical Psychology, 59,* 27–37.

Hollingshead, A. B. (1975). *Four factor index of social status.* New Haven, CT: Yale University, Department of Sociology.

Jastak, S., & Wilkinson, G. S. (1984). *Wide Range Achievement Test—revised.* Wilmington, DE: Jastak Associates.

Liberman, I. Y., Shankweiler, D., & Liberman, A. M. (1989). The alphabetic principle and learning to read. In D. Shankweiler & I. Y. Liberman (Eds.), *Phonology and reading disability: Solving the reading puzzle* (pp. 1–33). Ann Arbor: University of Michigan Press.

Lindamood, C. H., & Lindamood, P. C. (1984). *Auditory discrimination in depth.* Allen, TX: DLM/Teaching Resources.

Lovett, M. W., Warren-Chaplin, P. M., Ransby, M. J., & Borden, S. L. (1990). Training the word recognition skills of reading disabled children: Treatment and transfer effects. *Journal of Educational Psychology, 82,* 769–780.

Lundberg, I., Frost, J., & Peterson, O. (1988). Effects of an extensive program for stimulating phonological awareness in pre-school children. *Reading Research Quarterly, 23,* 263–284.

Lyon, G. R. (1985). Identification and remediation of learning disability subtypes: Preliminary findings. *Learning Disabilities Focus, 1,* 21–35.

Morrison, F. J. (1987). The nature of reading disability: Toward an integrative framework. In S. Ceci (Ed.), *Handbook of cognitive, social, and neuropsychological aspects of learning disabilities* (pp. 33–63). Hillsdale, NJ: Lawrence Erlbaum Associates.

Rack, J. P. Snowling, M. J., & Olson, R. K. (1992). The nonword reading deficit in developmental dyslexia: A review. *Reading Research Quarterly, 27,* 29–53.

Ragosa, D. R. (1988). Myths about longitudinal research. In K. W. Schaie, R. T. Cambell, W. Meredith, & S. C. Rawlings (Eds.), *Methodological issues in aging research* (pp. 171–210). New York: Springer.

Shankweiler, D., & Liberman, I. Y. (1989). *Phonology and reading disability.* Ann Arbor: University of Michigan Press.

Share, D. L., & Jorm, A. F. (1987). Segmental analysis: Co-requisite to reading, vital for self-teaching, requiring phonological memory. *European Bulletin of Cognitive Psychology, 7,* 509–513.

Share, D. L., & Stanovich, K. E. (1995). Cognitive processes in early reading development: A model of acquisition and individual differences. *Issues in Education: Contributions From Educational Psychology, 1,* 1–35.

Snowling, M., & Hulme, C. (1989). A longitudinal case study of developmental phonological dyslexia. *Cognitive Neuropsychology, 6,* 379–401.

Stanovich, K. E. (1988). Explaining the diffrences between the dyslexic and the garden-variety poor reader: The phonological-core variable-difference model. *Journal of Learning Disabilities, 21,* 590–604.

Thorndike, R. L., Hagen, E. P., & Sattler, J. M. (1986). *Guide for administering and scoring, the Stanford-Binet Intelligence Scale: Fourth edition.* Chicago: Riverside.

Torgesen, J. K., Morgan, S., & Davis, C. (1992). The effects of two types of phonological awareness training on word learning in kindergarten children. *Journal of Educational Psychology, 84,* 364–370.

Torgesen, J. K., Wagner, R. K., & Rashotte, C. A. (1994). Longitudinal studies of phonological processing and reading. *Journal of Learning Disabilities, 27,* 276–286.

Vellutino, F. R. (1991). Introduction to three studies on reading acquisition: Convergent findings on theoretical foundations of code-oriented versus whole-language approaches to reading instruction. *Journal of Educational Psychology, 83,* 437–443.

Vellutino, F. R., & Scanlon, D. M. (1991). The preeminence of phonologically based skills in learning to read. In S. Brady & D. Shankweiler (Eds.), *Phonological processes in literacy: A tribute to Isabelle Liberman* (pp. 237–252). Hillsdale, NJ: Lawrence Erlbaum Associates.

Wagner, R. K., & Torgesen, J. K. (1987). The nature of phonological processing and its causal role in the acquisition of reading skills. *Psychological Bulletin, 101,* 192–212.

Wagner, R. K., Torgesen, J. K., & Rashotte, C. A. (1994). The development of reading-related phonological processing abilities: New evidence of bi-directional causality from a latent variable longitudinal study. *Developmental Psychology, 30,* 73–87

Wagner, R. K., Torgesen, J. K., Rashotte, C. A., Hecht, S. A., Barker, T. A., Burgess, S. R., Donohue, J., & Garon, T. (in press). Changing relations between phonological processing abilities and word-level reading as children develop from beginning to skilled readers: A five-year longitudinal study. *Developmental Psychology.*

Willett, J. B. (1988). Questions and answers in the measurement of change. *Review of Research in Education, 15,* 345–422.

Wood, F., Felton, R., Flowers, L., & Naylor, C. (1992). Neurobehavioral definition of dyslexia. In D. Duane (Ed.) *The reading brain: The biological basis of dyslexia* (pp. 1–25). New York: York.

Woodcock, R. W. (1987). *Woodcock Reading Mastery Tests—revised.* Circle Pines, MN: American Guidance Service.

14

The Etiology and Remediation of Phonologically Based Word Recognition and Spelling Disabilities: Are Phonological Deficits the "Hole" Story?

Richard K. Olson
Barbara Wise
Mina C. Johnson
Jerry Ring
University of Colorado, Boulder

The chapters in this volume reflect a general consensus on the central importance of phonological decoding and phoneme awareness in the etiology and remediation of reading disabilities. In addition to being the year in which the conference spawning this volume was held, 1995 was also marked by the publication of two important theoretical papers consistent with this perspective (Share, 1995; Share & Stanovich, 1995). In this chapter we provide support for the importance of phonological skills from our studies on genetic factors in reading and phonological deficits and the remediation of these deficits with talking computers. However, we question whether phonological deficits are the whole story in reading and spelling disabilities.

The question arises from two main sources. The first is the presence of individual differences in word recognition and orthographic coding skills that are independent from phonological skills. To examine this we briefly review evidence from identical and fraternal twins on genetic and environmental contributions to this independent variance. The second reason for questioning an exclusive role for phonological deficits in reading and spelling disabilities comes from the results of several recent and ongoing remediation studies comparing good phonological training with other methods.

The main goal of the chapter is to review our own and other recent research on training in phonological awareness and decoding for children with specific reading disabilities. We conclude that although trained improvement in phonological skills has been accompanied by strong gains in fluent word recognition, similar gains in fluent word recognition have usually also resulted from other well-designed programs, despite their lack of explicit training or comparable gains in phonological skills. This is quite puzzling, because Share (1995) and others (Jorm & Share, 1983; Share & Stanovich, 1995) persuasively argued that phonological recoding provides a "self-teaching" mechanism that is the primary engine driving the development of printed word recognition. We propose research on ways to improve children's use of their trained phonological skills in flexible and fluent word recognition.

Phonological skill is not the only factor influencing the development of word recognition, but there is strong evidence for its central role in the etiology of most reading disabilities. Before turning to the training studies, we now briefly review the results of behavioral-genetic analyses that reveal both common and independent genetic influences on deficits in word recognition, phonological, and orthographic skills.

BEHAVIORAL-GENETIC EVIDENCE
ON PHONOLOGICAL DEFICITS
AND READING DISABILITY

The Center for the Study of Learning Disabilities at the University of Colorado is conducting a behavioral-genetic study of reading disabilities in identical and fraternal twins. The twins are identified from school records and are invited to the laboratory for testing if either or both members of the pair have some record of a reading problem. A comparison of identical and fraternal twin-pair similarities provides estimates of the proportion of the group deficit in reading and related skills that is due to genetic factors, shared environment, and non-shared environment (DeFries & Fulker, 1985).

Many studies have reported strong correlations among word recognition, phonological decoding (nonword reading), and phoneme awareness (e.g., deletion and manipulation of phonemes within a syllable). Similarly high correlations are found in our sample of twins with and without reading disability. Most of our twins with reading disabilities also display the commonly reported group deficit in phonological decoding and phoneme awareness when compared with younger normal twins at the same level of word recognition (Olson, Wise, Conners, Rack, & Fulker, 1989; Rack, Snowling, & Olson, 1992). This correlational evidence and structural models of prereaders' phoneme awareness and later reading skill (Wagner, Torgesen, & Rashotte, 1994) have been used to argue that phonological deficits have a significant causal role in reading disability.

Our analyses of the twin data have shown that the correlations between word recognition and phonological deficits have a significant genetic basis (Olson et al., 1989; Olson, Forsberg, & Wise, 1994). Approximately half of the group[1] deficits in word recognition, phonological decoding, and phoneme awareness are due to genetic factors, and significant genetic correlations between these deficits indicate that common genes are involved across the variables. However, there is also phenotypic variability in each measure that is not caused by common genes. Some of this variability, particularly in word recognition, is due to shared-environment influences. In addition, there are significant *independent* genetic influences on word recognition and phonological skills.

The clearest separation of independent genetic influences has been found between phonological decoding and orthographic coding. Our orthographic tasks assess the precision and speed of subjects' access to word-specific orthographic patterns (e.g., "Quickly, which is a word? *Rain*" or *rane?*"; Which is an excavation? *Whole* or *hole?*"). A complete description of our orthographic measures can be found in Olson, Forsberg, Wise, and Rack (1994). Contrary to an earlier report (Olson et al., 1989), the twin data now indicate a strong genetic influence on the group deficit in orthographic coding. Part of this genetic influence is shared with phonological decoding, but an even larger part is independent.

Some of the independent variance in word recognition and orthographic coding is due to shared-environment differences in print exposure (Olson et al., 1994; Stanovich & West, 1989). In addition, independent genetic influence on word recognition and orthographic coding further supports our contention that phonological skills are not the only important factor in the development of word recognition. The results from remediation studies reviewed in the next section are consistent with this view.

REMEDIATION OF PHONOLOGICAL DEFICITS AND CONSEQUENCES FOR WORD RECOGNITION

Share's (1995) argument for the self-teaching role of phonological decoding is straightforward: Children who have relatively good phoneme awareness and phonological decoding skills should be able to decode unfamiliar

---

[1]The emphasis on the *group* deficit is to indicate that the present behavioral-genetic analyses do not provide information on the proportion of genetic and environmental influence for any individual within the group. Rather, we are only estimating the average proportions for genetic and environmental influences across the group. More specific statements about genetic influence at the individual level may ultimately be possible; for example, when a gene linked to reading disability on chromosome 6 is finally identified (Cardon et al., 1994).

words more accurately, attend to their orthographic detail, and ultimately establish more accurate and rapidly accessible orthographic codes for whole words. We have already noted that many children with reading disabilities tend to have substantial deficits in phonological decoding and phoneme awareness, suggesting a causal role in many cases of reading disability. But the evidence for a causal role is often only correlational: More convincing evidence would be provided by training studies showing that improvement in phoneme awareness and phonological decoding is followed directly by the more rapid growth of word recognition when compared to an appropriate control group with structured reading experience but no explicit instruction or comparable gains specifically in phoneme awareness and phonological decoding. In this section we first describe some results from our own training study that employed this basic design (Wise & Olson, 1995). We then review several recent studies from other laboratories showing a similar pattern of results.

The Colorado Remediation Studies

Our research on the remediation of reading disabilities began with the development of a talking-computer system to provide speech support for children's decoding difficulties (Olson, Foltz, & Wise, 1986). This system, later nicknamed "ROSS" (reading with orthographic and segmented speech feedback), provided high-quality synthetic speech (DECtalk) that pronounced words when children targeted them with a mouse while they were reading stories on the computer screen (Olson & Wise, 1992; Wise et al., 1989). The subject samples included children in the second through sixth grades who were below the 10th percentile locally in word decoding and met the usual exclusionary criteria for specific reading disability. The studies were run in the Boulder schools over a one-semester time period. Trained subjects were pulled from their remedial reading or language arts class rooms for an average of four half-hour sessions per week. Following several sessions of pretesting and 1 to 2 weeks of training subjects to target difficult words, the subjects independently read stories on the computer for three of the four weekly sessions. The difficulty level of the stories was adjusted for each subject, so that each child typically would not require feedback for more than 5% of the words on a screen. The computer was programmed to present occasional multiple-choice comprehension questions and to present some of the targeted words in a review test. The experimenter monitored each subject's oral reading and encouraged targeting of unknown words during one session each week. Total training time on the computer averaged 14 hours, and the time between pre- and posttests averaged about 12 weeks. A randomly assigned comparison group was pretested and posttested at the same times as the trained groups, but they otherwise remained with their normal reading or language arts classes.

Two main questions were addressed in our early studies with the ROSS program with children with reading disabilities. First, could reading stories on the computer with speech support improve gains in phonological decoding and word recognition more than gains in similar control subjects who remained in their remedial reading or language arts classes? The answer to this question was clearly *yes.* Trained subjects averaged about four times the gains in phonological decoding (nonword reading) and about twice the gains in word recognition on the Peabody Individual Achievement Test (PIAT; Dunn & Markwardt, 1970).

The second main question was whether there were unique benefits from different types of orthographic and speech segmentation in the feedback provided for targeted words. We compared groups that received *whole-word* feedback, with the word highlighted as a unit and then spoken as a unit; *syllable* feedback, with syllables successively highlighted as they were spoken with a brief separation; and *onset-rime* feedback, with the onset (initial consonant or consonant cluster) and rhyme [vowel and following consonant(s)] of each syllable successively highlighted and spoken. An initial study suggested that gains in phonological decoding were greater with segmented feedback (Wise et al., 1989), but this effect did not replicate in a much larger sample (Olson & Wise, 1992). We have also failed to find a segmentation advantage for gains in phonological decoding or word recognition in a home-based study with 50 to 60 hours of reading on the computer over 6 months. We recently found a small but significant advantage for segmentation when subjects are tested on the words they have targeted in the stories and when the colored segments appear in the tested words, possibly encouraging the children to apply their decoding strategies.

The Olson and Wise (1992) study has been mistakenly interpreted as arguing that children with reading disabilities do not benefit from training in the analysis of subword orthography and speech (Lovett, Borden, et al., 1994). However, we only concluded that there appeared to be no unique benefits for gains in phonological decoding or PIAT word recognition from segmented feedback for difficult words while reading stories. We were not surprised to learn of unique benefits from orthographic and speech segmentation while practicing a specific list of trained words or of improved generalization to similar words (Lovett, Barron, Forbes, Cuksts, & Steinbach, 1994). In fact, the segmental analysis of words and the training of phonological awareness has been a central focus of our subsequent remedial studies (Wise & Olson, 1995).

Olson and Wise (1992) noted that subjects who had the lowest initial levels of phoneme awareness (adjusted for initial level of word recognition) tended to gain significantly less from reading with speech feedback, and there was a marginally significant interaction suggesting that these subjects' gains were particularly low when their feedback was segmented into the smallest units (onset-rime). That result, along with our own and others' evidence for disabled readers' group deficit in phoneme awareness and phonological decoding, led us to focus our next group of studies on improving phonological skills prior to and concurrently with reading stories on ROSS (Wise & Olson, 1995). Our hope was that such improvement would advance the self-teaching mechanism hypothesized by Share (1995), and accelerate the development of subjects' word recognition.

The method we chose to improve phoneme awareness (PA) and phonological decoding was our adaptation of the Auditory Discrimination in Depth program (Lindamood & Lindamood, 1975). Briefly, the PA program begins by helping children to discover the distinctive articulatory movements associated with different speech sounds. For instance, the first session included motivation and introduction of the program's first three "quiet and noisy pairs": "Lip poppers /p,b/, tip tappers /t,d/, and back scrapers /k,g/." In small groups consisting of the trainer and three students, children used mirrors to help them discover what their mouths were doing for different phonemes, and they learned to associate appropriate mouth pictures, articulatory labels, and letters with those phonemes. They practiced these associations on the computer using programs under development at the Lindamood-Bell Company in California. They then spent 20 minutes in small groups ordering a sequence of mouth pictures to indicate the sequence of phonemes in a syllable. After that, they next used programs developed at the University of Colorado to develop phonological awareness and phonological decoding with letter symbols. In one program, subjects practiced sequencing and manipulating the letter symbols to correspond to changes in syllables spoken by the computer. In the second program, children explored English orthographic patterns and print-to-sound relations in a spelling exploration game in which the computer pronounced correct and incorrect attempts, and children could modify their attempts (Wise & Olson, 1992). In the third program, children selected printed nonwords to match nonwords spoken by the computer.

When students achieved 80% success over 2 days manipulating sounds and symbols in CVC words, they began spending half their computer time reading on ROSS. The ROSS speech support for targeted words was segmented at the onset-rime level for regular one-syllable words and at the syllable level for multisyllable words. (Exception words such as *said* were not segmented.) The subjects had to push the mouse button first to highlight each segment in different colors. They attempted to sound out the segments with help from the articulatory and phonics (letter-sound) knowledge they had developed from earlier training. Then they pressed another button to have the computer successively highlight and speak each segment. A third button could optionally be pressed last to get whole-word support if needed. The total training time of 25 hours consisted of 7 hours in small-group sessions learning the articulatory and phonics concepts, 10 hours in practice on related computer games, and 8 hours reading stories on ROSS.

A trained comparison group had an equal amount of small-group interaction with the trainer (7 hours), but their initial small-group sessions were focused on methods for developing the comprehension strategies (CS) of predicting, generating questions, clarifying, and summarizing. This approach has shown positive effects for improving reading comprehension in groups of poor comprehenders (Palinscar & Brown, 1984). Children in the CS group began reading stories from the beginning of training, whereas the PA group was occupied with practice in articulatory awareness and the manipulation of phoneme and letter sequences.

Our main goals for the CS comparison group were to first equate the level of group interaction, enthusiasm, and trainer involvement, and then to provide greater print exposure with speech and segmentation support for decoding assistance in stories. We wanted to contrast the effects of the phonological awareness and decoding training in the PA group while controlling also for teacher and school effects by having both methods taught by all teachers in all schools. The CS group spent 7 hours in the initial small-group sessions reading and discussing stories, and 18 hours reading stories on ROSS. Decoding and speech support for targeted words was segmented in the same way as in the PA group, and subjects were told they should sound out each segment before asking for speech support to help them read targeted words. The CS subjects varied widely in the degree to which they seemed to use the segments to aid decoding.

The results from the two training conditions showed significant gains in phoneme awareness and phonological decoding in both groups. The CS group made gains in these skills that were stronger than in previous ROSS studies, suggesting that the engaging strategies and the daily interaction with a teacher benefited both groups. The most important result for our theoretical discussion was that the PA group made much greater gains than the CS group in phoneme awareness (three times greater) and phonological decoding (nearly two times greater).

Based on Share's (1995) self-teaching hypothesis, we had expected that the PA group's substantially greater gains in phoneme awareness and phonological decoding would also yield gains in word recognition that were substantially greater than those in the CS group. Both PA and CS groups made gains in word recognition that were larger than in previous ROSS studies. However, the groups were not significantly different on standardized tests of untrained words, despite their strong differences in phonological awareness and decoding. There was a nonsignificant trend toward a PA group advantage on the PIAT word recognition test (gains of 1.1 vs. .9 grade levels). The PA group was significantly worse in an experimental test of word recognition that provided a time-limited 2 seconds of exposure for each word in the list. There were no significant group differences in gains on reading comprehension or spelling.

The PA group did show significant advantages in word recognition performance on all tests of subsets of previously targeted words from the ROSS stories. These tests were given at the end of each monitored session, after each month using words targeted during the month, and at the end of training for a subset of words targeted over the semester. However, the words in these tests were orthographically segmented, as they had been when originally targeted in the ROSS stories. It is not clear if the PA group's better performance was due to better initial encoding of the word when it was first targeted in the story, better decoding on the test, or both. In any case, the explicit task demands on the PA group during the initial encoding and testing of targeted words were unlike our pre- and posttest measures of word recognition. In these measures, unsegmented words were presented one at a time on the computer screen. Apparently, the students in the PA group tended not to use their improved phonological decoding skills in this more natural presentation of tested words.

Wise and Olson (1995) speculated that the PA subjects may not have had enough print exposure to integrate their superior phonological skills in reading and build the larger reading vocabularies needed to surpass the CS group's gains on our measures of word recognition. We also suggested that the PA group's significantly inferior performance on the time-limited word recognition test was caused by their slower and more analytic decoding approach. Following more print exposure and opportunity to automatize their phonological decoding, we suggested that the PA group would equal or surpass the CS group's gains in time-limited word recognition. We hoped that these predictions, based on the self-teaching hypothesis, would be confirmed by our planned longitudinal follow-up testing.

A Brief Comment on Results for Reading Comprehension

Before turning to our unpublished follow-up results, we briefly comment on the null results for group differences in reading comprehension. Children enjoyed the comprehension strategy (CS) training, with its high level of social interaction and discussion of stories. Although we achieved our goal of balancing the general level of group interaction and student motivation across conditions, we had also hoped to find a significant advantage for students' reading comprehension on the PIAT and the Gates MacGinitie Reading Comprehension of Passages (MacGinitie & MacGinitie, 1989). Surprisingly, nonsignificant trends in comprehension gains actually favored the PA group. The only measure indicating a significant comprehension advantage for the CS group was the percent correct on ROSS comprehension questions (90% PA vs. 95% CS) that were answered in sessions when subjects' oral reading was monitored by a trainer who promoted the CS subjects' use of comprehension strategies. There was no significant difference in sessions where subjects read silently without the trainer (both 86% correct). Apparently, the CS subjects did not spontaneously use their trained comprehension strategies when reading on their own. This suggests a transfer problem similar to that observed on our posttest measures of word recognition for the PA subjects, who may not have consistently applied their improved phonological decoding skills.

Johnson (1995) asked a subset of the Wise and Olson (1995) PA and CS subjects to give oral summaries of stories read silently as pre- and posttests. The CS subjects showed significantly better main idea representation and less intrusion of irrelevant details. (The CS subjects were explicitly trained to summarize main ideas.)

Results From a Long-Term Follow-Up to Wise and Olson (1995)

No Group Differences in Rate of Gain. About 9 months (including summer vacation) after the end of training in the Wise and Olson (1995) study, subjects were retested on phoneme deletion, nonword reading, PIAT word recognition, and time-limited word recognition. Ring (1995) analyzed the data for the pretest, midtest, posttest, and final 9-month follow-up test. Figures 14.1A, 14.1B, 14.1C, and 14.1D show the results for 47 subjects (PA, $N = 27$; CS, $N = 20$) from three of the four schools in the original study. The fourth school was excluded because those students received extra training in other experimental methods during the following year. In the other three schools, subjects maintained their advantage in phonological decoding (Fig. 14.1A) and slightly less so in phoneme awareness (Fig. 14.1B). However, the PA subjects still did not show significantly greater gains in either PIAT word recognition (Fig. 14.1C) or in time-limited word recognition (Fig. 14.1D), although the PA group was no longer significantly worse in time-limited word recognition.

Drop-Off in Rate of Gain Following Training. It is clear in Figs. 14.1C and 14.1D that the rate of gain in word recognition over the 9 months following training was substantially less than the rate during training. Ring (1995) found a significant quadratic function that reflected the decline

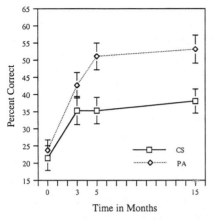

FIG. 14.1A. Gains in phonological decoding, percent correct.

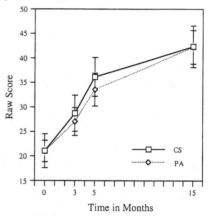

FIG. 14.1B. Gains in phoneme deletion, percent correct.

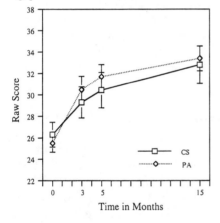

FIG. 14.1C. Gains in PIAT word recognition, items correct.

FIG. 14.1D. Gains in time-limited word recognition, items correct.

in growth rate following training. It appears that a continuation of structured reading practice similar to the ROSS program would be necessary to maintain the initial high rate of improvement observed during training. Subjects' print exposure during the 9 months following ROSS training may have been too limited and/or it lacked the corrective speech support subjects needed to decode difficult words and add them to their word-recognition vocabulary.

We have some evidence from an earlier unpublished study showing that the speech support provided while reading on ROSS and our emphasis on accurate word recognition are essential for producing the strong gains observed during training. Children were randomly assigned to either a group that read on ROSS with speech feedback for targeted words or a group that was encouraged to target difficult words and try to read them with help from the story context, but they received no speech support for unknown words. This type of independent reading was similar to what many of the children were doing with books in their "whole-language"-oriented remedial reading or language arts class rooms. Unfortunately, the study could not be completed because we had considerable problems motivating children in the no-feedback condition to continue with the training. The limited posttest data that was collected revealed minimal gains from the no-feedback condition.

Why Was There No Support for the Self-Teaching Hypothesis? Why didn't we find support for the self-teaching hypothesis (Share, 1995) in the PA group, with its significantly greater long-term gains in phoneme awareness and phonological decoding? There are several possible answers. Perhaps we had not trained subjects' phonological skills to a high enough level of accuracy, although their accuracy in nonword reading and phoneme awareness approached that of normal readers at their age level. Perhaps our encouraging the PA subjects' use of phonological decoding during their 8 hours of reading on ROSS was not enough to promote transfer of their new phonological skills to reading. It has been noted that learning-disabled children often do not use the strategies on which they have been successfully trained (Borkowski, Estrada, Milstead, & Hale, 1989; Kavale, 1980). Later in this chapter we continue this line of argument and discuss some other possible reasons for transfer failure. First we review some recent studies by other researchers that have also failed to find significantly greater gains in word recognition despite strong gains in phonological coding and phoneme awareness following successful phonological training, compared to well-trained reading-only control groups.

Other Studies With Similar Null Results for Word Recognition

The phonological training studies reported in this volume all seem to tell the same story across widely varying subject populations. Byrne, Fielding-Barnsley, Ashley, and Larsen's (chap. 12, this volume) training of phonological awareness in unselected preschoolers led to greater gains three years later in nonword reading and surprisingly in reading comprehension, but not generally in word recognition. Byrne et al. did find that there was a significant advantage for the trained group on five of the least frequent words in their regular word list. Torgesen, Wagner, and Rashotte's (chap. 13, this volume) articulatory-based phonological training of 52 unselected children from the second half of kindergarten through first grade led to better nonword reading but not significantly better word recognition, reading comprehension, or spelling at the end of first grade and in the second grade, compared to an implicit phonics group. Foorman, Francis, Shaywitz, Shaywitz, and Fletcher's (chap. 11, this volume) comparison of remedial teaching methods (potentially confounded by school and teacher) for 108 second- and third-grade children with reading disabilities included synthetic/analytic phonics, synthetic phonics, and the Edmark sight-word approaches. After controlling for group differences in memory and demographics, growth-curve analyses indicated that the synthetic phonics approach was most effective in training phonological processing, but the advantage in phonological processing did *not* lead to greater gains in word recognition when compared to the Edmark program. Finally, Nicolson (chap. 17, this volume) reviewed his remediation studies that showed greater gains in phonological skills (nonword reading) but no corresponding advantages in word recognition or passage reading.

Nicholson (personal communication, 1996) hypothesized that his phonologically trained subjects' advantage in nonword reading will eventually lead to better word recognition, but the follow-up data needed to support this hypothesis are not yet available. Nicholson also suggested that because word recognition tests typically contain many irregular words, they may not be a fair measure of subjects' gains in word recognition. This may be a valid criticism if the measures contain a disproportionate number of exception words compared to their distribution in the children's written language. We are now assessing this possibility in our own measures.

There were nonsignificant trends in an interesting study by Lovett, Borden, et al. (1994), suggesting that a letter-sound phonics approach may result in slightly better reading of simple regular words and poorer reading of exception words in children with severe reading disabilities. We are also interested in this study because both the authors of the Lovett, Borden, et al. study and Share and Stanovich (1995) described the results as providing clear evidence for the unique benefits of phonological training in the development of word recognition. However, a closer look at the Lovett et al. study actually reveals results for treatment differences in word recognition that are similar to those of Wise and Olson (1995).

Lovett, Borden, et al. (1994) trained three groups of 7- to 13-year-old children with severe reading disabilities from a clinic population, in a clinic setting, for a total of 35 1-hour sessions. Two of the treatment conditions were designed to promote the development of word decoding skills, but in different ways. A phonological analysis and blending/direct instruction (PHAB/DI) program (similar to Englemann & Bruner, 1988) focused on letter-sound correspondences and the segmentation and blending of phonemes in a corpus of regular words. A second treatment condition, the word identification strategy training (WIST) program, was based on part of a "metacognitive phonics" program developed by Gaskins and Elliot (1991). This program used a "whole-word" approach to train five key words each day (120 total) that contain a range of high-frequency spelling patterns. (These were the same words used in the PHAB/DI program.) Children were taught to use their knowledge of the spelling patterns in the key words to decode, by analogy, the parts of new words that contained similar spelling patterns. Other strategies included trying different vowel pronunciations and the "peeling off" of prefixes and suffixes to first decode the root word. Both methods promoted subword decoding skills, but the PHAB/DI program was oriented more toward the segmenting and blending of phonemes and their corresponding letters, whereas the WIST program emphasized larger spelling patterns and decoding by analogy.

Lovett, Borden, et al. (1994) trained a third "control" group in a variety of organizational and study skills to control for simple Hawthorne effects. However, it appeared that this training may have also displaced reading instruction that subjects would otherwise have had in the clinic. Thus, it is not surprising to learn that both of the trained groups gained significantly more than the control group on most reading measures, except reading comprehension. A control condition of reading with feedback but without special decoding instruction would have been needed to assess differences between decoding instruction and accurate reading practice. Nevertheless, a comparison of results from the two decoding programs in Lovett et al. can be used to make the same point.

When compared to the WIST program, the PHAB/DI program resulted in significantly greater improvement on phonological awareness and phonological decoding by the end of training. Unfortunately, as in our own study and in the other studies reviewed previously, the PHAB/DI group's better phonological performance did not generally lead to better word recognition compared to the WIST group. The Lovett, Borden, et al. (1994) study was remarkably well endowed with a broad array of word recognition measures. The pre- and posttest measures included the 120 trained key words, a list of 371 words similar to the key words, 105 multisyllabic words with embedded key-word spelling patterns, 298 regular words, 298 exception words, and 10 difficult low-frequency words for a grand total of 1,202 test words! Standardized measures of word recognition included the Wide Range Achievement Test—Revised (WRAT—R; Jastak & Wilkinson, 1984), and the Woodcock Reading Mastery Test—Revised (WRMT—R; Woodcock, 1987). On all but two of the measures, there were no significant training group differences. The WIST group did significantly better on the 10 difficult words, and the PHAB/DI group did significantly better on the WRAT—R test.

Lovett, Borden, et al. (1994) noted that the WRAT—R test allowed 10 seconds per word, and this may have given the PHAB/DI subjects the time needed to use their phonological decoding skills on the mostly regular words in this test. A group difference in response to word regularity was also suggested by trends in performance on the 298 regular and 298 exception word lists. The PHAB/DI group was slightly but nonsignificantly better on regular words, whereas the WIST group was nonsignificantly better on the exception words. Overall, the groups' average performance in word recognition was remarkably similar, in spite of the significant group differences in phonological skills. As in the Wise and Olson (1995) study and other studies reviewed earlier, there was a dissociation between growth in phonological skills and growth in word recognition that was inconsistent with Share's (1995) self-teaching hypothesis.

A Closer Look at Two Studies Showing Greater Gains in Word Recognition

Our review of the recent literature included two other studies that are frequently cited for showing a unique contribution from phonological training to word recognition for children with reading disabilities. The first study, by Brown and Felton (1990), identified children in kindergarten at risk for reading disability because of performance below the 16th percentile on three research measures of phonological processing. At the beginning of first grade, the children were randomly assigned to a "structured phonics" group (Lippincott Basic Reading 1981) or a "context" group (Houghton Mifflin Reading, 1986) for their reading instruction in the first and second grades. At the end of first grade, the structured phonics group was significantly better in nonword reading and spelling of regular words, but not in word recognition. At the end of second grade, there was still no significant difference in the standardized word recognition test given at the end of the first grade, and the previous differences in nonword reading and spelling were no longer significant. However, new measures included at the end of second grade revealed a significant advantage for the "structured phonics" group in monosyllable nonwords and polysyllable real words, but not monosyllable real words.

Felton (personal communication, 1996) collected follow-up data on a subset of the above subjects at the end of eighth grade. Some additional intervention of the "code" type had been given during the third grade to 4 of the 17 "code" and 6 of the 13 "context" subjects who were having the most trouble reading. This additional code instruction may have worked against any reading difference in the eighth grade, and there were no significant differences on the reading test. For example, grade equivalents on a composite based on the Woodcock Johnson word identification and passage comprehension tests were 5.6 GE ($N = 17$) for the "code" group, and 5.3 GE (N = 13) for the context group. However, the general efficacy of *both* groups' intense small-group instruction was shown by the significantly lower performance in the eighth grade for a passive control group (3.7 GE, N = 17).

We accept the authors' contention that trends in the data nearly always favored the "structured phonics" group, and that this is probably the superior method for these children. But we have two methodological concerns. First, the training methods were confounded by teacher, making it difficult to dissociate method effects from teacher effects. Second, the "context" group may have made many uncorrected decoding errors during their reading practice because word identity is often incorrectly predicted from context (Gough, Alford, & Holley-Wilcox, 1981). These uncorrected errors would reinforce inappropriate associations between print and speech. We return to this issue at the end of the chapter, and argue there that a more appropriate comparison group would include reading with corrective feedback for decoding errors.

A second study by Hatcher, Hulme, and Ellis (1994) was the only one we could find that appeared to show a clear advantage in several measures of word recognition from reading instruction that emphasized phonological analysis. A total of 124 7-year-old children with reading disabilities were assigned to supplemental training groups (40 30-minute sessions over 20 weeks) that included either phonological analysis plus reading instruction, reading instruction alone, or phonological analysis alone. A fourth control group received no supplemental instruction. The statistical analysis was limited because it only compared the trained groups against the untrained control group and not against each other. However, the phonological-analysis-plus-reading group was the only one that showed significantly greater gains compared to controls across all three measures of word recognition. These reading advantages were obtained in spite of the fact that the phonological-analysis-plus-reading group and the reading-only group were not significantly different from each other in their gains on four measures of phonological processing (sound deletion, nonword segmentation, sound blending, and sound categorization). Another concern is that without phonological training, the reading-only group generally showed little or no reading advantage over the untrained control group. Other studies typically do show significant advantages for all reading instruction groups versus untrained groups (cf., Lovett, Borden, et al., 1994; Olson & Wise, 1992). Thus, we are concerned that there may have been some problem with the reading comparison group beyond the absence of phonological training. The lack of significant group differences in phoneme awareness after phonological training raises questions about the contribution of this training to better word recognition in the phonological-analysis-plus-reading group.

Studies Showing Generalization to Word Recognition
for Unselected Samples

There have been a few recent studies with *unselected* samples of preschoolers, kindergarten, or first-grade beginning readers that have suggested generalization from better phonological skills to better word
recognition. Lundberg, Frost, and Peterson (1988) reported significantly
better word recognition in Danish children who had received substantial
training in phonological awareness, without print, as 6-year-old prereaders. The significant advantage in word recognition emerged in the second
grade but was not present in the first grade. Of particular relevance to
children at risk for reading disability, the benefits were significantly
stronger in those children whose initial phonological skills were unusually
low (Lundberg, 1994). This classic study is unique in showing the effects
of phonological training without the inclusion of print. It has a potential
confound of different teachers and different Danish islands for the treated
and control groups, although the authors carefully tried to equate the
samples on relevant demographic variables.

Uhry and Shepherd (1993) reported a study with unselected first graders that showed strong gains in word recognition and phonological awareness. They employed exercises in manipulating phonemes and letters in
spelling analysis and production as a key element in their experimental
training program. Children ($N = 11$) in this group also used several
computer games to foster the development of subword analysis in reading. A trained comparison group ($N = 11$) spent more of their time working
with print at a whole-word level of analysis, although they were encouraged to use decoding skills that were taught to both groups in the regular
classroom. In spite of the small samples and some common elements of
phonological decoding training for both groups in the regular classroom,
the spelling group showed significantly greater gains in phonological
awareness, phonological decoding, and word recognition. The small samples of children in the Uhry and Shepherd study were from college-edu-
cated families, most attended 3 years of preschool prior to kindergarten,
and their mean IQ score was 122.5. It would be very interesting to see if
the unique benefits of their spelling and sound manipulation program
would also generalize to a reading-disabled sample and to beginning
readers at risk for reading disability.

Ball and Blachman (1991) compared three groups of kindergarten children from inner-city schools. The two trained groups of interest here were
given 28 20-minute sessions of either letter-name-sound training and
general language activities (language activities group), or letter-name-
sound training plus exercises in manipulating phonemes within words
represented by tiles and ultimately individual letters (only one per word)

within words (phoneme awareness group). By the end of training, the phoneme awareness group improved significantly more on phoneme segmentation and on the mean number of words read correctly on the Woodcock Word Identification Subtest (3 words versus 1 word). A second kindergarten study compared phonological training with an untrained control group. The trained group was significantly better on posttests of phonological skills and regular word reading, but not on the Woodcock standardized measure of word recognition (Blachman, Ball, Black, & Tangel, 1994). During the first grade, the trained group participated in a reading program that emphasized the alphabetic code, whereas the control children participated in a basal reading program. At the end of first grade, and in a follow-up at the end of second grade, the trained group significantly outperformed the control group on measures of regular word reading. Differences between the two groups on the Woodcock standardized measure of word recognition also favored the trained children. These differences were marginally significant ($p = .056$) at the end of first grade and significant at the end of second grade.

The cited studies with unselected samples suggest that related advantages in phonological processing and word recognition can be found when comparing different methods of beginning reading instruction. A similar consensus has emerged from reviews of earlier studies of different training programs for beginning readers (Adams, 1990; Chall, 1983), although Adams cautioned that other confounding variables, such as teacher enthusiasm for a new and favored method or different time on task, may have influenced the results of some studies. It appears that the studies reviewed in this section were carefully controlled, but further research is needed to show that their methods can provide unique benefits for phonological skills *and* word recognition among children with reading disabilities.

SUMMARY AND THE WAY AHEAD

The studies of children with reading disabilities reviewed in the last section should not be used to argue the null hypothesis against *any* additional gains in word recognition from training in phonological skills. Sometimes there were nonsignificant trends favoring phonological training. Sometimes a significant advantage was found when task demands and/or the lack of time constraints seemed to favor the use of slow and deliberate phonological decoding for regular words, as in the Lovett, Borden, et al. (1994) study and our most recent training study. In our second training study with the PA and CS conditions (unpublished), a significant posttest advantage was found for PA subjects' gains in the WRAT—R test of word recognition, but not for gains on the PIAT test, our experimental measure of time-limited word recognition, or miscues on oral reading of paragraphs. Earlier we noted similar results from Lovett, Borden, et al. (1994). They reported that the liberally timed and largely regular-word WRAT—R test was the only one of their numerous word recognition measures that showed a significant advantage for the phonologically trained group. The question we turn to now is how to increase the effects of phonological training on the development of word decoding that is both fluent and flexible enough to deal with the irregularities of English orthography in normal reading.

Share (1995) may have been correct in his hypothesis that normally developing readers do use their superior phonological skills as a primary self-teaching mechanism to develop more accurate, fluent, and flexible word recognition. However, this mechanism may continue to be compromised in children with initially very weak phonological skills, even after training has produced better phonological awareness and decoding at the conscious level of processing required for greater accuracy in our measures (Bowey, 1995). Subjects' performance on our measures may provide only a rough index of the underlying phonological processes that are employed very rapidly and automatically (not requiring much attention) in normal readers' fluent word recognition (Perfetti & Bell, 1991; Van Orden, 1987). Training children with reading disability in conscious and deliberate phonological awareness and decoding may not automatically result in phonological processing that is fast and automatic enough to aid in the development and execution of fluent word recognition. If this hypothesized dissociation between levels of phonological processing is correct, then we may need to focus our efforts on training phonological processes beyond accuracy to a higher level of speed, automaticity, and flexibility.

One approach we are currently exploring is longer training time following the same PA training procedures and reading on ROSS used in Wise and Olson (1995). Recall that the PA group in Wise and Olson averaged only 8 hours reading stories on ROSS. We are currently training a small sample of children with reading disabilities over a full year and hope to reach a total of 40 hours training time, including at least 15 hours on ROSS, by the end of the spring semester. This longer training time should provide some additional boost in performance on our phonological measures. More importantly, it will provide much more time for the PA subjects to automatize and integrate their phonological processes with their reading of stories with speech support in the ROSS program.

For next year's study, phonological training will be followed by new computer exercises that encourage greater flexibility in trying different vowel pronunciations and stress patterns with real-word reading. Additional speed training will promote the rapid identification of printed words, particularly high-frequency exception words, and nonwords spoken by the computer.

We are optimistic that these procedures will result in more fluent and flexible word recognition for most children with reading disabilities when compared to similar children who receive CS training. We also hope that the self-teaching function of improved accuracy, speed, and automaticity of the PA group's phonological skills will result in more rapid growth in word recognition long *after* training. However, as our title implies, we do not think that phonological deficits are the whole story. The development of printed word recognition is also dependent on other factors such as general print exposure (Olson et al., 1994; Stanovich & West, 1989), accurate reading *with* speech support for decoding errors by person or computer (Olson & Wise, 1992; Wise & Olson, 1995), genetically based individual differences in orthographic skills that are independent from phonological skills (Olson, Forsberg, & Wise, 1994), lexical knowledge (Morton, 1989; Plaut, McClelland, Seidenberg, & Patterson, 1996), the use of context (Tunmer & Chapman, 1995), and speed of lexical access (Bowers & Wolf, 1993; Wolf, chap. 4, this volume). The effects of these factors on the growth of printed word recognition may often be largely independent from what we do for deficits in phonological processing.

We conclude with a critically important point for theory and practice in remediation: Our CS condition, with its comprehension strategy training and reading on the computer, was *not* like some whole-language approaches that encourage guessing based on context (cf., Houghton & Mifflin Reading, 1986). Gough et al. (1981) and others pointed out that guessing from context often yields errors in word decoding that can weaken the appropriate connections between orthography and speech (Jorm & Share, 1983). Instead, our CS subjects were trained to attempt all words and to use speech support when they were unsure of a word. We believe that this support and attention to correct decoding is necessary for the rapid development of accurate and fluent word recognition. Also, it is consistent with the essential role of corrective feedback in modern connectionist models of reading development (Adams, 1990; Plaut et al., 1996; Seidenberg & McClelland, 1989).

Children with reading disabilities usually require more trials with feedback than do normal readers to learn the correct decoding for unknown words, and they usually need more repeated exposures to develop fluent recognition (Ehri & Saltmarsh, 1995; Reitsma, 1983). Supportive parents and teachers may be the ideal source for this additional corrective feedback, but their availability is often limited. We have shown that our ROSS computer programs can provide the additional feedback and print exposure that is needed to substantially improve fluent and flexible word recognition, especially when used in a well-structured and motivated setting. A remaining challenge is to demonstrate whether and how intensive phonological training can significantly improve on these gains.

ACKNOWLEDGMENTS

This work was supported in part by program project and center grants from the NICHD (HD-11681 and HD-27802), and RO1 HD-22223. The contributions of staff members of the many Colorado school districts that participate in our research, and of the twins and their families, are gratefully acknowledged. We thank Benita Blachman, Brian Byrne, Carsten Elbro, Rebecca Felton, Barbara Forman, Ingvar Lundberg, Tom Nicolson, and David Share for their comments on an earlier draft.

REFERENCES

Adams, M. J. (1990). *Beginning to read: Thinking and learning about print.* Cambridge, MA: MIT Press.

Ball, E. W., & Blachman, B. A. (1991). Does phoneme awareness training in kindergarten make a difference in early word recognition and developmental spelling? *Reading Research Quarterly, 26,* 49–66.

Blachman, B. A., Ball, E. W., Black, R. S., & Tangel, D. M. (1994). Kindergarten teachers develop phoneme awareness in low-income, inner-city classrooms: Does it make a difference? *Reading and Writing: An Interdisciplinary Journal, 6,* 1–18.

Borkowski, J. G., Estrada, M. T., Milstead, M., & Hale, C. A. (1989). General problem solving skills relations between metacognition and strategic processing. *Learning Disability Quarterly, 12,* 57–70.

Bowers, P. G., & Wolf, M. (1993). Theoretical links among naming speed, precise timing mechanisms and orthographic skill in dyslexia. *Reading and Writing, 5,* 69–85.

Bowey, J. A. (1995). On the contribution of phonological sensitivity to phonological recoding. *Issues in Education, 1,* 65–70.

Brown, I. S., & Felton, R. C. (1990). Effects of instruction on beginning reading skills in children at risk for reading disability. *Reading and Writing: An Interdisciplinary Journal, 2,* 223–241.

Cardon, L. R., Smith, S., Fulker, D., Kimberling, W., Pennington, B., & DeFries, J. (1994). Quantitative trait locus for reading disability on chromosome 6. *Science, 266,* 276–279.

Chall, J. S. (1983). *Learning to read: The great debate* (2nd ed.). New York: McGraw-Hill.

DeFries, J. C., & Fulker, D. W. (1985). Multiple regression analysis of twin data. *Behavior Genetics, 15,* 467–473.

Dunn, L. M., & Markwardt, F. C. (1970). *Examiner's manual: Peabody Individual Achievement Test.* Circle Pines, MN: American Guidance Service.

Ehri, L. C., & Saltmarsh, J. (1995). Beginning readers outperform older disabled readers in learning to read words by sight. *Reading and Writing: An Interdisciplinary Journal, 7,* 295–326.

Engelmann, S., & Bruner, E. C. (1988). *Reading Mastery I/II Fast Cycle: Teachers guide.* Chicago: Science Research Associates.

Gaskins, I. W., & Elliot, T. T. (1991). *Implementing cognitive strategy training across the school: The Benchmark manual for teachers.* Cambridge, MA: Brookline.

Gough, P. B., Alford, J. A., Jr., & Holley-Wilcox, P. (1981). Words and contexts. In O. J. L. Tzeng & H. Singer (Eds.), *Perception of print* (pp. 85–102). Hillsdale, NJ: Lawrence Erlbaum Associates.

Hatcher, P. J., Hulme, C., & Ellis, A. W. (1994). Ameliorating early reading failure by integrating the teaching of reading and phonological skills: The phonological linkage hypothesis. *Child Development, 65,* 41–57.

Houghton Mifflin reading. (1986). Boston: Houghton Mifflin.

Jastak, S., & Wilkinson, G. S. (1984). *Wide Range Achievement Test—revised.* Wilmington, DE: Jastak Associates.

Johnson, M. C. (1995). *Effects of training in phonological awareness and reciprocal teaching on the comprehension of disabled readers.* Unpublished master's thesis, University of Colorado, Boulder.

Jorm, A. F., & Share, D. L. (1983). Phonological recoding and reading acquisition. *Applied Psycholinguistics, 4,* 103–147.

Kavale, K. A. (1980). The reasoning abilities of normal and learning disabled readers on measures of reading comprehension. *Learning Disability Quarterly, 3,* 34–45.

Lindamood, C., & Lindamood, P. (1975). *Auditory discrimination in depth.* Columbus, OH: Science Research Associates Division, Macmillan/McGraw-Hill.

Lippincott basic reading. (1981). Riverside, NJ: Macmillan.

Lovett, M. W., Barron, R. W., Forbes, J. E., Cuksts, B., & Steinbach, K. A. (1994). Computer speech-based training of literacy skills in neurologically-impaired children: A controlled evaluation. *Brain and Language, 47,* 117–154.

Lovett, M. W., Borden, S. L., DeLuca, T., Lacerenza, L., Benson, N. J., & Brackstone, D. (1994). Treating the core deficits of developmental dyslexia: Evidence of transfer of learning after phonologically- and strategy-based reading training programs. *Developmental Psychology, 30,* 805–822.

Lundberg, I. (1994). Reading difficulties can be predicted and prevented: A Scandinavian perspective on phonological awareness and reading. In C. Hulme & M. Snowling (Eds.), *Reading development and dyslexia* (pp. 180–199). London: Whurr.

Lundberg, I., Frost, J., & Peterson, O. (1988). Effects of an extensive program for stimulating phonological awareness in pre-school children. *Reading Research Quarterly, 23,* 263–284.

MacGinitie, W., & MacGinitie, R. (1989). *The Gates–Macginitie Reading Tests* (3rd ed.). Chicago: Riverside.

Morton, J. (1989). An information processing account of reading acquisition. In A. M. Galaburda (Ed.), *From reading to neurons* (pp. 43–86). Cambridge, MA: MIT Press.

Olson, R. K., Foltz, G., & Wise, B. (1986). Reading instruction and remediation with the aid of computer speech. *Behavior Research Methods, Instruments, and Computers, 18,* 93–99.

Olson, R. K., Forsberg, H., & Wise, B. (1994). Genes, environment, and the development of orthographic skills. In V.W. Berninger (Ed.), *The varieties of orthographic knowledge I: Theoretical and developmental issues* (pp. 27–71). Dordrecht, The Netherlands: Kluwer.

Olson, R., Forsberg, H., Wise, B., & Rack, J. (1994). Measurement of word recognition, orthographic, and phonological skills. In G. R. Lyon (Ed.), *Frames of reference for the assessment of learning disabilities: New views on measurement issues* (pp. 243–277). Baltimore: Brookes.

Olson, R. K. & Wise, B. W. (1992). Reading on the computer with orthographic and speech feedback: An overview of the Colorado Remedial Reading Project. *Reading and Writing: An Interdisciplinary Journal, 4,* 107–144.

Olson, R. K., Wise, B., Conners, F., Rack, J., & Fulker, D. (1989). Specific deficits in component reading and language skills: Genetic and environmental influences. *Journal of Learning Disabilities, 22*(6), 339–348.

Palincsar, A. S., & Brown, A. L. (1984). Reciprocal teaching of comprehension-fostering and comprehension-monitoring activity. *Cognition and Instruction, 2,* 117–175.

Perfetti, C. A., & Bell, L. (1991). Phonemic activation during the first 40 ms. of word identification: Evidence from backward masking and masked priming. *Journal of Memory and Language, 30,* 473–485.

Plaut, D. C., McClelland, J. L., Seidenberg, M. S., & Patterson, K. (1996). Understanding normal and impaired word reading: Computational principles in quasi-regular domains. *Psychological Review, 103,* 56–115.

Rack, J. P., Snowling, M. J., & Olson, R. K. (1992). The nonword reading deficit in developmental dyslexia: A review. *Reading Research Quarterly, 27*(1), 28–53.

Reitsma, P. (1983). Printed word learning in beginning readers. *Journal of Experimental Child Psychology, 75,* 321–339.

Ring, J. (1995). *A comparison of computer-based remedial reading programs: The effects of automaticity, phonological awareness, and comprehension strategy training on word recognition and phonological decoding skills.* Unpublished Master's thesis, University of Colorado, Boulder.

Seidenberg, M. S., & McClelland, J. L. (1989). A distributed, developmental model of word recognition and naming. *Psychological Review, 96,* 523–568.

Share, D. L. (1995). Phonological recoding and self-teaching: *Sina qua non* of reading acquisition. *Cognition, 55,* 151–218.

Share, D. L., & Stanovich, K. E. (1995). Cognitive processes in early reading development: Accommodating individual differences into a model of acquisition. *Issues in Education, 1,* 1–57.

Stanovich, K. E., & West, R. F. (1989). Exposure to print and orthographic processing. *Reading Research Quarterly, 24,* 402–433.

Tunmer, W. E., & Chapman, J. W. (1995). Context use in early reading development: Premature exclusion of a source of individual differences? *Issues in Education, 1,* 97–100.

Uhry, J. K., & Shepherd, M. J. (1993). Segmentation/spelling instruction as part of a first-grade reading program: Effects on several measures of reading. *Reading Research Quarterly, 28,* 219–233.

Van Orden, G. C. (1987). A ROWS is a ROSE: Spelling, sound, and reading. *Memory and Cognition, 15,* 181–198.

Wagner, R. K., Torgesen, J. K., & Rashotte, C. A. (1994). Development of reading-related phonological processing abilities: New evidence of bidirectional causality from a latent variable longitudinal study. *Developmental Psychology, 30,* 73–87.

Wise, B. W., & Olson, R. K. (1992). Spelling exploration with a talking computer improves phonological coding. *Reading and Writing, 4,* 145–156.

Wise, B. W., & Olson, R. K. (1995). Computer-based phonological awareness and reading instruction. *Annals of Dyslexia, 45,* 99–122.

Wise, B., Olson, R., Anstett, M., Andrews, L., Terjak, M., Schneider, V., & Kostuch, J. (1989). Implementing a long-term computerized remedial reading program with synthetic speech feedback: Hardware, software, and real-world issues. *Behavior Research Methods, Instruments, and Computers, 21,* 173–180.

Woodcock, R. W. (1987). *Woodcock Reading Mastery Tests—revised.* Circle Pines, MN: American Guidance Service.

15

The Use of Rime-Based Orthographic Analogy Training as an Intervention Strategy for Reading-Disabled Children

Keith T. Greaney
William E. Tunmer
James W. Chapman
Massey University, New Zealand

Recent research suggests that there is a level of structure in spoken words that is intermediate in size between syllables and phonemes (see Treiman, 1992, for a review). Several studies reported by Treiman indicate that the ability to segment into phonemes is preceded by the ability to segment syllable units into the intrasyllabic units of onset and rime, where onset is the initial consonant or consonant cluster, and rime is the vowel and any following consonants. Research further indicates that, for most children, sensitivity to the onset-rime division emerges spontaneously in development prior to exposure to reading instruction (Goswami & Bryant, 1990, 1992). In contrast, the ability to completely segment a word or syllable into its phonemic elements seems to develop only under certain learning conditions, such as when children are exposed to instruction in an alphabetic script (Bowey & Francis, 1991) or given specific training in phonemic segmentation skills (Lundberg, Frost, & Petersen, 1988).

These findings and the finding of a strong predictive relationship between preliterate onset-rime sensitivity and later reading achievement (Bradley & Bryant, 1985) have led to the hypothesis that beginning readers may initially link elements of written and spoken language at the level of onsets and rimes (Goswami & Bryant, 1990, 1992; Treiman, 1992). Because preliterate children are generally incapable of fully analyzing spoken words into phonemes, they may have trouble discovering correspondences between single letters or digraphs (e.g., *sh, th, oa*) and single phonemes in the beginning stages of learning to read. In support of these suggestions is research by Goswami (1986, 1988, 1991) indicating that beginning readers can use multiletter units corresponding to onsets and rimes when reading new words. This research also shows that the ability to make analogies on the basis of onsets and rimes precedes the ability to make analogies that cut across the onset/rime boundary or constitute a part of an onset/rime unit.

Although Goswami's work clearly showed that children are capable of using analogies as soon as they start to read, there remains the question of whether children spontaneously use analogies from the outset of reading acquisition without being prompted to do so and without the presence of trained "clue" words. Opponents of Goswami's view argue that, although beginning readers have the *potential* to use analogies, they will not be able to use this strategy until they have developed a sufficiently large sight vocabulary on which to base analogical inferences. In addition, a significant amount of letter-sound knowledge may be needed to store the base (analog) words in memory in sufficient detail to recognize identical orthographic units in known and new words.

In support of these claims Muter, Snowling, and Taylor (1994) found that, for children not exposed to clue words at posttest, the size of the analogy effect was greatly reduced and correlated with reading ability. Ehri and Robbins (1992) found that children with little or no phonological recoding skills were unable to read unfamiliar words by analogy. Rack, Hulme, Snowling, and Wightman (1994) showed that beginning readers learned to read their first words by means of partial letter-sound cues, suggesting that words are initially underspecified in semantic memory. These findings suggest that analogy mechanisms cannot come into play until later in reading development.

An alternative view to the two just described proposes that there is a reciprocally facilitating relationship between the development of phonological recoding skills, sight word knowledge, and the ability to make use of rime-unit analogies. Some phonological recoding skills (especially knowledge of initial letter sounds in words; Goswami, 1994) and basic sight word knowledge may be necessary to use rime-based analogies. However, the process of dividing words at the onset/rime boundary itself may help children to learn to isolate and recognize individual phonemes (Treiman, 1992). This, in turn, would enable children to utilize one-to-one correspondences between graphemes and phonemes *within* onsets and rimes. Consistent with this suggestion are the findings of three studies. Bowey and Hansen (1994) obtained results indicating that rime-unit knowledge and knowledge of grapheme–phoneme correspondences develop simultaneously during the first year of reading instruction. Goswami (1993) found that the use of vowel analogies (e.g., using the vowel in the known word *bug* as the basis for reading the unknown word *cup*) emerges gradually as reading develops and follows an initial phase in which children's use of analogies is restricted to spelling patterns corresponding to onsets and rimes. A path analysis of data from a longitudinal study by Bryant, Maclean, Bradley, and Crossland (1990) indicated that preliterate onset-rime sensitivity at age 4 influenced reading at age 6 both directly and through phonemic awareness at age 5.

THE USE OF RIME-UNIT ANALOGIES
BY DISABLED READERS

In addition to research on the use of analogies by normally developing readers, research has also been reported on the use of rime-based analogies by disabled readers. Findings reported by Lovett, Warren-Chaplin, Ransby, and Borden (1990) suggested that dyslexic children have difficulty abstracting spelling-to-sound pattern invariance, irrespective of the size of the units. Lovett et al. gave two groups of dyslexic children systematic word identification training. One group received letter-sound training, and the other group received whole-word training. Although both groups made substantial gains on the instructed words, the children did not profit differentially from letter-sound over whole-word training, and neither group showed significant transfer to uninstructed vocabulary. Moreover, when presented with uninstructed words (e.g., *cart, peak*) that shared rime spelling units with the taught words (e.g., *part, weak*), neither training group performed better than a matched control group. These findings suggest that dyslexic children do not spontaneously use rime-based orthographic analogies to identify unfamiliar words. Lovett et al. speculated that the cause of this difficulty is most likely dyslexics' inability to parse a syllable into subsyllabic units. The inclusion of a reading-level control group of normally developing readers and appropriate measures of onset-rime segmentation ability in the design of the study would have helped to clarify this point.

An alternative explanation is that disabled readers possess the necessary skills (viz., onset-rime segmentation ability, knowledge of initial letter sounds, basic sight vocabulary) to take advantage of rime-unit analogies, but do not make use of such knowledge when confronted with unfamiliar words. Instead, they rely on ineffective or inappropriate learning strategies, such as partial letter-sound cues. Consistent with this possibility are the results of studies by Reitsma (1983) and Ehri and Saltmarsh (1995). Reitsma gave a group of normally developing first-grade readers and a reading-level control group of older disabled readers varying amounts of practice at recognizing a set of words with standard spellings, and later tested their recognition of these words and a matched set of homophonic spellings of these words (the experiment was carried out in Dutch; an example pair of homophonic words in English would be *reach* and *reech*). He found that after four trials of practice the normal readers performed better on the standard spellings than on the homophonic spellings, whereas no such differences were found for the disabled readers, even after six trials of practice. Normal readers appear to develop better-quality orthographic representations of words than do disabled readers.

In extending this work, Ehri and Saltmarsh (1995) found that disabled readers were particularly deficient in remembering letter details in the middle of words. These results suggest that the reading progress of disabled readers plateaus in what Ehri (1991, 1992) described as the phonetic cue reading stage of development. This is the stage in which children rely primarily on initial and/or final consonant information to help identify words, rather than making full use of sound-symbol correspondences. A likely consequence of the continued use of partial letter-sound cues is the development of more poorly specified lexical representations in semantic memory. If disabled readers are not sufficiently analytic in their "word attack" skills to achieve normal progress in reading, they may need intensive strategy training in word decoding to develop the habit of making greater use of the letter-sound information that is available in unfamiliar words.

In a more recent intervention study, Lovett et al. (1994) tested both explanations (i.e., deficits in phonological skills versus deficits in decoding strategies) of dyslexic children's difficulties in acquiring invariant spelling-to-sound patterns and their limited transfer to uninstructed words. Two intervention programs were developed. The first focused on instruction in word segmentation and sound-blending skills followed by direct instruction of letter-sound correspondences. The second focused on instruction in the acquisition, use, and monitoring of four metacognitive decoding strategies, with particular emphasis on the use of rime-based analogies in identifying unfamiliar words.

Both training programs resulted in large positive effects, transfer to uninstructed materials, and generalized achievement gains. However, several questions remain unanswered. First, because no measures of phonological awareness were taken, it is unclear whether the success of the two programs was due largely to increasing dyslexics' phonological awareness skills or to increasing their word decoding skills and strategies. Second, as Lovett and colleagues noted, because both programs were successful, it is possible that some combination of the two programs would result in even greater benefits for dyslexic children. Finally, as Lovett and colleagues further noted, the optimal level of spelling-to-sound units for children with dyslexia is not known. As they put it, "The developmental sequence by which children use larger and smaller spelling-to-sound units is not obvious" (p. 819).

Regarding the latter issue, although the question of the developmental sequence by which *normally* developing readers use larger and smaller spelling-to-sound units is unresolved (see previous discussion), the situation may be more straightforward for disabled readers. In learning to recognize words, normally developing readers make greater use of grapheme–phoneme correspondences to form sublexical connections between specific letters seen in words and sounds detected in their pronunciations (Adams & Bruck, 1993; Ehri, 1991, 1992; Perfetti, 1992). In contrast, disabled readers rely more on partial word-level information (e.g., partial visual cues, partial letter-sound cues) and contextual guessing to identify words and, as a consequence, have less fully developed sublexical connections between the orthographic and phonological representations of words in semantic memory. Because there is less interaction between orthographic and phonological codes in the word processing of disabled readers who rely mostly on partial word-level cues, the development of awareness of individual phonemes and knowledge of correspondences between graphemes and phonemes may not be promoted to the same extent as in normally developing readers (Bruck, 1992). In support of this suggestion, Bruck (1992) found that disabled readers showed deficits in phonemic awareness at all ages and reading levels, but eventually acquired appropriate levels of onset-rime sensitivity.

Because rimes appear to be more accessible to disabled readers than phonemes, an initial focus on teaching orthographic units corresponding to rimes may be an effective intervention strategy for these children. Moreover, if the word recognition skills of dyslexic children are weak because of their use of ineffective or inappropriate learning strategies (such as relying on sentence context and partial word-level cues to guess words), then teaching these children to use rime-unit analogies may be a very useful first step in making them more aware of sublexical relationships between written and spoken words. In particular, it may help disabled readers to overcome their tendency to focus on boundary letters at the expense of medial information. Finally, another advantage of initially teaching disabled readers rime spelling units is that the complexity and variability of vowel spelling-to-sound correspondences is greatly reduced. Analyses of children's oral reading errors by Shankweiler and colleagues (Fowler, Liberman, & Shankweiler, 1977; Shankweiler & Liberman, 1972) showed that vowel spelling patterns are particularly difficult for beginning readers (and may even be more so for dyslexic children, given that vowel spelling patterns typically map onto single phonemes within rimes). However, because of the nature of English orthography, vowel sounds are generally quite stable in the rime segments of words that appear in beginning reading materials. Wylie and Durrell (1970) showed that knowledge of only 37 rime spelling patterns (or phonograms) would enable beginning readers to recognize 500 of the most frequently occurring words in beginning reading materials.

In summary, the major unresolved questions arising from the research on the use of rime-unit analogies by disabled readers are as follows: Why is it that disabled readers do not spontaneously use rime-based analogies to identify unfamiliar words? Is it because they lack the phonological skills necessary for taking advantage of rime-unit analogies, such as onset-rime segmentation ability? Or is it because they possess the requisite knowledge but do not make use of such knowledge when confronted with unfamiliar words, relying instead on ineffective or inappropriate strategies, such as partial letter-sound cues and contextual guessing? Given that there may be important advantages for disabled readers in initially linking print and speech at the level of onsets and rimes, a related set of questions arise: Can procedures be developed to help disabled readers make use of rime spelling units and, if so, do the positive effects of such training generalize to other reading skills and materials? More specifically, would some combination of skills training and metacognitive strategy training in the use of rime spelling units provide the basis for an effective intervention program for children with reading disability?

RIME-BASED ORTHOGRAPHIC ANALOGY
TRAINING FOR DISABLED READERS

To investigate these questions further, two studies were carried out (Greaney & Tunmer, 1996; Greaney, Tunmer, & Chapman, in preparation). Each employed a combination of a reading-level-match design and a follow-up intervention study.

Study 1

In the first study (Greany & Tunmer, 1996), 30 disabled readers, with a mean age of 11.24 years (S.D. = 0.93), were closely matched with 30 normal readers, with a mean age of 7.49 years (S.D. = 0.28), on a standardized measure of context free word recognition ability. The children in both groups were then given four tests measuring onset-rime sensitivity (a rhyme knowledge questionnaire, a rhyme oddity task, and two rhyme detection tasks) and an analogical transfer task. The rhyme knowledge questionnaire assessed children's understanding of the concept of rhyme; the rhyme oddity task measured children's ability to judge which word out of four orally presented words did not rhyme with the other three; the rhyme detection (in word lists) task measured children's ability to detect pairs of rhyming words within groups of four words; and the rhyme detection (in poem) task assessed children's ability to detect pairs of rhyming words in the context of a poem (in the latter two tasks, the experimenter read aloud the material presented individually to the children as they read along silently). The analogical transfer task measured children's ability to take spontaneous advantage of analogical units when reading two lists of words (each containing 20 groups of five words each) that varied in whether the words containing the common unit were presented contiguously (e.g., *book, took, look, shook, hook*) or noncontiguously (where order of presentation of all words in the list was randomized), and in whether the unit constituted the rime portion of the words (e.g., *b-all, t-all, w-all, h-all, f-all*) or was embedded in the rime portion of the words (e.g., *m-oo-n, r-oo-m, n-oo-n, sh-oo-t, b-oo-t*).

Results indicated that the younger, normal readers outperformed the older, disabled readers on the two rhyme detection tasks but not on the rhyme knowledge questionnaire or rhyme oddity task. Because the magnitudes of the differences on the two rhyme detection tasks were not great, the overall results seemed to suggest that, although the disabled readers were somewhat behind the reading-age controls in the development of onset-rime sensitivity, they appeared to have sufficient awareness of onsets and rimes in spoken words to be able to use rime-based analogies. On the analogical transfer task, the reading-age controls performed significantly better overall than did the reading-disabled children, which suggests that disabled readers are less likely than normal readers to take advantage of orthographic analogies when reading words containing common analogical units, large or small. This finding is consistent with the results of Lovett et al. (1990), who found that dyslexic children do not spontaneously use rime-based analogies to identify unfamiliar words (see previous discussion). The children in both groups performed better when the words containing a common unit were presented contiguously rather than noncontiguously. This result is similar to Muter et al.'s (1994) finding (discussed previously) that beginning readers were better able to use analogies when the clue word was exposed than when it was not exposed. The results from the analogical transfer task further indicated that the children performed better when the analogical unit constituted the rime portion of the word than when it was embedded within the rime portion of the word. This finding provides further support for the claim that beginning readers are better able to use multiletter units corresponding to rimes than to use smaller units corresponding to sounds within rimes.

A follow-up intervention study was carried out to determine whether the poor readers could be taught to use analogies when they encountered unfamiliar words while reading connected text. The poor readers were divided into two carefully matched groups. The treatment group received instruction in the use of orthographic analogies, whereas the comparison group received remedial instruction emphasizing context cue usage.

The children in both training groups were asked to read graded prose passages until a reading accuracy rate of 90% to 94% was achieved. The selected passage was read twice, once before and once after the training procedures. The first time the children read the passage their errors were underlined by the experimenter on a copy of the passage. The children were informed prior to the reading that any errors they made would be underlined by the experimenter, but the experimenter provided no prompting or feedback during the reading.

The purpose of the analogy training was to encourage the reading-disabled children to use, where applicable, relevant analogical unit knowledge to decode unfamiliar words. The training focused mainly on rime units, but occasionally included training on units within rimes. The assumption underlying the procedure was that poor readers would be better able to identify unfamiliar words when they became metacognitively aware that unfamiliar words often contained units that were analogous to units in known words (see Iversen & Tunmer, 1993). The experimenter first wrote down the words that were not read correctly by the child during the first reading in a column immediately to the right of the passage. In the next column the child was asked to spell a frequently occurring word provided by the experimenter that contained an analogical unit identical to one that appeared in the misread word. If all spelling attempts were incorrect (which was rare), the experimenter wrote down a word for the child that contained the relevant orthographic unit. The child was then asked to locate the common analogical unit in the spelling(s) and the misread word, to pronounce the corresponding sound, and then to copy the unit in a separate column.

For example, one child missed a total of 19 words in the target passage, including *garden*, *stake*, and *dew*. For the word *garden*, the child was asked to spell *car* and *far*, and then to identify, say, and write down the common unit *ar*. For the word *stake*, the child was asked to spell the words *make* and *take* and to identify the common unit *ake*. For the word *dew*, the child was asked to spell the words *new* and *few* and to identify the common unit *ew*. This procedure was repeated for as many of the children's errors as possible (some of the errors did not contain suitable analogical units from which example spellings could be based). Although no specific attempt was made to encourage the children to decode the reading errors *at this stage*, many of the words were instantly recognized as soon as the analogical unit was pronounced. Following the completion of the training procedure, the children were asked to read the passage a second time and to attend to the spellings and common sound units of the words previously misread.

In contrast, when reading the target passage the second time, the children in the control group were encouraged to make use of context cues to identify the words misread during the first reading of the passage. For each error they were given prompts in accordance with the procedures of a commonly used remedial reading program in New Zealand called "Pause, Prompt and Praise" (see Smith & Elley, 1994). If the children made an error that did not make sense, they were prompted with clues about the meaning of the story. If the children could offer no response to an unfamiliar word, they were asked to read on to the end of the sentence and start again and put in a word that made sense. If the children produced a word that made sense but was incorrect (a relatively rare kind of error), they were prompted to look at some of the letters in the word. This approach to remediation is based on the assumption that the meaning cues in the sentence and a minimal amount of word-level information are sufficient to enable beginning readers to recognize unfamiliar words in text (Smith & Elley, 1994).

The results indicated that there were no significant differences in mean number of pretreatment reading errors between the analogy training group ($M = 20.20$), and the context cue usage training group ($M = 21.00$), and that both groups showed significant reductions in the mean number of posttreatment errors. However, the children in the analogy training group made considerably fewer posttreatment errors ($M = 7.13$) than did the children in the context cue usage training group ($M = 13.20$). This finding suggests that reading-disabled children can be taught to use analogies to identify unfamiliar words, and that analogy training is much more effective in increasing the error corrections of disabled readers than training in context cue usage. Although these results were promising, further research was needed to determine the amount of training that was required to ensure that these positive effects were maintained and generalized to other reading materials.

Study 2

In the second study (Greaney, Tunmer, & Chapman, in preparation) a combined reading-level-match design and follow-up intervention was again used. Fifty-seven reading-disabled children, with a mean age of 8.52 years (S.D. = 1.02), were closely matched with 57 normal readers, with a mean age of 6.69 years (S.D. = 0.42), on two standardized tests, one a measure of context free word recognition ability and the other a measure of word recognition accuracy in graded passages. The children in both groups were then given tests measuring general verbal ability, onset-rime segmentation ability, phoneme segmentation ability, pseudoword reading, identification of words containing common rime spelling units, and rime spelling unit identification.

General verbal ability was assessed by a standardized test of children's hearing vocabulary. To measure onset-rime segmentation ability, a sound matching task was used that comprised two subtests, an onset matching subtest and a rime matching subtest. The children were asked to indicate which two of three orally presented words sounded "the same" (e.g., *sail, nail, boot*). Picture support was provided to reduce the load on working memory. To measure phoneme segmentation ability, the children were asked to use counters to represent the phonemes in orally presented nonword syllables of varying length (one to four phonemes). A pseudoword reading task was used to assess children's knowledge of letter-sound patterns. Thirty items (e.g., *jit, prew, thrain*) were scored in two ways, first according to the total number of items correctly pronounced and then according to the total number of sounds pronounced correctly in the items (provided the sounds in the item were blended together into a single syllable). The task requiring children to identify words with common rime spelling units was similar to the analogical transfer task used in the first study. The children were asked to read 72 monosyllabic words comprising 18 groups of words, each containing a common rime spelling unit (e.g., *cat, hat, bat, fat*). The 72 words were presented in 18 rows of 4 words each. In half the rows the words containing the common rime unit were presented contiguously (e.g., *back, sack, pack, tack*). In the remaining rows, the words were distributed such that no two words containing a common rime unit appeared in the same row (e.g., *pay, seat, lick, cot*). Manner of presentation (i.e., contiguous vs. noncontiguous) of each of the 18 word groups was counterbalanced across two forms of the test. In the rime unit identification task the children were asked to circle in each of 20 printed words a rime spelling pattern presented orally by the examiner (e.g., "ack", "est", "ick"). Each of 10 rime units appeared twice, once as the final segment of the word (e.g., *cr-ack*) and once embedded within the word (e.g., *p-ack-age*). The words containing the rime units were not used in the training phase of the study (discussed later in the chapter).

Results indicated that although the older, disabled readers performed better than the younger, normal readers on the receptive vocabulary task, they performed significantly less well on all other tasks. Particularly robust differences were obtained on the measures of phoneme segmentation ability, pseudoword reading, identification of words with common rime spelling units, and rime spelling unit identification.

The poorer performance of the disabled readers on the phoneme segmentation and pseudoword reading tasks is consistent with the findings of others (for reviews of research, see Adams & Bruck, 1993; Rack, Snowling, & Olson, 1992). As noted earlier, because disabled readers do not make full use of sound-symbol correspondences in identifying words (relying instead on partial word-level strategies), there is less interaction between orthographic and phonological representations in semantic memory. As a consequence, the development of awareness of individual phonemes and knowledge of grapheme–phoneme correspondences is not promoted to the same extent as in normally developing readers. Unless poor readers become more analytic in their word identification strategies, it is highly unlikely that they will ever acquire appropriate levels of phonemic awareness and phonological recoding ability, because the development of these skills depends on the normal use of phonological information in learning to read. Moreover, the continued use of contextual guessing and partial word-level cues at the expense of phonological information will result in progressive deterioration in the rate of reading development as these children grow older, because they do not develop as rich a network of sublexical connections between orthographic and phonological representations in semantic memory as normally developing readers. These connections are thought to provide the basis for rapid and efficient access to the mental lexicon, which in turn frees up cognitive resources for allocation to comprehension and text integration processes (Ehri, 1991, 1992; Perfetti, 1992).

Similar to what was found in the first study, the normal readers performed significantly better than did the poor readers when asked to read words containing common rime spelling units. This finding provides further evidence that disabled readers are less likely than normal readers to take advantage of analogies when reading unfamiliar words. As was also observed in the first study, the children in both groups performed better when the words containing a common rime unit were presented contiguously rather than noncontiguously.

A prediction that follows from the finding that disabled readers are less likely than normal readers to make use of analogies is that disabled readers will have had fewer opportunities to derive implicit orthographic rime correspondence rules (i.e., "large-unit" rules) for commonly occurring rime spelling units. In support of this suggestion, the poor readers performed less well than the normal readers on the rime unit identification task.

Although the normal readers significantly outperformed the poor readers on the measure of onset-rime segmentation ability, both groups performed reasonably well. Out of a maximum score of 18, the poor readers averaged 14.00 items correct and the normal readers averaged 15.28 items correct. This finding, combined with the results of the first study, conflicts with the suggestion by Lovett et al. (1990) that the failure of dyslexic children to make spontaneous use of analogies can be attributed to their inability to parse syllables into onsets and rimes. Rather, it appears that dyslexic children have sufficient onset-rime segmentation ability to read words by analogy but generally do not make use of this ability when attempting to read unfamiliar words, relying instead on ineffective word identification strategies.

A follow-up intervention study was carried out to determine whether a combination of skills training and metacognitive strategy training in the use of rime spelling units would produce positive effects that generalized to other reading skills and materials. If the word recognition skills of very poor readers are weak because of their continued use of compensatory strategies at the expense of phonological information, it may be necessary to provide them with explicit instruction in the use of more effective learning strategies, such as the use of rime-unit analogies. As noted earlier, the use of such an instructional strategy may be a very useful first step in making these children more aware of sublexical relationships between written and spoken words, and in helping them to overcome their tendency to focus on boundary letters at the expense of medial information. Learning to take advantage of rime-unit analogies may, in turn, facilitate further progress in reading by helping children to isolate and recognize individual phonemes and acquire one-to-one correspondences between graphemes and phonemes within onsets and rimes.

Most of the 57 disabled readers were in their third or fourth year of schooling and had already received remedial reading instruction at an earlier point (i.e., Reading Recovery). They were selected by the school system for additional remedial instruction by reading specialists called Resource Teachers of Reading (RTRs). The children were divided into three matched groups and received 30 minutes of individual instruction three or four times per week during a 12-week school term. In one group the children received the standard instruction provided by RTRs. In the two remaining groups additional training procedures for identifying unfamiliar words were incorporated into the lesson format. In one group the training focused on systematic strategy training in the use of rime spelling units, whereas in the other group the training focused on item-specific learning and sentence-level strategies. For these two groups possible effects due to differences in teacher characteristics were controlled by having each RTR use both modified interventions, one with half the children with whom they were working, and the other intervention with the remaining half. Possible effects due to differences in materials were controlled by using the same materials in the two training procedures incorporated into the RTR lesson format.

For the rime analogy training group, systematic training in the use of rime spelling units to identify words was incorporated into the 30-minute lesson format of RTRs. Three assumptions guided the instructional approach used with the rime analogy training group. First, reading-disabled children must become *active* problem solvers with regard to graphic information. Considerable emphasis must therefore be placed on developing self-improving strategies for acquiring spelling-sound relationships rather than on just teaching individual spelling patterns per se. As the reading attempts of the disabled readers become more successful, they will begin making greater independent use of letter-sound information to identify words from which additional spelling-sound relationships can be induced without explicit instruction. Second, reading-disabled children must learn to use their newly acquired word decoding strategies to identify unfamiliar words while reading connected text. Although reading-disabled children should receive explicit and systematic instruction in word recognition strategies outside the context of reading connected text, they must also be taught how and when to use these strategies during text reading. Third, reading-disabled children must be made aware that successful attempts at decoding unfamiliar words are a direct consequence of the appropriate and effortful application of taught skills and strategies. Disabled readers have been using for a considerable period of time ineffective learning strategies that may be very difficult to unlearn. Moreover, as a consequence of repeated learning failures, many poor readers develop negative reading-related self-perceptions of ability, and therefore do not exert as much effort as other children because of their low expectations of success (Chapman & Tunmer, 1995a, 1995b). Emphasis must thus be placed on making these children aware that they *can* achieve success by using more effective learning strategies.

For each 3- (or 4-) day training cycle, three pairs of target nouns were presented to each child to read. The words of each pair contained one of the 37 rime spelling units identified by Wylie and Durrell (1970). For one word of each pair, the rime unit constituted the final segment of the word (e.g., *m-eat*). For the other word of the pair, the rime was embedded in the word (e.g., *h-eat-er*). On Day 1 of each training cycle (which was often extended to 2 days), the child was asked to read aloud each of the six target words and was given feedback in the form of a tick or cross immediately after each word was attempted (but no corrective feedback was given). The child was then given three groups of words to spell, each group comprising three words (e.g., *seat, beat, neat*). The words of each group contained a common rime unit that also appeared in one of the three pairs of target words. Corrective feedback was given according to the particular pattern of responses arising from the child's initial spelling attempts. There were four possible response scenarios, but in each case the aim was to encourage the child to identify the common rime unit in the three spelling primes, to write the rime unit in an egg-shaped space above the words on the worksheet, and then to pronounce the rime unit.

On Day 2, the child was asked to read the same six target words that were attempted on Day 1, but in scrambled order. However, the child was first asked to study the "eggs" (rime units) that were learned during the previous day's lesson (and entered on the worksheet) and then circle the identical parts in the Day 2 words before attempting to decode them. Corrective feedback was given where necessary. Because the child's responses to the target words on Day 1 were visible on the worksheet, it was possible to make the child directly aware that the use of the "eggs" was helpful in improving word identification.

On Day 3, the child was again asked to read the six target words (in scrambled order) but no assistance was given, and the Day 1 and 2 material was not visible. After the test was completed, corrective feedback and further instruction in the use of "eggs" was provided. For each day of the training cycle the number of target words correctly identified was recorded.

The rime analogy training that was incorporated into the 30-minute RTR lesson generally did not exceed 5 minutes in duration. However, a standard feature of the RTR lesson is the introduction of unfamiliar reading material (i.e., "instructional" text) at the end of the lesson. While reading this new material, the children in the rime analogy training group were encouraged, wherever possible, to use their newly acquired strategic knowledge to help them identify unfamiliar words. Following Gaskins et al. (1988), the children were also encouraged to develop a "set for diversity." For example, if the child was unable to read the final word of the sentence, "He drank a glass of cold water," the child was asked to search for familiar "eggs" in the word (i.e., *at* and *er*) and then to generate a pronunciation for the word. In this instance an incorrect response was produced, but one that was a very close approximation to the actual word. The child was therefore encouraged to generate alternative pronunciations of the word until one was produced that matched a word in his or her listening vocabulary and was appropriate to the sentence context. In summary, although the children were taught specific skills in the rime analogy training program (i.e., knowledge of commonly occurring rime spelling units), considerable emphasis was also placed on the development of metacognitive strategies for knowing how and when to apply such skills.

For the item-specific training group, systematic training in the use of sentence context cues to identify unfamiliar words was incorporated into the 30-minute lesson format of RTRs. The children in this intervention group were presented with the same material that was used in the rime analogy training group, but with one exception. On Day 2 of the training cycle the target words were presented in underdetermining sentence contexts (e.g., "The *heater* made them warm").

On Day 1 of the training cycle for the item-specific training group (which was often extended to 2 days), the child was asked to read aloud each of the six target words and was given feedback in the form of a tick or cross immediately after each word was attempted. The child was then given three groups of words to spell (the same words that were used in the rime analogy training procedure), but this time the words containing the common rime unit were not presented contiguously. Corrective feedback was given immediately after each word was attempted, with the teacher orally spelling the correct version of the word as the child wrote it on the worksheet next to his or her initial response.

On Day 2, the child was asked to read aloud six sentences, each containing one of the six target words that were presented on Day 1. For each error the child was given prompts in accordance with the "Pause, Prompt and Praise" procedures that were used in the first study. As noted previously, this program focuses primarily on encouraging children to use sentence context cues in identifying unfamiliar words.

On Day 3, the child was again asked to read the six target words but this time in isolation. No assistance was given, and the Day 1 and 2 material was not visible. After the test was completed corrective feedback and further instruction in associating sentence meaning cues with the target words was provided.

The item-specific training that was incorporated into the 30-minute RTR lesson generally did not exceed 5 minutes in duration. However, similar to what occurred with the children in the rime analogy training group, the children in the item-specific training group received additional instruction in the use of the pause-prompt-praise procedures while reading the new material presented at the end of the RTR lesson.

The data obtained from the intervention phase of the study indicated that there were no differences between the rime analogy and item-specific training groups in either the mean number of lessons received or the mean number of training cycles completed. However, an analysis of the mean number of target words correctly identified at different points in the training cycle (averaging across the number of training cycles completed) revealed that, although there were no differences between the two training groups on Day 1 of the training cycle, the rime analogy training group significantly outperformed the item-specific training group on both Days 2 and 3 of the training cycle. This finding was consistent with the results of the first study and suggested that the rime analogy training procedures were more effective than the item-specific training procedures in helping the disabled readers to identify unfamiliar words.

Following the training, the children in the three intervention groups (i.e., the two modified intervention groups and the standard intervention control group) were given the same tests that were administered prior to the training, with the exception of the receptive vocabulary test, which was not included in the posttreatment test battery. Results indicated that gains were made by all groups, but that the rime analogy training group significantly outperformed the other two groups on the standardized measure of context free word recognition ability, the pseudoword reading test (both scoring procedures), the test of identifying words containing common rime spelling units, and the rime spelling unit identification test. Although the children in the rime analogy training group achieved a higher mean posttreatment score on the standardized measure of word recognition accuracy in graded passages than did the children in the item-specific training group, the difference did not reach statistical significance, most likely because the children in the item-specific group were able to use compensatory strategies when reading words in connected text. Of greater importance, the raw score gains achieved by the children in the rime analogy training group on the two standardized tests of reading both translated into 6-month increases in reading age, suggesting that the word identification strategies acquired by these children generalized to reading unfamiliar words in context as well as in isolation.

One third of the items on the test of identifying words with common rime units were not included in the training materials. A separate analysis of the scores for these words indicated that the superior posttreatment performance of the rime analogy training group was maintained. This finding combined with the results from the pseudoword reading test and the standardized test of context free word recognition ability provided converging evidence that the training these children received in recognizing and using commonly occurring rime spelling units generalized to uninstructed words. The superior posttreatment performance of these children on the rime unit identification task further indicated that the rime analogy training facilitated the acquisition of orthographic rime correspondence rules. Overall, the findings from the intervention study demonstrated that the positive effects of training in the use of rime spelling units were maintained and generalized to other reading materials.

CONCLUDING REMARKS

The results of the two studies on the effects of rime analogy training suggest that reading-disabled children have the requisite knowledge for taking advantage of rime-unit analogies, and that a combination of skills training and metacognitive training in the use of rime spelling units provides the basis for an effective intervention program for these children. Given that (older) disabled readers appear to possess a sufficient amount of onset-rime segmentation ability to make use of rime-unit analogies, there remains the question of why these children continue to rely on such ineffective word recognition strategies as partial letter-sound cues and contextual guessing when normally developing readers abandon these strategies early in development.

One possibility is that most children who *become* reading disabled do not possess an adequate level of phonological sensitivity at the outset of learning to read. This weakness in the phonological domain may be due to one or more factors (e.g., lack of prior exposure to certain kinds of language activities that promote phonological sensitivity, a delay in the development of the control processing skills required to perform cognitive operations on the structural subcomponents of spoken words, and/or a genetically linked deficiency in the phonological processing module of the left dominant cerebral hemisphere; see Tunmer & Hoover, 1993). Regardless of the source of the difficulty, children with deficiencies in phonological skills at the outset of learning to read may eventually overcome their initial weakness in the phonological domain and gradually develop along normal lines as they mature. However, a more likely possibility is that most children who do not possess adequate phonological skills at the outset of formal reading instruction will not await phonological development but will rely increasingly on ineffective word recognition strategies to such an extent that these strategies become consolidated and very difficult to unlearn. As noted previously, the continued use of such strategies at the expense of phonological information will result in progressive deterioration in the rate of reading development as the children grow older. This suggests that the early identification and remediation of children with weaknesses in the phonological domain may be the key to reducing the incidence of severe reading difficulties in children.

REFERENCES

Adams, M. J., & Bruck, M. (1993). Word recognition: The interface of educational policies and scientific research. *Reading and Writing: An Interdisciplinary Journal, 5*, 113–139.

Bowey, J. A., & Francis, J. (1991). Phonological analysis as a function of age and exposure to reading instruction. *Applied Psycholinguistics, 12*, 91–121.

Bowey, J. A., & Hansen, J. (1994). The development of orthographic rimes as units of word recognition. *Journal of Experimental Child Psychology, 58*, 465–488.

Bradley, L., & Bryant, P. E. (1985). *Rhyme and reason in reading and spelling* (International Academy for Research in Learning Disabilties Monograph Series, No. 1). Ann Arbor: University of Michigan Press.

Bruck, M. (1992). Persistence of dyslexics' phonological awareness deficits. *Developmental Psychology, 28*, 874–886.

Bryant, P. E., Maclean, M., Bradley, L. L., & Crossland, J. (1990). Rhyme and alliteration, phoneme detection, and learning to read. *Developmental Psychology 26*, 429–438.

Chapman, J. W., & Tunmer, W. E. (1995a). The development of young children's reading self-concept: An examination of emerging subcomponents and their relationship with reading achievement. *Journal of Educational Psychology, 87*, 154–167.

Chapman, J. W., & Tunmer, W. E. (1995b, April). *Reading self-concept, reading self-efficacy and beginning reading achievement.* Paper presented at the annual conference of the American Educational Research Association, San Francisco, CA.

Ehri, L. C. (1991). Development of the ability to read words. In R. Barr, M. L. Kamil, P. B. Mosenthal, & P. D. Pearson (Eds.), *Handbook of reading research* (Vol. 2, pp. 383–417). New York: Longman.

Ehri, L. (1992). Reconceptualising the development of sight word reading and its relationship to recoding. In P. Gough, L. Ehri, & R. Treiman (Eds.), *Reading acquisition* (pp. 107–143). Hillsdale, NJ: Lawrence Erlbaum Associates.

Ehri, L. C., & Robbins, C. (1992). Beginners need some decoding skill to read by analogy. *Reading Research Quarterly, 27,* 13–26.

Ehri, L. C., & Saltmarsh, J. (1995). Beginning readers outperform older disabled readers in learning to read words by sight. *Reading and Writing: An Interdisciplinary Journal, 7,* 295–326.

Fowler, C., Liberman, I., & Shankweiler, D. (1977). On interpreting the error pattern in beginning reading. *Language and Speech, 20,* 162–173.

Gaskins, I. W., Downer, M. A., Anderson, R., Cunningham, P. M., Gaskins, R. W., Schonmer, M., & the Teachers of the Benchmark School. (1988). A metacognitive approach to phonics: Using what you know to decode what you don't know. *Remedial and Special Education, 9,* 36–41.

Goswami, U. (1986). Children's use of analogy in learning to read: A developmental study. *Journal of Experimental Child Psychology, 42,* 73–83.

Goswami, U. (1988). Orthographic analogies and reading development. *Quarterly Journal of Experimental Psychology, 40A,* 239–268.

Goswami, U. (1991). Learning about spelling sequences: The role of onsets and rimes in analogies in reading. *Child Development, 62,* 1110–1123.

Goswami, U. (1993). Toward an interactive analogy model of reading development: Decoding vowel graphemes in beginning reading. *Journal of Experimental Child Psychology, 56,* 443–475.

Goswami, U. (1994). Reading by analogy: Theoretical and practical perspectives. In C. Hulme & M. Snowling (Eds.), *Reading development and dyslexia* (pp. 18–30). London: Whurr.

Goswami, U., & Bryant, P. E. (1990). *Phonological skills and learning to read.* Hillsdale, NJ: Lawrence Erlbaum Associates.

Goswami, U., & Bryant, P. E. (1992). Rhyming, analogy and children's reading. In P. B. Gough, L. Ehri, & R. Treiman (Eds.), *Reading acquisition* (pp. 49–63). Hillsdale, NJ: Lawrence Erlbaum Associates.

Greaney, K. T., & Tunmer, W. E. (1996). Onset-rime sensitivity and orthographic analogies in normal and poor readers. *Applied Psycholinguistics, 17,* 15–40.

Greaney, K. T., Tunmer, W. E., & Chapman, J. W. (in preparation). *The effects of rime-based orthographic analogy training on the word recognition skills of reading disabled children.*

Iversen, S., & Tunmer, W. (1993). Phonological procesing skills and the Reading Recovery Program. *Journal of Educational Psychology, 85,* 112–126.

Lovett, M. W., Borden, S. L., DeLuca, T., Lacerenza, L., Benson, N., & Brackstone, D. (1994). Treating the core deficits of developmental dyslexia: Evidence of transfer of learning after phonologically- and strategy-based reading training programs. *Developmental Psychology, 30,* 805–822.

Lovett, M. W., Warren-Chaplin, P. M., Ransby, M. J., & Borden, S. L. (1990). Training the word recognition skills of reading disabled children: Treatment and transfer effects. *Journal of Educational Psychology, 82,* 769–780.

Lundberg, I., Frost, J., & Petersen, O. P. (1988). Effects of an extensive program for stimulating phonological awareness in preschool children. *Reading Research Quarterly, 23,* 263–284.

Muter, V., Snowling, M., & Taylor, S. (1994). Orthographic analogies and phonological awareness: Their role and significance in early reading development. *Journal of Child Psychology and Psychiatry, 35,* 293–310.

Perfetti, C. A. (1992). The representation problem in reading acquisition. In P. Gough, L. Ehri, & R. Treiman (Eds.), *Reading acquisition* (pp. 145–174). Hillsdale, NJ: Lawrence Erlbaum Associates.

Rack, J., Hulme, C., Snowling, M., & Wightman, J. (1994). The role of phonology in young children learning to read words: The direct-mapping hypothesis. *Journal of Experimental Child Psychology, 57,* 42–71.

Rack, J. P., Snowling, M. J., & Olson, R. K. (1992). The nonword reading deficit in developmental dyslexia: A review. *Reading Research Quarterly, 27,* 28–53.

Reitsma, P. (1983). Printed word learning in beginning readers. *Journal of Experimental Child Psychology, 75,* 321–339.

Shankweiler, D., & Liberman, I. Y. (1972). Misreading: A search for causes. In J. F. Kavanagh & I. G. Mattingly (Eds.), *Language by ear and by eye: The relationships between speech and reading* (pp. 293–317). Cambridge, MA: MIT Press.

Smith, J. W. A., & Elley, W. B. (1994). *Learning to read in New Zealand.* Auckland: Longman Paul.

Treiman, R. (1992). The role of intrasyllabic units in learning to read and spell. In P. B. Gough, L. Ehri, & R. Treiman (Eds.), *Reading acquisition* (pp. 65–106). Hillsdale, NJ: Lawrence Erlbaum Associates.

Tunmer, W., & Hoover, W. (1993). Components of variance models of language-related factors in reading disability: A conceptual overview. In M. Joshi & C. K. Leong (Eds.), *Reading disabilities: Diagnosis and component processes* (pp. 135–173). Dordrecht, The Netherlands: Kluwer.

Wylie, R. E., & Durrell, D. D. (1970). Teaching vowels through phonograms. *Elementary English, 47,* 787–791.

Toward Distinguishing Between Cognitive and Experiential Deficits as Primary Sources of Difficulty in Learning to Read: The Importance of Early Intervention in Diagnosing Specific Reading Disability

Frank R. Vellutino
Donna M. Scanlon
Edward R. Sipay
The University at Albany

BACKGROUND[1]

Specific reading disability, as an etiological concept, carries with it the implicit assumption that reading problems in beginning readers are caused primarily by constitutional factors such as organic disorder or genetic limitations that adversely affect cognitive abilities that underlie reading ability. Yet, notwithstanding commonly used exclusionary criteria designed to distinguish between factors that lead to relatively circumscribed learning difficulties and factors that lead to general learning difficulties (e.g., low general intelligence, sensory deficits, emotional disorder, environmental impoverishment), there are no definitive criteria that would allow us to distinguish between constitutional causes of reading disability and experiential causes such as inadequate instruction and/or inadequate preliteracy experience. And, whereas psychological studies conducted in recent years have provided highly convergent evidence that reading disability may be caused by language deficits of one description or another rather than visual–spatial or occulo-motor deficits, as was once believed to

---

[1]The longitudinal study briefly discussed in this chapter is described in greater detail elsewhere (Vellutino et al., 1996).

be the case, there is not uniform agreement as to which of the language systems is a preeminent cause of the disorder. Results from genetic, neurological, and electrophysiological studies are also consistent with a language deficit explanation of reading disability, but results from these studies are yet inconclusive.

Regarding psychological research, the most compelling and convergent evidence suggests that reading disability is caused by phonological coding deficits that impair the acquisition of facility in word identification, letter-sound mapping, and spelling, as basic reading subskills. The evidence for this suggestion comes from a large number of cross-sectional studies that have found robust and reliable differences between both age-matched and reading-level-matched poor and normal readers, not only on tests evaluating these reading subskills, but also on tests evaluating phonological skills, such as phoneme segmentation, name encoding, name retrieval, and verbal (working) memory, all of which are presumed to underlie reading ability (e.g., Brady & Shankweiler, 1991; Bruck, 1990, 1992; Liberman & Shankweiler, 1979; Mann, Liberman, & Shankweiler, 1980; Stanovich, 1988; Tunmer, 1989; Vellutino & Scanlon, 1987a, 1987b; Vellutino, Scanlon, Small, & Tanzman, 1991; Vellutino, Scanlon, & Spearing, 1995; Vellutino, Scanlon, & Tanzman, 1994). Also supportive are results from: longitudinal studies demonstrating that these and other phonological skills, such as letter naming and rapid automatized naming, are reasonably good predictors of achievement in reading (Blachman, 1984; Bradley & Bryant, 1983; Liberman, Shankweiler, Fischer, & Carter, 1974; Lundberg, Olofsson, & Wall, 1980; Vellutino & Scanlon, 1987a; Wolf, 1984); and regression studies documenting that tests evaluating phonological skills, such as alphabetic mapping and phoneme segmentation, account for much more variance on measures of word identification than do tests evaluating other language-based skills or tests evaluating visual processing abilities (Vellutino et al., 1991, 1994). But especially impressive are results from training studies demonstrating that instruction in phoneme segmentation and alphabetic mapping has a positive effect on reading and spelling ability (Blachman, 1994; Blachman, Ball, Black, & Tangel, 1994; Bradley & Bryant, 1983; Byrne & Fielding-Barnsley, 1991, 1993; Foorman, Francis, Novy, & Liberman, 1991; Lundberg, Frost, & Petersen, 1988; Torgesen, Wagner, & Rashotte, this volume; Vellutino & Scanlon, 1987a; Williams, 1980).

Yet, despite the wealth of evidence supporting the view that phonological skills deficiencies are preeminent causes of reading disability, some have suggested that the disorder may, in some cases, be caused by deficiencies in semantic and/or syntactic development (Byrne, 1981; Donahue, 1986; Flood & Menyuk, 1983; Fry, Johnson, & Muehl, 1970; Loban, 1963; Scarborough, 1990; Vellutino, 1979, 1987). These suggestions are largely based on studies finding differences between poor and normal readers on tests of semantic and syntactic competence, but the conclusions drawn from such studies are compromised by the fact that most of them employed interme-diate- or adolescent-age subjects, thus presenting the possibility that reader group differences on tests of semantic and syntactic abilities are a conse-quence of longstanding reading difficulties, rather than a primary cause of such difficulties (Stanovich, 1986). In the semantic domain, this possibility is supported by the finding of strong and reliable reader group differences on tests of vocabulary knowledge and other semantic abilities, but only in adolescent-age children, and not in elementary-age children (Vellutino et al., 1995; Vellutino & Scanlon, 1987b; Vellutino, Scanlon, & Tanzman, 1988). Vellutino et al. (1991, 1994) replicated this pattern in the syntactic domain. Moreover, several studies have provided documentation that syntactic deficits of the types observed in poor readers (e.g., comprehending syntac-tically complex sentences, judging grammaticality, using sentence contexts for word identification) may be caused by more basic deficits in phonologi-cal coding (Mann, Shankweiler, & Smith, 1984; Shankweiler & Crain, 1986; Shankweiler, Crain, Brady, & Macaruso, 1992; Shankweiler, Smith, & Mann, 1984). These issues, nevertheless, remain open.

Finally, there is now abundant evidence that poor readers tend to perform as proficiently as do normal readers on tests evaluating visual–spatial and occulo-motor abilities (Olson, Kliegl, & Davidson, 1983; Stan-ley, Smith, & Howell, 1983; Vellutino, 1979, 1987), thus undermining visual deficit theories of reading disability.[2] However, most of these stud-ies evaluated children who were not beginning readers, and at least one

---

[2]A number of investigators have, more recently, theorized that reading disability may be caused by a deficit in the "transient visual system" (Badcock & Lovegrove, 1981; Breitmeyer, 1989; Lovegrove, Martin, & Slaghuis, 1986). The transient system is a functional component of the visual system that is operative during saccadic movements and is believed to be responsible for inhibiting the visual trace that normally persists for a short duration (approximately 250 milliseconds) after a visual stimulus has been terminated. Poor readers are presumed to suffer from a deficit in the inhibitory function of the transient system, producing a visual trace of abnormal longevity that creates masking effects and, thus, visual acuity problems when the children are reading connected text. Some experimental evidence to support this theory is provided by studies showing that poor and normal readers process high and low spatial frequency grids differently and that they have different contrast sensitivity functions, such that the poor readers require greater luminosity than the normal readers for distinguishing low frequency grids (Badcock & Lovegrove, 1981; Martin & Lovegrove, 1984). However, as pointed out by Hulme (1988), the trace persistence theory of reading disability predicts that poor readers should be impaired only when they are reading connected text and not when they encounter printed words one at a time under foveal vision conditions. Yet, we know that poor readers have as much or more difficulty identifying printed words encountered one at a time, under foveal vision conditions, as they have identifying words encountered in connected text. Moreover, there is no evidence that poor readers are impaired by visual masking and visual acuity problems under normal reading conditions. We, therefore, doubt that visual trace persistence is a significant cause of reading disability.

prominent theory of reading disability suggests that visual deficits, which might be causally related to the disorder, would be observed very early in the child's development, but perhaps not later (Satz, Taylor, Friel, & Fletcher, 1978).

Regarding the possibility that reading disability may be caused by constitutional deficits of one description or another, suggestive evidence is provided by neuroanatomical (Galaburda & Kemper, 1979; Galaburda, 1983), electrophysiological (Shucard, Cummins, Gay, Lairsmith, & Welanko, 1985), and neuroradiological (Filipek, 1995; Hynd & Semrud-Clikeman, 1989) studies demonstrating structural and functional anomalies in the brains of impaired readers, although results to date are conflicting. More impressive are results from genetic studies documenting that reading difficulties occur more often among family members of reading-impaired individuals than in the population at large. Furthermore, reading difficulties have a higher concordance rate in twins than in other siblings, especially monozygotic twins (Olson, Wise, Conners, & Rack, 1990). Moreover, a recent study has tentatively located a gene for reading disability on chromosome 6 (Cardon et al., 1994), although this finding has not yet been replicated. Additionally, twin studies have shown that measures of reading ability as well as measures of phonologically based skills—such as phoneme segmentation, letter-sound mapping, and rapid naming—have high degrees of heritability, thereby providing the most compelling evidence to date for a direct link between genetic endowment and cognitive abilities underlying reading ability.

However, as clearly articulated in a very penetrating paper by Clay (1987), virtually all studies concerned with the etiology of reading disability are equivocated by the fact that none have controlled for or evaluated the early literacy experiences or the school histories of the impaired readers who were the objects of inquiry. At the same time, early intervention studies suggest that most reading-impaired children, who might be diagnosed as "reading disabled," are not truly "disabled" in the sense in which this term is typically used (i.e., implying organically based cognitive deficits), but may simply have gotten off to a poor start because of experience and/or instruction that did not adequately prepare them for success in beginning reading (Clay, 1985; Iversen & Tunmer; 1993; Pinnell, 1989; Wasik & Slavin, 1993). Yet, results from these studies are, themselves, inconclusive, because none compared the cognitive abilities of children who were difficult to remediate with the cognitive abilities of children who were readily remediated, in order to ascertain whether cognitive deficits presumed to be causally related to reading disability are found more often in the former than in the latter group. Moreover, none attempted to evaluate rudimentary literacy and other precursor skills acquired by the children in these two groups before they had any formal instruction in reading.

DESIGN OF THE STUDY

To accomplish these objectives, we conducted a longitudinal study that incorporated an early intervention component designed as a "first cut" diagnostic to aid in distinguishing between children whose reading difficulties are caused by basic cognitive deficits and children whose reading difficulties are caused by inadequate experience and/or instruction (Vellutino et al., 1996). Of special interest was the question of whether or not these two groups would differ on the types of tasks that have consistently distinguished between poor and normally developing readers in previous research; in particular, tasks that depend heavily on phonological coding ability. Accordingly, kindergartners from several participating school districts (n = 1,407) in middle- to upper-middle-class neighborhoods in the Albany, New York, area were administered a large battery of psychological tests evaluating relevant cognitive abilities and rudimentary literacy skills. In mid-first grade, subsamples of poor readers (n = 118) and normal readers (n = 65) were selected from the population that remained following attrition (n = 1,284). Selection was based upon teacher recommendations, achievement testing, and the application of exclusionary criteria typically employed in reading disability research. (The number of poor readers identified by these exclusionary criteria represents 9% of the total population of available children.)[3] The poor and normal reader groups were studied in depth from kindergarten through fourth grade. In winter of first grade, the poor readers were randomly assigned to either a "tutored" or "nontutored" group. The children in the tutored group (n = 76) were given daily (one-to-one) tutoring (½ hour per day) for a minimum of one and a maximum of two school semesters, depending on progress. Children in the nontutored group were given school-based remediation, which typically entailed small-group instruction (n = 26). However, in given

---

[3]To qualify for the poor reader sample, children had to be identified by their classroom teacher as experiencing substantial difficulties with reading and had to have a score at or below the 15th percentile on either the Word Identification or Word Attack subtests of the Woodcock Reading Mastery Test—Revised (Woodcock, 1987). To qualify as a normal reader, children had to be identified by their classroom teacher as progressing at an average or above-average level in reading and had to score at or above the 40th percentile on both subtests. All (prospective) subjects also had to have an IQ of at least 90 or above on either the Verbal or the Performance Scales of the Wechsler Intelligence Scale for Children—Revised. These criteria were employed only after initial screening using the exclusionary criteria previously referred to.

instances, it entailed some amount of one-to-one instruction ($n = 16$). All target children (both poor and normal readers) were given annual achievement tests through fourth grade. They were also evaluated in first and third grades on a large battery of tests assessing cognitive abilities believed to underlie reading. A few additional measures were administered in second grade. The various tests discussed in this chapter are briefly described in Fig. 16.1.

The tutoring program was tailored to individual needs and the degree of emphasis placed on given remedial activities varied in accord with the child's strengths and weaknesses. However, in each session, some time was spent: helping the child acquire facility in whole word identification, helping him or her acquire phoneme awareness, attuning him or her to the alphabetic principle, and facilitating phonetic decoding and writing skills. In addition, each session typically included approximately 15 minutes devoted to reading connected text, both to facilitate reading for meaning and fun, and to foster deliberate and interactive use of a variety of strategies for word identification, in particular sentence and/or thematic contexts for prediction and monitoring, external aids (e.g., picture clues), and phonetic (letter-sound) decoding. Instruction was provided by teachers ($n = 14$) who were certified in either elementary education or in reading. All but one had at least 2 years of teaching experience. Tutor training consisted initially of a 30-hour seminar supplemented by reading of theoretically and practically relevant materials. To ensure fidelity of treatment, all tutoring sessions were recorded on audiotape, and 1 out of every 10 tapes was randomly selected for review and feedback by one of the authors, each of whom met weekly with one or another tutor on a rotating basis. There were also biweekly meetings with all of the tutors as a group, during which relevant issues and problems were discussed.

SUMMARY OF SALIENT FINDINGS

Our primary interest in the current study was in comparing children who were initially identified as poor readers but were readily remediated, with similarly identified children who were difficult to remediate, relative to normally developing readers. Thus, the results summarized in the ensuing sections focus on the target poor readers who received daily (one-to-one) tutoring and the normal reading control subjects. We discuss only the data collected during the period from kindergarten through second grade because data collection beyond this grade has only recently been completed. Growth rate in reading ability was estimated by calculating the slope for the line of best fit for the reading outcome measures using Rasch-based ability ("W") scores on the Basic Skills Cluster (BSC) of the

KINDERGARTEN BATTERY

A.   Intellectual Ability (estimated)

 .1.   Wechsler Preschool and Primary Scale of Intelligence-Revised (WPPSI-R).

        a.   Information subtest - asks child questions evaluating general
knowledge.

        b.   Block Design subtest - requires that the child assemble blocks to
reproduce abstract geometric designs under time constraints; evaluates visual-spatial
analysis and reasoning ability.

        c.   Concrete Operations - measures of conservation, seriation and class
inclusion were administered to determine whether the child had attained the concrete
operational stage (Piaget, 1952).

B.   Concepts of Print

     1.   Print Awareness - assesses understanding of the communication value of
print. For example, the child is asked to indicate which would be the best way to
find out what is in a can: read the label or open the can.

     2.   Print Conventions - assesses understanding of left/right sequencing of
print, concept of word and letter, etc.

C.   Achievement Measures

     1.   Rudimentary Reading Skills - measured by subtests of the Woodcock Reading
Mastery Test-Revised (WWRMT-R)

        a.   Letter Identification
        b.   Word Identification (naming whole words at sight)
        c.   Word Attack (pronouncing nonsense words)

     2.   Arithmetic

        a.   WPPSI-R Arithmetic subtest - evaluates ability to solve "story
problems" presented auditorily.

        b.   Experimental test evaluating basic number concepts and simple
arithmetic operations. Subtests included:

            (1)   Counting by 1s
            (2)   Counting by 2s
            (3)   Number Identification (identifying numbers on sight).

D.   Language Measures

     1.   Phonological Processing

        a.   Initial Deletion - say the word that remains after deleting the
initial sound of a word (e.g., cup - up).

        b.   Final Deletion - say the word that remains after deleting the final
sound of a word (e.g., plate - play).

        c.   Articulation - vocalize the different sounds in minimally
contrasted word pairs (/f/ and /c/ for fat and cat).

     2.   Syntactic/Grammatical Processing

        a.   The Linguistic Concepts subtest of the Clinical Evaluation of
Language Fundamentals-Revised - children hear sentences directing them to perform
certain operations ("Point to the red line after you point to the blue one.").

     3.   Semantic Development

        a.   Peabody Picture Vocabulary Test-Revised - evaluates recognition of
vocabulary words depicted pictorially.

     4.   Naming and Fluency

        a.   Rapid Automatized Naming - requires child to name simple objects
presented in a 5 x 10 array as quickly as possible. Score reported is total amount
of time taken (in seconds) to complete the array.

        b.   Rapid Articulation - requires child to repeat word pairs as quickly
as possible. Score reported is mean time (in seconds) to complete seven repetitions.

FIG. 16.1. Assessment batteries administered to target children.

353

5.   Verbal Memory and Visual-Verbal Learning

         a.   Sentence Memory - child hears sentences and must repeat each
verbatim.

         b.   Word Memory - child hears strings of randomly ordered words and
must repeat each verbatim.

         c.   Visual-Auditory Learning subtest from the Woodcock Reading Mastery
Test-Revised - child learns to associate novel symbols with words and learns to
"read" sentences made up of these symbols.

E.   Visual Skills

    1.   Visual-Spatial Reasoning

         a.   The Block Design subtest from the WPPSI-R - evaluates analysis and
synthesis of spatial relations, visual-spatial reasoning, visual-motor coordination,
etc. Child assembles blocks to reproduce geometric designs.

    2.   Visual Memory

         a.   Child is asked to reproduce dot patterns from memory on a magnetic
drawing board. Patterns are either labelable (e.g., dots form a "T") or non-
labelable (randomly arrayed).

F.   Executive Functions (Attention, Concentration, Planning and Vigilance)

    1.   Visual matching (Matching Familiar Figures Test-Modified) - the child is
asked to find the identical match for a line drawing in a group of four similar
drawings.

    2.   Visual Search (Target Search Test) - the child is asked to look at a
large group of geometric designs and put a line through all those that are identical
to a target design.

FIRST GRADE BATTERY

A.   Intellectual Ability

    1.   The full Wechsler Intelligence Scale for Children-Revised (WISC-R) was
administered to all target subjects.

B.   Achievement Measures

    1.   First Grade Selection Measures

         a.   Woodcock Reading Mastery Test-Revised

              (1)   Word Identification - evaluates whole word naming.

              (2)   Word Attack - evaluates ablity to decode nonsense
                    syllables.

    2.   First Grade Outcome Measures

         a.   WRMT-R Word Identification - see above

         b.   WRMT-R Word Attack - see above

         c.   Text reading - evaluates oral reading accuracy using narrative text
presented in short paragraphs

    3.   Math Achievement (Woodcock-Johnson Tests of Achievement)

         a.   Calculation - assesses ability to perform written math calculations
such as addition and subtraction.

         b.   Applied Problems - assesses the ability to solve math "story
problems."

C.   Language Measures

    1.   Phonological Processing

         a.   Phonemic Awareness - initial phoneme deletion, final phoneme
deletion, phoneme articulation (see Kindergarten measures for descriptions).

         b.   Phonological Memory - memory for six nonsense syllables assessed
over eight presentation/recall trials.

FIG. 16.1. (Continued)

354

2. Syntactic/Grammatical Processing

a. Token Test (Parts IV and V) - evaluates the ability to comprehend spoken directions.

b. Test of Language Development-Primary:2 (TOLD-P:2) Grammatic Understanding subtest - evaluates sentence comprehension.

c. Grammaticality Judgment - the child hears sentences, some of which contain grammatical errors; the child's task is to indicate whether sentences are grammatically well formed.

d. Oral Cloze - the child listens to paragraphs containing sentences from which given words are deleted; as each sentence is presented, the child is asked to fill in missing words using sentence contexts and story themes to aid in doing so.

3. Semantic Processing

a. Vocabulary subtest of the WISC-R - the child is asked to define spoken words.

b. Similarities subtest of the WISC-R - the child is asked to detect and characterize commonalities in verbally presented concepts.

4. Naming and Fluency

a. Rapid Naming of Letters, Numbers, Colors and Objects arrayed in a 5 x 10 matrix (see kindergarten battery for description).

b. Boston Naming Test - evaluates the ability to retrieve the names of objects presented pictorially.

5. General Language Processing

a. Listening Comprehension component of the Spache Diagnostic Reading Scales - evaluates ability to answer factual and inferential questions about narrative text presented auditorily.

6. Verbal Memory

a. Digit Span subtest of the WISC-R - evaluates verbatim recall of randomly presented digits.

b. Sentence Imitation subtest from the TOLD-P:2 - evaluates verbatim recall of sentences.

c. Memory for Words - evaluates recall of concrete and abstract words under immediate and delayed recall conditions.

d. Syntactic Word Order - child hears sentences presented in scrambled order and must repeat each sentence in correct order.

e. Phonological Memory - see Language Measures, Phonological Processing for task description.

D. Visual Processing Skills

1. Performance Scale of the WISC-R - measures a variety of visual processing abilities (e.g., visual recognition, visual coding, visual-spatial analysis and synthesis, visual-spatial reasoning, visual-motor coordination, etc.)

2. Visual Memory - child reproduces a pattern of dots from memory. (see kindergarten battery for task description).

SECOND GRADE BATTERY

A. Achievement Outcome Measures

1. WRMT-R Word Identification

2. WRMT-R Word Attack

3. Silent Reading Comprehension subtest of the Spache Diagnostic Reading Scales - evaluates ability to answer factual and inferential questions about narrative text presented in print.

B. Executive Functions (Attention, Concentration, Planning and Vigilance)

1. Target Search Test (Symbols) - see kindergarten battery

2. Target Search Test (Letters) - child searches a 14 x 10 array of CVC syllables through which he/she is to draw a line.

3. Target Search Test (Numbers) - child searches an array of 3 digit numbers for all occurrences of a target number.

FIG. 16.1. (Continued)

Woodcock Reading Mastery Test—Revised (WRMT—R), which combines the Word Identification and Word Attack subtests. The BSC served as the dependent variable, and time of test (in months from entry into kindergarten through fall of second grade) served as the independent variable (Bryk & Raudenbush, 1987; Rogosa & Willet, 1985). Growth rates were computed for each child separately based on four data points: fall of kindergarten, winter of first grade, late spring of first grade, and fall of second grade. The slopes for the entire poor reader group were then rank ordered, and four (roughly) equal groups were formed based on relative status on the slopes continuum. The four groups were designated as follows: very limited growth (VLG), limited growth (LG), good growth (GG), and very good growth (VGG). To more fully evaluate the possible effects of IQ on the various dependent measures, the normal reader group was partitioned into two groups by dividing it at the normal reader mean IQ (WISC—R Full Scale IQ; Wechsler, 1974), yielding an average IQ normal reader group (AvIQNorm) and an above-average IQ group (AbAvIQNorm).

In the ensuing sections, we organize the exposition as follows. We first present results on the sample selection measures in order to provide baseline data on reading subskills prior to remediation, and to document that results on our reading achievement and intelligence measures conform with acceptable psychometric criteria for defining specific reading disability. We next present results on the reading achievement outcome measures used to evaluate growth in reading over time to provide documentation for the utility of early intervention as a "first cut" diagnostic in distinguishing between problem readers impaired primarily by basic cognitive deficits and problem readers impaired primarily by experiential deficits. We thereafter summarize the most important findings on the preintervention kindergarten and first-grade assessment batteries, and present evidence that the cognitive profiles of readily remediated problem readers are more like those of normal readers than are the cognitive profiles of difficult to remediate problem readers.

Selection Measures

Table 16.1 presents results on the measures used for sample selection. It can be seen that the children in the various tutored groups performed well below the children in both normal reader groups on the word identification and phonetic (pseudoword) decoding tests (respectively, WRMT—R Word Identification and WRMT—R Word Attack). In contrast, the two normal reader groups performed at comparable levels on these tests. Note, however, that among the tutored groups, those who manifested the most limited growth in reading had the lowest scores on the word identification subtest at the outset, whereas those who manifested

TABLE 16.1

Scores Obtained by Tutored Poor Readers (Grouped in Accord With Growth in Reading Over Time) and by Normal Readers on the Reading and Intelligence Measures Administered for Sample Selection Prior to Intervention

	Raw Scores	Normal Readers		Tutored Groups*			
		AvIQNorm n = 28	AbAvIQNorm n = 37	VLG n = 19	LG n = 18	GG n = 18	VGG n = 19
VIQ	X	106.14	121.51	100.89	101.11	104.11	105.42
	S.D.	6.70	8.57	14.47	10.19	10.46	12.01
PIQ	X	107.00	119.03	102.32	102.67	106.11	105.26
	S.D.	9.03	5.97	9.84	9.59	13.35	9.43
FIQ	X	106.89	122.86	101.37	101.94	105.56	105.58
	S.D.	6.57	5.33	10.17	7.66	12.53	10.24
Word Identification raw score	X	37.39	38.81	4.42	6.89	11.56	11.53
	S.D.	12.91	10.83	3.34	4.59	4.62	5.51
Word Identification grade equivalent	X	2.20	2.22	.96	1.07	1.26	1.25
Word Attack raw score	X	12.79	13.73	.74	1.06	.78	1.32
	S.D.	8.36	7.46	2.28	1.86	.94	1.67
Word Attack grade equivalent	X	2.01	1.97	.60	.67	.65	.73

Note. From Vellutino et al. (1996). Reprinted with permission.

*Grouped by slopes for W scores obtained on the Basic Skills Cluster of the WRMT—R from kindergarten through fall of second grade.

Key for Abbreviations Used in All Tables and Figures

AvIQNorm = Average IQ normal readers
AbAvIQNorm = Above-average IQ normal readers
VLG = Very limited growth group
LG = Limited growth group
GG = Good growth group
VGG = Very good growth group

the greatest amount of growth in reading had the highest scores at the outset. In contrast, virtually all tutored children had inadequate facility in phonetic decoding at the outset. It is also worth noting that the poor readers in respective tutored groups and the average IQ normal readers performed at comparable levels on the intelligence measures.

Reading Achievement Outcome Measures

In accord with results obtained in previous intervention studies (Clay, 1985; Iversen & Tunmer, 1993; Pinnell, 1989; Wasik & Slavin, 1993), most of the children given daily tutoring (67.1%) scored solidly in the average range (>30th percentile) on the Basic Skills Cluster (BSC) after only one semester of remediation. In fact, 44.7% of these children scored above the 45th percentile on the BSC, whereas only 19.2% of the children given small-group instruction scored in this range. At the same time, 26.9% of the children given small-group instruction scored at or below the 15th percentile on the BSC, whereas only 15.8% of the children given daily tutoring scored in this range. This pattern of results indicates that, in most cases, daily tutoring was a more effective intervention procedure than was small-group instruction. (Note that two of the children initially given daily tutoring were subsequently lost through attrition. Thus, analyses reported in the ensuing sections are based on a total of 74 tutored children.)

More important, for present purposes, are results from the growth curve analyses comparing the progress of children who were found to be difficult to remediate with that of children who were more readily remediated, relative to the progress made by the normal readers. Figures 16.2 and 16.3 present growth curves for raw score averages on the WRMT—R Word Identification and Word Attack subtests (respectively) for children in the two normal reader groups and children in each of the tutored groups. (Although the tutored groups were partitioned on the basis of slopes for BSC W scores obtained from kindergarten through fall of second grade, we also present data for winter and spring of second grade to demonstrate stability in the rank ordering of these respective groups following remediation.) It can be seen that the slopes representing growth in word identification in the AvIQNorm and AbAvIQNorm groups (Fig. 16.2) are virtually identical throughout the period evaluated. And, as would be expected, the growth rates for these two groups, prior to initiation of the intervention program (fall of kindergarten to winter of first grade), are much greater than the growth rates for the tutored groups during the same period. However, after only one semester of remediation (winter to spring of first grade), the performance levels for respective tutored groups rose dramatically, indicating that the intervention program had a positive effect on children in each of these groups. Yet, it is apparent, from both group

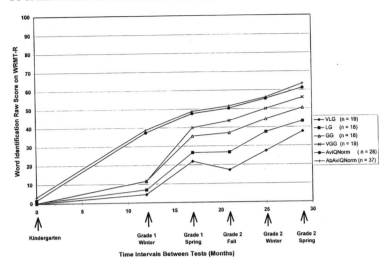

FIG. 16.2. Growth curves for raw scores on the WRMT—R Word Identification subtest for normal readers and tutored poor readers. From Vellutino et al. (1996). Reprinted with permission.

differences in the performance levels representing initial response to the intervention program and the consistency of the rank ordering of these performance levels over the period following intervention, that children in the VGG group were best able to profit from remediation, whereas children in the VLG group were least able to do so. Children in the GG group did not profit as much from remediation as did children in the VGG group, but

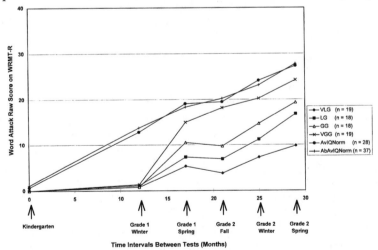

FIG. 16.3. Growth curves for raw scores on the WRMT—R Word Attack subtest for normal readers and tutored poor readers. From Vellutino et al. (1996). Reprinted with permission.

profited more than children in the LG group, who, in turn, profited more than children in the VLG group. Essentially, the same pattern of results emerged in assessment of growth in phonetic decoding ability.

It can be seen (Fig. 16.3) that the growth curves depicting change in phonetic (pseudoword) decoding ability are similar to the growth curves depicting change in word identification, insofar as the tutored children made little or no progress in acquiring this skill prior to initiation of the intervention program. However, their growth rates increased sharply from winter of first grade to spring of first grade, after one semester of remediation. In contrast, growth rates for the AvIQNorm and AbAvIQNorm groups increased sharply from kindergarten to winter of first grade, and continued to increase steadily thereafter. And, as was true of word identification, the growth rates in these two groups were virtually identical. In addition, the rank ordering of respective groups was maintained throughout the period following intervention. Note also that, following intervention, the performance level of the VGG group was more like that of the two normal reader groups than like those of the other tutored groups. Indeed, the disparity between the VGG group and the other tutored groups, vis-à-vis growth in phonetic decoding ability, is greater than the disparity between these groups, vis-à-vis growth in word identification. Given the heavy reliance of alphabetic mapping on phonological coding ability, these results lead one to expect that the VGG group would also be closer to normal readers than to the other tutored groups on nonreading cognitive tasks that also depend on phonological coding ability. As is seen further in this discussion, this expectation was essentially realized.

Finally, because respective tutored groups were partitioned on the basis of Basic Skills Cluster (BSC) W scores, Table 16.2 presents the BSC percentile ranks corresponding with these scores to allow norm-based comparison of the general reading abilities of respective groups, beginning with the BSC percentile ranks achieved just prior to initiation of the intervention program (winter of first grade). Table 16.2 also presents: raw score means and standard deviations for the oral (text) reading test administered to the children in each of the groups at the end of first grade, and grade equivalents on the test of reading comprehension administered at the end of second grade. It can be seen that the rank orderings of (respective) group means on the BSC obtained in first and second grade are cross-validated by the rank orderings of group means on both the text reading and reading comprehension tests, each of which provides an independent measure of reading ability.

It should be clear, from the stability of the results yielded by the reading achievement measures, that, following intervention, the reading subskills of children in the VGG group were much closer to those of the normal readers than were the reading subskills of children in the other three

TABLE 16.2

Reading Achievement Outcome Measures Administered to Normal Readers and Children in Respective Tutored Groups During the Winter and Spring of Their First-Grade Year and During the Fall, Winter, and Spring of Their Second-Grade Year

	Raw Scores	Normal Readers		Tutored Groups*			
		AvIQNorm n = 28	AbAvIQNorm n = 37	VLG n = 19	LG n = 18	GG n = 18	VGG n = 19
First Grade (Winter)							
Basic skills cluster percentile rank	X	72.21	72.65	8.58	13.56	18.72	22.26
	S.D.	16.68	16.99	9.99	8.15	6.99	10.92
First Grade (Spring)							
Basic skills cluster percentile rank	X	74.21	76.11	19.84	29.11	47.83	62.63
	S.D.	22.19	19.13	12.47	8.31	9.78	11.99
Text reading (raw score)	X	33.18	33.72	6.32	13.74	22.00	28.58
	S.D.	9.16	8.49	5.02	7.83	7.33	6.18
Second Grade (Fall)							
Basic skills cluster percentile rank	X	70.35	73.69	5.47	17.11	35.72	60.16
	S.D.	24.04	23.38	3.29	5.75	8.15	13.49
Second Grade (Winter)							
Basic skills cluster percentile rank	X	72.31	73.42	9.00	22.56	38.83	58.21
	S.D.	20.84	21.03	7.92	11.06	14.65	17.64
Second Grade (Spring)							
Basic skills cluster percentile rank	X	74.62	79.11	14.37	27.56	43.50	63.79
	S.D.	20.57	15.96	16.66	12.12	16.83	15.08
Reading comprehension grade equivalent	X	3.84	4.81	2.03	2.81	3.27	3.31

Note. From Vellutino et al. (1996). Reprinted with permission.

*Grouped by slopes for W scores obtained on the Basic Skills Cluster of the WRMT—R from kindergarten through fall of second grade.

tutored groups. It should also be clear that the reading subskills of children in the VLG group were farthest from those of the normal readers following intervention. Adding weight to this dichotomy is the fact that all children in the VGG group received only one semester of remediation, whereas all children in each of the other groups received two semesters of remediation. It would therefore seem that the strongest test of the hypothesis that reading disability, in some cases, may be caused by basic deficits in cognitive abilities underlying reading would be provided by comparison of the VGG and VLG groups, relative to the normal readers, on the tasks designed to evaluate these abilities. Accordingly, in the next two sections, we focus on these two groups in reporting results on such tasks, although results from the GG and LG groups are also presented for purposes of comparison.

Kindergarten Battery

Table 16.3 presents results on kindergarten measures of foundational literacy skills and cognitive abilities that distinguished between the tutored children and the normal readers, and in some instances, between the VGG and the VLG groups. Raw score means and standard deviations are presented for the average IQ normal readers. For all other groups, the data are presented as effect sizes computed relative to the performance of the average IQ normal reader group. Because of space constraints, the tables present data only for measures that produced statistically significant differences between given groups.

Not surprisingly, the normal readers performed significantly better ($p < .05$) than did children in both the VLG and VGG groups on the measures of letter and word naming administered in kindergarten. The normal readers also performed better on the tests (respectively) evaluating counting by 1s and number naming, although their performance was significantly better than that of the VGG group only on the number naming test. These latter results are significant because each of these tasks involves many of the same cognitive processes as letter and word naming, in particular, name encoding, name retrieval, phonological coding, and visual–verbal association learning. Thus, it is not surprising that the normal readers also performed significantly better than did children in the VLG group on WPPSI—R Arithmetic, (which also evaluates counting, as well as the ability to solve simple math "story" problems, among other rudimentary number skills) and on tests evaluating rapid naming of objects, fluency in articulation, sentence memory, word memory, and visual–verbal learning.

In contrast, the normal readers performed significantly better than did children in the VGG group only on WPPSI—R Arithmetic and on the

TABLE 16.3

Measures of Foundational Literacy Skills and Cognitive Abilities Evaluated in Kindergarten That Distinguished Between Tutored Children and Normal Readers and Between Tutored Children Who Were Difficult to Remediate and Tutored Children Who Were Readily Remediated[a]

	Raw Scores	Normal Readers		Tutored Groups[b]			
		AvIQNorm n = 28	AbAvIQNorm n = 37	VLG n = 19	LG n = 18	GG n = 18	VGG n = 19
Letter naming*@+	X	27.57	.11	-2.93	-2.17	-1.73	-1.52
	S.D.	5.69					
Word naming*@	X	1.71	.62	-.62	-.52	-.58	-.60
	S.D.	2.68					
Counting by 1s*+	X	7.89	.15	-1.20	-1.00	-1.00	-.45
	S.D.	2.28					
Number naming*@+	X	9.48	-.06	-2.31	-1.67	-1.02	-1.24
	S.D.	1.65					
Arithmetic (WPPSI—R)*@	X	15.61	.48	-1.07	-.95	-.85	-.70
	S.D.	2.74					
RAN[c] objects time*	X	68.98	-.15	.84	.69	.67	.53
	S.D.	16.69					

(Continued)

363

TABLE 16.3
(Continued)

	Raw Scores	Normal Readers		Tutored Groups[b]			
		AvIQNorm $n = 28$	AbAvIQNorm $n = 37$	VLG $n = 19$	LG $n = 18$	GG $n = 18$	VGG $n = 19$
Rapid articulation time*	X	6.95	.19	1.34	.33	1.42	.57
	S.D.	1.35					
Sentence memory*	X	4.96	.71	-.88	-.50	-.61	-.27
	S.D.	1.04					
Word memory*@	X	1.50	.36	-1.03	-.56	-.77	-.76
	S.D.	.79					
Visual-verbal learning*@+	X	41.52	.17	-2.13	-1.22	-1.13	-1.04
	S.D.	4.44					

[a]Raw score means and standard deviations are presented for average IQ normal readers. For all other groups, data are reported as effect sizes computed relative to the performance of the average IQ normal reader group.

[b]Grouped by slopes for W scores obtained on the Basic Skills Cluster of the WRMT—R from kindergarten through fall of second grade.

[c]RAN—rapid automatized naming—time reported in seconds.

*Significant differences between AvIQNorm vs. VLG.

@Significant differences between AvIQNorm vs. VGG.

+Significant differences between VGG vs. VLG.

tests evaluating word memory and visual–verbal learning. At the same time, children in the VGG group performed significantly better than did children in the VLG group on the tests evaluating letter naming, counting by 1s, number naming, and visual–verbal learning. These latter results provide substantial support for the possibility that the reading-related cognitive abilities of children in the VGG group are more like those of normal readers than like those of children in the VLG group. Furthermore, it is of some significance that the tasks that distinguished among the groups compared either depend on or are, in some way, related to name encoding, name retrieval, working memory, and phonological coding ability in general.[4] The only phonological task that did not distinguish these groups in kindergarten was that evaluating phoneme segmentation ability. However, in an additional analysis involving the worst- and best-achieving tutored groups, along with the average IQ normal reader group (VLG + LG vs. GG + VGG vs. AvIQNorm), significant differences ($p < .05$) did emerge on the phoneme segmentation test, but only between the average IQ normal reader group and the two worst-achieving groups combined (AvIQNorm vs. VLG + LG). Thus, the failure to obtain group differences on the initial analysis was probably due to lack of power.

It is also important to note that there were no significant differences ($p > .05$) between and among respective reader groups on tests evaluating semantic, syntactic, and visual abilities, nor were there significant group differences on tests evaluating print awareness, knowledge of print conventions, conceptual development, and various "executive functions," such as attention, concentration, and organizational ability (data not shown). These results accord quite well with our finding of no differences among the tutored groups, or between each of these groups and the average IQ normal readers, on the intelligence measures. The combined results are important, not only because they indicate that our tutored children were specifically disabled readers rather than "garden variety" poor readers who were generally impaired in learning, but also because they provide support for the assumption that semantic, syntactic, visual and/or executive function deficits are unlikely causes of reading difficulties in such children.[5] And, when this pattern of results is viewed in light

---

[4]The finding of significant differences between the VLG and AvIQNorm groups, on the rapid articulation task, raises the question of whether speech/motor programming may covary in some way with naming speed or reading ability. However, rapid articulation was not found to be significantly correlated with growth in reading ability in either the tutored children or the normal readers, nor was it reliably correlated with naming speed. Stanovich, Nathan, and Zolman (1988) obtained similar results. These investigators also asserted that although articulation speed may serve as a "marker variable for phonological problems at deeper levels" (p. 72), it is doubtful that it is causally related to reading disability. Our data are consistent with this assertion.

of that obtained on the tests evaluating rudimentary reading and related phonological skills, it seems reasonable to infer, in accord with results obtained in previous research, that phonological skills are primary determinants of success in learning to read; and, conversely, that deficiencies in such skills are causally related to difficulties one might encounter in learning to read. Results on the first-grade battery provide additional support for these inferences.

First-Grade Battery

Table 16.4 presents results from the first-grade cognitive measures that distinguished between tutored children and normal readers and between tutored children who were difficult to remediate and tutored children who were readily remediated. Once again, raw score means and standard deviations are presented for the average IQ normal readers, and effect sizes are presented for all other groups.

It can be seen that the tests that reliably distinguished between the AvIQNorm and VLG groups and quite frequently between the VGG and VLG groups are those that depend, in some measure, on name encoding, name retrieval, working memory, and phonological coding ability in general. Yet, these tests distinguished less reliably between the AvIQNorm and VGG groups. To be more specific, children in the AvIQNorm group performed significantly better ($p < .05$) than did children in the VLG group on tests that evaluated phoneme segmentation; rapid naming of objects, colors, letters, and numbers; naming of pictures; memory for digits; memory for sentences; memory for concrete and abstract words; and memory for nonsense syllables (Phonological Memory). At the same time, children in the VGG group performed significantly better than did children in the VLG group on the tests evaluating phoneme segmentation, rapid naming of letters and numbers, naming of pictures, and memory for concrete and abstract words. Moreover, the VGG and AvIQNorm groups did not differ significantly on any of the naming measures, nor were they found to differ on the measures evaluating sentence memory, word memory, and memory for nonsense syllables. Neither did they differ on the phoneme segmentation measure administered in spring of first grade. This pattern of results is quite in keeping with that obtained on the kindergarten battery, and it adds considerable weight to the idea that the cognitive abilities of children in the VGG group are more like those of normal readers than like those of children in the VLG group.

---

[5]Additional evidence that the poor readers in our sample were "specifically disabled" readers rather than "garden variety" poor readers is provided by the fact that group means for respective tutored groups on measures of math ability were all within the average range.

TABLE 16.4

Measures of Cognitive Abilities Evaluated in First Grade That Distinguished Between Tutored Children and Normal Readers and Between Tutored Children Who Were Difficult to Remediate and Tutored Children Who Were Readily Remediated[a]

	Raw Scores	Normal Readers		Tutored Groups[b]			
		AvIQNorm $n = 28$	AbAvIQNorm $n = 37$	VLG $n = 19$	LG $n = 18$	GG $n = 18$	VGG $n = 19$
Phoneme segmentation							
Winter*@+	X	9.63	.23	-1.59	-.86	-1.28	-1.08
	S.D.	4.88					
Spring*+	X	21.64	.37	-1.36	-.57	-1.24	-.59
	S.D.	7.23					
RAN^c objects time*	X	55.38	-.14	.93	.40	.49	.64
	S.D.	12.04					
RAN^c colors time*	X	52.92	-.18	1.53	.15	.53	.87
	S.D.	8.60					
RAN^c letters time*+	X	37.36	-.19	1.44	1.10	.90	.04
	S.D.	10.80					
RAN^c numbers time*+	X	40.83	-.37	.79	.54	.39	-.19
	S.D.	12.25					
Boston naming test (correct)*+	X	35.39	.41	-1.35	-.80	-.82	-.54
	S.D.	5.79					
Token sentence comprehension (IV)*@	X	8.00	.36	-1.94	-.81	-1.35	-1.39
	S.D.	1.44					
Token sentence comprehension (V)*+	X	16.07	.34	-1.13	-.41	-.14	-.23
	S.D.	2.85					
Oral cloze@	X	17.14	.64	-.34	-.81	-.33	-.91
	S.D.	2.77					
Listening comprehension*@	X	40.14	.66	-.60	-.63	-.57	-1.03
	S.D.	11.86					
WISC—R digit span*@	X	8.22	.45	-1.70	-.93	-1.47	-1.65
	S.D.	1.44					

(Continued)

367

TABLE 16.4
(Continued)

Raw Scores	Normal Readers		Tutored Groups[b]			
	AvIQNorm n = 28	AbAvIQNorm n = 37	VLG n = 19	LG n = 18	GG n = 18	VGG n = 19
TOLD sentence imitation*						
X	18.89	.61	-1.24	-.55	-.92	-.72
S.D.	4.72					
Syntactic word order*@+						
X	20.04	.09	-2.15	-1.71	-1.01	-1.00
S.D.	2.04					
Phonological memory*						
X	14.50	.52	-.76	-.50	-.65	-.22
S.D.	5.40					
Delayed recall concrete words+						
X	3.04	.10	-.39	-.11	.31	.45
S.D.	1.32					
Immediate recall abstract words*+						
X	14.32	.55	-.61	-.26	-.17	.17
S.D.	5.16					
Delayed recall abstract words*+						
X	1.96	.01	-.95	-.80	-.55	-.25
S.D.	1.35					
Visual memory labelable*@						
X	5.39	.15	-1.38	-1.29	-.81	-1.60
S.D.	1.17					
Target search letters correct*+						
X	12.54	.04	-1.31	-.59	-.83	-.06
S.D.	1.92					

[a]Raw score means and standard deviations are presented for average IQ normal readers. For all other groups, data are reported as effect sizes computed relative to the performance of the average IQ normal reader group.

[b]Grouped by slopes for W scores obtained on the Basic Skills Cluster of the WRMT—R from kindergarten through fall of second grade. All but the target search tasks were administered in winter and spring of first grade. The latter tasks were administered in second grade.

[c]RAN—rapid automatized naming—time reported in seconds.

*Significant differences between AVIQNorm vs. VLG.

@Significant differences between AVIQNorm vs. VGG.

+Significant differences between VGG vs. VLG.

However, children in the AvIQNorm group also performed significantly better than did children in the VLG group and, in some instances, better than children in the VGG group, on auditory tasks evaluating sentence comprehension (Token Tests IV and V), general language (listening) comprehension, the ability to use linguistic context to insert missing words in sentences (Oral Cloze), and the ability to reorder scrambled words to construct grammatically well formed sentences (Syntactic Word Order). In addition, children in the VGG group performed significantly better than did children in the VLG group on the Syntactic Word Order task and one of the sentence comprehension tasks (Token Test V). Furthermore, they performed as well as the children in the AvIQNorm group on the latter task. Because each of these tasks depends, to some extent, on semantic and syntactic knowledge and abilities, these findings might well be interpreted as an indication that semantic and syntactic deficits are causally related to difficulties in learning to read. It should be pointed out, however, that, in addition to their dependence on semantic and syntactic knowledge and abilities, all of these tasks make heavy demands on working memory and phonological coding ability. Thus, reader group differences on each could have been due to group differences in the latter rather than the former abilities. This is a likely possibility, because there were no significant differences between and among respective groups on semantic and syntactic measures that did not make heavy demands on working memory and phonological coding ability (e.g., WISC—R Vocabulary, WISC—R Similarities, Grammaticality Judgments). This pattern was also evident in the case of like measures administered to children in these groups when they were in kindergarten. It would, therefore, appear that syntactic and semantic deficits are unlikely causes of reading difficulties in children such as those studied in the present investigation.

Regarding results on the visual processing and executive function measures, there were no significant differences between respective groups on either the visual measures administered in first grade (including WISC—R Performance Scale subtests) or the executive function measures administered in second grade, with but two exceptions. The two exceptions emerged on a task evaluating memory for labelable dot patterns, on which the AvIQNorm group performed significantly better than did both the VGG and VLG groups, and on a visual scanning task evaluating accuracy in searching for pronounceable nonsense syllables, on which the AvIQNorm and VGG groups performed significantly better than did the VLG group. However, performance on both of these tasks entailed verbal coding, and it is not surprising to find differences between poor and normal readers on visual tasks when the visual stimuli can be assigned a verbal code (Katz, Shankweiler, & Liberman, 1981).

Finally, significance tests conducted to evaluate observed differences between the average IQ and above-average IQ normal reader groups produced statistically significant differences ($p < .05$) between these groups on experienced-based and cognitive tasks such as those typically included on intelligence tests (e.g., general knowledge, vocabulary, visual–spatial abilities). However, there were few significant differences between these groups on measures of phonologically based skills of the types that distinguished between the normal readers and children in the tutored groups. Only one such measure achieved statistical significance ($p < .05$) in kindergarten (Sentence Memory) and four did so in first grade (Oral Cloze, Immediate Recall of Abstract Words, TOLD Sentence Imitation, and Listening Comprehension).

SUMMARY AND CONCLUSIONS

The longitudinal study briefly summarized in this chapter addresses three related and important questions that had not been fully addressed in previous research evaluating the etiology of reading disability. The first question is whether early and labor intensive intervention would significantly reduce the number of poor readers who might be diagnosed as "learning disabled," relative to the number diagnosed solely on the basis of the exclusionary criteria typically employed in reading disability research. The second is whether such intervention would allow one to distinguish between poor readers whose reading difficulties are caused by basic cognitive deficits and poor readers whose reading difficulties are caused by experiential and/or instructional deficits. The third question is whether the types of cognitive abilities that had been found in previous research to distinguish between poor and normally developing readers would also distinguish between poor readers who were found to be difficult to remediate and poor readers who were found to be readily remediated. The results of the study provide an affirmative answer to all three questions.

In accord with results from early intervention studies conducted by Clay (1985) and others (Iversen & Tunmer, 1993; Pinnell, 1989; Wasik & Slavin, 1993), we found that most children who might have been classified as "learning disabled" prior to intervention would not have been so classified following intervention. In the present study, the largest percentage (67.1%) of the total number of poor readers who received daily one-to-one tutoring ($n = 76$) scored within the average or above-average ranges on standardized tests of reading achievement after only one semester of remediation. In contrast, a much smaller percentage (32.9%) of these children scored below the average range, and the smallest percentage (15%) scored in the severely impaired range (<15%). And, if we put these figures in terms of percentages based on the total number of children in the population from which the tutored children were drawn ($n = 827$),[6] $n = 12$ or only 1.5% of this population scored below the 15th percentile on a composite measure of reading ability after one semester of remediation, whereas $n = 25$ or only 3% scored below the 30th percentile after one semester of remediation. These figures represent a substantial reduction over the 9% figure ($118/1,284 = .09$) that was our original estimate of the percentage of reading-disabled children in the population when we used only the exclusionary criteria that are typically used to identify such children. Moreover, when the tutored children were grouped on the basis of growth in reading ability during the periods preceding and immediately following intervention (operationally defined by individual slopes on a composite measure of reading ability), we found that the groups were rank ordered such that the group that manifested the most accelerated rate of growth in reading subskills, as a function of intervention, approached the level of the normal readers and maintained their advantage over children in all other tutored groups thereafter. In contrast, children in the tutored group that manifested the least accelerated rate of growth in these subskills performed well below the children in all other groups thereafter, with each respective group maintaining its relative status throughout the period evaluated. These results make it clear that the sole use of exclusionary criteria to identify "disabled readers" does not guarantee that children so identified are truly "disabled" in the stereotypic sense of this term (i.e., having organically derived cognitive deficits), even if they are severely impaired readers.

Regarding the question of whether early intervention would aid in distinguishing between basic cognitive deficits and experiential/instructional deficits as root causes of reading disability, the present findings provide strong support for the possibility that reading problems in some, but not all, poor readers may be caused by basic deficits in cognitive abilities underlying reading ability. This possibility is, of course, supported by our finding that normal readers performed significantly better than the worst-achieving tutored children (VLG group) on various measures of such abilities. But especially impressive is our finding that the best-achieving tutored children (VGG group) also performed significantly

---

[6]To calculate the percentage of tutored children who continued to fall within the "disabled" category following intervention, we used as the population base the total number of children yielded by multiplying the number of children, in the total population of available children after attrition ($n = 1,284$), by the percentage corresponding with the total number of identified poor readers who received one-to-one tutoring ($76/118 = 64.4\%$; $1,284 \times 64.4\%$ = 827). Accordingly, the number of tutored children who scored below the 15th percentile on the Basic Skills Cluster (BSC) after one semester of remediation represents 1.5% ($12/827$) of the population from which these children were drawn, whereas the number of tutored children who scored below the 30th percentile on the BSC after the same period represents 3% ($25/827$) of the population from which they were drawn.

better than the worst-achieving tutored children on many of the same measures. Moreover, observed differences between the normal readers and the best achieving tutored children on these measures in many instances failed to achieve statistical significance, suggesting that reading-related cognitive abilities in the latter group were more like those of the normal readers than like those of the worst achievers. It would, therefore, appear that early and labor-intensive intervention can be an important vehicle for distinguishing between poor readers impaired by basic cognitive deficits and poor readers impaired by experiential and instructional deficits, and would ideally become a prerequisite for rendering a diagnosis of "specific reading disability."

Finally, our data strongly indicate that the types of cognitive abilities that have been consistently found to differentiate poor and normally developing readers in previous research can also differentiate poor readers who are difficult to remediate and poor readers who are readily remediated. In accord with convergent findings generated by previous research (see earlier discussion), we found that phonologically based skills—such as phoneme segmentation; rapid naming; and memory for words, sentences, and nonsense syllables—reliably and robustly differentiated not only the normal readers from the tutored children who were the most difficult to remediate, but, in many instances, the most difficult and the most readily remediated tutored children as well. And although the normal readers generally performed better on many of the same measures than even the most readily remediated tutored children, observed differences between these two groups were not always statistically significant. In contrast, observed differences between and among respective groups on semantic, syntactic, and visual measures were not found to be statistically significant, with the exception of syntactic measures that place a heavy load on working memory. This pattern of results emerged on both kindergarten and first-grade testing, which is significant because the data attest to the reliability of our findings. They also add to the growing body of evidence supporting the view that phonological deficits are preeminent causes of reading difficulties in beginning readers from the population of children studied herein, that is, otherwise normal children from middle-to upper-middle-class backgrounds who are not generally impaired in academic learning.

However, we should point out that, to conclude from our data that difficulties in learning to read may often be associated with phonological deficits is, quite simply, to acknowledge the heavy dependence of reading in an alphabetically based orthography on the phonology of language (Vellutino, 1991). In our view, phonological coding ability is a primary determinant of the child's success in mastering the alphabetic code and in learning to attach names to printed words as wholes. The child must acquire facility in both subskills in order to learn to read. Yet, these assertions in no way deny the importance of the semantic, syntactic, and visual components of written language as partial determinants of the child's ability to learn to read. Knowledge of word meanings and knowledge of syntax contribute, directly or indirectly, to the acquisition of facility in word identification, and both are critically important for reading comprehension. Similarly, the beginning reader must distinguish the graphic and orthographic attributes of printed words in learning to identify them, but because of the formidable load on visual memory occasioned by the alphabetic properties of written English the success of this enterprise is determined primarily by the child's ability to master the alphabetic code. This ability depends, in turn, on phonological coding ability. This, of course, suggests that semantic, syntactic, and visual abilities carry less weight, as determinants of success in beginning reading, than do phonological abilities, and there is independent evidence to support this suggestion (Vellutino et al., 1991, 1994). Thus, the pattern of results obtained in the present study would seem to be coherent.

Implied in each of the questions specifically addressed by the present investigation is the more general question of whether deficiencies in phonological abilities that (presumably) impair the acquisition of reading subskills are of constitutional origin. Our results, in general, provide indirect support for this possibility. Especially supportive is the fact that reader group differences were reliably observed on tasks evaluating phonological abilities, whereas no reliable differences were observed on tasks evaluating semantic, syntactic, and visual abilities when children in our target groups were at the beginning stages of literacy development and before the cumulative effects of reading disability began to take hold (what Stanovich, 1986, called "Matthew Effects"). Yet, we do not believe that phonological deficits of constitutional origin necessarily emanate from neurological damage, although this possibility cannot be ruled out in any given case. Rather, we suggest that both reading ability and the phonological skills underlying reading ability might better be placed on continua, such that those who have the strongest phonological skills will tend to have the greatest amount of success in acquiring basic reading subskills, whereas those who have the weakest phonological skills will tend to have the least success in acquiring basic reading subskills. The consistency of the rank ordering of respective reader groups, on all of the reading tests administered after initiation of the intervention program, provide the strongest support for this suggestion (see Figs. 16.2 and 16.3, and Table 16.2). Moreover, it is of some significance that performance on tests evaluating phoneme segmentation, naming, verbal memory, and other measures that entail phonological coding not infrequently approximated a linear trend across groups.

However, it has probably not escaped the reader's notice that the normal readers generally performed above the level of the children in each of the tutored groups on most of the measures included on our kindergarten and first-grade batteries when it might have been expected that children in at least the best-achieving tutored group (VGG group) would perform as well as the normal readers on most of these measures, in particular on those evaluating cognitive abilities that are especially important for learning to read. Yet, as is evident from a brief perusal of Table 16.2, most of the normal readers were considerably better than average-level readers, whereas most of the children in the VGG group became average-level readers as a consequence of remediation. We interpret this circumstance as an indication that the normal readers were endowed with a near-optimum mix of the cognitive abilities underlying beginning reading, whereas children in the VGG group were endowed with something less than a near-optimum mix of such abilities. Thus, the data, in general, speak for the validity of a continuum based conceptualization of reading ability and disability (see Shaywitz, Escobar, Shaywitz, Fletcher, & Makuch, 1992, for additional evidence in support of this conclusion).

Finally, in contrast to the positive implications of our findings, vis-à-vis the use of early intervention as a diagnostic tool, our data question the utility and widespread use of IQ/achievement discrepancy definitions of reading disability based on commonly used tests of intelligence such as the WISC—R (Rutter & Yule, 1975). Given that IQ scores predicted neither reading achievement in normal readers nor response to remediation in poor readers, we are at liberty to infer that there is not the kind of linear relationship assumed by IQ/achievement discrepancy definitions of reading disability, such that an average IQ implies average reading ability, a high-average IQ implies high-average reading ability, and a very high IQ implies superior reading ability, at least not when reading is simply defined as the ability to learn to "decode" print. Our data also allow us to infer that many of the skills and abilities evaluated by intelligence tests, such as the WISC—R, are not as important for success in beginning reading as are phonological skills, such as phoneme segmentation, phonetic decoding, and name encoding and retrieval. These inferences are given independent support by research reported elsewhere (Fletcher et al., 1994; Siegel, 1988, 1989; Stanovich & Siegel, 1994), and if they are ultimately found to be correct, then the IQ/achievement discrepancy definition of reading disability would be invalidated, and it might better be discarded as a basic criterion for diagnosing specific reading disability.

In sum, the results of the present study speak for the utility of using early and labor-intensive intervention as the primary vehicle for evaluating the etiology of specific reading disability. Our data suggest that reading difficulties in most children from middle- to upper-middle-class backgrounds are, quite likely, caused by experiential and instructional deficits. However, it is also clear from the results that there are substantial numbers of children whose reading difficulties are caused by phonological skills deficiencies that may well be of constitutional origin. The data also have important implications for our theoretical understanding of the etiology of reading disability as well as for the definition and diagnosis of the disorder, and these issues were discussed in some detail.

ACKNOWLEDGMENTS

The study discussed in this chapter was a component of a project funded under the auspices of a special Center grant from the National Institute of Child Health and Human Development (#P50HD25806) to the Kennedy Krieger Institute of the John Hopkins University. Martha Bridge Denckla was the Principal Investigator overseeing the various research projects initiated under this Center grant. The present study was part of Project IV (The Reading and Language Project) under a subcontract directed by Frank R. Vellutino and Donna M. Scanlon of the Child Research and Study Center of the University at Albany, State University of New York.

We wish to thank Melinda Taylor and Judith Moran for their assistance in editing and typing the manuscript. Thanks are due, as well, to Sheila Small, Diane Fanuele, Alice Pratt, Robin Parker, Deborah Tuohy, and Margaret Feldman for their invaluable assistance in collecting and processing the data for this study. We are especially indebted to the children, teachers, secretaries, and administrators in the many schools in the Albany, New York, area that participated in this research. Without their cooperation, this project would not have been possible.

REFERENCES

Badcock, D., & Lovegrove, W. (1981). The effects of contrast stimulus, duration and spatial frequency in visual persistence in normal and specifically disabled readers. *Journal of Experimental Psychology: Human Perception and Performance, 1*, 495–505.

Blachman, B. A. (1984). Relationship of rapid naming ability and language analysis skills to kindergarten and first-grade reading achievement. *Journal of Educational Psychology, 76*, 610–622.

Blachman, B. A. (1994). Early literacy acquisition—the role of phonological awareness. In G. Wallach & K. Butler (Eds.), *Language learning disabilities in school-age children and adolescents: Some underlying principles and applications* (pp. 253–274). Columbus, OH: Merrill.

Blachman, B. A., Ball, E. W., Black, R. S., & Tangel, D. M. (1994). Kindergarten teachers develop phoneme awareness in low-income, inner-city classrooms. *Reading and Writing: An Interdisciplinary Journal, 6,* 1–18.

Bradley, L., & Bryant, P. E. (1983). Categorizing sounds and learning to read—a causal connection. *Nature, 303,* 419–421.

Brady, S., & Shankweiler, D. (1991). *Phonological processes in literacy.* Hillsdale, NJ: Lawrence Erlbaum Associates.

Breitmeyer, B. G. (1989). A visual based deficit in specific reading disability. *Irish Journal of Psychology, 10,* 534–541.

Bruck, M. (1990). Word recognition skills of adults with childhood diagnoses of dyslexia. *Developmental Psychology, 26,* 439–454.

Bruck, M. (1992). The persistence of dyslexics' phonological awareness deficits. *Developmental Psychology, 28,* 874–886.

Bryk, A. S., & Raudenbush, S. W. (1987). Application of hierarchical linear models to assessing change. *Psychological Bulletin, 101,* 147–158.

Byrne, B. (1981). Deficient syntactic control in poor readers: Is a weak phonetic memory code responsible? *Applied Psycholinguistics, 2,* 201–212.

Byrne, B., & Fielding-Barnsley, R. (1991). Evaluation of a program to teach phonemic awareness to young children. *Journal of Educational Psychology, 83,* 451–455.

Byrne, B., & Fielding-Barnsley, R. (1993). Recognition of phoneme invariance by beginning readers. *Reading and Writing: An Interdisciplinary Journal, 5,* 315–324.

Cardon, L. R., Smith, S. D., Fulker, D. W., Kimberling, W. J., Pennington, B. F., & DeFries, J. C. (1994). Quantitative trait locus for reading disability on chromosome 6. *Science, 226,* 276–279.

Clay, M. M. (1985). *The early detection of reading difficulties* (3rd ed.). Auckland, New Zealand: Heinemann.

Clay, M. M. (1987). Learning to be learning disabled. *New Zealand Journal of Educational Studies, 22,* 155–173.

Donahue, M. (1986). Linguistic and communicative development in learning disabled children. In S. J. Ceci (Ed.), *Handbook of cognitive, social and neuropsychological aspects of learning disabilities* (Vol. 1, pp. 263–289). Hillsdale, NJ: Lawrence Erlbaum Associates.

Filipek, P. A. (1995). Neurobiologic correlates of developmental dyslexia: How do dyslexics' brains differ from those of normal readers? *Journal of Child Neurology, 10,* 862–869.

Fletcher, J. M., Shaywitz, S. E., Shankweiler, D. P., Katz, L., Liberman, I. Y., Steubing, K. K., Francis, D. J., Fowler, A. E., & Shaywitz, B. A. (1994). Cognitive profiles of reading disability: Comparisons of discrepancy and low achievement definitions. *Journal of Educational Psychology, 86,* 6–23.

Flood, J., & Menyuk, P. (1983). The development of metalinguistic awareness and its relation to reading achievement. *Journal of Applied Developmental Psychology, 4,* 65–80.

Foorman, B. R., Francis, D. J., Novy, D. M., & Liberman, D. (1991). How letter-sound instruction mediates progress in first-grade reading and spelling. *Journal of Educational Psychology, 83,* 456–469.

Fry, M. A., Johnson, C. S., & Muehl, S. (1970). Oral language production in relation to reading achievement among select second graders. In D. J. Bakker & P. Satz (Eds.), *Specific reading disability: Advances in theory and method* (pp. 123–146). Rotterdam, The Netherlands: Rotterdam University Press.

Galaburda, A. M. (1983). Developmental dyslexia: Current anatomical research. *Annals of Dyslexia, 33,* 41–53.

Galaburda, A. M., & Kemper, T. L. (1979). Cytoarchitectonic abnormalities in developmental dyslexia: A case study. *Annals of Neurology, 6,* 94–100.

Hulme, C. (1988). The implausibility of low-level visual deficits as a cause of children's reading difficulties. *Cognitive Neuropsychology, 5,* 369–374.

Hynd, G. W., & Semrud-Clikeman, M. (1989). Dyslexia and brain morphology. *Psychological Bulletin, 106,* 447–482.

Iversen, S., & Tunmer, W. (1993). Phonological processing skills and the reading recovery program. *Journal of Educational Psychology, 85,* 112–126.

Katz, R. B., Shankweiler, D., & Liberman, I. Y. (1981). Memory for item order and phonetic recoding in the beginning reader. *Journal of Experimental Child Psychology, 32,* 474–484.

Liberman, I. Y., & Shankweiler, D. (1979). Speech, the alphabet and teaching to read. In L. Resnick & P. Weaver (Eds.), *Theory and practice of early reading* (Vol. 2, pp. 109–132). Hillsdale, NJ: Lawrence Erlbaum Associates.

Liberman, I. Y., Shankweiler, D., Fischer, F. W., & Carter, B. (1974). Explicit syllable and phoneme segmentation in the young child. *Journal of Experimental Child Psychology, 18,* 201–212.

Loban, W. (1963). *The language of elementary school children* (NCTE Research Report No. 1). Urbana, IL: National Council of Teachers of English.

Lovegrove, W., Martin, F., & Slaghuis, W. (1986). A theoretical and experimental case for a visual deficit in specific reading disability. *Cognitive Neuropsychology, 3,* 225–267.

Lundberg, I., Frost, J., & Petersen, O. P. (1988). Effects of an extensive program for stimulating phonological awareness in preschool children. *Reading Research Quarterly, 23,* 263–285.

Lundberg, I., Olofsson, A., & Wall, S. (1980). Reading and spelling skills in the first school years predicted from phonemic awareness skills in kindergarten. *Scandinavian Journal of Psychology, 21,* 159–173.

Mann, V. A., Liberman, I. Y., & Shankweiler, D. (1980). Children's memory for sentences and word storage in relation to reading ability. *Memory and Cognition, 8,* 329–335.

Mann, V. A., Shankweiler, D., & Smith, S. T. (1984). The association between comprehension of spoken sentences and early reading ability: The role of phonetic representation. *Journal of Child Language, 11,* 627–643.

Martin, F., & Lovegrove, W. (1984). The effects of field size and luminance on contrast sensitivity differences between specifically reading disabled and normal children. *Neuropsychologia, 22,* 73–77.

Olson, R. K., Kleigl, R., & Davidson, B. J. (1983). Dyslexic and normal readers' eye movements. *Journal of Experimental Psychology: Human Perception and Performance, 9,* 816–825.

Olson, R., Wise, B., Conners, F., & Rack, J. (1990). Organization, heritability, and remediation of component word recognition and language skills in disabled readers. In T. H. Carr & B. A. Levy (Eds.), *Reading and its development: Component skills approaches* (pp. 261–322). New York: Academic Press.

Pinnell, G. S. (1989). Reading recovery: Helping at risk children learn to read. *Elementary School Journal, 90,* 161–184.

Rogosa, D. R., & Willett, J. B. (1985). Understanding correlates of change by modeling individual differences in growth. *Psychometrika, 50,* 203–228.

Rutter, M., & Yule, W. (1975). The concept of specific reading retardation. *Journal of Child Psychology and Psychiatry, 16,* 181–197.

Satz, P., Taylor, H. G., Friel, J., & Fletcher, J. M. (1978). Some developmental and predictive precursors of reading disabilities: A six year follow-up. In A. L. Benton & D. Pearl (Eds.), *Dyslexia: An appraisal of current knowledge* (pp. 313–348). New York: Oxford University Press.

Scarborough, H. S. (1990). Very early language deficits in dyslexic children. *Child Development, 61,* 1728–1743.

Shankweiler, D., & Crain, S. (1986). Language mechanism and reading disorder: A modular approach. *Cognition, 24,* 139–168.

Shankweiler, D., Crain, S., Brady, S., & Macaruso, P. (1992). Identifying the cause of reading disability. In P. B. Gough & L. C. Ehri (Eds.), *Reading acquisition* (pp. 275–305). Hillsdale, NJ: Lawrence Erlbaum Associates.

Shankweiler, D., Smith, S. T., & Mann, V. A. (1984). Repetition and comprehension of spoken sentences by reading-disabled children. *Brain and Language, 23,* 241–257.

Shaywitz, S. E., Escobar, M. D., Shaywitz, B. A., Fletcher, J. M., & Makuch, R. W. (1992). Evidence that dyslexia may represent the lower tail of a normal distribution of reading ability. *New England Journal of Medicine, 326,* 145–150.

Shucard, D. W., Cummins, K. R., Gay, E., Lairsmith, J., & Welanko, P. (1985). Electrophysiological studies of reading disabled children: In search of subtypes. In D. Gray & J. F. Kavanagh (Eds.), *Biobehavioral measures of dyslexia* (pp. 87–106). Parkton, MD: York Press.

Siegel, L. S. (1988). Evidence that IQ scores are irrelevant to the definition and analysis of reading disability. *Canadian Journal of Psychology, 42,* 201–215.

Siegel, L. S. (1989). IQ is irrelevant to the definition of learning disabilities. *Journal of Learning Disabilities, 22,* 469–479.

Stanley, G., Smith, G. A., & Howell, E. A. (1983). Eye movements and sequential tracking in dyslexic and control children. *British Journal of Psychology, 74,* 181–187.

Stanovich, K. E. (1986). Matthew effects in reading: Some consequences of individual differences in the acquisition of literacy. *Reading Research Quarterly, 21,* 360–407.

Stanovich, K. E. (1988). Explaining the differences between the dyslexic and the garden-variety poor reader: The phonological-core variable-difference model. *Journal of Learning Disabilities, 21,* 590–612.

Stanovich, K. E., Nathan, R. G., & Zolman, J. E. (1988). The developmental lag hypothesis in reading: Longitudinal and matched reading-level comparisons. *Child Development, 59,* 71–86.

Stanovich, K. E., & Siegel, L. S. (1994). Phenotypic performance profile of children with reading disabilities: A regression-based test of the phonological-core variable-difference model. *Journal of Educational Psychology, 86*(1), 24–53.

Tunmer, W. E. (1989). The role of language related factors in reading disability. In D. Shankweiler & I. Y. Liberman (Eds.), *Phonology and reading disability: Solving the reading puzzle* (pp. 91–131). Ann Arbor: University of Michigan Press.

Vellutino, F. R. (1979). *Dyslexia: Theory and research.* Cambridge, MA: MIT Press.

Vellutino, F. R. (1987, March). Dyslexia. *Scientific American,* 34–41.

Vellutino, F. R. (1991). Introduction to three studies on reading acquisition: Convergent findings on theoretical foundations of code-oriented versus whole-language approaches to reading instruction. *Journal of Educational Psychology, 83,* 437–443.

Vellutino, F. R., & Scanlon, D. M. (1987a). Phonological coding, phonological awareness, and reading ability: Evidence from a longitudinal and experimental study. *Merrill-Palmer Quarterly, 33,* 321–363.

Vellutino, F. R., & Scanlon, D. M. (1987b). Linguistic coding and reading ability. In S. Rosenberg (Ed.), *Advances in applied psycholinguistics* (Vol. 2, pp. 1–69). New York: Cambridge University Press.

Vellutino, F. R., Scanlon, D. M., Sipay, E. R., Small, S. G., Pratt, A., Chen, R., & Denckla, M. B. (1996). Cognitive profiles of difficult to remediate and readily remediated poor readers: Early intervention as a vehicle for distinguishing between cognitive and experiential deficits as basic causes of specific reading disability. *Journal of Educational Psychology, 88*(4), 601–638.

Vellutino, F. R., Scanlon, D. M., Small, S. G., & Tanzman, M. S. (1991). The linguistic basis of reading ability: Converting written to oral language. *Text, 11,* 99–133.

Vellutino, F. R., Scanlon, D. M., & Spearing, D. (1995). Semantic and phonological coding in poor and normal readers. *Journal of Experimental Child Psychology, 59,* 76–123.

Vellutino, F. R., Scanlon, D. M., & Tanzman, M. S. (1988). Lexical memory in poor and normal readers: Developmental differences in the use of category cues. *Canadian Journal of Psychology, 42,* 216–241.

Vellutino, F. R., Scanlon, D. M., & Tanzman, M. S. (1994). Components of reading ability: Issues and problems in operationalizing word identification, phonological coding, and orthographic coding. In G. R. Lyon (Ed.), *Frames of reference for the assessment of learning disabilities: New views on measurement issues* (pp. 279–324). Baltimore, MD: Brookes.

Wasik, B. A., & Slavin, R. R. (1993). Preventing early reading failure with one-to-one tutoring: A review of five programs. *Reading Research Quarterly, 28,* 179–200.

Wechsler, D. (1974). *Wechsler intelligence scale for children—revised.* New York: Psychological Corporation.

Williams, J. P. (1980). Teaching decoding with an emphasis on phoneme analysis and phoneme blending. *Journal of Educational Psychology, 72,* 1–15.

Wolf, M. (1984). Naming, reading, and the dyslexias—a longitudinal overview. *Annals of Dyslexia, 34,* 87–115.

Woodcock, R. W. (1987). *Woodcock reading mastery tests—revised.* Circle Pines, MN: American Guidance Services.

Closing the Gap on Reading Failure: Social Background, Phonemic Awareness, and Learning to Read

Tom Nicholson
University of Auckland

WHY ISN'T LEARNING TO READ LIKE LEARNING TO WATCH TELEVISION?

Learning to read should be easy. There are TV shows such as *Sesame Street* and the *Electric Company* that give lots of attention to the ABCs. Even supermarkets sell children's books, magnetic letters, crayons, and pencils. Yet strangely enough, the vast majority of children start school with only a very basic idea of what reading is about. They may recognize a few signs in the street, such as McDonalds and Pizza Hut. They may also know that books tell a story and that books contain "words." But most preschoolers have not yet figured out the alphabetic principle, that is, that there is a set of letter-sound rules, and these rules enable us to read the print on the page.

In short, when children start school most are in the same boat, in that hardly any of them can read or write. For example, in a classic study conducted in the United States, Durkin (1966) found that only 229 out of 9,568 school beginners (about 2.4%) were able to read 18 or more words on a list. The list was made up of familiar words like *mother*, *look*, and *funny*. Yet, even though most children start school unable to read or write, there are still some who are much more aware of books than others. These are children who come from print-rich environments, where they have already learned a great deal about literacy. As Adams (1990) noted: "They sit with books, often upside down, leafing through the pages as they talk aloud. They make you feel silly as they imitate the exaggerated intonation and funny voices with which you read stories to them. . . . They scribble and make letter like forms and tell you what it says" (pp. 334–335).

CHILDREN WHO ARE EARLY READERS

Research on children who *can* read before starting school also indicates that these children themselves, and their home environments, are not "run of the mill." A study of six children who learned to read before they got to school (Anbar, 1986) found that each of the six children went through similar stages. First, there was a period of time in which they became familiar with books. The children turned pages, their parents read to them daily, they played with magnetic letters and with alphabet blocks. Second, they went through a stage in which they learned to recognize letters and some sight words. Third, they showed interest in the sounds of letters, using ABC books, invented sound games, and alphabet letters. Fourth, they started to use this knowledge to "make words," using plastic letters, blocks, or cards. Fifth, they got interested in sounding out new words, as long as the words contained only a few letters. Then they started reading for themselves.

These stages were developed as a result of a series of extensive interviews with the parents of the six children. In the interviews, the parents reported reading stories to their children every day and helping with the alphabet, spelling, sound games, and "making words." According to Anbar (1986):

> Parents eagerly helped their children with spelling attempts and encouraged efforts in "making words." They daily read books to and with the child, often pointing at each word, and with much patience and enthusiasm listened to the children read aloud to them. They also enjoyed making rhymes with words. "What rhymes with Mommy?" one of the mothers used to ask. (Her son's favourite response would be "salami"). (p. 75)

These comments show the enormous amount of time that these parents willingly put into their children's preschool reading. They seemed to have a massive armory of books, alphabet letters, flash cards, dictionaries, workbooks, electronic games, and more (Anbar, 1986). Another interesting finding was that these parents, except for one, were not deliberately trying to make their children better readers than other children. Instead, the picture was more complex. For example (Anbar, 1986, p. 80):

Sean
In the case of Sean, it appears that reading development became something of a hobby for his parents.

Betty
In the case of Betty, early reading development seemed to have justified for the mother the resignation from her 12-year-long career.

Victor
In the case of Victor, the parents related how reading activities were used by them at first as a means of keeping him calm. This requirement was imposed on them by the child's paediatrician due to the child's asthmatic condition.

Marna
In Marna's case, reading activities seem to have been the lifeline between the child and her parents, who felt guilty about leaving her with a sitter so much of the time.

The point of these anecdotal data is to suggest that learning to read does not just happen. These parents actively instructed their children. This probably explains why early readers are so rare, in that most parents are unable to provide the countless hours of instruction that are needed.

In another study of 32 children who could all read fluently when they started school (Clark, 1976), it was found that many of the parents also had a highly personal interest in their children's progress. These data, as in the Anbar (1986) study, suggest that early readers do not acquire their skills naturally. Unlike learning to talk (or learning to watch TV), learning to read requires *instruction*.

MIDDLE-CLASS AND LOW-INCOME FAMILIES

Yet even though learning to read does not happen naturally, few would deny that a child who comes from a print-rich environment must have a head start. In Japan, for instance, where reading levels are very high, 36% of parents are already reading stories to their children when they are only 12 months old (Sakamoto, 1976, cited in Mason & Allen, 1986). According to Adams (1990), this may be a middle-class phenomenon, because this is what she did with her own child: "Since he was six weeks old, we have spent 30 to 45 minutes reading to him each day. By the time he reaches first grade, at age six and a quarter, that will amount to 1,000 to 1,700 hours of storybook reading, one on one, with his face in books. . . . I believe that John's reading related experience is quite typical of that of his middle-class peers in general" (p. 85).

Some middle-class parents are even more enthusiastic than this. Phillips and McNaughton (1990) studied a group of 10 parents who were avid story readers. They read an average of four books a day to their pre-schoolers, usually at bedtime. These parents also reported that they visited the library often, and estimated that they possessed in their homes an average of 300 children's books (range was from 50 to a massive 500). Interestingly, these parents hardly ever talked to their children about print-related aspects of books, even though they spent many hours reading to them. Talking about the print was not part of the bedtime experience. Instead, the focus was on the story, which perhaps explains why these children were still unable to read for themselves. Durkin (1966), mentioned earlier, also found that only 2 or 3 children in every 100 could read when they started school, even though many were well prepared for reading instruction.

In contrast to the experience of children of middle-class parents, children in low-income families may have had very different early literacy experiences. Teale (1986), in a study of 24 preschoolers from low-income families, found that they were only read to an average of 5 times a year. For these children, the experience of storybook reading was virtually nonexistent. Similar findings were reported by Feitelson and Goldstein (1986) in a study of 102 families. They found that 60% of kindergartners in areas where school achievement was poor did not own any books and were not read to at all. In contrast, kindergartners in areas where children did well at school each had an average of 54 books at home and, beginning at an early age, were read to, on average, for half an hour each day.

These differences in home experiences help to explain why there are such differences among children when they start school. Some children are much more ready for instruction than others. Gibbons (1981) was able to document these differences in a small sample of eight preschoolers who were categorized as either 100-book kids or 1,000-book kids. The 1,000-book kids had been read to at least once each night from the time of their first birthday. The findings revealed dramatic differences between the two groups in emergent reading, especially in knowledge of book conventions (e.g., turning pages, reading "words") and how stories are told (i.e., that books have a special language of their own). Also, the 1,000-book kids were better than the 100-book kids at print-related skills, such as knowing the alphabet.

Differences in home environment were also documented by Nicholson (1980a, 1980b) in a survey of 689 parents who participated in a course on beginning reading. This survey provided anecdotal evidence that some families were unable to provide the print-related experiences that can be found in many middle-class families. The reasons are probably economic. To get to libraries, parents need transport; to buy children's books, parents need disposable income. For example, the following written comments are from a parent who had to use public transport to attend a course on reading at a local play center (Nicholson, 1980b): "Leave home at 8.30 am with two toddlers to wait for school bus in frosts. Arrive at school. Wait in play centre which I had to light old-fashioned stove for heat. Meantime baby is crying cause of cold. So I couldn't stand my children getting cold. So rather than face a freezing cold play centre dropped out as did other mothers without cars" (p. 19).

Some parents lack the education to know what books to buy. For example, the following written note is from another parent who was also contacted about the course on reading (Nicholson, 1980b): "Yes I have two children how need books bad. They are very backwood in their readying at school. How do I get the right books for them. I am give you my name and address would you let me know about the books for my children I hope so" (p. 21).

The effects of social class have also been documented in an interview study of 12 low-achieving female students from economically disadvantaged backgrounds, who attended a single-gender, urban high school (Wilson & Dupuis, 1992). These students were compared with high-achieving female students who were either from low-income backgrounds or from middle-class backgrounds. The study found that the low-achieving female students from poor families (Group A) were more limited in terms of home facilities than were high-achieving students from low-income families. Wilson and Dupuis (1992) found that: "In general the standard of housing was poor, lacking space and privacy. Most of the girls shared a bedroom and there was no quiet place for them to do homework. . . . Half of the girls' families had no car, therefore, activities that required a car were out of the question" (p. 3).

In addition, these low-achieving female students came from large families (average number of children = 4.0) and did a great deal of domestic work (e.g., cleaning, ironing, cooking, babysitting). These work activities, on average, consumed 12 hours a week. All these students had reading difficulties and had experienced general academic difficulties from earlier years of schooling. Of the 12, 7 of their parents had been to the school, but only one of the seven parents had been able to get help for their daughter. Wilson and Dupuis (1992, p. 5) reported that some parents did not go to the school for help because they felt they were the ones to blame ("I thought it was me at fault"; "I was on a benefit in those days and there wasn't much money").

In contrast, female students who were from low-income homes but who were doing well at school (Group B) were better off in terms of home facilities. Also, parent income levels of the high-achieving female students, although low, were higher than those of parents in Group A. Most of the students had their own room, most of the families had a car, and family size was smaller (average = 2.9). In addition, these students had less domestic work to do (average = 2.5 hours per week).

Although these students (Group B) were now doing well at school, this had not always been the case. All their parents had contacted the school at some point, but with better results (Wilson & Dupuis, 1992). For example, one pupil (Helen) commented as follows, "I had trouble with maths. I couldn't understand how to do fractions, so Mum went and talked to the teacher. I got extra books and that helped" (p. 8). The mother of another pupil (Melissa) commented that: "Melissa had trouble with learning to read. I was told she was a trouble stirrer. Her teacher was very inadequate. After underachieving she was put into the bottom Standard 1 [grade 2]. Luckily she had a teacher who put a lot of time into her and got her up to the top of the class within a year" (p. 8).

In the middle-class group of high-achieving students (Group C), the study found that facilities were better than for Group A. Wilson and Dupuis (1992) remarked that, "Every girl had her own room, and a specific area in which to do her homework, including a desk with adequate lighting. The average family size was 2.75. Each family had a car, sometimes two" (p. 9). When it came to domestic duties, the average time spent per week was 1.5 hours for these middle-class high-achieving students (compared with 12 hours for Group A). Five of these students had experienced learning problems early in their school careers, and their parents had been to the school about these difficulties. Parents who received a negative response (2 out of the 5), however, had the resources to seek outside help (e.g., private tutoring), options that were less feasible for parents of Group A students.

In summary, the study showed that although children from low-income backgrounds *can* be successful in school, the odds are often very much against them. Their parents are likely to be under a lot of financial and social stress (e.g., living on unemployment benefits while raising a large family) and are less able to provide the kind of support available in middle-class homes (e.g., parents able to drive their children to another school, or pay for private tutoring). Also, the fact that low-income parents are often less well educated themselves, and have jobs with lower status, seems to reduce their confidence in approaching the school. As Wilson and Dupuis (1992) put it:

> Inequalities of power are clear in the parents' reactions to news that their daughter was doing badly at school. Most low income parents were unable, or unwilling, to approach the school or teacher, or did not realise that they could. Those who did approach the school, did not get help. Only one high-income parent got no help when she approached a school, and she knew where (and had the money) to look for outside help. Maybe the schools were reacting, unfairly, to signs of wealth and academic expecta-tions, but the most depressing discovery is that low-income parents blamed themselves for their daughters' lack of achievement. (p. 11)

These social-class differences are also reflected in the poor performance of low-income students at the end of their schooling. In a study of 2,000 secondary school students, from low-income and middle-class backgrounds, Hughes and Lauder (1991) found that 36% of students from low-income homes left school without any basic formal qualifications (e.g., a certificate showing C grades or higher in academic school subjects), whereas only 11% of middle-class students did so.

These statistics also seem related to levels of reading achievement. In their survey of 1,451 pupils who were in their first year of high school (13-year-olds), Nicholson and Gallienne (1995) found that more than 90% of students from low-income homes were below average on a standardized reading test. In contrast, students from middle-class homes showed a pattern more in line with a normal distribution, with 50% above and 50% below the national average. These incoming differences in reading levels appear to be associated with low levels of high school achievement by pupils in economically disadvantaged areas. For example, in 1993, low-income schools in the Nicholson and Gallienne study had success rates that ranged from 9% to 33% in "school certificate," which is a minimum formal qualification attempted by 15-year-olds. In contrast, middle-class schools in the study had success rates that ranged from 60% to 69%.

This high failure rate of pupils in low-income schools may be related to the way in which reading is taught in New Zealand. The mainstream approach is whole language, which has a high failure rate. In 1993, 27% of 6-year-old pupils received remedial reading tuition (Kerslake, 1994). This early experience of failure seems to create a gap in achievement between good and poor readers that gets wider and wider (Stanovich, 1986). Such Matthew effects (rich get richer and poor get poorer) may not be unique to New Zealand. Other evidence suggests similar problems in other countries. In California, for example, 26% of 6-year-olds receive remedial tuition (Hiebert, 1994). In England (Beard & Oakhill, 1994) and in Canada (see Levine, 1994), there is also evidence of a high failure rate associated with the whole-language approach. Although these other data do not look at socioeconomic differences, it may well be that the pattern is consistent with New Zealand, in that pupils from low-income backgrounds experience higher failure rates. Hiebert (1994), for example, cited preliminary data showing that the Reading Recovery program is less effective in schools with low-income students, which may indicate that it is harder to bridge the reading gap for pupils from low-income backgrounds.

In a longitudinal study of 32 children from low-income homes, including some who were successful in school and some who were unsuccessful, Chall, Jacobs, and Baldwin (1990) found that the academic problems of these children increased as they went through school. This was especially the case by fourth grade (9-year-olds), where the more academic demands of text material led to a decline in reading achievement. In a parallel study of the same children, Snow, Barnes, Chandler, Goodman, and Hemphill

(1991) also noted that these children's problems were not picked up by parents, due to miscommunication by the school when studying home report cards. As they put it, "Parents in our study expected to be contacted when problems arose, but they received report cards full of A's and B's and little information indicating problems even when their children's academic performance was poor" (p. 140).

According to Chall et al. (1990), the explanation for such high grades may have been that the teachers were giving children credit for the *extent* of improvement made during the school year, rather than their *actual* level of achievement. Whatever the reason, school report cards misled parents about their children's progress. Snow et al. (1991) noted that:

> The low-income families in our study had, in general, high expectations and high aspirations for their children's educational achievement, but their understanding of what level of achievement their children's grades reflected often differed from the teachers'. As a result, parents interpreted grades of B's and C's as reflecting adequate progress, whereas teachers often gave these grades to children in academic trouble. (p. 169)

Stanovich (1986) pointed to other disadvantages facing pupils from low-income homes. These relate to the effects of growing up and going to school in a predominantly low-income area. Why should this be so? Stanovich (1986) argued that pupils who attend schools where most of their classmates are also from low-income backgrounds are unable to take advantage of the ability-composition effect. To support this point, Stanovich cited Rutter (1983), who studied 12 inner-city secondary schools in London. Rutter concluded that "A child of any level of ability is likely to make better progress if taught in a school with a relatively high concentration of pupils with good cognitive performance" (p. 19). Stanovich also cited a study by Share, Jorm, Maclean, and Matthews (1984), who found similar effects to those in Rutter's study. Share et al. tested 500 children (5- and 6-year-olds) and found that the ability mean of the school accounted for an extra 9% of the variance, even after taking account of 30 cognitive and home background variables. The classroom mean also accounted for an extra 5% of the variance. These findings are in line with those of Nicholson and Gallienne (1995), who found that the socioeconomic location of the school (i.e., in a middle- or low-income area) accounted for an additional 6% of the variance, even after taking account of factors such as ethnicity and parent occupational status.

To summarize, data from a number of studies indicate that children from low-income homes are less likely than children from middle-class homes to do well in school. There are a number of factors that militate against success for low-income pupils, including the need to help out more at home, the lack of study facilities, and attendance at schools that are predominantly composed of other students from low-income homes. Low-income parents are more likely to experience stress and feelings of inadequacy when dealing with the school, and miscommunication with teachers when trying to interpret the grades their children have been given on their report cards.

In addition to these social-class differences, there appear to be linguistic differences as well. It appears that children from low-income backgrounds start school with less knowledge of rhyme and alliteration than do middle-class children. Such differences may reflect less opportunity to pick up such linguistic skills (e.g., nursery rhyme books, playing "I spy") in low-income homes. A study by Wallach, Wallach, Dozier, and Kaplan (1976), which compared 76 disadvantaged and 76 middle-class kindergarten children (5-year-olds), found that the disadvantaged children did much more poorly on tests that required phonemic analysis (e.g., deciding which of two pictures, as in *cat* and *mouse*, started with the sound /m/). Raz and Bryant (1990), however, found that disadvantaged children did not start to lag behind middle-class children until they started school. As the school year went on, the disadvantaged children fell further and further behind. A possible explanation for this result is that the middle-class children had many more books at home. Also, the number of books at home correlated with their progress in phonemic awareness. This correlation suggests that when middle-class children start school, the instructional assistance of parents at home is likely to gear up, as they help their children learn to read. Thus, as parents help their children with letters and sounds, they also facilitate the development of phonemic awareness skills. As already discussed, this is less likely to happen in low-income families. As we see in the next section, phonemic awareness skills are very important for reading acquisition, and may be yet another explanation for the academic difficulties faced by children from low socioeconomic backgrounds.

THE SIGNIFICANCE OF PHONEMIC AWARENESS

Phonemic awareness involves being aware that words are themselves made up of sound segments. For example, it has been found that many preschoolers are not able to think about whether or not the *length* of a spoken word is short or long. Rather, they think about whether its meaning is short or long. For example Papandropoulou and Sinclair (1974, cited in Foss & Hakes, 1978), reported that children will say a "train" is long and a "dandelion" is short, which is true about their meanings, but not about their sounds. Preschoolers are also not very good at playing with sounds in words. For example, many have trouble spotting the odd one out, when given a series of words like *mat, mop, man,* and *cat.* In this case, the odd one out is *cat,* because it does not start the same way as the others (Bradley, 1980; Bradley & Bryant, 1983). Even simpler tasks than this can prove difficult. What is interesting, however, is that such tasks also seem important for learning to read. For example, Bowey (1991) reported the following results: "Children were shown three pictures (e.g., the sun, a crab, a skate). They were told that 'sun' begins with /s/, and asked 'Which begins with /s/, crab or skate?' At the end of the school year, only 26% of preschoolers who could not yet read passed this task. Of those who could read a little, 90% passed" (p. 140).

The emergence of phonemic awareness is something that occurs late in the preschool years, and not all children have it when they start school. It is part of a general change in children's thinking ability, when they are able mentally to stand back from a situation, or from their own thinking, and comment on it. In reflecting on their own speech, children are also able to "play" with their speech, manipulate it, and think about what it might mean in other contexts. In the early stages of literacy acquisition, phonemic awareness seems to be very important. Without it, children seem unlikely to become good readers and spellers.

The extent to which children have phonemic awareness skills when they start school seems related to home experiences with literacy, but there are also developmental differences among children. Phonemic awareness seems obvious to adults, but it is not at all obvious to children. Children who score well on phonemic awareness tests also score well on reading tests (for a summary of many of these studies, see Stanovich, 1992). A typical finding, for example, is that children about to start school who show good phonemic awareness skills are likely to be making good reading progress a year later, when compared to children who start school lacking such skills.

For example, in a New Zealand study by Milina (1991), 112 kindergarten children (4-year-olds) were tested on sound categorization tasks just before entering their first year of formal schooling. The tasks involved the "odd-one-out" procedure, using a test devised by Bradley (1980). The child was asked to spot the word that did not have the same rhyme (e.g., *fan, cat, hat*), or which did not start with the same sound (e.g., *cat, man, map*), or which did not share the same middle sound (e.g., *pet, nut, cut*). The testing was preceded by a discussion using large nursery rhyme books to ensure that children understood what the term *rhyme* meant. About 4 months after the initial testing, the children were given the reading and spelling subtests of the Wide Range Achievement Test (Jastak & Wilkinson, 1984). Milina found significant correlations between initial phonemic awareness scores and later reading ($r = .59$) and spelling ($r = .56$) achievement, that is, nearly one third of the total variation in later reading and spelling success for these children could be explained by their preschool scores on a phonemic awareness test.

I have reanalyzed Milina's (1991) data, as shown in Fig. 17.1. The interesting point is that of the 112 preschoolers (4-year-olds) she tested, 46 were initially above the group average on a test of phonemic awareness (these pupils are represented on Fig. 17.1 with the letter X). Of these 46, only 8 (17%) were below the group average on a word reading test after a few months in school. And only 4 (9%) of the 46 were below the group average on tests of both word reading and spelling. In contrast, of the 66 remaining preschoolers who were initially at or below the total group

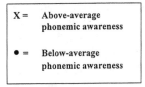

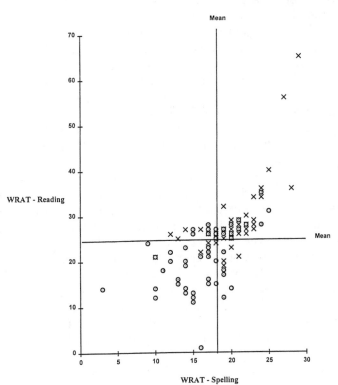

FIG. 17.1. Reading and spelling scores of children who entered school with either below-average or above-average levels of phonemic awareness.

average on the test of phonemic awareness (shown in Fig. 17.1 with the letter O), 40 (61%) of the 66 were later below the group average on a test of word reading, and 35 (53%) out of 66 were later below average on tests of both word reading and spelling. This visual analysis of Milina's (1991) data adds to the argument that children who start school with above-average levels of phonemic awareness appear to have a better prognosis in terms of later reading and spelling progress than do those who have lower levels of this metalinguistic skill.

Figure 17.1 also demonstrates that some children who had below-average phonemic awareness as preschoolers were nevertheless able to make above-average progress in reading and spelling. It appears that some children will discover this principle for themselves. What the data indicate, however, is that children who start school with high levels of phonemic awareness have a better prognosis in terms of learning to read and spell.

The importance of phonemic awareness skill in learning to read and spell reflects the way in which English uses an alphabetic writing system. The child has to become aware that letters in words stand for little segments of sound. If the child lacks phonemic awareness, it will be difficult to do simple things like learn the sounds of letters, "sound out" words in reading, or write words the way they sound. This, of course, is not to say that phonemic awareness is all there is to learning to read, but it does seem to be the hardest hurdle for some children to get over. Learning the alphabet is a visible task, in that the letters are in front of the child and can be seen. Yet phonemes, or sounds in words, are fused together in the speech stream, glued together within words. To become aware of phonemes is difficult, unless someone points them out.

However, many preschoolers do learn about phonemes, and the starting point is probably when they learn about nursery rhymes at home. To really understand rhymes, children have to be able to break a word into onset and rime (*rime* is a technical term in linguistics). As Bowey (1991, p. 141) explained: "The onset is the optional consonant or consonant cluster preceding the vowel (/p/ in pie, or /sk/ in sky). The rime is the vowel and the optional consonant or consonant cluster following (/ee/ in free or /ast/ in mast)." Words that rhyme usually start differently but end the same, so the child has to match up the common endings of each word. Doing this is a lot easier than separating out single phonemes, and it may help children start to read and spell. Bowey (1991) pointed out that having a sense of rhyme will help children notice letter-sound patterns between parts of words that have the same rhyme and are also spelled the same (e.g., *cat*, *rat*). They may also take the next step of noticing single-sound similarities between similar words (e.g., *cap*, *rat*).

Thus, although rhyme awareness is only a simple kind of phonemic awareness, it may be a natural step toward a more complex understanding of the phonemic structure of words. There is support for this from a study by Bryant, Bradley, Maclean, and Crossland (1989). They found that preschoolers who could recite nursery rhymes at 3 years of age were likely to be better readers at age 6. Thus, it seems that language games like nursery rhymes, "I spy," and rhyming stories like *Cat in the Hat* may help children figure out the alphabetic principle. Other support for the notion that knowledge of rhyme and alliteration is an important intermediate step toward full phonemic awareness comes from Treiman (1993) and Goswami (1994).

TEACHING PHONEMIC AWARENESS

There have been a number of attempts to teach phonemic awareness, both to preschoolers and to children in their first year of school. For example, Elkonin (1973) used slowed pronunciation (e.g., *m-ou-se*) to unpack sounds in words. Children were then taught to represent each sound in sequence with counters. Other researchers have used the iteration technique as a way of segmenting sounds, especially for consonants that don't stretch (i.e., they can't be said slowly without distortion), such as *p-t-d-b-k-g*. This technique is used, for example, in "What's the first sound in *d-d-d-doggie?*" (Lundberg, Frost, & Peterson, 1988; Zhurova, 1963). Fox and Routh (1975) used the "little bit" technique, as in "Say a little bit of the word *cat*." A variation is, "Instead of *hem*, let's say *h, em*" (Treiman & Baron, 1983). Another example of a phoneme awareness activity is asking a child "Which picture (cat, mouse) starts with /k/?" (see Wallach & Wallach, 1979).

Other segmentation approaches include deleting phonemes (e.g. *tape* → *ape*, *meet* → *me*) or adding phonemes (e.g., *and* → *sand* → *stand*). These adding and deleting activities are harder than segmenting activities. Lewkowicz (1980) suggested that segmenting activities be combined with slowed pronunciation, so as to make the task easier. A number of researchers have tried the earlier-cited techniques with some success (for reviews, see Olson, 1990; Stanovich, 1992; Tunmer, 1991). Training programs have usually shown gains in reading and/or spelling. It has also been found that 6-year-olds in the remedial reading program Reading Recovery finished 30% faster when extra phonemic awareness training was added to their remedial instruction (Iverson & Tunmer, 1993). Center, Wheldall, Freeman, Outhred, and McNaught (1995) also found that children who made progress in Reading Recovery had started their remedial training with higher levels of phonemic awareness than children who did not make progress. A summary of various training studies is shown in Table 17.1.

TABLE 17.1
A Cross-Cultural Comparison of Phonemic Awareness Training Studies

Country	Authors	Sample Size (N)	Grade	Age	Size of Training Group	Number of Sessions	Control for Hawthorne Effects	Focus of Study	Training Effects
Russia	Elkonin (1973)	15	kindergarten	5 & 6	Whole class	14	No	Reading	Yes
England	Bradley & Bryant (1983)	64	1	5 & 6	Single case	40	Yes	Reading and spelling	Yes
	Hatcher, Hulme, & Ellis (1994)	128	1-2	6 & 7	Single case	40	No	Reading and spelling	Yes
Sweden	Olofsson & Lundberg (1985)	83	kindergarten	6	Whole class	32	Yes	Reading and spelling	Yes
Denmark	Lundberg, Frost, & Petersen (1988)	390	kindergarten	6	Whole class	160	Yes	Reading and spelling	Yes
Norway	Lie (1991)	208	1	7	Whole class	90	Yes	Reading and spelling	Yes
Australia	Byrne & Fielding-Barnsley (1991, 1993)	126	kindergarten	4	4-6	12	Yes	Reading	Yes

United States	Wallach & Wallach (1979)	80	1	6	Single case	50	No	Reading	Yes
	Williams (1980)	102	Learning disabled	7–12	3	120	No	Reading	Yes
	Cunningham (1990)	84	kindergarten and 1	5 & 6	4–5	20	Yes	Reading	Yes
	Ball & Blachman (1991)	89	kindergarten	5	5	28	Yes	Reading and spelling	Yes
	Iverson & Tunmer (1993)	96	1	6	Single case	42	Yes	Reading	Yes
	Whitehurst et al. (1994)	167	Preschool	4	Whole class	60	No	Reading and writing	Yes
	Brady, Fowler, Stone, & Winbury (1994)	96	kindergarten	5	Whole class	54	No	Reading and spelling	Yes
	Tangel & Blachman (1992, 1995); Blachman, Ball, Black, & Tangel (1994)	159	kindergarten	5	4–5	41	No	Reading and spelling	Yes
	Weiner (1994)	79	1	6	4–5	12	No	Reading	No
Argentina	Manrigue, cited in Manrigue & Signorini (1994)	Single classroom	kindergarten	5	Whole class	Whole year	No	Reading and spelling	Yes
New Zealand	Castle, Riach, & Nicholson (1994)	Exp. 1:30	1	5	5	20	Yes	Spelling	Yes
		Exp. 2:45	1	5	3	15	Yes	Reading	Yes

In addition to the success of training studies, the correlation between phonemic awareness and reading progress is so strong that it is hard to doubt the value of phonemic awareness for reading success (for reviews, see Juel, 1986; Nicholson, 1994; Stanovich, 1994; Tunmer, Herriman, & Nesdale, 1988; Tunmer & Hoover, 1993). In a 4-year follow-up of 54 children, Juel (1988) reported that all the children who became poor readers had entered first grade with low levels of phonemic awareness. Wimmer, Landerl, Linortner, and Hummer (1991) also reported that children with high phonemic awareness at the beginning of grade 1 had high reading and spelling levels at the end of grade 1. Furthermore, Griffith, Klesius, and Kromrey (1992) reported that beginning-of-year levels of phonemic awareness were more important for reading success than method of instruction (they compared phonics and basal reading approaches). Finally, Stanovich (1992) reported a mean correlation of .54 between level of phonological awareness and reading achievement, averaged across more than 40 correlations, reported in 14 studies. In summary, the results of both correlational and training studies suggest that children who start school with high levels of phonemic awareness will get off to a better start in reading (and spelling). This suggests that children with low levels of phonemic awareness on entry to school may benefit from specific instruction in segmenting, blending, deleting, and adding phonemes in words.

A still unanswered question is whether phonemic awareness training will be any better than training in alternative strategies, such as "process writing" and the teaching of "prediction" skills, which are part of the whole language approach. Evidence is starting to accumulate on this question. For example, Castle, Riach, and Nicholson (1994) recently reported two experiments on phonemic awareness training carried out in whole-language classrooms. Details of activities used in these experiments are in Nicholson (1994). In the first experiment, 15 school beginners were taught phonemic awareness for 20 minutes, twice weekly for 10 weeks, in small groups of 5. A matched control group of 15 new entrants did "process writing," also in small groups of 5, where they wrote their own stories and were encouraged to invent their own spellings, for example, "hv" for *have* or "kt" for *cat*. Total training time was 6.7 hours for both groups.

Each experimental group lesson covered specific activities aimed at increasing phonemic awareness, such as slowed pronunciation, the iteration technique, phoneme substitution (e.g., what would *cat* say if it ended with *b* instead of *t*—answer is *cab*), phoneme deletion (e.g., say *cat* without the /k/), and rhyme (e.g., which pictures rhyme—show picture of *log*, *dog*, *sun*). The phonemic awareness teaching also included games such as "concentration," wherein children were asked to spot matching pairs of picture cards that had the same initial, final, or middle phoneme. This game was derived from Wallach and Wallach (1976). Another game was "say it and move it" (Ball & Blachman, 1991), in which children had to represent phonemes in a given word by moving counters from the bottom half of a card to an appropriate position in a series of square boxes above as they said the word aloud. This activity was based on work by Elkonin (1973) and Clay (1985). Sound-letter rules were also taught using the concentration game (e.g., playing the game so that children could match picture cards to alphabet letter cards).

As indicated previously, the control group received the same amount of instructional time (to control for Hawthorne effects), but they engaged in "process" writing activities wherein they wrote their own stories and invented their own spellings. To help them with their spellings, each group had an alphabet card, about the size of a regular page, with each letter of the alphabet accompanied by a picture that started with the "sound" of that letter (e.g., the letter *a* had a picture of an apple).

The findings of the first experiment were that the phonemic awareness training group achieved significantly higher scores than did the control group on a test of phonemic awareness (Roper, 1984). The phonemic training group also showed greater gains than the control group in word spelling, as measured by the Wide Range Achievement Test (WRAT) and by an informal spelling test, especially on words in the latter test that had regular spellings. In summary, the study looked at whether children in the experimental group improved in spelling more than those in the control group, even though both groups got equal amounts of extra teaching. The findings indicated that children in the experimental group did indeed improve more than did the control group in spelling skill.

The second experiment also involved teaching phonemic awareness to school beginners, but with a focus on the improvement of reading. In the experimental group, 15 children were taught phonemic awareness. One matched control group of 15 other new entrants did alternative activities, such as categorizing pictures (e.g., "Which pictures are animals?"), and a second matched control group of 15 children got no extra instruction at all. This study looked at whether the experimental group gained more in reading than did the other groups. The training was also done in small groups of three, 20 minutes per week, for 15 weeks. Total training time in this second experiment was 5.0 hours for each of the three groups.

The phonemic awareness training group focused on segmentation and blending skills. As in the spelling experiment, activities included alliteration, using the "odd one out" procedure (e.g., pictures of *piano*, *pig, fish*—where *fish* is the odd one out). Segmentation training involved use of the Elkonin (1973) technique wherein children placed tokens into squares to represent each of the phonemes in a specific word (e.g., *duck* → | • | • | • |).

Other activities (based on Williams, 1980) involved games in which children decided which picture cards had the same beginning, middle, or ending sounds (e.g., "Do these pictures start the same?" Show pictures of *flag* and *fish*, and children say "Yes"). Children were also taught to blend sounds (e.g., mooo = moo) and to delete sounds (e.g., *meat* without *m* says *eat*). As the training progressed, more attention was paid to letter-sound relationships. Counters were replaced by plastic letters (as in Bradley & Bryant, 1983; Bryant & Bradley, 1985).

The control group that participated in alternative activities was included to act as a control for Hawthorne effects. They engaged in similar activities, but the focus was on the meaning of words rather than their phonemic structure. For example, cards were used for categorization activities (e.g., show pictures of *cat*, *bag*, *elephant*, *sun*—which cards are animals?). When plastic letters were used, their names rather than their sounds were used. This group was also read stories by the researcher. The mix of activities took up the same amount of training time as the experimental group, but differed in that phonemic awareness instruction was avoided. As mentioned earlier, the second control group was not seen at all. These children were pretested and posttested. Otherwise, they received only their regular classroom instruction.

The findings of the second experiment were that the phonemic awareness training group achieved significantly higher scores on a test of phonemic awareness (Roper, 1984) than did the two control groups. They also gained more than the other groups in both a dictation test that assessed invented spelling (Clay, 1985) and a pseudoword reading test in which children had to read words such as *buf* or *maz* (Bryant, 1975). In summary, the results indicated that training effects did occur in both spelling and in reading of pseudowords. Also, a later follow-up of the progress of the children found that the children who did *not* receive training in this skill were more likely to receive Reading Recovery remediation (i.e., an intensive individual remediation program that begins after one year of schooling). This indicated that children who received phonemic awareness training got off to a better start in reading and spelling than did children in the two control groups. Finally, it is worth restating that training in both of these studies was not confined just to phonemic awareness but also included attention to letters (e.g., children learned that *c* is the letter that starts *cup*). Such training is consistent with other research on the value of teaching phonemic awareness as a routine part of the regular reading program as soon as children start school.

Phonemic awareness training of this kind may be even more important for children from disadvantaged backgrounds, especially if such children are taught with whole-language methods. Morais (1991), in a study of the reading progress of Belgian pupils from contrasting backgrounds, found that low-income pupils made virtually no progress with the whole-word method. As Morais put it, "No child taught according to a pure whole-word method and coming from a family with low educational attainment could read. For culturally underprivileged children, the whole-word method is a threat" (p. 19). Morais also found that middle-class children did better with the whole-word approach, although the parents of these children had usually taught them the alphabetic principle at home. This had not happened with underprivileged children in his study.

In order to test the effectiveness of phonemic awareness instruction for children from low-income backgrounds, I recently conducted a study that replicated Castle et al. (1994). In the Castle et al. study, training was given to 5-year-old pupils from middle-class backgrounds who entered the study with at least some minimal phonemic awareness skills. In my own study (Nicholson, 1996), however, pupils had very low entry levels of phonemic awareness.

The study began with 113 pupils in seven different schools. Pupils who participated in the training ($n = 88$) came from six of these schools. In each school, pupils were matched on verbal ability. They were then randomly assigned either to experimental ($n = 44$) or control ($n = 44$) groups. In each school there were two experimental and two control subgroups. The pupils, all 5-year-olds, were trained in small groups (2 to 4 pupils) for 10 minutes each day, over a 12-week period. At the end of the study, due to attrition, the original sample had dropped to 60 pupils, with 30 pupils in the experimental group and 30 pupils in the control group. In addition to the two training groups, there was a contrast group of pupils ($n = 25$) from a school in a middle-class suburb of Auckland. This group was not trained, but received pretests and postests. At the start of the study, pupils from the low-income area had only been at school for three months. Almost all pupils were from Pacific Island and Maori backgrounds. All pupils were born in New Zealand and spoke English.

The experimental group received 8 weeks of training in phonemic awareness and letter recognition. The training was carried out by tutors who were university students. The phonemic awareness training was based on "Sound Foundations" (Byrne & Fielding-Barnsley, 1991). The program, originally designed for 4-year-olds, used large posters containing lots of colourful illustrations, all starting with the same sound or ending with the same sound. The posters covered words that either began or ended with nine separate sounds: S, M, P, L, T, G, SH, A, E.

Other phonemic awareness activities included the "yes–no" game (Wallach & Wallach, 1976), in which pupils were shown two picture cards and had to decide whether they started or ended with the same sounds. Another activity was the "bag game" (Lewkowicz, 1994). In this game, two bags were used, each containing the same five objects (e.g., a toy mouse, dog, frog, sheep, and pig). One child would locate a particular toy in the bag and say its beginning sound. A second child, with the other bag, would look inside and locate the toy that started with that sound.

Apart from phonemic awareness training, time was also spent teaching pupils to recognize alphabetic characters. Children would say the sounds represented by the alphabetic characters, copy them, and write them from memory. They also wrote stories using their own invented spellings. Story writing occurred once each week. Finally, pupils were read stories that contained alliteration and rhyme (e.g., "How many trucks can a tow truck tow?"). This was also done once each week. Tutors had access to a number of books of this type, based on recommendations in Griffith and Olson (1992) and Nicholson (1994).

The "Sound Foundations" program took 4 weeks to complete. It was then repeated, to reinforce the concept of beginning and ending sounds. In the final four weeks of the study, Fun Fit (Nutshell, 1993) alphabet cards were used to teach pupils how to make and read simple, regular words (e.g., *big, ran, pot*). The materials consisted of 12 sets of 15 alphabet cards. Each set of cards had 10 different consonants and 5 vowels. Tutors used the cards to practice alphabet recognition and to construct simple regular words.

The control group used the same materials as the experimental group (e.g, "Sound Foundations" program and "Fun Fit" alphabet cards) to control for Hawthorne effects. The control group children completed the same activities but without the same emphasis on sounds. They were taught alphabet names, wrote stories, listened to the same stories, and worked with the same posters. Tutors would talk about the meanings of the poster illustrations rather than their sounds. Pupils would look for illustrated items in the posters that were edible, or items that were alive, and so on. When the alphabet was taught, letter names were used, but not letter sounds. Children also wrote a story once each week. The control group received all the "special" elements of the program but without the emphasis on sounds.

Total training time for each group was 10 hours. The findings were that the experimental group achieved significantly higher scores than did the control group in invented spelling, dictation, and standardized test spelling as measured by the Wide Range Achievement Test (WRAT), but only when a scoring system was used that gave credit for number of phonemes correct. This is a more sensitive way of scoring spelling ability than assessing spelling attempts as either correct or incorrect. Using the phoneme scoring method, the experimental group also outperformed the control group on a test of pseudoword reading and reading of short regular words (e.g., *cat, mat, at*).

Because the experimental group was slightly older (1 month) than the control group, the groups were compared using age as a covariate. When this was done, the basic pattern of results remained the same, except that the experimental group was also better than the control group on dictation (correct spelling) and in terms of the spelling quality of their story writing (i.e., the extent to which invented spellings matched the number of phonemes represented in each word attempted).

At the end of the study, when the results for the two training groups were compared with the middle-class contrast group, the middle-class group was still well ahead of the two training groups. However, the gap between the middle-class group and the experimental group was *smaller* after training than the gap between the middle-class group and the control group in those areas in which the training had been of benefit to the experimental group (i.e., invented spelling, and decoding of short regularly spelled words and pseudowords). Figure 17.2 shows results for those measures that were administered as pretests and posttests (the dictation and regular word reading measures were given as posttests only).

The effects of the training did not extend to text reading, or word recognition as measured by a standardized test. This lack of transfer has been observed in other studies (e.g., Blachman et al., 1994). On the one hand it may be that children who receive phonemic awareness and simple phonics training also need training in speeded recognition of irregular words (as in *the, was, come*, etc.) to assist them in the transition to text reading (see Olson, Wise, Johnson, & Ring, chap. 14, this volume). On the other hand, it may be that the effects of such training take time to appear. For example, Lundberg et al. (1988) found that phonemic awareness training did not impact on reading until a year after their study ended.

In all, the results of this training study with 5-year-old pupils from low-income areas indicated that phonemic awareness and simple phonics instruction could help to bridge the gap between pupils from different socioeconomic backgrounds. Compared with the Castle et al. (1994) study, which involved pupils from mostly middle-class backgrounds, pupils in the Nicholson (1996) study did not make the same rate of improvement. Yet pupils from the Nicholson (1996) study were from low-income backgrounds and started school with much lower readiness skills than did children in the Castle et al. (1994) study.

These results, when combined with those of Castle et al. (1994), suggest that children from disadvantaged backgrounds would benefit from early instruction that focused on the development of phonemic awareness skills. Even children taught with a whole-language approach would get off to a better start in reading and spelling. Learning to read requires phonemic awareness skills. Children who start school with phonemic awareness

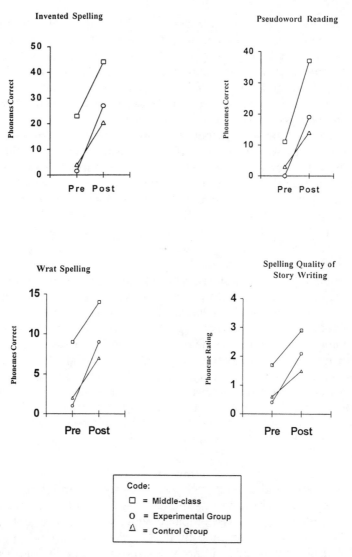

FIG. 17.2. Differences among middle-class, experimental, and control groups in invented spelling, WRAT spelling, pseudoword reading, and spelling quality of story writing.

skills are more likely to learn to read and write. These skills may be more important even than the method of instruction (Griffith, Klesius, & Kromrey, 1992; Juel, 1988, 1994; Tunmer & Nesdale, 1985; although see Johnston, Connelly, & Watson, 1995, who reported that Scottish children taught with phonics made better progress than did New Zealand children taught with whole language).

CONCLUSION

Children in middle-class families are often read to daily from the time they are 12 months old. These children, when they get to school, already know a great deal about what stories are like, what print is for, and how books work. They are not yet able to read or write as adults do (and, in fact, may not be able to read or write at all), but, for many, their home background has given them an excellent start on the path to literacy. In particular, such children are also likely to have important language skills, such as phonemic awareness, which is now known to be an essential prerequisite to literacy acquisition. Children with phonemic awareness are good at language rhymes and know how to separate sounds in words, for example, to say that /kat/ without the /k/ is /at/. This knowledge helps them to associate letters with sounds and, ultimately, learn to read and spell.

In contrast, many children from low-income families do not get such preschool advantages. They may come to school knowing much less about print and have less skill in the area of phonemic awareness. Their parents may not earn enough money to buy them books, and may have insufficient education themselves to feel comfortable about joining libraries, using these facilities, and providing all the other kinds of language and reading experiences that tend to occur in middle-class homes. Such pupils are very much at risk of not learning to read and spell, especially if they are taught with a whole-language approach presupposing that pupils have phonemic awareness. Thus, although all children seem likely to benefit from early instruction in phonemic awareness, children from low-income families may be the ones who benefit most.

REFERENCES

Adams, M. J. (1990). *Beginning to read: Thinking and learning about print.* Cambridge, MA: MIT Press.

Anbar, A. (1986). Reading acquisition of preschool children without systematic instruction. *Early Childhood Research Quarterly, 1,* 69–83.

Ball, E. W., & Blachman, B. A. (1991). Does phoneme awareness training in kindergarten make a difference in early word recognition and developmental spelling? *Reading Research Quarterly, 26,* 49–66.

Beard, R., & Oakhill, J. (1994). *Reading by apprenticeship? A critique of the "Apprenticeship Approach" to the teaching of reading.* Slough, England: National Foundation for Educational Research.

Blachman, B. A., Ball, E. W., Black, R. S., & Tangel, D. M. (1994). Kindergarten teachers develop phonemic awareness in low-income, inner-city classrooms. Does it make a difference? *Reading and Writing: An Interdisciplinary Journal, 6,* 1–18.

Bowey, J. A. (1991). Early reading: Rime and reason. *Australian Journal of Reading, 14,* 140–144.

Bradley, L. (1980). *Assessing reading difficulties: A diagnostic and remedial approach.* London: Macmillan Education.

Bradley, L., & Bryant, P. E. (1983). Categorizing sounds and learning to read—a causal connection. *Nature, 301,* 419–421.

Brady, S., Fowler, A., Stone, B., & Winbury, N. (1994). Training phonological awareness: A study with inner-city children. *Annals of Dyslexia, 44,* 26–59.

Bryant, N. D. (1975). *Bryant test of basic decoding skills.* New York: Teachers College Press.

Bryant, P. E., & Bradley, L. (1985). *Children's reading problems.* Oxford, England: Blackwell.

Bryant, P. E., Bradley, L., MacLean, M., & Crossland, J. (1989) Nursery rhymes, phonological skills, and reading. *Journal of Child Language, 16,* 407–428.

Byrne, B., & Fielding-Barnsley, R. (1991). *Sound foundations.* Sydney, Australia: Peter Leyden Educational.

Byrne, B., & Fielding-Barnsley, R. (1993). Evaluation of a program to teach phonemic awareness to young children: A 1-year follow-up. *Journal of Educational Psychology, 85,* 104–111.

Castle, J. M., Riach, J., & Nicholson, T. (1994). Getting off to a better start in reading and spelling: The effects of phonemic awareness instruction within a whole language program. *Journal of Educational Psychology, 86,* 350–359.

Center, Y., Wheldall, K., Freeman, L., Outhred, L., & McNaught, M. (1995). An evaluation of Reading Recovery. *Reading Research Quarterly, 30,* 240–263.

Chall, J. S., Jacobs, V. A., & Baldwin, L. E. (1990). *The reading crisis: Why poor children fall behind.* Cambridge, MA: Harvard University Press.

Clark, M. M. (1976). *Young fluent readers: What can they tell us?* London: Heinemann.

Clay, M. M. (1985). *The early detection of reading difficulties.* Auckland, New Zealand: Heinemann.

Cunningham, A. (1990). Explicit versus implicit instruction in phonemic awareness. *Journal of Experimental Child Psychology, 50,* 429–444.

Durkin, D. (1966). *Children who read early.* New York: Teachers College Press.

Elkonin, D. B. (1973). U.S.S.R. In J. Downing (Ed.), *Comparative reading* (pp. 551–579). New York: Macmillan.

Feitelson, D., & Goldstein, Z. (1986). Patterns of book ownership and reading to young children in Israeli school oriented and nonschool oriented families. *The Reading Teacher, 39,* 924–930.

Foss, D., & Hakes, D. (1978). *Psycholinguistics: An introduction to the psychology of language.* Englewood Cliffs, NJ: Prentice-Hall.

Fox, B., & Routh, D. K. (1975). Analyzing spoken language into words, syllabus, and phonemes: A developmental study. *Journal of Psycholinguistic Research, 4,* 331–342.

Gibbons, J. (1981). *The effects of book experience on the responses of four-year-olds to texts.* Unpublished master's thesis, University of Waikato, Hamilton, New Zealand.

Goswami, U. (1994). Phonological skills, analogies, and reading development. *Reading, 28,* 32–37.

Griffith, P. L., Klesius, J. P., & Kromrey, J. D. (1992). The effect of phonemic awareness on the literacy development of first-grade children in a traditional or a whole language classroom. *Journal of Research in Childhood Education, 6,* 85–92.

Griffith, P. L., & Olson, M. W. (1992). Phonemic awareness helps beginning readers break the code. *The Reading Teacher, 45,* 516–523.

Hatcher, P. J., Hulme, C., & Ellis, A. W. (1994). Ameliorating early reading failure by integrating the teaching of reading and phonological skills: The phonological linkage hypothesis. *Child Development, 65,* 41–57.

Hiebert, F. (1994). Reading Recovery in the United States: What difference does it make to an age cohort? *Educational Researcher, 23,* 15–25.

Hughes, D., & Lauder, H. (1991). Human capital theory and the wastage of talent in New Zealand. *New Zealand Journal of Educational Studies, 26,* 5–20.

Iverson, S., & Tunmer, W. E. (1993). Phonological processing skills and the Reading Recovery Program. *Journal of Educational Psychology, 85,* 112–126.

Jastak, S., & Wilkinson, G. S. (1984). *Wide range achievement test—revised.* Wilmington, DE: Jastak Associates.

Johnston, R., Connelly, V., & Watson, J. (1995). Some effects of phonics teaching on early reading development. In P. Owen & P. Pumfrey (Eds.), *Emergent and developing reading: Messages for teachers* (pp. 32–42). London: Falmer Press.

Juel, C. (1986). Support for the theory of phonemic awareness as a predictor in literacy acquisition. In J. A. Niles & R. V. Lalik (Eds.), *Solving problems in literacy: Learners, teachers and researchers* (pp. 239–243). Chicago: National Reading Conference.

Juel, C. (1988). Learning to read and write: A longitudinal study of 54 children from first through fourth grades. *Journal of Educational Psychology, 80,* 437–447.

Juel, C. (1994). *Learning to read in one elementary school.* New York: Springer-Verlag.

Kerslake, J. (1994). A summary of the 1993 data on Reading Recovery. *Research Bulletin, 3,* 68–72.

Levine, A. (1994, December). The great debate revisited. *Atlantic Monthly,* 38–44.

Lewkowicz, N. A. (1980). Phonemic awareness training: What to teach and how to teach it. *Journal of Educational Psychology, 72,* 686–700.

Lewkowicz, N. A. (1994). The bag game: An activity to heighten phonemic awareness. *The Reading Teacher, 47,* 508–509.

Lie, A. (1991). Effects of a training program for stimulating skills in word analysis in first-grade children. *Reading Research Quarterly, 26,* 234–250.

Lundberg, I., Frost, J., & Peterson, O. (1988). Effects of an extensive program for stimulating phonological awareness in preschool children. *Reading Research Quarterly, 23,* 263–284.

Manrigue, A. M. B., & Signorini, A. (1994). Phonological awareness, spelling and reading abilities in Spanish-speaking children. *British Journal of Educational Psychology, 64,* 429–439.

Mason, J. M., & Allen, J. (1986). A review of emergent literacy with implications for research and practice in reading. *Review of Research in Education, 13,* 3–48.

Milina, T. (1991). *Preschool screening as a means of predicting children at risk of experiencing reading and spelling difficulties.* Unpublished master's thesis, University of Auckland, New Zealand.

Morais, J. (1991). Constraints on the development of phonemic awareness. In S. A. Brady & D. P. Shankweiler (Eds.), *Phonological processes in literacy* (pp. 5–27). Hillsdale, NJ: Lawrence Erlbaum Associates.

Nicholson, T. (1980a). Why we need to talk to parents about reading. *The Reading Teacher, 34,* 19–21.

Nicholson, T. (1980b). *An evaluation study of the radio series "On the way to reading."* Hamilton, New Zealand: University of Waikato, Education Department.

Nicholson, T. (1994). *At the cutting edge: Recent research on learning to read and spell.* Wellington: New Zealand Council for Educational Research.

Nicholson, T. (1996). *Can the poor get richer? Some effects of phonemic awareness and simple phonics instruction on the reading and writing development of children from low-income backgrounds.* Auckland, New Zealand: University of Auckland, Department of Education.

Nicholson, T., & Gallienne, G. (1995). Struggletown meets middletown: Reading achievement levels among 13-year-old students in low and middle socioeconomic areas. *New Zealand Journal of Educational Studies, 30,* 15–23.

Nutshell Products. (1993). *Fun fit.* Kalbar, Australia: Author.

Olofsson, A., & Lundberg, I. (1985). Evaluation of long-term effects of phonemic awareness training in kindergarten: Illustrations of some methodological problems in evaluation research. *Scandinavian Journal of Psychology, 26,* 21–34.

Olson, M. W. (1990). Phonemic awareness and reading achievement. *Reading Psychology, 11,* 347–353.

Phillips, G., & McNaughton, S. (1990). The practice of storybook reading to preschool children in mainstream New Zealand families. *Reading Research Quarterly, 25,* 196–212.

Raz, I. T., & Bryant, P. (1990). Social background, phonological awareness and children's reading. *British Journal of Developmental Psychology, 8,* 209–225.

Roper, H. D. (1984). *Spelling, word recognition and phonemic awareness among first grade children.* Unpublished doctoral dissertation, University of Texas, Austin.

Rutter, M. (1983). School effects on pupil progress: Research findings and policy implications. *Child Development, 54,* 1–29.

Share, D. L., Jorm, A. F., Maclean, R., & Matthews, R. (1984). Sources of individual differences in reading acquisition. *Journal of Educational Psychology, 76,* 1309–1324.

Snow, C. E., Barnes, W. S., Chandler, J., Goodman, I. F., & Hemphill, L. (1991). *Unfulfilled expectations: Home and school influences on literacy.* Cambridge, MA: Harvard University Press.

Stanovich, K. E. (1986). Matthew effects in reading: Some consequences of individual differences in the acquisition of literacy. *Reading Research Quarterly, 21,* 360–407.

Stanovich, K. E. (1992). Speculations on the causes and consequences of individual differences in early reading acquisition. In P. B. Gough, L. C. Ehri, & R. Treiman (Eds.), *Reading acquisition* (pp. 307–342). Hillsdale, NJ: Lawrence Erlbaum Associates.

Stanovich, K. E. (1994). Romance and reality. *The Reading Teacher, 47,* 280–291.

Tangel, D. M., & Blachman, B. A. (1992). Effect of phoneme awareness instruction on kindergarten children's invented spelling. *Journal of Reading Behavior, 24,* 233–261.

Tangel, D. M., & Blachman, B. A. (1995). Effect of phoneme awareness instruction on the invented spelling of first grade children: A one-year follow-up. *Journal of Reading Behavior, 27,* 153–185.

Teale, W. H. (1986). Home background and young children's literacy development. In W. H. Teale & E. Sulzby (Eds.), *Emergent literacy: Writing and reading* (pp. 173–206). Norwood, NJ: Ablex.

Treiman, R. (1993). *Beginning to spell: A study of first grade children.* New York: Oxford University Press.

Treiman, R., & Baron, J. (1983). Phonemic-analysis training helps children benefit from spelling-sound rules. *Memory and Cognition, 11,* 382–389.

Tunmer, W. E. (1991). Phonological awareness and literacy acquisition. In L. Rieben & C. A. Perfetti (Eds.), *Learning to read: Basic research and its implications* (pp. 105–119). Hillsdale, NJ: Lawrence Erlbaum Associates.

Tunmer, W. E., Herriman, M. L., & Nesdale, A. R. (1988). Metalinguistic abilities and beginning reading. *Reading Research Quarterly, 23,* 134–158.

Tunmer, W. E., & Hoover, W. A. (1993). Language-related factors as sources of individual differences in the development of word recognition skills. In G. B. Thompson, W. E. Tunmer, & T. Nicholson (Eds.), *Reading acquisition processes* (pp. 123–147). Clevedon, Avon, England: Multilingual Matters.

Tunmer, W. E., & Nesdale, A. R. (1985). Phonemic segmentation skill and beginning reading. *Journal of Educational Psychology, 77,* 417–427.

Wallach, M. A., & Wallach, L. (1979). Helping disadvantaged children to learn to read by teaching them phoneme identification skills. In L. A. Resnick & P. A. Weaver (Eds.), *Theory and practice of early reading* (Vol. 3, pp. 227–259). Hillsdale, NJ: Lawrence Erlbaum Associates.

Wallach, L., Wallach, M. A., Dozier, M. G., & Kaplan, N. E. (1976). Poor children learning to read do not have trouble with auditory discrimination but do have trouble with phoneme recognition. *Journal of Educational Psychology, 69,* 36–39.

Wallach, M. A., & Wallach, L. (1976). *Teaching all children to read*. Chicago: University of Chicago Press.

Weiner, S. (1994). Effects of phonemic awareness training on low- and middle-achieving first graders' phonemic awareness and reading ability. *Journal of Reading Behavior, 26,* 277–300.

Whitehurst, G. J., Epstein, J. N., Angell, A. L., Payne, A. C., Crone, D. A., & Fischel, J. E. (1994). Outcomes of an emergent literacy intervention in Head Start. *Journal of Educational Psychology, 86,* 542–555.

Williams, J. P. (1980). Teaching decoding with an emphasis on phoneme analysis and phoneme blending. *Journal of Educational Psychology, 72,* 1–15.

Wilson, C., & Dupuis, A. (1992). Poverty and performance. *Set* [Research information for teachers] available from New Zealand Council for Educational Research, P.O. Box 3237, Wellington, New Zealand.

Wimmer, H., Landerl, K., Linortner, R., & Hummer, P. (1991). The relationship of phonemic awareness to reading acquisition: More consequence than precondition, but still important. *Cognition, 40,* 219–249.

Zhurova, L. E. (1963). The development of analysis of words into their sounds by preschool children. *Soviet Psychology and Psychiatry, 72,* 17–27.

18

Early Intervention and Phonological Awareness: A Cautionary Tale

Benita A. Blachman
Syracuse University

During the past 25 years, investigations that have focused on the relationship between speech and reading have provided critical insight into the factors that influence early reading ability. Specifically, the identification of deficits in phonological processing has helped explain the discrepancy between the *ease* with which most children acquire spoken language and the *difficulty* many of these same children have in learning to read (Brady & Shankweiler, 1991; Goswami & Bryant, 1990; I. Y. Liberman & Shankweiler, 1985; Wagner & Torgesen, 1987). In response to overwhelming evidence that phonological processing plays such a central role in reading acquisition, many researchers have focused reading intervention studies on aspects of phonological processing, especially phonological awareness (see Blachman, 1994a, for a review).

Phonological awareness—an awareness of the phonological segments in speech, the segments of speech that are more or less represented in an alphabetic orthography—has been the focus of sustained scientific inquiry, due, in large measure, to the insights of Isabelle Liberman some 25 years ago. She observed that one of the fundamental tasks facing the beginning reader is understanding that speech can be segmented and that these segmented units can be represented by printed forms (I. Y. Liberman, 1971, 1973). In collaboration with her colleagues at Haskins Laboratories, she was able to explain and to demonstrate why it is difficult for the young beginning reader to become aware of the phonological structure of spoken language, and why failure to achieve this awareness is a major stumbling block in learning to read (I. Y. Liberman, 1971; I. Y. Liberman & Shankweiler, 1979; I. Y. Liberman, Shankweiler, Fischer, & Carter, 1974). The difficulty stems from the fact that the phonemes are coarticulated or "merged" during speech production (A. M. Liberman, Cooper, Shankweiler, & Studdert-Kennedy, 1967; I. Y. Liberman, 1971), thus obscuring the segmental nature of the speech stream. As I. Y. Liberman and Shankweiler explained (1991):

> Though the word "bag," for example, has three phonological units, and, correspondingly, three letters in print, it has only one pulse of sound: The three elements of the underlying phonological structure—the three phonemes—have been thoroughly overlapped and merged into that one sound—"bag." . . . [Beginning readers] can understand, and properly take advantage of, the fact that the printed word *bag* has three letters, only if they are aware that the spoken word *"bag"* . . . is divisible into three segments. (p. 6)

The results of a large body of research, grounded in a common theoretical framework, provide unequivocal evidence that:

1. Children who lack phonological awareness are likely to become poor readers (Bradley & Bryant, 1983; Fletcher et al., 1994; Juel, 1988; Share, Jorm, Maclean, & Matthews, 1984; Vellutino & Scanlon, 1987).

2. Instruction that enhances phonological awareness has a facilitating effect on beginning reading and spelling (e.g., Lundberg, Frost, & Petersen, 1988) and is even more effective when combined with instruction that connects the phonological segments to letters (Ball & Blachman, 1991; Blachman, Ball, Black, & Tangel, 1994; Bradley & Bryant, 1983; Byrne & Fielding-Barnsley, 1991, 1993, 1995; Castle, Riach, & Nicholson, 1994; Iversen & Tunmer, 1993; Williams, 1980).

3. Instruction that emphasizes the alphabetic code promotes accuracy and fluency of word identification—skills that are essential to becoming a proficient reader (Adams, 1990; Beck & Juel, 1995; Chall, 1989; I. Y. Liberman & Liberman, 1990; Stanovich, 1986; Vellutino, 1991).

Despite this convergence of opinion regarding practices most likely to facilitate beginning reading acquisition, there is much to be learned. Even within the realm of phonological awareness—the area of phonological processing about which we have the greatest consensus—many questions remain unanswered. Some of the most pressing are identified here, and each is discussed in turn in this chapter:

1. At what age and level of developmental readiness should phonological awareness instruction begin?
2. What are the most appropriate and beneficial tasks for our earliest intervention efforts?
3. How much phonological awareness is needed?
4. How do we measure phonological awareness?
5. What are the characteristics of the reading instruction that should follow an early emphasis on phonological awareness?
6. What are the long-term outcomes of our early intervention efforts?
7. Who are the treatment resisters?
8. What other phonological factors (e.g., problems in the retrieval of phonological information) play a role in treatment success?

But this, after all, is a cautionary tale. After addressing each question, I share some thoughts on the need for caution now that "phonological awareness" has become one of the educational buzzwords of the 1990s. Although for some time researchers have suggested that phonological awareness activities should be incorporated into the kindergarten and first-grade classroom before children have had a chance to fail in reading and spelling (Adams, 1990; Blachman, 1989; Juel, 1988; Williams, 1980), it is only recently that this idea has been widely disseminated (e.g., as part of the *Learning to Read/Reading to Learn* public awareness campaign that began July 9, 1996, funded by the U.S. Office of Education, Office of Special Education Programs; NCLD, 1996). It is especially important at this critical juncture not to lose sight of the unanswered questions.

AT WHAT AGE AND LEVEL OF DEVELOPMENTAL READINESS SHOULD INSTRUCTION IN PHONEME AWARENESS BEGIN?

For those of us interested in early intervention and the prevention of reading failure, it might, at first glance, seem that the answer to the question of when instruction should begin would be obvious. The answer is, of course, "the earlier, the better." But is that always true? We know from studies like those by Byrne and Fielding-Barnsley (1991, 1993, 1995) that the phonological awareness skills of 4-year-olds can be heightened and that children who enter school with heightened awareness, whether from direct training or because they were able to develop these insights from environmental stimulation (e.g., being read to), are more successful as readers and spellers. Does that mean that all 4-year-olds should be participating in programs to develop phoneme awareness?

An article by O'Connor, Jenkins, Leicester, and Slocum (1993) triggered this question for me. The researchers evaluated a program to heighten phoneme awareness in young children with developmental delays, including children as young as 4 years of age. Children were randomly assigned to rhyming, blending, or segmenting conditions. Although children gained in phonological awareness, there was little transfer to skills other than the skill on which the child was trained, and little generalization within a skill, such as blending, to untrained items. A review of the characteristics of the children in this study revealed that 80% had significant language delays and some had additional disabilities, such as behavior disorders and mental retardation. The mean IQ of the children on the McCarthy Scales of Children's Abilities was about 70, with an average mental age of 3 years, 8 months. Although this well-designed study answered some questions about the feasibility of teaching these skills to young children with significant developmental delays, I couldn't help but wonder if phonological awareness training was the highest priority for these children. Did it represent good pedagogy? Just because we know how to do something does not mean that is what we should be doing. When is a child developmentally ready for this instruction?

WHAT ARE THE MOST APPROPRIATE TASKS FOR OUR EARLY INTERVENTION EFFORTS?

At least part of the answer to the question of a child's developmental readiness depends on the appropriateness of the tasks that are selected for instruction. Which activities are most beneficial, the optimal order of presentation, and amount of classroom time that should be spent on each, depends on several variables, including age and developmental level of the child (for research-based, clinical suggestions, see Snider, 1995). To help prereading children discover sound similarities in spoken language, it has been suggested that young children would benefit from extended word play in the form of nursery rhymes and rhyming games. There is evidence from longitudinal research by Bryant and his colleagues (Bryant, Bradley, MacLean, & Crossland, 1989; Bryant, MacLean, Bradley, & Crossland, 1990; MacLean, Bryant, & Bradley, 1987) to support these suggestions. Beginning when children were 3 years old, the researchers made periodic assessments of knowledge of nursery rhymes, ability to detect and produce rhyme and alliteration, and ability to identify letters and read highly frequent words. The results indicated that knowledge of nursery rhymes at age 3 was related to the child's ability to detect rhyme more than 1 year later. This was true even after differences in IQ and social background were controlled. Performance on rhyme and alliteration detection tasks was also related later to beginning word reading.

Teaching children to detect and produce rhyme and alliteration may be particularly useful in the development of phonological awareness when working with preschool and kindergarten children. Treiman (1992) pointed out that tasks requiring rhyme and alliteration also provide an opportunity to assess the child's awareness of intrasyllabic units—specifically, onsets and rimes (e.g., in the syllable *trip*, the onset is *tr* and the rime is *ip*). It has been suggested (Goswami & Bryant, 1990; Treiman, 1992) that helping children gain access to onsets and rimes, the two primary parts of the syllable, might help children negotiate the transition from syllable awareness to awareness of phonemes.

To help kindergarten children learn to analyze simple words into their constituent phonemes, we (Ball & Blachman, 1991; Blachman et al., 1994) have used a very simple task we call "say-it-and-move-it" (adapted from Elkonin, 1973) to teach children to move disks to represent the sounds in words. Children are taught to move disks from the top half of an 8½" × 11" sheet of paper to a black line at the bottom of the sheet to represent the sounds in spoken words. The program begins by modeling for children the representation of one sound /i/ with one disk and then introduces the child to the representation of a single sound that is repeated (e.g., /i/ /i/ with two disks). Eventually, children learn to represent two-phoneme (e.g., *up*) and three-phoneme items (e.g., *fan*) by moving disks to represent individual sounds as they say each word slowly. After segmenting an item into its constituent phonemes, the children repeat the original word as a whole unit. Once successful at this level of representation, children learn to connect the phonological segments to the letters that represent those segments. Although we have shown in our research that phonological awareness can by heightened using this structured phoneme segmentation task—and others have demonstrated that phonological awareness can be developed using different activities (see, e.g., the sound categorization activities developed by Bradley & Bryant, 1983, 1985)—this does not mean that the question of the right beginning task for a particular group of children has been resolved. It is possible that the children in any given training study might have been more (or less) successful if a different training task or combination of tasks had been chosen. We need more information about the relative merits of these tasks when used with comparable groups of children.

Several recent studies with kindergarten children have begun to address this question (see, e.g., Cary & Verhaeghe, 1994; O'Connor, Jenkins, & Slocum, 1995; Torgesen, Morgan, & Davis, 1992). Although reading was not directly assessed in the two studies reported by Cary and Verhaeghe (1994), these researchers compared the benefits to metaphonological development of training programs that focused on different levels of linguistic analysis. In their first study, one of the training programs emphasized only rhymes and syllables, whereas the second program emphasized rhymes, syllables, *and* phonemes. In a second study, the training programs focused on either syllable awareness *or* phoneme awareness, and a third program trained children in visual analysis of nonlinguistic stimuli. The important finding was that in both studies, training that included *phonemic analysis* was the most beneficial. Training at this level of analysis generalized to tasks involving rhymes and syllables, but training in rhyme manipulation and syllabic analysis did not generalize to tasks involving analysis at the level of the phoneme. Given that phonemic analysis appears to play a greater role in reading acquisition than other levels of linguistic analysis (Hoien, Lundberg, Stanovich, & Bjaalid, 1995), it may be especially important during kindergarten (and with older children) to include explicit instruction at the level of the phoneme. Observations of classroom practice indicate that this level of analysis is not always included. Learning to recognize and produce rhyming words, an activity often recommended in kindergarten curriculum guides, is probably not, by itself, adequate to induce the level of awareness of the phonological structure of words needed for maximum benefit when learning to read and spell.

The evaluation of individual training components within specific programs also awaits investigation. Olson (1995) and Wise and Olson (1995), for example, suggested that phoneme awareness training studies that use the Auditory Discrimination in Depth program (Lindamood & Lindamood, 1984) should, in the next wave of intervention studies, compare the effectiveness of the program with and without the use of articulatory gestures (e.g., children are taught to observe their mouth movements while producing individual sounds, and then are taught specific labels that characterize these movements, such as "lip popper" for /p/ and /b/). How important is the use of these articulatory gestures to the success of the program? Does this component make more of a difference for those with severe phonological processing problems than for those with more modest deficits? Is there an optimal combination of tasks for children who experience different degrees of difficulty when learning to read?

HOW MUCH PHONOLOGICAL AWARENESS IS NEEDED?

How good do you have to be to be good enough? From studies that have investigated the relationship between phonological awareness and reading development in somewhat older children and adults (see, e.g., Pratt & Brady, 1988), we know that tasks such as phoneme deletion (e.g., say *stale*, now say it again, but don't say the /t/; example from Rosner, 1975), and phoneme manipulation with colored blocks can be used to discriminate between good and poor older readers. Does this mean that older children should work on phoneme awareness activities (outside the context of reading and spelling) until complex phoneme manipulations can be performed successfully? Will such a program result in a greater degree of reading success for these students?

I am reminded by some of the visual motor activities that were so prevalent in the 1960s and 1970s that it is possible to get carried away with an idea that might originally have had some academic relevance. Two items from the spatial relations subtest of the Developmental Test of Visual Perception (Frostig, 1963), a test given to children between the ages of 4 and 8, can be used to illustrate this point. Items 3 and 8 from this 8-item subtest have been reproduced in Figs. 18.1 and 18.2, respectively. It is possible that a clinician might learn something about the fine motor skills of a young child just learning to print by evaluating a child's performance on Item 3 (see Fig. 18.1). It is much more difficult to determine what could be learned from performance on Item 8 (see Fig. 18.2). What does it mean if a child can't reproduce this complex design? Unfortunately, failure on Item 8, or more specifically, a low score on this subtest, was often translated into a set of activities designed to remediate the perceived deficit in spatial relations. One component of the remediation program was to practice reproducing designs as complicated as the design in Item 8. Such activities were included in The Developmental Program in Visual Perception (Frostig & Horne, 1972), the popular Frostig remediation program. Children spent valuable hours becoming more competent at activities that we eventually learned had little real-world value (Hammill, 1972; Masland & Cratty, 1971; Vellutino, Steger, Moyer, Harding, & Niles, 1977).

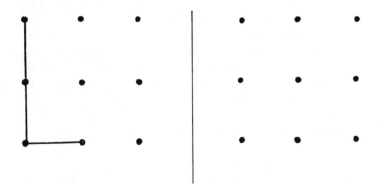

FIG. 18.1.   Item 3 from the Spatial Relations subtest of the Developmental Test of Visual Perception (Frostig, 1963). Reprinted by permission of ProEd.

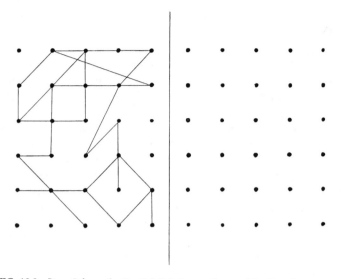

FIG. 18.2. Item 8 from the Spatial Relations subtest of the Developmental Test of Visual Perception (Frostig, 1963). (This item was not administered until the child was in first grade or higher.) Reprinted by permission of ProEd.

The problem for educators developing a program in phoneme awareness is not totally unrelated to issues raised by the Frostig materials. How good do you have to be at phonological awareness activities (as measured by which task) to get the maximum advantage out of these important insights about the phonological structure of words? The ability to perform more complex manipulations (e.g., deletion and rearrangement of phonemes) is likely the *result* of learning to read and spell and of being able to visualize the orthographic structure as an aid in making complex phonological judgments (Adams, 1990; Ball, in press; Bruck, 1992; Ehri, 1989, 1991; Wagner, Torgesen, & Rashotte, 1994). When does additional teaching of phoneme awareness per se stop becoming productive? Do you need to be able to say *stale* without the /t/? My clinical instincts suggest that once children are aware that speech can be segmented and that these segmented units can be represented by letters (as demonstrated, e.g., by relatively simple phoneme identity or phoneme segmentation), children should be engaged in reading and spelling instruction that utilizes these insights in developing knowledge of the alphabetic code and in building accurate and fluent word recognition.

This is not meant to suggest that the development of phoneme awareness is complete or even adequate at the point that children can demonstrate success on the simpler phoneme awareness tasks. Given the reciprocal relationship between phonological awareness and reading (Ehri,

1979; I. Y. Liberman, Liberman, Mattingly, & Shankweiler, 1980; Perfetti, Beck, Bell, & Hughes, 1987; Stuart & Coltheart, 1988), we know that as children become readers and spellers their awareness of the phonological structure of words becomes more sophisticated (but see Bruck's 1992, 1993, accounts of the persistence of phoneme awareness deficits among adults with childhood diagnoses of dyslexia—even among those who attain relatively high levels of word recognition). As pointed out by Brady and her colleagues, "Phoneme awareness is a *gradual* attainment, rather than an all-or-none phenomenon. The refinement of phoneme awareness continues for an extended period, well after the critical discoveries that words have an internal structure and that letters represent phonemes" (Brady, Fowler, Stone, & Winbury, 1994, p. 50). The question is how best to facilitate the development of phoneme awareness after those early discoveries. There is no evidence that it is advantageous to continue to develop phoneme awareness *outside* the context of learning to read and spell words, once those early discoveries have been made.

HOW DO WE MEASURE PHONOLOGICAL AWARENESS?

In order to determine the degree of phonological awareness needed to learn to read, we need some agreed-upon guidelines for the measurement of phonological awareness (Stahl & Murray, 1994) and more research-based information about the essential characteristics (e.g., memory load) of different tasks (Vellutino, Scanlon, & Tanzman, 1994). Two studies of task comparability (Stanovich, Cunningham, & Cramer 1984; Yopp, 1988) provide information regarding a hierarchy of task difficulty. Among the phonological awareness tasks evaluated, rhyming proved to be the easiest and phoneme deletion the most difficult, with phoneme counting and segmenting falling in between (also see Adams, 1990, for a discussion of task complexity). More recently, in a large study ($n = 1,509$; Hoien, Lundberg, Stanovich, & Bjaalid, 1995) of the factor structure underlying six phonological awareness tasks, three separable components were identified (i.e., syllable awareness, rhyme awareness, and phoneme awareness), with the phoneme awareness factor making the greatest contribution to the prediction of reading. To more accurately characterize the different degrees of phonological awareness required by different tasks, Stanovich (1992) suggested terminology—specifically, *shallow phonological sensitivity* and *deep phonological sensitivity*—that reflects the changing nature of phonological awareness over time.

Researchers have also proposed looking at additional dimensions of complexity when assessing phonological awareness. For example, it has been suggested that we look not just at task complexity but at the linguistic complexity of items within and across tasks as well (Stahl & Murray, 1994; Treiman, 1992). Another task that has considerable potential for use in measuring what children know about phonology and morphology is spelling, particularly early invented spelling. Documenting systematic changes in spelling may be one of the most sensitive methods for monitoring changes in a young child's awareness of the phonological structure of words (Ehri, 1989; Mann, Tobin, & Wilson, 1987; Stage & Wagner, 1992; Tangel & Blachman, 1992, 1995; Treiman, 1993). As Treiman so persuasively points out in chapter 9 of this volume, we really haven't begun to take advantage of spelling as an important source of information, particularly with reading-disabled children. As we increase our understanding of the tasks used to measure phonological awareness, we need to be sensitive to the fact that the lack of consensus among researchers regarding how phonological awareness (and other aspects of phonological processing) should be measured may limit our ability to translate what we have learned from research into educational practice.

WHAT ARE THE CHARACTERISTICS OF THE READING INSTRUCTION THAT SHOULD FOLLOW AN EARLY EMPHASIS ON PHONOLOGICAL AWARENESS?

How do we get from phonological awareness to word recognition? What are the characteristics of the reading instruction that should follow an early emphasis on phonological awareness? For children at risk for reading failure, the evidence appears incontrovertible that explicit instruction in the alphabetic code is essential to the development of accurate and fluent word recognition (Adams, 1990; Chall, 1989; Vellutino, 1991). Without accuracy and fluency, there will always be constraints on comprehension and, ultimately, on becoming a skilled reader (Perfetti, 1985; Vellutino, 1991). As Adams and Bruck (1995) explained, "Reading fluency and comprehension depend not merely on knowing about these relationships [between spellings and sounds] but on using them, on overlearning, extending, and refining them, such that word recognition becomes fast and nearly effortless" (p. 15). Yet, knowing that children need to develop accurate and fluent word recognition is not the same as knowing how best to teach these skills.

    In our own research, we (Blachman, 1994a; Blachman, Ball, Black, & Tangel, 1996) followed our kindergarten phonological awareness activities with a five-step program (see Blachman, 1987, for a description) in first grade that continued to emphasize phonological awareness and understanding of the alphabetic code and included: (a) a brief review of sound–symbol associations; (b) instruction in phoneme analysis and blending by manipulating individual letters on a small pocket chart (e.g., changing *sat* to *sam*, *sam* to *ham*, *ham* to *him*); (c) a brief review of regular words and high-frequency irregular words to develop fluency; (d) reading stories from phonetically controlled readers, basal readers (basal workbooks were not used), and trade books; and (e) written dictation of regular words and sentences. A primary goal was to develop accurate and fluent recognition of the six basic syllable patterns in English (i.e., closed syllables—*sun*; open syllables—*he*; final "e" syllables—*like*; vowel team syllables—*train*; vowel + *r* syllables—*car*; consonant *le* syllables—bub*ble*). At the end of first grade, the treatment children significantly outperformed the control children on measures of phoneme awareness and letter-name and letter-sound knowledge, regular word and nonword reading, a developmental spelling test, and a standardized spelling measure.

The instructional framework I've just described shares characteristics with many programs designed to help children understand the alphabetic principle. However, as is the case with programs designed to develop phonological awareness, the programs that might follow early phonological awareness training require research-based answers to a number of questions regarding specific instructional variables. For example, how does a program that teaches children to recognize the six basic syllable patterns in English compare to one that emphasizes learning to read words by analogy (see, e.g., Greaney, Tunmer, & Chapman, chap. 15, this volume; Lovett et al., 1994). Is one or the other a better instructional framework for drawing the child's attention to the internal structure of words and developing the recognition of orthographic patterns that facilitates accurate and fluent word recognition (Ehri, 1992, chap. 8, this volume; Share & Stanovich, 1995; Vellutino, Scanlon, & Tanzman, 1994)?

Another unresolved issue concerns instruction in the reading of nonwords. The nonword reading deficit in dyslexic children has been well documented (Rack, Snowling, & Olson, 1992). To what extent should the reading of nonwords (or *pseudowords*, as they are also called) be included in beginning reading instruction? In two intervention studies described in this volume (see chap. 14 by Olson, Wise, Johnson, & Ring, and chap. 13 by Torgesen, Wagner, & Rashotte), some instructional time in the early grades is devoted to teaching children to read nonwords. Both of these studies include aspects of the Auditory Discrimination in Depth program (Lindamood & Lindamood, 1984), and nonword reading instruction is part of that program. As is true with any instructional decision, each decision, whether it is to include instruction in reading nonwords or additional practice in complex phoneme manipulations, represents a trade-off between time spent in that activity and time spent doing something else. Is the trade-off worth it? To date, we lack information regarding the value of using nonwords in instruction.

Clinicians have frequently used nonwords when teaching older reading disabled students. The clinical justification has been that the use of nonwords allows the instructor to bypass the student's sight vocabulary (which might be considerable in an adolescent or adult dyslexic) and forces the student to use phonological coding skills. For example, an adolescent who is seriously delayed in reading might be able to read *can* because it is in his or her sight vocabulary but unable to read *paf*. The failure to read simple nonwords might also be reflected in the student's inability to read multisyllable words (e.g., *insipid*)—words that become increasingly important beyond the primary grades. In order to get an older student to attend to the phonological structure of words, it may be helpful to include nonwords in instruction. Can the same rationale be used to support the use of nonwords in beginning reading instruction? Basically, all written words are, at least initially, "nonwords" for a first grader who has no sight vocabulary. One does not have to use nonwords to find words that are novel for purposes of instruction. For the young beginning reader, we need to ask what can be accomplished by instruction in the reading of nonwords that cannot be accomplished as well or better with the use of real words.

Another important consideration is the appropriate balance between decontextualized and contextualized instruction. In order to develop fluency, children with reading disabilities who are learning to decode need extensive practice reading words in connected text, but often don't get the practice they need. It has been proposed that each successful decoding experience acts as a self-teaching mechanism (Jorm & Share, 1983; Share & Stanovich, 1995), yet, for poor readers, attempts to decode words during independent practice often result in a high rate of errors and inconsistent responses that are likely to undermine rather than support self-teaching. Phonetically controlled readers and predictable texts are two sources of practice that can provide opportunities for successful decoding, but the constraints on the selection of words used to create these texts also limits the student's exposure to a more varied word pool. Computer-based reading programs that furnish speech feedback for unknown words may get around some of these problems by offering valuable practice opportunities that reinforce accurate decoding. Olson and his colleagues (Olson & Wise, 1992; Olson, Wise, Johnson, & Ring, chap. 14, this volume; Wise & Olson, 1995) have found substantial gains in word recognition and nonword reading for poor readers who were trained to request synthetic-speech feedback for unknown words while reading stories on a computer.

WHAT ARE THE LONG-TERM OUTCOMES
OF OUR EARLY INTERVENTION EFFORTS?

Do the benefits of early phonological awareness training last? This question seems particularly important in light of the evidence (Wagner, Torgesen, & Rashotte, 1994) that individual differences in phonological processing abilities are remarkably stable from kindergarten through second grade (see also Byrne, Freebody, & Gates, 1992). Wagner and his colleagues (1994) suggested "that stability may make it difficult to alter the course of development in this area through interventions such as phonological awareness training" (p. 26).

Data to respond to the question of long-term benefits are still rather limited, although the results are very promising. After an intensive program to heighten the phonological awareness of preliterate children in kindergarten, Lundberg and his colleagues (Lundberg, Frost, & Petersen, 1988) followed the children in their kindergarten study until the end of second grade. They found that phonological awareness training in kindergarten resulted in significant differences in reading and spelling at the end of grade 2. Bradley (1988) also reported a follow-up study, almost 5 years after their original study ended (Bradley & Bryant, 1983), and found that children who were taught in the primary grades to make the connections between phonological segments and letters, in combination with instruction in sound categorization, were still significantly ahead of the untrained control group in reading and spelling at age 13. Given the relatively limited nature of the intervention (i.e., 40 10-minute lessons spread over a 2-year period), it is impressive that there were still measurable group differences almost 5 years later. In a more recent study to document long-term benefits, Byrne and Fielding-Barnsley (1995) found that 3 years after an intervention to train preschoolers in phoneme identity and recognition of the letters that represented the target phonemes, the trained children demonstrated a significant advantage in reading comprehension and pseudoword decoding (see Byrne, Fielding-Barnsley, Ashley, & Larsen, chap. 12, this volume, for additional details).

Thus, there is evidence that the positive effects on reading of early intervention in phonological awareness are still apparent in follow-up studies. Although some researchers have raised questions about the magnitude of the gains (Crowder & Wagner, 1991; Wagner, Torgesen, Laughon, Simmons, & Rashotte, 1993), others have argued that even modest early gains can positively influence the course of later reading development (Stanovich, 1986, 1992). The authors of several of the chapters in this volume (see, for example, chap. 12 by Byrne et al.; chap. 11 by Foorman, Francis, Shaywitz, Shaywitz, & Fletcher; chap. 14 by Olson et al.; chap. 13 by Torgesen et al.; and chap. 16 by Vellutino, Scanlon, &

Sipay) have built extensive follow-up studies into their research programs and will be able to provide information about the long-term benefits of a variety of early intervention programs. As researchers gather this information, it becomes possible to use the results to fine-tune early intervention efforts to maximize outcomes. Will early phonologically based intervention programs, in general, result in significant clinical (as well as statistical) differences that withstand the test of time? In order to maximize the chances that there will be long-term benefits, what should our programs look like?

WHO ARE THE TREATMENT RESISTERS?

It is important to look at both the children who are successful in our training programs and those who are not successful. Byrne and Fielding-Barnsley (1991) provided a good example of this by identifying a small subgroup of children who, despite success in phoneme identity and letter knowledge, were not successful on their word recognition task. This observation drew the authors' attention to the fact that phonological awareness and letter knowledge, although necessary, are not sufficient to learn to decode. Others (Torgesen, Morgan, & Davis, 1992) were also explicit about individual differences among their subjects in response to treatment. Torgesen and his colleagues reported, for example, that although as a group the children who received instruction in both segmenting and blending skills performed significantly better than did the controls on posttests of these skills and on a reading analog task, approximately a third of the treatment children made almost no improvement on the segmenting posttest. What modifications in treatment might have had a positive influence on the outcome for this subgroup of treatment children? It has been reported (Blachman, 1994b; Torgesen, 1995) that increasing the length and complexity of our interventions can have a positive influence on reducing the number of children resistant to treatment. We need to know more about treatment variables—such as length, intensity, timing, and combination of instructional components—that will influence treatment effectiveness for our most resistant learners.

The first in-depth analysis of the characteristics of children who are "treatment resisters" was provided by Vellutino and his colleagues (Vellutino et al., chap. 16, this volume; Vellutino et al., 1996). After giving an extensive battery of cognitive and early literacy measures to a large sample of unselected children during kindergarten and the first semester of first grade, poor readers were identified from the sample in the middle of grade 1. Poor readers then received either one or two semesters of one-to-one tutoring (depending on progress). After the tutoring ended, data from the battery of preintervention measures were used to identify the cognitive characteristics of the tutored children who had made the *most growth* in reading and the tutored children who had made the *least growth* in reading (i.e., the treatment resisters). Results indicated that those children who were the most difficult to remediate were significantly different from normal readers on phonological, fluency, and verbal memory measures. On the other hand, those poor readers who were the easiest to remediate had profiles more like the normal developing readers on these preintervention tasks. Vellutino et al. suggested that the provision of appropriate treatment *and* the child's responsiveness to that treatment should be important considerations in the diagnosis of a reading disability. Establishing a database that includes the characteristics of our treatment resisters could add considerably to the knowledge acquired from each intervention study.

WHAT OTHER PHONOLOGICAL FACTORS PLAY A ROLE IN TREATMENT SUCCESS?

What other phonological factors influence the effectiveness of our reading instruction? More specifically, how might limitations in various aspects of phonological processing (e.g., problems in the retrieval of phonological information, deficits in the phonological processes needed for efficient storage of information in working memory) interact to influence the effectiveness of reading instruction? There is considerable evidence, for example, that there is a pervasive problem among poor readers in the retrieval of phonological information, as demonstrated by slowness on rapid naming tasks (Bowers & Swanson, 1991; Denckla & Rudel, 1976; Felton, Naylor, & Wood, 1990; Wolf, 1986, 1991). It is important to note that not all researchers agree that performance on rapid naming tasks is dependent primarily on phonological processing. Bowers and Wolf (1993; see also Wolf, chap. 4, this volume) discussed the independence of deficits in naming speed and deficits in phonological processing, and posited that slowness on rapid naming tasks reflects an underlying deficit in timing mechanisms.

Despite the disagreement among researchers about underlying mechanisms, there does seem to be relative agreement that measures that tap speed of lexical access consistently show poor readers to be slower. To what extent do phonological awareness and naming speed deficits co-occur in children? Are these children more impaired than other poor readers and, if so, are they more resistant to treatment (see Blachman, 1994b, for a discussion of this point)? Evidence presented by Wolf (chap. 4, this volume) and Bowers and Wolf (1993) suggests that poor readers who exhibit phonological decoding deficits (i.e., nonword decoding) and naming speed deficits are, indeed, more impaired than are poor readers without these "double deficits." The development of effective strategies to develop word reading accuracy and fluency in children who have pronounced naming-speed difficulties presents a formidable challenge for both researchers and practitioners.

A question related to the interaction of phonological deficits and treatment effectiveness is whether treatments that result in changes in one aspect of phonological processing (e.g., phonological awareness) have an influence on any other aspect of phonological processing. Most training studies have failed to include measures that would be sensitive to such changes and, as such, this is a relatively unexplored area. Brady, Fowler, Stone, and Winbury (1994; see also Brady, chap. 2, this volume) presented data from a kindergarten phoneme awareness training study demonstrating that improved phonological awareness was accompanied by greater accuracy on a measure of speech production that required quick, multiple repetitions of two-syllable nonwords. These changes occurred despite the fact that the treatment did not include any emphasis on accurate or rapid word repetition. The authors hypothesized that the "development of phonemic awareness reflects and/or has consequences for the nature of underlying phonological representations" (p. 52). If phonologically based interventions result in changes in underlying phonological representations, one might expect changes in other aspects of the phonological system (see Fowler, 1991, for an extensive discussion of this point). One way to investigate this hypothesis is to include multiple measures of phonological processing in our training studies.

FINAL THOUGHTS

Answers to many of the questions I've raised are being actively pursued, as demonstrated by much of the research presented in this volume. Although gaps in our scientific understanding of reading acquisition, specifically the role of phonological processes in reading, are being filled in rapidly, it is necessary to exhibit caution in the educational arena. As new research is translated into educational practice, the tendency is to lose sight of the questions, complexities, and qualifications associated with the research. For example, "invented spelling" is now a term that many teachers use indiscriminately to describe, and to justify acceptance of, almost any incorrect spelling (no matter how bizarre), by almost any elementary age child. This is not what linguist Charles Read had in mind in his 1971 analysis of the invented spellings he observed in a group of preschool children. By analyzing their written productions, Read concluded that the children's initial attempts at spelling were strongly influenced by their awareness of speech sounds and the relationships among speech sounds, particularly articulatory features. With considerable consistency, most of the children Read studied created a phonetically reasonable written notation of our sound system. As discussed previously, early invented spellings, if analyzed systematically, can tell us a great deal about the child's understanding of the internal structure of words. Yet, today, the term *invented spelling* is used to justify an educational practice of questionable pedagogical benefit.

We have reason to be concerned that now that *phonological awareness* has moved into the educational mainstream and become one of the educational buzzwords of the 1990s, it may suffer the same fate. It is not uncommon, for example, to hear phonological awareness confused with phonics or, in the case of a recent article for teachers (Richgels, Poremba, & McGee, 1996), to have phonological awareness confused with aspects of print awareness. Recently, states such as California (1995) have called for changes in the whole-language practices that have dominated the teaching of reading for the last decade and asked, instead, for balanced beginning reading programs that include literature-based reading and writing instruction *and* instruction in phonological awareness, letter-sound knowledge, and the alphabetic coding skills needed to develop word reading accuracy and fluency. It is important to ask, however, how teachers will gain the knowledge needed to implement these practices. Understanding why children have difficulty accessing the phonological segments in spoken words and understanding how this insight is connected to learning to read an alphabetic writing system requires knowledge of the internal structure of spoken and written language that is not included in teacher training programs (I. Y. Liberman, 1987; Moats, 1995). There is no reason to believe that efforts to change practice will be successful without significant changes in teachers' understanding of reading acquisition. The challenge remains to translate the research in phonological awareness into appropriate educational practices that remain grounded in theory and that are flexible enough to absorb new research as it becomes available.

REFERENCES

Adams, M. J. (1990). *Beginning to read: Thinking and learning about print.* Cambridge, MA: MIT Press.

Adams, M. J., & Bruck, M. (1995). Resolving the "great debate." *American Educator, 19*(2), 7, 10–20.

Ball, E. W. (in press). Exploring implications drawn from phonological awareness research for whole language and emergent literacy programs: This is not an oxymoronic exercise. *Topics in Language Disorders.*

Ball, E. W., & Blachman, B. A. (1991). Does phoneme awareness training in kindergarten make a difference in early word recognition and developmental spelling? *Reading Research Quarterly, 26*(1), 49–66.

Beck, I. L., & Juel, C. (1995). The role of decoding in learning to read. *American Educator, 19*(2), 8, 21–25, 39–42.

Blachman, B. (1987). An alternative classroom reading program for learning disabled and other low-achieving children. In R. Bowler (Ed.), *Intimacy with language: A forgotten basic in teacher education* (pp. 49–55). Baltimore: Orton Dyslexia Society.

Blachman, B. (1989). Phonological awareness and word recognition: Assessment and intervention. In A. G. Kamhi & H. W. Catts (Eds.), *Reading disabilities: A developmental language perspective* (pp. 133–158). Boston: College-Hill Press.

Blachman, B. (1994a). Early literacy acquisition: The role of phonological awareness. In G. Wallach & K. Butler (Eds.), *Language learning disabilities in school-age children and adolescents: Some underlying principles and applications* (pp. 253–274). Columbus, OH: Merrill/Macmillan.

Blachman, B. (1994b). What we have learned from longitudinal studies of phonological processing and reading, *and* some unanswered questions: A response to Torgesen, Wagner, and Rashotte. *Journal of Learning Disabilities, 27*, 287–291.

Blachman, B., Ball, E., Black, S., Tangel, D. (1994). Kindergarten teachers develop phoneme awareness in low-income, inner-city classrooms: Does it make a difference? *Reading and Writing: An Interdisciplinary Journal, 6*, 1–17.

Blachman, B., Ball, E., Black, S., Tangel, D. (1996). [Promising practices for improving beginning reading instruction]. Unpublished raw data.

Bowers, P. G., & Swanson, L. B. (1991). Naming speed deficits in reading disability: Multiple measures of a singular process. *Journal of Experimental Child Psychology, 51*, 195–219.

Bowers, P. G., & Wolf, M. (1993). Theoretical links among naming speed, precise timing mechanisms and orthographic skill in dyslexia. *Reading and Writing: An Interdisciplinary Journal, 5*, 69–85.

Bradley, L. (1988). Making connections in learning to read and spell. *Applied Cognitive Psychology, 2*, 3–18.

Bradley, L., & Bryant, P. (1983). Categorizing sounds and learning to read: A causal connection. *Nature, 30*, 419–421.

Bradley, L., & Bryant, P. (1985). *Rhyme and reason in reading and spelling.* Ann Arbor: University of Michigan Press.

Brady, S., Fowler, A., Stone, B., & Winbury, N. (1994). Training phonological awareness: A study with inner-city kindergarten children. *Annals of Dyslexia, 44*, 26–59.

Brady, S., & Shankweiler, D. (Eds.). (1991). *Phonological processes in literacy: A tribute to Isabelle Y. Liberman.* Hillsdale, NJ: Lawrence Erlbaum Associates.

Bruck, M. (1992). Persistence of dyslexics' phonological awareness deficits. *Developmental Psychology, 28*, 874–886.

Bruck, M. (1993). Word recognition and component phonological processing skills of adults with childhood diagnosis of dyslexia. *Developmental Review, 13*, 258–268.

Bryant, P. E., Bradley, L., MacLean, M., & Crossland, J. (1989). Nursery rhymes, phonological skills and reading. *Journal of Child Language, 16*, 407–428.

Bryant, P. E., MacLean, M., Bradley, L. L., & Crossland, J. (1990). Rhyme and alliteration, phoneme detection, and learning to read. *Developmental Psychology, 26*, 429–438.

Byrne, B., & Fielding-Barnsley, R. (1991). Evaluation of a program to teach phonemic awareness to young children. *Journal of Educational Psychology, 83*, 451–455.

Byrne, B., & Fielding-Barnsley, R. (1993). Evaluation of a program to teach phonemic awareness to young children: A 1-year follow-up. *Journal of Educational Psychology, 85*, 104–111.

Byrne, B., & Fielding-Barnsley, R. (1995). Evaluation of a program to teach phonemic awareness to young children: A 2- and 3-year follow-up and a new preschool trial. *Journal of Educational Psychology, 87,* 488–503.

Byrne, B., Freebody, P., & Gates, A. (1992). Longitudinal data on the relations of word-reading strategies to comprehension, reading time, and phonemic awareness. *Reading Research Quarterly, 27,* 141–151.

California Department of Education. (1995). *Every child a reader: The report of the California Reading Task Force.* Sacramento: California Department of Education.

Cary, L., & Verhaeghe, A. (1994). Promoting phonemic analysis ability among kindergartners: Effects of different training programs. *Reading and Writing: An Interdisciplinary Journal, 6,* 251–178.

Castle, J. M., Riach, J., & Nicholson, T. (1994). Getting off to a better start in reading and spelling: The effects of phonemic awareness instruction within a whole language program. *Journal of Educational Psychology, 86,* 350–359.

Chall, J. S. (1989). *Learning to read: The great debate* 20 years later: A response to "Debunking the great phonics myth." *Phi Delta Kappan, 70,* 521–538.

Crowder, R. G., & Wagner, R. K. (1992). *The psychology of reading: An introduction* (2nd ed.). New York: Oxford University Press.

Denckla, M. B., & Rudel, R. G. (1976). Rapid "automatized" naming (R.A.N.): Dyslexia differentiated from other learning disabilities. *Neuropsychologia, 14,* 471–479.

Ehri, L. C. (1979). Linguistic insight: Threshold of reading acquisition. In T. G. Waller & G. E. MacKinnon (Eds.), *Reading research: Advances in theory and practice* (Vol. 1, pp. 63–144). New York: Academic Press.

Ehri, L. C. (1989). Development of spelling knowledge and its role in reading acquisition and reading disabilities. *Journal of Learning Disabilities, 22,* 356–365.

Ehri, L. C. (1991). Learning to read and spell words. In L. Rieben & C. A. Perfetti (Eds.), *Learning to read: Basic research and its implications* (pp. 57–73). Hillsdale, NJ: Lawrence Erlbaum Associates.

Ehri, L. (1992). Reconceptualizing the development of sight word reading and its relationship to recoding. In P. B. Gough, L. C. Ehri, & R. Treiman (Eds.), *Reading acquisition* (pp. 107–143). Hillsdale, NJ: Lawrence Erlbaum Associates.

Elkonin, D. B. (1973). U.S.S.R. In J. Downing (Ed.), *Comparative reading* (pp. 551–580). New York: Macmillan.

Felton, R. H., Naylor, C. E., & Wood, F. B. (1990). Neuropsychological profile of adult dyslexics. *Brain and Language, 39,* 485–497.

Fletcher, J. M., Shaywitz, S. E., Shankweiler, D. P., Katz, L., Liberman, I. Y., Stuebing, K. K., Francis, D. J., Fowler, A. E., & Shaywitz, B. A. (1994). Cognitive profiles of reading disability: Comparisons of discrepancy and low achievement definitions. *Journal of Educational Psychology, 86,* 6–23.

Fowler, A. E. (1991). How early phonological development might set the stage for phoneme awareness. In S. A. Brady & D. P. Shankweiler (Eds.), *Phonological processes in literacy: A tribute to Isabelle Y. Liberman* (pp. 97–117). Hillsdale, NJ: Lawrence Erlbaum Associates.

Frostig, M. (1963). *Developmental test of visual perception.* Palo Alto, CA: Consulting Psychologists Press.

Frostig, M., & Horne, D. (1972). *The developmental program in visual perception* (rev. ed.). Chicago: Follett.

Goswami, U., & Bryant, P. (1990). *Phonological skills and learning to read.* Hillsdale, NJ: Lawrence Erlbaum Associates.

Hammill, D. (1972). Training visual perceptual processes. *Journal of Learning Disabilities, 5,* 552–559.

Hoien, T., Lundberg, I., Stanovich, K. E., & Bjaalid, I. (1995). Components of phonological awareness. *Reading and Writing: An Interdisciplinary Journal, 7,* 171–188.

Iversen, S., & Tunmer, W. (1993). Phonological processing skills and the Reading Recovery Program. *Journal of Educational Psychology, 85,* 112–126.

Jorm, A. F., & Share, D. L. (1983). Phonological recoding and reading acquisition. *Applied Psycholinguistics, 4,* 103–147.

Juel, C. (1988). Learning to read and write: A longitudinal study of 54 children from first through fourth grades. *Journal of Educational Psychology, 80*(4), 437–447.

Liberman, A. M., Cooper, F. S., Shankweiler, D., & Studdert-Kennedy, M. (1967). Perception of the speech code. *Psychological Review, 74,* 731–761.

Liberman, I. Y. (1971). Basic research in speech and lateralization of language: Some implications for reading disability. *Bulletin of the Orton Society, 21,* 72–87.

Liberman, I. Y. (1973). Segmentation of the spoken word and reading acquisition. *Bulletin of the Orton Society, 23,* 65–67.

Liberman, I. Y. (1987). Language and literacy: The obligation of the schools of education. In W. Ellis (Ed.), *Intimacy with language: A forgotten basic in teacher education* (pp. 1–9). Baltimore: The Orton Dyslexia Society.

Liberman, I. Y., & Liberman, A. M. (1990). Whole language vs. code emphasis: Underlying assumptions and their implications for reading instruction. *Annals of Dyslexia, 40,* 51–76.

Liberman, I. Y., Liberman, A. M., Mattingly, I. G., & Shankweiler, D. (1980). Orthography and the beginning reader. In J. Kavanagh & R. Venezky (Eds.), *Orthography, reading and dyslexia* (pp. 137–153). Baltimore: University Park Press.

Liberman, I. Y., & Shankweiler, D. (1979). Speech, the alphabet, and teaching to read. In L. B. Resnick & P. A. Weaver (Eds.), *Theory and practice of early reading* (Vol. 2, pp. 109–134). Hillsdale, NJ: Lawrence Erlbaum Associates.

Liberman, I. Y., & Shankweiler, D. (1985). Phonology and the problems of learning to read and write. *Remedial and Special Education, 6,* 8–17.

Liberman, I. Y., & Shankweiler, D. (1991). Phonology and beginning reading: A tutorial. In L. Rieben & C. A. Perfetti (Eds.), *Learning to read: Basic research and its implications* (pp. 3–17). Hillsdale, NJ: Lawrence Erlbaum Associates.

Liberman, I. Y., Shankweiler, D., Fischer, F. W., & Carter, B. (1974). Explicit syllable and phoneme segmentation in the young child. *Journal of Experimental Child Psychology, 18,* 201–212.

Lindamood, C. H., & Lindamood, P. C. (1984). *Auditory discrimination in depth.* Allen, TX: DLM/Teaching Resources.

Lovett, M. W., Borden, S. L., DeLuca, T., Lacerenza, L., Benson, N. J., & Brackstone, D. (1994). Treating the core deficits of developmental dyslexia: Evidence of transfer of learning after phonologically- and strategy-based reading training programs. *Developmental Psychology, 30,* 805–822.

Lundberg, I., Frost, J., & Petersen, O. (1988). Effects of an extensive program for stimulating phonological awareness in preschool children. *Reading Research Quarterly, 23*(3), 263–284.

MacLean, M., Bryant, P., & Bradley, L. (1987). Rhymes, nursery rhymes, and reading in early childhood. *Merrill-Palmer Quarterly, 33,* 255–281.

Mann, V., Tobin, P., & Wilson, R. (1987). Measuring phonological awareness through the invented spellings of kindergarten children. *Merrill-Palmer Quarterly, 33,* 365–391.

Masland, R. L., & Cratty, B. J. (1971). The nature of the reading process, the rationale of non-educational remedial methods. In E. O. Calkins (Ed.), *Reading forum* [NINDS Monograph No. 11, DHEW Publication No. (NIH) 72–44; pp. 141–175].) Washington, DC: United States Government Printing Office.

Moats, L. C. (1995). The missing foundation in teacher education. *American Educator, 19*(2), 9, 43–51.

National Center for Learning Disabilities (NCLD). (1996, Summer). Learning to read, reading to learn: NCLD joins in a national campaign to prevent reading failure among young children. *NCLD News,* p. 6.

O'Connor, R. E., Jenkins, J. R., Leicester, N., & Slocum, T. A. (1993). Teaching phonological awareness to young children with learning disabilities. *Exceptional Children, 59*, 532–546.

O'Connor, R. E., Jenkins, J. R., & Slocum, T. A. (1995). Transfer among phonological tasks in kindergarten: Essential instructional content. *Journal of Educational Psychology, 87*, 202–217.

Olson, R. K. (1995, May–June). *Phonological deficits in the etiology and remediation of reading and spelling disabilities: But is that the whole story?* Paper presented at a conference sponsored by the National Dyslexia Research Foundation: "Cognitive and Linguistic Foundations of Reading Acquisition: Implications for Intervention Research," Kauai, Hawaii.

Olson, R. K., & Wise, B. A. (1992). Reading on the computer with orthographic and speech feedback. *Reading and Writing: An Interdisciplinary Journal, 4*, 107–144.

Perfetti, C. A. (1985). *Reading ability.* New York: Oxford University Press.

Perfetti, C. A., Beck, I., Bell, L., & Hughes, C. (1987). Phonemic knowledge and learning to read are reciprocal: A longitudinal study of first grade children. *Merrill-Palmer Quarterly, 33*, 283–320.

Pratt, A. C., & Brady, S. (1988). Relation of phonological awareness to reading ability in children and adults. *Journal of Educational Psychology, 80*, 319–323.

Rack, J. P., Snowling, M. J., & Olson, R. K. (1992). The nonword reading deficit in developmental dyslexia: A review. *Reading Research Quarterly, 27*, 29–53.

Read, C. (1971). Pre-school children's knowledge of English phonology. *Harvard Educational Review, 41*, 1–34.

Richgels, D. J., Poremba, K. J., & McGee, L. M. (1996). Kindergarteners talk about print: Phonemic awareness in meaningful contexts. *The Reading Teacher, 49*, 632–642.

Rosner, J. (1975). *Helping children overcome learning difficulties.* New York: Walker.

Share, D. J., Jorm, A. F., Maclean, R., & Matthews, R. (1984). Sources of individual differences in reading achievement. *Journal of Educational Psychology, 76*(6), 1309–1324.

Share, D. L., & Stanovich, K. E. (1995). Cognitive processes in early reading development: Accommodating individual differences into a model of acquisition. *Issues in Education: Contributions From Educational Psychology, 1*, 1–57.

Snider, V. (1995). A primer on phonemic awareness: What it is, why it's important, and how to teach it. *School Psychology Review, 24*, 443–455.

Stage, S., & Wagner, R. (1992). Development of young children's phonological and orthographic knowledge as revealed by their spellings. *Developmental Psychology, 28*, 287–296.

Stahl, S. A., & Murray, B. A. (1994). Defining phonological awareness and its relationship to early reading. *Journal of Educational Psychology, 86*, 221–234.

Stanovich, K. E. (1986). Matthew effects in reading: Some consequences of individual differences in the acquisition of literacy. *Reading Research Quarterly, 21*, 360–407.

Stanovich, K. E. (1992). Speculations on the causes and consequences of individual differences in early reading acquisition. In P. B. Gough, L. C. Ehri, & R. Treiman (Eds.), *Reading acquisition* (pp. 307–342). Hillsdale, NJ: Lawrence Erlbaum Associates.

Stanovich, K. E., Cunningham, A. E., & Cramer, B. B. (1984). Assessing phonological awareness in kindergarten children: Issues of task comparability. *Journal of Experimental Child Psychology, 38*, 175–190.

Stuart, M., & Coltheart, M. (1988). Does reading develop in a sequence of stages? *Cognition, 30*, 139–181.

Tangel, D., & Blachman, B. A. (1992). Effect of phoneme awareness instruction on kindergarten children's invented spelling. *Journal of Reading Behavior, 24*, 233–261.

Tangel, D. M., & Blachman, B. A. (1995). Effect of phoneme awareness instruction on the invented spelling of first grade children: A one year follow-up. *Journal of Reading Behavior, 27*, 153–185.

Torgesen, J. K. (1995, May–June). *Instructional alternatives for children with severe reading disabilities*. Paper presented at a conference sponsored by the National Dyslexia Research Foundation: "Cognitive and Linguistic Foundations of Reading Acquisition: Implications for Intervention Research," Kauai, Hawaii.

Torgesen, J. K., Morgan, S. T., & Davis, C. (1992). Effects of two types of phonological awareness training on word learning in kindergarten children. *Journal of Educational Psychology, 84,* 364–370.

Treiman, R. (1992). The role of intrasyllabic units in learning to read and spell. In P. B. Gough, L. C. Ehri, & R. Treiman (Eds.), *Reading acquisition* (pp. 65–106). Hillsdale, NJ: Lawrence Erlbaum Associates.

Treiman, R. (1993). *Beginning to spell*. New York: Oxford University Press.

Vellutino, F. R. (1991). Introduction to three studies on reading acquisition: Convergent findings on theoretical foundations of code-oriented versus whole-language approaches to reading instruction. *Journal of Educational Psychology, 83,* 437–443.

Vellutino, F. R., & Scanlon, D. M. (1987). Phonological coding, phonological awareness, and reading ability: Evidence from a longitudinal and experimental study. *Merrill-Palmer Quarterly, 33*(3), 321–363.

Vellutino, F. R., Scanlon, D. M., Sipay, E. R., Small, S. G., Pratt, A., Chen, R. S., & Denckla, M. B. (1996). Cognitive profiles of difficult-to-remediate and readily remediated poor readers: Early intervention as a vehicle for distinguishing between cognitive and experiential deficits as basic causes of specific reading disability. *Journal of Educational Psychology, 88,* 601–638.

Vellutino, F. R., Scanlon, D. M., & Tanzman, M. S. (1994). Components of reading ability: Issues and problems in operationalizing word identification, phonological coding, and orthographic coding. In G. R. Lyon (Ed.), *Frames of reference for the assessment of learning disabilities: New views on measurement issues* (pp. 279–332). Baltimore: Brookes.

Vellutino, F. R., Steger, B. M., Moyer, S. C., Harding, C. J., & Niles, J. A. (1977). Has the perceptual deficit hypothesis led us astray? *Journal of Learning Disabilities, 10,* 375–385.

Wagner, R. K., & Torgesen, J. K. (1987). The nature of phonological processing and its causal role in the acquisition of reading skills. *Psychological Bulletin, 101,* 192–212.

Wagner, R. K., Torgesen, J. K., Laughon, P., Simmons, K., & Rashotte, C. A. (1993). Development of young readers' phonological processing abilities. *Journal of Educational Psychology, 85,* 83–103.

Wagner, R. K., Torgesen, J. K., & Rashotte, C. A. (1994). The development of reading-related phonological processing abilities: New evidence of bi-directional causality from a latent variable longitudinal study. *Developmental Psychology, 30,* 73–87.

Williams, J. (1980). Teaching decoding with an emphasis on phoneme analysis and phoneme blending. *Journal of Educational Psychology, 72,* 1–15.

Wise, B. W., & Olson, R. K. (1995). Computer-based phonological awareness and reading instruction. *Annals of Dyslexia, 45,* 99–122.

Wolf, M. (1986). Rapid alternating stimulus naming in the developmental dyslexias. *Brain and Language, 27,* 360–379.

Wolf, M. (1991). Naming speed and reading: The contribution of the cognitive neurosciences. *Reading Research Quarterly, 26,* 123–141.

Yopp, H. K. (1988). The validity and reliability of phonemic awareness tests. *Reading Research Quarterly, 23,* 159–177.

Author Index

431

Subject Index

443